THE BIG BOOK OF

How to Say It®

includes the complete texts of

How to Say It® by Rosalie Maggio

&

How to Say It® *At Work* by Jack Griffin

Prentice Hall Press

 A member of Penguin Putnam Inc.
375 Hudson Street
New York, New York 10014

| www.penguin.com |

Previously published as *How to Say It®: Choice Words, Phrases, Sentences, and Paragraphs for Every Situation,* copyright © 2001 by Rosalie Maggio and *How to Say It® at Work,* copyright © 1998 by Jack Griffin

Library of Congress Cataloging-in-Publication Data available upon request

Special Markets ISBN: 0-7352-0403-9

Printed in the United States of America

10 9 8 7 6 5 4 3 2 1

Most Prentice Hall Press Books are available at special quantity discounts for bulk purchases for sales promotions, premiums, fund-raising, or educational use. Special books, or book excerpts, can also be created to fit specific needs.

For details, write: Special Markets, Penguin Group (USA), Inc., 375 Hudson Street, New York, New York 10014.

Contents

How To Say It®

How To Say It® At Work

Introduction

How to Say It® is a practical, easy-to-use book that tells you what to say and how to say it. Its flexible approach helps you fashion compelling letters in little more time than it takes to handwrite or type them.

Although an impressive amount of business and social interaction takes place today over the telephone and fax, by e-mail, or in person, the well-written letter remains a staple of business success and one of the strongest connecting links between human beings.

Most of us are capable of writing a satisfactory letter, but few of us have the time and mental energy to deal with the countless letters that life today seems to demand of us—especially since all of them should have been written yesterday.

How to Say It® features comprehensive, versatile lists of words, phrases, sentences, and paragraphs that allow you to express yourself on any subject in your own voice and style.

Thesaurus-like, these lists provide you with terms relating to your topic. Whether you want to sound formal or casual, traditional or contemporary, businesslike or lighthearted, distant or intimate, you'll find here the words for every letterwriting occasion—from powerful, cogent business letters to warm, sensitive personal letters.

An important message of this book, delivered indirectly in its pages, is that there is rarely "one right way" to write a letter. You may follow, adapt, or ignore the guidelines given here; after all, you know more about your message and your reader than any letterwriting manual. Except for someone like Napoleon, who apparently wrote more than 50,000 letters in his lifetime (and nobody ever said to him, "Get a life!"), almost everyone can use this book to write letters with increased speed, individuality, success—and enjoyment!

How to Use This Book

Begin by skimming the table of contents to familiarize yourself with the fifty letter topics available to you (for example, sales letters, thank-you notes, references, apologies, acknowledgments, letters dealing with employment).

Next, flip through the Appendixes so that you know what kind of help waits for you there: Appendix I deals with the mechanics of letterwriting (what kind of stationery to use, how to address an envelope, the four most common ways of setting up a letter on the page) while Appendix II deals with the content of your letter (writing tips, grammar and usage, frequently misspelled or confused words, redundant words and phrases, correct forms of address).

To find advice about the letter you want to write, either turn to the chapter that deals with that kind of letter or check the index in the back of the book. Its one thousand entries ensure that you will find the help you need.

Each chapter includes a brief introduction, a list of occasions for writing that type of letter, what to include in each letter, what not to say, comments on special situations, and what format to use.

At the heart of each chapter are the lists of words, phrases, sentences, and paragraphs you can use to construct your letter. Sample letters are also given.

The lists "prime the pump"—they start you thinking along the lines of that letter topic. They also provide those who want to compose their own letter with a number of appropriate words, or they allow those using the sample letters as guides to substitute words that fit their needs.

To compose a letter:

- Read through the "How to Say It" section, note the elements your letter should include, and personalize them to reflect your situation.
- Choose from the lists of words, phrases, sentences, and paragraphs those terms that are useful to you.
- Study the sample letters to see if one can serve as a model.
- Combine your checked-off words, phrases, sentences, and paragraphs to produce a letter that says what you need it to say.
- Check your rough draft against the list of what not to say. Have you written something inappropriate? At this point, you may have a question about format or grammar or a social title. Check the Index to locate the answer in one of the Appendixes.

After writing your first few letters using this book, you may find that it is not, after all, so difficult or time-consuming to write your share of the billions of letters mailed each year.

Acceptances

1

*The mind gives us thousands of ways to say no, but there's
only one way to say yes, and that's from the heart.*

—SUZE ORMAN

Once you decide to accept an invitation or grant a request, simply say so; this is one of the easiest letters to write.

A "yes" that doesn't come from the heart results in an unenthusiastic acceptance and you may even find yourself backing out later. Writing the acceptance is not as difficult as being sure you want to say "yes" in the first place.

Write Acceptances for

- admissions requests: schools/clubs/organizations
- franchise applications
- invitations: dinner/meeting/party/luncheon/hospitality
- job offers
- membership offers: board/commission/organization
- proposals
- requests: contributions/favors/help
- speaking invitations: conference/workshop/banquet
- wedding invitations (see WEDDINGS)

- Express your pleasure in accepting the invitation/offer/proposal/bid or agreeing to do what was asked.
- Repeat the details of what you are accepting (meeting date and time, amount of the bid or of your contribution, the precise nature of your assistance, the duties you agree to assume).
- Inquire about particular needs: receipt for a tax-deductible contribution, directions to your host's home, wheelchair accessibility, equipment for your speech, list of other organizers.
- Close with an expression of pleasure to come (seeing the person, working for the company, being part of the group) or of future action (what you want to accomplish, actions you intend to take, a reciprocal invitation).

- Avoid ungracious amplifications: you are busy but you suppose you can manage it; you have two other events on the calendar that evening but you will try to stop by; you probably won't be a good speaker but, sure, you'll try. Let your "yes" be a simple "yes." If you have reservations about your acceptance, it may be better to decline.

Tips on Writing

～ Send acceptances as soon as possible. If you are late, apologize, but do not dwell on it.

～ Acceptances are brief and generally deal only with the acceptance.

～ Noted usage expert Rudolf Flesch says, "If your answer to an inquiry is yes, it's a good idea to make yes the first word of your letter."

～ Be enthusiastic. It is entirely proper to simply state your acceptance and repeat the details of the invitation, but your stock with hosts, employers, or friends will go up if you add a sentence saying something personal, cheerful, or lively.

~ When your invitation is issued in the name of more than one person, mention all of them in your reply. Mail your reply either to the person listed under the R.S.V.P. or to the first name given.

~ Always respond promptly to an invitation marked "R.S.V.P." or "Please reply." This is mandatory, obligatory, required, compulsory, imperative, and essential.

Special Situations

~ When offered a position you want, write an acceptance letter that expresses your enthusiasm and pleasure and that confirms the details of your employment.

~ When writing to offer a job to an applicant, include: a congratulatory remark about being chosen and something complimentary about the person's credentials, experience, or interview; information about the job—duties, salary, supervisor's name, starting date; the name and telephone number of someone who can answer questions; an expression of goodwill about the person's employment with the company. Highlight some of the advantages of working for the company to influence the person's decision to accept the offer.

~ In some situations (large weddings, for example), one of a couple may accept an invitation while the other declines. In other cases (large dinner parties), check with your host to see if this is acceptable.

~ White House invitations include the phone number of the Social Office where you telephone your acceptance and can ask questions about protocol, where to park your car, what to wear, how to respond to the invitation. General guidelines are: send your reply within a day of receiving the invitation; write the reply yourself (do not have a secretary do it); handwrite your reply on plain or engraved personal stationery; use the same format and person (first person or third person) to reply but insert "have the honor of accepting"; if the invitation was sent by the President's or First Lady's secretary (in the case of an informal invitation), reply to that person and write "Would you please tell/convey to . . ."

~ Children can write brief acceptances for invitations: "Thank you for inviting me to your Halloween party. Wait till you see my costume!"

Format

∼ Model your reply on the format used in the invitation or letter. If it is handwritten, handwrite your reply. If letterhead stationery is used, reply on your letterhead. If the invitation is e-mailed, e-mail your acceptance. When the language of the invitation is informal, your reply is also informal. When replying to a formal invitation, use nearly the same words, layout, and style as the invitation:

Mr. and Mrs. Masterson Finsbury
request the pleasure of
Mr. and Mrs. Edward Bloomfield's company
at a dinner-dance
on Saturday, the seventh of February
at eight o'clock
Gideon Country Club

Mr. and Mrs. Edward Bloomfield
accept with pleasure
the kind invitation of
Mr. and Mrs. Masterson Finsbury
to a dinner-dance
on Saturday, the seventh of February
at eight o'clock
Gideon Country Club

WORDS

accept	gratifying	satisfying	touched
approve	pleased	thoughtful	welcome
certainly	pleasure	thrilled	willing
delighted			

PHRASES

able to say yes
accept with pleasure
agree to
glad to be able to vote yes
happy to let you know

I am pleased/happy/honored to accept
it is with great pleasure that
it was so thoughtful of you to
it will be a pleasure to

pleased to have been invited
thank you for asking me to
thank you for nominating me for
we are delighted to accept

we are sincerely happy to join you
we have accepted your bid of
we look forward with pleasure

SENTENCES

After reviewing your application, we are pleased to be able to offer you the funding requested.

I accept with pleasure the position of senior research chemist.

I am happy to be able to do this.

I appreciate very much (and accept) your generous apology.

I'll be happy to meet with you in your office March 11 at 10:30 to plan this year's All-City Science Fair.

In a word, absolutely!

In response to your letter asking for support for the Foscari Children's Home, I'm enclosing a check for $500.

Thank you for inviting me to speak at the Chang-Ch'un Meditation Center next month.

We accept your kind invitation with great pleasure.

We are happy to accept your estimate for refinishing our Queen Anne dining room suite.

We are pleased to grant you the six-week extension you requested to complete your work.

We are pleased to tell you that your application for admission to the Emmet School has been approved.

We look forward to working with you.

PARAGRAPHS

I will be delighted to have dinner with you on Friday, the sixteenth of March, at seven o'clock. Thanks so much for asking me. I can hardly wait to see you and Anders again.

Thanks for telling me how much the children at St. Joseph's Home liked my storytelling the other night. I'm happy to accept your invitation to become a regular volunteer and tell stories every other Thursday evening. Do you have a record player or tape deck so that I could use music with some of the stories?

I'm looking forward to your graduation and the reception afterwards. Thanks for including me.

Your bid of $6,780 to wallpaper our reception rooms has been accepted. Please read the enclosed contract and call with any questions. We were impressed with the attention to detail in your proposal and bid, and we are looking forward to your work.

SAMPLE LETTERS

Dear Selina,

Vickers and I accept with pleasure your kind invitation to a celebration of your parents' fiftieth wedding anniversary on Saturday, July 16, at 7:30 p.m.

                                              Sincerely,

Dear Dr. Cheesewright:

Thank you for inviting me to speak at your county dental society's dinner banquet on October 26 at 7:00. I am happy to accept and will, as you suggested, discuss new patient education strategies.

I'm not sure how much time you have allotted me—will you let me know?

                                              With best wishes,

Dear Ms. Thirkell,

I am pleased to accept your offer of the position of assistant director of the Gilbert Tebben Working Family Center.

I enjoyed the discussions with you, and I look forward to being part of this dynamic and important community resource.

The salary, hours, responsibilities, and starting date that we discussed during our last meeting are all agreeable to me. I understand that I will receive the standard benefits package, with the addition of two weeks' vacation during my first year.

                                              Sincerely yours,
                                              Laurence Dean

Dear Dr. Bennett,

I would be most happy to perform twenty minutes of magic tricks at the Five Towns Children's Hospital annual fair to be held on Saturday, November 8. As the date approaches, we can discuss details.

All the best,
Anna Tellwright

Dear Mr. Grandby:

We are pleased to accept for publication your self-help book, tentatively entitled *Don't Give Up*. All of us are excited about its possibilities.

Enclosed are guidelines from the production editor to help you prepare the final manuscript. Also enclosed is a preliminary draft of the book contract. Please look it over, and I will call next week to discuss it.

Sincerely yours,

Dear Ms. Unwin:

Congratulations! Your franchise application has been approved. Welcome to the Sunshine family.

Enclosed is the contract, which we suggest you discuss with your attorney, and a packet of informational materials.

Please call this office to set up an appointment to discuss any questions.

Sincerely,

Dear Violet,

Yes! I will be delighted to stay with the twins while you and Gordon take the horses to the state fair. A week is *not* too long for me. And thanks for the offer of the plane ticket—I accept with pleasure.

Love,

Dear Mr. Van Druten,

In response to your letter of February 10, we are pleased to grant you a two-month extension of the loan of the slides showing scenes of our amusement park. We appreciate being able to help you add, as you said, "a bit of amusement" to your corporate meetings.

We offer this extension with our compliments.

Cordially,
Laura Simmons

Dear Richard,

    I will be happy to write you a letter of reference, and I'm delighted that you thought to ask me. You were one of my favorite students, and I'll enjoy explaining just why to Forey, Harley and Wentworth.

Yours truly,

~

Mr. Clarence Rochester
accepts with pleasure
William Portlaw and Alida Ascott's
kind invitation to dinner
on the sixteenth of June at 7:30 p.m.
but regrets that
Dr. Maggie Campion
will be absent at that time.

~

See also: REFUSALS, RESPONSES.

Acknowledgments and Confirmations

2

Life is not so short but that there is always time enough for courtesy.

—RALPH WALDO EMERSON

Letters of acknowledgment and letters of confirmation resemble each other. The letter of acknowledgment says, "I received your letter (telephone call, gift, materials)." The letter of confirmation says, "I received your letter (message, contract) and we agree about the matter"; this letter can serve as an informal contract.

Sometimes a letter of acknowledgment also serves as a "thank you." Or it says you received the message or materials but will respond later, or that you passed them on to the appropriate person. Sometimes, too, "acknowledgment" letters are really sales letters that use the excuse of acknowledging something (an order, a payment) to present an additional sales message.

You always acknowledge expressions of condolence. You generally acknowledge anniversary or birthday greetings, congratulations, apologies, or divorce announcements.

Acknowledge or Confirm

- anniversary/birthday greetings
- apologies
- complaints
- condolences
- congratulations
- divorce announcements

9

- documents/reports/files/materials received
- gifts (thank-you note to follow)
- information received
- inquiries/requests (will respond as soon as possible)
- letters from constituents
- letters of introduction
- letters received (action underway, will let you know)
- mail in supervisor's absence (assistant writes that message/letter has been received and will be dealt with later)
- manuscripts (under consideration, will give decision later)
- oral agreements, telephone discussions/agreements
- orders (see also ORDERS)
- payments
- proposals
- receipt of orders/merchandise (see also ORDERS)
- receipt of wedding gifts (see WEDDINGS)
- reports
- reservations, speaking dates, invitation times
- sympathy messages

- State precisely (reservation, amount, letter, order) what you are acknowledging or confirming.
- Refer to the date and occasion of your last contact (telephone conversation, previous letter, in-person discussion).
- Describe what action, if any, is being taken.
- Tell when the reader will hear further from you or from someone else.
- If indicated, explain why you are not able to respond fully to the letter/request/gift at the moment.
- Express appreciation for the previous contact, for the kindness of the person in writing you, or for the business.
- Close with a courtesy or forward-looking statement.

What Not to Say

- Don't belabor explanations; letters of acknowledgment and confirmation are brief.
- Avoid a negative tone ("thought I'd make sure we're both talking about the same thing"). Repeat matter-of-factly the details of the items you're acknowledging or confirming.

Tips on Writing

∽ Write promptly. Acknowledgments are, by their very nature, sent immediately. One exception is acknowledging expressions of sympathy. Because of the hardships involved, responses may be sent up to six weeks later. Or, a close relative of the bereaved may write the acknowledgment: "Mother asked me to tell you how much she appreciated the loving letter of sympathy and the memorial you sent for Dad. She will be in touch with you as soon as she is able to."

Special Situations

∽ When a letterwriter asks about an issue better handled by someone else, acknowledge the letter and provide the name, address, and telephone number of the appropriate person. You can also forward the letter to the proper department and so notify your correspondent.

∽ Timely and regular business transactions need no acknowledgment: orders are received, merchandise is delivered, payments are sent. You would, however, acknowledge receipt in unusual situations. If the previous order went astray, you will want the sender to know that this one arrived. When you receive payment from someone to whom you've been sending collection letters, let the person know that payment has been received (and, by implication, that there will be no more collection letters). Acknowledge large or important payments, orders, and shipments—or those from first-time customers or suppliers. Acknowledge letters, requests, orders, manuscript submissions, or complaints that cannot be responded to immediately so that the person knows that action is being taken.

∽ Acknowledge mail that arrives in a supervisor's or co-worker's absence. Mention the absence without offering apologies or explanations. Do not refer to the contents of the letter; an exception is made for the announcement of a death or serious illness. Express sympathy on behalf of the other person and say that a letter will follow as soon as possible.

~ Organizations receiving memorial donations acknowledge receipt of the contribution and also notify the family so it can thank the donor personally.

~ Domestic hotel and motel reservations are often made and confirmed entirely by phone. Occasionally, however, written confirmation is necessary because of special conditions or changes of plans. Include your requirements: date, length of stay, kind of accommodation, price, extras requested (crib in a room, for example), wheelchair accessibility, availability of pool, HBO, entertaining facilities. Request written confirmation from foreign hotels or resorts. Include an International Reply Coupon (IRC) for any response or include your e-mail address or fax number.

~ If someone announces a divorce, avoid expressing either congratulations or sympathy (unless you know which is called for); in most cases, simply acknowledge the information.

~ An apology is acknowledged to let the other person know that you have received it (and accepted it, if that is the case).

~ If you cannot respond to a proposal, report, or manuscript right away, acknowledge its receipt to the sender and assure the person that you will communicate further as soon as you have evaluated it. People spend time writing reports, proposals, and manuscripts and are naturally eager for results. They will wait more patiently if their mailing has been acknowledged.

~ When you cannot make an immediate decision among job applicants, acknowledge receipt of their applications or résumés or thank them for their interviews. Tell them you will let them know as soon as a decision has been made. (If you have an idea of when this will be, say so.) Thank them for their interest in your organization.

Format

~ Routine acknowledgments and confirmations (receipt of applications, manuscripts, requests, payments) can be handled with preprinted cards or a simple form letter. Fill in the item received and the date of receipt.

~ For numerous wedding gifts or expressions of sympathy, send printed acknowledgment cards indicating that you'll respond soon. In the case of a public figure whose death inspires many messages of sympathy from people unknown to the family or deceased, printed or engraved cards or foldovers are sent (with no personal follow-up).

~ Use e-mail for routine acknowledgments and confirmations. For business records, keep hard copies or back-up file copies of these transactions.

~ For complicated business acknowledgments or confirmations, use letterhead stationery or memo paper.

~ Personal acknowledgments and confirmations are handwritten on informal personal stationery; e-mail can be used for casual situations.

WORDS

accept	approve	ensure	reassure
acknowledge	assure	indicate	receipt
affirm	confirm	notice	reply
agreed-upon	corroborate	notify	respond
appreciate	endorse	reaffirm	settle

PHRASES

as I mentioned on the phone

as we agreed yesterday

I enjoyed our conversation of

in response to your letter

I sincerely appreciated

look forward to continuing our
discussion

thank you for the package that

this will acknowledge the receipt of

to confirm our recent conversation

want to confirm in writing

we have received

will respond as soon as

SENTENCES

I enjoyed speaking with you this afternoon and look forward to our meeting next Thursday at 2:30 at your office.

Just a note to let you know that the printer ribbons arrived.

Thank you for remembering my ten-year anniversary with Lamb and Company.

Thank you for the wallpaper samples, which arrived this morning.

Thank you for writing me with your views on socialized medicine.

Thank you for your order, which we received yesterday; it will be shipped to you this week.

The family of Annis Gething gratefully acknowledges your kind and comforting expressions of sympathy.

The members of the Board of Directors and I appreciated your presentation yesterday and want you to know that we are taking your concerns under serious advisement.

This is to acknowledge receipt of the rerouted shipment of Doncastle tennis rackets, catalog number AE-78573.

This is to confirm our recent conversation about the identification and removal of several underground storage tanks on my property.

This will acknowledge receipt of your report on current voter attitudes.

This will confirm our revised delivery date of November 6.

We are proceeding with the work as requested by Jerome Searing in his May 3, 2002, telephone call.

We hereby acknowledge that an inspection of the storm drain and street construction installed by the Bagshaw Company in the Rockingham subdivision has been completed.

PARAGRAPHS

Your letter of July 16 has been referred for review and appropriate action. We value you as a customer and ask your patience while a response is being prepared.

Thank you for the update on the preparation of the Price-Stables contract. I appreciate knowing what progress you're making.

Thank you for your workshop proposal, which we have just received. Ms. Bramber is out of the office for the next two weeks but will contact you soon after she returns.

Thanks for the samples. As soon as we've had a chance to get them under the microscope and run some tests, we'll let you know what we find.

I've received your kind invitation to join the Friends of the Library committee. I need to review other commitments to be sure that I can devote as much time to the Friends as I'd like. I'll let you know next week. In the meantime, thanks for thinking of me.

The information you sent was exactly what I needed. It will take several weeks to reach a decision, but I'll call as soon as I do. In the meantime, thanks for your promptness.

Thanks for the call this morning, Janet. I'll see you on May 23 at 10:00 a.m. and will bring the spring lists with me.

I wanted you to know that I received your letter this morning, but as I'm leaving for Dallas later today I won't have time to look into the billing problem with the contractor for another week or so. If you need action sooner than that, give Agnes Laiter a call.

I'm glad we were able to reach an agreement on the telephone this morning. I'll have the contracts retyped—inserting the new delivery date of March 16, 2003, and the new metric ton rate of $55—and sent to you by the end of the week.

Thank you for telling me about the divorce. It's been too long since I've seen you. Can we get together sometime? How about breakfast Saturday morning? That used to work for us.

Thank you for your letter of June 9, describing the employee behavior you encountered on three different visits to our store. We are looking into the situation, and will let you know what we find. In the meantime, please accept our apologies for any embarrassment or unpleasantness you experienced.

Thank you for your letter of application and your résumé. We have received numerous responses to our advertisement, which means you may not hear from us immediately. Beginning March 1 we will call qualified applicants to arrange interviews.

We received your request for information on estrogen replacement therapy and for a sample of the placebo skin patch. Because of the enthusiastic response to our advertisement, we have temporarily exhausted our supplies of the skin patch. I'm enclosing the literature you requested, and will send the skin patch in approximately two weeks.

SAMPLE LETTERS

Dear Edna Bunthorne:

This will acknowledge your letter of August 6 addressed to Francis Moulton. Mr. Moulton is on a six-month medical leave of absence, and his interim replacement has not yet been named.

I am enclosing materials that will answer some of your questions, and I will refer the others to the new director as soon as possible.

If the delay is unacceptable to you, you may want to contact Kate Croy at the Lowder Foundation.

Sincerely,

Dear Professor Erlin:

Thank you for your paper, "The Rise and the Fall of the Supercomputer," which we received this week. Because of an overwhelming response to our call for symposium papers, our editorial staff will not be able to respond within the usual two to three weeks. It may be five to six weeks before you hear from us. Thanks for understanding.

Yours truly,

Dear Member,

Thank you for your order.

Unfortunately, we're temporarily out of stock on the item below. We've reordered it and expect to have a new supply in a few weeks. We'll ship it as soon as it arrives.

Sincerely,

Dear Dr. Breeve,

This is to confirm that you have permission to use the Great Organ of St. Luke's Church for an organ recital March 30 at 7:30 p.m. As agreed, you will be responsible for the expense of any organ repairs necessary for the recital.

Please call me to arrange for an extra key when you need to begin practicing.

We're delighted that someone of your talent will be using our wonderful old—but often forgotten—organ.

With best wishes,

Dear Geraldine Dabis:

We have received your loan application and will process it as quickly as possible. However, because of the complex nature of the application, it is being reviewed and evaluated by loan officers from two different divisions. This may delay our response somewhat.

If you have questions about the delay or about our process, please call me at 555-1216.

Yours truly,

See also: ACCEPTANCES, APPOINTMENTS, FOLLOW-UP, RESPONSES, SALES, THANK YOU, TRAVEL, WEDDINGS.

Letters of Adjustment

3

A reputation for handling customer claims quickly and fairly
is a powerful public relations tool for any firm.

—L. SUE BAUGH, MARIDELL FRYAR, DAVID THOMAS

Write a letter of adjustment in response to a customer's letter of complaint (also called a claims letter). Business imperfections—incorrect bills, damaged merchandise, late payments—are not as rare as we'd like. In most instances, adjustments are handled routinely. "Keeping an old customer is just as important as gaining a new one." (N.H. and S.K. Mager)

An adjustment letter serves to (1) correct errors and make good on company inadequacies; (2) grant reasonable full or partial adjustments in order to maintain good customer relations; or (3) deny unwarranted claims so tactfully that the customer's goodwill is retained.

In his classic *Handbook of Business Letters*, L.E. Frailey advises treating a complaint with as much respect as an order, letting customers know you are as eager to serve them as to sell them.

"Every unhappy customer will tell ten others about a bad experience, whereas happy customers may tell three." (Lillian Vernon)

The only thing worse than customers who complain are customers who don't complain—and take their business elsewhere. A claims letter gives you the opportunity to win the customer back. You will know when you have written a good letter of adjustment because the customer will return.

(To request an adjustment, see COMPLAINTS; this chapter deals only with making them.)

Kinds of Adjustment Letters

- billing/invoice errors
- credit
- damages
- exchanges
- explanations: oversight/error
- newspaper corrections
- refunds/discounts
- refusing to make (see REFUSALS)
- repairing damages
- replacements
- time extensions

- Open with a cordial statement ("Thank you for your letter of June 3"), a thank you for bringing the matter to your attention, or a sentiment such as "We were sorry to hear that . . ."
- Refer to the error, specifying dates, amounts, invoice numbers.
- If the customer was correct, say so.
- State your regret about the confusion, mix-up, or error.
- Explain your company's policy of dealing with customer claims, if appropriate.
- Describe how you will resolve the problem or what you've already done. Sometimes you give customers the choice of a replacement, a refund, or a credit to their account.
- Mention when you expect the problem to be resolved, even if it is only "immediately," "at once," or "as soon as possible."
- Reassure the customer: this error is rare; you do not expect a repeat occurrence of it; the company works hard to satisfy customers.
- Close by acknowledging the customer's patience, asking for continued customer loyalty, offering further cooperation, reaffirming the company's good intentions and the value of its products, or expressing your expectation that the customer will continue to enjoy your services and products for years to come.

What
Not to
Say

- Don't use the words "claim" or "complaint" even though that's how these incoming letters are commonly identified. To customers, the terms sound accusatory and judgmental, and the majority of them honestly believe they are due an adjustment. Instead of "The damage that you claim was due to improper packing" or "Your complaint has been received," substitute a word like "report" for "claim" and "complaint."

- Don't say how "surprised" you are ("I can't believe this happened"; "Not once in twenty years have we encountered this problem")— unless it truly is an exceptional occurrence. Customers assume that if the error happened to them, it could happen (and probably has) to anyone. You lose credibility.

- Don't repeat all the details of a problem or overemphasize it. A passing reference is sufficient. Focus on the solution rather than on the error. You want the latter to quickly become a vague memory for the customer.

- Avoid long explanations. Customers generally don't care about your difficulties with suppliers, employees, or shippers; they simply want an adjustment. Restrict your explanation, if you wish to include one, to several words ("due to a delayed shipment" or "because of power outages last week").

- Don't be excessively apologetic. A simple "We regret the error" is adequate for most slip-ups.

- Don't blame "computer error." By now people know that human beings run the computers, not vice versa, and this weak and obviously untrue excuse irritates people. And don't imply that these things are bound to happen from time to time. Although this may be true, it makes your company look careless.

- Don't make an adjustment grudgingly, angrily, impatiently, or condescendingly, and don't imply that you're doing the customer a big favor. This cancels the positive public relations effect of righting the error. Make your adjustment graciously or at least matter-of-factly even when the customer is angry or rude. Your attitude must be friendly and understanding; the "high road" leads to goodwill and customer satisfaction.

- Don't end your letter by mentioning the problem ("Again, we are so sorry that our Great Southwest Hiking Holiday was such an unpleasant experience for you") because it leaves the problem, not your goodwill and adjustment, uppermost in the reader's mind.

- Don't overstate company culpability or indicate in writing that the company was negligent. When negligence is involved, your lawyer can suggest the best approach for your letter.

Tips on Writing

∾ Respond promptly; this establishes your good intentions.

∾ Be specific: about the problem, about the steps you are taking, about what the customer can expect in the future. Vagueness leaves customers expecting more than is offered and unhappy when they don't get it.

∾ Assume responsibility when appropriate. Use the active voice ("We sent the wrong monitor") rather than the passive voice ("The wrong monitor was sent to you").

∾ When the customer has been inconvenienced, be generous with your sympathy. Sometimes out of fear that the customer will "take advantage" of such openness, businesses fail to give customers their due—and then pay for it in reduced customer satisfaction.

∾ In some cases, add a goodwill gesture: a discount coupon or gift certificate, or a reduction on the next order.

∾ Adjustment letters are easier to write when your company has a codified strategy for managing customer complaints. You can then follow and appeal to policy and handle similar situations evenhandedly; you will not have to reinvent the wheel for each claims letter.

∾ Old but still good advice: "Legalistic quibbles have no place in the answer to a complaint. The customer is rightly or wrongly dissatisfied; business is built only on satisfied customers. Therefore the question is not to prove who is right but to satisfy the customer. This doctrine has its limitations, but it is safer to err in the way of doing too much than in doing too little." (Mary Owens Crowther, *The Book of Letters*, 1923)

∾ An excellent resource for those who write letters of adjustment is Cheryl McLean, *Customer Service Letters Ready to Go!*, MTC Business Books, 1996.

Special Situations

~ Some problems are partly or wholly the customer's fault (failure to read installation instructions, excessive or inappropriate use). If you decide to grant the adjustment (most companies give customers the benefit of the doubt), don't assign blame to the customer; it undoes the goodwill you are establishing. When neither the company nor the customer is completely at fault, suggest a compromise adjustment or offer several solutions ("Because this item is not manufactured to be fire-resistant, we cannot offer you an exact exchange, but we would be glad to replace the fielder's glove at our wholesale cost, offer you a 30% discount on your next purchase, or repair the fire-damaged nylon mesh back"). "A compromise is the art of dividing a cake in such a way that everyone believes that he or she has got the biggest piece." (Ludwig Erhard)

~ When you deny the requested adjustment (a complete refund, for example), explain why: an investigation of the matter did not support it (include documents or itemize findings); standard company policy does not allow it (and violating the policy in this case is not possible); the item is no longer under warranty; the item was used in a specifically prohibited manner. Be gracious but firm. Express your sympathy for the customer's point of view, explain that their letter was considered carefully, appeal to their sense of fair play, and close with a positive statement (expressing your appreciation of past business and cooperation, offering a coupon, saying that this was a difficult letter to write but the only response consistent with your values of fairness and responsibility).

~ Before mailing a product recall notice, consult with your attorney since the wording is important. Most recalls are announced in a form letter that describes the recalled product, tells what the problem is, and explains how the consumer can receive an adjustment, replacement, or refund.

Format

~ Adjustment letters dealing with nonroutine problems are typed on letterhead stationery. For routine adjustment matters, use a half-sheet size memo or form letter with blanks to insert the details.

~ Small companies may return a copy of the customer's letter with a handwritten note: "We apologize for the error. Enclosed is a check for the difference."

~ If you learn of the problem by e-mail or fax, respond that way.

WORDS

accommodate	correct	refund	replace
amend	credit	regulate	return
apologize	rebate	reimburse	satisfaction
arrange	rectify	remedy	settle
compensate	redress	repair	solution

PHRASES

appreciate your pointing out
corrected invoice/statement/bill
greatly regret your dissatisfaction
I'm sorry to learn that
make amends for
our apologies
please disregard
prevent a recurrence

reduce the price
sincerely sorry to hear that
sorry for the inconvenience/
    misunderstanding
sorry to learn that
until you are completely satisfied
will receive immediate credit
you are correct in stating that

SENTENCES

I'm sorry about the error in filling your order—the correct posters are being shipped today.

Thank you for bringing to our attention the missing steel pole in the tetherball set you ordered from us.

Thank you for giving us the opportunity to correct the erroneous information published in the last issue of Tallboys' Direct Mail Marketer.

Thank you for your telephone call about the defective laser labels—you will receive replacement labels within two to three business days.

We appreciate the difficulties you have had with your Deemster Steam Iron, but all our appliances carry large-print, bright-colored tags alerting consumers to the safety feature of the polarized plug (one blade is wider than the other and the plug fits into a polarized outlet only one way).

We are pleased to offer you an additional two weeks, interest-free, to complete payment on your formal-wear rental.

We hope to continue to serve your banking needs.

We regret the difficulties you had with your last toner cartridge.

We're sorry you had to write; this should have been taken care of some time ago.

We were sorry to learn that you are dissatisfied with the performance of your Salten personal paper shredder.

Your business and goodwill are important to us.

You're right, the self-repairing zippers on your Carradine Brent Luggage should not have seized up after only two months' use.

You will receive immediate credit for the faulty masonry work, and we will send someone to discuss replacing it.

PARAGRAPHS

Thank you for responding to our recall notices and returning the Small World farm set to us for a refund. Small World has been making quality toys for children since 1976, and we regret the design error that made this set potentially dangerous to young children.

Thank you for calling to our attention the pricing error on our Bluewater automatic pool cleaners. Enclosed is a check for the difference. We look forward to serving you again.

Thank you for your telephone call. You are correct in thinking that you should not have been charged interest this past month. We have credited $2.85 to your account.

After carefully reading your letter of August 4, I consulted our shipping department. It appears that we did comply with the terms of the contract (documents enclosed).

I am sorry that your order was filled incorrectly. Enclosed are the back issues that you ordered. Please keep the others with our apologies.

Thank you for taking the time to let us know of your recent experience with one of our products. We are always interested in hearing from our customers but regret that it was this type of occurrence that prompted your letter.

SAMPLE LETTERS

Dear Mr. Stefanopoulos:

Thank you for your letter requesting a correction of several statements that appeared about you and your company in the most recent issue of *Small Business Today*. The information we were given was not double-checked; we apologize.

The correction appears on page 4 of this month's issue.

Sincerely,

Dear Eva Steer:

I am sorry that the Irish linens you purchased from us proved to be flawed.

Please return the order to us, complete with packaging. We will replace it at once and also refund your mailing costs.

I notice that you have been a loyal customer for the past eight years, so you know that our quality control people don't let something like this happen very often. I'm enclosing a discount good for 20% off your next order as our way of apologizing for your inconvenience.

Best regards,

~

Dear Gabriel Bagradian,

Thank you for your letter of July 7, appealing the $50 charge for the non-emergency use of the Werfel Community Hospital emergency room.

A review of the records shows that your son Stephan visited the emergency room on March 19 with a collapsed lung, not for treatment of acne. We regret the error that was made in coding the reason for the visit and have made an adjustment to your account.

We appreciate your spotting the error and letting us know about it so courteously.

Sincerely,
T. Haigasun
Billing Department

~

Dear Mrs. Painter,

Thank you for telling us about the infestation in our Wheatley cereal. We are sorry you had this experience and want you to know we share your concern.

Consumer satisfaction is most important to us, and we sincerely regret your recent experience with our product. Our company has strict standards of quality control. We carefully examine each lot of raw materials when it arrives. Sanitarians inspect our manufacturing plant continually and, in addition, make periodic checks of our suppliers' facilities. Food samples are collected all through the manufacturing process and are analyzed in our laboratories. We enforce these stringent procedures to ensure the production of high-quality, insect-free products.

The information you gave us about our product is being brought to the attention of the appropriate company officials.

Again, thank you for writing.

Yours truly,

~

Dear Mr. Steinmetz,

No, the motor on your vacuum should not have "worn out" six months after you purchased it. We can't be sure what the problem is, but this is unusual for our top-of-the-line Costello vacuum.

Please take the vacuum to one of our repair shops (see attached list to find the one closest to you). The personnel there will examine the machine and if they can repair it, they will do so and bill us. If they find that the machine is defective, we will arrange to have a replacement shipped to you.

Please accept our apologies for the inconvenience this has caused you.

~

Dear Mr. Ramsdell:
Re: Claim 02018-1134 WB 753

Enclosed is a check in full settlement of your claim.

Because Shipper's Transit Insurance was not purchased, the carrier's liability is limited to $1.25 per pound times the weight of the load. This conforms with tariff regulations.

To obtain full reimbursement for damages or loss you must file a claim with your corporation traffic department or its insurance carrier. Please check with them about this.

Thank you for your patience and cooperation during the necessary delays in processing your claim.

Sincerely,

~

Dear Mr. Magnus,

We were unhappy to hear that you felt the installation of your fiber-optical cable was "sloppily done" and the electricians "unprofessional."

We now have the report of two inspectors, one from our company and one from an independent oversight bureau, who visited your offices on November 11 and 12. Their evaluations indicate that the installation was meticulously done, that code standards were met or exceeded, that site cleanup was faultless, and that, in fact, there was no findable cause for objection.

Interviews with your staff members who had contact with the electricians turned up no negative information about their behavior.

In the light of these reports, we are unable to offer you the requested deep discount on our services.

~

See also: ACKNOWLEDGMENTS, APOLOGIES, BELATED, COMPLAINTS, CREDIT, REFUSALS, RESPONSES.

Advice

4

Advice . . . is a habit-forming drug. You give a dear friend a bit of advice today, and next week you find yourself advising two or three friends, and the week after, a dozen, and the week following, crowds!

—CAROLYN WELLS

Ask for advice only when you are open to it, not when you already know the "advice" you want to receive. That isn't fair to the person who spends time on a response. In addition, you may be unpleasantly surprised.

If you are the advice-giver, respond only to the issues raised by the other person; don't venture further afield.

If you have not been asked for advice, you are on shaky ground to volunteer it. "It is well enough when one is talking to a friend to hedge in an odd word by way of counsel now and then, but there is something mighty irksome, in its staring upon one in a letter where one ought only to see kind words and friendly remembrances." (Mary Lamb)

In general, give advice only when you have been sincerely asked for it.

Kinds of Letters Dealing with Advice

- asking for/requesting
- giving unsolicited
- offering suggestions
- rejecting
- responding to request for
- thanking for

- To ask for advice, briefly outline the issue. Tell what you expect from the other person and perhaps why you chose them in this situation. If you need the advice by a deadline, say so. Reassure them that they are not obliged to respond. Thank them for being available to you.

- To give advice, begin by rephrasing the other person's request ("You asked my advice about your college plans") or by explaining why you are writing (something came across your desk you thought might be of interest, or you had an idea that might be useful). State your opinion, advice, or suggestion. Explain your reasoning, if necessary. Tell what, if any, action you think the person might take. Include a disclaimer: "this is only my opinion," "I know you will use your own good judgment," "just an idea . . ." Finally, assure your reader of your confidence that they will make a good decision, deal with the situation, succeed at any task.

- To thank someone for advice, express your gratitude as you would for any gift, but tell how the advice was useful to you. If you didn't take the advice, thank the person for their time, effort, and concern. When you receive inappropriate or unwanted advice, assume—for politeness' sake—that they meant well and acknowledge their attention.

- Don't over-explain. Outline your suggestion or course of action in a few sentences. "Whatever advice you give, be short." (Horace) Brevity is difficult in a letter giving advice. We are tempted to offer all the wisdom accumulated over a lifetime. Resist. After writing your letter, delete half of it. The person who wants to know more will ask.

- Avoid "should" as in "I think you should . . ." No one can say what anyone else "should" or "ought to" do. Find a more flexible way of phrasing your suggestion.

- Don't imply that you've found the one, correct answer. Offer instead alternatives, possibilities, fresh approaches.

Tips on Writing

 ✎ When giving advice, use tact, tact, and more tact. Read your letter as though it had been sent to you. How does it make you feel? Have someone read it to make sure it isn't abrasive or patronizing. "Advice is like snow; the softer it falls, the longer it dwells upon, and the deeper it sinks into the mind." (Samuel Taylor Coleridge)

 ✎ Start with a compliment or upbeat remark to frame your advice in a positive context.

 ✎ Be specific. "Get a grip!" or "Shape up!" or "Try harder!" is not advice. Mignon McLaughlin wrote: "'Pull yourself together' is seldom said to anyone who can." When possible, include names and telephone numbers of resources, costs of what you're recommending, clear-cut steps to the goal.

 ✎ When possible, attribute the advice to someone else. Especially when your advice is unsolicited, consider getting another person to offer the advice you want to give. Advice that is unwelcome from a parent is often accepted from a third party. Advice from a superior may be better received from a colleague—or vice versa.

 ✎ When giving unsolicited advice, be respectful and low-key, mildly suggesting that this is something the person might want to think about. In this instance, passive voice or indirect phrasing is useful ("If the loans could be consolidated" instead of "If you would consolidate your loans"). An intermediate step might be to write, "I noticed that . . ." or "Do you need any help?" and, without giving advice then and there, indicate that you are willing to do so.

Special Situations

 ✎ Letters giving professional advice (a lawyer advising a client, a doctor outlining a program of patient health care, a teacher suggesting tests for a child) is written much more carefully than most advice letters. The advice must be professionally defensible and might include references or sources for the advice. Keep copies of the letter (and sometimes send them to third parties). On occasion, another person's opinion may be needed to reinforce the advice and protect yourself. Ours is a litigious society; good Samaritans enjoy no protection under the law for their good works and intentions.

 ✎ If you request advice about investing money or about a situation with significant consequences, emphasize that the other person will not be held responsible for the outcome. With a written absolution, the recipient might feel easier about giving advice. You get what you pay for, however, and you might be better off seeing a professional (financial counselor, psychologist, lawyer, realtor).

~ If your first letter of advice is ignored or poorly received, let it be your last letter of advice to that person. "The true secret of giving advice is, after you have honestly given it, to be perfectly indifferent whether it is taken or not, and never persist in trying to set people right." (Hannah Whitall Smith)

~ Don't give advice warning against individuals, companies, or products; you could create legal problems for yourself. It's generally not a problem to recommend a person or an organization although, if you are a public figure, you might get asked pretty smartly to explain why you didn't mention certain others.

Format

~ Use letterhead stationery to write a business associate outside the firm, memo paper or letterhead to write someone inside the firm, and informal stationery for social relationships.

~ The choice of a handwritten or typewritten letter of advice can set the tone of your letter. A handwritten note to an employee might be perceived as too personal and a bit apologetic, where the typewritten message appears objective and matter-of-fact. On the other hand, writing a personal note in some sensitive business situations indicates that you are writing as a friend as well as a customer, client, or supervisor.

WORDS

advantageous	consult	forethought	precaution	suitable
advisable	counsel	guidance	principle	urge
advocate	debate	guidelines	prudent	useful
appropriate	desirable	insight	rational	valuable
apt	direction	instructions	reasonable	warn
beneficial	encourage	open-minded	recommend	weigh
careful	examine	opinion	resource	wisdom
caution	expedient	persuade	sensible	worthwhile
consider	fitting	practical	study	

PHRASES

alert you to the possibility	look into
as I understand it	might want to
backseat driver	piece of advice
compare notes	so far as I know
consider carefully	speak for
I am convinced that	take care of
I don't like to interfere, but	take into account
I feel/assume/presume/think	take it amiss/the wrong way
I have the impression that	take to heart
if you don't mind	think about
in my estimation/judgment/	think through
opinion/view	to my way of thinking
I noticed that	to the best of my knowledge
I take it that	weigh both courses of action
it seems to me	what you could do
just wanted to suggest/recommend	whether you take my advice or not
keep a lookout for/an eye on	you've probably already thought of
kick around this idea	this, but

SENTENCES

Although I liked what you wrote about switching your major from Physics to Astronomy, I have a suggestion you might want to consider.

Do you have any advice about how I can raise morale in the Accounting Department?

Ever since you asked my opinion about the Middlemarch line, I've been mulling over the situation, weighing the benefits against the rather considerable cost.

I don't usually give unsolicited advice, but this seems to me to be a special case.

I hope this is the sort of advice you wanted.

I'm considering a switch from the technical to the management ladder—do you have any wise, helpful words for me?

I'm writing to you for advice.

I thought I should mention this.

I took your excellent advice and I'm grateful.

I will appreciate any comments or advice you'd care to give.

I would be grateful for your frank opinion about our registering Jermyn for kindergarten this year (he won't be five yet) instead of waiting another year.

I wouldn't ordinarily presume to tell you your business, but I'm concerned.

Thank you for your unerring advice about our hot rolling equipment—we're back on schedule.

There is one thing you might want to consider.

We are unable to take your advice just now, but we're grateful to you for thinking of us.

Would you be willing to tell me quite frankly and confidentially what you think about my interpersonal skills?

You asked for my opinion about switching service providers—here it is.

You must, of course, use your own judgment, but I would suggest this.

Your counsel and advice have meant a great deal to me.

Your idea is excellent and I may regret not going that route, but I'm going to try something else first.

You were kind enough to ask my advice about the Hexam-Riderhood merger—this is what I think.

PARAGRAPHS

You asked what I thought of the new store hours. They are certainly more convenient for customers and will bring us the early evening business that can make a difference in our year-end numbers. However, I wonder if it is profitable to stay open so late on Saturday evenings. Could we keep a record of Saturday evening sales for a month?

We suggest that, instead of external motors and vacuum seals around the drive-shafts, you install internal, pancake motors to handle the required tension ranges. Let us know if this takes care of the problem.

You might want to hire an investment banking firm to help with your financial restructuring. Such a firm can assist you in exploring strategic alternatives to rebuild your liquidity and improve value for shareholders.

Have you noticed that the newsletter is not carrying its own weight? I wonder if we ought to continue to subsidize it. I suggest we put it on a subscription basis. This will also oblige it to become more responsive to readers, one of the current complaints being that it isn't. If it can't survive on the income from subscriptions, I question its necessity.

I would like to suggest that you examine the issue of cooperation versus competition in the school environment. In the three years our children have been students here, I've noticed the school is strongly oriented toward competition, with little value assigned to cooperative learning, cooperative sports, and cooperative activities. I'm enclosing several reports and studies on this issue. May I stop in and speak to you about this next week?

I'm flattered that you want my advice on choosing a college. However, you seem interested in the eastern colleges, and I know little about them. I wonder if you wouldn't want to talk to Ling Ch'ung, who in fact knows quite a bit about them.

Thanks so much for your advice on the hip roof and preparing for the building inspector. I doubt if she would have given me the building permit the way I was going about things!

I'm grateful to you for the time you took to outline a solution to our current problem. We are interested in your ideas. However, we just started working on another approach last Thursday and I'm going to wait and see how that develops. I'll let you know if we are later able to consider your plan. In the meantime, thanks for your helpful suggestions.

SAMPLE LETTERS

Dear Mr. Brimblecombe:

I was present at the Music Educators' Conference when your elementary school jazz band performed. I was impressed to hear that out of a school population of 640, you have 580 students in your instrumental music program. This is unusual, as I'm sure you know.

Do you have any advice for other elementary music directors trying to increase the number of student musicians? If you do not have the time to respond by letter, perhaps you could indicate on the enclosed postcard a time and date when I could call you long-distance. I'd appreciate any tips you might have.

Gratefully,

Dear Walter,

I hope you will forgive this unasked-for intrusion into your business affairs, but I felt I would be less than a friend if I didn't say something after visiting one of your gift shops last week (the one on Lewis Street).

I was surprised to see the china jumbled together on the shelves, the collector's dolls looking dusty and wrinkled, and some of the figurines chipped and dirty. This hasn't seemed to hurt business—customers were lined up at both counters when I was there—but over the long term it might be unfortunate. I just wondered if you were aware of the situation.

With best wishes,

Dear Tony,

As one of our most aggressive sales representatives, you have an enviable record and I expect you will be up for an award at the end of the year. The flip side of this aggressiveness is, unfortunately, a certain abrasive attitude that has been reported by several customers lately.

I'd like to suggest two things. One, come in and talk this over with me. I can give you some idea of how people are responding to you and why it's a problem over the long term if not the short term. Two, spend a day or two with Tom Jerningham. He has a manner that is effective without being too insistent.

Let me hear from you.

Sincerely,

Dear Shreve,

We are both proud of how well you're doing in college—your grades, your job, your friends. I think we've told you often how much we love you and admire the way you handle things. BUT . . . (did you know there was a "but" coming?) we are extremely concerned about one new thing in your life: cigarettes. Will you please think about what it will mean if you let this habit take hold?

I'm enclosing some literature on the subject.

We won't nag you about this, but we had to speak up strongly at least once and say that, based on our experience, knowledge, and love for you, this is not a good choice.

Love,

Dear Marion and Leopold,

Thanks so much for driving all the way into the city just to look over the situation with the house. The decision whether to repaint or put on all new siding was really getting us down. Your advice was excellent, and we feel good about our decision. It was also wonderful to see you again!

Love,

Dear Hazel,

I appreciate your concern, and I am sure you have good reasons for feeling that we ought to move as soon as possible. However, after careful consideration of your proposal, I have decided that the situation is fairly stable at present and we should stay put.

Let me know if you have further information that would affect this decision.

Yours truly,

Dear Uncle Thorkell,

Thank you for your letter. I appreciated your advice about my earrings. I know it doesn't seem "manly" to you, but my friends and I like earrings. I'm coming home at the end of the month for a visit, and I don't want you to be disappointed when you see that I still have them. Although I am grateful for your concern, I am going to keep wearing earrings. I hope this won't hurt our good relationship.

Love,

See also: EMPLOYMENT, INSTRUCTIONS, REFUSALS, REQUESTS, SENSITIVE, THANK YOU.

Anniversaries and Birthdays

5

*I know a lot of people didn't expect our relationship to last—but we've
just celebrated our two months' anniversary.*

—BRITT EKLAND

With the availability of attractive greeting cards today, few people send personal anniversary or birthday notes and letters. However, anyone who has received a commercial card with only a signature knows how much pleasure could have been added with a handwritten line or two. For most people, finding a letter enclosed in the card is as good as receiving a gift.

Anniversaries once referred primarily to wedding anniversaries. Today, people celebrate business, service, personal, and other anniversaries and they appreciate being remembered on their special day.

Some businesses send birthday and anniversary cards to their customers as a goodwill gesture.

Send Letters or Cards for

- anniversary of a death
- birthday
- business goodwill (see GOODWILL)
- business or business association anniversary
- customers' birthdays or anniversaries (see SALES)
- invitations to birthday or anniversary celebrations (see INVITATIONS)
- personal achievement or service anniversary
- wedding anniversary (spouse, parents, family members, friends)

- Mention the occasion (if you don't know the number of years, refer to "your service anniversary," "your birthday," or "the anniversary of Beryl's death").

- Include, whenever possible, an anecdote, a shared memory, good-hearted humor, or a sentence telling why the person is important to you.

- End with good wishes for another anniversary period or for the coming years and with assurances of your affection, love, admiration, warmth, interest, delight, pleasure, continued business support, or other appropriate sentiment.

- Don't detract from your greetings by including other information or news; remain focused on the anniversary or birthday. The exception is the newsy letter to a family member or close friend.

- Don't include "joking" references to advancing age, incapacity, passing years, the difficulties of married life, becoming a fixture at the office. Clever cracks about age and marriage and length of service may evoke reluctant smiles, but they carry little warmth. Avoid negative greeting cards that assume all 21-year-olds can hardly wait to get to a bar, that "the big 4-0" is depressing, and that 50-year-olds are over the hill.

Tips on Writing

～ Birthday or anniversary greetings can be personalized with a quotation: "The great thing about getting older is that you don't lose all the other ages you've been." (Madeleine L'Engle) "The fact was I didn't want to look my age, but I didn't want to act the age I wanted to look either. I also wanted to grow old enough to understand that sentence." (Erma Bombeck) "The marriages we regard as the happiest are those in which each of the partners believes that he or she got the best of it." (Sydney J. Harris)

～ Keep a supply of greeting cards on hand. At the beginning of the year, note dates to remember on the calendar or in a computer file (the gathering of dates is time-consuming only the first time you do it). On the first of each month, choose and address cards to all those celebrating that month. On the upper right hand corner of the envelope (which will later be covered by a stamp) pencil in the date of the birthday or anniversary—and mail each one a few days before the date.

〜 Collect small, flat, useful gifts that can be inserted in a greeting card: handkerchiefs, bookmarks, postage stamps, lottery tickets, art postcards, dollar bills. You can also plump up a birthday or anniversary card with photographs, newspaper clippings, and recipes.

〜 A number of Internet sites allow you to choose and personalize greeting cards to be sent by e-mail.

Special Situations

〜 Keep track of service anniversaries in your company; sending a note to mark the date creates company loyalty, especially if you add a complimentary remark about the person's work. In the case of colleagues, personalize the note with a recalled shared experience. Goodwill is also built when you remember the anniversary of your relationship with important suppliers or customers.

〜 Birthday and anniversary goodwill cards are sometimes sent to individual customers. William B. Dudley, financial adviser, says sending these cards is a way of keeping in touch with people; he sends more cards to people with whom he has not done business than he does to clients. "It is one way of marketing my services and keeping my name in front of people."

〜 In her book *The Bestseller*, Olivia Goldsmith points out, tongue-in-cheek, that it is considered bad form to wish authors on their birthdays "many happy returns" since to a writer "returns" are unsold books returned to the publisher.

〜 Congratulations are appreciated on the anniversary of a significant personal achievement—abstaining from smoking or drinking, for example—but only between people who know each other well.

〜 Write close friends and relatives who have lost someone on the anniversary of the death. Don't worry about "bringing up sad memories." In one of her columns Ann Landers wrote, "I was among those who had the mistaken notion that it was painful for family members to hear references to a loved one who had died. Many readers called me on it, and I know better now." The person is well aware of the date, and will be grateful that others remember. When someone close to you has lost a spouse after many years of marriage, you might want to send the survivor a special note on the couple's wedding anniversary.

Format

∾ For business, sales-oriented, or official letters, send typed or handwritten messages on letterhead or personal-business stationery.

∾ Commercial greeting cards are appropriate for non-business uses, as long as you add a handwritten note.

∾ E-mailed birthday and anniversary wishes are also received happily.

∾ Many newspapers have columns where family and friends can publish birthday or anniversary congratulations (usually for a fee). Often this is done in conjunction with an open house or reception to celebrate the anniversary.

WORDS

celebration	heartfelt	milestone	remember
congratulations	honored	progress	special
delighted	landmark	prosperity	successful
future	memorable	red-letter day	unique
happy	memories	remarkable	

PHRASES

all good wishes	important day
anticipate another period of success	look forward to the next ten years
celebrate with you	on the occasion of
convey our warmest good wishes	send our love
great pleasure to wish you	

SENTENCES

Congratulations on forty years of outstanding contributions to Heaslop-Moore Plastics.

Congratulations on the tenth anniversary of Stanley Graff Real Estate—it has been a pleasure serving all your stationery needs!

Every good wish to both of you for much health, happiness, prosperity, and many more years of togetherness.

Here's a question for you from Ruth Gordon: "How old would you be if you didn't know how old you were?"

May you enjoy many more anniversaries—each happier than the last.

May you live as long as you want, and never want as long as you live! (traditional birthday wish)

May you live long and prosper!

On the occasion of your 25th wedding anniversary, we send you our best wishes for continued love and happiness together.

Today marks the fifth anniversary of Archie's death, and I wanted you to know that we still miss him and that you are in our thoughts today.

PARAGRAPHS

Best wishes for a happy anniversary to a couple we have long admired and loved. May your relationship continue to be a blessing to both of you as well as to all those who know you.

This marks the tenth anniversary of our productive and happy business association. In that time, we have come to appreciate Fausto Babel Inc.'s prompt service, reliable products, and knowledgeable staff. I'm sure the next ten years will be equally happy and productive. Congratulations to all of you.

Happy 1st Anniversary! I have such lovely memories of your wedding day. I hope you have been gathering more happy memories of your first year of married life.

Barbara and Dick Siddal celebrate their 50th wedding anniversary on February 14. They have four children, nine grandchildren, and many wonderful friends. Love and congratulations from the whole family.

Sunday is the first anniversary of Emily's death, and I couldn't let the day go by without writing to see how you are getting along and to tell you that all Emily's friends here in Groves Corners miss her very much.

SAMPLE LETTERS

Dear Muriel Joy,

Happy birthday! I'm sending you 6 quarters, 6 colored bows for your hair, 6 teddybear stickers, and 6 tiny horses for your collection.

How old did you say you are today?

Love,
Aunt Dinah

Dear Dr. Arnold,

On behalf of the governing board, I would like to congratulate you on ten years of outstanding service as headmaster. Under your leadership the School has established itself among the premier ranks of such institutions.

Be assured of our continued admiration and support.

Very sincerely yours,

Dear Winnie and Ed,

Congratulations to you both on the fifteenth anniversary of Leitner's Heating & Plumbing. As you know by now, you're our best (our only!) supplier, and the reason is simple: you're a class act. Quality and competence have paid off for you, and nobody could be happier for you than I. Best wishes with the next fifteen years.

Dear Auntie Em,

I send you love and hugs on your 80th birthday. If only I were there to celebrate with you!

I read this once: "Years in themselves mean nothing. How we live them means everything." (Elisabeth Marbury) I hope I live my years as well as you've lived yours!

Speaking of which, how is the bridge group? the golf foursome? the church cleaning crew? your birthday luncheon friends? your bowling game? your Monday night dinners with the family? And are you still going to Las Vegas in February?

(Watch the mail for a small package from me!)

Love,
D.

Dear Rabbi Wassermann,

On behalf of the members and officers of the Adath Women's League, I send you best wishes for a joyous birthday and a happy, healthy year!

Karen Engelschall
President
Adath Women's League

Dear Martin,

All of us here at Eden Land Corporation congratulate you at Chuzzlewit Ltd. on your twenty years of solid contributions in the field of architecture.

We know that when we do business with you we can count on superior designs, reasonable costs, and dependable delivery dates.

May the success of these first twenty years lead to an even more successful second twenty.

With best wishes,

Dear Penrod,

Congratulations on your twelfth birthday. I hope you have a wonderful time and get everything you want (although, from what your father tells me, I hope you don't want another slingshot).

Your uncle and I are sorry we can't be there to celebrate with you, but I'm sending you a little something in a separate package. Have a good time and give everyone a hug for us.

Happy birthday!

Dear Grandma Annie,

I know you and Grandpa Oliver would have been married 65 years today—and that you still miss him. I love my photograph of the two of you taken at your 60th wedding anniversary party. I think about him—and about you—a lot.

I hope this day isn't too sad for you. Fortunately you have a lot of happy memories—maybe they'll be some comfort.

Just thinking about you . . .

Love from
Monica

See also: ANNOUNCEMENTS, BELATED, CONGRATULATIONS, FAMILY, GOODWILL, INVITATIONS, THANK YOU.

Announcements

6

It is good news, worthy of all acceptation! and yet not too good to be true.

—MATTHEW HENRY

Announcements, whether formal or informal, make an art of stating essential facts in the fewest possible words. A little like this paragraph.

Announcements Are Made for

- acquisition
- address change
- anniversary: business/wedding (see ANNIVERSARIES)
- baby birth or adoption
- change in benefits (reduced/increased/additional), policies (purchasing/hiring), regulations, procedures (billing dates)
- collection actions on overdue account (see COLLECTION)
- company merger/reorganization
- death
- divorce
- engagement (see WEDDINGS)
- graduation
- layoff (see EMPLOYMENT)
- marital separation
- meeting/workshop/conference
- merger or acquisition

- new company policy/directions/administration/management
- new division/subsidiary
- new home/house/apartment/condo
- new office/business/professional practice/service/career
- new partner/executive/associate/employee
- open house: school/business
- price/rent increase/reduction
- product recall
- promotion
- resignation/retirement (see also EMPLOYMENT)
- wedding (see WEDDINGS)

- Express pleasure in making the announcement.
- List key details of the news or event: who, what, when, where, why.
- To announce a meeting, include: the name of the organization, sub-committee, or group; the date, time, place, and purpose of the meeting; a request to notify a contact person if unable to attend. This can be done by preprinted postcard or by in-house memo or e-mail. To announce a directors' meeting, follow the format fixed by corporate by-laws or by state or federal laws; a waiver of notice or a proxy card is often enclosed along with a postage-paid reply envelope.
- To announce the opening of a new business or store, use an invitation format to ask customers to an open house or special sales event.
- To announce changes in company policies, benefits, procedures, or regulations, include: an expression of pleasure in announcing the change; a description of the change; a reference to the former policy, if necessary for clarification; an explanation of what the change will mean for employees or customers; printed instructions or guidelines if appropriate; the reason for the change and why it is an improvement; the deadline for implementing the change; the name and telephone number of a contact person for questions; an expression of your enthusiasm about the change; appreciation for help in effecting the change.
- To announce a birth or adoption, use engraved, printed, hand-lettered, commercial, or designed-by-you notes. Include: the baby's full name

and, if not obvious from the name or if still unnamed, whether it's a boy or girl; birthdate (and time, if you wish) or age (if the baby is adopted); parents' full names; siblings' names (optional); some expression of happiness ("pleased to announce"). Baby announcements are made by unmarried parents ("Julia Norman and Basil Fane announce the birth of their son, Alec Norman-Fane"), by single parents ("Jean Emerson announces the birth of her son, Howard Thede Emerson"), and by married couples where each uses a separate name. Newspaper birth announcements include: the date of birth; sex of child and name, if known; parents' names and hometowns; grandparents' names. Some newspapers allow weight and height information and such sentiments as "welcome with love" or the mention of "many aunts, uncles, and cousins" in listing the baby's relatives. Check with your newspaper about its guidelines.

- To announce a change of address, use forms available from the United States Postal Service, commercial change of address notes, or printed cards: "As of July 1, Sybil Knox (formerly Sybil Coates or Mrs. Adrian Coates) will be living at 15 Morland Drive, Houston, TX 77005, 713/555-1234."

- To announce a graduation, use the printed announcements available through most high schools and colleges. Since space at graduation ceremonies is often limited, announcements are more common than invitations. There is no obligation to send a gift in response to an announcement (a congratulatory card is usually sent), but since many people feel so obligated, it is kinder to send announcements only to those close to the graduate.

- To announce a separation or divorce to family and friends (which is a personal decision), state the news briefly ("We regret to inform you that our divorce was finalized on December 1") or frame the news as a change of address, telling where each person and the children will live after a certain date. If the woman resumes her birth name, identify her that way. You are not obliged to explain what has happened; if people sense from your announcement that you are retaining some privacy, it will be easier to cope the next time you see them. Notify banks, businesses, charge accounts, and creditors of the changed circumstances.

- Deaths are announced in several ways: (1) a death notice is inserted (usually for a fee) in the obituary section of the newspaper; (2) a news article describes the person's achievements and contributions; (3) printed announcements are sent to out-of-town friends and acquaintances; (4) handwritten notes are sent to close family and friends who live out of town. The deceased person's address book will indicate who should be notified. The newspaper obituary notice includes: name of deceased, including a woman's birth name if she wasn't already using it; address; date of death; age at time of death; names, relationships, and hometowns of survivors; affiliations; personal or career information; date and place of services and interment; whether services are private or open to friends and relatives; suggestions for flowers or memorial contributions; name, address, and telephone number of funeral home. Since the death announcement appears in the paper almost immediately, hand-deliver it or read it over the phone.

What Not to Say

- Don't include unrelated information or news. Although there are some exceptions (changes in company policy, for example), an announcement is not meant for lengthy explanations, instructions, or descriptions. An announcement can become diluted when part of a longer communication.

Tips on Writing

〰 Send your announcement as soon as possible after the event. "The first rule of thumb about announcing an event . . . is that *your* announcement reaches the reader before the news travels by other means. If your announcement is old news, it has arrived too late." (Dianne Booher)

〰 Ask someone to double-check your spelling and the general content. The announcement with errors in it is announcing something very different from what was intended.

Special Situations

〰 Combine routine announcements (new type of billing statement, new address, or meeting notice) with goodwill or sales messages.

~ A news release announces information of interest to the general public (product recall; annual or quarterly financial report; business anniversary; fundraiser; new programs, policies, executives; company achievements, mergers, or acquisitions). Sent to newspaper editors and to radio and television station news directors, the news release includes, along with the announcement, your organization's name and address and the name and telephone number of a contact person. Address the news release to a specific person; call and ask for a name if you don't have one. Double or triple space, leaving wide margins, and answer the who-what-when-where-why-how questions in the first paragraph or two. Double-check accuracy of your facts and explain any unfamiliar terms. News releases traditionally have "more" typed at the bottom of each page except the last, which has "- 30 -" or " # # # " to indicate the end.

Format

~ Business announcements are made in traditional letter format typed on letterhead stationery. When sent to large numbers of people, form letters are used.

~ Use a memo format for interoffice announcements (new benefits package, change in flex-hours procedures). Sometimes e-mail is a good choice.

~ Formal announcements are printed or engraved in black ink on a white or cream-colored card (with matching envelopes). Stationery stores and printers have sample announcements ranging from traditional to modern in a variety of fonts, papers, inks, and formats.

~ Announcements made to close friends and family are handwritten on foldovers or personal stationery.

~ Postcards are appropriate for announcing changes of address, meetings, and special sales.

WORDS

announce	inform	reveal
celebrate	introduce	share
delighted	mention	signal
gratified	notice	
happy	pleased	
honor	report	

PHRASES

announces the appointment of

are pleased/proud/happy to announce

give notice that

happily announce the merger of/a new subsidiary

have the honor of announcing

it is with great pleasure that we announce

joyfully announce the birth/ adoption/arrival of

make known/public

notice is hereby given that

public announcement

take pleasure in announcing

wish to announce/inform/ advise you

SENTENCES

A meeting of the Broadway-Aldine Community Council will be held October 3 at 7:00 p.m. in the NewBank boardroom to elect board members and officers for the coming year.

Ben Bowser announces that by permission of the court of Ramsey County, New Jersey, April 18, 2002, he will now be known as Benjamin Middleton.

Broadbent Civil Engineering, Inc., is proud to announce the opening of offices in Denver and Salt Lake City.

Dolores Haze (formerly Mrs. Richard F. Schiller) has changed her address to 155 Carol Avenue, Gilberts, IL 60136.

Important notice of change in terms: Effective January 1, 2004, your credit card agreement will be amended as follows.

Isabel Wahrfield and Frank Goodwin announce the dissolution of their marriage, effective July 15.

Mrs. Rachel Dean announces the engagement of her daughter Susan to Richard Tebben.

Nguyen Van Truy and Tran Huong Lang are proud and happy to announce the birth of their son Nguyen Van Tuân on March 11, 2002.

Please be advised that your payment due date has been changed to the sixteenth day of each month.

Vanderhof Industries, Inc. is pleased to announce the acquisition of the Connelly-Smith-Dulcy Energy Group, a Gordon-area company with ninety-seven employees that specializes in energy development services.

With great sadness we announce the death of our husband and father, Leon Gonsalez.

PARAGRAPHS

Fairford Corporation, Cooper City, announces that it has reached a distributorship agreement with Antoine-Lettice, based in Paris, France, granting them exclusive marketing rights for its Superbe! ultra-high-pressure waterjet equipment in France and Italy, with nonexclusive rights for the rest of Europe.

Averill Airlines will now serve Paris's Charles de Gaulle Airport (previously Orly). Airport transfers included in any of our vacation packages will provide convenient motorcoach transportation between Charles de Gaulle Airport and Port Maillot Station in Paris (formerly Montparnasse Station).

Miles and I have decided that we would make better friends than spouses. As of last week, we have canceled our engagement. We are both, I think, quite relieved, although we still think the world of each other. I know how happy you were for me when I wrote about our engagement, so I wanted to let you know right away that you can still be happy for me—but not because I'm engaged.

Carrie and Frederick Josser, New London, celebrated their twenty-fifth wedding anniversary on March 2. An open house was hosted by Cynthia and Ted Josser of Collins. Eight proud children and many friends and relatives were there.

I'm sorry to tell you that Mother died on July 11 of a heart attack. I know how much your friendship and your lively letters meant to her over the years. She spoke of you often.

We regret to announce that our Davy Jones Aquarium Pump, Model no. 686, has been found to be defective. It is possible that it could deliver a fatal shock. Please return your pump as soon as possible to the store where you purchased it or call the toll-free number below for instructions.

Eggerson Power Equipment Company is proud to announce the opening of a new store on County Road B and Highway 47. One of the largest power equipment sources in the state, the new store specializes in an exhaustive in-store stock and a forty-eight-hour "we can get it" guarantee.

Cornelia (Kay) Motford, George and Gladys are now living at 1941 Knowles Avenue, Centralia, KY 42330 (502/555-4590). Henry Moulton Pulham is living at 332 Riverside Drive, Lexington, KY 40507 (606/555-2441).

Montford Estates is pleased to announce the expansion of its commercial construction division. The division offers cost-efficient, high-quality commercial construction with emphasis on interior detailing.

Georgina Gardner has been promoted to director of retail leasing for Pelham Development Properties. She will be responsible for leasing Pelham Mall in downtown Brandon.

Due to the rapid rise in labor and operating costs, Ames Fast Maintenance finds it necessary to increase service charges as of September 1. Service charge increases will vary, depending upon the type of service your company uses: on call, when needed, monthly preventive maintenance.

The Board of Directors of the Fiske Corporation will meet on Wednesday, December 3, at 10:00 a.m. at the Company's central office in Harrington. New contracts for executives will be discussed, and such other business as may come before the meeting will be acted upon. If you cannot attend, please sign the enclosed waiver of notice.

Thanks to you, and the orders that have been pouring in for our special line of children's clothing, we are able to make greater bulk purchases of raw materials and thus manufacture at a lower cost. We are proud to announce that we are passing on these savings to you. Enclosed is our current catalog, but please note the new low prices printed in red.

Francis Getliffe, age 44, of Cambridge. Survived by wife, Katherine March Getliffe; son, Francis, Jr.; brother Herbert; also nieces and nephews and good friends from C.P. Snow, Inc. Special thanks to the staff at Cambridge Lutheran Hospital. Memorial service Sunday at 2:00 p.m. at the Hillside Memorial Funeral Home. Family will receive friends one hour prior to service. Interment Hillside, with reception following in the Hillside Community Room. Memorials preferred. Hillside Memorium, 555-1216.

SAMPLE LETTERS

Dear Friend,

We have moved! During the past fifteen years we were so crowded in our old location that sometimes customers had to stand shoulder to shoulder or squeeze through the aisles. Nowadays you'll find it much easier to call on Taylor & Company.

Easy parking facilities in our parking lot and pleasant offices will make it simple for you to meet all your printing needs.

Enclosed is a map showing the new location, along with a one-time 10% discount coupon. Come in and see us while the paint's still fresh!

Sincerely yours,

Announcements

Brangwen International
is pleased to announce
that Lydia Lensky
has joined the firm
as a partner.
She will direct the
Southeast Asia Operations.

〜

FOR: Immediate Release

Boorman, Inc. of Menzies announces the recall of its fresh and frozen sandwiches because of the discovery of bacterial contamination during a recent Food and Drug Administration (FDA) test. Some of the sandwiches were found to contain *Listeria monocytogenes*, a bacterium that can endanger fetuses, infants, pregnant women, the elderly, and people with weakened immune systems.

No illnesses have been reported.

Please destroy all Boorman QuickWich sandwiches from lot 480032 or return them to Boorman for a refund.

〜

Paul J. Maggio, D.D.S.
and Matthew J. Maggio, D.D.S.
announce the opening
of their new office
at 1099 Kenyon Road
Fort Dodge, Iowa 50501
(515/576-1981)
and an open house
on July 15, 2004

〜

Dear Bondholder:

This letter is to inform you that a portion of the July 1, 2003, debt service payment for the above-referenced bond issue was made with monies transferred from the Reserve Fund established pursuant to Section 4.09 of the Indenture of Trust dated December 1, 1997, between Simmons International and Herbert Banking & Trust, as Trustee. Use of such monies in the Reserve Fund does *not* constitute an Event of Default under the indenture. However, the Trustee considers this information may be of interest to bondholders and potential bondholders.

Sincerely,

〜

Bonnie and Steven Goldsmith
are most happy to announce
the arrival of their daughter
Emily Virginia
born in Korea May 23, 1989
welcomed home October 11, 1989

Dear Customer:

As of May 1 of this year, your garbage hauling fee will be increased by $1.95 per month. We are always reluctant to raise prices, but are obliged to do so in this case by a recent ruling of the Silvius County Board of Commissioners.

In order to conserve landfill space, all garbage collected in Silvius County since July of 1989 has been required to be taken to the new recovery facility in Shepard rather than to landfills. However, it costs more to "tip" a load of garbage at Shepard than at a landfill, so the County agreed to subsidize haulers until April 30 of this year.

Although other haulers may be raising the householder's portion of the bill more than $1.95 (due to inflation and haulers' additional operating expenses), we are going to try to keep the price increase as low as possible.

It is only fair to warn you, however, that there may be more increases in sight. The current legislature is considering raising landfill surcharges and putting a sales tax on hauling fees, which could further increase garbage bills.

There are several ways you can lower your garbage bills. Enclosed are flyers with information on using a volume-based garbage hauler, recycling, composting yard waste at home or at one of the County composting sites, and disposing properly of household hazardous waste.

For further information, call 555 1567.

Sincerely,

See also: COVER LETTERS, GOODWILL, SALES, WEDDINGS.

Apologies

7

An apology is the superglue of life. It can repair just about anything.

—LYNN JOHNSTON

A letter is often better than a face-to-face or telephone apology because you can take your time getting the words right. It's also better to write when you don't know if the other person is willing to speak to you. A letter doesn't oblige them to respond immediately; there's time to absorb the message and decide how to react.

Whether you think of apologies as etiquette, ethics, justice, or even good business, they are an inevitable by-product of being alive. Because we all make mistakes, people are generally less bothered by your errors than you are; write your apology with dignity. "If you haven't made any mistakes lately, you must be doing something wrong." (Susan Jeffers)

Occasions That Call for Apologies

- belated response to a gift, favor, invitation, or major event in someone's life
- billing, credit, or financial errors
- business errors: incorrect information given, order mix-ups, contract misunderstandings, merchandise that is defective, dangerous, ineffective, damaged, delayed, or that is missing parts, instructions, or warranties
- children's misbehavior or damage to property/pet
- damage to another's property
- employee problems: rudeness, ineptness, dishonesty, poor service, unsatisfactory work
- failure to keep an appointment, deadline, shipping date, payment schedule, or promise

- insulting or insensitive remarks
- personal errors: giving someone's name and phone number to a third party without permission, forgetting to include someone in an invitation, betraying a secret
- pets that bite, bark, damage property, or are otherwise nuisances
- sexual harassment
- tactless, inappropriate, rude, or drunken behavior

- Briefly specify the fault and apologize for it ("I'm so sorry about the damaged book") or, in the case of a customer complaint, summarize the problem ("I understand you were twice given incorrect information"). In most cases, use the words "I apologize" or "I am sorry."
- Thank the person for writing or calling or for bringing the problem to your attention.
- When appropriate, convey understanding of the other person's position: "I can see how disappointing this must have been"; "You have every right to be upset."
- Tell what corrective action you're taking, if appropriate ("I will replace the shovel"; "A refund check is being sent"), or offer to make amends. Suggest several possible solutions and ask which the person prefers.
- Assure the person this won't happen again.
- In a business context, end the letter with a forward-looking comment about serving their future needs.

- Don't apologize for more than the specific incident. Avoid generalizations about what a klutz you are or how these things always happen to you.
- Don't be overly dramatic ("You will probably never want to see me again after what I did." "I wish I were dead after the way I behaved last night." "I am very, very, very sorry." "This is the worst thing I've ever done in my whole life"). Apologize briefly once instead of apologizing many times in different ways.

- Don't defend or excuse yourself, justify your actions, or sidestep an apology ("I'm sorry, but I still think I was right"). If you are going to apologize, do so cheerfully and wholeheartedly. "A stiff apology is a second insult." (G.K. Chesterton) Ethicist Jeremy Iggers says an apology must be made unilaterally. When we begin to stray into the area of what the other person did to us, we lose the ethical base of making an apology. Whatever anyone did to us is a separate matter from whatever mistake we made.

- Don't imply that the other person is at fault. Some people's apologies read like accusations. In business, it is probably better not to write than to insinuate that the customer is at fault. With some ingenuity, you can express regret without accepting responsibility for a situation that is not entirely your fault. When the other person is partly responsible, apologize only for your share of it. Don't mention anything else.

- Don't blame the computer. By now everyone knows that some human had its fingerprints all over the guilty computer; this patently untrue excuse only irritates people. And don't say that these things are bound to happen from time to time. Although this may be true, it makes you look careless.

- Don't admit negligence in writing. If negligence is a factor, consult with your attorney, who can suggest the best approach for your letter. In his article, "Saying You're Sorry in a Litigious Society" (in *The International Journal of Medicine and Law*, no. 7/8, 1992), Ralph Slovenko advises doctors to be careful about how they sympathize on a patient's death. An expression of sympathy at a funeral, for example, "could lead to an utterance which, in the hands of a skillful lawyer, might be turned into an admission of wrongdoing."

Tips on Writing

~ Write as soon as possible. Procrastination turns writing an apology into a major effort and you end up apologizing twice, once for the infraction and once for the delay.

~ Sometimes there are mitigating circumstances—for example, a shipment delayed because of a strike or flu outbreak. At other times, however, explanations weaken your apology—when, for example, you try to explain why you were rude or why a child said something tactless but truthful.

Special Situations

~ Parents of a child who annoys or hurts others or damages property write a note of apology. However, the child should also apologize in some age-appropriate manner. The adult's note might say, "Of course, Drusilla will want to apologize to you herself."

~ Employees apologizing to their boss for work-related errors or behavior provide a written, detailed account of what happened because their boss most likely reports to another higher-up and will need all relevant information.

~ The problem of sexual harassment has become increasingly visible and is no longer categorized as "just fooling around" or "having a good sense of humor." Making sexual remarks, threats, innuendoes, or passes is illegal. Anything that can be construed as sexual harassment requires a heartfelt apology that shows that the offender has some real (as opposed to expedient) understanding of what was done. The apology may not avert a company reprimand or even legal action, but then again it might. In any case, an apology is owed to anyone who has been sexually harassed. In addition to exhibiting contrition, the offender should promise not to repeat the behavior. Individuals being sued for sexual harassment are generally repeat offenders who still don't understand how unacceptable their actions were. Few people will pursue a first-time offender who didn't fully realize the harm done and who is now contrite and reformed.

~ The apology may have a special place in customer relations. "Two words will get you through many bad times in the business world: *I'm sorry*." (Mary A. De Vries) A well-written apology for a business problem can make a satisfied customer out of an unsatisfied one. Sometimes you may add a refund, discount, free pass, or other material apology for your customer's inconvenience. When writing an apology to a customer, end with a positive statement: "We look forward to continuing to serve you" or "We value your patronage and your friendship."

Format

~ Use personal stationery or notecards for apologies dealing with social situations. A few greeting cards charmingly or amusingly say "I'm sorry," but you still need to add a handwritten message.

~ Use business stationery for all apologies to customers, clients, and suppliers. If, however, the situation has personal overtones (a manager has publicly slighted someone or a supervisor has unjustly docked someone's pay), the apology might be handwritten on business-personal stationery.

~ Routine apologies (shipping delays, out-of-stock merchandise) are handled with a form letter.

~ An e-mailed apology would probably not be the most persuasive, unless you needed to get the apology to the other person immediately and the telephone wasn't an option.

WORDS

absentmindedly	ill-advised	misleading	repay
accidental	imperfect	misprint	responsible
acknowledge	imprudent	misquote	restitution
admit	inaccurate	mistaken	restore
awkward	inadequate	misunderstanding	sheepish
blunder	inadvertent	muddle	short-sighted
careless	incomplete	negligence	slip
compensate	inconsiderate	omitted	tactless
distressed	inconvenience	overlooked	thoughtless
disturbed	incorrect	pardon	unaware
embarrassed	insufficient	rectify	unfortunate
erroneous	irresponsible	red-faced	unhappy
error	lax	redo	unintentional
excuse	miscalculation	regrettable	unsatisfactory
explain	misconception	reimburse	unsound
failure	misconstrued	remiss	unwarranted
fault	misinterpreted	repair	unwise

PHRASES

absolutely no excuse for

accept the blame for

admit that I was wrong

angry with myself

appreciate your calling our attention to

asleep at the wheel/on the job/
   at the switch

avoid this in the future

breach of good manners

correct the situation

express my regret

feel sorry/terrible/bad about

how can I apologize for

I am most upset about

I am not excusing our/my errors, but

I am so sorry for

I don't know how it happened that

I have thoroughly investigated/
looked into the matter and

I'm sorry you were dissatisfied with

it was embarrassing to discover that

it was most understanding of you to

I was distressed to hear/read/
discover/learn that

make amends/restitution

make right with you

much to my regret

my apologies for any inconvenience

owe you an apology for

please accept my/our apology/
apologies for

presumed where I shouldn't have
presumed

prevent a recurrence

put to rights

reproach myself

sincerely regret/apologize

sorely regret

sorry for the inconvenience/confusion/
mix-up/misunderstanding

the least I can do is

to compensate for

under the mistaken impression that

until you are completely satisfied

weighs on my mind

we regret to inform our customers
that

you were entirely right about

SENTENCES

Although I apologized to you last night for our guests blocking your
driveway, I want you to know how sorry we are and to assure you that it
won't happen again.

As you rightly pointed out, a mistake has been made on your July bill.

I am extremely embarrassed about my behavior last night.

I am sincerely/very sorry.

I apologize for Jimmy's behavior.

I can only hope you will forgive this serious lapse of good taste on my part.

I don't blame you for being upset.

I don't like being on the outs with you, particularly since it was my fault.

I hope this situation can be mended to everyone's satisfaction.

I'm sorry for telling everyone in the office your good news before you could
tell them—I don't know what I was thinking.

I'm sorry you were treated so disparagingly by the salesclerk.

I only realized later how insulting my remarks might have appeared.

I understand how disappointed you must have been to receive only half your order.

I've taken steps to ensure that it doesn't happen again.

I was totally out of line this morning when I insisted on knowing what your salary is—I can only hope you will forgive my poor taste and insensitivity.

My face gets red every time I remember that night.

Please accept my apology for the oversight.

Please excuse my inattention/shortsightedness/thoughtlessness.

Please forgive me.

Thank you for advising us of this error/for bringing the matter to my attention.

Thank you for your letter of July 15 telling us about the unfortunate remark made by one of the security guards.

Thank you for your patience and understanding.

This will not, of course, happen again.

We apologize for the delay—it is unfortunately unavoidable.

We are sorry/apologize for any embarrassment this has caused you.

We look forward to continuing to serve you.

We owe you an apology.

We were caught napping on this one.

You were right, I was wrong, and I'm sorry.

PARAGRAPHS

We are unable to deliver the spring fabric samples by the date promised. The product supervisor promises me that you will have them by January 5. If this is unsatisfactory, please telephone me. It isn't often we have to renege on a delivery date, and we're not happy about it. Please accept our apologies for the delay.

Please accept our apologies for what's recently happened at your house. We're all working hard to find other homes for the bunnies. When Hillel assured you that both bunnies were female, he relied on the green-striped ribbons they wore around their necks. None of us knew that a four-year-old neighbor had switched a green-striped ribbon for a yellow polka-dotted ribbon that the male rabbits were wearing. I know this doesn't make up to you for what you've been through, but I thought you should know that our intentions were good. Again, we're sorry and we'll let you know as soon as we've found ten good homes.

We were sorry to hear that the track lighting fixture you ordered was defective, as described in your letter of April 29. Please return it to us using its original mailing box and the enclosed label, and we will send you a replacement by return mail. All Midlothian merchandise is inspected twice before leaving the factory, but with a recent 45% increase in production, we have a few rough spots to work out yet. I'm sorry that you were inconvenienced, and hope that you will continue to use our fine Midlothian products—products that we proudly back with our full-service Midlothian guarantee.

It occurred to me in a dream, or maybe it was in the shower, that you had asked for the return of your baby books some time ago. I suppose the friend's child has gone off to college by now. I'm sorry for the tardiness— they're in today's mail.

We erroneously mailed you the same order you placed last month. This month's order has been sent this morning, and we've marked the box plainly with AUGUST written in large red letters. If you will please refuse acceptance of the first box, the carrier will bring it back to us. We apologize for the error.

We were sorry to hear that the last neon tetras you bought from us were infected with ich and subsequently infected your entire aquarium. As tropical fish enthusiasts ourselves, we appreciate how devastating this has been. I immediately spoke to our supplier about the problem, and she has assured me this was an isolated slip-up. In the meantime, please restock your aquarium at our expense. Thank you for your understanding. I hope you will continue to be one of our most valued customers.

SAMPLE LETTERS

Dear Dorothea,

I feel dreadful about ruining your lovely luncheon yesterday by arguing with Celia about Will Ladislaw. You certainly did everything you could to save the situation, and I apologize most humbly for ignoring good taste, old friendship, and common sense in pursuing a "discussion" that was completely inappropriate.

I talked to Celia first thing this morning and attempted to mend my fences there, but I feel a great deal worse about what I did to you. The luncheon was delicious, and the first two hours were delightful. I hope you will someday be able to forgive me for blighting the last half-hour.

Your friend,

Dear Mr. Ravenal:

As editor of the Cotton Blossom newsletter, I want to apologize for omitting your name in the last issue. Captain Hawks asked me how I could have possibly forgotten to include our hottest new actor! In proofreading the copy, my eyes failed to notice that your name wasn't where my brain expected it to be. I'm sorry. A correction will appear in the next issue.

Regretfully,

Dear Hsiao-Wei,

I apologize for not showing up at the meeting this afternoon. Although there is no excuse for such a thing, I will say that I was involved in an automobile accident on the way to work and what with filling out forms, notifying my insurance company, and arranging for a rental car, I completely forget about the meeting.

Can we reschedule for this Thursday, same time? Thanks—and again, I'm sorry.

Regards,

Dear Merton Denscher,

Thank you for your letter of March 19. I am sorry that the background research I submitted was unusable. A careful re-reading of your instructions showed me at once where I'd gone wrong. I do apologize.

With your permission, I would like to resubmit the work—this time correctly. I believe I can get it to you by the end of next week since I am already familiar with the relevant sources for your topic.

Please let me know at once if you prefer me not to go ahead.

Sincerely,

Dear Annette,

I must beg your forgiveness for my outspoken and insensitive remarks last night about your religious convictions. I'm afraid I got carried away in the heat of the discussion. I certainly feel that each of us has a right to our own beliefs, and I in no way meant to belittle yours.

I would be happy if you would accept an invitation to dinner at my house on Saturday, August 3, at 7:00 p.m. I'm just having a few friends, most of whom you know.

Hoping to see you then, I am

Yours truly,

See also: ACKNOWLEDGMENTS, ADJUSTMENTS, BELATED, COMPLAINTS, RESPONSES, SENSITIVE.

Letters of Application

8

The nearest to perfection most people ever come is when
filling out an employment application.

— KEN KRAFT

There are three ways to persuade a prospective employer to invite you for an interview:

1. Fill in one of the company's application forms and submit it alone or with a cover letter (a brief letter stating that the application is enclosed and mentioning a point or two indicating you are a good candidate for the job).

2. Send a résumé (a businesslike and detailed summary of your work and educational history, your skills, and your career goals), also accompanied by a cover letter.

3. Write a letter of application, which is a combination cover letter and résumé—longer than a cover letter, shorter and less formal than a résumé. (The letter of application is also known as a broadcast letter or a letter of interest.)

Which approach is best? The clue comes from the prospective employer: "Fill out an application form"; "Send or fax a résumé"; "Apply to the following department."

In addition to applications that are solicited (there is a definite opening being advertised), there are unsolicited applications (you know of no opening but you would like to work for that company). In the latter case, with no directions from the employer as to how to apply, a letter of application—a powerful one-page letter that includes résumé material—may be more effective than a conventional résumé and cover letter.

Some organizations continue to rely on letters of application to gauge an applicant's overall self-presentation and command of the written language.

The purpose of the application letter is to attract and hold the reader's attention long enough to get your letter placed in the short pile of those candidates who will receive an invitation to an interview. (The other pile is much, much taller.) A letter of application is thus a sales letter in which you are both seller and product.

Send an Application Letter to

- camps
- clubs and organizations
- colleges, universities, technical schools
- franchise companies
- internships
- private elementary and secondary schools
- prospective employers
- volunteer organizations

- Address your letter to a specific individual, after verifying the person's title and double-checking the spelling of the name (even if it's simple—"Gene" could be "Jeanne," "John" could be "Jon").
- Open with an attention-getting sentence or paragraph.
- Tell why you are seeking this position, why you have chosen to apply to this particular company, and why you believe you are qualified.
- List the skills, education, and experience that are most relevant to the opening. Leave the rest for the interview.
- Request an interview ("I will be in Burbank next week and would like to arrange an interview").
- Provide an address, daytime phone number, fax number, and e-mail address.
- Close with a pleasant or forward-looking statement: "I appreciate your time and consideration"; "I look forward to discussing this position with you."

What Not to Say

- Don't indulge in generalities or the vague "etc."; specify exactly what you can do or have done.
- Don't use gimmicks, fancy language that you don't normally use, a "humorous" approach, or any attention-getting device that could backfire. Conservative (which is not the same as boring) is better here.
- Don't refer to yourself as "the writer" ("The writer has had six years' experience as a heavy equipment operator").
- Don't emphasize how much the company can do to further your career goals. Emphasize rather how your abilities can benefit the company. Instead of the message "Here is what I can do," fashion the message to say, "Here is what I can do for you."
- Don't mention negative aspects of your present or past employment.
- Don't belittle your qualifications.
- Don't base your request on your need for the job or on an appeal to sympathy ("I am the only support of my family"); focus on what you have to offer.
- Don't mention salary in your letter (even when an ad asks you to state salary requirements); save that discussion for the interview.

Tips on Writing

↬ Don't use your present company's letterhead stationery for your letter of application.

↬ Re-read your letter before mailing to see if it sounds confident, professional, and persuasive. If you were the employer, would you want to interview the person who wrote this?

↬ Be concise. The letter of application should be no longer than one page.

↬ Use action verbs when describing your abilities and accomplishments (see RÉSUMÉS for a list of effective verbs).

↬ Tailor your message to a specific company. Employers can spot a generic or boilerplate letter; it tells them you are more interested in a job, any job, than in a job with them. Personalize your letter. When prospective employers receive a letter that has been written especially for them, they will give it more than the sixty seconds most letters get.

∼ The most critical factor in getting an interview is how closely you match the prospective employer's needs. You already know what you have to offer; you also have to know what the company needs from you. Call the company and ask questions; research the company at the library; speak to people who work there or who know the company. By presenting as clear a picture of yourself as you can, couched in terms of what the company needs, you make it easy for an employer to determine quickly whether there is a match.

∼ It's not necessary to say "References available upon request." It is understood by both parties that references will be offered and checked.

∼ Avoid spelling or grammar errors, low-quality paper, smudged or hard-to-read print, and poor spacing on the page. In the case of a fax, use the "fine resolution" setting to send as sharp a copy as possible.

Special Situations

∼ To apply for a franchise, study FTC guidelines. You may want a lawyer to help you with some of the correspondence.

∼ Most applications to colleges, universities, community colleges, or technical schools are routine and codified. If, however, you are a student at the very high or very low end of your graduating class or if you have special needs (for financial assistance, for example), seek help from your high school counseling office, private counseling services, or some of the numerous publications available. For some students, the process of applying for admission to college can take many months and require specialized information.

∼ If you are on the other side of the desk and are asked to design a job application form, familiarize yourself with state and federal antidiscrimination laws. You may not ask applicants for such information as age, race, sex, height and weight, color of eyes, hair, or complexion; birthplace; dates of public school attendance; arrest record, type of military discharge, past workers' compensation claims; whether they own their own home, have ever been sued, or had a surety bond or government clearance denied; work transportation arrangements; non-job-related handicaps; activities, memberships, and hobbies not directly related to the job; how they heard about the job opening. Have a lawyer check the rough draft of your application form to ensure that it complies with state and federal laws.

Format

∽ Letters of application are typed, preferably on letterhead stationery.

∽ Some prospective employers suggest that applicants fax materials to them. Unless a résumé is specifically requested, you may fax a letter of application, either with a cover sheet or leaving space at the top of the letter for the faxing information (see FAXES).

WORDS

abilities	education	opportunity	skills
apply	experience	professional	suitable
background	goals	qualified	
credentials	objectives	responsible	

PHRASES

applying for the position of

arrange a meeting at your convenience

experience that qualifies me for

extensive experience with

good candidate/match for the job

in response to your advertisement

interested in pursuing a career with

may I have fifteen minutes of your time to discuss

meet and exceed your criteria

serious interest in

similar to my most recent position

skills that would be useful to

ten years' experience with

well suited for

SENTENCES

According to this morning's paper, you are seeking a storm restoration contractor.

After eight years as a senior analog engineer at Blayds-Conway, I am seeking a position in this area because of a family move.

At the suggestion of Wilhelmina Douglas-Stewart, I am writing to request an interview for the project leader position in your long haul fiber optic communications department.

Because I believe you would find me to be an efficient, experienced, and dedicated legal administrative assistant, I am applying for the position at Wilson & Bean.

Dr. Breuer has informed me that you are currently looking for a part-time veterinary technician.

I am applying for the position of credit research analyst that you advertised in today's paper.

I look forward to hearing from you.

I understand from Dr. Demetrius Doboobie that you have an opening for a medical records supervisor.

I understand that there is currently no opening in your office, but I would like you to keep my résumé on file and to consider me for any openings that occur.

I was happy to learn that there is an opening for an insurance underwriting coordinator at the Daffyd Evans Marine Insurance Agency.

I was pleased to see your advertisement in this morning's paper for a floral designer because I have just moved here and am looking for a position after having worked as a floral designer in Chicago for the past six years.

I will call you Thursday to discuss setting up an interview.

My eight years as a food microbiologist at Samuel Braceweight, Inc., make me eminently suitable for the responsibilities of the position you are currently advertising.

Please consider me as an applicant for your advertised part-time position as clerical assistant in your business office.

Roger Brevard told me that you are looking for a real-time software engineer.

Thank you for considering my application.

The skills and duties outlined in your advertisement in today's paper are almost a perfect match for the position I held until recently at Geoffrey Bentley Publishers, Inc.

PARAGRAPHS

I have held a position as head teller very similar to the one you are currently advertising. Employed for the past five years at Jethway State Bank, I was promoted to head teller last January. Because of a family situation, I am obliged to move to Swancourt. My immediate supervisor, Felix Jethway, said he would be happy to discuss my work with you if you would like to telephone him (515/555-1000).

As you know, I have been managing the Albany branch of your Woodstock Bookstore for three years. I understand that you plan to franchise several of your bookstores, and I would like to apply for the franchise for this store, if it is available.

Your neighbor, Gina Gregers, who is a friend of mine from high school, told me yesterday that you are seeking a lunch-hour delivery driver for your catering company. I have a valid driver's license, have never had a moving violation, and, as a twenty-year resident of Werle Heights, know my way around the city and suburbs.

My career accomplishments include: setting a fifteen-year collection record during the first two months of employment as a collector of delinquent medical accounts; being promoted to unit manager as a result of high achievement levels and later to office collection manager; maintaining my record as the leading collector at the Denver branch of the Montjoy Agencies.

I would like to be considered for your customer service representative position. You requested experience in the transportation industry; I was employed from 1998–2001 as customer service representative for Coldstream Transport and from 1995–1998 as dispatcher for Steenson Intermountain Express.

SAMPLE LETTERS

Dear Ms. Rondabale,

I would like to apply for the position of surgery scheduler for your ophthalmology practice.

I received a two-year degree in office administration from Beckford Business College in 2000. Since then, I have worked full-time for Alasi Surgical Associates as a surgery scheduler.

The work here has been more than satisfactory to me, but your clinic is half an hour closer to my home and I would like to shorten the commute.

I can come for an interview any Saturday, or any weekday during the lunch hour, or after 5:30. If you leave an interview date and time on my home answering machine (555-1234), I will call to confirm.

Thank you.

Dear Ms. Saverne,

As the result of a telephone call to your office this morning, I learned that Duval International is seeking someone to manage the security operations of its office complex, and that you are the person to contact about the position.

I have eleven years' experience as a security services supervisor and broad experience with access control and with most security systems, including CCTV alarms. I also have an AA degree in law enforcement.

I was employed by Stanislas & Sons from 1989–1994, and by Barr Associates from 1994 to the present. Favorable references are available from both companies.

I would like to set up an interview to discuss the position with you. I have 24-hour voice mail at 555-1234.

Dear Ms. Jocelyn,

I am looking for a position as an electrical engineer. Several people have mentioned your employment agency as being outstanding in placing people in this field.

I have an MS in Electrical Engineering and seven years' experience in the design of lighting and power systems; the last two years I was also project manager.

I believe my qualifications make me someone you can place, both to my satisfaction and to a future employer's satisfaction.

I will call next week for an appointment and can then bring in my résumé, list of publications, and references.

I look forward to meeting you.

                                        Sincerely,

Dear Mr. Squales,

As someone with three years' telemarketing experience and two years' experience as office manager of a small business, I think I am a good candidate for your convention sales and marketing coordinator position.

My strengths include effective oral and written communication skills and an aptitude for interpersonal business relationships. I am considered a good team player and am precise and detail-oriented in my work.

I would like to bring my résumé and references in and discuss this opening with you.

Dear Margaret West,

Libraries have been a second home to me for years, and I will be majoring in library science. In the meantime, I would like to apply for the summer job opening in your children's room.

Although my work background is slight (see résumé), I think I can offer you a deep and genuine interest in library science, a strong desire to excel at this kind of work, and library skills that come from many hundreds of library visits. As the oldest of five children, I also have considerable experience and a high comfort level in dealing with young people.

Thank you for your time and attention.

Dear Mr. Baillie:

The requirements for the branch manager position you advertised describe almost perfectly my own background.

As assistant manager of Gulliver Travel, I have been responsible for overseeing eight full-time agents. I am a travel school graduate (Charlson International) with a great deal of experience and a good working knowledge of the travel industry in all its phases— from issuing tickets and seat assignments and assisting with ticket assembly to PARS computer experience. I have two years of experience in domestic reservations, one year of experience working with corporate international travel operations, and a thorough understanding of international tariffs.

I would like to discuss this position with you and will be happy to come in for an interview at your convenience.

Sincerely yours,

See also: COVER LETTERS, EMPLOYMENT, FOLLOW-UP, RÉSUMÉS.

Appointments and Interviews

9

Showing up is 80% of life.

—WOODY ALLEN

Many appointments, interviews, and meetings arranged by telephone are often confirmed by letter, fax, or e-mail.

Some appointment letters are simple: confirming or altering an appointment; reminding someone of an appointment; refusing or canceling an appointment.

When you want someone's time in order to sell your company's product or service, however, the letter requesting an appointment must be an outstanding sales letter, persuading the person that it is in their interest to see you.

To secure a job interview, send some combination of carefully crafted résumé, cover letter, or letter of application (see APPLICATIONS, RÉSUMÉS).

Letters About Appointments Include

- accepting
- asking for/requesting
- canceling
- changing/postponing/delaying
- confirming/following up
- refusing
- thanking for

- When asking for an appointment: identify yourself if you're unknown to the person; explain why you want to meet with them; mention a benefit to them in meeting with you; suggest a length of time for the appointment ("fifteen minutes" or "no more than half an hour of your time"); offer possible dates, times, and places; mention others who will be present; give your address, phone number, e-mail address, and fax number; express your appreciation for the person's attention to your request. In some cases, tell when you will call for their response.

- When agreeing to meet with someone: say "yes" to the meeting; repeat the purpose, date, time, place, and length of meeting; express your pleasure or thanks (see also ACCEPTANCES, ACKNOWLEDGMENTS).

- When confirming arrangements made in person or by telephone: refer to your previous discussion; repeat the meeting specifics— date, time, place, purpose; close with an expression of pleasure ("look forward to discussing this").

- When changing or postponing an appointment: mention the original time, date, and place; state your alternatives; apologize for the inconvenience; ask for confirmation of the new time.

- When refusing a request for an appointment: thank the person for their letter or telephone call; say "no" politely and neutrally; if appropriate, offer an alternative way to meet the goals of the proposed meeting; if you wish, indicate why you cannot accept, although a simple "I am unable to meet with you" should suffice.

- When canceling arrangements: repeat the time, date, place; state that you must cancel; briefly explain why; apologize for the inconvenience; offer a substitute action, if appropriate.

- When sending a follow-up letter after an appointment: give the date of the meeting; state your pleasure at all that was accomplished; enclose promised information or materials; refer to your hope for future meetings/contacts/business.

- Don't "postpone" or "delay" a meeting that you are actually canceling. If you have no intention of ever meeting with the person, use the word "cancel" and omit all references to the future.

- Don't over-apologize for canceling or changing an appointment unless the situation is special (you've requested the meeting and the company has invited upper-level management and arranged for refreshments and video equipment). Usually all you need is a brief "I'm sorry to have to cancel/change/postpone . . ." For more complex situations, see APOLOGIES.

Tips on Writing

~ Be assertive about making appointments; if you leave it to the other person ("I'd appreciate hearing from you") you may not get a response.

~ Thank the person who sets up the meeting when there are more than two people getting together.

~ Some people are persistent about wanting your time, from the neighbor who is determined to learn everything you know about genealogy or playing bridge to the sales representative who won't take no for an answer. When it's someone you will continue to deal with (the neighbor), write a note, using equal doses of tact and firmness: "I know you will understand, but I must say no." In the face of persistence, never give a reason for your "no." The moment you say why you are unable to meet with them ("I'm really busy just now"), they will have a response ("It will only take a minute"). When you offer another reason, they will have another rebuttal. Engaging you in wearying debate is part of the strategy; you wouldn't be the first person to say "yes" just to avoid being harangued. A simple "I'm sorry, but no" repeated many times is most effective—and putting it in writing doubles its effect.

Special Situations

~ When requesting a sales or job interview, use your letter to pique the person's curiosity. Make them want to see you. Sell your product or yourself, but don't tell so much that the person thinks nothing more will be gained by an interview.

~ If you forget an interview, appointment, or meeting, write an immediate, sincere apology. Ask what you can do to make amends.

Format

~ Correspondence about business appointments, interviews, and meetings is typewritten on business letterhead or personal-business stationery.

~ Interoffice and some out-of-house communications about meetings are handled by memo or e-mail.

~ Letters regarding personal appointments can be either typed or handwritten. The more formal or personal the appointment is, the stronger the indication for a handwritten message.

WORDS

accept	consult	examine	pleasure	session
arrange	contact	interview	postpone	unable
confer	discussion	notify	review	

PHRASES

already committed/have plans	meet with you
another engagement	move up the date to
an unexpected complication	of interest to you
can't keep our original date	previous commitments
convenient time	set a time and date
introduce you to	unfortunately obliged to
looking forward to seeing/ meeting you	when you are able
	won't be free
may I suggest	would be convenient for me

SENTENCES

Can we change our meeting on July 15 from 2:00 p.m. to 4:30 p.m.?

I am unfortunately obliged to change the date we set earlier.

I don't believe a meeting would benefit either of us.

If you're unable to make the meeting on the tenth, please let my assistant know as soon as possible.

If you would like to discuss this, I could meet with you at a time convenient for you.

I'll give you a call in a couple of days to see if you can schedule a meeting with me.

I'm not able to meet with you for several months—please contact me again in late January.

I would be happy to meet with you in my office on Friday, November 8, at two o'clock to discuss your invention.

I would appreciate twenty minutes of your time this week.

I would like to meet with you to discuss Jackie's progress so far on the new medication.

I would like to review with you my current salary, which I believe no longer reflects my responsibilities and contributions.

Let me know as soon as possible if this is convenient for you.

May I stop by your office for a few minutes next week to drop off our latest samples and catalog and to explain how our new service contract works?

Mr. Patterne is seriously ill and will be unable to keep his appointment with you on June 23 at 1:30.

Thank you for your time yesterday—I enjoyed meeting with you.

This will confirm your appointment with Ms. Tucker on Tuesday, December 18, at 3:00 p.m.

We would like to discuss with you, either in person or over the telephone, our concerns about the academic progress of our daughter, May Bracknel.

PARAGRAPHS

After you have evaluated my application and résumé, I hope we can arrange an interview at a mutually convenient time. I note several areas where the company's areas of emphasis and my areas of expertise overlap, and I would like to discuss these aspects of the position. You will no doubt have questions for me as well. I look forward to hearing from you.

Charlotte Moulin, managing director of Hardy's Cycle Supply, will be in Alberta the week of August 4, and would like to tour Wheels Unlimited while she is there. Please let me know if something can be arranged.

I understand you are looking for acreage east of town. May I come in and speak with you sometime this week about the property I have for sale?

Thank you for the copies of the contracts, which we received October 31. As we review them with our lawyer, a few questions occur to us. We would appreciate being able to sit down with you and your lawyer to discuss a few of them. When would this be possible?

Did I have the date wrong? I thought we had a meeting scheduled for 1:30 yesterday. I'm afraid I won't be free again until late next week, but maybe we can arrange something then. Please let me hear from you.

May I have fifteen minutes of your time next week to show you some large colored photographs of what Office Greenery has done for other area businesses? Offices that use our services report increased customer and employee satisfaction, and I think you will be glad you investigated our unique, effective, and cost-efficient program. I will call your secretary on Monday to see if you are available for a brief meeting.

We are interested in replacing the decorative stone brick on our home and would like you to give us an estimate on your lightweight "cultured stone." Please call either of us at work during the day or at home during the evening (see enclosed business cards) to set up an appointment. Thank you.

SAMPLE LETTERS

Dear Mr. Stobbs:

I've received your letter of June 16 requesting an appointment to see me about your Handley Cross computer software.

We have been using the Surtees line of software for all our business needs for the past three years, and we are very satisfied with it. I don't see a meeting benefiting either of us.

Thanks anyway.

Yours truly,

Dear Lionel,

I have to cancel the meeting we set up for Friday, September 3, at 2:30 p.m., as we've got a little trouble at the Valliscourt plant. I should be back on September 6 and will call you then to set up another appointment.

Thanks for understanding.

Sincerely,

Dear Ms. Vulliamy:

People with disabilities get hired for one very special reason: they're qualified.

I would like to tell you about some of the highly qualified people listed with the Ogilvy Employment Agency who could make a positive and energetic contribution to your organization.

May I meet with you sometime next week?

Sincerely,

Dear Laura Payton:

Our longtime supplier of plastic tubing has recently informed us that they are discontinuing their plastic tubing division. Our vice-president of purchasing will be visiting several plastic tubing manufacturers in your area next week.

Would it be possible for you to schedule a meeting and plant tour for him on Tuesday or Wednesday of next week? Enclosed are data on our projected needs for plastic tubing, our production schedules, and delivery requirements that may be helpful to you in preparing for his visit.

Thank you.

Sincerely,

See also: ACCEPTANCES, ACKNOWLEDGMENTS, EMPLOYMENT, FOLLOW-UP, INVITATIONS, REFUSALS, REQUESTS, THANK YOU.

Letters of Appreciation

10

I have yet to be bored by someone paying me a compliment.

—OTTO VAN ISCH

Letters of appreciation are the easiest, most delightful letters to write. You are never obliged to write them, there is no deadline, and the only rule is sincerity. One of life's small pleasures is to be able to be kind and generous with little cost to yourself.

Letters of appreciation are related to letters of acknowledgment, congratulations, and thanks. In the latter cases, we are not surprised to hear from others, whereas a letter of appreciation is always unexpected. When Aunt Estrella gives you a gift, you thank her. When Aunt Estrella sends your son a graduation gift, he thanks her, but you write a letter of appreciation, saying how much her support of your children has meant to you over the years.

You don't need to thank someone for prompt payment, for turning in a report, for giving you a bonus based on performance, or for returning your lost wallet intact. In all these cases people are doing the expected thing. However, it is entirely appropriate to show your appreciation. As Abraham Lincoln said, "Everybody likes a compliment."

Letters of appreciation are sent to employees who do "ordinary" work, but do it well; to strangers you encounter who demonstrate above-average efficiency and service; to friends and relatives who go the extra mile for you; to people who have referred work or clients to you; perhaps to people you've read about in the newspaper who have contributed something to your community.

Write Letters of Appreciation for

- awards/honors
- bonuses
- commendations/compliments/encouragement/praise
- community service
- complimentary letters about company/employee/service/product
- customer referrals
- customers to whom you extend privileges in appreciation of their business/prompt payments/new accounts
- customers whose business you want to acknowledge
- employers for a bonus/raise/promotion
- employees for their good work
- financial contributions
- group efforts
- helpful advice/suggestions/tips
- introductions
- prompt payments
- public figures whose work you admire
- speeches/workshops/conferences
- sympathy (see also ACKNOWLEDGMENTS, THANK YOU)
- volunteers

- State what you appreciate (a talent, the business lunch, the plans for the new building).
- Use a key word early in your note: "appreciation," "congratulations," "gratitude," "admiration," "recognition."
- Be specific about the person's work, talent, or actions: "You're a delight to work with because . . ." or "Your work has meant a lot to the company because . . ." In some cases, relate an anecdote, a shared memory, or reflection that bolsters your good wishes.
- Close with wishes for continued success or with some forward-looking remark about your future business or personal association.

What Not to Say

- Don't add information, a meeting reminder, or a sales message; for maximum impact your upbeat message should stand alone.
- Don't express more than you feel. People know when your sentiments are insincere. Use language that feels genuine and comfortable to you; avoid effusiveness, exaggeration, and excessive flattery.
- Don't talk about "luck" when expressing appreciation; it implies that chance rather than talent and hard work was responsible for the person's achievements.
- Don't use letters of appreciation to customers as an excuse to solicit more business or for your future advantage; a meaningful letter of appreciation has only one purpose.

Tips on Writing

↝ Be brief, warm, and sincere. The "brief" part is easy, but if you have trouble being warm and sincere, you might want to think about why you're writing. Perhaps it is not a letter of appreciation that you need to send.

↝ Be slightly formal. Even when you know well the person to whom you're writing, a certain formality increases its impact.

↝ Be positive. Instead of writing, "I never thought you could do it," say "You've shown us what a person can do with enough energy and determination."

↝ When someone sends you a letter of appreciation, reflect on what pleases you about it. Remember this the next time you write one.

Special Situations

↝ Letters of appreciation sent to customers, present and potential, are more sales letters than letters of appreciation (see SALES).

↝ Enormous goodwill can be generated for your business by writing brief, sincere notes of appreciation to employees, customers, or suppliers. Once you start looking for ways to appreciate people, you will see them everywhere; make a habit of sending off appreciative notes several times a month.

↝ Sometimes you need to turn down something—a gift, an invitation, a membership—but you are flattered and pleased at the thought behind it, so you write a letter that is part appreciation, part refusal (see also REFUSALS).

∼ Letters of appreciation can be written to several employees at once—teams, divisions, branch offices, sectors, and other groups that have performed particularly well or solved a problem.

∼ "A fan letter is an enduring testament to excellence, which puts it in a category of its own—perhaps somewhere between a valentine and an honorary degree." (Jennifer Williams) When writing a fan letter to a movie star or public figure, be brief (no more than one page). There is little point in asking for the person to call you or see you—as they say, "only in your dreams." Requesting a photograph is acceptable, although not everyone will respond. Don't send a gift; it's unlikely that the person will ever see it (it will be donated to a nonprofit organization). Addresses for most celebrities can be obtained at the library.

∼ If your company gives corporate gifts, attaching handwritten notes of appreciation will double their impact. Seventy-five years ago, Agnes Repplier wrote, "Letterwriting on the part of a busy man or woman is the quintessence of generosity." In today's fast-lane business culture, this generosity is even more highly regarded. Unlike the spoken compliment, this one can be read and re-read.

Format

∼ Use postcards for one- or two-sentence notes of appreciation. In just minutes you can dash off notes rich in public relations potential. Consider postcards featuring scenery from your area for people outside it, art postcards, reprints from old movies that might relate to your business or your interests, or even an especially attractive picture of your factory, office, building, or other installation.

∼ Personal notes of appreciation are handwritten on foldovers or personal stationery.

∼ Business letters of appreciation are typed on letterhead stationery if you have a somewhat formal relationship with the person. In more casual contexts, jot an appreciative message on memo paper.

∼ E-mail, which wouldn't be appropriate for a standard thank-you note, is often useful for the quick note of appreciation. Some things seem too trivial to warrant notepaper and pen, but are just right for e-mail: "Great presentation!" (from a colleague; from a superior, a handwritten note would be preferable); "I noticed your rose garden when I drove by the other day—fabulous!"; "Heard you got another patent—way to go!"

WORDS

admire	honor	recommend	thoughtfulness
appreciate	impressive	refreshing	thrilled
commendable	inspired	remarkable	touched
delightful	kindness	respect	treasure
engaging	knowledgeable	satisfying	triumph
enjoyable	large-hearted	sensational	unique
fascinating	memorable	sincere	valuable
favorite	one-of-a-kind	special	welcome
generous	overwhelmed	stunned	
gracious	pleased	superb	

PHRASES

appreciate your contributions to

as a token of our gratitude/appreciation

delighted to learn about

grateful to you for

heard about your success

held in high regard

hope I can return the favor someday

I am impressed by/with

I appreciate the time and effort you expended on

important contribution

it was thoughtful of you to

I want you to know how much we/I appreciate

job well done

let me tell you how much I liked

offer my compliments

realize the worth of

set great store by

think highly of

we can point with pride

wish you well

without your dedication and expertise

would like to compliment you on

SENTENCES

As principal of Jerome Elementary School, you might like to know that we think Miss Eurgain is an absolute treasure.

Can you stand one more compliment?

Customers like you are the reason we stay in business.

I'd like to express my appreciation for the knowledgeable and sympathetic care you gave me during my hospitalization for bypass surgery.

I don't know how I would have managed without your help.

If I can repay your kindness, let me know.

I'm impressed!

I sincerely appreciate your time and attention.

I want to express my appreciation to all of you for the extra hours and hard work you put in last week to secure the Gryseworth contract.

I want to tell you how much I appreciate what you are doing for the recycling program in our neighborhood.

My hat's off to you!

Thanks again for your clever and useful suggestion.

The Ridley County School Board would like to add its thanks and appreciation to those of the recipients of the scholarships you made possible.

This past year has been a banner year for the company, and you have contributed significantly to its success.

We are all happy for you.

Well done!

Your efforts have made this possible.

Your support is greatly appreciated.

You've done it again!

PARAGRAPHS

As Bette Midler once said, "People are not the best because they work hard. They work hard because they are the best." And you are the best! Know that we appreciate you!

You've been a valued cardmember with Stuyvesant Bank since 1990, and we thank you for the exceptional manner in which you've handled your account. To show our appreciation, we've preapproved you for our premier bankcard, the Gold 100. We think you will find it to be the ultimate in credit card performance.

Please accept the enclosed token of our appreciation for your five years as one of our most dependable and delightful volunteers. We don't know what we would do without you!

Thank you for your timely and excellent solution to the problem of tangled hoses. Only those of us who have struggled with this annoying and time-consuming inconvenience can appreciate what a delight the new boom system will be. You will be receiving an Outstanding Contribution award in May, but I didn't want to wait that long before telling you how pleased and impressed we all are.

All of us here at Legson, Ltd. enjoyed your enthusiastic letter about the quality of our lace goods. We are proud to offer such a wide selection of fine handiwork from all four corners of the globe. Please accept with our appreciation the enclosed 20% discount coupon good on your next order.

Appreciation and thanks go to Angela Messenger and her Documentation Department for a successful transformation of the tracking system. The new equipment and its faster, more accurate method of record-keeping will help keep us in the forefront of the Stout, Old, Mild, Bitter, Family Ales market. Our success here at Marsden & Company is due to an exceptional group of talented employees.

SAMPLE LETTERS

Dear Dr. Rowlands,

Your suggestions for next year's technical forum are much appreciated. I've turned them over to the steering committee, although I suspect you'll be invited to join them. I hope you will accept—your ideas seem as workable as they are useful.

Sincerely yours,

Dear Ms. Lees-Noel:

I'm told that you were the good-hearted soul who kept my desk from overflowing during my sick leave (while still keeping up with your own work).

Instead of the chaos I expected to return to, I was able to start back with a clear slate. I am most appreciative of everything you did. I don't know whether this is a compliment or not, but you did things just the way I would have!

Do call on me if I can ever return the favor.

Sincerely,

Dear Mr. Fitzmarshall:

We were pleased to learn that you received such outstanding service from one of our employees. Be assured that we have passed on your compliments to Ms. Stretton. You will perhaps enjoy knowing that in recognition of her talent and managerial skills, Ms. Stretton has just been promoted to floor supervisor.

We appreciate your taking the time to write us.

Yours truly,

⁓

Dear Mrs. Sixsmith,

Thank you for accompanying the fifth and sixth graders to Language Camp last weekend. I understand you chaperoned the group on your own time. Since Ronald arrived home, I've heard dozens of stories of your helpfulness, good humor, and ability to make the camp a home-away-from-home for these youngsters.

We felt a lot better knowing you would be with the group, and we appreciate Ronald's opportunity to spend time with a dynamic adult who's a good role model.

With best wishes,

⁓

Dear Ms. Stanley,

The entire department joins me in thanking you for the superb workshop on hard disk filing systems. We all learned a great deal (I was fascinated by your introductory description of early Abyssinian slate files).

I am passing on your brochure to George Hickson in Building 201-BE in case he would be interested in having you speak to his department.

Yours truly,

⁓

Dear Judge Whipple,

Congratulations on the editorial you wrote for Sunday's op-ed page. I have followed your career over the years and have been impressed by your passion for justice, especially for society's most vulnerable people: children, the homeless, and those with disabilities.

My best wishes to you for professional and personal happiness.

Sincerely,

⁓

See also: ACKNOWLEDGMENTS, CONGRATULATIONS, GOODWILL, THANK YOU.

Belated Letters 11

People who are late are often so much jollier than
the people who have to wait for them.

—Edward Verrall Lucas

One of the most difficult letters to write is the one that is overdue. Every day that passes magnifies our guilt and intensifies our resistance to writing; too often we end up not writing at all.

Centuries ago, Titus Livius advised, "Better late than never." In the case of a letter, "late" is inconsiderate. "Never" can be unpardonable. Your effort in writing, even though belated, will be appreciated.

Belated Letters Include

- letters dealing with sensitive issues (see also SENSITIVE)
- letters to family and friends who have written us such lovely, long, newsy letters that we don't know where to begin to answer them (see also FAMILY)
- refusal and rejection letters (see also REFUSALS)
- sympathy notes for which we feel we have no words (see also SYMPATHY)
- thank-you notes for gifts we didn't like or that were so generous we were overwhelmed by them (see also THANK YOU)

• Avoid the situation in the first place by organizing letters to be answered in order of importance. Don't respond to less difficult letters until you have taken care of those on top of the pile.

• Briefly acknowledge your tardiness and then go directly to the main message.

• Don't go into a long song and dance about how sorry you are for your tardiness, or an even longer explanation of exactly why you couldn't write earlier. "Don't fill *more* than a page and a half with apologies for not having written sooner!" (Lewis Carroll) Egocentric agonizing about your shortcomings only takes the spotlight off the other person and focuses it on you.

• Don't imply the tardiness is somehow the other person's fault ("I'm always nervous about writing you because you write such beautiful letters" or "I didn't want to hurt your feelings with our rejection, so I put off writing").

Tips on Writing

～ Keep a selection of interesting postcards on hand. When you realize you're going to have trouble writing a letter, send a brief note on a postcard acknowledging the issue and saying you'll write soon. This does away with the sense of something hanging over you. The letter will be twice as easy to write when you get to it because you'll feel virtuous for having sent the postcard.

～ Knowing that "the path of later leads to the house of never" (Donald E. Walker), set yourself up for success. Address an envelope to the person. Open a computer file or pick up pen and paper. You'll feel the weight of a half-begun task pulling at you and you will find it easier to finish it, just to get that envelope off your desk.

～ Don't feel you have to write three times as much and four times as charmingly because you're late; this kind of pressure will keep you from ever writing. Write the letter you would have written had you written it earlier.

~ We aren't the only ones behind in our correspondence. Oscar W. Firkins (in Ina Ten Eyck Firkins, ed., *Memoirs and Letters of Oscar W. Firkins*, 1934) was often late:

> "I want to write a word to you this morning to thank you for the kind letter I received some months ago, and to assure you that my silence has meant neither forgetfulness nor indifference."

> "Again delay has overtaken me in the matter of response to your letter. Examination time and the preparations for my trip must shoulder part of the responsibility, and the rest must be referred to that immemorial scapegoat, human nature."

> "I have long had in mind a letter to you, postponed by the foolish wish we all have to write more and better tomorrow instead of less and worse today."

Sylvia Townsend Warner (in William Maxwell, ed., *Letters: Sylvia Townsend Warner*, Viking Press, 1982) did her share of apologizing:

> "It is disgraceful that I have meant for so long to write to you, and put it off for equally long."

> "I have begun many letters to you in my mind, and some even on paper, but never finished them."

> "I have been a Hog with Bristles not to have written to you before—though I got back ten days ago I have not had a moment to turn around in since, not to turn around with any feelings of leisure and amplitude, such as I would want when I write to you."

> "You must have thought me very ungrateful in not writing before to thank you for taking so much trouble about my poems. My time has been taken up with visitors."

Special Situations

~ Although in principle there is zero tolerance for business tardiness—late deliveries, unanswered letters, unfilled orders—it happens. Frequently. Advice in this chapter is useful, but for industrial-strength help, see ADJUSTMENTS and APOLOGIES.

~ When late with a "thank you," don't take more than a phrase or a sentence to apologize ("My thanks are no less sincere for being so unforgivably late"; "I am sorry not to have told you sooner how much we enjoyed your homemade chutney"). There are not many good excuses for being late with a thank-you note, so don't offer one—it's bound to appear feeble. It's better to say you have no excuse and you're sorry. Then continue with an expression of your thanks, which should probably be more fervent and well-crafted than if you'd written at once. "The obligation to express gratitude deepens with procrastination. The longer you wait, the more effusive must be the thanks." (Judith Martin, "Miss Manners")

Format

∾ All belated letters take the format of the letter as it would originally have been written: a handwritten belated thank-you note; a typewritten apology on letterhead stationery for a business tardiness.

WORDS

absentminded	forgive	overlook	remiss
apologies	inadvertently	pardon	sheepish
distressed	negligence	regret	sorry
embarrassed			

PHRASES

accept my apology

asleep at the wheel/on the job/
  at the switch

delayed answering your letter
  because

embarrassing to discover that

excuse the delay

feel sorry/terrible/bad about

forgive my tardiness

I am upset about

I don't know how it happened that

intended to write immediately

much to my regret

no excuse for

not from any lack of

pardon my late response

reproach myself

slipped my mind

SENTENCES

I apologize for not having responded sooner.

I hope my tardiness in answering your question has not greatly
  inconvenienced you.

I imagine that everyone but me has written by now to congratulate you on your promotion and exciting move to Los Angeles.

I'm sorry for the delay in getting back to you—I've been out of town the past three weeks.

I'm sorry—this letter is badly overdue.

I've been writing you in my head for weeks—it's time to get it down on paper.

My delay in acknowledging the touching gift of your father's stamp collection is simply inexcusable.

My tardiness is due to bouts of extreme busyness and bouts of extreme laziness—I don't know which is worse.

Our best wishes for your 75th birthday are no less warm and heartfelt for being so late.

Our holiday greetings are late this year, frankly for no good reason.

Please forgive me for not writing sooner to thank you for the unique and useful fleur-de-lis letter-opener.

Please forgive the delay in responding to your letter of June 14.

PARAGRAPHS

Well, yes, it's me responding with my usual promptness. I wish that I had any kind of excuse (I've been hospitalized, I've been imprisoned, I've been on a secret mission, I'm a finalist with Publisher's Clearing House), but sadly I do not.

I might have to borrow Groucho Marx's explanation for his belated letter: "Excuse me for not answering your letter sooner, but I've been so busy not answering letters that I couldn't get around to not answering yours in time."

Many and fervent (but, alas, belated) good wishes to you on your birthday. I've got a bad sector in my brain, and can't remember if it was this year or last year that I sent you the birthday card with the warthogs on it. However, I'm betting on last year.

We apologize for the delay in scheduling your tree trimming. The cleanup after the May 30 storm left us shorthanded for everything else. A crew is available at 8 a.m. on the following dates: June 6, 9, 10. Please call with a day that is convenient for you.

SAMPLE LETTERS

Dear Maurice Garcia,

Please accept our apology for not letting you know that the Carlist desktop organizer (# CL-5521) you ordered on February 11 is temporarily out of stock. You are correct: three weeks is a long time to wait for something billed for same-day shipping. In the normal way, you would have received a postcard asking whether you wished to wait until we had the item in stock or wished to change or cancel your order.

As you've ordered the organizer from another company, we will cancel your order with Wallace Office Supply. In the meantime, I am enclosing a coupon good for 20% off your next Wallace order. We regret the inconvenience to you and look forward to serving you more effectively in the future.

Dear Roberta Alden,

Please excuse the delay in sending you your copy of the signed contract (enclosed). Mr. Dreiser will be calling you next week about the schedule.

Sincerely,
Clyde Griffiths

From: "PT"<akadoc@email.net>
To: "Mary"<MMM@email.net>
Date: Tue, 15 Aug 2000 11:26:14 -0500

Hi, I have a good excuse for not writing. I've been thinking. For example, did you hear about the guy who collected paste jewelry? He was hooked on faux onyx! Ha, ha, ha . . .

Dear Reverend Charwell,

I said I would notify you as soon as we made a decision on filling our associate position. I imagine that, not having heard from us, you assumed correctly that we had offered the position to another candidate. However, I am sorry to be so late letting you know myself.

We were impressed with your credentials, especially with your achievements in Porthminster and with the references from Hubert Conway and Jean Tasbrugh. In the end, however, we decided in favor of the candidate with more experience in homiletics.

Best wishes to you for continued good work in your ministry.

From: BJZG@email.net
To: RMK@email.net
Date: Fri, 7 Jul 2000 12:33:33 EDT
Subject: a major case of guilt—yea, a boatload

Oh, right. I neglect you shamefully and what do you do in return? You send me a present! I am scheduling hari-kiri for next Wednesday at 11:20. Be there.

~

Dear Dorcy Aldrich,

Please forgive our tardiness in thanking you for your generous and valued donation to the Hatcher Ide Community Affairs Fund. Because moneys received in our current fundraising drive are being matched, your contribution is a significant one for us.

Thank you for being one of our most consistent and openhanded supporters.

~

See also: ACKNOWLEDGMENTS, APOLOGIES, SENSITIVE, THANK YOU.

Collection Letters 12

The object of collection letters is to get the money without losing the customer.

—N.H. AND S.K. MAGER

When writing collection letters you have two goals that work against each other: you want the customer to pay the overdue account and you want to keep the customer's goodwill and business. Well-written, effective collection letters pay off handsomely, not only because of the retrieved income but also because of the delinquent accounts that become dependable accounts.

Collection attempts most often begin as past-due reminders from a company's billing office, accounting department, or credit division. When the account is thirty, sixty, or ninety days overdue, the first of a series of collection letters will be sent. Only when the company's series of increasingly aggressive collection letters is ignored is the account turned over to a collection agency. Many large firms use statistical models to predict which accounts need more aggressive action early on. Remember, too, that given a large population of overdue accounts, the single most effective collection method may be a pleasant telephone reminder.

Collection Letters Include

- announcements that the account is being turned over to lawyer/collection agency
- letters to lawyer/collection agency
- personal collection letters: friend/relative
- reminders
- series of increasingly insistent letters
- thank you for payment

- Collection letters can reach levels of high art in their quest to collect on an overdue bill without losing the customer's goodwill. They are always courteous and in the beginning they assume that the customer intends to pay but has been forgetful. Each letter sent to an overdue account is written as though it is the last; you are optimistic, appreciative, confident. Include: customer, order, or invoice number; date and amount of purchase; items purchased; original payment due date; date by which you expect payment now; references to previous letters about the outstanding balance; suggested payment plan; other descriptive information. Leave enough time (two to three weeks between letters) to give the customer a chance to pay. End each letter with a definite request as well as a statement that if payment has been sent this letter can be ignored. Include a postage-paid reply envelope to encourage prompt response. A suggested plan featuring six collection letters is given below. Your own needs may be met by a series of four or ten, or you may prefer to vary the messages.

- Collection letter 1: After sending several statements indicating the past-due status of the account (perhaps with a stamped message or reminder sticker that says "Past Due" or "Second Notice"), you send a gentle, friendly letter pointing out the overdue payment. Your letter is brief, saying simply that a stated amount is so many weeks or months overdue. You pleasantly request payment.

- Collection letter 2: You are a little more insistent and remind the customer that payment still hasn't been received. In a second paragraph, ask for explanations or suggest several face-saving reasons why the person hasn't paid (bill was overlooked, was lost in the mail, customer was away). Close with an expression of your confidence that the payment will be sent at once.

- Collection letter 3: Your tone becomes more urgent, your letter is longer, and you give the customer one or more good reasons to pay the bill: it will protect their credit rating and reputation; it is a matter of fairness/justice/conscience; it is the responsible thing to do; it will make them feel good; it is a matter of their self-respect; it is in their own best self-interest. In this or the next letter, propose two payment schedules that are acceptable to you, and offer the customer a choice. Divide the past-due amount into weekly, semi-monthly, monthly, or two lump-sum payments.

- Collection letter 4: Your message is increasingly stern, and you present additional arguments for payment: you have carried out your obligations by providing the service or shipping the goods and now they must carry out theirs; the amount is too small to lose their credit rating over it; the customer wouldn't want to be placed on your delinquent list; they wouldn't want to be reported to the trade credit bureau; they will not be able to place any future orders with you. For the first time, you mention the possibility of turning their account over to a collection agent or attorney for collection.

- Collection letter 5: By now you assume the customer is aware of the problem and is deliberately avoiding payment. In a strong message, you announce that you're obliged to take other action, to turn the account over to a collection agency for collection or to a lawyer for legal action. (If you opt for legal action, word your letter with your attorney's advice.) Even now, however, give the customer ten days in which to make arrangements to settle the account before taking action. Be clear that the action can be avoided if the customer responds at once.

- Collection letter 6: The final letter represents your belief that the customer will pay only if compelled. You say that the account is being transferred to a stated collection agency or to a stated law firm as of a stated date. This letter simply announces the action you're taking; you no longer try to get the customer to pay.

- When you write to the collection agency, give complete information: name, address, telephone numbers, account number, copies of all correspondence, statements, data sheets.

What Not to Say

- Don't threaten the customer with a collection agency or legal action until you are ready to pursue these avenues. If you say you are turning the account over to a collection agency in ten days, do so.

- Don't use words like "failure" ("your failure to respond," "failure to pay"); "ignore" ("you have ignored our letters"); "insist" or "demand" ("we insist that you send payment at once"). They make the other person feel small, which will not endear you to them.

- Don't use negative tactics (insults, name-calling, bullying, sarcasm, arrogance, and verbal wrist-slapping); they produce only negative results and tarnish your company's reputation.

- Avoid the arch, pseudo-puzzled, and ineffective tone sometimes seen: "We simply cannot comprehend why someone with such a good credit rating . . ." "We are at a loss to understand why we have not heard from you." "We've been scratching our heads . . ."
- Don't say anything that could be construed as libelous.

Tips on Writing

∼ Be tactful. Even people with poor credit histories often feel they are doing a good job given their circumstances. A poorly written collection letter can inspire feelings of anger, self-pity, or helplessness, none of which leads to the writing of a check.

∼ Space collection letters. In the beginning send them monthly, immediately after a payment date is missed. Allow enough time for the customer to respond or for delays caused by illness, busy periods, or vacations. Later, send letters every ten days to two weeks. The more stubborn the account, the closer together you space the letters. When the account has a good credit history, you don't send letters quite as often.

∼ Credit and financial matters are, theoretically at least, confidential. Make every attempt to safeguard the credit information you give and receive.

∼ Don't send collection letters to a person's place of business where others might open the mail. For the same reasons of privacy, don't use postcards to send collection messages. You don't want to embarrass your customer or leave yourself open to complaint or legal action.

Special Situations

∼ When trying to collect from a customer who reports adverse circumstances (illness, unemployment, financial reverses), work out a feasible payment program even if it is a generous one. A background check will indicate whether the person is experiencing difficulties that merit special attention. Reducing a debt by even a small amount is a success for both creditor and debtor and is worthy of your best efforts.

∼ To remind a friend or family member of an overdue loan, help the person save face by including an excuse ("I know how busy you are . . ."; "I wonder if you forgot about . . ."; "Am I mistaken, or did we agree that you'd repay the loan September 1?"). It will be helpful if you have drawn up a loan agreement or a letter stating the terms. When writing a second time, include a photocopy of your agreement.

Format

~ Collection letters are always typed on letterhead stationery.

~ Form letters are used for the first few collection letters in a series. The first can be a simple reminder with spaces to fill in the amount and due date.

WORDS

action	explanation	propose
advise	extend	reminder
arrangement	liability	repayment
balance	misunderstanding	request
circumstances	necessitate	require
collect	nonpayment	satisfy
concerned	notice	settle
cooperation	outstanding	statement
creditworthiness	overdue	terms
debt	overlooked	unpaid
disappointed	oversight	urge
embarrass	past-due	

PHRASES

account past due

accounts receivable

act upon

amount/balance due/owed

appreciate hearing from you

at least a partial payment

be good enough to/so good as to

behind with your payments

call/direct your attention to

clear your account before the next statement period

credit rating/standing/record

damaging to your credit record/ standing/rating

delinquent status of your account

despite our notice of a month ago

did not respond

discuss this with you

easy payment plan
escaped your attention
final opportunity
friendly reminder
have heard nothing from you
how can we work together to
immediately payable
important to resolve this matter
in arrears
it is our policy
I understand and appreciate your position, but
just a reminder/to remind you
legal action/advice/steps
let us hear from you right away
mail today
must hear from you
mutually satisfactory solution
no activity on your account
not made a payment since
now due on your account
official notice
outstanding balance
overdue account
past-due amount
perhaps you didn't realize

please let us hear from you by
please mail/send us
pressing need for action
prompt payment/remittance
reasonable payment arrangement
recourse to legal action
reduce your balance
resolve this matter
review of our files/your account shows
seriously delinquent
several statements and letters
since you haven't replied to our last letter
so that you can maintain your credit standing
special appeal
strongly suggest
suggested payment plan solution
to avoid additional expenses, delays, and unpleasantness
unacceptable delay
valued customer
we haven't heard from you
we would appreciate your sending us
without further delay

SENTENCES

After 120 days, we normally/routinely/automatically turn an account over to our attorneys for collection.

A postage-paid envelope is enclosed for your convenience.

Despite our last three reminders, your account remains unpaid.

Enclosed is a copy of your last statement, showing a balance of $457.89 that is ninety days overdue.

I am sorry, but we are unable to extend you any more time for the payment of your outstanding balance of $896.78.

If we do not hear from you at once/within the next ten days, we will be obliged to pursue other collection procedures/we will have no choice but to engage the services of a collection agency.

If you have already sent your check/paid your balance of $324.56, please ignore this notice.

If you haven't already mailed in your payment, won't you take a moment to mail it today?

If your financial circumstances make it impossible to pay the full amount at this time, please let us know as I am sure that we can work out an acceptable schedule of installment payments.

If your payment is not received by June 1, we will be obliged to turn your account over to the Costello Collection Agency.

It is important that you take some action before this unpaid balance affects your credit rating.

Just a reminder: your account balance of $106.87 is thirty days past due.

May we have your check for $89.43 by return mail?

Our records show your account to be seriously in arrears.

Please call or write to make arrangements.

Please forward payment in the amount of $269.89 promptly.

Please mail your check by May 5 so that no future action will be necessary.

Thank you for your cooperation/attention to this matter/for taking care of this at once.

Thank you for your recent remittance, which has allowed us to reactivate your account.

There may be a good explanation for your lack of response to our requests for payment of your overdue account—won't you tell us about it?

This matter must be resolved without further delay.

Unfortunately your payment has not been received.

We are disappointed not to have heard from you about your overdue balance of $1785.97.

We ask for your cooperation in paying the balance due.

We expect to hear from you by July 15 without fail.

We have sent a number of friendly requests for payment but have had no response from you.

We hope that you will take advantage of this last invitation to settle your account and to avoid further damage to your credit rating as well as the costs of any possible legal action.

We look forward to hearing from you.

We must know your intentions immediately.

We provide prompt service, and we expect prompt payment.

We resort to legal action with the greatest reluctance.

We would be happy to work with you to arrange an easy payment plan suited to your circumstances.

Why not take care of this matter right now?

You are a much-appreciated customer, and we hope there is no problem.

You may not realize that your account is ninety days past due.

Your account has been turned over to Darley and Havison, our attorneys, for collection and, if necessary, legal action.

Your payment of $876.23 will be appreciated.

Your prompt payment will protect your good credit rating.

You will want to mail your check today so that you can continue using your credit privileges.

PARAGRAPHS

Enclosed are copies of your statements, year to date. Please check them against your records, and let us know if they do not agree with ours. We show an outstanding balance of $1,236.90.

The nonpayment of your balance is expensive for both of us: it is costing you your excellent credit record as well as monthly service charges and it is costing us lost revenues and extra accounting expenses. We strongly urge you to make out a check right now for the balance due on your account (a self-addressed stamped envelope is enclosed for your convenience). If you wish to discuss some financial difficulty or arrange for a special payment schedule, please call 800/555-1331 today so that we can avoid reclassifying your account as delinquent.

The Locksley-Jones Collection Agency has been authorized by Elliot Lumber to collect the $980.54 past due amount on your account. According to information turned over to us by Elliot, you have not responded to requests for payment made over a period of eight months. This letter serves as your official notice that collection proceedings will begin ten days from the date of this letter unless you contact us to make some satisfactory arrangement for payment.

Thank you for your payment of $763.21, received today. We are happy to be able to remove you from our collection system and to re-establish your line of credit. We do this with the understanding that you will keep your account current in the future. We hope to continue to serve you with all your plumbing and electrical needs.

SAMPLE LETTERS

Dear Ms. Phippard:

Your account is now ninety days overdue in the amount of $85.89. As you are one of our longtime customers with an excellent credit rating, we assume this is a simple oversight.

Thank you for taking care of this matter promptly.

Sincerely,

~

Dear Mr. Landauer,

We would like to remind you once again that we have not received any payment on your account balance of $597.45. If you need additional time or would like to arrange a special payment schedule, please call the credit department today or tomorrow at extension 91. Otherwise, we will expect to receive a check in the mail.

We appreciate your prompt attention to this matter.

Sincerely,

~

TO: Nolan Associates

FROM: Charney Office Supplies

DATE: March 6, 2002

RE: Past-Due Account

We have alerted you several times (see our statements of November 4 and December 7 and our letters of January 6 and February 5) that your account has a balance of $1,059.32

outstanding. Because your credit rating could be adversely affected by continuing non-payment, we hope that you will send us something on account immediately.

We need to hear from you this week concerning your plans for repayment. Thank you.

Sincerely,

~

Dear Ms. Seebach:

We are concerned about your past-due account of $473.23 and your lack of response to our inquiries about it. We would like to hear from you within the next ten days so that we are not obliged to seek other, more serious means of satisfying this debt.

Please consider protecting your credit rating by sending us a check promptly. You will be glad you did.

Sincerely,

~

Dear Stephen Bracebridge:

Your account (# 8103-484-2329) is seriously in arrears. As we have had no response to our reminders, we are obliged to consider collecting the past-due amount of $12,489.19 with the help of a collection agency.

We like to avoid this way of removing unpaid accounts from our books—both for your sake and ours. Your credit standing will be affected by such action, and we lose time and money trying to collect money that is, in all justice, owed to us.

We will transfer this account to a collection agency on April 3. We would, however, be happy to work out a payment schedule with you if you will call before then.

Sincerely,

~

Dear Algy,

I dislike reminding you yet again, but it's now been six weeks since I lent you $200 "for just a few days." If I could just forget about it, I would, but as it happens I need that money myself—right away.

Shall I stop by after work to pick it up or do you want to drop it off at the house? Let me know.

Sincerely,

~

See also: CREDIT, FOLLOW-UP, REQUESTS.

Complaints

13

If you don't write to complain, you'll never receive your order. If you do write, you'll receive the merchandise before your angry letter reaches its destination.

—ARTHUR BLOCH

If you're writing a letter of complaint, you're not alone. Millions write them every year. One multifoods corporation receives three hundred thousand complaining phone calls and letters per year.

Some complaints can be handled by telephone. In general, however, a letter of complaint (also known as a claim letter or consumer action letter) is more effective. First, you've put something tangible on someone's desk—eventually it must be dealt with. Second, you can be more tactful in a letter. Third, the details are conveyed in an accessible form (it's hard to imagine someone on the other end of the telephone taking down dates, names, and invoice numbers as carefully as you would spell them out in a letter). Fourth, you have a record of your complaint.

When you have a general, community-wide complaint, see LETTERS TO THE EDITOR. If you are responding to a complaint, see ADJUSTMENTS or even APOLOGIES.

Write Letters of Complaint About

- billing/collection/financial/ordering errors
- children: misbehavior/damage by
- community or neighborhood problems: adult bookstores/ unkempt property/noisy parties
- delays: late shipment/refund/merchandise/supplies/payment

- employees: incompetent/rude/inappropriate behavior
- legislative problems: high taxes/unfair laws/pending bills
- merchandise: defective/damaged/dangerous/overpriced/missing parts, misleading advertising, bait-and-switch tactics
- mistakes, misunderstandings, personal errors
- neighbors (see also NEIGHBORS)
- pets: damage by/attacks by
- policies: unfavorable/restrictive/discriminatory
- schools: undeserved reprimands/undesirable programs

- State the problem: what it is, when you noticed it, how it inconvenienced you.
- Provide factual details. For a problem with merchandise: date and place of purchase, sales slip number, description of product, serial or model number, amount paid, name of salesperson, your account number or charge card number. For a problem with a rude or inefficient service person: date and time of the incident, name of person involved (if you know it), where it occurred, names of witnesses, description of behavior. For a problem with printed inaccuracies, misstatements, or incomplete information: date, section, page, column, and incorrect material; correct data; your phone number. For a problem with the airlines: flight number, dates of flight, points of origin and termination, description of problem or incident, where and when it occurred.
- Include relevant documentation: sales slips, receipts, warranties or guarantees, previous correspondence, pictures of damaged item, repair or service orders, canceled checks, contracts, paid invoices. (Send photocopies of your documents.)
- Tell why it's important to resolve your problem.
- State clearly what you expect from the person or company: refund, replacement, exchange, repair. If you want money, state how much. Request a reasonable solution.
- Suggest a deadline for the action.
- Give your name, address, and home and work telephone numbers.

- Close with your confidence in the other person's desire to do the right thing and ability to take care of the problem to your satisfaction ("I am sure you will find a solution for this problem"; "I am confident that you will want to replace this defective answering machine"). Assume that the person who receives your letter will be helpful and let this assurance show.

What Not to Say

- Don't use subjective phrases like "I want," "I feel," and "I need." Figures, dates, facts, photographs, and documentation are more persuasive.

- Don't indulge in sarcasm, accusations, abuse, recriminations, blaming, smart remarks, exaggerations, or emotional outbursts—unless, of course, your only aim is to vent your anger on someone. If you want an adjustment, an apology, or other positive response, avoid antagonizing the person who is in the best position to help you. Negative letters are not only ineffective, they make you look foolish (and feel foolish later, when you think about it).

- Don't be negative ("I don't suppose you'll do anything about this"). Assume the other person wants to be helpful (at least until you find out otherwise).

- Don't threaten to sue. This is generally seen as a bluff; people who actually sue leave this to their lawyers. You might—if you mean this—say that you are going to take the case to small claims court. Sometimes this can lead to a quick, inexpensive resolution. (Note that there are time limits on certain legal actions.)

- Don't accuse anyone of lies, unprofessionalism, cheating, stealing, or misrepresentation. You may be creating legal problems for yourself.

- Don't hint for free products or "compensation" beyond what you are due.

Tips on Writing

∼ Write your letter soon after the incident or problem; details are fresher in your mind, and your chances of getting a good response are greater.

∼ Be brief: a one-page letter has the best chance of being read.

∼ Be courteous: the person to whom you are writing may have had nothing to do with the error and will be more willing to help you if you are calm and reasonable. When appropriate, include positive remarks: why you chose that product, how long you've used the company's services or products, that you think this incident must be an exception to the rule.

∼ Focus on one complaint or issue per letter. When you report in the same letter a rude salesperson, insufficient parking, a mispriced item, and a can opener too dull to open anything, you are likely to get (at most) a blanket apology and no particular action on any of the individual problems.

∼ Place more emphasis on how the problem can be resolved and less emphasis on the details of the mix-up, your reactions and feelings, and what a disaster it has all been. Your letter should be oriented toward resolving the problem or arriving at a solution.

∼ Help the other person save face. If you act as though only your threats and string-pulling are bringing about a settlement, you deny the other person their sense of themselves as decent, generous people.

∼ If your complaint has several components (list of ordered items missing, series of events), set off these items in a numbered or bulleted list.

∼ Keep a record of every phone call, letter, or other action you take, along with the dates, the names and titles of those you dealt with, and a summary of the results.

∼ Keep the originals of all correspondence, canceled checks, sales slips, and supporting documents.

∼ Don't send copies to third parties when you first write a company; give it a chance to settle the problem. If you receive no satisfaction, subsequent letters can be copied to regulatory agencies, trade associations, or consumer advocate offices. On your letter to the company, use "cc:" to indicate those who are receiving a copy.

∼ "Complain to one who can help you." (Yugoslavian proverb) There's nothing less effective than writing a great letter to the wrong person. In general, send a complaint letter to a specific person. A letter addressed to nobody in particular ends up on nobody's list of responsibilities. When writing to lawmakers or government officials, check the library reference department for listings in *U.S. Government Manual* (new edition every year), *Who's Who in American Politics*, and state and federal handbooks and directories. *Federal Information Centers*, which lists contacts across the country when you need assistance from the federal government, is available free from Consumer Information Center, Pueblo, CO 81009. When writing businesses, obtain names and titles of company officials by calling the company or from directories of U.S. businesses in the reference section of your library. Addressing a letter to the company's consumer affairs department is a good choice; these departments specialize in problems like yours. If you receive no satisfaction from the company, pursue the matter with: your local Better Business Bureau; a local, county, or state consumer agency; the consumer division of the state attorney general's office; your state representatives; a relevant consumer group; trade association; the appropriate regulatory government agency. When appealing to one of these groups, include a description of the problem, a list of the steps you've taken, and the names and titles of those you've contacted. If you're involved in a disagreement with a professional, write the state board that licenses the person.

~ *The Consumer Action Handbook* is a useful 144-page publication updated yearly and available free by writing: Handbook, Federal Consumer Information Center, Pueblo, CO 81009 or by calling 800/688-9889 (for weekly updates click on Handbook at www.pueblo.gsa.gov). In addition to preventive advice (consumer tips on car repair, purchase and leasing; shopping from home; avoiding consumer and investment fraud; home improvement and financing; choosing and using credit cards wisely), the handbook tells you where to direct complaints, listing contact information for national consumer organizations, corporate consumer relations departments, automobile manufacturers, better business bureaus throughout the country, trade associations, third-party dispute resolution programs, federal agencies as well as state and local consumer protection offices. You can also go to http://www.pueblo.gsa.gov/complaintresources.htm where the Federal Consumer Information Center offers a list of resources for consumer complaints about medicines, drugs, and medical devices; health clubs and exercise equipment; veterinary products; airline baggage and service; auto dealers; banking; online services, spam or junk e-mail; telephone service.

~ If you write many complaint letters, you might like *Shocked, Appalled, and Dismayed! How to Write Letters of Complaint That Get Results* by Ellen Phillips.

Special Situations

~ In a dispute about a credit-card purchase, contact the credit card company to withhold payment while the problem is being resolved (read the information on the back of your statement for details). Most companies have forms for this, asking for your name, account number, credit card statement reference number, amount, store where purchased, and description of the item and the problem.

~ To protest an increase in rent or in auto, medical, or homeowner insurance, include: name, address, telephone number, apartment or policy number, years you have been renting or insured with that company, history of rates, reasons for your objection. Ask that someone call you to discuss the matter.

~ When there are issues with your child's school, assume nothing at the outset. Begin your letter with questions: "Can you tell me . . . ?" "Is it true that . . . ?" Too often, misunderstandings crop up somewhere between school and home. Clarify the issues before asking for changes or apologies.

~ When schools relay complaints to parents, phone calls are the first avenue of communication, but sometimes letters must be sent. In writing parents, the school official's points of reference will be "tact" and "fact." State what happened briefly and objectively. Suggest a date and time for a meeting or ask that the parent call you. Enclose a copy of the school regulations the child violated or refer the parent to the student handbook. State what action is being taken or may be taken by the school.

~ When you are one of a large group protesting an action, product, service, or corporate behavior, send individual, personalized letters rather than form letters or group-generated complaints. Organizations are more likely to respond to one well-written, original letter than to hundreds of mimeographed postcards. In some cases, the great number of complaints is persuasive, but in general you may be wasting time and postage on mass-produced complaints.

~ When writing to an elected official to recommend a course of action, mention the issue or legislation you're writing about in the first sentence or in a subject line ("Re: property taxes" or "Subject: HR4116"). State your opinion clearly ("I strongly disapprove of . . . /I urge you to . . ."). Give reasons for your position. If there are several, list them separately, set off by numbers, asterisks, or bullets. Indicate the course of action you would like the person to take or the response that you expect. Offer to serve as a resource if the issue is something you are particularly knowledgeable about. End with an expression of appreciation for their interest and time.

~ Sometimes apologies are necessary on both sides of a dispute. Even when you have a legitimate complaint, it's possible that you have in some small way aggravated the situation. Making your own apology is not only honest (if called for) but is often helpful in eliciting the response you want.

Format

∿ Business letterhead, business-personal stationery, or personal letterhead are all good choices for a complaint letter.

∿ Type the letter if possible. If you must handwrite it, be sure it is legible and neat.

WORDS

action	inaccurate	misprint	resolve
adjustment	inadequate	misquote	restore
agreed-upon	inappropriate	misrepresented	short-sighted
compensation	incident	missing	slipshod
concerned	incomplete	misstatement	thoughtless
damaged	inconsistent	mistake	uncooperative
defective	inconvenient	misunderstanding	unfortunate
disagreement	incorrect	nonfunctioning	unfounded
disappointed	inexperienced	off-putting	unjustifiable
displeased	inferior	omission	unpleasant
dispute	insufficient	overcharged	unprofessional
dissatisfaction	lax	overestimated	unqualified
embarrassing	misapprehension	overlooked	unreasonable
exasperating	miscalculation	oversight	unreliable
experience	misconception	regrettable	unsatisfactory
fault	misconstrued	reimburse	unsound
flaw	mishandled	remake	untidy
grievance	misinformed	repair	untrue
ill-advised	misinterpreted	repay	unwarranted
impolite	misleading	replace	

PHRASES

a mix-up in my order
appealing to you for help
are you aware that
as a longtime customer
call to your immediate attention

correct your records
defective upon arrival
does not meet our performance
    standards
expect to hear from you soon

has not met my expectations

hope to resolve this problem

I am concerned about

I feel certain you would want to know that

it has come to my attention that

it is with reluctance that I must inform you

it was disconcerting to find that

I was displeased/distressed/disturbed/ offended/disappointed by

I wish to be reimbursed for

I would like to alert you to

may not be aware that

not up to your usual high standards

register a complaint about

serious omission/problem

under the conditions of the warranty

unpleasant incident

unsatisfactory performance

we were unhappy with

with all possible speed

would like credit for

you have generally given us excellent service, but

SENTENCES

Anything you can do to speed matters up/resolve this problem will be greatly appreciated.

Here are the facts.

I am confident that you can resolve this.

I am expecting the courtesy of a prompt reply.

I am writing regarding my last bill, invoice # G4889, dated August 15, 2002.

I believe that an apology is due us.

I expect an adjustment to be made as soon as possible.

I hope you will take this complaint in the helpful spirit in which it is meant.

I know you will want to see that such an incident does not occur again.

I like your product but I object strongly to your advertising.

I'm concerned about Coach Ingelsant's angry, abusive manner with the junior soccer players.

I'm confident that we can resolve this matter to our mutual satisfaction.

I regret/am sorry to inform you of the following unpleasant situation.

I strongly oppose your position on this weapons system.

It is my understanding that it will be repaired/replaced at your expense.

I will send a check for the balance as soon as I receive a corrected statement.

I wish to receive credit on my account for this item.

I would appreciate a telephone call from you about this situation.

I would like a refund in the amount of $49.99.

I would like to clear up this misunderstanding as soon as possible.

Let me know what is being done.

Please call the principal's office to arrange a meeting with the principal, the school counselor, and myself regarding Christie's suspension.

Please contact me within three business days to make arrangements for rectifying the situation.

Please let me hear from you at your earliest convenience.

Please let me know what options are available to me.

Thank you for your prompt assistance with this situation/problem.

The following situation has come to my attention.

The most satisfactory solution for us would be for you to send us a replacement lamp and reimburse us for the cost of mailing the defective lamp back to you.

There was too little feedback to us during the design of the #2 unit.

This product has been unsatisfactory in several respects.

We experienced the following problem in your store/restaurant/hotel last week.

We would like to resolve this situation without delay/without having recourse to the Better Business Bureau or Small Claims Court.

Will you please check on this?

PARAGRAPHS

I received the leather patchwork travel bag today (copies of catalog page and invoice enclosed), but the matching billfold was not included. Please send me one as soon as possible, in burgundy to match the bag. Thank you.

Five weeks ago I mailed you my check for our stay at the Vörös Csillig in Budapest, and I have not yet received confirmation of our reservations. As the rest of my itinerary depends on whether we are able to stay in Budapest, I would appreciate an immediate phone call from you.

Channel 12's insistence on running inappropriate programming between 5:00 p.m. and 7:00 p.m., when many young people are watching, means that this family at least will no longer turn to Channel 12 for any of its news, entertainment, or programs.

Please find enclosed a bracelet, a necklace, and a pair of earrings. We would appreciate either repair or replacement of these items. The bracelet has a broken clasp, the gold on the earrings appears to be chipped, and the silver finish is overlaying the gemstone on the necklace. In each case, dissatisfied customers of our store returned the items to us. Your immediate attention to this matter will be greatly appreciated.

I'm enclosing a photocopy of a collection letter I received from your agency. This is the sixth letter I have received about this account. Although my first initial and last name are the same as the person responsible for it, we have nothing else in common. I marked each of the earlier letters "incorrect address" and returned them to you. Please verify the correct address of your correspondent. I will expect a letter from you stating that my name and address have been removed from your files and that my credit rating has not been affected by this error.

My order (# 578942-E) for two dozen Shipley short wave radios, placed three weeks ago, has not yet been received. I was told to expect them within the week. Will you please check to see if the order has gone astray? We need them immediately.

I object to the tactics used in your telephone sales efforts. Today a caller identified herself as someone from the credit bureau. After hearing the words "credit bureau" I stayed attentively on the line. It was only after several minutes of trying to understand what was wrong with my credit rating that I realized I was being asked to buy life insurance. I think your approach is deceitful. Enclosed is a copy of the letter I have written to the Better Business Bureau complaining of it.

Thank you for your fifty-six-page report on your department's activities over the past six months. The graphics are outstanding. However, while there is much to reflect on in the text, I find many questions unanswered and several important issues left unaddressed. I would like to discuss with you the kinds of information I need to see in a departmental semiannual report. Please phone my secretary to set up an appointment.

Imagine our embarrassment when we served one of your Paramount Hams for Easter, and none of our guests were able to eat it because it was excessively salty. I would like a refund for the inedible ham (label and store receipt enclosed). Also, can you give me any good reasons for ever buying another Trotter and Duff Paramount Ham? I don't like writing someone off on the basis of a single error, but one bad ham is one too many.

The Abbeville Faxphone 200 that I ordered from you two weeks ago receives documents but will not transmit them. Several phone calls to your service department (I was, of course, unable to fax them) about this serious problem have been unhelpful. The only information I was given was that I was not to return the machine without prior approval. Please send such approval immediately.

SAMPLE LETTERS

Dear Mr. Tallant:

As you know, a great deal of our work is coordinated with Harvey Crane Construction. They must complete their paving and other operations before the median work on Pearl Street can begin.

I have seen no progress on their part for about a month. Their delays mean that we incur such damages as loss of production, lower profits, winter protection costs, remobilization, accelerated schedules (overtime), and barricade rental—to name just a few items.

As these costs and damages will necessarily be passed on to you, you may want to check into the situation.

Sincerely,

Dear Mr. Thornton,

This is the third time we have contacted you about your dog, Buck. The neighborhood children continue to be frightened of him, and refuse to play outdoors when he is in your yard. There have been several reports of him snapping at the children.

When would be a good time to discuss this situation with you? We would like to come to some agreement without going to the authorities.

I hope to hear from you very soon.

Sincerely yours,

dear cummings writing machine company,

i would like an immediate replacement for this typewriter. i bought it on june 3 of this year from 'tulips' in cambridge, massachusetts (sales slip enclosed), but, as you can see, it will not produce capital letters.

the 'tulips' people tell me that the manufacturer is responsible for all defects. please let me know at once how you plan to supply me with a typewriter that types capital letters.

yours truly,

Dear Mr. Abednego,

When I bought my first insurance policy with the Independent W. Diddlesex Insurance Company, I was told that buying my auto, homeowners, and life insurances from you would guarantee me a 20% reduction over the rates I would normally pay separately. Now that I have switched my life insurance to Diddlesex to obtain this complete coverage, I find that I am paying substantially the same rates as before.

Will you please check to see why I am not getting the lower rates, and let me know as soon as possible?

Sincerely,

Dear Mr. Bellman:

We have come to expect a high degree of judgment and integrity from the Calcutta Tape and Sealing Wax Office. It was therefore as surprising as it was distressing when the last shipment was found to be substandard.

Substitutions were made without our permission—invariably a substitution of an inferior product at the original price. In two instances, quantities were not the quantities ordered (they were smaller), with no equivalent adjustment made on the invoice. I am enclosing a copy of our order, a copy of your invoice, and a list of what we actually received. I would appreciate hearing from you immediately on what we can do not only to remedy the current shipment but also to ensure that this doesn't happen again.

Sincerely,

Dear Mr. Atterbury:

Before scheduling an appointment with you to discuss the incorporation of my business, I asked your secretary about your legal fees. He told me you charge $100 an hour. I was therefore very surprised to received a bill for $350 when I spent no more than one hour with you.

I will appreciate an explanation of my bill. Thank you.

Sincerely,

Dear Ms. Scanlon,

We have been renting Apartment 206 at 1935 Chicago Avenue for the past four years and have been pleased with our situation until just recently, when new tenants moved into Apartment 306.

We have spoken to Mr. Lonigan and Ms. Branahan about the frequent parties, arguments, and loud noises after 11:00 p.m., and we have also asked the building manager to do what she could. However, we think you need to look into this situation yourself.

Please let us know what we can expect.

Sincerely yours,

⌒

Dear Wheatley Office Products:

On April 3, I purchased your four-drawer, self-locking EZ-Open File Cabinet, serial number 007800, from your Wheatley outlet on Broadway. I paid a sale price of $329.99 plus tax for the unit.

Unfortunately, the file cabinet does not function as claimed. It self-locks arbitrarily; half the time it does, half the time it doesn't, and no one is able to predict just when it will do which. The one-touch unlocking mechanism does not work at all, which means that usually the drawers have to be unlocked manually with the "emergency only" key. Even when the drawers are not locked, they are difficult to open because of a design problem with overlapping inside shelving.

Mr. Denny Swinton, who sold me the unit, informs me that because the unit was on sale I am unable to return it. I am certain, however, that, sale price or no, I have a right to expect that the unit will perform as promised.

I would like to hear within the next several days that a truck will be coming from Wheatley to pick up the defective unit and that my purchase price will be refunded.

Sincerely,

⌒

Dear Dr. Blenkinsop,

As you know, we have been satisfied patients of yours for the past six years. However, I wonder if you are aware that the condition of your waiting room is off-putting. The carpet rarely appears vacuumed, the plastic plants are thick with dust, and the magazines and children's playthings are strewn about, apparently untouched from one of our visits to the next. Hygiene seems particularly important in a healthcare environment, and, although I know what an excellent physician you are, I can't help worrying about how clean everything else is.

I hope you find this letter helpful rather than unpleasant—it was written with the best intentions.

Sincerely,

⌒

See also: ACKNOWLEDGEMENTS, ADJUSTMENTS, APOLOGIES, NEIGHBORS, ORDERS, RESPONSES.

Congratulations 14

To hear how special and wonderful we are is endlessly enthralling.

—GAIL SHEEHY

Some of the most delightful words we receive—right up there with "I love you"—is the letter that begins, "Congratulations!" Because it is rarely obligatory and because its contents are wholly positive, the congratulations note adds a glow to any personal or business relationship. And you don't have to wait for big news to send one. Small landmarks and successes have a sweetness all their own, and the recipient of your note will long remember your thoughtfulness.

Occasions That Call for Letters of Congratulations

- achievements/awards/honors/prizes/speeches/publications/recognition
- adoption or birth of child
- anniversaries: business/years of service/wedding (see ANNIVERSARIES)
- birthdays (see ANNIVERSARIES)
- business: good business year, new store, new account, new contract, merger, opening own business, securing a franchise
- changes: new car/home/job
- customers: good news, major life events
- election to office: public/organization or club/professional society/ social group
- employees' work
- engagement (see WEDDINGS)

- graduation
- jobs: new job, promotion, new title
- loan payment (see CREDIT)
- religious milestones: christening/circumcision/bar mitzvah/bat mitzvah/ first communion/confirmation/ordination/taking of religious vows
- retirement
- sales messages: being selected to receive special offer/credit limit raised (see SALES)
- wedding (see WEDDINGS)

- Use the word "congratulations" early in your note.
- Mention the reason (graduation, promotion, honor, baby).
- Tell how happy, pleased, proud, or impressed you are—and why. "The art of pleasing consists in being pleased." (William Hazlitt)
- If appropriate, tell how you learned about the good news. If you read it in the newspaper, enclose the clipping or a photocopy of it.
- Relate an anecdote, shared memory, or reflection that has some bearing on the occasion.
- In closing, wish the person continued success and happiness; express your confidence in a bright future; assure them of your affection, love, admiration, warmth, interest, delight, pleasure, or continued business support.

- Don't indulge in excessive flattery ("watch out, Corporate America—here she comes," "I can see that I'll soon be writing to congratulate you on the Nobel Prize"). It makes people uncomfortable. A simple "Congratulations!" and a few personal remarks bring quite enough joy.
- Don't make your congratulatory note do double duty: don't include questions, information, sales messages, or work matters that aren't relevant to the good news.

- Don't compare the recipient's news to something you once did or to something you read in the paper; let the person enjoy a moment in the sun—alone.
- Don't talk about "luck" when congratulating someone; it implies that chance rather than talent and hard work was responsible for the success.
- Beware of inadvertently putting a negative spin on your congratulations. Instead of "I never would have thought you could do it" or "After all this time, you finally did it," say "I'm so impressed with your energy and determination" or "Congratulations on your hard work and perseverance."

Tips on Writing

◞ Written congratulations are optional except when you have received an announcement of personal news (a graduation, for example).

◞ Write soon after hearing the news. Congratulations are best served up warm. If you're late, apologize only briefly.

◞ Even when you're close to the person to whom you're writing, make your congratulatory letter brief and somewhat formal; this increases its impact.

Special Situations

◞ Sending notes of congratulations to customers, clients, colleagues, and other business associates about their good news (births, weddings, promotions, new business) is a thoughtful goodwill gesture.

◞ When a branch office, department, or division has enjoyed a collective success, write to them as a group, naming each employee ("Congratulations on surpassing this year's collection goal/securing the new account/your speedy inventory reduction/a new sales volume record/a smooth departmental reorganization").

◞ Your response to news of an engagement is pleasant and congratulatory. If you have reservations about the relationship, deal with them in person or don't write at all; cautionary or qualified congratulations are worse than none. Traditionally "congratulations" were offered to the engaged man and "best wishes" to the engaged woman; you may properly use either expression for women or men.

〜 The news of a divorce can elicit a simple acknowledgment, a letter of sympathy, or a letter of congratulations. The latter is sent rarely, and then only to someone you know well. You might, however, want to congratulate someone not on the divorce itself but on surviving the upheaval of a difficult period.

〜 Baby announcements inspire some of the happiest congratulations. When the baby is premature, send congratulations, gifts, and good wishes in the normal way; do not wait to see how the baby does. In the event of multiple births, don't ask if the woman took fertility pills and don't say or imply, "You poor things!" Just say "Congratulations!" When a child is born with medical problems or a disability, write that you've heard they have a new little one, that you are thinking of them. Avoid commercial "new baby" cards and conventional congratulations on the one hand, and expressions of sympathy on the other. Some of the unfortunate remarks that these new parents hear include: "You're not going to keep it, are you?" "I think you should sue the hospital." "Is one of you a carrier for this?" "Maybe the baby won't live; that would be best all around." "Whose fault was it?" "Did you drink while you were pregnant?" "I guess it could have been worse." "God only sends burdens to those who can bear them." Until you know how the parents are feeling (devastated, concerned but optimistic, happy to have the child at any price), don't reveal your feelings—they may be wide of the mark. Later, when you know how the parents are feeling, you can respond on a more emotional level. When congratulating someone on an adoption, do not write, "I'll bet you get pregnant now." People adopt for reasons other than fertility and adoption is not, in any case, a cure for infertility (pregnancies occur after adoption at approximately the same rates as they occur in couples dealing with problems of infertility). Don't ask about the child's background or biological/birth parents (never write "real parents"; you are writing to the real parents). Don't say that you "admire" your friends for adopting anymore than you would "admire" a biological parent for having a child. What *do* you write? Ask the parents to tell you about the child and the great arrival day. Say that you can't wait to come visit, and wish them much happiness.

〜 Sometimes a "congratulations" approach is used in sales letters (see SALES).

Format

〜 Most congratulations take the form of a note—on personal stationery, foldovers, or notecards.

~ Commercial cards are available for almost every occasion that calls for congratulations. However, use the inside or back of the card to add your own message.

~ In some contexts (business, politics, clubs and organizations), congratulations may be sent on business letterhead, business-personal paper, or memo stationery, depending on the degree of closeness between sender and recipient and the importance of the good news.

~ Some congratulations may be e-mailed, particularly in office settings among colleagues.

WORDS

accomplishment	excellent	leadership	success
achievement	exceptional	legendary	superb
admire	exciting	meaningful	superior
applaud	extraordinary	memorable	superlative
appreciate	feat	milestone	talent
asset	finest	momentous	thrilled
brilliant	foresight	occasion	tradition
celebration	future	outstanding	tremendous
cheer	generous	peerless	tribute
commend	genius	performance	triumph
compliment	gift	perseverance	unforgettable
congratulate	gratifying	pleasure	unique
contribution	happy	progress	unparalleled
creative	hero	prolific	unrivaled
dazzling	honor	proud	valuable
début	imaginative	recognize	victory
dedicated	impressed	resourceful	vision
delighted	incomparable	respected	vital
dependable	innovative	salute	well-deserved
distinguished	inspiring	satisfying	winner
effort	invaluable	sensational	
enterprising	inventive	skillful	
esteem	kudos	special	

PHRASES

accept my heartiest congratulations
    on

achieved your goals

all possible joy and happiness

an impressive record/achievement

another success

beyond all expectations

cheerful/cheering news

continued health and happiness/
    success

couldn't let this happy occasion go
    by without

delighted/happy/thrilled to hear/
    read/receive the news

good/great/sensational/joyful/
    thrilling news

high quality of your work

I especially liked the way you

impressed with this latest award/
    honor/prize/achievement

in awe of all that you've done

joins me in sending best/good/
    warm wishes

know that you're held in high esteem

many congratulations and much
    happiness

offer my warmest/sincerest/heartiest
    congratulations

red letter day

rejoice with you

sharing in your happiness

significant/valuable contribution

sincere wishes for continued success

spectacular achievement

take great pleasure in sending
    congratulations to you

take this opportunity to wish you
    every happiness

were thrilled to hear about

wishing you all the best/
    much success/continued success

with all good wishes to you in your
    new venture

wonderful ability to get things
    done—and done well

your important contribution

you've done a superb job of

SENTENCES

Baxter called this evening to tell us that the two of you are engaged to
    be married, and we wanted to tell you immediately how happy we are
    for you.

Best wishes from all of us.

Congratulations on opening your own chiropractic office!

Congratulations on the littlest Woodley—may she know health, happiness,
    and love all her life.

Good news travels fast!

Hear hear!

I am almost as delighted as you are with this recent turn of events.

I couldn't be happier if it had happened to me.

I hear wonderful things about you.

I hope we will enjoy many more years of doing business together.

I just heard the news—congratulations!

I'm proud to know you/to be your friend!

I'm so impressed!

It was a splendid performance/great triumph/brilliant speech.

I understand that congratulations are in order.

I've just heard from Choi Nam-Sun that two of your poems will be included in the next issue—congratulations!

I very much admire your organizational skills/perseverance/many achievements/ingenuity/calm in the face of difficulties.

I wanted you to know how proud and happy I was to hear that your short will be shown at the Brooklyn Film Festival.

I wish I could be with you to share in this happy occasion.

My hat's off to you!

My heartiest congratulations to you both.

My thoughts are with you today as you celebrate.

My warmest congratulations on your graduation from Columbia!

This is the best news I've heard in a long time.

We are pleased with your work on ethics-in-government legislation.

Well done!

We've all benefited from your expertise and creativity.

What terrific news!

With best wishes for fair weather and smooth sailing in the years ahead.

You certainly haven't let the grass grow under your feet.

Your reputation had preceded you, and I see you intend to live up to it.

You've done it again!

You've topped everyone in the store in sales this past month—congratulations!

PARAGRAPHS

I was delighted (although not surprised) to hear that you won the Schubert piano concerto competition this year. Congratulations! I've watched you develop as a fine pianist over the years, and it is a thrill to see you rewarded for your talent—and, above all, for your hard work.

Please accept the congratulations of everyone here at Avonia-Bunn Title Insurance Company on your Outstanding Service Award. Your industry, your attention to detail, and your creative problem-solving have been an inspiration to all of us.

You remind me of something I read long ago, written by Elinor Smith: "It had long since come to my attention that people of accomplishment rarely sat back and let things happen to them. They went out and happened to things."

I well remember your diffident début twenty-five years ago. Who would have guessed that your "awkward little offspring" would grow to be the successful business it is today?

In the past ten years, the company has grown beyond all recognition—a complete line of new products, computerization of all departments, financial growth beyond our wildest expectations—and wherever there has been innovation, development, progress, you've been in the front ranks. We wouldn't be the company we are today without you. Please accept the enclosed bonus as a sign of our gratitude and appreciation for ten wonderful years.

Aunt Evalina told us about your "dramatic" success. Congratulations on what was evidently a stunning performance! I'm so proud of you, not only for this latest accomplishment, but for all your hard work of the past four years.

SAMPLE LETTERS

Dear Professor Arronax,

Heartiest congratulations on the recently published accounts of your discoveries. I have read them with the greatest fervor and admiration.

With all best wishes, I am

Faithfully yours,

Dear Briggs,

I was happy to hear about your promotion to division credit manager. Let's celebrate!

Your cousin,

Dear Raoul,

Congratulations on being named this year's Outstanding Manager. Having recently visited one of your division branches, I know that you very much deserve this honor.

I'm looking forward to seeing you at the May banquet when you accept your plaque. Until then, best wishes.

Sincerely,

Dear Governor Peck,

Congratulations on your landslide election. All of us who campaigned for you in this area are proud and pleased to have been part of your victory.

Please accept my best wishes for a distinguished, productive, and happy term of office.

Respectfully yours,

Dear Mr. Dodsworth:

Congratulations on the opening of your newest branch of the Revelation Motor Company. We have always appreciated doing business with you, and expect to enjoy it even more now that your new office is only two blocks from us.

Best wishes for happiness and success to all of you at Revelation.

Sincerely,

Dear Synnöve,

Congratulations on receiving the Granliden award! That's terrific. I was so happy for you when I saw the announcement in the paper.

I hope everything else in your life is going as well.

Best,

Dear William,

I've just heard from Katherine that you are finally a full-fledged chemical engineer—congratulations! I've admired you as I've watched your struggles these past few years to acquire an education. Katherine and I said some rather flattering things about you and concluded that you're going to go far in this world.

My best wishes to you for a bright and happy future.

Fondly,

Dear Mr. Rochester,

Congratulations on your election to the Thornfield School Board. I hope that after running such a vigorous and inspiring campaign you still have enough energy to carry out some of your sound and needed ideas.

Be assured of our continued support, and do not hesitate to call on us if we can do anything to help.

With best wishes,

Dear Ms. Hubbard,

Congratulations on an outstanding first year at Grattan Public Relations, Inc. A growing company like ours needs and appreciates people with your energy, expertise, and intuition. We are all predicting a brilliant future for you.

Congratulations and best wishes.

Sincerely,

Dear Helen and Arthur,

So little Laura has arrived at last. It has been such a long process, and I know it's been hard for you wondering if there would ever be an end to the red tape and waiting. But all that's over now, and the three of you can begin your life together.

From what I hear, this is definitely an adoption made in heaven. I know that Laura will add a great deal to the joy you two already find in each other.

With every good wish,

See also: APPRECIATION, EMPLOYMENT, FAMILY, GOODWILL, RESPONSES, SALES, WEDDINGS.

Letters That Serve As Contracts

15

The degree of miscommunication regarding what's been agreed upon in a business deal tends to increase in direct proportion to the amount of money involved.

—ROBERT J. RINGER

A letter can serve as a short, informal contract. Whether you need an attorney to check such letters depends on the complexity of the contract and the possible negative outcomes if it is poorly written.

Contract Letters Deal with

- agreements
- cancellations of agreements/contracts
- changes in terms
- leases
- rentals
- work orders

- Identify the nature of the contract in a subject line ("Re: Tuckpointing at 1711 Grismer Avenue").
- Begin with a phrase such as "This letter will serve as a contract between . . ."
- Give names and addresses of both parties to the agreement or contract.

- State what each party will give and receive.
- Specify dates by which the work must be completed and by which payment must be received.
- Mention whether and under what conditions the contract may be canceled.
- Specify date by which you expect the letter to be signed and returned.
- Leave lines and blank spaces at the bottom for both parties to sign and date the letter.

What Not to Say

- Don't include anything that doesn't bear on the contract; this is a focused document.
- Don't use legal-sounding terminology to make a contract look more legal (unless you are a lawyer). Use simple, standard English to avoid later charges that the other party "didn't understand" part of the contract.

Tips on Writing

~ Before writing, list all factors that will protect your agreement (for example, time limits, price ceilings, independent inspector). Have someone familiar with the situation double-check it for you.

~ Don't be afraid to write as though you were speaking. Use personal pronouns and ordinary grammar and sentence structure ("I promise to . . . in exchange for . . ."). On the other hand, maintain a businesslike tone to inspire confidence and to strengthen the letter's use as a contract.

~ The main body of the contract can be as short as a paragraph or long enough to be divided into many paragraphs. In the latter case, organize the information into clear, logical units.

Special Situations

~ If timing is important to your agreement, contract, or the cancellation of either, send your letter return receipt requested so that you can verify the date that the letter was received. If your lease requires you to give thirty days' notice, you will be glad to have a receipt stating that the notice was received within the time limit.

∼ When submitting a proposal that you expect to be accepted, turn it into a contract or binding agreement by adding at the bottom, "Approved by [signature] on [date] by [printed name and title]."

∼ When lending money to family or friends, all parties will benefit from having a letter contract spelling out amounts, dates, and responsibilities.

Format

∼ All contracts and letters dealing with contracts are typed on business letterhead, personal letterhead stationery, or good bond stationery.

∼ Forms are used when your business habitually contracts for the same kind of work.

WORDS

agreement	conditions	negotiation	transaction
arrangement	confirm	obligations	understanding
assure	conform	provisions	underwrite
bind	consent	settlement	verify
certify	endorse	stipulation	warrant
clauses	guarantee	terms	

PHRASES

agreed-to terms	mutual satisfaction
articles of the agreement	on condition that
as of the agreed-upon date	please sign and date
comply with	reach an understanding
considered complete when	return this letter by
effective as of/until	terms listed below
in return, you agree to	

SENTENCES

Enclosed is a check for $500, which will serve as earnest money for apartment # 37 in the 131 Park Drive building.

In the event of disagreement about the quality of the work, the dispute will be submitted to independent arbitration with costs being shared equally by both parties.

Note: This contract may be withdrawn by us if not accepted within 10 days.

Paragraph N of the contract is irrelevant to the matter at hand; please delete it and initial and return this letter.

The enclosed forward currency contract constitutes an agreement to deliver or receive a present stated amount of currency at a future specified date.

This letter serves as a contract between Madge Allen and Cain & Sons for sheetrock and plaster repair to the property at 35 James Court, with the following conditions and specifications.

This letter will serve as an informal agreement between us covering the period from January 1, 2002, to December 31, 2003, for the following services.

PARAGRAPHS

I am happy to lend you the money to buy the truck. As we discussed, you will repay the $9,000 loan over a period of 36 months in the amount of $250 per month. There will be no interest. Please sign and date the second copy of this letter and return it to me.

I agree to translate your Moroccan contracts, letters, faxes, and other messages for the fee of $35 per hour. I further agree to complete the outstanding translations by February 10. You will pay messenger service fees between your office and mine, parking fees for consultations at your offices, and postage for mail or overnighting services.

Acceptance of contract: The above prices, specifications, and conditions are satisfactory and are hereby accepted. You are authorized to do the work as specified. Payment will be made upon completion. Date of acceptance: May 6, 2004. Authorized signature: Bernard Boweri

SAMPLE LETTERS

Dear Mr. Bowling,

As required by our lease, we hereby give you thirty days' notice of our intention to move from Apartment 2 at 619 Fourth Street.

Please call any evening after 6:00 p.m. to let us know when you need to show the apartment.

Our rent deposit of $450 will need to be refunded to us as we have not damaged the apartment in any way during our tenancy.

We have enjoyed our two years here very much, and will be sorry to move.

Sincerely yours,

Dear Ms. Hart:

Pryke Financial Services, Inc. will be happy to act as Investment Adviser to the Collins Foundation and, as such, will assist with cash management and investment of foundation funds with the exception of the initial investment of the bond issue proceeds from certain bond issues.

We agree to provide the following services:

1. A complete review and analysis of the Collins Foundation's financial structure and conditions.
2. The preparation of written investment objectives outlining preferable investments, portfolio goals, risk limits, and diversification possibilities.
3. The establishment of preferred depository or certificate arrangements with banks or savings and loans.
4. Soliciting bids for guaranteed investment agreements.
5. Monitoring fund transfers, verifying receipt of collateral, completing documentation.
6. Working with a governmental securities dealer to execute governmental security transactions.
7. Meeting with your treasurer and financial adviser periodically and with your board of directors as requested.
8. Providing monthly portfolio status reports with sufficient detail for accounting and recording purposes.

Pryke Financial Services, Inc. will submit quarterly statements for services. Our fees will be billed in advance and calculated by multiplying .000375 times the Collins Foundation's invested portfolio at the beginning of each calendar quarter (.0015 annually). Fees will be adjusted at the end of each quarter to reflect the rate times the average invested balance for the previous quarter. Adjustments will be included in the next billing.

  Fees can be reviewed and adjusted annually on the anniversary date of this contract.
  This agreement will run from June 1, 2004, through June 1, 2005, but may be canceled by either party without cause with thirty days' written notice.

        Sincerely,
        Grace Bloom
        President

The above agreement is accepted by the Collins Foundation (blanks for date, signatures, titles).

~

Dear Mr. Golspie,

  This letter will serve as an informal agreement between us. On Feb. 7 from 4:00–5:00 p.m. you agree to provide entertainers for my daughter's birthday party consisting of one clown, one magician, and one facepainter. I understand that the clown and magician portion of the entertainment will last about 20 minutes, and the facepainter will remain for the rest of the hour.

  I agree to pay you a $50 deposit (check enclosed) and the remaining $200 on Feb. 7. As requested a room will be available for your use. Also enclosed is a detailed map with directions to our home.

  We're all looking forward to this, adults as well as children!

~

See also: ACCEPTANCES, ACKNOWLEDGMENTS, ADJUSTMENTS, ORDERS.

Cover Letters 16

It is estimated that the average piece of business correspondence gets less than thirty seconds of the reader's attention. Even a truly great cover letter will not get much more.

—Martin Yate

Cover letters (also called transmittal letters) accompany résumés, application forms, manuscripts, documents, product literature, payments, charitable contributions, contracts, reports, samples, data, and other materials.

They may be as short as two sentences, telling what is enclosed and why, or as long as two pages, highlighting important points in the enclosures, explaining something that is not immediately obvious, or developing a sales message to accompany the report, sample, document, information, or package.

The main purpose of the cover letter is to direct the reader quickly and persuasively to the enclosed materials.

Distinct from a cover letter, the cover sheet accompanies a fax and lists the person sending the fax, the person receiving it, the fax number, and the number of pages being faxed (see FAXES).

Cover Letters Accompany

- application forms
- brochures/booklets/catalogs/pamphlets (see SALES)
- checks unaccompanied by statements or invoices
- contracts/agreements
- contributions to charitable causes

- documents
- faxes (see FAXES)
- information/instructions
- manuscripts
- product literature (see SALES)
- proposals
- questionnaires
- résumés
- samples (see SALES)
- surveys

- Address your letter to a specific person.
- State what is enclosed, attached, or mailed under separate cover. If there are several items, list them. Give number and type of items ("three brochures"), amount of payment, or other descriptive information.
- Mention why you're sending the material (in response to a request, to introduce the person to a new product, for their information).
- If necessary, explain what the item is and how to interpret or use it.
- Summarize the main points of the enclosure, highlight strong qualifications on your résumé, or otherwise orient the reader toward the most important issues of your material.
- Tell what response you're expecting from the other person or what future action you'll be taking.
- Include your name, address, telephone number, e-mail address, and fax number.
- Close with an expression of appreciation or a forward-looking statement.

- Don't duplicate the enclosed material. Summarizing a document or mentioning the salient points of a contract is helpful, but repeating sentences and paragraphs may lead the reader to skip over those parts later.

- Don't close on a weak note. Words like "hope," "wish," "if," "should," "could," and "might" signal a lack of confidence ("If you wish, I could come for an interview at your convenience"; "Call me if you're interested").

- Don't try to attract attention with "cute" stationery, humor, multiple question marks or exclamation marks, smiley faces, or other gimmicks. You want to personalize your letter and make it stand out, but there's a fine line between an enthusiastic, confident letter and one that makes the reader wince. If you're in any doubt as to which your letter is, ask someone to evaluate it for you.

Tips on Writing

～ Cover letters aren't needed for routine orders, payments, shipments, recommendations, references, or when the recipient has requested or is expecting your enclosure. Include a cover letter when the materials are not expected, do not speak clearly for themselves, or benefit from an accompanying persuasive message.

～ Double-check names, titles, and addresses for accuracy; this is crucial when applying for a position or sending a manuscript to an editor.

～ Be brief. Shakespeare's advice was to use "few words, but to effect." Except when the cover letter is a sales letter accompanying samples, product literature, or catalogs, it is only a side dish, not the main course. A good cover letter is usually not more than one page long (five or six paragraphs) and it will make the reader want to set it aside quickly in order to get to the enclosure.

～ Cover letters are exquisitely clean and attractive, with generous margins and no spelling, grammar, or usage errors. "The old aphorisms are basically sound. First impressions *are* lasting." (Jessie Fauset)

～ In *Cover Letters That Will Get You the Job You Want* (Better Way Books, 1993) Stanley Wynnett says, "The last two words of every cover letter I have ever written are *thank you*." Some authorities think that it is presumptuous to say thank you in advance, that it is trite, and that it signals the end of an exchange rather than an intermediate step. However, few people object to being thanked, so use your own judgment.

～ For more assistance with cover letters, see the excellent *Cover Letters That Knock 'Em Dead* by Martin Yate, 3rd ed. (Adams Media Corporation, 1998) and *Cover Letters* by Taunee Besson, 2nd ed. (John Wiley & Sons,

1996). For cover letters that accompany résumés, see *The Perfect Cover Letter* by Richard H. Beatty, 2nd ed. (John Wiley & Sons, Inc., 1997) and for cover letters that accompany manuscript submissions, see *How to Write Attention-Grabbing Query & Cover Letters* by John Wood (Writer's Digest Books, 1996).

Special Situations

〜 A well-written cover letter for your résumé is a powerful selling instrument. "Very seldom will you write a letter more important to you than that accompanying a résumé." (Margaret McCarthy) Open by mentioning the person who referred you, the ad you're responding to, or something complimentary about the company you're applying to (and the more specific you are about what you like about the company the more effective it is). Identify the position or kind of work you're applying for. Emphasize how your qualifications match those the company is seeking (but don't repeat phrases or dates or specific material from the résumé). Don't focus on what you want, but generate interest in you by telling how you can contribute to the company. Don't write more than a page; you may want to include everything, but a long cover letter is offputting to a busy person and your résumé may not get read at all. Don't send a one-size-fits-all cover letter. Tailor each letter to a specific company; recipients often look to see if there is anything related to their company; few are impressed by mass-produced letters. Close by requesting an interview, which is the purpose of your cover letter and résumé: "I will call you next week to arrange an interview appointment after you have had a chance to review my résumé"; "I look forward to meeting with you to discuss the match between your requirements and my qualifications." See APPLICATIONS for additional ideas for writing the cover letter.

〜 The cover letter you send to an editor with a manuscript is brief. Its main purpose is to introduce your submission (type of book or article, title, word count) and yourself (past publishing credits or credentials for writing the material). A good cover letter includes a tightly written paragraph that reads like catalog copy. Your best writing skills are used to describe or give the flavor of your book or article. Always (that's "always") include a SASE and close with a courtesy.

〜 The cover letter that accompanies a report identifies the report by title; mentions why it was prepared, who authorized it, and who wrote it; provides a summary (based on the report's introduction, abstract, or summary). If the report is formal, the transmittal letter is placed after the title page and before the table of contents.

~ A note that accompanies a gift has a purpose similar to that of a cover letter. Identify the enclosure ("a little something for your birthday") and include your greetings and best wishes. To accompany a corporate gift, mention the occasion for the gift, if there is one (service anniversary, completion of a major project). Be specific about the person's work, talent, anniversary, or award: "I'm particularly grateful because . . ." or "You've been a delight to work with because . . ." or "Your work has meant a lot to the company because . . ." Relate an anecdote, a shared memory, or reflection that bolsters your good wishes. End your note with pleasant wishes for continued success or with some forward-looking remark about your future work association. The same type of note is written when the gift is being sent to the person from the shipper or from an Internet company, except that the writer mentions sending "a little something" or "something I thought you'd like" or "something for your desk" and, when possible, estimates when it will arrive. The impact of a corporate gift is magnified one-hundredfold when it is accompanied by a handwritten note of appreciation. Employees who receive such a note from a busy executive feel valued in a personal, memorable way.

~ A cover letter accompanying a sample or product literature is more properly considered a sales letter (see SALES).

Format

~ Except for notes accompanying gifts or the most informal transmittals, cover letters are typed on business letterhead or on memo paper (for in-house materials or for those outside people and firms with which you have a high-volume and casual correspondence).

~ When asked to fax or e-mail a résumé, you will also be faxing or e-mailing your cover letter. In the case of a fax, write it as you would a regular letter on letterhead stationery and use the "fine resolution" setting to ensure that it is as attractive and readable as possible when it arrives.

~ Use form cover letters to accompany requested information. To give them a more personal appearance, use good quality paper, address the person by name (instead of "Dear Friend" or "Dear Subscriber"), and sign each letter individually. For potentially important customers, write a personal cover letter.

WORDS

announce	enclosed	policy	provisions
attached	illustrate	project	report
deliver	notice	proposal	summarize
document	outline	prospectus	terms
draft			

PHRASES

acquaint you with

as promised

at your request

brochure that presents/details/
  describes/outlines/explains

call with questions

complimentary copy

direct your attention to

enclosed is/are

for further information

here are/is

I am sending you

if you need/want additional
  information

I'm also enclosing

in response to your advertisement

please note that

rough draft

SENTENCES

After you have reviewed the enclosed proposal, please call me (or Bess Beynon if I'm out of town) to discuss it.

As a June graduate of Cleveland College with a BA in business, I am looking for employment and wanted to check first with you because I so enjoyed working for The Clement Group as an intern in your marketing department.

As you will see from my résumé, I have a great deal of experience in program development, administration, contract development, and budget planning.

At your request, I am enclosing three copies of the Empire State Film Festival program.

Complete medical records from the office of Dr. Anna Lakington for Mr. Barnabas Holly are enclosed.

Enclosed are copies of the recorded deeds and easements for the above-referenced properties.

Enclosed is a completed application form—please note my four years' experience as an installation technician.

Enclosed is a copy of the survey on equipment rental in the six-county metro area.

Enclosed is a quitclaim deed conveying the new Fort Road from Faulkland County to the City of Sheridan.

Enclosed is the requested report on the Heat Treatment Seminar, held July 14–17.

Here are the molding samples we'd like you to evaluate.

I am enclosing the damaged belt from my twenty-year-old Bannister vacuum in the hopes that you can locate a replacement for it.

I am interested in your part-time position for a truck unloader.

I am responding to your advertisement in Sunday's paper for a senior analyst programmer.

I am writing to introduce myself and inquire about openings for a Tae Kwon Do instructor.

I believe I am well qualified to apply for your opening for a water quality extension agent.

I'm sending you a copy of the article on the Minnesota twins study that we discussed last week.

In response to your ad for a website producer/editor, I'm enclosing my résumé, which details my considerable experience in this area.

I understand you are looking for a form tool grinder.

I will telephone your assistant Monday morning to see if you can schedule an interview next week to discuss the position.

I would like to bring my commercial interior design skills to work for Engelred Offices, Inc.

Ms. DeGroot suggested I contact you about the development grant writer and board liaison position.

Please sign both copies of the enclosed letter of agreement and return them to us.

Prentice Page suggested I write you about the wallpapering specialist position.

Thank you for your patience—enclosed please find the replacement part for your Noyes Intercommunication System.

Under separate cover I'm sending you samples of our new line of Natural
Solution products for the hair.

We are pleased to send you the set of deck plans you requested.

Will you please look over the enclosed rough draft of your will and let me
know if it needs any changes or corrections?

PARAGRAPHS

I note that you are seeking a warehouse manager with five years of supervisory or managing experience and five years of experience in shipping, receiving, and inventory control. This almost precisely describes my qualifications.

Enclosed is a sample (ref. #4467-AB) of the film that Alwyn Tower and
I discussed with you last Thursday. Please keep in mind that the sample was
produced under laboratory conditions. If you have any questions about this
material or variations of it, please call Alwyn or me.

Enclosed is an Agreement and Release between you and Lakely
Associates, which gives the terms of the settlement for the redevelopment of
your well. When you sign the Agreement and present written proof of the
adjudication of the well to Lakely Associates, we will send you a check for the
agreed-upon amount.

Our check for $15,223.92 is enclosed and constitutes full payment for all
items listed on Invoice # 68-331982. Thank you for your help in getting the
airconditioners to us so quickly.

Today I am shipping approximately one square foot each of 0.090 to
0.100 inch thick sheets of Fe-3% Si (hot-rolled) and IF (niobium-containing
interstitial-free; hot-rolled, one sheet, cold-rolled, one sheet). The rolling
direction is marked on each sheet.

I am currently employed in an engineering environment by a large independent transportation firm, but I am interested in making a career change
into the investment/financial services field. I have recently obtained my CFP
designation and hope to find a position as a broker trainee. I am enclosing my
résumé for your review and consideration for such a position.

Enclosed is the complete report on the foreign language survey conducted last fall. Vice-presidents and personnel directors of one hundred of the
nation's largest corporations were asked which foreign language would be
most important for a successful business career during the next twenty years.
The results may surprise you!

Thank you for your interest in Griffiths Collar and Shirt Company. I'm enclosing a packet of materials that will describe our range of products and services. I will call you next week to see if you have any questions and to discuss how we might be of help to you. You are, of course, always welcome to visit our offices and factory here in Lycurgus.

You've been buying Ponderevo's Cough Lintus and our line of Mogg's soap for years. Now we proudly announce a new product that is sure to become a household word: Tono-Bungay! Enclosed are several samples. Try Tono-Bungay yourself and share some with friends. Our Order Line is available to you 24 hours a day, and orders are shipped within 48 hours.

The attached set of project plans covers work through the end of 2004. The plans have been generated in consultation with each of the key people involved. We expect to review progress the first of each month and to adjust the work accordingly. You will note that we are dependent on the work of others in the office and that they are in turn dependent on us. Please review the scheduled work and give me your comments.

SAMPLE LETTERS

Dear G.E. Challenger,

I was intrigued with the ad in Sunday's paper seeking someone experienced with high pressure liquid chromatography—first, because there aren't that many openings in this field and, second, because my experience and background match almost precisely what you appear to need.

I was further intrigued when I called the number given in the ad and discovered that this is your company. I have never forgotten several of your research papers that were required reading when I was in college.

After you have a chance to read my résumé, I hope you will agree that an interview might be interesting for us both.

Dear Kurt,

Enclosed is a copy of the letter of recommendation I wrote for you. I've sent the original on to the academic dean in the envelope you provided. I thought you might like a copy for your files.

I am so pleased you asked me to do this. I just hope I was of some small help. Let me know as soon as you hear the good news!

With best wishes,

Dear Dr. Cheesewright,

Your office manager, Ms. Sherriff, mentioned to me that you might soon have an opening for a dental hygienist. She suggested I send you my résumé.

You may not remember, but I was a patient of yours when I was growing up here, and even as a youngster I thought it would be "fun" to work in your office! I've been living in Chicago for the past ten years, but am planning to move back here because of my father's health.

After you've had a chance to look at my résumé, you can reach me at 555-1234 to schedule an interview.

Dear Maria,

I received the film sample (#18-1A) from Julian Silvercross and am impressed. We are excited about the performance improvement that we think this technology may offer us. As Nancy Sibley explained to you on the phone, we are interested in using it for our silicon detector assembly, which is an integral part of sensors used for various industrial purposes.

I'm enclosing three of these detector assemblies for your review. Feel free to dissect them to locate the detector assemblies.

We ask that you respect the confidentiality of our product and interest in your film. Please give me a call after you have had a chance to look at the sensors.

Yours truly,

Dear Mr. Oakley:

Enclosed is your copy of the contract between Sullivan Press and Eaglesham Publications. Several of the clauses are being revised, and I will see that you receive the amended version as soon as it is ready.

If you have any questions about your obligations under the contract, please check with our attorney, Mary Jane Reed, in the Legal Services Department.

Sincerely yours,

See also: APPLICATIONS, QUERIES, RESUMES, SALES.

Letters About Credit

17

The world is a puzzling place today. All these banks sending us credit cards. . . .
Imagine a bank sending credit cards to two ladies over a hundred years old!
What are those folks thinking?

—SARAH AND A. ELIZABETH DELANY

Much of the paperwork involved in obtaining and granting credit has been standardized and codified into forms reflecting federal, state, or institutional rules and guidelines. However, nonroutine matters require carefully written letters.

Letters About Credit Include

- approving loans
- canceling an account
- collecting past-due accounts (see COLLECTION)
- congratulations: fine record/payment (see also SALES)
- credit bureaus: letters to and from
- delinquent account
- denying/refusing credit or loan applications (see REFUSALS)
- errors in credit history
- explaining credit/loan refusals/conditions
- extending payment deadlines
- family members and friends: lending/borrowing
- inviting new accounts/reviving inactive accounts
- obtaining one's own credit history
- requesting credit/bankcard/loan

- When asking a credit bureau for a copy of your credit report: give name, address, social security number, and telephone number. Use letterhead stationery or enclose a business card to substantiate that you are the subject of the check. When requesting a credit report on another person: supply the person's name, address, and social security number; give a reason for asking (you are renting property to the person, selling them a car, co-signing a contract for deed with them).

- When writing an individual or a business to ask for a credit reference, give the name and address of the person under consideration, request any pertinent credit information, explain briefly why you want it ("we are discussing a partnership"), state that you will treat the information confidentially, express your appreciation for the information, and enclose a self-addressed stamped envelope for their reply. In some cases, mention how you were referred to them (for example, by the person under consideration). Ask specific questions: How long have you known the person? In what capacity? What kinds of credit have you extended? What is the current balance? The person's payment pattern? How long have they been employed there? What is their income?

- When requesting correction of an inaccurate credit record, identify yourself by full name and address, state the incorrect portions of the record, and explain why they are incorrect. Include copies of documents (statements, loan papers, tax returns, paycheck stubs) substantiating your position. Ask that a corrected copy of the report be sent to you. Thank the person; they most likely were not responsible for the errors and can, in fact, be helpful to you.

- When denying credit or a loan: thank the person for their interest; express regret that you are unable to extend credit; assure them that you considered their request thoroughly; suggest an alternate course of action (layaway, paying cash, smaller loan) that will allow a continued relationship; encourage them to re-apply later. If questioned further, list your credit criteria, mentioning the problems presented by the person's credit background, and telling what sources you used to determine creditworthiness. For smaller, more routine credit requests, use forms stating simply, "Your request for a loan has been denied," followed by a check-off list of possible reasons: length of employment, lack of information, excessive credit obligations, newcomer to the area with no credit record, poor payment record, garnishment. Leave a blank to fill in the name of the credit bureau where you obtained your information.

- When approving a loan application or granting credit, state that you've approved the request, indicate the amount approved and the effective date, and explain credit or loan payoff procedures. Enclose forms needing signatures along with instructions on how to complete them. Welcome new customers to your lending institution or business, express appreciation for their business, and suggest they bring all their credit needs to you.

What Not to Say

- Don't write anything that cannot be documented. Phrases like "misses payments" or "habitually late with payments" must be substantiated by records of such payment patterns.

Tips on Writing

～ Credit matters are confidential. Take every precaution to safeguard the credit information you give or receive.

～ Accuracy is essential when providing information on someone's credit history. Double-check your facts as well as spellings of names and account numbers.

～ Be tactful. Even people with poor credit histories want to hear good of themselves and often feel they are doing a decent job given their circumstances. In her 1923 book, Mary Owens Crowther writes, "Tactless credit handling is the most effective way known to dissipate good-will."

Special Situations

～ Loans between family members or friends often come with hidden financial and personal costs. When requesting a loan, be businesslike and factual: tell how much you need and why; suggest a repayment plan and the amount of interest you will pay. Always offer the other person a face-saving "out" ("You may have financial problems of your own, for all I know," "This may not be a good time for you," or "You may disapprove, on principle, of loans between friends"). Reassure them that there is no reason to feel guilty or uncomfortable about turning you down. Do not beg or play on their sympathies; pressuring a person who is not willing to lend you money won't get you the money—and it will lose you a friend. When refusing a request for a personal loan, be brief: "I wish I could help you, but it's not possible just now." Don't overexplain or apologize or hedge. If you like, close by asking if there is some other way you could help. When granting a request for a loan from a friend or family member, put it in writing: state the loan amount, the terms and dates of repayment, the interest, and any other information. Send two copies of your letter and ask that the person sign and date one and return it to you. To remind a friend or family member of an overdue loan, be gentle at first: "I know how busy you are . . ."; "I wonder if you forgot about . . ."; "Am I mistaken, or did we agree that you'd repay the loan September 1?" If you write a second time, include a photocopy of your original agreement letter and word your expectation of getting your money back more strongly.

∽ If you can't make a loan or installment credit payment on time, write the company at once. Apologize for being overdue, tell them you intend to pay as soon as possible, and enclose whatever portion of the balance you can. If you have a good reason for being overdue (illness, layoff), mention it. Otherwise, don't go into lengthy excuses; your creditor is more interested in knowing that you are taking responsibility for the account.

Format

∽ There are virtually no handwritten letters dealing with credit matters. Routine correspondence may be handled with form letters. Others will be typed on business letterhead.

WORDS

application	default	lessor	reimburse
approval	finance	lien	repay
arrangement	funds	loan	requirements
balance	guarantee	mortgage	verify
collateral	installment	nonpayment	
creditworthy	IOU	receipt	
debt	lender	regretfully	

PHRASES

after careful consideration

although you have only occasional payment problems

apply for credit privileges

as much as we would like to extend credit to you

cannot justify approval

cash basis only

consistently on-time credit payments

credit application/history/record/ standing/rating/limit

current/up-to-date financial statement

due to a rise in the number of uncollectable past-due accounts

due to cash flow difficulties

excellent credit rating

financial difficulties/needs/services

in checking your credit background

it is our policy

I understand and appreciate your position, but

late payments

must delay payment

one of our credit requirements is

pattern of late payments

pay in advance/in full

pleased to be able to accommodate you

poor payment history

preferred customer

regret that we are unable to

responsible use of credit

review of our files

steady credit payments

subject only to normal credit requirements

unable to accommodate you at this time

unpaid balance

we are happy/pleased to approve

will you please run a credit check on

SENTENCES

Because our inquiries disclosed a number of past-due and unpaid accounts, we are unable to extend the line of credit you requested.

Could you could see your way clear to lending me $200 for approximately three weeks, until I receive my income tax refund (enclosed is a copy of my return, showing the amount I will be receiving)?

Cressida Mary MacPhail, 1968 Taylor Avenue, Bretton, IN 47834, has applied to the Maxwell Credit Union for a loan, and gave us your name as a reference.

Eileen Schwartz has had an excellent credit history with this company, and we recommend her highly as a credit customer.

I appreciate your courtesy in allowing me to pay off the balance of my account in small installments.

I'm writing to notify you of an error in our credit history and to request an immediate correction.

I would appreciate your raising my credit limit from $10,000 to $20,000.

Please close my Fortis-Pryde account, effective immediately.

Please keep us in mind for your other credit needs.

The credit bureau cites repeated credit delinquencies.

We are pleased to report that our credit dealings with Angela Crossby have been excellent.

We are puzzled that our application for a home equity line of credit has been refused—please send us a copy of our credit report, if that was the problem, or your explanation for this refusal.

We are unable to furnish you with any current credit information on Emerson-Toller—they have not been a credit customer of ours for over ten years.

We expect to be making large purchases of office furniture from your firm as well as routine purchases of office supplies and would like to open a credit account with you.

We have run into some difficulties checking the references you supplied.

We note a persistent pattern of nonpayment in your credit history.

We suggest you reapply for the loan once you have resolved some of these problems.

We will appreciate any credit information you can give us about Walter Tillotson.

PARAGRAPHS

Enclosed please find a check for $457.32, which will bring my account up to date. I am sorry that I let the account become past due. I expect to keep it current in the future.

I would like to see the credit record you currently have on me. I am applying for a second mortgage on my home next month, and would not want to be unpleasantly surprised by anything that may be on file. Thank you.

I am pleased to report that we were able to approve your loan request for the amount of $5,000. A check is enclosed, along with a payment booklet and a packet of payment envelopes. Please read your repayment schedule carefully.

We are sorry to report that your loan application has not been approved. Our decision was based primarily on information received from the Carnaby Reporting Services credit bureau. You may want to look at their record on you to verify that it is correct. If it is, we suggest working with a financial counselor, something that has been helpful to several of our customers. We will be happy to review your loan application at a later date if your circumstances change.

In order to set up a credit account for you with Copper Beeches, we need the following information: company name and tax identification number; a copy of your annual report; the names of banks with which you currently have accounts and those account numbers; names and phone numbers of at least three companies from whom you have purchased materials in the past six months. We appreciate your business and look forward to serving you.

Because of an electrical fire at our main plant three months ago, we have been experiencing some temporary financial difficulties and have fallen behind on our payments to you. We expect to rectify the situation by the end of the year. In the meantime, please accept the enclosed check on account. We thank you for your understanding.

We must report that our business experiences with the Baroness de la Cruchecassée have been less than satisfactory. Over a period of eighteen months we have failed to collect anything on a fairly large outstanding balance. We trust you will keep this information confidential.

SAMPLE LETTERS

TO: Dudley Credit Data
FROM: Eustace Landor, Landor First Banks
DATE: September 3, 2003
RE: Edith Millbank

Will you please run a credit check for us on:

Edith Millbank
1844 Coningsby
Oswald, OH 45042
Social Security # 000-00-0000

Ms. Millbank is taking out a loan application with us, and we wish to verify the information she has given us with regard to her credit history.

Thank you.

Dear Ms. Panzoust,

Thank you for your letter of March 16 requesting our opinion of the creditworthiness of Valmouth Fiber Arts.

We have had only the most limited business transactions with them and, since they have always been on a cash basis with us, we have no idea of their financial standing. I would not feel comfortable expressing an opinion on so little information.

I'm sorry I couldn't have been more helpful.

~

Re: Loan # 211925
Dear Ms. Parry-Lewis,

We have reviewed your request for a renewal of your home equity loan, as required by Raine National Bank every five years. In addition to a pattern of late payments and frequent disagreements about interest payments, we find that your current financial obligations seem excessive for your stated income. As a result, we are unable to grant you a renewal.

We would be happy to serve your banking needs in the future. If you meet our criteria for a home equity loan renewal in six months, please re-apply and we will waive the new-loan fees.

Sincerely,

~

Dear Michael Dunne,

We noticed that you have not used your Pearson Charge Card in some time now. If you do not use it before it expires in March of 2004, we will be unable to issue you a new card for the following year.

We would be sorry to lose you as a good charge customer, but we think that you would lose too—lose out on such benefits as the $250,000 flight insurance that is yours every time you charge an airline ticket on your card . . . the twice-yearly newsletter that saves you money by offering discounts on motels, car rentals, and vacation packages . . . the low annual rate . . . the variable interest rate . . . and the flexibility of a card that can be used at over 15,000 places of businesses!

We hope that you will rediscover the many uses and benefits of the versatile Pearson Charge Card!

Sincerely yours,

~

See also: ACKNOWLEDGMENTS, ADJUSTMENTS, ANNOUNCEMENTS, APOLOGIES, COLLECTION, COMPLAINTS, ORDERS, REFUSALS, REQUESTS, RESPONSES, THANK YOU.

18

Letters of Disagreement

Anyone who thinks there aren't two sides to every argument is probably in one.

—THE COCKLE BUR

There are people who thrive on conflict, and there are those who spend enormous energy avoiding it. If they live in the real world, both types will sooner or later have to write a letter about a disagreement. Disagreement is neither good nor bad, but the way you handle it affects subsequent events, feelings, and relationships.

Letters of Disagreement May Concern

- contracts
- decisions
- oral agreements
- payments
- personnel problems
- policies/programs/procedures/regulations
- property lines

- Refer to the previous correspondence or to the event responsible for the present letter.
- Outline the two opposing views or actions.

- Give clear (perhaps numbered) reasons for your stand, using statistics, quotations from an employee handbook, supportive anecdotal material, or names of witnesses or others who agree with you (with their permission).

- If appropriate, suggest an intermediate stage of negotiation: a reply to specific questions in your letter; further research; a meeting between the two of you or with third parties present; visits to a lawyer, accountant, or other appropriate expert.

- If the disagreement has reached the stage where you can effectively do this, state clearly the outcome you desire.

- End with your best wishes for a solution acceptable to both of you and a reference to good future relations.

What Not to Say

- Don't put the person on the defensive. Use more "I" than "you" phrases ("you" statements tend to sound accusatory). Make sure your letter doesn't make the person feel bad, shamed, inept, or weak; people who have been made to feel small are not likely to give you what you want.

- Avoid language that escalates the situation ("ridiculous," "egregious," "brainless"). This is counterproductive as well as unconvincing. "Neither irony nor sarcasm is argument." (Rufus Choate) It also betrays vulnerability. "Strong and bitter words indicate a weak cause." (Victor Hugo)

- Avoid emotional statements. Concentrate on facts instead of feelings. For example, saying, "I don't feel this is fair" does not carry as much weight as saying, "I believe it is unfair that only one out of seven secretaries is consistently asked to work overtime—and without overtime pay."

Tips on Writing

∾ The tone of your letter can make all the difference between being heard and not being heard. Strive for a letter that is factual, dispassionate, considerate, and even-handed.

∾ Be clear about your goal. Before writing, think about the end of this sentence: "I want them to . . ." Do you want a rebate, an exchange, repairs? Do you want an apology, a corrected statement, a credit? Do you want to convince the person that their facts, statistics, opinions are wrong? Do you want something redone?

∾ Help the other person save face. Set up the situation so that the person can do what you want in a way that makes them feel generous, gracious, powerful, and willing.

∾ Although active voice is usually preferred to the passive voice, consider using the more tactful passive voice when involved in a disagreement. Instead of saying, "You did this," say, "This was done."

∾ Examine your position for possible areas of negotiation. Can you trade one point for another? Can you accept anything less than what you originally wanted?

∾ When writing to disapprove the passage of legislation, note whether the bill is state or federal and then write the appropriate lawmakers. Federal bills have numbers prefixed by HR (House Resolution) or SR (Senate Resolution). State bills are usually denoted HF (House File) and SF (Senate File).

Special Situations

∾ You will handle most disagreements yourself or with the help of family or co-workers. However, in situations like the following you may want to consult with a lawyer: in marital separations where letters contain admissions, demands, or threats; where you need to reduce informal, oral agreements to written agreements; when family disagreements about an estate become heated; when you are being accused of something; when the disagreement escalates to threats of lawsuits.

∾ Sometimes groups use letterwriting campaigns on controversial issues. A sample letter is distributed for proponents to copy over their own signature. When representatives are interested in the number of people on each side of an issue, such letterwriting campaigns have value. Most often, however, form letters do not get much attention. One well-written original letter will carry more weight with a lawmaker than a hundred form letters. Know when a group effort is effective and when it is not. "If you were the Establishment, which would you rather see coming in the door: one lion or five hundred mice?" (Florynce B. Kennedy)

~ When you write to lawmakers to inform them of your opinion on an issue, you often don't need to receive a three-page reply outlining their position—a position with which you're already familiar from the newspapers. In this case, end your letter with, "Please do not respond to this letter. I know your views; I wanted you to know mine."

Format

~ Letters dealing with business disagreements are typed on letterhead stationery.

~ When writing about personal disagreements, your letter will appear friendlier and a little more open to negotiation if you handwrite it. If you wish to appear firm and not open to negotiation, typing is best.

WORDS

argument	dilemma	friction	quarrel
break	disapprove	impasse	reconcile
conflict	displeased	incompatible	regrettable
contention	dispute	infuriated	rift
contradiction	dissatisfaction	irritating	stalemate
controversy	disturbing	misunderstanding	standstill
dead-end	estrangement	object	unfortunate
deadlock	faction	offense	unhappy
differ	feud	protest	

PHRASES

agree to differ/disagree

as I understand it

at cross purposes

be at odds with

believe you should know that

bone of contention

bury the hatchet

come to terms

complicated situation

conduct an inquiry

difference of opinion

direct your attention to

disputed point

do a disservice to

fail to agree

I am convinced that

I assume/presume/think/have no
    doubt that

I have the impression that

in my estimation/judgment/
    opinion/view

in the best interests of

I take it that

it seems to me

matter/point in dispute/at issue/
    under discussion/in question

my information is

part company with

point of view

question at issue

register my opinion

strongly oppose

take into consideration

think differently

to my way of thinking

to the best of my knowledge

wonder if you are aware that

SENTENCES

Are we ready to put this to a vote?

Do you think it would help to call in an arbitrator?

Enclosed please find several abstracts that may be helpful.

I agree with the necessity of fundraising for the purchase and maintenance of band instruments, but I disagree with the fundraising program adopted for next year.

I am convinced that the passage of this bill would do more harm than good/is not in the best interests of the state/would be a grave error.

I disagree with the store policy of filling prescriptions with generic drugs without notifying the customer.

I found the language and tone of your last letter completely unacceptable; please put us in touch with someone else in your organization who can handle this matter.

If you would like some background reading on this issue, I would be happy to furnish you with some.

I received your letter this morning and am sorry to hear that you cannot accept our terms.

Several of the points you mention are negotiable; some are not.

We are submitting this matter to an independent referee.

We still have one major area of disagreement.

What would make the situation more agreeable to you?

PARAGRAPHS

I realize that there is technically no more to be said about the Dillon-Reed merger, but I would like to state for the record that I strongly oppose the move. I refer you to the enclosed independent report that we commissioned from Elkus, Inc. This is the classic situation where one owns a dog but persists in barking oneself. The Elkus people, acknowledged experts in the field, advised us against the merger. Do we have strong enough grounds for rejecting their conclusions? I think not.

I know we've talked about this until we're both blue in the face, but I feel strongly that Great-Aunt Elsie is not yet ready for a nursing home. It would make her unhappy and shorten her life to be placed in one prematurely. What changes would you need to see before you could feel comfortable about her remaining in her apartment?

My lawyer requested the addition of the following clause to the contract: "Clause S. This agreement will expire ten years from the date of execution." The clause does not appear in the final contract. I know this issue was in dispute at one time, but I understood that you had finally agreed to it. I am returning the unsigned contracts to you for correction.

We seem to be at an impasse on determining the boundary line between our properties. Would you be interested in sharing the costs of hiring a surveyor?

SAMPLE LETTERS

Dear Ms. Burling-Ward:

I enjoy working for Stegner Publishing, and you in particular have been most helpful in introducing me to people and showing me around.

When I was interviewed for the job, Mr. Oliver consistently used the term "production editor," and the job duties he listed were those generally associated with the position of production editor.

During my three weeks on the job, I have done nothing but copyediting. After speaking to you yesterday and discovering that this was not just a training stage but my permanent position, I suspect there has been a misunderstanding.

I would like to meet with you and Mr. Oliver sometime soon to clarify this situation.

Sincerely,

Dear Nandie and Victor,

Our jazz trio has been so compatible and has had such a good time these last three years that I'm uncomfortable with our present disagreement. I think we're used to getting along and thus don't know how to handle it when we don't agree.

Here's my suggestion. Next Thursday night, instead of rehearsing, let's meet at Saduko's Restaurant for dinner. Each of us will bring three 3 x 5 cards with our reasons for changing the trio's name.

After a good meal and some non-work conversation, we will exchange cards so that each of us is holding the three viewpoints. I hope we can then come to a good decision.

What do you think?

Angelo

Dear Mr. and Mrs. Archibald Craven,

Thank you for your letter of November 30, disputing the payment of interest charges on your "12-month interest-free" purchase of furniture from us.

When you purchased your sofa, chair, and ottoman last November 18, we offered to carry the full amount of the purchase, $1,574.97, interest-free for one year—and you accepted our offer. The terms of the offer were explained at that time.

Each month thereafter you received a statement from us, noting the amount of the original purchase, the accruing finance charges, and stating clearly, "If you pay the pay-off amount by the expiration date listed below, you will be credited for the amount of interest accumulated on that purchase."

You did not pay the payoff amount by the expiration date of our agreement, November 19 of this year; thus you now owe the payoff amount plus the accrued interest of $272.61.

Please note that interest will continue to accrue until all charges are paid.

For further questions, call Mary Lennox in the Accounts Due Department at 555-1234.

See also: COMPLAINTS, NEIGHBORS, REFUSALS, SENSITIVE.

Letters to
the Editor

19

*It were not best that we should all think alike;
it is difference of opinion that makes horse-races.*

— MARK TWAIN

Letters to the editor constitute some of people's favorite reading. Knowing this, almost every newspaper and periodical prints a limited number of letters in each issue. A daily newspaper publishes as many as 30 to 40 percent of the letters it receives; a national weekly newsmagazine publishes only 2 to 5 percent of its incoming letters. Fortunately, there are ways of increasing the chances of your letter being chosen for publication.

Write a Letter to the Editor When

- you agree or disagree with a story, article, news item, editorial stance, or other letterwriter
- you have an opinion about a topic of current national or local interest
- you want to correct published information
- you want to reach a large number of people with information that you think would interest them

- In the first sentence, refer to the issue that prompted your letter ("the Nov. 1 editorial opposing a new hockey arena") so that readers know immediately what you're talking about.

- State your position ("I agree with," "I oppose," "I question").
- Briefly support, defend, or explain your position. Most publications have word limits for these letters; if you exceed them, editors may trim your letter in ways you don't like. Aim for around 100 to 300 words.
- Include facts (statistics, studies, articles, items of record, quotes) rather than feelings and impressions. If you have specific knowledge or a professional connection with an issue, mention it; this often makes publication likelier and your opinion more useful.
- Indicate what action, if any, you want readers to take (form neighborhood block watches, call legislators, boycott a product, sign a petition, stop littering).
- Close with a startling, memorable, or powerful sentence, if possible—something that makes the reader want to go back and read your letter again.
- Give your first and last name, or at least two initials and a last name, address, and daytime phone number. Sign your name. Almost all publications insist on this. When letters to the editor are signed by a number of people, usually only one or two of the names are published (followed by a note "and 16 others"); most publications prefer to use that space for opinions, not lists of names.

What Not to Say

- Don't begin your letter with, "You won't dare print this letter." Editors generally delete such sentences because, in fact, they dare to print a wide range of opinion, including letters critical of themselves.
- Avoid whining ("It's not fair," "It always happens to me"). It does not make interesting reading.
- Don't expect newspapers or magazines to print letters that are thinly disguised advertisements for your business or your group. If you want people to know about a nonprofit, community-wide event, editors are generally willing to include it in an events column.
- Avoid half-truths or inaccuracies. Letters are subject to editing for length, libel, good taste, newspaper style, and accuracy. Editors will check the facts in your letters.

- Don't write anything that can be proved malicious (even if it's true) and don't write anything that can't be proved (even if there's no intent to harm); publishers won't print anything libelous.

- Don't use threats, bullying language, pejorative adjectives ("stupid," "ridiculous," "redneck," "bleeding heart liberal"), or stereotypes ("what can you expect from a lawyer," "labor unions have always looked out for themselves first," "another anti-male feminist"). Certain readers will agree with your sentiments. Most, however, will see, quite properly, that such language indicates a weak argument. Margaret Thatcher once said, "I always cheer up immensely if an attack is particularly wounding because I think, well, if they attack one personally, it means they have not a single political argument left."

- Don't end your letter with "Think about it!" One editor says this line shows up routinely in letters and is just as routinely deleted. If your letter appears on the opinion-editorial (op-ed) page, the implication is that you want people to think about it.

- Don't submit poetry, lost-and-found announcements, or personal messages ("I'm looking for descendants of Jenny Treibel").

Tips on Writing

↝ Check the area near the letters-to-the-editor column for guidelines; most publications have requirements.

↝ Address your letter "To the Editor," rather than to the person responsible for the article, cartoon, or letter you're writing about.

↝ Although regional publications might accept letters commenting on a previously published letter, most national publications have policies against publishing letters about letters.

↝ Your topic should be timely; editors rarely run letters about issues that are weeks or months old.

↝ Limit yourself to one topic, to one main thought. If you don't stick to the point, your letter will probably be edited so that it does.

↝ Your topic should be important to more than one person (you). Readers may not care how awful your neighbors are, unless you can tie their behavior to a larger issue (people who don't shovel their walks).

∾ To get a letter accepted in a competitive market, aim for pithiness, humor, unusual information, or a twist on conventional thinking. Editors like letters of interest to other readers, opinionated letters on a controversy, letters reflecting a unique point of view on a broad topic, and letters that are clear, entertaining, and thought-provoking.

∾ When you feel strongly about an issue, get others to write too so that the letters to the editor column reflects that many people feel the way you do.

∾ Have others read your letter; oftentimes you are too close to the problem to see how your letter may affect others.

∾ Most papers won't print letters from the same individual more frequently than every month or two, so if you've just had a letter published there's no point in writing again soon.

∾ Some publications want letters original to them, not copies of letters sent to other publications. Check your publication's editorial policy.

Special Situations

∾ Anonymous letters aren't often printed as most publishers believe their readers have a right to know whose views are being expressed. However, some circumstances (prospect of physical harm to the writer or loss of a job) justify anonymous letters. Editors will print such letters over a "Name Withheld." Call first to be sure this is possible. When you write, specify that the letter is to be published only if your name does not appear.

∾ Letters-to-the-editor columns become especially popular just before elections. Some publications print letters that support one candidate or criticize another; others ban election-related letters during a period immediately preceding an election or on Election Day in order to avoid being used to launch last-minute offensives. Blatant politicking usually never makes it to the printed page; editors have learned to spot letters that are thinly disguised publicity efforts or those that are part of an effort to create a bandwagon effect.

∾ When asking for a correction or retraction of an inaccuracy, begin by identifying the erroneous article by date, section, page, and column. Be polite, factual, firm. Offer to supply correct data, proofs of your assertion, and phone numbers to call for verification.

∾ Write letters to the editor commending civic groups or individuals who have contributed to the common good in ways that may not be known to everyone. Letters like these not only add welcome relief to the usual fare of the letters column, but they build positive community feelings and often engender more of the same productive activities. Note, however, that "nice" letters don't often get published; this kind of letter needs an extra dash of humor, wit, or color.

Format

∾ Editors prefer typewritten letters. If you handwrite a letter, it must be legible.

∾ Most publications accept e-mailed or faxed letters.

WORDS

advice	disagree	insulting	prejudiced
aspect	disapprove	judgmental	premise
assume	dissatisfied	misunderstanding	provocative
attitude	disturbing	notion	slant
bias	doctrinaire	offensive	stand
commentary	dogmatic	omission	suppose
conclude	embarrassing	one-sided	surmise
conjecture	examine	partisan	unfortunate
consensus	express	perspective	view
consider	impression	persuade	
contradict	infer	position	
controversy	inflammatory	posture	

PHRASES

after reading your Sept. 29 article on

a May 3 *New York Post Dispatch* article spoke of

an affront to those of us who

cartoonist Humphry Clinker should be aware that

did a slow burn when I read

difference of opinion

fail to agree

how can anyone state, as did Laetitia Snap (June 3), that

I agree wholeheartedly with

I am horrified by the Aug. 11 report

I am one of the many "misguided" people who was outraged by

I am puzzled by the reference to the long-term effects of

I am writing on behalf of

I disagree with the Reverend Septimus Crisparkle's premise (Feb. 7)

I found the short story in your September issue to be

I must take issue with

infuriating to see that

in response to a July 3 letterwriter who said

I really enjoyed

I strongly object

I take exception to the opinions expressed by

it seems to me

I was disturbed/incensed/pleased/angry/disappointed to read that

letterwriter Muriel McComber's suggestion (Aug. 9) was intriguing, but

made me see red

neglected to mention

one side of the story

on the one hand/on the other hand

point in dispute

presented a false picture

read with great/considerable interest

recipe for disaster

regarding Senator Sam Blundel's new bill for the hearing-impaired

several letterwriters have commented upon

the article on women in trades did much to

your editorial position on

your Sept. 17 editorial on

SENTENCES

A Dec. 9 writer is incorrect in saying that the Regional Transit Board was abolished several years ago; we are, in fact, alive and well.

I am writing to express my appreciation for your excellent coverage of City Council meetings on the local groundwater issue.

I commend you for your Aug. 11 editorial on magnet schools.

I disagree with Elizabeth Saunders' Apr. 5 column on city-supported recycling.

I look forward to seeing a published retraction of the incorrect information given in this article.

In Hennie Feinschreiber's Dec. 9 column on the living will, she uses statistics that have long since been discredited.

In his December 1 Counterpoint, "Tax Breaks for the Rich," Gerald Tetley suggests that out of fear of giving the rich a break, we are actually cutting off our noses to spite our face.

I was disappointed that not one of the dozens who wrote to complain about the hike in municipal sewer rates noticed that the rates are actually lower than they were ten years ago.

Many thanks for your unpopular but eminently sane editorial stand on gun control (July 2).

Please consider the cumulative effect of such legislation on our children.

Please do not drop Flora Lewis/Cal Thomas/Ellen Goodman/George Will from your editorial pages.

Several important factors were omitted from your Apr. 6 article on wide-area telephone service.

The writer of the Mar. 16 letter against triple trailers seemed to have little factual understanding of semi-truck traffic and professional truck drivers.

Your Aug. 3 editorial on workers' compensation overlooked a a crucial factor.

Your June 29 editorial on child care failed to mention one of the largest and most effective groups working on this issue.

PARAGRAPHS

Has anyone noticed that the city has become overrun with dogs in the last several years? Most of these dogs have no collars and run in packs of five to eight dogs. If I had small children, I'd worry when they played outdoors. Where have these dogs come from? Whose problem is it? The city council's? The health department's? The police department's?

Letter writer Charles Shandon neglected to mention in his long, rather hysterical diatribe against mayoral candidate Hugh Desprez that he is running Mary Shandon's bid for the mayor's office. He is also her husband.

Your story on the newest technology in today's emergency rooms featured the views of hospital administrators, medical care-givers, and manufacturers' representatives. Nowhere was a patient mentioned. Is overlooking the patient also a feature of today's emergency rooms? (If it is, it's not new.)

To those of you who have been expressing yourself in these pages about the presence of wild geese in the city parks: Hello! A park is supposed to be natural. It is not meant to be as clean as your kitchen floor. It has messy leaves and gravel and bugs and, yes, goose grease. If you can't handle nature in the raw, there's always your back yard.

Count at least six women (the undersigned) who were outraged at your "news story" on the recently appointed Episcopalian bishop for our area. You devoted several lines early on in the story (thus implying their relative importance) to Ms. Dinah Morris's clothes, hairstyle, and even the color of her fingernail polish. Do you do this for new male bishops?

There was an error in your otherwise excellent article about the Lamprey Brothers Moving and Storage. In addition to brothers Henry, Colin, and Stephen (whom you mentioned), there is also brother Michael, a full partner.

A flurry of letter writers urges us to rally against the proposed congressional pay raise. I wonder if they understand the protection that such a raise would give us against special interest groups. Let's give this one a closer look. It may actually be a sheep in wolf's clothing.

I commend Meg Bishop for the use of "people first" language in her Jan. 2 column. By using expressions such as "people with severe disabilities" rather than "the severely disabled" and "people with quadriplegia" rather than "quadriplegics," Bishop helps change the way society views people with disabilities.

SAMPLE LETTERS

Dear Mr. Scott,

What happened to the ecclesiastical crossword puzzle you used to have every month in *The Abbot*?

To the Editor:

Several months ago, you announced a "bold new look" for the paper. Could we perhaps have the timid old look back?

Sometimes I find the financial pages behind the sports pages, sometimes in a section of their own, and occasionally with the classified ads. Usually the advice columnists and funnies are run together in their own section, but more often they are separated and positioned variously with the sports pages, the community news, the feature section, or the food pages.

I have tried to discern a method to your madness—perhaps on Mondays the sports have their own section, on Tuesdays they appear with the financial papers. No such luck. Somebody down there must just roll dice and say, "Ha! Let them try to find the foreign exchange rates today!"

Is there any hope for a more organized future?

Dear Mr. Burlap:

The excerpt from *Point Counter Point* in your June issue was excellent. I hope you will continue to offer us selections from lesser-known but high-quality literature.

~

Dear Business Editor:

An article in the Aug. 3 morning edition reported sales for our company in the billions. Naturally that would be nice, but it should have read millions. We would appreciate your printing a correction in the next edition of the paper.

Enclosed is our most recent annual report.

~

Dear Editor:

I read with interest the proposal to add four stories to the downtown public library building at a cost of $5.3 million.

I am concerned, however, that no provision has been made for user access. As it now stands, hundreds of thousands of books are all but useless since no one can get to them. There are a handful of metered street parking spaces, but you must be lucky to find one. And then you must not forget to run out every hour and insert four more quarters (the meter readers are particularly active in this area).

How many of you have driven around and around and around hoping for a parking place? How many of you have walked five or six blocks carrying a back-breaking load of books? How many of you have gotten $10 tickets because you forgot to feed the meter on time? It is utterly pointless to spend $5.3 million on a facility that no one can use.

~

To the Editor:

The front page of your Nov. 3 issue carried a full-color picture of a car accident victim who later died.

We, the undersigned, worked with Hilda Derriford—some of us for only two years, some of us for as long as sixteen years. To see our good friend and co-worker displayed in her last moments for an unknowing and uncaring public was one of the most painful things we can describe. How her husband and children felt about the picture is another story, but we can't think they were any less devastated than we were.

What is the point of using a photo like that? Can you defend such a practice in any logical, compassionate way?

~

See also: APPRECIATION, COMPLAINTS, DISAGREEMENTS.

E-mail

20

Admitting you don't have an e-mail address these days is almost like admitting you still listen to eight-track tapes.

—Tom McNichol

Less intrusive than the telephone and simpler than writing a letter, e-mail has been adopted by millions.

The hallmark of the e-mailed message is its conversational tone. Because questions and answers can be exchanged rapidly, it resembles a dialogue; a regular letter resembles a monologue. Senders dash off e-mails, knowing that if they make a mistake or omit information, they can send another e-mail in seconds.

E-mail has inspired a surge in communicating. People who haven't written a letter in years use e-mail because of its simplicity, directness, and speed. When contacting someone in another time zone or on another biorhythmic pattern, there is no fear of waking them with a phone call. When working late, you can send information to another person's electronic mailbox for retrieval first thing in the morning. E-mail is particularly useful when you have a thirty-second message to send someone who usually involves you in a fifteen-minute phone call. It also encourages the sending of quick notes that wouldn't, in themselves, warrant the effort of a regular letter.

E-mail When Your Message Is

- brief
- informal
- sent to a number of people
- timely
- urgent

- Double-check every e-mail address before sending your message. The system is absolutely unforgiving. "Almost correct" doesn't cut it.
- Use a subject line, a word or brief phrase to tell your reader right away what the e-mail is about. Most e-mail servers have their own format, but all will have some sort of space for this purpose. Examples of subject lines:

  Re: Welcome back!
  Re: newsletter error
  Re: benefits hotline
  Subject: the check's in the mail
  Subject: fundraising meeting
  Subject: new corporate library hours

- Start with "Hi" or "Hello," or the person's name followed by a comma or dash. The "Dear" convention of letters is generally too formal for e-mail.
- State your message succinctly. (Some people suggest limiting e-mail messages to one screen.)
- If appropriate, tell what action you expect: a telephone call, an e-mail response, attendance at a meeting. When the e-mail is simply for their information, indicate this.
- Close with a courtesy, if you wish, or with just your name. Formal closings ("Sincerely," "Truly yours") aren't necessary.
- In some cases, include your full name, title, telephone number, and e-mail address. This identifies you quickly and is useful if the e-mail is forwarded to a third party who needs to contact you.

- Don't send high-impact news (a death, new company president, serious illness) by e-mail.
- Don't write anything you don't want the whole world to know. E-mail is far from private and it is easily forwarded or misrouted. It was never meant for confidential messages.

- Don't send an urgent message by e-mail unless you know the person is expecting it or you call to say it's coming; there's no guarantee it will be read immediately. Some people check their e-mail frequently and in many offices users are notified when e-mail comes in, but other people may not read an e-mail for days.
- Don't write angry e-mails; it's too easy to fire off our first thoughts and regret them afterwards.
- Don't use all capital letters unless you want the recipient to understand that you are YELLING.

Tips on Writing

~ An e-mail address consists of (1) a name identifying the individual or group ("xyz"); (2) the "at" sign ("@"); (3) the name of the server (for example, "earthling"); (4) a code that identifies the mailer by type (domain): .com (commercial); .net (network); .gov (government); .edu (educational institution); .org (organization—usually nonprofit); .mil (military); .st (state government). Thus: xyz@earthling.org

~ Include one topic per e-mail.

~ Use everyday, informal language. In a letter you might write "I will"; in an e-mail you write "I'll."

~ Check for accuracy, spelling, and punctuation before transmitting; once it's gone, it's gone.

~ When you send copies of an e-mail (listing the copied recipients' names under "cc") be aware of the possible effect on your recipient. E-mail has made copying so easy that it is sometimes done unnecessarily and counterproductively. When appropriate and not detrimental to your original recipient, protect other people's privacy by copying the message to them "bcc" (blind carbon copy).

~ Certain options don't work in e-mail (italics, underlining, foreign accents). To indicate italics, put asterisks before and after the word or phrase ("I'm sending you *two* instead of three").

~ Don't waste people's time with trivial e-mails—jokes or idle thoughts that we'd never consider typing, signing, and sending through the regular mail.

~ Before forwarding an e-mail, obtain the original sender's permission and delete the headers and extraneous material.

~ Do not pass on others' e-mail addresses without their permission. And never give your password or user ID to anyone you don't know well.

~ Abbreviations are popular with some e-mailers. Others never use them and even find them annoying. Examples include:

ASAP = as soon as possible

FYI = for your information

BTW = by the way

TIA = thanks in advance

LOL = laughed out loud

FAQ = frequently asked questions

OIC = Oh, I see

WTG = way to go

~ Emoticons are also used by some people, shunned by others. For example, :-) stands for a happy face (look at it sideways) and :(for an unhappy face; :) for a smile, ;-) for a wink, :-D for a laugh, and :'(for crying.

~ Graphics may not be able to be read by everyone so skip them when unnecessary.

~ Acknowledge e-mail, especially in work situations. When you can't respond immediately, send a reply saying the message was received and you will write later. Some systems send an automatic electronic acknowledgment of every e-mail that comes in.

Special Situations

~ If you use e-mail at work, familiarize yourself with your company's policies on e-mail usage, privacy, security, and archiving. The e-mail system is company property and most organizations have guidelines about its use by employees.

~ The American Management Association recommends documenting your business e-mail transactions so that you can retrace your steps if necessary.

~ Attachments (long files hooked onto your e-mail "cover letter") are iffy. If you work for a large company where your computers are effectively protected against viruses, you send and receive attachments worry-free. Individuals using computers in small businesses or at home may decide not to open an attachment because of the possibility of importing a virus. When you must send an attachment, be sure your recipient will open it.

~ An estimated 15 to 30 percent of the e-mail received in the United States is spam (an unsolicited and generally unwanted e-mail sent to thousands of e-mail addresses, the electronic equivalent of junk mail). Chain letters are both spam and scam; do not indulge. Eliminating spam has so far not been successful. Some software will block certain addresses so that you don't receive their mail, but the e-mailers get around this by inventing random and unfathomable new e-mail addresses, many of which are not even the correct addresses. In addition, should you respond to their invitation to tell them you want your address removed from their files, they will rejoice because they have found a "live" one and send you more spam than ever. Just delete them. Don't even sigh, just delete.

~ Sometimes a friend or acquaintance stuffs your e-box with jokes (that you've heard before), chain letters, maudlin anecdotes, canned advice, virus scares, and notices of websites that you absolutely must visit. Letitia Baldrige, former White House social secretary, advises sending the person an e-mail saying, "I really appreciate your thinking of me and keeping me on your routing list, but I'm sorry to say I'm so darned busy, I can't read my necessary, urgent mail, much less amusing mail. I think it's time you substituted my name with someone else's because Father Time won't let me enjoy your e-mails."

Format

~ The format will depend upon your server although you will have some choices (length of your lines, whether to include the other person's message in your e-mail).

~ Making a hard copy of an e-mail message (that is, printing it) gives it the same permanence and nearly the same validity as a letter or memo.

WORDS

announce	explain	inform	remind
answer	following	inquire	reply
attachment	forwarding	notify	respond

PHRASES

alert you to the possibility	just a note to let you know
ask your help	please let me know ASAP
do you know	send me a copy of
for your information	speedy response
here are	wanted to follow up
in answer to your question	will you please send
information you wanted/requested	

SENTENCES

A dear friend of mine would like to ask you a couple of questions—may I forward your e-mail address to her?

Did you see the article on hog confinements in today's *Des Moines Register*?

Do you have a phone number for Joe Mangles?

Just a reminder about the conference call with Eusabio International this afternoon at 3 p.m.

New surge protectors are now available for anyone who needs one.

Subject: Small-diameter sleeve tools

Tax forms are available in the lobby from now until April 15, thanks to Courtenay Brundit, who obtained them for us.

We've been notified that Highway 36 will be closed from July 9–15; you may want to plan alternate routes to work.

Will you be home tomorrow around 5:15 so I can drop off the skis?

You asked if the company store currently has sandpaper seconds: yes, it does.

PARAGRAPHS

Please mark your calendars. William Denny, industrial engineer at our new high tech data entry facility in Porter, will explain the latest technology on Thursday, Jan. 21 at 3 p.m. in Building 201B, Room 43. A question-and-answer period will follow.

You wanted to know who keeps my Harley in such great shape? I do! Okay, okay, I know what you mean. The greatest Harley repair and service east of the Mississippi is The Caloveglia Shop on South Douglas.

Thanks for the new programmable multifunction mouse that you sent over. I'm having a good time with it!

In response to your question about the community organizer position, yes, benefits are included. In addition, the deadline for applying has been changed to September 30.

Would you please let me know the name of the contractor who did your deck? We're inspired enough to get going on ours.

SAMPLE LETTERS

From: burb@email.com
To: realty@email.com
Date: Fri, 16 Aug 2002 12:41:00
Subject: Purchase agreement for 1711 Grismer

Yes, draw up a purchase agreement at the asking price and fax me a copy at 651/555-1234. Thanks.

~

From: info@ducksfordinner.com
To: foxes@email.com
Date: 20 Nov 2000 14:30:01
Subject: Order confirmation # 82654560

This is an automated message acknowledging acceptance of your online order. You may check your order status by writing to: info@ducksfordinner.com

~

From: clubred@aol.com
To: juliagotrocks@email.com
Date: Tue, 18 Jan 2002 16:53:31 EST
Subject: Thank you!

Hello Julia—I received your check. Thanks! I put $30 toward dues, and $50 as a contribution to our latest fundraising drive. You'll be getting a fundraiser letter but it will be fyi only—not to ask you to give again. Netty

~

From: sgk@email.com
To: rmk@email.com
Date: Wed, 29 Mar 2003 17:02:35 +0400
Subject: Help—April 1

Hello from Russia! I'm planning my April 1 English class around the idea of practical jokes and I'd appreciate your help. (1) Could you describe this tradition as far as you know it from your own experience? (2) Do you remember a really successful April 1 practical joke? (3) In Russia the joke ends with the cliche "S pervym aprelya!" which means "Congratulations on April 1!" What do they say in the circumstances in your part of the world? Thanks!

From: hcalverly@email.com
To: thewhitecompany@email.com
Date: Tue, 29 Jul 1997 17:34:08 (EDT)
Subject: ATTN: Doyle

I received the fax of the essay. It was above and beyond the call of duty, and yes, I still needed it. I owe you one. Best, Hugh

From: msadlier@email.com
To: kcairns@email.com
Date: 07 Apr 2001 13:01:21
Subject: favor

Kitty, would you be willing to spend fifteen minutes or so speaking with a high-school senior in your area who's interested in the Fanny Gaslight School of Design? Thanks!

See also: ACKNOWLEDGMENTS, FAMILY, FOLLOW-UP, MEMOS.

Letters Dealing with Employment

21

It's strange how unimportant your job is when you ask for a raise, and how important it is when you want a day off.

—HOWIE LASSETER

Robert Orben said, "Every morning I get up and look through the Forbes list of the richest people in America. If I'm not there, I go to work." Most of us go to work.

While we're there, letters between employers and employees contribute to (or undermine) workplace morale, efficiency, and rapport.

The employee is affected, directly or indirectly, by letters that range from requesting a raise to asking for clarification of retirement benefits. The employer depends on well-written letters to maintain good employee relations and to resolve personnel problems that interfere with the company's goals.

Employment Letters Deal with

- acknowledgments: applications/proposals/suggestions (see also ACKNOWLEDGMENTS)
- advice/complaints/reprimands (see ADVICE, COMPLAINTS)
- announcements: layoffs/changes/company policies (see ANNOUNCEMENTS, INSTRUCTIONS)
- approvals: raise/promotion/projects/requests/changes (see also ACCEPTANCES)
- congratulations/commendations (see also CONGRATULATIONS)

173

- getting a job (see APPLICATIONS, COVER LETTERS, REFERENCES, RÉSUMÉS)
- interviews (see APPOINTMENTS, FOLLOW-UP, RÉSUMÉS)
- invitations: retirement parties/service anniversaries/awards ceremonies/speaking engagements (see also INVITATIONS)
- meetings: announcing/canceling/changing/postponing (see also APPOINTMENTS)
- networking (see INTRODUCTIONS)
- references and recommendations (see REFERENCES)
- refusals: raises/promotions/proposals/requests (see REFUSALS)
- requests: raise/promotion/project approval/interview/meeting (see REQUESTS)
- resignations
- résumés and letters of application (see RÉSUMÉS)
- retirement (see also ACKNOWLEDGMENTS, ANNOUNCE-MENTS, CONGRATULATIONS, INVITATIONS)
- terminations

- Date every memo or letter.
- When responding to job applicants: (1) If you are unable to make an immediate choice among applicants, acknowledge receipt of their materials or thank them for their interviews. If possible, say when you will notify them of your decision. Thank them for their interest in your company. (2) In the case of a rejection, express appreciation for the applicant's time and interest and state simply that you are unable to make an offer. If appropriate, briefly explain the decision. Close with positive comments on the person's application, an invitation to re-apply at a later time (if you mean it), and your confidence of success in the person's search for a suitable position. (3) When offering someone a position, open with congratulatory and compli-mentary remarks. Include confirmation of the job description and the name and telephone number of someone who can answer further questions. Repeat a selling point or two about the company to influ-ence the person's decision to accept the offer. Close with an expres-sion of goodwill about the person's future with your organization.

- When announcing a change in company policies, procedures, or regulations, include: description of the new policy; reference to the old policy, if necessary for clarification; brief reason for the change; expected benefits of the change; deadline for the change implementation; instructions or enclosures that further explain the change; name and telephone number of someone to answer questions or help with problems; expression of your enthusiasm about the change.

- When you arrange an in-house meeting by memo or e-mail: explain the purpose of the meeting, offer possible dates and times, and express your appreciation for the person's attention to your request. To change a meeting time, always mention the original date and time and ask for acknowledgment of the new time. To cancel a meeting, repeat the time and date, state that you must cancel (briefly explaining why), and apologize for the inconvenience. If you miss a scheduled meeting, write an immediate, sincere apology.

- When writing to request a raise, be brief and factual, supplying as much supporting material as possible (letters of commendation, sales records, copies of patents, research papers, evaluations, list of awards). No one ever has a "right" to a raise; do not let this attitude color your letter. Avoid threatening to leave unless you mean it. Don't compare your salary to others'; it is tactless, usually meaningless, and puts your reader on the defensive. Instead, show how your work has become more valuable to the company or speak of an "adjustment" to reflect additional hours, duties, or productivity.

- When writing a reprimand, begin with a positive or complimentary remark. Describe factually the employee behavior and, if necessary, tell why it is unacceptable. If appropriate, tell how this came to your attention. Suggest how the employee can change. State the consequences of continuing the behavior. Close with an expression of confidence that the situation will be handled successfully. A reprimand is brief, respectful, encouraging, and positive (instead of writing, "Do not make personal phone calls while patients are in the waiting room," say, "Please confine personal phone calls to times when the waiting room is empty."). Your goal in writing a letter of reprimand is not to get revenge or blow off steam; it is to change employee behavior. Avoid condemning, belittling, haranguing, preaching, scolding, or patronizing the employee.

- Notifying employees of layoffs or terminations has become codified—because of labor unions, because of legal ramifications, and because it is most effective for large organizations to follow a uniform manner in dealing with them. When a letter is written, it is brief and might include: a statement about the layoff or termination; an expression of regret at the necessity of taking this measure; the date on which the layoff or termination becomes effective; details on severance pay, profit sharing, retirement benefits, and medical coverage; in the case of a layoff, the possible length of the time, if known; details on company layoff and termination policies, career counseling, letters of recommendation, available public assistance, and other information that helps employees cope with the layoff or termination; the name and telephone number of someone who can answer questions. When the termination is due to the employee's poor work record or behavior, you will want to follow company and legal guidelines carefully. Tell why they're being fired and document previous warnings.

- When resigning, an oral notice may be all that is necessary. Generally, however, it is useful for both employer and employee to have a written record of the resignation. The common practice is to resign in person and follow up with a letter. Begin by writing something positive about the position, company, or organization you're leaving. Give the effective date of your resignation. In most cases, give a reason for resigning: poor health; age; family move; work-related health problems; greater opportunities for advancement, higher salary or more desirable location with another company; wish to change careers; recent changes that have affected your position. If you're leaving because of problems with management, co-workers, restrictive company policies, or other negative reasons, be vague: "For personal reasons, I am resigning effective March 1." Don't use your letter as a dumping ground for complaints. Take your leave in a polite, dignified manner—even if the truth lies elsewhere. For one thing, you may need a letter of reference. For another, despite confidentiality, angry letters have a way of following you about in your professional community. And you don't know when you might have dealings with the company in the future. If you're leaving because of illegal or dishonest practices, take your information (with as much documentation as possible) to outside bureaus or agencies. If you've been asked to resign, your letter doesn't refer to this; state simply that you are resigning, so that it appears that way in the official records. Offer to help find or train a replacement, if appropriate. End on a pleasant note, expressing appreciation for what you have learned, for your co-workers, for being associated with such a dynamic company, for being part of a new development. In some situations, write a one-sentence letter of resignation, giving no explanation.

- In responding to a letter of resignation, include a statement of acceptance "with regret," positive comments on the person's association with your organization, and an expression of good wishes for the person's future.

What Not to Say

- Don't write anything in letters to employees or prospective employees that could be considered actionable. Common sense will provide some guidance, but in questionable instances, consult an attorney on the phrasing of sensitive letters (reprimands and terminations, for example).

- Don't express negative emotions. Negative facts may have to be outlined, but your letter remains objective rather than angry, vengeful, irritated, judgmental, hurt, or contemptuous. When you are overly involved emotionally, ask another person to write the letter.

Tips on Writing

～ Be brief. Your memos and letters will be more popular (and more quickly answered) if they are concise. Check your correspondence for words, sentences, and paragraphs that can be cut without loss of clarity.

～ Be professional and courteous. Even when writing someone you know well, maintain a businesslike tone. Anything that gets put on paper can be saved and re-read. Although a careless remark can be forgotten, a carelessly written sentence lives forever.

～ Use parallel name forms. If you begin a letter, "Dear Hazel Marston" your name at the bottom is "John Reddin." When she is "Hazel," you are "John." If you feel a first name is appropriate after a job interview ("Dear Henry"), sign your first name ("Ferris") over your typed full name (just as the other person's name is spelled out in full in the address block).

Special Situations

～ Send goodwill notes of congratulations and commendation to: employees who complete a project, obtain a new account, or otherwise contribute to the good of the company; co-workers and employees who are promoted or receive awards; workers marking service anniversaries; employees, co-workers, and managers celebrating personal milestones (birth of baby, marriage). These notes are the least obligatory and the most influential of office correspondence. Something as brief as "Thanks, Tom. You're terrific" can inspire people to new heights of accomplishment.

Format

∽ Most in-house correspondence consists of memos. More official communications (promotions and resignations, for example) or letters that go in people's files are typed on letterhead stationery.

∽ E-mail is useful for brief nuts-and-bolts communications. Nothing confidential or important is sent this way, however.

WORDS

accomplishments	cutback	policies	regulations
achievement	goals	position	success
behavior	morale	procedure	supervise
capable	objectives	process	training
competent	operation	recognize	
conduct	outstanding	regret	

PHRASES

accepted another position

after much deliberation

an opportunity has recently arisen

appreciate having had the opportunity to work

ask you to accept my resignation

cannot presently offer you any encouragement

company cutbacks/merger

considered for the position of

due to economic conditions

eliminate certain positions

expect to fill the vacancy

financial problems/difficulties have forced/obliged us

have no other option but to

highly motivated

must advise/inform you

not adding to/expanding our staff at the moment

proposed termination date of

submit/tender my resignation

under consideration

value your contributions

with great personal regret/great reluctance/mixed feelings

SENTENCES

According to the terms of my contract, I hereby give four weeks' notice that as of April 18 I am terminating my employment as freight transportation manager with Sweedlepipe, Inc.

Although your credentials are impressive, we are offering the position to someone who also has the grain futures experience we are looking for.

Because Don Rebura Associates was not awarded the Marryat contract, we are obliged to consider employee layoffs.

I accept with pleasure the offer to join Potticary Dairy Products as institutional services manager.

I am proud to be part of such a creative and enthusiastic team—I hope you are too.

I'll be happy to recommend you highly to potential employers.

I'm concerned about the infractions of our safety regulations.

I'm looking forward to a long and challenging association with Willard Electronics.

I've seen your wonderfully creative and appealing display windows and want to congratulate you on your excellent work.

I would like to meet with you to review the circumstances leading to my termination notice.

On behalf of the management of Steenson Engineering, I am happy to inform you that you have been promoted to Senior Research Engineer, effective March 1.

Our decision in no way reflects on your excellent qualifications.

Thank you for applying for the position of commercial plant specialist with Calvert Tropical Plants.

The award properly belongs to the entire department.

The position for which you have applied has already been filled.

This is to advise you that you are being laid off in compliance with Article XXXI, Section 6, of our current labor agreement.

This letter will give formal notice of my resignation from Toddhunter Associates as Media Specialist effective April 1.

Unfortunately we are not able to offer you a position with Roehampton, Ltd. at this time.

We accept your resignation with regret, and wish you well in future endeavors.

We are pleased to offer you the position as warehouse attendant for Landor Textiles.

We are sorry to see you leave.

We have received a number of responses to our advertisement, and we ask your patience while we evaluate them.

We hope to be able to consider you for another position soon.

We hope you will be available for recall.

We will let you know/contact you/notify you/be in touch with you/write or call you about the status of your application sometime before June 1.

PARAGRAPHS

We have carefully considered your letter of application, résumé, and portfolio, and have been most favorably impressed. Please call the Human Resources Office at 555-6790 to arrange an interview with Enoch Emery, the Art Director.

Thank you for offering me the opportunity to work for Wedderburn Printers and Lithographers as manager of bindery services. I am delighted to accept this position with such a distinguished and forward-looking company.

We are seeing more travel expenses turned in after the fact, whereas company policy states that all travel expenses must be preapproved. If you have questions about how to handle travel expenses, call Michael Lambourne in Human Resources, extension 310.

We've received complaints that employee attempts to guard against receiving bad checks have become overly intrusive, hostile, and humiliating. Several customers have said they will not return to the store. While we encourage every effort to prevent the writing of bad checks, your actions must be tactful, courteous, and respectful. Please reread your employee handbook for specific acceptable measures and for suggested phrases and actions for handling this situation.

Last month, we lost $3,780 worth of clothing to shoplifters. There is an informational seminar on shoplifting scheduled for June 16 at 3:00 p.m. In the meantime, we ask all employees to be especially vigilant.

I am obliged to resign my position with the Van Eyck Company because of ill health. I appreciate the good employer-employee relationship we have enjoyed over the years and will be watching the company's growth with much interest. If I can be of any assistance to my successor, I will be glad to help out.

We are sorry to announce that Jeanne Beroldy has resigned from the firm effective July 1. She has accepted the position of Managing Director with Christie Packaging Corp. Although we will miss her, we wish her every success in her exciting new position.

It is with much regret that we advise you that we are unable to continue your employment after September 1. As you are no doubt aware, the company is experiencing severe—but temporary, we hope—difficulties. We believe the layoff will also be temporary, although for the moment it is not possible to promise anything. In the meantime, please check with Personnel for information on letters of reference, company layoff policies, public assistance available to you until you find other employment, and career counseling.

With regret we accept your resignation, effective March 1. You have been one of the company's strongest assets for the past five years. Please accept our best wishes in your new position.

SAMPLE LETTERS

Dear Mr. Karkeek:

Thank you for your letter seeking employment with our firm.

You have an interesting background. However, we feel your qualifications and experience do not match the needs of the account executive/trainee position presently available in our Chicago office.

We thank you for your interest in Lessways International and wish you success in the attainment of your career objectives.

Sincerely yours,

Dear Elizabeth Firminger,

Thank you for applying for the position of insurance adjustor with the Raybrook Adjusting Service. Your work history is outstanding, and you made a good impression at your interview. As you know, however, we were looking for someone with experience in the inland marine area, and we did find a candidate with that qualification.

We appreciate your interest in our company, and would like to suggest that you re-apply to us in six months when we expect to have several other positions open. We will keep your application on file until then.

It is clear that you will be an asset to the company that eventually hires you—good luck in finding the right place.

Sincerely,

Dear Marguerite Lambert,

Thank you for your application for the position of litho stripper, your résumé, and your work samples. They are being carefully considered by our Human Resources Department.

We received a number of other applications, so it may be three or four weeks before we can make a decision. You will be notified either way as soon as we do.

Thank you for your interest in Greatheart Printing Company.

Sincerely yours,

Dear Ms. Moncada:

As you know, I just celebrated five years with Tresham Paper Products. In that time, I've been stimulated by my work, supported by co-workers, and encouraged by management. I've enjoyed being part of the Tresham team.

The recent reorganization has changed things for me, however, and I question whether the next five years will be as fruitful for me as the last five and whether I'll be as useful to the company in my new situation. Because of this, I am accepting a position with Walter & Co., Inc., where I am assured of opportunities for advancement as well as exceptional laboratory support.

Please accept my resignation, effective November 1, along with my appreciation for a satisfying and rewarding five years.

Sincerely,

∼

TO: All Employees
FROM: Lawrence Mont, Head Librarian
DATE: August 14, 2002
RE: Library usage

As of September 1, all library books will be due one month from the checkout date (the previous loan period was two months). For the first several months, we will be calling this change to your attention as you check out books.

∼

TO: Dr. Betti Lancoch
FROM: Caradoc Evans
DATE: February 3, 2003
RE: Biodegradable plastics technology

We continue to be very interested in your biodegradable plastics technology, which appears to be the cornerstone for several new products. I understand you're pursuing patents for this technology. We'd like to see your patent applications filed by May 1, 2003, so that we could begin customer contact to clarify performance criteria for several of the products.

I want to emphasize our need for your technology along with appropriate patent protection. If you require additional support, please call. Thanks.

∼

See also: ANNOUNCEMENTS, APPOINTMENTS, APPRECIATION, CONGRATULATIONS, COVER LETTERS, FOLLOW-UP, REFERENCES, REFUSALS, RESPONSES, RÉSUMÉS, THANK YOU WELCOME.

Letters to Family and Friends

22

Do let me hear from you even if it's only a twenty-page letter.

—Groucho Marx

Although inexpensive long-distance dialing has replaced some letters to family and friends, millions are still sent every year. E-mail has probably fueled writing among family and friends like nothing since the pony express.

Start talking about the joy of personal letters and people will tell you about their family round-robin letter, about the grandmother who returned years of correspondence to each of her children and grandchildren, about the couple celebrating their anniversary who read aloud their first letters to each other, about high school friends who saved their letters for twenty-five years.

And there are serious letters: the man whose friends flood him with letters before each chemotherapy appointment; the young woman who chooses her baby's adoptive parents by reading letters written to her from each candidate couple; the weekly letters that are read with such pleasure by a ninety-year-old uncle who can no longer hear.

"How eagerly in all times and all places, have people waited for mail from home! How wistfully have they repeated, over and over again, that old familiar question: 'Any mail for me?'" (Lillian Eichler Watson)

Letters to Family and Friends Include

- annual form letters (see HOLIDAYS)
- correspondence with friends and relatives
- letters to young people: birthdays/congratulations on an achievement/ away from home

- love letters (see LOVE LETTERS)
- pen pals
- special-event letters (see CONGRATULATIONS, HOLIDAYS, SYMPATHY, WEDDINGS)
- welcoming prospective or new in-laws (see also WELCOME)

- Open with a cheerful remark indicating you're happy to be writing the other person.
- Ask questions about the other person's life, without, however, sounding like an interviewer.
- Write about what you've been doing lately; books you've read; movies or plays you've seen; sports events you've participated in or attended; local or national politics and issues you care about; news of mutual friends; something that made you laugh; an item you just bought; plans for summer, fall, next year; the weather; changes at work; pets' behavior; hobbies or collections. Or, choose a recent event (it needn't be terribly important) and tell it like a story.
- Close with an expression of affection or love and with a forward-looking statement about seeing or hearing from the person.

- Don't begin with "I don't know why I'm writing, because I don't have anything to say," or "You know how I hate writing letters" or "I'm sorry for not writing sooner"—unless, of course, you can say it with wit and originality. Start your letter with a cheerful, positive, interesting remark.
- Don't write only questions and comments on the other person's life and last letter ("Your remodeled kitchen sounds fantastic!"; "The new car sounds great." "Your party must have been a lot of fun." "I'll bet you were proud of Cicely."). Mark Van Doren says, "The letter which merely answers another letter is no letter at all." And Sigmund Freud said, "I consider it a good rule for letterwriting to leave unmentioned what the recipient already knows, and instead tell . . . something new." D. H. Lawrence added, "I love people who can write reams and reams about themselves: it seems generous."

- Don't complain or be negative, unless you can do it entertainingly. A cheerful, positive tone is welcome (except when you or your reader have been facing difficulties).
- Don't end with "I've bored you long enough" or "I'd better quit before you fall asleep." Instead, say how much you'd enjoy hearing from them when time allows or how much you miss them or, again, how happy you are about their news.

Tips on Writing

~ Write when it is a pleasure and not a chore (unless, of course, this is never the case for you). The casual guideline about letters to family and friends is that short and frequent is better than long and infrequent. However, this is a matter of temperament. The general feeling is that it is delightful to get personal mail at all, and never mind whether it is short and infrequent, or otherwise.

~ Remember your writing teacher's advice to "Elaborate! Elaborate!" Instead of merely reporting that you went camping, tell a story or describe something you saw so that the other person can almost see it. Almost any sentence lends itself to some kind of elaboration.

~ Include cartoons, newspaper clippings, snapshots, bookmarks, or other materials that are satisfying to receive and make your letter look like more than it is.

~ Postcards help you keep in touch when you haven't time for a letter. Keep a stack of colorful, funny, or oldtime postcards near your letterwriting area and get in the habit of sending off a couple a week. This will make you popular and will relieve you of the guilt that unanswered mail produces in most people.

Special Situations

~ One of the best letters to family doesn't even need postage: the notes or drawings put in children's lunchboxes; the note in a traveling spouse's luggage; the letter of congratulations to a hardworking student; the simple "I love you" pinned to a bedspread. These are worth many times their weight in the gold of family harmony.

❧ When children are in the care of adults other than their parents or guardians, they should have with them a letter authorizing emergency medical help. In the case of summer camps or day-care providers, a form for this purpose is generally provided. But if you leave your children with someone for the weekend, write: "I [name] give permission to [name of person caring for your children] to authorize any necessary medical emergency care for [name of child or children] from [date] to [date]." Sign and date the letter and give a telephone number where you can be reached.

❧ While it is rarely a good idea to write to unknown individuals who are incarcerated, it is generally a good idea to remember family and friends who are in jail or in prison—and with whom you have a close relationship. They appreciate mail. The first several letters will be awkward, but if you can establish some neutral subjects (books, interests, hobbies, mutual friends, social issues), the letters will become easier to write with time and practice.

❧ When dealing with strong feelings, letters are effective because they distance people from each other and from the problem while obliging them to think clearly enough to put their thoughts down on paper. However, letters can also worsen a problem. Written words are not as easily forgotten as words spoken in the heat of anger; they can be reread many times by a grudgeholder. Words without accompanying gestures, smiles, and apologetic looks are colder and more inflexible. Think carefully about the temperament of the person to whom you are writing and determine an approach that the person will be able to "hear"; do not write in the heat of your strongest feelings—that is, it is good to write then, but do not mail it; reread and rewrite your letter several times over a period of days.

❧ When writing to children: Print or type your letter; it's easier to read. Include a stimulating, challenging, or curious statement. Relate a bit of trivia, thought problem, word puzzle, anecdote. Children enjoy being let into the adult world; tell them about something important to you—a job problem, your garden, the next election. Share your thoughts, discuss ideas, ask questions. Avoid the word "kids" ("I'm so proud of you kids!"). For their reply to you, enclose a few postcards or a self-addressed envelope with an unattached stamp (so the stamp isn't wasted if they don't write back). Or, construct a letter for the child to return to you that consists of boxes to check off with various made-up statements and "news." This technique will probably net you a letter at least once. Very young children appreciate mail even if they can't read. Keep in mind that a parent will be reading your letter aloud; things sound different that way. Include a colorful drawing or cut-out picture along with the child's name (which many youngsters recognize early on), a picture of you, a fancy pencil, a small toy.

~ When writing a child who is away from home for the first time, you can say lightly, "We miss you!" but don't emphasize how empty the house seems; some children feel responsible for their parents' feelings. Don't detail what everyone at home is doing; that too can make a child sad. Instead, ask questions that will provide something to write back about: What time do you get up? What do you usually eat for breakfast? Do you have a swimming class? Who else lives in your cabin? Are there any animals there? Have you been in a canoe yet? What is your favorite activity? Who is your counselor? Have you made new friends?

~ To help your children become letterwriters: see that they receive mail themselves; supply them with small sheets of wide-lined paper and interesting pens; sit with them during the writing of their first two dozen brief notes—being with you is part of the fun; make the writing of a thank-you note a requirement for using the gift or spending the money, but let them do it at their own pace and, whenever possible, make a mini-party out of it, writing thank-you notes of your own at the same time.

~ Although the term "pen pal" suggests youthful letterwriters, it includes not only dedicated young correspondents but thousands of adults who write with great enthusiasm to people they've never met. A better term might be "pen friend." In the beginning, be discreet about giving personal information; start with facts that most people know about you and reserve more private details for later in the correspondence. The main "rule" for pen friends is to be yourself. Where one person is put off by a ten-page letter from a new correspondent, another person is delighted. The person who talks only about self-centered news fascinates one person, bores the next. The letterwriter who never tells anything personal is considered discreet by some, too uptight by others. When you are being yourself you'll find those who like you just as you are. To find a pen pal, contact one of the following organizations. International Pen Friends, based in Dublin, Ireland, has members of all ages; send a self-addressed stamped envelope to: International Pen Friends, Box 290065, Brooklyn, NY 11229-0001. Young people (ages twelve to twenty) who want to write a foreign pen pal can contact World Pen Pals, International Institute of Minnesota, 1690 Como Avenue, St. Paul, MN 55108. Also for young letterwriters are: The Student Letter Exchange, Box 2465, Grand Central Station, New York, NY 10163, and The International Friendship League, 55 Mount Vernon Street, Boston, MA 02108. Some organizations charge fees.

Format

~ Letters to family and friends can use any format you like. Acquaintances are a little different; the less well you know a person, the more formal (personal stationery, handwritten) the letter or note will be.

WORDS

activities	friendship	news	tell
affectionately	funny	pleased	vacation
announce	goings-on	proud	weather
busy	happy	recently	
events	healthy	satisfying	

PHRASES

a warm hello
did you know
good to hear from you
have you ever thought about
have you heard
how did you manage to
I enjoyed hearing about
I hope that by now
I meant to tell you
in your last letter you didn't mention
I thought you might like to know

missing you
remember the time
sympathize with
thinking of you
we were so happy to hear that
we wondered if
what did you think of
whatever happened to
what would you say to
when are you going to

SENTENCES

Are you planning to travel this summer?
Have you read any good books lately?
I can't tell you how much I appreciated your letter.
I'll be counting the minutes till I see you.
I'm wondering how your finals went.
I think of you every day/so often.
I've never written to anyone I didn't know before, so let's see how this goes!

I was so glad to see your handwriting again.

Please write and tell me all the news.

We'd love to see pictures of the new house.

We thoroughly enjoy your letters—you can't write often enough for us.

What a dear letter!

Write when you have time, will you?

You must send the quickest of moral support notes to me because I'm having an absolutely dreadful time at the office.

You're in my thoughts every minute of the day.

Your last letter was priceless/delightful/a pleasure to receive.

Your letters always brighten my day.

Your letter was such fun to read—thanks!

PARAGRAPHS

Hello! My name is Henry Earlforward and in addition to being your new pen friend I'm a bookseller by vocation and a bibliophile by avocation. I hope you like books as much as I do.

I can hardly wait for summer to get here. What's that you say? Summer has come and gone? The kids are back in school? But . . . but . . . I really don't know where the time goes.

Please say hello to everyone and tell Audrey thanks again for taking us out. We had a great time! Your family is so warm and fun to be around—so much energy and self-assurance! I miss you all!

I'm sorry about this one-size-fits-all letter, but my negligence in corresponding with all of you finally got so oppressive that I had to take immediate steps. These immediate steps have taken me almost three weeks. Meanwhile, my brand-new personal computer was crying out, "Use me! Use me!" Then . . . Poof! Voilà ! Eureka! Hoover! . . . this letter was conceived and executed.

Will wonders never cease? Hannah is finally sprouting some teeth—believe it or don't. I mean she's only seventeen months old! I was beginning to wonder if kids need teeth to get into first grade. Well, those teeth may have been slow in coming but at least they brought out the monster in her for four months. Actually she's been pretty good considering how sore her mouth must be.

This evening we're having our first interview with a private adoption agency—at home, in my natural habitat. Next week we start paying them money and attend a two-day workshop. Then the following week there's another two-day workshop, then more interviews—all this to complete a home study. After that the search begins and could take anywhere from one day to eighteen months. It makes me nervous in the service because it's such a big step, but I think we're ready for it. Keep us in your thoughts!

SAMPLE LETTERS

Dear Angela and Tom,

Parlez-vous français? That means "Sorry I haven't written lately." It all started when I ran out of lined paper at my office. I hate trying to write on this blank stuff, it's like trying to drive on a snow-covered road, only a little safer.

So how's the world treating you these days? We are winding down from another busy summer and hoping for a beautiful and serene fall. Whoever coined the phrase "lazy days of summer" ought to have their vital signs checked. I mean, who are we kidding here?

Both Kalli and Lauren are taking a gymnastics class, so we spend a lot of after-dinner time in the yard practicing what they are learning, with me as their "equipment." But it's fun, at least until the mosquitoes begin setting up their derricks.

I had a busy summer at the office, but September is slow as usual. The kids are back in school, the farmers are busy, and bow-hunting season is here. It's actually a nice pace although hard on the budget. I think I would enjoy dentistry a lot more if I didn't have to make money at it.

I'm manager of our softball team this season. It's one of those things that doesn't sound like much, and shouldn't be, but is. I'd rate it about a 9.8 on the headache scale (of 10). We are winning at 11-3 and tied for first in our twelve-team league, but, honestly, the manager has nothing to do with that. Now if we were losing, then it would be my fault. The hardest part is collecting money from people for various things and making a lot of phone calls.

Well, that's all for now. Say hello to the kids for me.

With love,

～

Dear Mrs. K.,

It was so nice to hear from you. I wish we could have had a longer visit at Easter. This semester has gone by so quickly—there are only three weeks left. Maybe we can get together when I come home for the summer.

I know you don't watch TV, so I'll tell you what Oprah Winfrey said. The average cost of a wedding is $13,000. Can you believe that? Mom tried to break the news to Daddy. He guessed the average wedding cost was $700 to $1,000. Poor Daddy.

Because there *is* going to be a wedding! We think next year. Can you believe I've written a whole page and haven't mentioned the love of my life? Jeff is fine, and sends his love too.

With a hug,

～

Subj: Just keepin' in touch
Date: 04-05-05 13:43:52 EDT
From: md@email.com
To: rm@email.com

Hi mom. Of course I'm alive. Had you doubts? I hardly think that three days without hearing from me justifies using capital letters.

～

Dear Fritz,

And how is my favorite uncle? Your letter came the other day and it was one of the nicest I've gotten in a long time. It was great seeing you over Christmas break.

Baseball is now in full swing (get it?), and we're running sprints every morning by 6:00 a.m. By 10:00 we're hitting off the machine. I can't wait for the weather to clear up so we can go outside to do all this.

Tell everybody "Hi" for me, and if Liz has any questions about college, she can write me. I can't answer them all but tell her the first quarter of the first year is the toughest, and it's all downhill after that!

Love,

～

Dear Lettie,

We all enjoyed your last letter, and have taped the cartoons up on the refrigerator.

Somewhere I read that life, to a five-year-old, is full of alternatives. Tommy is forever asking, "Mommy, would you rather have me get eaten by an alligator, bonked on the head, or fall out of a skyscraper window?"

I went bargain hunting at some rummage sales last weekend. I guess you could say I got my limit. The Lamberts were here for two days along with their poodle, Muffy (French for "lint ball," isn't it?).

I bought a generic fruit punch that says one of its ingredients is "natural punch flavoring." What is a punch? I assume it grows on trees, and I'm guessing it needs a warm climate.

We're having a party Friday night—twenty-two people. It's been the best way I've discovered to get the spring cleaning done.

This letter is more disjointed than most. I guess I don't try often enough to harness a thought, and now that I'm trying, my fingers are too weak to hold the reins. You like my metaphor? I ought to be a writer.

Give my love to everyone!

~

Subj: Friday morning
Date: 96-02-23 13:24:46 EST
From: mdk@email.com
To: rmk@email.com

I will medley for you when I plane in to the Cities. Who's going to car me home from the airport? I'm going to go CD now.

~

Dear Wu Sung,

This is my first experiment with writing to someone I've never met. It's a good thing that you speak (and write) English or this wouldn't be possible. Unfortunately I don't speak any other languages, not even Spanish, which I took for two years in high school.

To help us get to know each other, I'm sending you a few things that show my little corner of the world: a road map, postcards, a small travel book about Chicago, some pages from this morning's newspaper that tell what's going on in Chicago these days, and some pictures of my family, my apartment, and our cat, Mulch.

I work in a bank, so in my next letter I'll send a picture of the bank, some brochures describing its features, and tell you a little about what I do there.

I look forward to hearing about you and your corner of the world!

~

Dear Christopher,

Congratulations on doing such a good job on your term paper. I read it through twice and learned so much. I'm not surprised you got an A+ on it. I especially liked the way you paced yourself on this long drawn-out project. I remember you starting your note cards back in February, and then working on it steadily all spring. I'm impressed!

Love,
Mom

~

See also: ADVICE, ANNIVERSARIES, APOLOGIES, CONGRATULATIONS, "GET WELL," HOLIDAYS, LOVE LETTERS, SYMPATHY, THANK YOU, WEDDINGS, WELCOME.

Faxed Letters

23

*With the only certainty in our daily existence being change, and a rate of change
growing always faster in a kind of technological leapfrog game,
speed helps people think they are keeping up.*

—GAIL SHEEHY

The fax (short for facsimile machine) has become indispensable to many individuals and businesses, increasing the speed of communication and changing our idea of "response time" from days to minutes. It scans letters, converts the words and graphics to signals that can be sent over telephone lines, and transmits them to a machine at the other end, where the process is reversed. Like a photocopying machine, it works only with already prepared documents.

A letter sent by fax is like any other letter. However, once it's been typed or printed and signed, it's inserted in the fax machine. No folding it, addressing an envelope, putting the letter in the envelope, sealing it, stamping it and waiting several days for it to reach your addressee. The appeal is obvious.

However, the virtue of the faxed page is its speed, not its good looks. Some fax paper is not appealing aesthetically. The print can be blurry or smudged or at times illegible, depending on the quality of the original document and the machines used to transmit it.

Fax Letters When

- communicating overseas
- someone is difficult to reach by phone
- speed is the principal factor

- the appearance of the document is not an issue
- you've been requested to

- Determine whether faxing is indicated. If you and your addressee agree you need a speedy transferal of data or information, it is the best choice.
- Write your letter as carefully as you would if you were putting it in an envelope and sending it by mail.
- Include on a cover sheet or the first page of your fax: the recipient's name, department, and fax number; your name along with information on how to contact you (fax number, e-mail address, company name and address, phone number); the number of pages being faxed (include the cover sheet in your count).

- Don't send thank-you letters by fax unless you know the other person well; doing it this way parcels out the cost of the thank you between sender and recipient. It's also not very heartwarming.
- Don't send confidential or sensitive information by fax, unless you're certain your intended recipient will collect it on the other end. Anyone can read your letter while the fax machine is printing it or while it waits to be picked up by your recipient. Ads may say, "Please fax confidential résumé," but it is better to assume that confidentiality is not absolute.

Tips on Writing

~ Handwritten letters or notes don't make satisfactory faxes; printed copy is the norm.

~ Use a readable font. A 10-point size is the minimum; 12-point is better.

~ When the page being faxed is important, send the fax for instant reception but mail the hard copy at the same time so the other person has a decent-looking original. (You may want to note at the bottom of the letter that this is a confirmation of a fax sent on such-and-such a date.)

~ Read over faxes before sending; they can constitute legally binding documents.

~ Don't fax something that has been faxed several times; each transmission reduces its sharpness, making it hard to read and unappealing. Any fax that looks a little fuzzy when you get it is going to look worse after you send it on. To see what your letter will look like when faxed to the recipient, run it through your fax machine on copy mode. The result is about what they'll get.

~ When faxing letters or documents with small, dense print, adjust your resolution to "superfine." The document will be easier to read and the transmittal time will be increased only slightly.

~ Keep in mind that the fax machine reads everything. Heavy fonts, graphics, borders, icons all increase transmission time and, on the other end, gobble up ink.

~ If you rely heavily on the fax machine, it is thrifty and efficient to design letterhead stationery that will accommodate information needed for faxing. Experiment with different ink colors, letterheads, fonts, and logos in order to find the ones that look best after being faxed. You can then do away with the cover page, saving yourself and your recipient time, paper, and phone costs.

~ For fine-tuning your faxed letters, see Audrey Glassman's *Can I Fax a Thank-You Note?*

Special Situations

~ Faxing is useful for correspondence with people in other time zones. Many foreign hotels now routinely request that reservations be made by fax. Faxes have all the immediacy of a telephone call but are less expensive.

~ Faxes are being used for sending routine information quickly: receiving/confirming/changing orders, invoices, shipping information, specifications, quotes, and corrections to contracts or proposals in process. When faxes are legible, this has proved to be convenient and cost-effective.

~ Faxing has made possible long-distance business transactions where documents are sent to someone to be signed or initialed and faxed back. In many cases an original signature is eventually needed, but this allows the transaction to proceed in a timely manner.

~ Faxing unrequested sales messages is not appreciated. Theoretically someone could fax a sales letter to all the fax numbers they find. However, this means recipients pay to receive something they didn't request. Although most of us have learned to live with unsolicited third-class mail, we would not be pleased to have to pay to receive it. Because it costs the recipient to receive a fax, be sure the person welcomes it.

~ Faxing résumés and application letters has become acceptable to many companies and actively solicited by others. Faxing a résumé or letter of application in such cases is appropriate and probably necessary since other applicants will be faxing theirs. However, at this stage in the technology of fax machines, your résumé won't look as professional as a mailed original.

~ Faxes can be sent to anyone who has a fax machine—and to anyone who doesn't. People without a machine of their own send and receive faxes at photocopy centers. To send, bring in the letter or pages to be faxed while you wait. Don't take stapled items; this annoys copy shop personnel since pages are sent one at a time. To receive, notify your correspondent of the store's fax number and advise them to put your name and phone number at the top of the fax so the store can call you when it arrives.

Format

~ A faxed letter uses standard letterhead or memo stationery.

~ Small preprinted fax information forms are available to stick onto the first page of your letter or memo, thus making the cover sheet unnecessary. This only works, however, when there's room on the page for the form.

WORDS

attached	forward	quickly	speedy
confirm	immediately	request	transmittal
correction	instructions	rush	urgent
following	prompt	send	

PHRASES

additional instructions	by return fax
as soon as possible	by this afternoon
as you requested/at your request	happy to be able to send
because of the tight deadline	I need a response by

pass along
please acknowledge receipt
price quotation
prompt reply
the information you requested

to advise you
to speed your application
transmittal problems
via facsimile transmission and
U.S. mail

SENTENCES

Below are the figures you need for the meeting this afternoon.

Here is the missing paragraph for my newsletter piece.

I authorize you to debit my credit card in the amount of $4000 (card number, signature, and date below).

I'd appreciate a call at 555-4234 when you receive this.

I'm sorry about the rush, but I'd appreciate it if you could look over this press release and let me know by noon if it's all right with you.

In response to your ad for an estimator at your headquarters office, I am faxing you my résumé.

Let me know if you have any problems reading this.

Please have the current owners and the buyers sign below to indicate that they have received this disclosure, and then fax it back to this office.

Please read and initial the attached rider to your contract # 007945.

This will confirm the arrangements for delivery of order # C18803 made on the telephone this morning.

We were ready to starting printing when Itzik Landsman pointed out that these figures don't make sense—will you check them and get back to us right away?

You may use this form to respond.

Your Peterkin Turkeys will be delivered today between 2 p.m. and 4 p.m. Please check the delivery against the attached order, sign to acknowledge receipt, and return the signed order form to us.

PARAGRAPHS

Your good faith estimate of closing costs is attached. Please read it and call me with any questions. I'd like to get a final copy typed up this afternoon. Thanks.

Bettina Vanderpoel has provided us with the necessary figures and documents. Please check the attached statement for errors or inconsistencies and fax it back with your corrections as soon as you can. Before 3:00 today would be helpful. Thanks!

O.A. Pardiggle Termite, Inc. Wood destroying pests and organisms inspection report for 1711 Grismer # 6. Please read, sign, and return ASAP.

Can you let us know by this afternoon if you can supply us with one hundred (100) pool-testing kits from stock? We need them immediately. Is there a possibility of one- or two-day delivery? I assume this purchase would fall under your bulk-rate (10%) discount.

I'm faxing both you and your lawyer a copy of the revised contract. If you leave a message on my voice mail or fax me back with an okay, I can overnight the original copies of the contract to you for your signature first thing Monday morning. I'm looking forward to working with you.

Please complete the attached Uniform Commercial Loan Application, responding to all fields marked with an X. Sign and return by 9/23.

SAMPLE LETTERS

TO: William Marling, Manager
FAX: 715/555-2033
FROM: Lettice Watson
TELEPHONE/FAX: 715/555-4355
PAGES FAXED: 2

I've just learned that you have an immediate opening for a sales associate in your casino products store.

As indicated on the résumé on the next page, I've worked in sales for the past four years.

I would like to set up an appointment to discuss this position with you.

Thank you for your time and attention.

~

Dr. Grimesby Roylott
Fax # 818/555-3232
February 7, 2001

Dear Dr. Roylott,

I'm working on the brochure for our next conference on plastic and reconstructive surgery and I don't have a professional bio for you. Will you fax us one (about a paragraph in length) as soon as possible? Thanks. Our fax number is 616/555-4687.

~

FROM: Valentine Wannop
Security Systems
Fax # 212/555-1443

TO: Christopher Tietjens
Fax # 212/555-4877

PAGES SENT: 2

Chris, I need to turn in the attached meeting announcement this afternoon. Is everything correct? Thanks. Val

~

TO: Customer Service, Vesson Jewelers
FROM: Mary Webb
DATE: August 12, 2003
RE: Order # 189441, catalog item # 43A-8215
PAGES SENT: 2

The second sheet of this fax is the page from your catalog that shows the wristwatch I recently ordered. Although the catalog number agrees with the catalog number of the watch I received, the watch itself bears no resemblance to the one pictured. Instead it matches the description of your catalog item # 431-8255. I need this watch for a birthday gift on August 16. Please send instructions immediately on how to rectify the situation before then. Thank you.

~

TO: Lambert Strether
        Strether Medical Supply
        Fax 612/555-2566
FROM: Chadwick Newsome
        Newsome Mfg. Co., Inc.
        Fax 715/555-2534
RE: Order # LSX-655-12211
DATE: Oct. 12, 2002

The above-referenced shipment should have arrived before noon today and did not. Are we scheduled to receive it this afternoon? Let me know. We were assured we would have it today. Thanks.

~

See also: MEMOS.

Follow-Up Letters 24

Bulldogs have been known to fall on their swords
when confronted by my superior tenacity.

—Margaret Halsey

Writing a follow-up letter on the heels of an earlier letter, conversation, or meeting is a graceful way of tying up a loose end, reminding someone to carry through on a promised action, or building on something that went before. Sometimes you need to write several follow-up letters. Combine your bulldog tenacity with charm and originality, and you will achieve your goal.

Letitia Baldrige, the New York writer of etiquette books and former White House social secretary, encourages following up meetings and lunches with letters. "This little personal touch, which takes three minutes, makes an enormous impression," she says. "The ones who do it regularly in business are such standouts. They're the ones who jump ahead."

Write a Follow-Up Letter to

- amplify material in your original sales letter after it brings a response (order, expression of interest, request for more information)
- confirm a meeting date, a telephone or other oral agreement, a message left with a third party
- express appreciation and acknowledge what was accomplished at a business lunch, dinner, or meeting
- express appreciation and the hopes that they are interested to someone who has visited your school, university, college, or organization as an applicant

- express your appreciation and impressions after a visit to a school, university, or college or after attending a meeting as a guest or potential member
- inquire whether your unacknowledged gift arrived
- reinforce sales visits or demonstrations
- remind someone of an appointment, meeting, favor, request, inquiry, invitation, payment, or work deadline
- remind someone that you are waiting for answers, information, confirmation, or merchandise that you wrote about earlier
- send omitted or supplemental material or to revise an earlier correspondence
- someone who has not responded to a sales letter or product literature
- someone who hasn't returned your telephone call
- sum up what was accomplished in a meeting or interview so that there is a record and so that your view of what went on can be verified by others
- thank someone for a job interview
- verify with a customer that a shipping problem or missing order has been settled to their satisfaction

- State why you are writing ("I haven't heard from you"; "I wanted to remind you").
- Refer to the key idea (the meeting, your last letter, the unacknowledged gift).
- Thank the person for the interest shown or tie your purpose in writing to your last contact with them. If necessary, remind the person who you are ("We met last week at the performance boats trade show") or what your telephone discussion was about.
- Tell what you want the person to do: acknowledge receipt of merchandise, telephone you, send payment, reply to an earlier letter.
- Close with an expression of appreciation for the person's time and attention, or with a forward-looking statement about further business or contacts.

What
Not to
Say

- Don't imply your reader is thoughtless or negligent when writing about an unanswered letter or unacknowledged gift. Although the possibility of mail going astray is slim, you must allow for it. Even if the recipient is at fault, it is neither good manners nor good business to point this out.

- A follow-up letter should not simply repeat earlier information (except in the case of confirming an oral agreement or discussion). You need an identifiable reason for writing, such as sending new information, requesting a response, making a special offer, thanking for a previous order or meeting.

Tips on Writing

〜 When writing a follow-up letter to an unanswered request, query, or letter, repeat your original message (or include a copy of it). Go into a little more detail on the importance of the person's response.

〜 Some offices maintain a tickler file. When sending a letter (inviting someone to speak at the awards banquet, for example), make a note on the calendar a week or two later to verify that you've heard from the person. Letters awaiting responses can be kept together, arranged by the date when a follow-up letter should be sent.

〜 When sending a follow-up letter to an unacknowledged statement or invoice, include the necessary information (amount, account number, date due, days past due) with a simple notice, "A brief reminder." This is often all it takes since some late payments are oversights. (If this letter brings no response, see COLLECTION.)

Special Situations

〜 After interviewing for a job, send a follow-up letter immediately, before a decision has been reached. "A follow-up letter after a job interview can often be the extra push that gets you the job." (Harold E. Meyer) State that you enjoyed the interview and restate your abilities and your interest in the position. Emphasize a particular strong point. If there were any misunderstandings or any points you failed to clarify during the interview, you can remedy the situation in this letter. Close with your thanks and a courtesy such as "I look forward to hearing from you."

~ If, following an interview, you are not offered the position, write a follow-up letter anyway. Thank the person for their time, tactfully express your disappointment, ask that they keep your résumé on file, and close with an appreciation of the person and the company.

~ When someone fails to acknowledge your gift, write a follow-up letter (about eight weeks after sending the gift). Describe the gift. Business gifts are often opened by staff rather than by the intended recipient and wedding gifts can be easily misidentified. Adopt a neutral tone, emphasizing your concern about receipt of the gift rather than negligence in acknowledging it.

~ When a meeting or event has been scheduled months in advance, it's helpful to send follow-up notes reminding people. Repeat all the information along with a pleasant remark about hoping to see them.

~ Follow-up sales letters are essential. Write promptly, while the customer is still thinking about the presentation, earlier sales message, or visit from a sales representative. Write after a customer requests a brochure, stops by your booth at a trade fair, calls with a question, or responds to an ad. Follow-up letters are also sent when you receive no response to a sales letter. Refer to the earlier contact ("I wrote you several weeks ago to tell you about . . ." or "Did you receive the certificate we sent you, good for . . . ?"), thank the person for their interest or the time they gave you, add something new to the overall message, emphasize the one or two features the person seemed most taken with during your presentation, reinforce your original strong selling points, and suggest an action: place an order, call you, call a toll-free number, accept a trial subscription, use the enclosed discount offer. If this is a second letter, emphasize a different benefit or aspect of your product or service. This letter is also shorter or longer than the first and perhaps different in tone. Although all these can be called follow-up letters, they are primarily sales letters.

~ Successful businesses keep in touch with customers after they purchase products or services, sending follow-up letters to see how things are working out, to inform customers of new product lines, to remind them that you appreciated their business in the past and hope to serve them again.

~ After a meeting or conference call, write a follow-up letter to the other participants. Outline the issues discussed and decisions made in order to provide a written record of what was said. In *The 100 Most Difficult Business Letters You'll Ever Have to Write, Fax, or E-mail*, Bernard Heller recommends writing a follow-up letter or memo when you want to be certain the ideas you contributed in a meeting are credited to you. He suggests saying that you've had some further thoughts on the ideas you submitted and that you think it's a good idea to get all of them down on paper; "This is the gist of the ideas I offered. A detailed explanation of each one is on the pages that follow." Patricia King (*Never Work for a Jerk!*) suggests giving a written summary of meetings and conferences to your boss and keeping one in your own file.

Format

∽ Most business follow-up letters are typed on letterhead or memo stationery. Social letters or brief reminder-type notes can be handwritten.

∽ Although not widely used, "to remind" cards can be sent to follow up a telephone invitation. Handwrite the information in regular invitation format on printed cards, foldovers, or personal stationery: "This is to remind you that Mr. and Mrs. Louis Rony expect you on . . ."

WORDS

acknowledge	mention	remind	review
confirm	notify	repeat	suggest
feedback	prompt	reply	summarize
inform	remember	response	

PHRASES

about a month ago, we sent you/wrote you about
a little/brief reminder
am writing to remind you that
appreciate your interest in
as I have not heard from you
as I mentioned on the phone this morning
as mentioned in your letter
as we agreed yesterday
beginning to wonder if you received
I am still interested in
if you want further documentation on

I know how busy you are, so
in reference/reply/response to
jog your memory
just a note to remind you
make sure you're aware of
now that you've had time to consider/review/familiarize yourself with
prompt you to
since we haven't heard from you
thank you for your letter telling us about
thought you might like to be reminded

SENTENCES

After visiting with you at the textile trade convention last week, I telephoned Yvonne Dorm, our representative in your area, and asked her to call on you.

Did you receive the Blake River catalog and discounted price list that you requested?

I am writing to follow up on our conversation about the three-party agreement among Clara Hittaway, Amelia Fawn, and Georgiana Fawn.

I appreciate the time you gave me last week to demonstrate our unique Lammeter Integrated Phone Service System.

I enjoyed visiting with you last week when you stopped in to pick up some brochures at Spina Travel Consultants.

If you did not receive my materials, I would be happy to send you another set.

I'm wondering if you received my telephone message last week.

It occurred to me that I haven't received confirmation that you received the report mailed on June 4—could you let me know on the enclosed, self-addressed postcard?

It's so unlike you not to have responded that I suspect you didn't receive the wedding invitation.

I wanted to follow up on our phone conversation of yesterday.

I wanted to make sure you're aware of the service warranty on your new microwave.

Just a note to see if you received the message I left for you Friday.

Now that you have had a chance to tour the proposed site, I'd like to set a date to discuss our options.

On February 7, I sent a questionnaire to you on the departmental reorganization.

Reminder: staff meeting 3:30 p.m. Thursday in the teachers' lounge.

Thank you for letting me help you with the purchase of your new home, which I hope you are enjoying—I'm enclosing my business card in case I can be of further service to you or to anyone you know.

Thank you for taking the time this morning to describe the media buyer position, to show me around the complex, and to introduce me to other members of your staff.

PARAGRAPHS

I was delighted to meet with you at your home and hear your thoughts about our community. The best part of running for the Bonville City Council is the opportunity to talk with neighbors like you about our future. Please call my office with your concerns, and remember to vote on November 7!

On October 26, I submitted to you a letter of application in response to your advertisement for a moldmaker. I hope you have not yet filled the position and that you are considering my application. Could you please let me know where you are in this process? Thank you.

I'm looking forward to having dinner with you Friday evening. I'll be waiting in the lobby of the Rosalba Hotel at 7:00 p.m. See you then!

Several weeks ago we sent you a packet of informational materials on Topaz Island Resort. Now that you've had a chance to look over the color photographs of our unique vacation paradise, would you like to reserve vacation time in one of the ultra-modern cabins? Our spaces fill up quickly after the first of the year, so make your choice soon!

Thank you for the courtesy and interest you showed me yesterday when I stopped in to inquire about the opening for a child care advocate. I didn't expect to do more than pick up an application form, so it was a pleasure to discuss the job with you. As you could probably tell from our conversation, I am very interested in the position and believe I am well qualified for it. I'll have my references and résumé in the mail to you by the end of the week.

As you know, the Norrington Trolley and Lunch Tour will begin its expanded summer schedule on June 2. Please let me know if we are on schedule to have the new seat covers installed by the May 25 date we agreed on. Thank you.

I know you've been especially busy these last few weeks trying to settle into your new home, but I'd like to make sure that you received a package I mailed you a month ago. It was a housewarming gift, of course. I did insure it, so if it's lost I can have a tracer put on it. Do let me know, won't you, if it hasn't shown up?

SAMPLE LETTERS

TO: Johannes Rohn
FROM: Oren Cornell
DATE: February 10, 2003

We have not yet received your year-end report. I'm enclosing a copy of my original letter and another copy of the report form. Please complete it and turn it in as soon as possible. We now have all the evaluations but yours, and need to process them before the winter recess.

Dear Ms. Collen:

We hope you are as pleased with your Safe-Home Security System as we were pleased to install it for you. Let us know if you experience any problems in these first few months. Very few of our customers do, but we're available if anything should come up.

You did not choose to purchase our Monthly Inspection Service at this time. However, if you change your mind, we can easily arrange it for you.

It was a pleasure doing business with you!

Sincerely yours,

Dear Mr. Ayrton,

Just a note to remind you that I still haven't received my copy of the Brodie contract. It's probably in the mail, but with December being such a busy month, I thought I'd mention it.

Sincerely,

Dear Julia Avery:

I'm wondering if you received my letter of January 14 asking you to speak at the Society of Professional Engineers meeting to be held May 3. We are still interested in having you present your recent work to the group.

If you did not receive my letter or if you would like additional information, please call me collect at 612/555-6613. We expect to send the program to the printers by the end of the month.

Sincerely yours,

Dear Ms. Edelman:

On September 16, I sent you my résumé and reprints of several articles I have authored in response to your classified ad for a career services specialist.

As I have had no response, I wonder if you received my materials. Enclosed is a self-addressed stamped postcard. Would you please indicate whether my materials were received by you and, if not, if you are still interested in seeing them?

Thank you.

Sincerely,

See also: ACKNOWLEDGMENTS, APPRECIATION, CREDIT, EMPLOYMENT, RESPONSES, SALES, THANK YOU.

Fundraising Letters

25

In the end, raising money is basically a matter of going out there and asking. There are no shortcuts.

—GEORGETTE MOSBACHER

Intense and growing competition for the charitable dollar means that your fundraising letter has to pack the maximum of persuasion and appeal in the minimum of words. In the average home mailbox, fundraising appeals will out-number every kind of letter except sales letters. How do you convince readers to set *your* letter aside for a contribution?

It helps if you are writing on behalf of a long-established organization with a good reputation. Beyond that, your best strategy is vigorous writing: compelling anecdotes, easily grasped and persuasive statistics, thought-provoking metaphors, testimonials from familiar public figures, dynamic verbs, and well-worded appeals to heart and purse. One way of learning to write strong fundraising letters is to study effective sales letters.

Fundraising Letters Include

- asking for volunteers to help fundraise
- follow-up letters after initial appeal (see FOLLOW-UP)
- invitations: benefits/balls/banquets/fundraising events
- political campaign fundraising
- requests for contributions
- responses to fundraising letters (see ACCEPTANCES, REFUSALS, RESPONSES)
- thanks for contributing (see THANK YOU)

- Excite the reader's interest with an attention-getting opening.
- Clearly identify the organization.
- Describe the organization quickly and colorfully enough to retain the reader's interest: what it does and for whom, how it is unique, what its most impressive achievements are.
- Establish a compelling and urgent need for the reader's help.
- Appeal to the heart by the use of anecdotes, quotations, testimonials, case histories, descriptions.
- Appeal to the head by use of facts, statistics, information.
- Tell specifically how the person's contribution will be used ("With your help, we want to offer college scholarships to an additional twenty students this year").
- Mention the benefits of contributing (personal satisfaction, alleviation of suffering, improving the community, bettering someone's prospects, offering a tax deduction, providing entry to a select group of givers, resulting in recognition or publicity, allowing them to share some of their surplus, responding to a cause they believe in).
- Establish the credibility of the organization and assure readers that their contributions will be used effectively.
- Thank readers for their interest, attention, time, concern.
- Make it easy to give by including a postage-paid reply envelope or a toll-free number where contributions can be made by credit card.
- Have the letter signed by the highest-ranking member of your organization or by a well-known public figure.
- Add a postscript emphasizing a new or strong point.

- Don't ask questions or suggest that your reader think about something. Build from one strong message to another without interrupting your sequence to give the reader a chance to reflect, "argue back," or rationalize.
- Don't allow a subtly harassing or moralizing tone to creep into your letter. People who feel strongly about a cause often think others "should" contribute, and this attitude colors their message. Potential

contributors cannot be shamed or manipulated into giving; they prefer to believe their contribution is a free-will offering springing from their own higher impulses, not from your pressure.

- Don't use clichés if you can help it: "We need your help"; "Why read this letter?"; "You don't know me, but . . ."; "Send your check today!"; "Please take a few minutes to read this letter." You can distinguish clichés only by reading hundreds of fundraising letters, but it is worthwhile to do so to see what works and what doesn't.

- Don't use gimmicks such as unusual typefaces, extensive underlining or capitalization, colorful inks, or odd page layouts. A strong message is key, and gimmicks will not help a weak one and will undercut a strong one. Fundraising appeals today, however, are using strategies such as what appears to be a handwritten note on the envelope, a smaller enclosed letter, or an incentive that is either enclosed or offered.

Tips on Writing

∼ Be positive. Rather than describe how bad the situation will be if the reader doesn't contribute, describe how much improved the situation will be if the reader does contribute.

∼ Be specific. Your support evidence is specific (instead of "Every night in this country children go to bed hungry," write, "Every night in this, the richest country in the world, one child in four goes to bed hungry"). Make a specific request ("Please send a check today") or ask for a specific amount ("Your $100 will plant four new trees").

∼ Be as brief as possible. You have only seconds to make an impact.

∼ Convey a sense of urgency. The reader must not only give, but give *now*. The letter that gets set aside to be dealt with later often doesn't get dealt with at all. Ask for an immediate response and include at least one good reason for doing so.

∼ Establish a bond between you and your reader or between your organization and the reader ("As a parent/teacher/physician, you understand what it means to . . .").

∼ Herschell Gordon Lewis, author of *How to Write Powerful Fund Raising Letters*, says, "The strongest word in fundraising is 'you.'" Check your letter to see which occurs more often: "you" or "we" (or "I").

~ Divide your message into two parts. First, give the reader a vivid picture of what is possible: healthy, well-nourished children; an active community center; eradication of a disease; a new library. Second, tell the reader exactly how you plan to arrive at the previously painted picture. Your vision statement has an emotional, subjective appeal; your mission statement is factual and objective.

~ A fundraising letter can begin by asking the reader to take some action (sign a petition, call a legislator, vote on an issue, participate in a letter-writing campaign) and then later in the letter ask for a contribution as well.

~ Most serious contributors are interested in how organizations use their money. Enclose an annual report or fact sheet telling what percentage of funds go to administrative costs and what is spent on the organization's main activities. Credibility and accountability are serious issues for fundraisers.

~ The P.S. is more likely to be read than any other part of your letter, and letters with a P.S. have higher response rates than those without. The attention-getting P.S. is brief (less than five lines) and urges the person to take action immediately, expresses appreciation for the person's help and interest, or adds one more persuasive bit of information. More is not better in this case; two postscripts are weaker than one.

~ A series of fundraising letters, each with a different emphasis, is often effective because when one angle doesn't rouse an individual, another might.

Special Situations

~ When inviting people to benefits and fundraising events, use the appropriate invitation form (see INVITATIONS), but be clear about what is expected of those who accept ("$100 donation suggested" or "Tax-deductible contribution of $500 per couple suggested"). Your wording may be limited by the allowable meanings of "tax deductible" and "donation."

~ When writing to ask someone to be part of a fundraising committee, spell out exactly what you expect of the person as well as a description of the fundraising efforts and the overall campaign goals (financial and publicity).

Format

~ The vast majority of fundraising letters are form letters. Although one might not expect people to respond to a generic request, these letters do in fact raise large sums for their organizations. Well-written form letters are not only acceptable but effective. The audience you target with this form letter is important to your success, however. Direct mail solicitation will be less effective than letters directed to members of specific groups or personal letters written to individuals.

∼ Personal letters of appeal on business letterhead are effective but questionable. They should be written only with the express approval of your employer.

∼ Fundraising letters are not sent by e-mail or fax.

WORDS

advocate	cooperation	help	request
aid	donation	humane	rescue
appeal	donor	necessity	share
ask	encourage	need	solicit
assistance	endow	offer	sponsorship
auspices	essential	open-handed	subsidy
backing	favor	participate	supply
befriend	foster	partnership	support
benefactor	furnish	patronage	tribute
benefit	generous	petition	unsparing
bequest	gift	philanthropic	urgent
charity	give	promote	
compassionate	grant	public-spirited	
contribution	grateful	relief	

PHRASES

a campaign to stop/protect/
   encourage/support
acquaint you with
adopt the cause of
all you have to do is
as generous as possible
as soon as you can
be good enough to
broad program of services

call upon you for
can bring comfort to those in need of
champion of
come to the aid of
consider carefully
continue our efforts
counting on your contribution
deserves your thoughtful
   consideration

direct your attention to
financial backing
for the sake of
give assistance
good/guardian angel
have the goodness to
helping hand
humanitarian interests
I am confident that we can
in order to provide the necessary funds
it can make all the difference for
join forces
make room in your heart for
make this possible
on account/behalf of
our immediate needs are
please join your friends and neighbors in supporting
pressing need

rising costs
shaping the future
special cause/program/need
struggling with a worldwide shortage of
there are no funds presently available for
the time has never been better to/for
this program really works because
those less fortunate than you
urgently need you to
welfare of others
with open hands
without your contribution
working together, we can
your contribution will enable
your donation will make it possible for
your past/unselfish generosity
your tax-deductible gift

SENTENCES

Almost all the money we need to help preserve the Bradgate River Valley comes from people like you.

Any amount/contribution is most welcome/appreciated.

Before we can begin raising funds for the new annex, we need volunteers to help with the mailing—will you consider giving several hours of your time to help out?

But without your help, it cannot be done.

Do it now, please!

Help us work for a solution to this most tragic disease.

Here's how you can help.

I am troubled by the growing incidence of violence in our society, and I know you are too.

If each family gave only $7.50 we could meet our goal of $5,000.

I'll call you next week to see if you can help.

I'm writing to ask you to join our campaign.

I need your immediate help to make sure our legislation continues to progress despite a fierce lobbying campaign against it.

In order to take advantage of bulk prices, we need to raise $10,000 before May 1.

It can be done!

I thank you from the bottom of my heart.

It is people like you who make the world a better place.

I want to share a story with you that illustrates for me what heroism is all about.

I want to tell you about the progress you have made possible.

I will truly appreciate whatever you can give, and I know these young scholars will too.

Join us today.

Last year, your contribution helped more than 3,000 students come closer to their dream of a liberal arts education.

Not a dime of your contribution will be wasted.

Now, more than ever, your continued support is needed to help keep the doors open.

Only by working together can we make a difference.

Our deadline for raising $50,000 is April 1—could you please send your gift by then?

Please be as generous as you can.

Please encourage your friends and neighbors to call legislators, sign a petition, contribute funds.

Please mail your tax-deductible check in the enclosed postage-paid envelope.

Please respond quickly and generously.

Please take some time to read the enclosed brochure.

P.S. Write your check and make your phone call today.

Thanks for whatever you can do.

The Cypros Food Shelf presently faces a crisis.

The people of Port Breedy are counting on you.

The Raybrook Foundation is at a financial crossroads this year and we critically need your generous giving to sustain the important work we've begun.

We are looking to people like you to help us provide the dollars we need to continue out hospice program.

We invite you to become part of the Annual Giving Campaign.

We've accomplished a great deal, but much more must be done.

Whatever you decide to send, please send it today—the situation is urgent.

When you contribute to the Belknap Foundation, you invest in the future.

You don't have to give until it hurts—just give until it feels good.

Your contribution will help us expand our resources and do a far more extensive job of protecting our vulnerable waters.

Your donation is tax deductible.

Your generosity to the Boyle County Library Fund will ensure not only that we can preserve existing books, manuscripts, and archives, but also that we can continue to supplement the rising acquisitions budget for new books and periodicals.

Your generosity will be recognized in *The Anchor*, the monthly organization newsletter.

Your telephone calls, letters, and checks have made all the difference.

PARAGRAPHS

Many alumni and friends have "shared the wealth" of their Jarrett education by contributing to the tuition aid fund. Some of these tax-deductible gifts have been given directly to the development office, while others have been donated in memory of a loved one. This funding is available for students who are unable to pay all the necessary tuition fees and is a satisfying way of feeling that you have passed on some of what you have received.

I'm asking you to do two things. First, write your congressional representatives and senators and tell them you want a change. Second, help us meet the rising costs of lobbying and publicizing this issue with a gift of $10, $25, $50, or more.

Please indicate if your gift will matched by your employer. (Your personnel office will provide the necessary information and forms.)

Will you be breathing cleaner air next year, or not? It's up to you. A bill currently before the state legislature (SF1011) will set new, lower levels of tolerable pollution for rural and urban areas. To convince lawmakers of the importance of this bill, I need you to sign the enclosed petition and return it to me at once. Time is running out—the bill comes out of committee later this month.

A successful petition drive requires your signed petition . . . and your dollars. Along with your signed petition, I'm asking you to return a contribution of $25 or $50 to support lobbying efforts for this important measure. But please hurry!

Because the School Enrichment Council is organized for the purpose of lobbying and influencing legislation, your gift or donation is not deductible under current IRA guidelines as a charitable contribution. It may, however, be deductible as a business expense. If you have questions, please contact the SEC or your tax accountant.

The challenges we face this year are substantially greater than those of the past. We need your support, and you need the benefits of our important work.

Please try to send at least $15. Our only source of support is the voluntary dollars of those like yourself who are concerned about our vanishing wildflowers.

A sizable percentage of Clara Hibbert's campaign funding consists of small individual contributions from people like you who live in the Fifth Ward. She is not the candidate of special interests. She is the candidate of the people who live and do business in your ward.

SAMPLE LETTERS

Dear Mrs. Farrinder:

The Board of Directors of the James Area Community Councils recognizes your invaluable help to the J.A.C.C. in various capacities over the years. We also note with great interest your successful fundraising efforts last year on behalf of the public library system.

We are asking for your support for the J.A.C.C. in a special way this year: Would you consider chairing the 2004 fundraising campaign?

This is of course a major commitment and you may have questions about it. Last year's chair, several members of the committee, and the Board of Directors will be happy to meet with you at your convenience to discuss what this position might involve.

We think you would be an effective and inspiring campaign chair, and we hope very much that you will say "yes."

Sincerely,

Dear Monty Brewster:

On behalf of the Board of Directors of the McCutcheon Foundation and all those who benefit directly and indirectly from its work, I thank you for your most generous contribution. I think I can safely say we have not seen its like in all the years we have been asking individuals to help us with this important work.

Hundreds of people's lives will be materially and positively affected by the kindness and charity we have witnessed today.

Thank you, and may you reap one hundredfold the goodness that you sow.

Sincerely,

Dear Mr. and Mrs. Claggart:

You may wonder if people with severe disabilities really can live independently. Isn't it easier for a disabled person to be taken care of rather than to struggle with the day-to-day decisions about how and where to live? Isn't institutional living cheaper for the taxpayer? The answer is a resounding NO to both questions!

Consider Eva, a thirty-three-year-old woman with developmental disabilities who has lived with her parents all her life. She came to the Denver Center for Independent Living last March and asked for assistance so she could live in an apartment in the community. She *wanted* to be independent. And her parents were concerned about what would happen to Eva when they could no longer care for her.

DCIL staff went to Eva's home, evaluated her situation, and helped her decide exactly what special help she needed to live independently. One-on-one training in laundry, cooking, cleaning, money management, and job interviewing skills was provided. Additionally, Eva participated in our recreation program and found a great buddy to do things with.

Today Eva has a job washing dishes, her own checking account, a best friend, and a roommate with whom she will be sharing an apartment as soon as she has saved up her share of the rent deposit. Her family is delighted with the self-confidence and independence Eva has developed through her work with DCIL.

DCIL provides training and support services to any person with a physical, emotional, or developmental disability who wants to live in the community or who is in danger of being placed in an institution. A recent study by the Colorado Department of Social Services shows a 40% savings to the taxpayer when severely disabled people live independently in the community. DCIL services help make that independence possible.

With your help, many more people like Eva can live productive lives. Please consider a tax-deductible end-of-year gift to DCIL to continue this important work. Your contribution directly enables persons with disabilities to become independent, contributing members of our community.

Thank you for your generosity, and happy holidays!

Sincerely,

See also: ACCEPTANCES, ACKNOWLEDGMENTS, COVER LETTERS, FOLLOW-UP, GOODWILL, INVITATIONS, REFUSALS, REQUESTS, RESPONSES, THANK YOU.

"Get Well" Letters 26

I work for myself, which is fun. Except for when I call in sick. I know I'm lying.

—RITA RUDNER

Most of us rely on "get well" cards, but if you've ever received a card with nothing but a signature below the commercial message, you know how disappointing it is. You're grateful for the kindness, but you would have loved a personal, handwritten message.

Some "get well" messages are easy to send—the illness isn't serious or we know the person only casually and aren't too involved emotionally. At other times, however, our feelings of helplessness, anxiety, and even pity either keep us from writing altogether or produce letters we feel are awkward.

The main purpose of "get well" letters is to remind people that they are not alone in their trouble, to offer them the undoubted power of love and friendship as a force for healing. Your "encouraging word" does not have to be lengthy, literary, or memorable; a few warmhearted sentences will do.

Send "Get Well" Letters to

- business customers, clients, and colleagues who are ill or who have an illness or accident in the family
- family members, friends, co-workers, neighbors, or acquaintances who are ill, hospitalized, recovering from an accident, undergoing tests, or having surgery
- friends or relatives in chemical dependency treatment or in treatment for depression, eating disorders, or other conditions

218

- State simply that you are sorry about (or sorry to hear or learn about) the illness, accident, surgery, hospitalization.

- Express concern for the person's well-being ("I want you to be comfortable and on the mend").

- Be pleasant, positive, optimistic.

- Offer to help in a specific way: to make the person's most critical sales calls the next week, finish a project, sit in on a meeting, bring in library books, take children for the weekend or chauffeur them to school events, make calls canceling a social event, provide meals for the family, bring mail to the hospital and help answer it, read aloud to the person, run errands. A vague "Let me know if there's anything I can do" isn't helpful. Someone who is ill often can't even think how you can help or muster the energy to call you. Check with a family member or neighbor to see what needs doing. "People seldom refuse help, if one offers it in the right way." (A.C. Benson)

- In some cases, offer to visit if the person is laid up for a long time or if you think they would welcome company. Generally it's better not to visit those who are hospitalized or seriously ill at home. The point of a "get well" message is to stand in for you when someone isn't well enough to see you. Make it easy for the person to refuse your visit in case they aren't feeling up to it.

- Assure the person of your affection, concern, warm thoughts, best wishes, love, or prayers.

- End with your hopes for less discomfort, speedy recovery, rapid improvement, better health, a brighter tomorrow.

- Avoid being unnecessarily and tactlessly specific about the illness or accident. Say "your car accident" instead of "that horrible accident that took two lives," or "your surgery" instead of "your ileostomy."

- Avoid such words as "victim," "handicapped," and "bedridden" with their unnecessary overtones of tragedy, helplessness, and self-pity. Also avoid dramatic words such as "affliction," "torture," "nightmare," or "agony" unless the situation truly calls for them. Take your cue from the patient and do not jump to conclusions as to how they might perceive their situation. Be sympathetic without overstating the facts or dramatizing your own reaction to them.

- Don't resort to empty phrases, clichés, and false cheeriness like "It's probably for the best" (it doesn't feel "best" to the patient); "I know how you feel" (no, you don't); "God only gives burdens to those who can carry them" (this is arguable); "Every cloud has a silver lining" (not when the cloud is hovering over *your* bed); "At least you don't have to go to work" (the person might prefer the office to the sickbed); "You'll be up and around again in no time" (the patient is sure of no such thing, and the time passed in bed does not feel like "no time"). Re-read your letter to see how you, in the same situation, would feel about it.

- Don't criticize or question the patient's care or medical choices unless there is a good reason for doing so. Most people already have doubts about whether they are being cared for as effectively as possible; it's upsetting when friends add to these doubts.

- Don't compare the person's situation, illness, or surgery to anyone else's. Even if you have gone through something almost identical, wait until the person is fully convalescent and distanced from the present discomfort and danger to bring it up. Each person's experience is unique and generates its distinctive woes.

Tips on Writing

~ Write as soon as you hear the news. Although "get well" letters are welcome at any time, prompt ones carry a stronger message.

~ Focus more on the other person's situation than on your own feelings of inadequacy. If you feel helpless and upset, say so, but don't dwell on it. The situation is more about the patient's feelings than about yours.

~ Address the person in the same manner you did before the illness. Jean Kerr once wrote, "One of the most difficult things to contend with in a hospital is the assumption on the part of the staff that because you have lost your gall bladder you have also lost your mind." It is wounding when friends and family treat the patient as someone who is not quite what she or he used to be. The recipient of your letter is still a person, with all the usual human hopes, interests, relationships, and emotions.

~ Be brief if the person is seriously ill; later you can send a longer note or letter. Your note shouldn't be a chore to read; someone just out of surgery may not be up to deciphering illegible handwriting. The person convalescing at home, however, usually welcomes a long, newsy letter. Consider enclosing a few amusing or intriguing clippings from the paper ("What do you think about THIS?!"), photographs, a pressed flower, a cartoon, a sachet of potpourri, a quotation, a child's drawing, or colorful postcards or pictures. Enclosures are also a good idea when the usual words don't come easily—in the case of the terminally ill, for example.

Special Situations

~ Reassure hospitalized or ill employees that their jobs are secure and that their work is taken care of. If appropriate, reassure them about sick-leave policy and medical benefits. People often don't read the small print until they are too sick to do anything but worry about it. The person's immediate supervisor or someone from the human resources office can send information about insurance, sick leave, and company policies. If you know the person well, your simple assurance that there is nothing to worry about may be sufficient. "Get well" messages from managers or executives—even when the employee is not personally known to them—inspire loyalty and are a good idea on both the personal and business levels.

~ When writing to a sick child, say you're sorry to hear about the sickness and enclose something colorful, entertaining, and age-appropriate: a word puzzle, riddles, a cartoon or clipping from the paper, a story you made up or found in a magazine, a sticker book. Hand-letter a "coupon" good for a stack of library books that you will bring over and pick up several weeks later, a carry-in meal from a favorite fast food place (if parents approve), thirty minutes of being read to, chauffeuring of friends to and from the patient's house or the hospital. If you think the child will write back, help them along by asking a few questions: What's the hospital room like? Who is the doctor? What is the best thing about being sick? The worst thing? What is your day like, from morning to night? What is the first thing you're going to do when you get well?

~ Don't send a get-well message to someone who isn't going to get well. And don't write to say how sad you are. Instead, send your love along with an upbeat note ("I'm glad you're resting comfortably now" or "It sounds as if you're getting excellent care" or "I see your grandson's math team is going to the finals"). Don't mention death until the other person brings it up. Some people do not want to discuss it; others do. Follow their lead. Reread your letter to see that you have not subconsciously written a "sympathy" card to the person about their anticipated death. An appropriate letter says you are thinking about your friend and (if this is true) that you are praying for them. Include a shared memory, but avoid telling it as an epitaph ("I will never forget . . ." "I will always remember you as the one who . . ."). You might say instead, "I'm still thinking about your giant pumpkin. I'll bet it would have won first prize at the State Fair." Focus on those pleasures that are still possible for the terminally ill patient, for example, letterwriting, visits with family and friends, reading, old movies, card games, dictating memoirs.

∽ Those who are living with AIDS are your friends, neighbors, and relatives first, and only second are people with a usually terminal illness. Write as you would to anyone with a serious illness, and don't assume the person's time is short; medical advances are adding years of high-quality life for some people with AIDS. Being supportive and sending a card is more important than saying exactly the right thing. Focus on the person, rather than on the illness. You might also suggest a visit. Because of the false perception of the nature of AIDS, some people distance themselves from friends living with it, adding another hardship to the illness.

∽ When writing those in treatment for chemical dependency, eating disorders, and other such diseases, choose commercial cards that say "thinking of you" rather than "get well." Add a handwritten note that says in your own words "I care about you" or "You are important to me."

∽ When a friend or relative is injured or ill enough to need constant care, write not only to the patient but to the person responsible for their care—spouse, parent, child, relative—and offer your emotional support as well as some practical help (running errands, chauffeuring, bringing meals, spending time with the patient so the caregiver has some free time).

Format

∽ Commercial cards are appropriate for many different "get well" situations and their use is almost standard today. Some recipients skip the printed verse to read your handwritten message, but others read every word of the commercial message as though you had written it for them; for this reason, select your card with care. Always write something personal on the card—either a brief message at the bottom of the inside right-hand page or a longer message on the (usually blank) inside left-hand page.

∽ Use personal stationery, notepaper, or engraved note cards for handwritten notes.

⌁ For business contacts or close friends, a typed message on business letterhead, personal-business stationery, or memo paper is as welcome as a handwritten note.

WORDS

accident	disheartening	painful	treatment
affection	disorder	recovery	uncomfortable
cheer	distressed	relapse	undergo
comfort	heal	saddened	unfortunate
concerned	health	sickness	unwelcome
convalescence	hope	sorry	
diagnosis	illness	support	
discomfort	optimistic	sympathy	

PHRASES

be up and about	have every/great confidence that
bright prospects	quick return to health
clean bill of health	rapid/speedy recovery
devoutly hope	regain your health
early recovery	restore/return to health
encouraging news	sorry/very sorry/mighty sorry to hear
felt so bad to hear	thinking of you
fervent/fond hope	unhappy to hear about
good prospects	wishing you happier, healthier days
greatly affected by the news that	ahead

SENTENCES

Although we'll miss you, don't worry about your work—we're parceling it out among us for the time being.

Best wishes for speedy recovery.

Don't worry about the office—we'll manage somehow.

Fawnia says you're doctoring that annoying shoulder again.

From what I understand, this treatment will make all the difference/will give you a new lease on life.

Hearing about your diagnosis was a shock, but we're hoping for better news down the road.

Here's hoping you feel a little better every day.

I am concerned about you.

I hope you'll soon be well/back to your old self/up and around/up and about/back in the swing of things/back on your feet.

I hope you're not feeling too dejected by this latest setback.

I'm glad to hear you're getting some relief from the pain.

I'm sorry you've had such a scare, but relieved to know you caught it in time.

It's no fun being laid up.

I was so sorry to hear about your illness/that you were in the hospital.

Knowing your unusual determination and energy, we are anticipating a speedy recovery.

The news of your emergency surgery came as quite a shock.

The office/this place is not the same without you!

We expect to see you as good as new in a few weeks.

We're all rooting for you to get better quickly.

We're hoping for the best of everything for you.

We're thinking of you and hoping you'll feel better soon.

What a bitter pill to come through the heart surgery with flying colors and then to break your hip!

You're very much on my mind and in my heart these days.

PARAGRAPHS

I'd love to hear from you when you feel up to writing. Until then, be patient with yourself and don't try to do too much too soon. I'm thinking about you every day.

We're relieved you came out of the accident so lightly—although from your point of view, it may not feel all that good at the moment. I hope you're not too uncomfortable.

I was sorry to hear about your arthritis. I hope you don't mind, but I made a contribution in your name to the Arthritis Foundation and asked them to send you informational brochures.

Can I help with anything while you're out of commission? Because of my work schedule and the family's activities, I'm not as free as I'd like to be. However, some things I would be delighted to do are: pick up groceries for you on my way home from work (about 5:30), run the children to evening school events, have them over on Saturday or Sunday afternoons, make phone calls for you, run errands on Saturday mornings, bring over a hot dish once a week. I'd really like to help. You'd do the same for me if our positions were reversed. I'll be waiting for your call.

I'm sending you some old *Highlights for Children* magazines and one new scrapbook. I thought you could cut out your favorite pictures and stories and paste them in the scrapbook. It might help pass the time while you have to stay in bed.

SAMPLE LETTERS

Dear Harry,

What a shock to get to work this morning and have Louie tell me that the only reason I punched in earlier than you for once was that you'd been in an accident. It was pretty gloomy around here until we got some information from the hospital. Your doctor evidently thinks the general picture looks good and you shouldn't be laid up too long.

Louie has divided up your work between Max and Charlie so don't worry about anything at this end.

Best wishes,

Dear Mrs. Gummidge,

We were sorry to learn that you have been hospitalized. I took the liberty of stopping your newspaper and mail delivery for the time being (the mail is being held at the post office). Since I had a copy of your house key, I went in to make sure the faucets were off and the windows shut (except for leaving one upstairs and one downstairs open an inch for air). I've been going in at night and turning on a few lights so it doesn't look empty.

I wasn't sure you were up to a phone call, but I thought you'd want to know that the house is being looked after.

We're praying for your speedy recovery.

With best wishes,

Dear Ms. Melbury,

The staff and management at The Woodlanders join me in wishing you a speedy recovery from your emergency surgery. We are relieved to hear that the surgery went well and that you'll be back among us before long. For one thing, you are the only one who can ever find the Damson files.

Don't even think about work. Giles Winterborne is taking over the outstanding projects on your desk, and Felice Charmond is answering your phone and handling things as they come up. Marty South will send you a copy of company policy on sick leave and hospitalization costs (both are generous, I think).

Sincerely yours,

∽

Dear Jay,

I hear you've been under the weather lately. As soon as you feel up to it, let me know and I'll call Daisy and Tom and Nick—there's nothing like a party for lifting the old spirits.

Best,

∽

Dear Eliza,

Grandma and I were so sorry to hear that you've got the chicken socks. We didn't know chickens wore socks, so we were surprised. What's that? You say you have the chicken fox. What kind of an animal is a chicken fox anyway? What's that? You say you have a chicken box. Are you going to raise chickens in it? Oh, excuse me, you have the chicken rocks. We've never heard of them. Are they the latest fad, like pet rocks? Oho! We've got it now. You've got the CHICKEN POX. Maybe by the time you've read this long letter, you will be feeling a little better.

Grandma said to tell you to be sure not to scratch, but I'm sure you won't.

In a few days when you feel better we'll give you a call and you can tell us yourself how you're feeling.

Love,

∽

Dear Olivia,

You realize, of course, that there will be no further bridge games until you are well! None of us is willing to invite a substitute—"Replace Olivia? As Sam Goldwyn put it in two words: Im Possible."

Don't worry about the homefront. George has things under control, and we are all taking turns entertaining your house guest, that nice Mr. Pim.

Give us the high sign when you are ready for phone calls or visits—or a game of bridge!

Love,

∽

Dear Goldie,

I was sorry to hear about Abraham's accident yesterday. Your daughter seemed to think that although he was facing some surgery and was fairly uncomfortable, the outlook was good. I hope all goes well and that he can look forward to coming home soon.

You have taken no compassionate leave in the eight years you have been with us, so there is no problem with your taking as long as you like to be with Abraham. Patsy Tate assumed responsibility for your station; she may call you from time to time with a question, but otherwise the situation is well in hand.

Although our hospitalization insurance is based on a pre-admit system, this doesn't apply in the case of an emergency, such as Abraham's hospitalization. However, there are a few steps you should take in the next several days to regularize the situation. I've asked someone from Human Resources to call you about this.

If there is anything we can do to make things easier for you, let us know. In the meantime, you are very much in our thoughts.

Sincerely,

See also: ACKNOWLEDGMENTS, BELATED, FAMILY, SENSITIVE, SYMPATHY, THANK YOU.

Goodwill Letters 27

It is not enough to collect today's profits, for your competitor
is collecting tomorrow's good will.

—THE SYSTEM COMPANY, *HOW TO WRITE LETTERS THAT WIN*, 1906

Goodwill letters are sales letter, but you aren't selling a product or service directly. You "sell" the recipient on your company's worth, reputation, friendliness, integrity, and competence. You want the reader to think well of your company and to keep you in mind for future purchases and services.

Although sales are generally based on price, color, dimensions, length of service contract, and other measurable properties, many other sales are based on feelings or attitudes. Goodwill letters appeal to the nonmaterial aspects of customer choice.

Kinds of Goodwill Letters

- anniversaries: service/wedding
- announcements: change in prices/personnel/policies/address (see also ANNOUNCEMENTS)
- appreciation: good payment record/past business/customer referral (see also APPRECIATION)
- congratulations (see CONGRATULATIONS)
- customers' and employees' life events (see appropriate topic)
- holiday greetings (see HOLIDAYS)
- special events and offers: open houses/sales/discounts/gifts/samples/certificates/coupons
- surveys/questionnaires

- thank you: previous business/current purchase/suggestions/ assistance/good work (see also THANK YOU)
- welcome/welcome back (see also WELCOME)

- Open with a friendly or complimentary remark.
- State your main message (congratulations, thank you, keeping in touch, happy holidays, "just want to see how you're doing"). Almost any occasion is reason enough to show interest in your customers or employees.
- Expand on the message ("I'm particularly grateful because . . ." or "You've been a delight to work with because . . ." or "I hope the New Year is a happy and healthy one for you and your family").
- When possible, focus on the other person's situation, interests, concerns; this is a "you" letter.
- Close with pleasant wishes for success and a mention of future or continued contact.

- Don't include a strong sales message in a goodwill letter. Mention your products or services only lightly or not at all.
- Don't dilute the impact of a goodwill letter by asking for business, or for a favor, or for higher work outputs, or by including business news or comments. Save them for another letter.
- Don't be too effusive. Use a natural, informal tone that conveys a genuine friendliness.

Tips on Writing

~ Send goodwill letters within your organization. Although it is never mandatory to congratulate an employee on a service anniversary, for example, you encourage good morale and company loyalty by doing so. Holidays are an excellent occasion for goodwill letters written to employees on behalf of company management, firm officers, or board of directors.

~ Take advantage of routine announcements (new type of billing statement, new address, meeting notice) to develop a goodwill letter (thanking customers for their business or employees for a good year).

~ The end-of-the-year holiday season is an excellent time to send a goodwill letter, but mail it early so that it doesn't get lost in the other December mail and so that customers haven't already spent their gift budget elsewhere.

Special Situations

~ A survey or questionnaire about the customer's use of your products or services is helpful to you; it also serves as a goodwill letter as most people like being asked for an opinion and thanked for their help. To ensure that it is a pleasure instead of a burden, the survey must be brief, easy to complete, and returnable with a postage-paid envelope.

~ Goodwill gifts—samples, trial sizes, the first in a series, something the customer can keep whether they purchase anything or not—are accompanied by a cover letter. The sales message is not too strong as the free product is theoretically the message. However, follow up this mailing with a letter a few weeks later. At that time you can intensify the sales message. (See also COVER LETTERS, SALES.)

Format

~ All goodwill letters are typed on letterhead stationery, except for brief congratulatory notes to employees and colleagues that may be typed, or possibly handwritten, on memo paper.

~ When sending holiday greetings to employees, or customers, or other general-message letters, a well-written form letter is customary and acceptable.

WORDS

appreciate	kindness	sensational	unique
delighted	memorable	special	valuable
enjoyed	pleased	superb	
grateful	remarkable	terrific	
inspired	satisfying	thoughtful	

PHRASES

happy/pleased to hear	look forward to your next
how are you getting along with	pleased to be able to
just thinking about you	show our gratitude for
just to let you know	wanted you to know
keep us in mind	wishing you all the best
let us know if	would be glad to have you stop in again when
like to keep in touch with	

SENTENCES

All of us here at Larolle International send you warmest holiday greetings and our best wishes for a happy, healthy new year!

As one of our longtime customers, you may be interested in our new, faster ordering procedures.

Because we appreciate the responsible handling of your account, we are raising your credit limit to $15,000.

Congratulations on your ten years with us—you're a key player on our (thanks to you!) successful team.

Enclosed is an article on retirement savings that we thought you'd like to see.

I heard something pretty special is going on over there!

Sawbridge Training Services, Inc. now has a special customer hotline—at no charge to the calling party—for all your questions and concerns.

The Pig and Whistle invites you to a customer appreciation sale, but bring this card with you as the sale is "invitation only."

PARAGRAPHS

You used to order regularly from us, but we haven't heard from you for some time now. To help you remember how easy it was to order and how much you enjoyed our high-quality camping merchandise, we're enclosing a "welcome back" certificate good for 15% off your next order. We hope you use it—we've missed you!

I noticed the handsome photograph of you and your husband in Sunday's paper—congratulations on twenty-five years of marriage! Do stop by the office the next time you're in the store so I can congratulate you personally.

Thank you so much for referring Stanley Purves to us. It is because of generous and appreciative customers like you that Dorset Homes has been growing by leaps and bounds. We will give Mr. Purves our best service—and we are always ready to help you in any way we can. Thanks again for passing on the word!

You are cordially invited to an Open House on January 29 from 5:00 to 8:00 p.m. to celebrate our fiftieth anniversary. We are taking this opportunity to show our appreciation to our many fine customers. Do come—we will have a small gift waiting for you!

SAMPLE LETTERS

Dear Jules,

I see that the bank is celebrating an important birthday—congratulations! You must be proud to see what a success Mignaud et Fils has become one hundred years after its founding by your great-grandfather.

All of us here at Philips Deluxe Checks wish you continued success and prosperity.

Sincerely,

Dear Mr. and Mrs. Charles:

It has been three months since your new floor tiles were installed. I hope you've been enjoying them. We have customers who still rave about floor tile they bought from us thirty years ago.

If we can be of service to you in the future, keep us in mind. We're planning a storewide three-day sale on all floor coverings in late January in case you're interested in doing any other rooms.

Thanks again for choosing a fine floor product from Geiger Tiles.

Yours truly,

Dear Joanna Pryke,

We are delighted to note that Warner Maintenance Experts have been cleaning your office carpets four times a year for six years now. As a business executive yourself, you know the value of faithful, longtime customers.

To show our appreciation, we'd like to pass on to you a sample of an effective carpet spot cleaner that we recently discovered. Note that we are not selling this product nor do we make any recommendation for it other than that we ourselves like it. When we had a chance to buy some samples, we thought of our favorite customers and decided to share them.

Enjoy the spot cleaner, and I hope you continue to look forward to our thorough, deep-cleaning process that leaves your carpeting like new!

Dear Hilda Cherrington:

Over the years, you have ordered a number of our fine products. You're one of the reasons that Lee Gifts is the premier mail order house that it is.

To thank you for your business and to introduce you to a completely new line of Christmas ornaments, we are enclosing the "Christmas Star" for your enjoyment. We think we you will admire the fine craftwork that went into this delicate ornament. It makes a wonderful keepsake gift for friends and relatives. Also enclosed is a copy of our current catalog, which shows all twenty-five of the new "Memories" series of ornaments.

We hope you enjoy your ornament!

Sincerely,

See also: ANNIVERSARIES, APPRECIATION, CONGRATULATIONS, "GET WELL," HOLIDAYS, NEIGHBORS, SYMPATHY, THANK YOU, WELCOME.

Holiday Letters   28

A holiday gives one a chance to look backward and forward,
to reset oneself by an inner compass.

—MAY SARTON

With the proliferation of commercial greeting cards and holiday-oriented retail sales events (Memorial Day Sale! July Fourth Sale! Presidents' Day Sale! Labor Day Sale!), we are now conscious not only of such traditional holidays as New Year's or Thanksgiving, but also of dozens of others.

Businesses wanting to send goodwill letters to customers, colleagues, and employees can choose any holiday as a reason for writing. Family and friends generally send holiday greetings and newsy letters no more than once or twice a year, most often around the end of the old year or the beginning of the new one. Fundraisers know that people are more willing to give during the holidays and therefore schedule some of their most important appeals in late fall. It is not surprising that first-class canceled mail peaks substantially in December.

The United States Postal Service likes us to "mail early" to equalize the flow of holiday mail and reduce the expense of overtime hours for carriers. When not enough of us mail early, a metropolitan post office that ordinarily cancels eight or nine hundred thousand first-class letters per day will handle nearly three million per day just before December 25 (most of it scheduled for local next-day service).

Of all personal mail, 43 percent is accounted for by holiday cards (other greeting cards make up 21 percent and letters the remaining 36 percent).

Holiday Letters Include

- Christmas
- Columbus Day

- Easter
- Election Day

234

- Father's Day
- form/annual letters
- goodwill letters
- Halloween
- Hanukkah
- Independence Day
- Labor Day
- Martin Luther King, Jr.'s Birthday
- Memorial Day

- Mother's Day
- New Year's
- Pesach
- Purim
- Rosh Hashana
- St. Patrick's Day
- Thanksgiving
- Valentine's Day
- Veterans Day
- Yom Kippur

- Begin with an expression of the appropriate holiday greeting.
- Inquire about the other person and relate your own news if it is a personal letter. For a business letter, express appreciation for the other person and the hopes of being of service in the future.
- Wish the person happiness, success, health, prosperity.

- Don't let a greeting card do all your speaking for you. If you have nothing to say to the person beyond the sentiments of a mass-produced card followed by a preprinted or signed name, your gesture may be meaningless; most people are disappointed to open a card and find no personal message.
- When sending a goodwill letter to employees, don't use it to "get a point across," to chide the group, or to transmit office news.
- Don't send an aggressive sales message in a holiday letter (which is essentially a goodwill letter). An exception is a logical connection such as florists and Mother's Day or candy and Valentine's Day.

Tips on Writing

~ Not every household is a happy one. Among your friends, co-workers, and customers are people who have lost loved ones, who have financial worries, illnesses, or other burdens. Except for mass-produced business holiday letters, of which no one expects great sensitivity, choose seasonal greetings that are low-key and can convey your good wishes without an insistent and perhaps offensive cheeriness.

~ Because some holidays are also holy days, businesses try to respect customers' beliefs. This means avoiding religious cards and sentiments unless your audience is well known to you. Do not casually bring religious elements into your goodwill letters; it may be perceived as hypocritical and self-serving. Consult with adherents of different faiths to see how your message appears to them. Since the majority of holiday letters are mailed in December, a reference to the New Year is appropriate. Mention the year ("to wish you success and happiness in 2003") to avoid confusion with religious year beginnings. Otherwise, use terms such as "the holidays," "this season," "at this time of year."

~ When sending holiday letters to family and friends, you can piggyback other news onto your greetings: the announcement of a new address, an engagement, a baby, or a new job. In the case of a divorce, for example, it is convenient to append the news to year's-end letters. Be sure to mail your greeting early to save friends the minor embarrassment of sending their greetings to you as a couple.

~ When one member of the household writes the messages and signs the greeting cards for all, it doesn't matter if they put their name first or last.

Special Situations

~ Send holiday greetings to employees on behalf of company management, firm officers, or board of directors to generate goodwill and company identification. Wish the employees personal and professional happiness, offer congratulations for the good year just past, and express appreciation for the employees' contributions.

~ The most common customer goodwill letter is probably the year-end greeting. If your message is a general calling-to-mind letter or card (insurance agent, publisher, bank), send it anytime. But if December is an important sales or fundraising month for your organization, mail your greeting early in the month or even in November, before people shop or spend their donation dollars.

~ Some people (and letterwriting authorities) find holiday form letters unacceptable, while others (including yet other letterwriting authorities) enjoy writing and receiving them. Whatever one thinks of them, they are unlikely to disappear. After years of printing letters pro and con, Ann Landers polled her readers and then wrote, "The verdict is clear—100 to 1" in favor of the holiday newsletters. They are practical for those who must either send a form letter or not write at all. People used to live and die in the same town; their pool of friends and acquaintances was small and didn't require written communications. Today's family might have hundreds of names in its address file. Form letters don't have to be boring, and many aren't. In the polycopied part of your letter, tell your general news: the year's highlights, changes in your lives, travels, work and school happenings. You can organize your letter chronologically or by topic or by giving each family member a paragraph. A letter is more interesting if you discuss ideas as well as activities: your concerns about the environment, a good book you recommend, a lecture you attended, the state of television today, your political views. You can also include anecdotes, quotations, photocopied clippings of interest, or snapshots. Be specific. Instead of saying something was "wonderful" or "beautiful," give details. In the handwritten part of your letter (which is a "must," even if it's only a line or two), address the interests of that particular person, commenting on their last letter, asking about their life. If you receive a number of photocopied letters in your year's-end mail, you are probably safe sending one yourself. If none of your correspondents use this form, it's possible that you are marching to a different drummer—which may also be why they like you.

Format

⌁ The tremendously popular greeting card is always acceptable, but add a handwritten message to it. If your name is printed or engraved on the card, add a personal note. Don't use social titles when having your name printed. For example, "Eddie Swanson," "Goldie Rindskopf," "Bill and Sarah Ridden" (not "Mr. and Mrs. William Ridden") or simply "Bill and Sarah." Children's first names are usually listed on the second line. In the case of a single parent with a different name ("Grace Larkins"), the children's last name is given ("Annie, Miriam, and Minnie Wells").

⌁ Business letters conveying seasonal greetings are generally typed, although some companies send greeting cards, postcards, or specially printed letters with colorful graphics. A letter can be made more personal than a greeting card and can carry more information. Investigate the cost differences between greeting cards and letters. The latter are generally less expensive even if you use special effects, decorations, and a colored envelope. Keep an idea file of some of the clever seasonal creations other businesses have used over the years. Eye-catching letters are not, of course, appropriate for all purposes; banks, legal firms, insurance companies, and others are not helped by overly "creative" letters.

~ E-mail has a limited use in letting people know we wish them well on a holiday. Use it for people with whom you correspond almost entirely by e-mail.

WORDS

blessings	health	prosperity	serenity
celebration	joy	rejoice	success
gratitude	peace	remembrances	wishes
happiness	pleasure	season	

PHRASES

all the best of the season	magic of the holiday season
at this time of year	much to look forward to
compliments of the season	season's blessings/greetings
during this season and always	sincere wishes for
great/happy/festive time of year	this festive season
happy memories	warmest regards/wishes to you
have appreciated your patronage over the past year	wishes for a joyous season
	wishing you love
holiday greetings	with warm personal regards
in commemoration/celebration of	wonderful holiday season

SENTENCES

As we at the Bennett Company look back over 2001, we remember with appreciation our friendly, faithful customers.

Best wishes for a bright and beautiful season/for a New Year of happiness.

Everyone here at Taunton-Dawbeney sends you best wishes for happiness, health, and prosperity throughout the coming New Year.

"Here's to your good health, and your family's good health, and may you all live long and prosper." (Washington Irving)

Holiday greetings and best wishes for the New Year.

I hope that 2002 was a good year for you and that 2003 will be even better.

I hope the New Year brings you health, happiness, and small daily joys!

May the beauty and joys of this season stay with you throughout the year.

May you be inscribed and sealed for a happy, healthy, and prosperous year.

May your shadow never be less!

On Rosh Hashanah it is written . . . On Yom Kipper it is sealed.

Our best wishes to you for a Merry Christmas and a prosperous New Year.

Skip this part if you are allergic to form letters, if you don't care what we've been doing, or if you can't remember who we are.

The best part of this beautiful season is keeping in touch with special friends like you.

This is just a note to say we're thinking of you at Thanksgiving/Hanukkah/Christmas/Passover/Easter.

This time of year inspires us to count our blessings—and good customers like you are chief among them!

Though we can't be with you at the Thanksgiving table, our hearts are there.

Warm wishes to you and your dear ones this holiday season.

We're remembering you at Passover and wishing you happiness always!

We send our warmest wishes for health and happiness—and to borrow my Irish grandfather's blessing: "I hope we're all here this day twelve-month."

We wish for you the gifts of love, friendship, and good health.

We wish you all the best in the coming year.

PARAGRAPHS

They don't call them Easter "bonnets" anymore, but the idea is the same! Come in and see our chic selection of spring hats: delicate straws from Italy, smart little toques from France, wacky and colorful sun-skimmers from Haiti, elegant felts from England, and much more! Buy a hat before Easter and receive a free stuffed bunny (wearing the latest in bunny bonnets) for the special child in your life.

Eileen spent a month in Germany this summer, surviving a no-show on her luggage, a tick bite that required serum treatment, and a bomb threat on her return flight. As for me, I've been working with a local group to promote a recycling program here—we can talk trash, even in front of the children. Now you're thinking, "Great! I didn't have to hear about their latest remodeling project." Sorry. This year we turned the pantry into a bathroom, and . . .

To start the New Year off right and to show our appreciation for your patronage last year, I'm enclosing a certificate good for one free meal with the purchase of another of equal or greater price.

Mother's Day is coming soon, and Rowley Floral Shops (with twenty-three metro-area locations) are offering a Mother's Day special you'll want to consider. Choose from one of six stunning floral arrangements (and six surprisingly low prices) to tell that very important person in your life how much she means to you. Included in your one low price is delivery anywhere in the metro area and a special Mother's Day card with Anne Taylor's charming verse:

Who ran to help me when I fell
And would some pretty story tell,
Or kiss the place to make it well?
My Mother.

Come in today and see which of the six arrangements will bring a smile to YOUR Mother's face!

This Thanksgiving, as you reflect on your blessings, take a minute to consider those who have been overwhelmed by adversity. Help us provide traditional home-cooked Thanksgiving dinners with all the trimmings for the hungry and homeless during this Thanksgiving season. You can feed ten hungry people for $13.90, twenty for $27.80, or one hundred for $139. Won't you help?

SAMPLE LETTERS

TO: All Norton employees
FROM: Marda Norton, President
RE: Martin Luther King, Jr. Day

Beginning this year, Martin Luther King, Jr. Day will be a paid holiday for all employees. This day has particular significance for us as I believe Norton represents in many ways the lived-out reality of the dream for which Martin Luther King, Jr. lived and died.

We urge employees to devote at least a part of the day to some community service. Bob Gates in Personnel has a list of suggestions if you are interested.

Also, for this, our first holiday, you are invited to a potluck dinner in the upper cafeteria at 6:00 p.m. on January 16. Please call Bob Gates, ext. 42, with your reservation, and bring a covered dish. Depending on the interest shown in this year's potluck, we may continue the tradition.

Dear Homeowner,

It's not too late! If you haven't put in your shrubs and trees and perennials yet, Verrinder Garden Center's big Memorial Day sale will make you GLAD you didn't get around to it!

Enclosed is a checklist of our complete tree, shrub, perennial, and annual stock (helpfully marked to show sun/shade requirements) so that you can walk around your yard and note what you need. Bring the list with you and you won't forget a thing! Not only that, but when you check out, show your checklist and you will receive a 10% discount on your entire order!

Have a safe and happy Memorial Day weekend!

~

Dear Mr. and Mrs. Burdock,

Will you be entertaining family and friends over the Fourth of July weekend?

How about inviting just one more to the celebration? Galbraith Catering—a full-ser-vice, licensed, insured caterer—can provide you with box lunches, a full multi-course buf-fet, or anything in between. If you want to make the main course, we'll bring salads, breads, and desserts. Or vice versa!

Feel like a guest at your own party! We provide servers, clean-up crew, tables, chairs, linens, dishes, and expert advice and assistance.

We are glad to supply references, and as a concerned member of the community, we recycle all papers and plastics, and we donate extra food to the Vane County Food Shelf.

For special events, you may want to make an appointment to come taste some of our specialties and choose the ones you think your guests would like. For simpler events, you are only a phone call away from trouble-free hospitality!

Happy Fourth of July! And, remember, we can help with everything but the fire-works!

~

Dear Parent,

What perfect timing! Just as you're worrying about getting the children outfitted for the winter months, along comes Columbus Day! The children have a free day, and WE'RE having our lowest-prices-ever children's outerwear sale!

During our big Columbus Day sale (special hours 9 a.m. to 9 p.m.) we'll have free balloons and cookies for the children . . . and great prices and selections on over twenty name-brand children's coats and jackets.

Did we say it already? What perfect timing!

~

Dear Mrs. Gorsand,

If you're a kindergartener, Halloween can be scary. If you're a homeowner, it can also be scary—if you've gotten that far into fall without finishing your yard chores!

The MORGAN RENTAL BARN has everything you need to prepare for winter: leaf blowers, power rakes, lawn vacs, aerators, trimmers, chippers, shredders, drop spreaders, tillers—even lawnmowers if yours didn't make it through the season and you don't want to give a new one house room over the winter!

(And if you do finish your chores in time and want to celebrate Halloween with the kids, check out our rental party supplies!)

∽

December 2002

Greetings Dear Family and Friends,

Seasonal salutations to you! We hope this finds you in good health and spirits.

The year 2002 has been especially noteworthy for our family. We saw Kalli play the clarinet at Carnegie Hall, Lauren's soccer team win the World Cup, Leah awarded the Nobel Prize for Literature, and Paul discover the cure for cavities. Not bad for a year's efforts.

Wait a minute! Wait a minute! Just testing to see if you were really reading this. Actually, it has been a fine year, mostly filled with all of the usual family business—school, soccer, piano lessons, soccer, gymnastics, soccer, clarinet, soccer, and softball. Favorite activities included skiing, hiking, swimming, camping, golfing, eating in, and eating out.

As the wonderful holidays approach, we want to take this opportunity to send you our best wishes. Even though in miles you may be far away, in spirit you're close to our hearts.

All the best to you and yours in 2003!

Lots of love,
Paul, Terry
Kalli, Lauren, and Leah

∽

See also: CONGRATULATIONS, FAMILY, FUNDRAISING, GOODWILL, SALES.

Letters of Instruction

29

Most of us would rather risk catastrophe than read the directions.

—MIGNON McLAUGHLIN

Individual letters of instruction have been replaced by form letters, package inserts, owners' manuals, product brochures, drugstore medication printouts, and other computer-generated or preprinted materials.

Such instructions include equipment or appliance operating instructions, safety instructions, assembly instructions, and installation instructions as well as instructions on how to dispute a credit card charge, apply for admission, sign an enclosed contract or lease, return merchandise, obtain a refund or exchange, or order replacement parts. Because commercial instructions deal with matters involving possible injury, loss of money, damage, and of course customer goodwill and repeat sales, they must be precisely crafted. "Read the manufacturer's directions with care. . . . This is one of the hardest kinds of prose in the world to write. It must be factual, accurate, and crystal clear." (Virginia Graham)

Businesses occasionally write letters of instructions, generally in response to a customer query. Letters of instruction are also written inside a company, most often as a memo.

Written instructions are given to the couple staying with your children while you are out of town, the patient following a specific care regimen, the neighbor child who waters your garden, the day-care provider, the carpenters working on your house.

Write Letters of Instructions for

- agreements/contracts/leases
- babysitters/day-care providers

243

- changes to your will and other legal issues
- forms/applications/surveys
- house/plant/garden/pet care
- new policies/procedures/regulations
- operating instructions: appliances/tools/equipment
- payments
- product registrations/use/care
- return, repair, or replacement of merchandise
- samples
- shipping instructions

- Thank the person (if you are responding to a letter, phone call, or in-person query) or state the purpose of your letter ("To help you get the most out of your new software, we offer the following suggestions for use"; "These instructions will help you care for your instrument so that it will give optimum performance pleasure").
- Number or otherwise set off each step in the instructions.
- If appropriate, give a phone number, contact person and address, or other resource where further help can be obtained.
- End with a pleasant statement of appreciation or with a mention of future business or enjoyment of the new product.

- "Don't give instructions in the negative" is a negative statement. "Word your instructions positively" is a positive one. Use the positive form. When you see "don't," "never," and "should not" in your instructions, rephrase the sentence to read positively.
- Don't use words like "simple" and "obvious." Invariably, these words preface something that is neither simple nor obvious to readers, and they feel rebuked for not understanding something that apparently everyone else does.
- Don't use a condescending tone. For example, sometimes a "broken" appliance is simply not plugged in. The first in a list of trou-

bleshooting instructions generally advises seeing that the appliance is plugged in. State this neutrally so that the customer doesn't feel too stupid if that's the problem.

Tips on Writing

～ Be brief. After writing the instructions, pare them down to the essentials. "Explanations grow under our hands, in spite of our effort at compression." (John Henry Cardinal Newman)

～ Be specific. If you say "soak contacts overnight," give the desired number of hours in parentheses. "Overnight" means different things to different people. When advising that an appliance be cleaned regularly, describe products and procedures that work best and tell what "regularly" means. Explain or graphically identify parts, in case readers are not familiar with industry terminology.

～ Be intelligible. When preparing a form letter that will be used thousands of times, ask people outside your department to read it for clarity. Some of the worst instructions have been written by experts; because they know their field so well they cannot understand the mind of the uninitiated well enough to adequately explain anything. In her 1923 book, Mary Owens Crowther counsels, "It is well to remember that motion pictures do not accompany letters and hence to take for granted that if a way exists for getting what you mean wrong that way will be found."

～ Be diplomatic. Some requests for instructions may appear inane to you and the answers so obvious you hardly know how to phrase your response. But people's brains work in wonderfully odd and divergent ways, and the person may actually be looking at the situation in a way very different from the way you see it. Then, too, even if it is a "stupid" question, good public relations demands that you treat it as politely and helpfully as any other question.

～ When possible, explain *why* as well as *how*. For example, "Do not use this compound when there is danger of rain followed by temperatures below 32 degrees." Many people will accept this instruction without question. But others will wonder what rain and cold have to do with anything, and still others will ignore it, thinking it unimportant. If you add, "because the compound will absorb the moisture, freeze, expand, and probably crack," users are far more likely to follow the instruction—and you will receive fewer complaints. "I can never remember things I didn't understand in the first place." (Amy Tan)

Special Situations

~ Cover letters often contain instructions. When sending someone a sample, a contract, or a product, for example, explain how to interpret or use the item.

~ Any document that must be signed (contract, lease, stock transfer) is accompanied by a letter explaining where signatures or initials are needed, if the signatures need a medallion or notarization, which copy to retain for the person's files, where to send the other copies.

~ Assembly, installation, operating, and safety instructions are generally included in an owner's manual. However, you might accompany the manual with a cover letter emphasizing special cautions ("Please particularly note the section on fire hazards").

Format

~ Instructions to customers are typed on letterhead stationery.

~ Memos are used for in-house instructions and are typed except for the briefest and most casual instructions.

~ Form letters are used for routine letters of instructions.

WORDS

advice	explanation	method	simplify
carefully	guidelines	operation	steps
caution	how-to	policy	system
demonstrate	illustrate	precaution	warning
description	indicate	procedure	warranty
details	information	regulations	

PHRASES

alert you to	much more effective to
always check to see	note that
as the illustration shows	once you are familiar with
before you use your appliance	point out
commonly used to	recommend/suggest that you
important safety instructions	standard operating procedure
it requires that you	you will find that

SENTENCES

Caution: please read the rules for safe operation before plugging in your Villamarti "Thinking Bull" table lamp.

Follow the illustrated instructions to trim hair at home quickly and professionally with your Clavering Clippers.

I am not sure which model of the Thursley Electric Toothbrush you have, so I'm enclosing instructions for all of them.

If you have more questions, call our hotline at 800/555-5379.

If you plan to deliver your baby at Malmayne's Old St. Paul's Hospital, please note the following instructions for preadmittance.

Please note the following guidelines.

We are happy to be able to clarify this matter for you.

You don't need special tools to install this fixture, but follow the steps in the order given.

Your Aldridge electric knife will provide you with a lifetime of use if you follow these care instructions.

PARAGRAPHS

Enclosed is the final version of the contract, which constitutes the complete and entire agreement between us. Please read it carefully and consult with your attorney before signing all three copies on the bottom of page 5. Please also initial clauses C1 and D3 to indicate your awareness of the changes we have agreed upon. Return all three copies to me along with a check covering the agreed-upon amount. One copy of the contract will be countersigned and returned to you.

Thanks for taking care of the hamsters while we're away. If you can stop by once a day, that'd be great. Give everybody one-quarter cup of hamster food. Fill their water bottles. Give Furball an apple slice and Marigold a banana slice from the fruit in the plastic box (they don't care if it's old and brown). The others don't need any special treats. We'll be back before the cages need cleaning, so don't worry about that.

To obtain a credit card for another member of your immediate family, please complete the enclosed form, making sure that both your signature and the new cardholder's signature appear on the indicated lines.

Thank you for agreeing to complete the enclosed survey. It will take only a few minutes. Use a # 2 pencil and carefully fill in the circles corresponding to your answer. Do not write in the white box in the upper right-hand corner. Fold the form along the dotted lines and seal by moistening the flap. Do not use staples or transparent tape. Your name and address are optional. Thank you!

Please give Caddy a bottle around 8:30 (or earlier if she seems hungry). If she falls asleep with the bottle in her mouth, take it out. Leave her bedroom door open so you can hear her if she wakes up.

SAMPLE LETTERS

Dear Mrs. Dollery:

We were sorry to hear that your AutoAnswer communication system is unsatisfactory. All our equipment is carefully checked before leaving our Chicago factory. However, in rare cases, an intermittent problem may have been overlooked or something may have happened to the equipment during shipping.

Please return your system to us, following these steps:

1. Use the original carton and packing materials to ship the system back to us.

2. Address the box to: Customer Service, P.O. Box 1887, Woodlanders, IL 60031. (The California address is only for placing orders.)

3. Enclose a letter describing the problem (a copy of the letter you originally sent us would be fine) and mention whether the trouble occurred immediately or after use. The more information you can give us, the more quickly we can locate the problem.

4. Fasten the enclosed RUSH label to the top right-hand corner of your letter. This will ensure that you receive a fully functioning machine (your present system or a new one) within ten working days.

Thousands of satisfied customers are experiencing the delight and time-saving features of the AutoAnswer communications system every day; I want you to be one of them very soon.

⁓

TO: Estabrook County Residents
FROM: Estabrook County Board of Commissioners
DATE: October 2
RE: Yard Waste

The amount of garbage each of us produces is enormous, and so are the problems and costs of disposing of it. During the summer months grass clippings make up 24% of residential garbage.

Legislation passed earlier this year requires us to separate grass clippings and leaves—yard waste—from regular trash after January 1.

How do we do this?

1. Leave grass clippings on the lawn. This is the most cost-effective and environmentally sound way to deal with grass clippings. They decompose, returning nutrients to the soil, and never enter the waste stream.

2. Bag grass clippings and take them to one of the six County compost sites (list of compost sites is enclosed). Empty your bags of grass clippings and fill them with free compost for your garden.

3. Use grass clippings as mulch around trees and shrubs (if your grass has not been chemically treated).

4. Bag grass clippings and pay a trash hauler to collect them separately.

For additional information call 555-2117, Estabrook County's Compost Center.

P.S. We've had a number of calls asking if grass clippings will ruin the lawn if left on it. You can leave grass clippings on the lawn and still keep it healthy by (1) not letting the grass get too long before mowing (clippings should be no more than one inch long in order to filter down into the soil); (2) using a sharp mower blade (the sharper the blade the finer the clippings and the faster they decompose); (3) avoiding overfertilization (dense grass doesn't allow clippings to reach the soil to decompose); (4) removing excessive thatch (1/2 inch is ideal); (5) mowing the lawn when it's dry.

Dear William D. Carmichael,

Beginning January 1, we will be adopting an exciting new program of flexible benefits. To become part of this program, we ask that you:

1. Read the enclosed brochure, which explains the program.

2. Sign up for the informational meeting that is most convenient for you (list enclosed).

3. Schedule an appointment with one of the Human Resources staff to discuss the program and to ask any questions you might have. At that time you will be given a confidential record of your personal benefit program and an enrollment form to fill out specifying the way you want to "spend" your benefits.

4. Return the form by October 1. This date is important. If you fail to send in your enrollment form by October 1, you will automatically be enrolled in the "no choice" plan (see brochure for description).

If you have questions about this process, call Human Resources at ext. 43.

Dear Customer:

Thank you for your inquiry about home maintenance of your recently purchased VCR. We do not recommend that owners repair their own VCRs. Although it may be more costly, a professional repair job is a better choice in the long run.

However, if you are willing to accept the risks, there are some maintenance and small repair jobs you can attempt at home. You can clean the record and playback heads with a commercially manufactured cleaning cassette (read instructions before using). Note, however, that most of these special cassettes, particularly the dry kind, work by abrasion and can wear down your video heads. After unplugging your VCR, clean the interior with a soft painter's brush and—for hard-to-reach places—a can of compressed air. You can also replace belts, rollers, switches, and springs, and can lubricate gears, shafts, and other moving parts every few years. Using a light machine oil, *oil* parts that spin. *Grease* parts that slide or mesh (but don't use too much grease).

For further information, consult the manual that came with your VCR, check with a local repair shop, or write us with your specific question.

⌒

See also: ADVICE, RESPONSES.

Letters of
Introduction

30

Why is it that the person who needs no introduction usually gets the longest one?

—MARCELENE COX

Letters of introduction are not as common as they were. The telephone has largely replaced them as a means of putting two people in touch with each other. Then, too, most people have enough social and business contacts to last several lifetimes. They are reluctant to suggest additional ones to friends unless they're sure the proposed introduction will be genuinely beneficial to both parties.

Although letters introducing people to each other are still seen, today's letter of introduction is more commonly used to introduce a new sales representative, new product, or new service to customers.

Letters of introduction are related to references and recommendations in that A is vouching for B to C. However, a letter of introduction is more like the superficial introduction that takes place at a large party, whereas the recommendation is more like a serious talk about someone your friend wants to employ.

Write Letters of Introduction for

- business associates/employees
- friends moving/traveling to a city where you know people
- introducing business/product/services to newcomers in the area (see WELCOME)
- job seekers (see also REFERENCES)
- membership in clubs/groups/organizations
- new address/office/division/outlet/company (see also ANNOUNCE-MENTS, WELCOME)

- new billing procedure/statement/payment schedule
- new employees/associates/partners/programs/policies/prices (see also ANNOUNCEMENTS)
- new products/services (see also SALES)
- requesting an introduction to someone from a third party
- researcher working in the other person's field

- Begin by stating your reason for writing: to introduce yourself, to introduce someone to your reader, to suggest that your reader meet with someone visiting or new in their area.
- Give the person's full name, title, position, or some other "tag" to situate them for your reader.
- Tell something about the person being introduced—whether it is yourself or a third party—that will make your correspondent want to meet them ("she has collected paperweights for years, and I know this is a great interest of yours"). Mention people they both know, work or school connections, interests they have in common.
- Tell how you and the other person are related or acquainted.
- Explain why contact with this person is desirable.
- Suggest how the meeting can take place: the reader contacts the other person (include address and phone number); the other person calls your reader; you are inviting them both to lunch.
- Close with an expression of respect or friendship, and your thanks or appreciation ("I will be grateful for any courtesies you can extend to Chadwick").

- Don't organize introductions lightly. They set in motion responsibilities, demands on time and energy, and consequences involving several people. Reserve introductions for special cases.
- Don't insist that two people meet or predict that they will like each other. No one can tell who will take to whom. By emphasizing what they have in common, your reader can decide how much interest there might be in meeting the other person.

- Don't make the person feel obligated to accommodate you. Unwilling hospitality or grudging meetings do not have good outcomes. Allow the person room to maneuver and provide a way to save face if they must refuse you ("I realize you may not be free just now").

Tips on Writing

↦ There are two ways of providing a letter of introduction. One is to give the letter to the person you're introducing; the person then calls upon the third party and presents the letter. The envelope is left unsealed, which means your letter will be tactful. The second way is to write directly to the third party, asking if they would be able to meet with, entertain, or help the person you're introducing.

↦ Be specific about what you would like the other person to do: invite your friend to dinner; make introductions in the neighborhood; explain work opportunities in the area.

Special Situations

↦ It used to be that the letter of introduction had to be offered, unlike a letter of reference or recommendation, which is requested. In their 1942 book, *How to Write Letters for All Occasions*, Alexander L. Sheff and Edna Ingalls write sternly, "The note of introduction is often requested for a friend, never for one's self." This still applies to social introductions, but networking has changed the rules in the business world. You may tell someone you plan to be in a certain area or that you're job-hunting and wait for the other person to suggest introducing you to friends or colleagues. But you may also actively seek introductions.

↦ When you want A to offer hospitality to B, write A directly and ask that they respond to you. This spares B the embarrassment of presenting a personal letter of introduction only to be rebuffed because of lack of time or interest. It also spares A the awkwardness of being caught off guard and pressured into doing something they don't really want to do.

↦ Write a letter of thanks or appreciation to anyone who has written a letter of introduction on your behalf. You also write to thank the person to whom you were introduced for any courtesies extended to you.

↦ Introduce new employees, business associates, or personnel to those with whom they'll be working with a paragraph or two: their names, new positions, starting dates, responsibilities and work relationships, highlights of their professional backgrounds, and a request for others to welcome them.

～ Introducing a new sales representative to customers before the first visit smoothes the representative's way. It also serves as a goodwill gesture, letting customers know that headquarters takes a personal interest in them. Express your confidence in the person's abilities.

～ When introducing a change in billing procedures (new due date, automatic deposit, windowed reply envelopes, new statement format), explain why you instituted the change and, if possible, enclose a sample procedure. Focus on the value of the change to the customer, not its value to you. When you express appreciation for the customer's business and say that the change will improve service, your letter of introduction becomes a goodwill letter or even a sales letter.

～ Letters introducing new products and services have strong sales messages. Only a phrase like "we are pleased to introduce" qualifies it as a letter of introduction (see SALES).

Format

～ Business introductions (requests for them, the letters themselves, and thank yous) are typed on business or personal-business letterhead. A personal touch is commonly added by a handwritten note on your business card to be included with the letter or given to the person requesting the introduction.

～ Handwriting social introductions used to be required, but it is not necessary today.

～ Form letters are useful when the same message of introduction must be conveyed to a number of people and the message is not particularly personal. For example, introducing a new slate of officers to a far-flung membership, or introducing a new product line or new payment schedules to thousands of customers.

～ E-mail is used for very informal introductions.

WORDS

acquaint	contact	meet	receive
announce	co-worker	notify	sponsor
associate	greet	pleasure	suggest
colleague	hospitality	present	visit
connections	introduce	propose	welcome

PHRASES

acquaint you with	please don't feel obliged to
bring together two such	present to you
bring to your attention/notice	shares your interest in
get together with	similar background
I'd like to introduce to you	the bearer of this letter
if you have time	this letter/note will introduce
I'm happy to introduce you to	we'd like to tell you about
I think you'll like	we're pleased to introduce
known to me for many years	you've heard me mention/talk about
longtime friend	

SENTENCES

Dr. Roselli plans to be in Rome for the next two years, so if you feel able to offer him any hospitality during that time, I would be most grateful—and I think you'd enjoy meeting him.

I'd appreciate any consideration you can extend to Mr. Chevenix.

I feel sure you would not regret meeting the Oakroyds.

I'll appreciate any hospitality you can offer Harriet.

I think you and Nathan would find you have a great deal in common.

I've always wanted to bring you two together, but of course it will depend on whether you are free just now.

I've asked Adela to give you a call.

Thank you for whatever you may be able to do for Ms. Ingoldsby.

There is little that Ms. Trindle does not know about the field; I suspect that you would enjoying talking to her.

This letter will introduce Nicholas Broune, president of our local professional editors network, who will be spending several weeks in New Orleans.

This will introduce a whole new concept in parent-teacher conferences.

We are pleased to introduce the Reverend Duncan McMillan, who will be serving as weekend presider as of June 1.

PARAGRAPHS

Hello! May I introduce myself? I'm Flora Mackenzie, and I'm running for city council from Ward 4. I'd like to give you a few reasons to vote for me on November 7.

Sarah Purfoy of Clark Machinery will be in San Francisco February 3, and I've given her my card to present to you. I wasn't sure if you knew that Clark is working on something that may solve your assembly problem. If you haven't time to see her, Ms. Purfoy will understand.

Dear friends of ours, Ellen and Thomas Sutpen, are moving to Jefferson later this month, and I immediately thought of you. They've bought one hundred acres not far from you, and their two children, Henry and Judith, are almost the same ages as your two. I know you're busy just now, so I'm not asking you to entertain them or to do anything in particular—I just wanted you to know that the Sutpens are delightful people, and I think you'd enjoy them. Remember us to them if you do meet them.

I would like you to meet Rachel Cameron, as I think she would be a wonderful person to run the Good Samaritan program. I'm having a small cocktail party Friday night, and I thought I could introduce you to her then. Will you come?

A friend of mine whom I admire very much, Dodge Pleydon, will be visiting various galleries in Atlanta this next week, and I suggested he see you. I think you would be interested in his work. He is rather shy, so if you do not like what he is doing, he will take the hint quickly. He is not at all like the artist you described who camped outside your office for days at a time trying to get you to change your mind!

I've just learned that our favorite babysitter has moved next door to you. Not only is it a small world but are you lucky! Bob Vincy is dependable, resourceful, and full of fun. I wish I could introduce you to him personally, but I hope this note will inspire you to go over and sign him up immediately.

I would like to arrange a meeting with Rosamund Redding to discuss setting up small investors' groups in rural areas. I know the two of you are good friends, and I thought it might mean something to her if I were to mention that you and I have been in the same investors' group and on the New Beginnings Center board of directors for several years. May I use your name when I write her for an appointment?

I don't often do this, but I'm going to stick my neck out and say that I think you ought to see an engineer named Alec Harvey. The man can do anything, and I think he may be just the person to unsnarl your transportation department. I've asked him to give you a call, but do feel free to tell him you're busy if you don't want to see him. It was I who urged him to call because I'm convinced it might be worth your while.

SAMPLE LETTERS

Dear Ms. Cardross:

The account you have established with us has been reassigned within our Telemarketing Department. I would like to introduce myself as your new representative at Chambers Office Supply and take this opportunity to ask if we can be of any service to you at this time.

You are currently set up with account AB 40021, and you receive a 15% discount on list prices.

I notice that the printer ribbons that you normally buy are on sale this month (25% off).

If you have questions regarding your account, or need assistance in any way, please contact me.

Thank you for your continued business. I look forward to working with you in the near future.

Sincerely,

Dear Edwin,

I'm going to be in New York for three weeks in June, trying to find a publisher for my book. I know that you have extensive publishing contacts there, and I wonder if you might know anyone in particular I ought to see and, if so, if you would be so kind as to provide me with a letter of introduction.

I hope this is not an imposition, and I wouldn't want you to do anything you're not comfortable with, so I'll understand perfectly if you don't feel you have any information that would be useful to me.

In grateful appreciation,
Henry

Dear Henry,

Congratulations on finishing the book! I'm so pleased for you. And, as a matter of fact, I do know someone I think you ought to see while you're in New York. Maud Dolomore has her own literary agency and she deals almost exclusively with biographies.

I'm enclosing a brief letter that will introduce you to her. In this case I feel that I am doing both you and Maud a favor by putting you in contact with each other—I suspect your book is something she would be pleased to handle.

Let me know how things turn out.

> With best wishes,
> Edwin

~

Dear Henry,

I'm pleased to hear that you've finished the book! Unfortunately, I've looked through my files but don't see anyone who would be particularly useful to you or to whom I'd feel comfortable writing a letter of introduction.

Most of my contacts are now older and retired, spending their limited time and energy on their own projects. I hope you understand.

> Sincerely,
> Edwin

~

Dear Edwin,

I am grateful for the letter of introduction you wrote to Maud Dolomore on my behalf.

I had lunch with her, and she decided to represent my book. From finding an agent to finding a book contract is a long way, but I am pleased that the manuscript is in good hands.

The next time you are in town for a conference, would you let me know ahead of time so I can take you to lunch?

I will let you know immediately if Maud manages to find me a book contract. Thanks again.

> Yours truly,
> Henry

~

Dear Mr. De Fontelles,

Thank you for your letter of August 16 asking me to introduce your son to my grandfather. Although I am sympathetic to his project, I must say no to your request. My grandfather is in very poor health.

I wish you luck interviewing some of the other former members of the Resistance.

> Sincerely yours,

~

Dear Gordon and Madeline,

Some good friends of ours, Nina and Charles Marsden, will be in Seattle August 18 to September 1. I usually hesitate to put strangers in touch with each other because it doesn't seem to work out. But in this case, I have a feeling you would enjoy meeting them. They are both officers of the Midwest Appaloosa Conference and are interested in arranging reciprocal shows with groups from outside the Midwest.

I've mentioned that I'd be writing you, but added that you are busy and may not even be in town during the last part of August, so there is certainly no obligation to call them. If, however, you have time and think you'd like to meet them, they'll be staying at the Horseshoe Inn on Murray Road.

All our best,

Dear Homeowner,

Let me take this opportunity to introduce you to Irmiter Contractors and Builders. Founded in 1921 by my great-grandfather, our sixty-eight years of experience have firmly established us in the home renovation, restoration, and remodeling industry.

We base our professionalism on the principles of old world craftsmanship and customer service. We are members of, actively participate in, and meet the requirements of the National Association of the Remodeling Industry (NARI) and the National Kitchen and Bath Association (NKBA). Our six decades and four generations of experience in the building trades assure you, the homeowner, of the best return for your home improvement dollar. We are dedicated to creating the perfect living space for you and your family. Irmiter Contractors does this by combining state-of-the-art products and up-to-date management techniques with time-honored traditions of quality workmanship and attention to your needs. We recently received a Regional National Kitchen Design Award from NARI and offer complete design and drafting services for any type of project. In short, we are the problem solvers for the modern family living in an older home environment.

We invite you to compare, to talk to our customers, visit our jobs in progress! You'll see what we've done, what we're doing, and what we can do for you!

Please send the enclosed card or give us a call today, and let's get started on our most important project this year—YOUR HOME!

Sincerely,
Tom Irmiter
President

P.S. We will accept invitations to bid on blueprints.

See also: ANNOUNCEMENTS, APPLICATIONS, REFERENCES, REFUSALS, REQUESTS, THANK YOU, WELCOME.

Invitations

31

Invitation is the sincerest form of flattery.

— MARCELENE COX

All major and many minor life events are marked by occasions to which we invite family and friends. Being gregarious animals, we also celebrate non-events for the pure fun of it. Social gatherings offer friendship, entertainment, and relaxation. Invitations can range from the casual "Come visit!" scrawled on a postcard to engraved, highly codified invitations to dinner-dances.

In the world of business, banquets, lunches, cocktail parties, receptions, and open houses offer opportunities to conduct business, to improve employee morale, and to encourage or solidify relationships with clients, customers, suppliers, and others.

Write Invitations to

- exhibitions/fashion shows/new equipment or product shows/trade shows/book fairs
- fundraising events
- hospitality: lunches/dinners/teas/receptions/open houses/cocktail parties/buffets/brunches/parties
- meetings/workshops/conferences
- open a store account/credit card account or to accept trial membership/subscription/merchandise
- overnight/weekend hospitality
- recitals/performances
- religious ceremonies

- reunions—class, family
- sales (see SALES)
- school events
- showers: baby/engagement/wedding (see also WEDDINGS)
- speaking engagements: conference/banquet/workshop
- tours: factory/office/plant
- weddings (see WEDDINGS)

- State the occasion (open house, awards banquet, anniversary celebration, dinner-dance, retirement party)..
- Give the date and time: month, day, year, day of week, a.m. or p.m. (In formal invitations, the time is written out: "Seven o'clock in the evening"; "a.m." and "p.m." are never used.)
- Give the address. If necessary, include driving instructions or a map.
- Mention refreshments, if appropriate.
- Include the charge, if any (for fundraisers and certain other non-social events).
- Enclose an engraved or printed reply card and envelope for a formal invitation ("R.S.V.P." is noted on the invitation). Slightly less formal invitations may have in the lower left corner of the invitation "R.S.V.P.," "R.s.v.p.," "Please respond," or "Regrets only," followed by an address or phone number. Informal invitations may also request a response and furnish a phone number. If appropriate, give a date by which you need a response.
- Indicate the preferred dress (black tie, white tie, formal, informal, casual, costume) in the lower right corner, when appropriate.
- Let overnight guests know when you expect them to arrive and leave, what special clothes they may need (for tennis, swimming, hiking), whether they will be sharing a room with a child, will need a sleeping bag, and whether there will be other guests. Ask whether they can tolerate animals, cigarette smoke, or other potential nuisances.
- Additional information might include parking facilities, alternate arrangements in case of rain, and an offer of transportation.
- Express your anticipated pleasure in seeing the person.

What Not to Say

- Don't use "request the honour of your presence" except on wedding invitations.
- Don't use abbreviations in formal invitations except for "Mr.," "Mrs.," "Ms.," "Dr.," "Jr.," and sometimes military rank. Avoid initials in names. In formal invitations, write out "Second" and "Third" after a name, although you may use Roman numerals: Jason Prescott Allen III. There is no comma between the name and the numeral. There is, however, a comma between the name and "Jr." States should be spelled out (Alabama, not Ala. or AL) as is the time ("half past eight o'clock").

Tips on Writing

∼ Invitations are issued in the names of all those hosting the event. Women use whatever name they prefer (married name, business name, birth name) on invitations. The invitee responds using that name. When unsure how to address the woman, call her office or home and ask. For business invitations, hosts often use their titles and company names. Friends issue invitations together. Even groups ("The Castorley Foundation invites you . . ." or "The Central High School senior class invites you . . .") issue invitations.

∼ The phrase "request(s) the pleasure of your company" is suitable for any invitation but the most casual.

∼ When you need to know who is coming, include a reply card. Of the same paper, style, and format as your invitation, this card is enclosed with a small envelope (at least 3½" × 5" inches to meet postal requirements) printed or engraved with your address and with postage on it. The card says, "M _____ [Ms., Mrs., Miss, Mr. Name to be filled in] _____ regrets _____ accepts [one is checked] for Saturday, November 20." In some cases, "accepts" and "regrets" stand alone, and the guest crosses out the word that doesn't apply or circles the one that does. The "M" is a puzzle to some people and contemporary usage often omits it. Printers have samples and can advise you on the format that fits your situation.

∼ When inviting a single person or someone whose personal life is unfamiliar to you, indicate whether the invitation (1) is intended for that person only; (2) includes a friend; (3) can be taken either way as long as you are notified ahead of time.

~ When issuing an invitation to a family with young children, list each child by first name on the envelope on the line underneath the parents' names; never add "and family." Adults living in the family home should not be included in their parents' invitation but should receive their own. Children approximately thirteen and up also receive their own invitations.

~ In an invitation, it is wholly inappropriate to suggest the kind of gift one wants (mentioning where one is registered or specifying that money is the gift of choice, for example). Sometimes, however, people want to specify that gifts not be given (for example, the person celebrating an eightieth birthday who has no need of gifts and no room for them). Ann Landers approved two of the solutions suggested by readers of her column: "Your friendship is a cherished gift. We respectfully request no other." Or: "We request your help in compiling a book recalling memories from our parents' first fifty years of marriage. On the enclosed sheet, we ask that you write one memory or event that you have shared with them and return it to us by April 26. We believe that the loving memories they have shared with you, their friends, would be the most treasured gift they could receive; therefore, we request that no other gift be sent."

~ Some sit-down dinner invitations specify the time guests are to arrive and the time dinner will be served. These are usually sent by people whose previous dinner parties have been spoiled by late arrivals.

~ When dress is indicated, the following formulas are used. White tie is the most formal dress: men wear a white tie, wing collar, and tailcoat while women wear formal gowns. Black tie or formal means, for men, a tuxedo with soft shirt and a bow tie (a dark suit is not acceptable) and, for women, dressy dresses, cocktail-length dresses, or long evening wear. Semiformal means sports jackets or suits for men and dresses (but not long gowns) or dressier tops and pants for women; jeans and T-shirts are never appropriate as semiformal wear.

~ Mail invitations to an important event involving out-of-town guests as early as six months ahead. Guidelines for mailing invitations include: four to six weeks before a formal dinner, ball, dance, charity benefit, reception, or tea; two to four weeks before a reception or cocktail party; three weeks before a bar mitzvah or bat mitzvah; two weeks before a casual dinner or get-together.

Special Situations

~ When issuing invitations to a casual in-house business event, send a memo or e-mail that includes: type of occasion (retirement, going-away, service anniversary, guest speaker); time, date, place; if refreshments will be served; if a collection is being taken up; an extension number to call for confirmation or information.

~ Invitations to religious ceremonies include: date, time, place, type of ceremony, information about reception or gathering afterwards. Invitations to a bar mitzvah or bat mitzvah can be engraved, printed, or handwritten, and should include: the young person's full name; time, date, place; details about reception or celebration afterwards.

~ Invitations to a daughter's début are issued by the parents, whether married, widowed, divorced, or separated: "Sir Arthur and Lady Dorcas Clare request the pleasure of your company at a dinner dance in honor of their daughter Millicent on Saturday . . ." When simply receiving, the invitation can read: "Mrs. Sybil Fairford and Miss Elizabeth Fairford will be at home Sunday the second of June from five until half past seven o'clock, One Cooper Row."

~ Invitations to a fundraising event should be clear about what is expected of those who accept ("$100 donation suggested" or "Tax-deductible contribution of $500 per couple suggested"). Your wording may be limited by the allowable meanings of "tax deductible" and "donation." Enclose a postage-paid reply envelope to make it easy for people to respond; if you don't, tell where to send the check and how to obtain tickets. Some fundraisers fail because potential donors are busy people who can't take the time to read the small print or guess how they should handle the request; make it easy for them. Invitations to benefits, public charity balls, and other fundraisers need no response; purchase of tickets constitutes acceptance.

~ When inviting a guest speaker include: the name of the event and sponsoring organization; the date, time, and place; the type of audience (size, level of interest, previous exposure to subject); the kind of speech wanted; the length of time allotted and the approximate time the speech will begin; equipment available for use; accommodation and transportation information or directions to the meeting site; whether there will be a question and answer session; a description of the program; meals available; name of the contact person; details of the honorarium; an offer of further assistance; an expression of pleasure at having the person speak to your group. At this time you also request biographical information from the speaker to use in the program.

~ Sales letters are sometimes phrased as invitations to a special showing, sale, open house, or demonstration or to become a member, account holder, or subscriber.

~ Annual meetings are usually announced with the formal notice required by corporation by-laws, but invitations may also be sent, especially if there is a banquet or dinner following. No reply is necessary to attend the meeting, but a reply is usually requested for the dinner.

~ When your invitees fail to "R.S.V.P." and you need to know how many will be attending your event, the written word is no longer useful. You will have to telephone and ask. A recently married woman wrote "Dear Abby" (Abigail Van Buren) that of the one hundred printed wedding invitations she and her fiancé sent, only three self-addressed, stamped response cards were returned, yet most of their invitees showed up at the wedding. "Dear Abby" suggested the preventive measure of replacing "R.S.V.P." with plain English: "Please let us know if you are able to attend—and also if you are *not*." Except for formal or large events, you are probably better off inviting your guests by telephone (or at least inviting their answering machines) and then following up with an invitation in the form of a reminder.

~ To cancel or postpone an invitation, follow the original invitation in format, style, and quality of paper. If there's time, the announcement is printed or engraved as the invitation was. Otherwise, handwrite the note, using the same style as the invitation: "Mr. and Mrs. Hans Oosthuizen regret that it is necessary/that they are obliged to postpone/cancel/recall their invitation to dinner on . . ." or "We must unfortunately cancel the dinner party we had planned for . . ." Urgent situations, of course, require the telephone.

~ To cancel an invitation that you have already accepted, call your host at once and then follow up with a note apologizing for the change of plans. Stress your regret and offer a believable excuse. When you cancel at the last minute or when your cancellation is an inconvenience, you may want to send flowers with your note.

Format

~ Formal invitations are engraved or printed on fine-quality notepaper, use a line-by-line style, and are phrased in the third person ("Terence Mulvaney requests the pleasure of your company at a dinner-dance in honor of his daughter . . ."). Printers, stationery stores, and large department stores offer a number of styles, papers, inks, and designs. Invitations may also be handwritten, using the same format and phrasing. The expression "requests the pleasure of your company" is appropriate for all invitations except formal weddings. Each invited person is mentioned by name and honorific (Ms., Mrs., Miss, Dr., Mr.) either on the envelope or in the invitation itself. All words, state names, and numbers less than 100 are spelled out. Abbreviations are not used. Telephone numbers and zip codes are never given on formal invitations. The zip code is usually available in the return address or on the reply envelope. Business formal invitations (awards banquet, for example) are issued in standard formal invitation format.

∽ Informal social invitations use either commercial fill-in cards or are handwritten on informal stationery or foldovers in usual letter style (first person, run-in format). The invitation is usually written on the first page of a foldover or, if this page has your name on it, you can add the details of the invitation below your name.

∽ Informal business invitations may be sent on letterhead stationery; in-house invitations may be issued via memo, even sometimes by e-mail.

∽ Invitations that are actually sales letters use a form letter format.

∽ Commercial fill-in-the-blank invitations are available; there is nothing wrong with using these for casual gatherings. Some of them are even quite cheerful and clever.

∽ If you entertain regularly you may want to order engraved or printed invitations with blank spaces to be filled in as needed: "Mr. and Mrs. Desmond Mulligan request the pleasure of [name's] company at [event] on [date] at [time] o'clock, 1843 Thackeray Street."

WORDS

attend	début	occasion	salute
cancel	fête	pleasure	solemnize
celebration	honor	postpone	welcome
commemorate	installation	rejoice	

PHRASES

accept with pleasure	in commemoration/celebration of
be our guest	in honor of
bring a guest	invite you to
cordially invites you to	kindly respond on or before
have the honor of inviting	looking forward to seeing you

obliged to recall/cancel/postpone
owing to the illness/death of
request the pleasure of your
   company

we are celebrating
we would like to invite you to
you are cordially invited

SENTENCES

A revolutionary new service is now available to valued customers—and you're among the first invited to enroll.

Are you free after work on Friday to join a few of us for dinner?

Business attire is suggested.

Come hear noted Reformation scholar and professor of history Dr. Margaret Heath speak on September 12 at the 8:30 and 11:00 services at Gloria Dei Lutheran Church, 1924 Forster Avenue.

Horseback riding will be available; dress accordingly.

I'm pleased to invite you to acquire the Golden American Bank Card.

It will be so good to see you again.

I urge you to look over the enclosed materials and consider this special invitation now.

Mr. and Mrs. Alex Polk-Faraday regret that it is necessary to cancel their invitation to brunch on Sunday, the sixteenth of August, because of the illness of their daughter.

Please confirm by June 6 that you can attend.

Please join us for a farewell party in honor of Veronica Roderick, who is leaving Wain International to pursue other business interests.

We invite you to apply for an account with Oxenham Leather Warehouse, Inc.

You are invited to a special evening showing of our new line of furniture from European designers.

PARAGRAPHS

The Jervis family invites you to help Laura and Frank celebrate their Golden Wedding Anniversary. An Open House will be held at the Russell Eagles Hall, from 1:00 to 4:00 p.m. on Sunday, March 10, 2002.

You are invited to attend the Fall Family Festival this Tuesday evening from 6:00 to 9:00 p.m. at Temple Beth Shalom, 14 Burnsville Parkway. There will be puppet shows, activity booths, games, and refreshments!

Kindly respond on or before
September 18, 2003

M_____
accepts/declines
Number of persons _____

You are invited to hear the National Liturgical Choir under the direction of Maugrabin Hayraddin at 4:00 p.m. Sunday, September 28, at Quentin Methodist Church, 1823 Scott Avenue. The sixty-voice chorus will sing Russian liturgical music by Gretchaninof and Kalinikof and selections by Bach, Shaw, and Schutz. The cost is $5 ($3 for seniors and students).

You are invited to join the Henderson Video Club for one month—at absolutely no cost to you. Tell us which four selections you want, and they will be sent the same day we receive your order.

The tenth annual Public Works Open House will be held on Tuesday, October 3, from 4:00 to 7:00 p.m. at the Evans Street yards, a block south of Owen Avenue. The whole family will enjoy it. Get your picture taken on a Public Works "cherry picker." Car buffs can tour the biggest maintenance and repair shop in the city. There will be drawings for prizes, music, food, and entertainment. Some lucky winner will take home an actual traffic signal used for fifty years on the corner of Blodwen and Marquand Streets.

SAMPLE LETTERS

Lucas-Dockery Importers, Inc.
cordially invites you to a
cocktail hour and reception
in honor of their merger with
Sheridan International Associates
Friday, the tenth of November
from five to half past eight o'clock
Mansfield Gardens
One Mansfield Commons

Dear James Ayrton,

You are invited to become a member of the Brodie Community Anti-Crack Coalition. Formed eight months ago, this coalition of three community councils and six community organizations was formed to oppose the activity and effects of illegal drug use and trafficking in Easdaile and especially in the Brodie neighborhood.

The Brodie Community Council already has two delegates to the coalition, but we believe it would be helpful to have one more. Your name has been mentioned several times as someone with the necessary experience and enthusiasm.

I'll call later this week to discuss the possibility of your participation.

⁓

Agnes Leslie Graham and Robert Graham
request the pleasure of your company
at a dinner-dance
on Saturday, the twenty-first of May
at seven-thirty o'clock
Harcourt Inn

R.S.V.P.

⁓

Dear Dr. Denny:

It is with great pleasure that I invite you to the 43rd Annual Engineering Society Conference. This year's Conference will be held at The Citadel Hotel in downtown Dallas from September 23 through September 27.

We are offering a valuable program with industry-wide applications, speakers who are recognized experts in their field, and topics with many implications for the future (see enclosed brochure). Ample time is scheduled for discussion periods. In addition, tours to two outstanding instructional materials centers have been arranged.

We have obtained special meeting rates from the management of The Citadel. Information on accommodations, transportation, and registration is enclosed.

If you have questions, please call the session coordinator, A.J. Cronin, at 610/555-1889.

⁓

Houghton-Maguire Marine
cordially invites you to its
First Annual Marine Electronic Equipment Exhibit
1:30 p.m. to 6:30 p.m.
Saturday, May 2, 2003
Highway 32 and County Road C

Refreshments
Drawings

⁓

Dear Mrs. Lucas,

We are having a reception on Sunday, May 5, from 1:00 p.m. to 4:00 p.m. to celebrate our joy in the adoption of our new son, Philip. It would mean a great deal to us to have you join us.

Sincerely,

❧

Haidée Czelovar Power and Raoul Czelovar
cordially invite you to a reception
celebrating the
Golden Wedding Anniversary of
Simone Rakonitz Czelovar and Karl Czelovar
Sunday, the second of April
at eight o'clock
Wyatt's Village Inn
Indianapolis

R.s.v.p.   Formal Dress
555-1980

❧

Special Savings Invitation!

Dear Martin Lynch Gibbon:

As one of our Preferred Customers, you are invited to save 10% on every purchase you make at Murdoch Jewelers on July 14 and 15. This discount applies to both sale-priced and regular-priced merchandise, and includes our line of dazzling Iris diamonds, the ever-popular Headliner watches for men and women, and our complete selection of wedding gifts.

You deserve the best, and for two days this month, "the best" comes with a discount just for you!

Note: The discount does not include labor or service charges.

❧

Dear Major and Mrs. Caswell,

We are planning to celebrate Mother and Dad's fortieth wedding anniversary with dinner at The Azalea Gardens on September 16, at 7:00 p.m. We would love to have you celebrate with us.

Please let me know if you can join us.

Fondly,

❧

Invitations   **271**

The Board of Directors
of the Finsbury United Aid Society
requests the pleasure of your company
at a wine and cheese reception
on Saturday, the fourteenth of May
at half past seven o'clock
Finsbury Community Ballroom
for the benefit of
The Finsbury Children's Home

Suggested Contribution $50   Black Tie

See also: ACCEPTANCES, ACKNOWLEDGMENTS, ANNIVERSARIES,
ORGANIZATIONS, REFUSALS, RESPONSES, SALES, THANK YOU, WEDDINGS.

Love Letters

32

*If valentines are the equivalent of a gentle rain, love letters have
all the power and unpredictability of a tropical storm.*

—JENNIFER WILLIAMS

The love letter is one of the most difficult and frustrating letters to write
because we want it to be perfect. Stunning. Memorable. Touching. Thrilling.
Witty. Tender. Intelligent. And—did we say?—perfect.

Nothing is too good for the person we love. We pick up the pen, imag-
ining the letter that will say it all, the letter that will do everything but sing.
But are our expressive skills equal to the grandeur and fineness of our love?
We fear not.

There are two kinds of love letters. One is written to someone who
returns your love. This letter carries an automatic guarantee of success; your
reader thinks everything you do is wonderful. In this chapter you can pick up
a few more high cards to go with the ace you already hold.

The second kind of love letter is written to someone you're courting,
someone whose love you want to win. "Special Situations" offers assistance for
this type of letter.

Write Love Letters to

- a man
- a woman

- Open with something simple, preferably your main thought ("Dearest Leslie, I miss you" or "Dear Jack, This has been the longest week of my life!").
- Expand on your thoughts and feelings about the other person.
- Recall happy times you've spent together in the past and mention future plans that include both of you.
- Tell what you've been doing, thinking, feeling. The other person is hungry for news of you. Self-revelation is appealing and will usually elicit similar revelations from the other person. "I have never told you this before, but . . .."; "When I was little, I always dreamed that . . .."; "One thing I'm really looking forward to (besides seeing you again!) is . . .."; "My favorite way of spending a Sunday afternoon is . . .."
- Use the person's name not too often, but several times anyway. There's nothing quite as wonderful as reading our name in our lover's handwriting (or typing).
- Say the words: "I love you." No one can hear it often enough, and lovers—especially new ones—have fears and doubts that crave reassurance.

- Don't be brief. "Brevity may be the soul of wit, but not when someone's saying, 'I love you.'" (Judith Viorst) The other person wants you to never stop talking or writing or saying how wonderful they are. Don't stint yourself.
- Don't use language that isn't natural to you. While you may be tempted to dress your letter in flowery or high-flown words, they will not sound like you, and you, after all, are the person your reader loves.
- Don't write a letter that requires a note at the end: "Tear this up as soon as you've read it." Recipients seldom do this. If it's a simple matter of your embarrassment, it won't make much difference, but if the letter falls into the wrong hands (as in the case of a romance involving infidelity), you may regret putting anything on paper.
- Don't ask another person to read your letter before you send it to see if it is "okay." The only people who know if the letter is good are you and the one you love. In 1901, Myrtle Reed wrote, "A real love letter is absolutely ridiculous to everyone except the writer and the recipient." This is still true.

Tips on Writing

∿ Before writing the letter, jot down ideas that will lead to sentences or paragraphs in your letter: What is special or unexpected about being in love? What is it about the other person that is endearing? What touches you deeply? What do you miss? What would you do if she walked into the room right now? When do you think about her most often? What things remind you of him? What would you like to give him if you could give him anything? Why do you admire her? Be specific. Give examples of times you were filled with love.

∿ Write from the heart. The most important quality of a love letter is its sincerity.

∿ Keep the other person in mind as you write. Try to imagine what she is thinking, feeling, and doing at this moment and to picture her later as she reads your letter.

∿ Fatten the letter with newspaper clippings or cartoons, a dried leaf or flower, bookmark, photographs, a half-completed crossword puzzle for him to finish.

∿ Include a new "why I love you" reason in each letter.

∿ If you expect to write more than a few love letters, buy a book of quotations on love. They can inspire you while supplying quotations that express your feelings. Some are good for discussion: "Do you agree with Antoine de Saint-Exupéry that 'love does not consist in gazing at each other but in looking outward together in the same direction'?" Bess Streeter Aldrich once wrote, "Love is the light that you see by." Aldrich would probably not mind if you wrote, "You are the light that I see by," and then tell why that is.

∿ For inspiration, read the letters from the world's great lovers.

↬ For passion and fire, read Juliette Drouet writing to Victor Hugo (in Louis Gimbaud, ed., *The Love Letters of Juliette Drouet to Victor Hugo*, 1914):

> "A fire that no longer blazes is quickly smothered in ashes. Only a love that scorches and dazzles is worthy of the name. Mine is like that."

> "I see only you, think only of you, speak only to you, touch only you, breathe you, desire you, dream of you; in a word, I love you!"

> "I love you *because* I love you, because it would be impossible for me not to love you. I love you without question, without calculation, without reason good or bad, faithfully, with all my heart and soul, and every faculty."

"When I am dead, I am certain that the imprint of my love will be found on my heart. It is impossible to worship as I do without leaving some visible trace behind when life is over."

⟜ For a deeply sincere but lighter touch see Ogden Nash's letters to Frances Rider Leonard (in Linell Nash Smith, ed., *Loving Letters From Ogden Nash: A Family Album*, 1990):

"I couldn't go to bed without telling you how particularly marvelous you were today. You don't seem to have any idea of your own loveliness and sweetness; that can't go on, and I shall see that it doesn't."

"Both your letters arrived this morning. Thank you. I had sunk pretty low in the eyes of the elevator man, to whom I have been handing a letter to mail nearly every night and who has evidently noticed that I have been getting nothing in return. I could sense his thinking, 'You have no charm, sir.' But now it's all right again—his attitude today is as respectful and reverent as I could wish."

"I've been living all day on your letter. . . . Have I ever told you that I love you? Because I do. I even loved you yesterday when I didn't get any letter and thought you hated me for trying to rush things. It ought to worry me to think that no matter what you ever do to me that is dreadful I will still have to keep on loving you; but it doesn't, and I will."

"I've been reading your letter over all day, it's so dear . . . . Haven't you a photograph or even a snapshot of yourself? I want to look at and touch it, as I read and touch your letters; it helps bring you a little closer."

"Do you know what is the most delightful sound in the world? I'm sorry that you'll never be able to hear it. It's when I'm sitting in your library, and hear you cross the floor of your room and open the door; then your footsteps in the hall and on the stairs. In four days now—."

⟜ For insight on a long-lasting, ever-green love, read Winston and Clementine Churchill's letters to each other (in Mary Soames, *Clementine Churchill: The Biography of a Marriage*, 1979):

Winston to Clemmie: "I love you so much and thought so much about you last night and all your courage and sweetness." "You cannot write to me too often or too long—my dearest and sweetest. The beauty and strength of your character and the sagacity of your judgment are more realized by me every day." "The most precious thing I have in life is your love for me." "Do cable every few days, just to let me know all is well and that you are happy when you think of me." "This is just a line to tell you how I love you and how sorry I am you are not here." "Darling, you can write anything but war secrets and it reaches me in a few hours. So send me a letter from your dear hand." "Tender love my darling, I miss you very much. I am lonely amid this throng. Your ever-loving husband W." "My darling one, I think always of you. . . . With all my love and constant kisses, I remain ever your devoted husband W." "Another week of toil is over and I am off to Chartwell in an hour. How I wish I was going to find you there! I feel a sense of loneliness and miss you often and would like to feel you near. I love you very much, my dear sweet Clemmie."

Clementine to Winston: "I miss you terribly—I ache to see you." "I feel there is no room for anyone but you in my heart—you fill every corner." "My beloved Winston, This is a long separation. Think of your Pussy now and then with indulgence and love. Your own, Clemmie." "My darling. My thoughts are with you nearly all the time and though basking in lovely sunshine and blue seas I miss you and home terribly. Tender love, Clemmie." "I'm thinking so much of you and how you have enriched my life. I have loved you very much but I wish I had been a more amusing wife to you. How nice it would be if we were both young again."

Special Situations

～ When writing to someone who doesn't (yet!) love you as you love them, be brief rather than long. Retain some emotional distance. While you might tell an amusing anecdote about something that happened at work, you wouldn't tell a story from your childhood that has high meaning for you. Don't move too quickly. Instead of inviting the other person to go camping with you, ask if they've ever done much camping, what they thought of it. Instead of sprinkling your letter with "you" and "I" (and especially "you and I" as if you were already a couple) keep it neutral. Your goal is much like that of a letter of application: you don't aim to get the job, you want to get the interview. You present yourself as a warm, bright, funny, interesting person so that you can keep the person's interest long enough to present yourself as a candidate for their love.

Format

～ Anything goes. However you choose to write (type of paper, envelope, stamp, fountain pen, felt-tip, computer, e-mail, even fax) will be an expression of who you are. You can write longhand on lined paper, on scented stationery, or on the back of your video rental receipt. You can use the same pen, ink, and paper every time so that your letters have a recognizable look even from a distance. Or you can vary your letters, sometimes on one kind of paper, sometimes typed, sometimes filling in the spaces on a greeting card. Use colorful postage stamps and rubber-stamp art on your envelopes. Or use perfectly decorous, conservative # 10 envelopes and say wild things in the letter inside.

〜 Is it a love letter if you send it by e-mail? Sometimes. In general, however, even the most romantic e-mailed words don't have the impact they have in a letter. A letter has come straight from the loved one's hands. It is personal, physical, an artifact. Rereading a printed-out e-mail doesn't do quite the same thing for us. Use e-mail for short "thinking of you" messages.

WORDS

attractive	fascinating	inspiring	promise
bliss	fate	intensely	remember
boundless	feelings	lasting	soulmate
charming	fiercely	lonesome	sweetest
cherish	forever	lovable	tenderness
dearest	handsome	lucky	treasure
delight	happy	memories	unceasing
desire	heart	miracle	undying
dream	heaven	paradise	unforgettable
endless	immeasurable	passionately	unique
eternal	incomparable	pleasure	

PHRASES

from the first moment

hardly wait for the day when

how I long to

how much you mean to me

if I had only one wish

if only you knew

in my heart

I often think of

make life worth living

memories that keep me going

miss you so much

one of the happiest moments of
my life

only love of my life

on my mind

remember the time

re-read your letter

so happy to get your letter

wait for the mail every day

want to hold you

whenever I think of you

when we're apart

without you, I feel

you make me feel

SENTENCES

I couldn't sleep last night—and you know why.

I'd give anything to be able to touch you right now.

I had to tell you how much I enjoyed being with you yesterday.

I'll never forget the first time I saw you.

It's too lonely without you!

I've been carrying your last letter with me everywhere and it's getting limp—will you write me another one?

Just when I think I know everything about you, there's a new and wonderful surprise.

Two more days until I see you—I'm not sure I can wait.

We're some of the lucky ones—our love is forever.

You are my whole world.

You're the answer to my prayers and my dreams.

PARAGRAPHS

You are the first thing I think of in the morning. You are the last thing I think of at night. And guess who's on my mind every minute in between!

There is nothing I want more to do and feel less able to do than write you a beautiful love letter. And yet when I try to write, I'm wordless. I've been sitting here, pen in hand, for half an hour trying to express what you mean to me. Will you accept some borrowed words? Jeremy Taylor once said, "Love is friendship set on fire." I feel them both, the fire and the friendship. Bless you for bringing them into my life.

I feel more intensely alive, more intensely real, more intensely myself since I met you. As if a dimming filter had been removed, the world suddenly shouts with bright colors, sharply outlined shapes, evocative scents, intriguing textures, music, laughter, flashes of joy. You.

SAMPLE LETTERS

Dear Nance,

Because of you, I find myself filled with love for the whole world. Ruth Rendell wrote in one of her mysteries, "It is not so much true that all the world loves a lover as that a lover loves all the world."

Yes! I do! I now pat grubby children on their grubby little heads. I no longer kill mosquitoes. I straighten up crumpled weeds in the sidewalk cracks. I let dogs sniff my ankles (and, well, you know). I line up the bars of soap on the shelves at K-Mart. The world is mine, and I am its, and I love it. Maybe this is a way of saying that I love you a whole world's worth!

Kisses from me

～

Dearest Oliver,

There's only time for a quick postcard between flights, but I wanted to tell you how I treasure my last sight of you waving at the window. All I have to do is shut my eyes and I see you again.

Three more days and I won't need to shut my eyes! Until then, all my love!

～

Dear Sophy,

Scientists seem unable to measure love. I—you will not be surprised to discover this, knowing how talented I am!—have found a way to do it.

When you go to your seminar in Denver next week, I am going to keep Traddles for you. Now you know that I am not, and have never been, a dog person. If I were a dog person, my tastes would not run to Mexican hairless dogs with bat-like ears, rat-like tails, wrinkled snouts, and, in this case, a cast on its leg.

Not only will I keep Traddles (we haven't taken the full measure of this love yet!), but I will let her sleep in my bed, I will be faithful to her finicky feeding schedule, and I will even—once or twice a day—kiss her on the lips. Or near the lips anyway. I will pet her, I will let her watch football with me and follow me around. I will take her for her daily walks, even though everyone who sees us will look at her cast, then look at me and think, "Ah, a man who abuses dogs!"

And all this because I love you. So, what do you think? Have I found a way to measure love?

Tom

～

See also: APPRECIATION, FAMILY.

Memos

33

Talk of nothing but business, and dispatch that business quickly.

—ALDUS MANUTIUS

Memos may be an endangered species.

The memo (short for memorandum—plural is memos, memoranda, or memorandums) grew out of a need to streamline correspondence—to communicate swiftly, directly, and concisely—among employees of the same company. There was little point in using letterhead stationery, "Dear," "Sincerely," and other complimentary openings and closings with co-workers, managers, and executives with whom you communicated constantly and who were well aware of what company they worked for.

E-mail meets the same criteria and has the advantage of being faster and easier.

The memo is still useful: in a small office where not everyone has access to e-mail; when the information is too confidential for e-mail; when you attach it to a report with too many pages and graphics to be easily sent electronically; when you want a message routed and signed or initialed or commented upon; for routine out-of-house communications with customers or suppliers (orders, transmitting material, acknowledgments, confirmations, inquiries).

In *How to Survive From Nine to Five*, Jilly Cooper writes, "The memo's chief function, however, is as a track-coverer, so that you can turn on someone six months later and snarl: 'Well, you should have known about it, I sent you a memo.'"

Write Memos About

- announcements
- changes in policy/procedure

280

- in-house events
- instructions
- meetings
- reminders
- reports

- The memo heading has four items. The most common arrangement stacks all four lines flush left:

    TO: Blanche Challoner
    FROM: Francis Levison
    DATE: Nov. 20, 2003
    SUBJECT: employee stock purchase

  Or, capitalize only the initial letter:

    To: Blanche Challoner
    From: Francis Levison
    Date: Nov. 20, 2003
    Subject: employee stock purchase

  You may also line up the information like this:

    TO: Blanche Challoner
    FROM: Francis Levison
    DATE: Nov. 20, 2003
    RE: employee stock purchase

  Or, arrange them in two columns:

    TO: Blanche Challoner   DATE: Nov. 20, 2003
    FROM: Francis Levison   RE: employee stock purchase

- Select a phrase for the subject line that will immediately tell the reader the main point of your memo: "new flexible tubing"; "personal telephone calls"; "medical benefits enrollment"; "change in library hours."

- Begin the body of your message two to four lines below the subject line and flush left. All paragraphs in the body begin flush left and are separated by one line of space (text is otherwise single-spaced).

- Close with a request for the action you want, if appropriate, and a date by which it should be carried out: "Please call me before Tuesday"; "Please inform others in your department"; "Send me a copy of your report by Oct. 13."

- Sign your name at the bottom of the memo or put your signature or initials next to your name in the heading.
- Reference initials and enclosure notation (if any) are typed under the memo flush left.

- Don't include salutations or complimentary closings or any of the wind-up or wind-down sentences used in a standard business letter. You are courteous, but you get straight to the point.
- Don't use the memo for official communications (promotions and resignations, for example); type those on letterhead stationery.

Tips on Writing

~ State the purpose of your memo in the first sentence.

~ Be concise. Use short, simple sentences with present tense and active verbs. Although memos can technically be any length, the one- or two-page memo is the norm, except for report or issue memos. The shorter the memo, the more likely it is to be read immediately.

~ Informality is the hallmark of memos. They are shorter and less complicated than letters. They use plainer language. Jargon and acronyms familiar to those in the company may be used. "We" is used instead of "Lamprey-Wutherwood Telecommunications, Inc."

~ When sending a memo to more than one person: (1) list each name, if you have only a few, after the word "To:"; or (2) list the principal recipient after "To:" and the others at the bottom of the memo after "cc:"; or (3) list all the names in a distribution list on the last page of your memo. After "To:" type "See distribution list on page 2." Names appear without courtesy titles (Ms., Mr.) but occasionally with professional titles (Dr.). When managers are listed, their names are often given in order of corporate rank. In some companies, alphabetic order is used.

Special Situations

~ An issue memo is a fact-oriented report that summarizes important information so that policy decisions can be made. An efficient organization of material includes some or all of the following: (1) stating what the issue is, putting it in context, providing history or background information; (2) listing available or suggested options or solutions, along with their pros and cons; (3) detailing the costs, fiscal impact, and effects on other programs of each of the options; (4) if appropriate and welcome, naming steps necessary to implement the various options; (5) offering your recommendations; (6) suggesting the next step in the process (further study, meeting, vote, management decision).

⁓ Employees can be invited to in-house events by memo, which is more "inviting" than an e-mail message. (See INVITATIONS for guidelines.)

Format

⁓ Memos are not sent on company letterhead. Some organizations have memo stationery with the company name or simply "Memo" at the top or forms preprinted with the headings. The use of computers (with a macro for memo headings) and e-mail, however, mean that dedicated memo stationery is less common.

WORDS

announcement	information	policies	report
attachment	instructions	procedures	request
deadline	listing	progress	status
feedback	notice	proposed	summary
guidelines	outline	reminder	

PHRASES

appreciate your comments on	request a response by
background information	route this message to
clarify recent changes in procedure	see below for
effective immediately	summarize yesterday's discussion
pleased to report	would like to announce the following

SENTENCES

Attached is a "get well" card for Ethel Ormiston—sign it if you like and pass
it on to the next name on the list.

I've had phone calls from the following people about the new hook lifting
   devices—will you please return their calls and let me know what the
   problem is?

Please initial this memo to indicate that you've read it.

Please read the attached proposal before tomorrow's meeting.

Please sign up below for staff lounge cleanup duty and route this memo as
   indicated.

The attached outline covers projected work through the end of the year.

There's been some confusion about the new procedures for travel
   reimbursements—please note and file the following guidelines.

This memo will serve to authorize the preparation and filing of a patent
   application in the United States Patent and Trademark Office for a
   Three-dimensional Blueprint Acrylic Viewer.

We are pleased to announce that last week's sales figures as reported by the
   branch offices (see below) constitute a record for us.

We suggest you keep these fire drill instructions posted near your desk.

PARAGRAPHS

As of January 1, all customer 612 area code numbers given on the
attached sheet will be changed to 651. Please correct your files. Note that 612
area codes not on this list remain 612. Also attached is a list of the three-num-
ber prefixes that take 612 and those that take 651 so that you can verify the
correct area code for any new numbers.

Devizes, Inc. will be selling company cars that are more than two years
old. Employees will be given priority. Please see the attached list of vehicles
with descriptions and prices.

The Pudney Summer Soccer Camp has approached Potter Commercial
Development Corp. to ask if some of our employees would be interested in
volunteering at the Soccer Camp this summer. Attached is a brochure
describing the camp and an application form for volunteers. Thank you for
considering their request.

Those of you who work with Priss Hartshorn will want to know that her
husband of eighteen years died suddenly last night. No other details are
known at present. Funeral services will be held on Saturday; for time and
place, please check the newspaper. Those who want to send a note or sympathy card can write to her home address: 1963 Vassar Street, 50501.

SAMPLE LETTERS

TO: Dick Phenyl
FROM: A.W. Pinero
DATE: March 3, 2002
SUBJECT: Internet training session on March 10

So far the following people have signed up for the class. Will you please arrange with their supervisors for their absence that day? It also looks as though we're going to need a larger room and a few more computers. Can you arrange it? Thanks.

~

TO: See routing list
FROM: Beck Knibbs
DATE: June 10
SUBJECT. Department picnic at Talbothays Farm

Listed below is everything we need for the picnic. Please pencil in your name after the item you're willing to bring and keep this memo moving! The last person should return it to me. Thanks.

~

TO: See distribution list
FROM: Human Resources
DATE: August 28
SUBJECT: Design department/reduced schedule

Elfine Hawk-Monitor will be working a reduced schedule in the design department for the next three weeks. She will be here on Mondays and Tuesdays only as she is preparing for her gallery exhibit of sculptures made solely from scrap metal. (See the current newsletter for dates and the location of her show.) We all certainly wish her weld . . . I mean well. This schedule is effective as of August 25 and I'll keep you posted on any changes. We will welcome Ms. Hawk-Monitor back full-time in mid-September and hope she won't have gotten rusty in the interim.

~

See also: ACKNOWLEDGMENTS, ANNOUNCEMENTS, E-MAIL, INSTRUCTIONS, REPORTS, REQUESTS, RESPONSES.

Letters to
Neighbors

34

While the spirit of neighborliness was important on the frontier because neighbors were so few, it is even more important now because our neighbors are so many.

—LADY BIRD JOHNSON

The search for harmony among neighbors is as old as human society. And there's been no dearth of advice on how to achieve it. In a much-consulted etiquette book written in 1902, *The Correct Thing*, Florence Howe Hall writes, "It is not the correct thing to take offense if a neighbor states civilly that he would prefer your children should cease from breaking his windows." Of course! Why didn't we know that?

Most troublesome issues between neighbors can be handled with common sense and good will. In *Miss Manners' Guide for the Turn-of-the-Millennium*, Judith Martin says, "The challenge of manners is not so much to be nice to someone . . . as to be exposed to the bad manners of others without imitating them."

Write Your Neighbors to

- alert them to neighborhood problems
- announce personal or business news
- complain (see COMPLAINTS)
- congratulate them
- express appreciation
- introduce your local business to them
- invite them to a neighborhood gathering (see also INVITATIONS)
- offer help

- send birthday or anniversary wishes (see ANNIVERSARIES)
- thank them for assistance or cooperation

How to Say It

- Be certain that writing is the appropriate road to take. If you've already had several unproductive in-person or telephone discussions about the issue, it probably is. Dealing with a problem face to face keeps it smaller; once the discussion escalates to a letter, the situation becomes complicated.
- State your message ("thank you," "congratulations," "we invite you," "have you heard"). If you're asking something, be specific: stay off our new grass, trim trees that extend onto our property, contribute toward repairing a common fence.
- When appropriate, offer to reciprocate or in some indirect way express your desire to be a good neighbor.
- Close with a pleasantry, compliment, or forward-looking remark.

What Not to Say

- Don't accuse. This will put your neighbor on the defensive, a position that rarely apologizes or changes. Use an indirect construction. Instead of "You never put the lids on your garbage cans properly—no wonder it all ends up here!" say, "I'm finding garbage in the alley every Thursday morning." Instead of "Your wind chimes are driving us crazy," say "We are having trouble sleeping at night because of the wind chimes."
- Don't generalize ("you always park in front of our house" or "you never shovel your walk"). It undercuts your position and angers the other person who can think of lots of times they shoveled their walk.

Tips on Writing

~ If you are in the habit of sending your neighbors notes of thanks, appreciation, congratulations, or just saying "I'm thinking about you," you will have a good basis on which to build when problems crop up.

Special Situations

~ Apartment living is grand when the owner and neighbors are. For letters about problems, see COMPLAINTS.

~ Noisy, aggressive, or trespassing pets are a common sore spot. In all but the most egregious cases (obvious animal abuse, for example), you will not get much help from police or other authorities. Know from the outset that the solution to the problem most likely depends on how well you deal person-to-person with the pet's best friend. At the least, try honey before you go for the vinegar.

~ Unruly, unsupervised, or otherwise troublesome children are a neighborhood perennial. "Give the neighbors' kids an inch and they'll take the whole yard." (Helen Castle) A letter is written only after you have spoken kindly with the child and, if that is not successful, with a parent. Describe how the situation appears to you, using "I" statements (not "you" statements, as in "you let her run wild"). Offer to help resolve it or show yourself willing to compromise, if possible.

~ In a dispute, attempt to see the issue from your neighbor's point of view. The more clearly you see the other person's side, the more effectively you can frame the discussion so that your neighbor derives some benefit or saves face in some way, thus opening the way to a solution.

~ Build a sense of community with invitations to an annual block party, picnic, or ice cream social. Prevention of neighborhood problems is much more fun than most cures.

Format

~ Handwritten or typed notes can be hand-delivered or sent by mail or even by e-mail.

WORDS

admire	concerned	helpful	share
agreement	considerate	kindness	socialize
appreciate	cooperation	neighborly	solution
attention	coordinate	respect	troubling
careful	generous	responsibility	upkeep

PHRASES

affecting the neighborhood

ask your help/cooperation

block watch

combined action

community council

coordinate our efforts

did you know

get together to discuss

happy to help with

hope you are willing to

important to all of us

inform you that

not really my business but

on behalf of the neighbors opposite you

reluctant to write

wanted you to be aware that

what would you think of

would you consider

SENTENCES

As a result of the fire last week at Opal and Paul Madvig's, they need warm school clothes for the kids, blankets and bedding, and kitchen utensils—if you can help, call me, will you?

On behalf of my family and several of the neighbors, I'm writing to ask you to make other arrangements for Cleo when you are at work during the day—her constant barking is a serious problem for the neighborhood.

Thanks for your comments on our new sod last week—it's about time we did something about the yard!

Thanks so much for taking care of things while we were away   we look forward to doing the same for you.

This is a long overdue note of appreciation to you for arranging the alley-plowing each winter.

We have corn coming out of our ears (and, oddly enough, ears coming out of our corn)—if you can use some, please help yourselves.

We've been so delighted to have you for neighbors that it's difficult to write this letter.

Your daughter is the most dependable newspaper carrier we've ever had—I'm writing her a note, but I also wanted you to know what a delight we think she is.

PARAGRAPHS

This is to let you all know that Ajax is having a graduation party for about twenty of his friends Friday night. Bill and I will be home all evening, but if it gets too loud for you give us a call (I'm hoping you won't need to do that).

I've just heard that Rosa Klebb is in the hospital with a broken hip. Would the seven families on this block want to buy a plant for her—perhaps something she could later plant in her garden? I'll be glad to buy it and take it to the hospital. I'll stop by tomorrow to see what you think and to have you sign the card.

I'm ordering trees to replace the ones we lost in the storm. I've found a great nursery in Wisconsin with the healthiest trees and the lowest prices of any place I've checked. There's a discount for bulk orders so if any of you are also thinking of buying trees now, check out the attached list of trees and prices available. If some of you ordered the same time I do we'd all save on delivery charges plus we'd get a more favorable rate.

I'd like to ask Olivia and Kate to feed the rabbit and play with her a little while we're gone. Would this be okay with you? I'd leave a key with them and they could come and go when they liked. I feel sure they'd be good about locking up behind them.

I wonder if you're aware of zoning regulations prohibiting small businesses in this area. I'm guessing it wouldn't be a problem for the neighbors if your students didn't take up all the street parking three nights a week.

SAMPLE LETTERS

Hello Neighbor!

The Darnel-Greaves Community Council (District 14) is celebrating its 10th anniversary in the green space Saturday, July 15, from 1 p.m. to 4 p.m. We invite you not only to enjoy the refreshments and some good conversation with your neighbors but to consider joining us in making our neighborhood a better place to live. (The only "cost" of belonging is to attend monthly meetings when you can.)

In the last ten years the Darnel-Greaves Community Council has organized a recycling program, offered free radon checks of your home, bought bulk quantities of longlife light bulbs, lobbied for three new "Stop" signs, AND saved the green space from development!

See you Saturday!

Hi Imogen and Jack!

I offered to take care of Winifred Forsyte's sidewalks this winter (oh, the pride and energy of the owner of a new snowblower!) but I've got to be out of town next week. Would you mind clearing her sidewalks when you do your own? Knowing you, you will generously say yes, but if there's a problem, give me a call before Friday, will you? Thanks!

~

Dear Mr. Ancrum,

My name is Dora Lomax and I live around the corner from you at 1892 Ward Avenue. I noticed that you have a large pile of red bricks and a stack of old picket fence sections in your backyard. If you have no use for them and are planning to get rid of them, I'd love to take them off your hands and use them for my own backyard and garden.

I will tap on your door and introduce myself in the next day or two. Otherwise I would be happy to hear from you (555-6755). You may have your own plans for the bricks and picket fencing or they may already be spoken for. Perhaps you had planned to sell them? But if not and if I may have them, I would be grateful.

Thank you very much!

Sincerely,

~

See also: ANNIVERSARIES, APOLOGIES, CONGRATULATIONS, INVITATIONS, REQUESTS, SENSITIVE, THANK YOU.

Letters Dealing with Orders

35

If it is good and I want it, they don't make it anymore.

—ELIZABETH C. FINEGAN

Standardized order forms, purchase forms, and requisition forms, along with 24-hour toll-free order lines and the convenience of buying and selling on the Internet, have almost entirely done away with letters dealing with orders. However, as long as human beings are ordering and filling orders, there will be errors, exceptions, special requests, and problems to write about.

Write Letters About Orders When

- acknowledging/confirming receipt of order/telephone order/delivery date (see also ACKNOWLEDGMENTS)
- asking for additional information (see also REQUESTS)
- canceling/changing an order
- complaining about an order (see COMPLAINTS)
- explaining procedures/policy changes/overpayments
- inquiring about order/delivery date/how to return merchandise
- instructing how to order/return goods (see INSTRUCTIONS)
- making adjustments (see ADJUSTMENTS, APOLOGIES)
- payments are late (see COLLECTION, CREDIT)
- placing an order
- refusing/returning an unsatisfactory order

- When ordering without a form, give: description of the desired item, quantity, size, color, personalization/monogram, and price. Include your name, address, zip code, daytime phone number, e-mail address, and method of payment. If you pay by bank card, include number, expiration date, and signature. When buying from a company in your home state, add sales tax to the total. Include stated handling charges and specify shipping directions or any special considerations.

- Indicate the date by which items must be delivered. You can thus generally cancel the order without forfeit if you don't receive it in time; the letter serves as an informal contract.

- To respond to orders received, use an all-purpose form for problems. Begin with "Thank you for your order. We are unable to ship your merchandise at once because . . ." and list possible problems so that one or more can be circled, underlined, or checked off. For example: "Payment has not been received." "We no longer fill C.O.D. orders. Please send a check or money order." "We cannot ship to a post office box. Please supply a street address." "We are currently out of stock—may we ship later?" "We no longer carry that item. May we send a substitution of equal value and similar style?" "Please indicate size (quantity, style, color)." "We must receive shipping and handling charges before processing your order."

- Don't include other business (request for new catalog, complaint about a previous order, request for preferred-customer status) when ordering. It may delay your shipment.

Tips on Writing

∼ When ordering, arrange your request so that it can be deciphered at a glance. Instead of phrasing an order as a sentence ("I would like to order six pairs of size 11 men's white sports socks and four pairs of size 11 men's black dress socks, at $7.95 per pair . . ."), type the information in columns or units of information, each on a separate line. Use Arabic numerals ("12 Menaphon harmonicas") instead of writing them out; they are more quickly read.

∼ Don't forget the niceties. In the nuts-and-bolts world of ordering it's easy to forget that real live people are on the other end. Buyers close their letters with, "Thank you for your prompt attention." Suppliers always say, "Thank you for your order" and indicate their readiness to be of service to the customer and an appreciation of their business; helpful, courteous responses serve as goodwill letters.

Special Situations

∼ If your first order wasn't received and you order the same items again, emphasize that it's a duplicate order. The first order may turn up later and also be filled.

∼ When canceling a prepaid order or asking for a refund, include: order, invoice, or reference number; date of order; description of merchandise. Specify whether the amount of the merchandise should be credited to your account, credited to your charge card, or returned to you as a check.

∼ To return merchandise, include in your cover letter: your name and address; item description; copy of sales slip, invoice, or shipping label; why you're returning it; request for a refund, credit to your account, or replacement merchandise; an expression of appreciation. If returning the merchandise is difficult because of its large size or fragility, write first and ask how it should be returned. Request (although you may not get) reimbursement for your shipping costs.

Format

∼ Orders were made for forms, and vice versa. Simplify dealing with orders by creating standardized forms for the original order, problem orders, refunds, returned merchandise, and any other routine correspondence. Include such items as: customer's name, business name or title, address, zip-code, telephone number with area code, e-mail address, fax number; customer's account number; description of merchandise, page where it appears in catalog, quantity, size, color, type; monogram or personalization; price per unit; total price for each item; shipping and handling chart; sales tax information; amount enclosed; shipping information (options available plus shipping time); space for bank card number, expiration date, and signature; spaces for signatures from purchasing department or other authorization.

∼ Individualized letters dealing with orders are typed on letterhead or memo stationery.

～ If writing about a personal order from your home, a handwritten note is acceptable if clearly written.

WORDS

billed	expedite	items	stock
cancel	freight	merchandise	underpayment
change	goods	overnight	urgent
charge	handling	overpayment	warehouse
confirm	immediately	receipt	
deposit	invoice	rush	

PHRASES

as soon as possible/at once	next-day delivery
being shipped to you	please advise us/let us know
confirm your order	please bill to
delivery date of	prompt attention
enclosed is my check for	retail/wholesale price
hereby confirm	return receipt requested
I would like to order	ship C.O.D.
must cancel my order of	shipping and handling charges

SENTENCES

Along with your order I'm enclosing our spring catalog as I think you'll want to know about our new lower prices (many are lower than last year's!) and our completely new line of Strato work clothes.

If you cannot have the storage cabinets here by October 3, please cancel the order and advise us at once.

Please bill this order to my account # JO4889 at the usual terms.

Please cancel my order for the Heatherstone china (copy of order enclosed)—the three-month delay is unacceptable.

Please charge this order to my Carlyle First Bank Credit Card # 333-08-4891, expiration date 11/04 (signature below).

Please check on the status of my order # 90-4657 dated March 1.

Please confirm receipt of this order by fax or telephone.

Please include your account number/invoice number/order number on all correspondence.

We acknowledge with thanks your order of August 19 for one Pumblechook self-closing, self-latching chain link gate.

We are pleased to inform you that both your orders were shipped this morning.

We are sorry to advise you that we will be out of that particular piano tuning kit (# P11507) indefinitely.

We are unable to fill your order dated June 3 because your account is currently in arrears.

We hope you enjoy your personalized stationery, and will think of us for your other stationery needs.

Your order # KR45G is being processed and should be shipped by August 1.

PARAGRAPHS

This is to confirm receipt of your order # 104-1297 dated June 17, 2002. It will be shipped on or about June 26. Please allow two to three weeks for arrival. If you need to contact us again about this order, use our reference number, 442-48895.

We appreciate your order # GR3315 for the exposed aggregate. However, we no longer ship C.O.D. Please send a check or money order for $782.11 so that we can expedite your order.

Please note that you received a special price on the sheet protectors. Your refund check for the overpayment is enclosed.

We are trying to match exactly the interior folders we use for our hanging files. The ones shown in your current catalog, page 217, look very much like ours. Could you please send us samples in several colors so that we can be sure before ordering?

With one exception, your order is being shipped to you from our Gregsbury warehouse this week. The six desktop calculators are coming from our Chicago warehouse, and we've been experiencing some delays from that warehouse recently. You may not receive the calculators until approximately March 8. Please let us know if this is acceptable.

Thank you for your purchase order (# K12291944) of July 9 for the Bascomb stairway elevator. Your order has been forwarded for fulfillment, and your Purchasing Department will be contacted with information about terms and shipping dates.

It was my impression that we agreed upon a delivery date of May 15. The confirmation I have just received gives June 15. This will unfortunately be too late for us. Please let me know at once if this was a clerical error or if we have a serious problem on our hands.

SAMPLE LETTERS

Dear Ritson Projectors:

We have just received the audio cassette front- and rear-screen slide projector we ordered from you on November 3 (copies of order and invoice enclosed). One of the lenses appears to have been broken in transit.

Please let us know whether we should return the entire projector to you, take it to a service center if you have one in the vicinity, or have it repaired and bill you.

Yours truly,

Dear Dr. Sturmthal:

Thank you for your purchase order # H459991, which we received on June 3, for the TEM-500 Transmission Electron Microscope. Your order has been sent to our Administration Department and your Purchasing Department will be advised directly as to the confirmation of terms and shipping dates.

Teresa Desterro, Manager of the Sales Department, located in our Gillespie office, will advise you of confirmed delivery dates and can provide you with answers to questions on order processing or shipment expediting. Alec Loding, National Service Manager, also located in our Gillespie Office, will send you complete information on the installation requirements of your new TEM-500. Both Ms. Desterro and Mr. Loding can be reached directly by calling 212/555-1212.

We appreciate your order and the confidence you have shown in our company and in our instruments. We look forward to hearing from you either now or in the future if there is any way in which we may be of assistance to you.

Sincerely yours,

TO: Conford Confections
FROM: Alexander Trott
DATE: June 3, 2003

I have been buying your Conford Confections for family, friends, and business acquaintances twice a year (Easter and Christmas) for many years. I will be traveling in Europe this summer and would like to take along Confections to offer friends and business acquaintances there.

My questions:

1. Do Confections need to be refrigerated, either to maintain good quality and appearance or to ensure that there is no product spoilage?

2. Do you have outlets for your product in Europe? (I would not like to cart them along as a "special treat" and then find them being sold everywhere over there.)

3. Is there any other reason that would prevent me from taking Confections with me? (Do they melt easily, for example?)

If you can reassure me on the above points, please place my order for:

| 6 boxes | 8 oz. Gift Box | $7.95 |
| 10 boxes | 14 oz. Supremes | $12.95 |

My check for $197.83 (including sales tax and shipping and handling) is enclosed. Please ship to the letterhead address.

If you think the Confections won't travel well, I'll appreciate your saying so and returning my check.

~

See also: ACKNOWLEDGMENTS, ADJUSTMENTS, APOLOGIES, COLLECTION, COMPLAINTS, CREDIT, INSTRUCTIONS, REFUSALS, RESPONSES.

Letters Related to 36
Organizations
and Clubs

Please accept my resignation. I don't want to belong to
any club that would accept me as a member.

—Groucho Marx

Over 20,000 organizations are listed in the *Encyclopedia of Associations* (Gale Research Company), and many other clubs, societies, and groups function in less formal ways to provide people with ways of sharing interests, goals, professional information, and recreational activities.

Most club or organization correspondence is brief, routine, and easily written. But every announcement, invitation, or letter also represents the organization to its members and to the public and thus needs to be accurately written and attractively presented.

Write Letters Dealing with Clubs/Organizations for

- announcements: meetings/changes/reminders (see also ANNOUNCEMENTS)
- invitations: organization events/speaking engagements (see also INVITATIONS)
- meetings: canceling/changing
- recommending new members (see also REFERENCES)
- recruiting new members
- requests: membership/sponsorship/applications/volunteers/ information/copies of agenda or minutes

- resignations
- welcoming new members (see also WELCOME)

- When announcing a meeting, include: the name of your organization; date, time, and place of the meeting; a phone number for further information; at least one reason why a person would want to attend the meeting (celebrity guest speaker, special election, panel discussion, book signing).
- When inviting a speaker, include: your organization's full title; an estimate of the audience size; a description of the group's interests so the speaker can tailor the talk to them; available equipment (overhead projector, microphone); directions or map; name and phone number of contact person.
- When recruiting new members, an attractive brochure describing the group and its goals and activities may best "sell" you to others. Send it along with a friendly cover letter that emphasizes the group's strong points and tells why your organization would be appropriate for this person.

- Avoid putting anything negative on paper. Personality conflicts, disagreements and disputes over policies, and shifting allegiances give groups their dynamism and distinct character, but they are best handled face to face. Committing delicate situations to letters that end up in public files is unwise.
- Avoid paternalistic, top-down language in letters. Most groups today have a collegial rather than hierarchical spirit. Although there may be officers or leaders, everyone in the organization feels some ownership of it.

Tips on Writing

~ Unless you write on behalf of a small, casual group, keep letters to members dignified, businesslike, and somewhat formal. Spuriously intimate letters are offputting to some people, whereas a reserved letter appears less warm but certainly not offensive.

~ Spell members' names correctly. The mutilation of our names on mailing labels has become routine, but no one likes to see it from their professional or social group.

Special Situations

~ You may be asked to do a favor or write a recommendation for someone in your club or society whom you don't know well. By virtue of association and club kinship, there is a subtle pressure to respond positively. But you are no more obliged in this case than in any other (see REFUSALS).

~ The word "chairman" has generally been replaced by "chair." (Other choices include moderator, committee/department head, presiding officer, presider, president, convener, coordinator, group coordinator, discussion/group/committee leader, head, organizer, facilitator, officiator, director, administrator.) Some people use "chairwoman" and "chairman," but "chairwoman" is perceived as a less weighty word and it is seldom used as an exact match for "chairman." "Chairperson" is a self-conscious term used mostly for women. The short, simple "chair" was the original term (1647), with "chairman" coming into the language in 1654 and "chairwoman" in 1685. Using "chair" as both noun and verb parallels the use of "head" for both noun and verb. (People who are upset about being called "a piece of furniture" apparently have no problem with the gruesome picture of a "head" directing a department, division, or group, nor is there evidence that anyone has confused people chairing meetings with their chairs.)

Format

~ Type all club or organization business correspondence. An exception might be a social club in which the members know each other well and handwrite notes to each other.

~ E-mail messages and postcards are wonderfully useful in getting out meeting notices, announcements, invitations, and short messages.

~ For an organization of any size, your mailing list should be computerized; combining such a list with the merge function of most word processing systems simplifies correspondence.

WORDS

action	constitution	legacy	qualifications
affiliation	contribution	nominate	regulations
agenda	establish	policies	rules
allegiance	generous	positive	society
alliance	guild	practical	support
association	headquarters	principles	unwavering
benefit	heritage	procedures	valuable
bylaws	ideals	program	welcome
coalition	improve	progress	worthwhile
committee	league	project	

PHRASES

a credit to the organization	join forces
affiliated/associated with	minutes of the meeting
all-out effort	service to the community
board of directors	slate of officers
committee chair	take pride in nominating
common goal	unfortunately must resign
cooperative spirit	worthwhile cause
credit to us all	would like to nominate you for
have been elected a member of	

SENTENCES

Enclosed please find names of hosts, meeting dates, and topics for the next six months.

I am sorry to inform you that family illness obliges me to step down from the club vice-presidency, effective immediately.

It is with great pleasure/regret that I accept/decline your nomination to the Board of Directors of Montmorency House.

I would be happy to discuss any questions you have about the Club over lunch some day next week.

I would like to recommend/wish to propose Brander Cheng for membership in the Burke Orchestra Society.

Join now and take advantage of this limited offer to new members.

Our annual fundraising meeting to plan events for the next year will be held August 3 at 7:00 p.m.—all are invited.

Please accept my resignation from the Rembrandt Society.

To join the Frobisher Society today, simply indicate your membership category on the enclosed form and return it with your check.

Would you be willing to staff the Club's concession stand at the High-Lake Street Fair?

Would you please place the following three items on the agenda for the November meeting?

PARAGRAPHS

The Belford Area Women in Trades Organization invites you to attend its next monthly meeting, Thursday, June 14, at 7:30 p.m. in the old Belford Union Hall. Get to know us. See what we're trying to do for women in trades in this area. And then, if you like what you see, join up! Introductory one-year membership is $45, and we think we can do as much for you as you can do for the Organization!

This is to acknowledge receipt of your membership application. You will hear from us as soon as we have received all your references and evaluated your application. Thank you for your interest in the Society.

I understand you and some other employees have formed several noon-hour foreign language clubs. I would be interested in joining your Italian-speaking group. Can you put me in touch with whoever is in charge of it? Thanks.

Congratulations to our new officers, elected at the September 12 meeting: Truda Silber, president; Martin Lynch Gibbon, vice-president; Andrew Davies, secretary; Maria Eleonora Schoning, treasurer. They will be installed at the beginning of the October 15 meeting. Our most sincere gratitude is extended to last year's officers, who saw the Club through a remarkable expansion and a rewriting of the bylaws. Thanks, Fran, Leo, Rose, and Dennis!

Notice: The Professional Educators Network will not hold its regularly scheduled monthly meeting on February 10 at 7:30 p.m. We regret any inconvenience this cancellation may cause you. The next meeting will be held March 8 at 7:30 p.m. in the Schley Library meeting room.

We are all, of course, very sorry to see you resign, but we understand that you have many other obligations at this time. We will be happy to welcome you back whenever your circumstances change. It's been wonderful having you with us.

Thanks so much for helping to clean up after the dance last Saturday. It's certainly not a popular job, which makes me appreciate all the more the good-hearted folks who did pitch in. The next time you're on the clean-up committee, you can put my name down!

SAMPLE LETTERS

Dear Hugh,

As a member and current secretary of the Merrivale Philatelic Society, I'm always on the lookout for other stamp collectors. Someone happened to mention yesterday that you have been collecting for years. Would you be interested in joining us?

Because some of the members have quite valuable collections, we are careful to accept newcomers only on the basis of three references in addition to the recommendation of a member.

I would like to propose you for membership, if you think it's something you would enjoy. I'm enclosing some information that will tell you a little more about the group and its activities.

Let me know if you're interested, because I'd be pleased to sponsor you.

Sincerely,

To: Board of Directors

It is with much regret that I resign my position as Secretary of the Macduff Drama Club. Family complications necessitate that I withdraw from any evening activities at least for the foreseeable future. If I can be of any help to my successor, I am available by telephone.

I have thoroughly enjoyed my association with the Macduff Club. Best wishes to all of you. I look forward to joining you again as soon as possible.

Dear Friend,

There is something remarkable and unique about the Tropical Fish & Aquarists Club. For one thing, it really is a club, not an organization whose "membership benefits" amount to little more than having your name on a mailing list and receiving a monthly magazine.

When you join the Tropical Fish & Aquarists Club, you don't belong to it—it belongs to you. You have the option of meeting with other hobbyists in large, small, or special-interest groups as often as you and your co-enthusiasts want. You are entitled to four free five-line ads per year in a magazine that reaches thousands of other hobbyists. We'll extend your subscription to the magazine for one year if you contribute an article for publication. And, at the end of each year, we share any profits from membership fees and magazine revenues with members.

You don't belong to the Club; it belongs to you!

Yours truly,

See also: ANNOUNCEMENTS, FUNDRAISING, INVITATIONS, REFERENCES, REFUSALS, REQUESTS, RESPONSES, WELCOME.

Query Letters

37

A query letter is really a sales letter without the hype.

—LISEL EISENHEIMER

A query is a brief, well-written letter that sparks an editor's interest in publishing your article or book and ideally results in a request to submit the manuscript. A combination request letter and sales letter, the query letter is also used to persuade a literary agent to represent you or to pique someone's interest in a business proposal.

Editors like the query letter because it allows them to decide quickly if the idea is suitable for them and if it's interesting enough to pursue. They also use a good query letter to help them sell the idea in turn to their colleagues at editorial meetings.

For unagented writers, the query letter is the only way to approach publishers who no longer accept unsolicited manuscripts. And it may be a good way to approach even those publishers who do. Once an editor responds to your query letter with an invitation to send your manuscript, you can mark the package "Requested Material" and your manuscript will not end up doing time in the slush pile. You'll also know in advance that they're looking for material like yours.

Write Query Letters for

- books
- business opportunities
- dramatic scripts
- filmscripts/screenplays

- journal and review articles
- literary agents
- magazine articles

- Address your query to the right person. Familiarize yourself with the periodical or publishing house so that you are certain your material is suitable for them. Obtain the name and title of the editor receiving queries for your type of book or article (from a market book, online source, friend, writing group). Call the publisher and verify that the person is still there, that the name is spelled the way you have it, and that the person's title is current. (Don't speak to the editor; an operator, receptionist, or editorial assistant can answer your questions.)
- Orient your reader quickly to the purpose of your letter ("Would you be interested in seeing a 10,000-word article on . . . ?").
- Establish a strong hook to keep the editor reading. Some query letters open with the first paragraph of the proposed article or book.
- Tell what type of book or article it is (reference, biography, children's), how long it is (in number of words), its intended audience, and its title. In a few sentences, describe the work so that the editor itches to read it; this paragraph must be your finest writing.
- Tell why your article or book is different from others on the same subject, why you're the best person to write it (mention relevant expertise or knowledge), and why you chose this particular publisher.
- List your past publications.
- Thank the person for their time and attention.
- Include a self-addressed stamped envelope (SASE). Always. Every time.

- Don't discuss payment, royalties, rights, or other business issues in the query letter; it isn't appropriate at this stage of the process.
- Don't include personal information (age, marital status, hobbies, education) unless it is highly relevant to the proposed work. You do,

of course, include your full name, address, telephone number, e-mail address, and fax number.

- Don't use gimmicks to attract an editor's attention. Editors know how to zero in on the heart of the work and are not swayed by colored typefaces, joke or riddle openings (unless, of course, it's a joke or riddle book), or glitzy approaches. They usually consider gimmicks the mark of an amateur.

Tips on Writing

∿ Follow instructions on how to query. Publishers that accept e-mail queries will say so; if they mention a self-addressed stamped envelope (SASE) they prefer a written query. Most publishers offer writer's guidelines; get a copy (either from their website or by writing and enclosing an SASE) for any publisher you are interested in selling to.

∿ In general, address your query to associate editors and assistant editors, who are more likely to read your letter than are executive editors or editors-in-chief.

∿ Your letter is one page long—two at the most. "A query letter is like a fishing expedition; don't put too much bait on your hook or you'll lose your quarry. Be brief and be tantalizing!" (Jane von Mehren)

∿ Convey your enthusiasm for the material.

∿ A clever, memorable, or intriguing title (as long as it's appropriate to the material) is helpful to your cause. It doesn't have to be your final title; select a working title or choose one solely for querying.

∿ Proofread your letter as many times as it takes to be certain there are no spelling, punctuation, grammar, or usage errors; they can be fatal.

∿ Multiple submissions involve sending the same manuscript to several editors at the same time. There is little agreement among authors and editors about the advisability of submitting multiply. In general, you can query several editors at the same time about the same project. A decision about submitting multiply is then made only if several editors reply to your query letter by asking to see the manuscript.

∿ For assistance on writing great query letters, see John Wood, *How to Write Attention-Grabbing Query & Cover Letters*, and Lisa Collier Cool, *How to*

Write Irresistible Query Letters, both published by Writer's Digest Books. There are also sections on query letters in books such as Judith Appelbaum, *How to Get Happily Published*, 4th ed., HarperPerennial, and Poets & Writers, Inc., *Into Print*, Quality Paperback Book Club.

Special Situations

∼ The query letter has traditionally been used for works of nonfiction, but it is also being requested today for works of fiction. In those cases, the query letter is actually a cover letter, and an outline or synopsis and sample chapters are attached. To query about a fiction project, follow the guidelines in this chapter except that plot, characters, conflict, and resolution are described in the paragraph outlining your story or novel.

∼ Unpublished writers commonly fear that someone at the publishing house will steal their idea after reading their query letter. This is an exceedingly rare and undocumented occurrence. In any case, there are no new ideas. What is always new—and saleable—is the way the idea is clothed and presented. Even two people working on the same idea (there are supposedly only thirty-six dramatic situations) will produce significantly different works. Then, too, how will you get published if you don't send a query letter? This is the way it's done.

∼ When selling a reader on a business venture or idea, attach copies of charts or reports showing past successes, your résumé, your credit and business references, and any other data that relate to your proposal. Your object is to persuade the person to meet with you and discuss the matter. This letter differs from the literary query letter; you might profitably check with the chapters on APPLICATIONS, REPORTS, RÉSUMÉS, SALES.

Format

∼ Query letters are always typed, preferably on personal letterhead stationery. Don't try to fit more than usual on the page by using a smaller typeface or reducing margin space.

∼ E-mail queries are being accepted by some editors (you can tell who they are because their e-mail addresses are listed in marketing reports). Check to see if there are any special e-mail requirements.

∼ Query by fax only if you have been invited to do so or if the market information suggests it.

WORDS

appeal	feature	nonfiction	round-up
audience	fiction	outline	summary
consider	interested	overview	synopsis
contemporary	manuscript	publication	viewpoint
expertise	material	review	

PHRASES

about 2,500 words

aimed at long-distance runners

first-person narrative

most recent publications include

mystery series

personal experience with

previous works include

professional background supports

publication credits include

sample chapters and outline

trade journal appeal

SENTENCES

As you do not currently accept unagented submissions, I'm writing to ask if you'd like to see a picture book manuscript.

Can the market stand one more book on weight control? If it's this one—written by a physician with thirty years' success in helping patients lose weight—it can!

Enclosed are three sample chapters and an outline.

Enclosed is a SASE for your response.

I can submit the article by e-mail, on disks, or as hard copy.

I could deliver a 5,000-word article by September 1.

I look forward to hearing from you.

It was a dark and stormy night—or was it?

Thank you for your time and consideration.

"The Invisible Dragons" is an original Japanese folktale in which two brothers who try to outdo each other are rescued from a predicament of their own making by a girl whose name is too big for her.

When *should* you "cry wolf?"

PARAGRAPHS

Francesca Lia Block once wrote, "Love is a dangerous angel." She added, "Especially nowadays." Would you be interested in seeing an 80,000-word manuscript on the physical, emotional, intellectual, and spiritual dangers of sex today, supported by my current research?

A man with amnesia tries to negotiate the tricky steps of the life he is told is his. A familiar plot? Not in this novel.

Thank you for sending the submission guidelines for *Stucco City*. Having studied the guidelines and having also been a subscriber to your magazine for more than five years, I believe the article I want to submit to you is as new as it is highly appropriate to your readership.

Do you still believe in the existence of high-yield, low-risk stocks? You may not be as naïve as you think.

We met at a writers' conference in Los Angeles last month and briefly discussed the point at which a writer might need an agent. I believe I have reached that point.

I've been a season ticket-holder for the past three years and have thoroughly enjoyed your theater company's vitality, intelligence, and creativity. I am also a playwright with a script that I think is particularly appropriate for your ensemble.

On November 27, 1910, Marie Marvingt set the first women's world records in aviation. Earlier that month she had obtained her pilot's license, the third woman in the world to do so. An outstanding athlete (in 1910 the French government awarded her a gold medal for being expert in *all* sports), she was also a nurse, inventor, traveler, and the most decorated woman in the world. I would be surprised if your readers had ever heard of her.

SAMPLE LETTERS

Dear Ms. Selston,

It's a question we'd all like answered: Is there life after death?

In September of 2000 I was pronounced clinically dead. As you might suspect, the diagnosis was correct only up to a point.

My experience fed a fierce curiosity to know how "normal" such experiences are. And what they mean. And whether they might be proof of anything.

Since that time, I have interviewed 184 people who have also been to the "other side" and returned.

Not since Moody's *Life After Life* has there been such a diverse collection of anec- dotal evidence that there is indeed more to life than life.

Would you be interested in seeing some or all of this 70,000-word manuscript? Enclosed is a SASE for your reply.

Thank you.

～

From: jhall@email.com
To: query@email.com
Date: 06/26/2000 01:41 PM MST
Subject: Query: Renting a villa in Sicily

Hello. For my third stay in Sicily this fall, I'm renting a villa. Would you be interested in a 1,200-word piece comparing the benefits of villa life with hotel life, using as exam- ples three of my favorite Sicilian hotels (one on the north coast, one on the south coast, and one in Taormina)? Travel information layered into the article includes getting to Sicily; the best times to visit; auto rental peculiarities there; the three best areas in which to rent villas and the daytrips that are possible from each; the sites that no visitor to Sicily should miss.

I've written eighteen books published by mainstream publishers as well as a number of magazine and other articles. I'll be in Sicily Oct. 13–Nov. 13 and could get the piece to you several weeks after that. Because Sicily is best traveled in spring or fall, the article might appear in the spring for fall travel.

Thanks for your time and attention.

～

Dear Randy Shepperton,

Would you be interested in seeing an 85,000-word novel, *The Boarding House*?

Wealthy, intelligent, and isolated, Marshall is a house divided against himself. Denying important and life-giving facets of his self from an early age, he surrounds him- self with shadows formed by his projected unacceptable imaginings. In this literary explo- ration of the divided self, Marshall struggles to resolve the four basic human conflicts—between freedom and security, right and wrong, masculinity and femininity, and between love and hate in the parent-child relationship. In daring to love with maturity and without reserve he is finally able to deal with the boarders living in his house and to trade his mask for a real face.

I can send the complete manuscript or, if you prefer, sample chapters and a detailed synopsis.

I am also the author of a number of short stories, one of which won the Abinger Prize last year, and I was recently awarded a grant by our state arts board based on a sample from this novel.

Enclosed is a SASE for your reply.

~

Dear Mr. Windibank,

My family and I have just spent two months on a small island with no human company but our own. The strange story of why we went there and what we did while we were there is one that I think would interest your readers.

Each one of us—48-year-old husband/father, 49-year-old wife/mother, and 17- , 15-, 12-, and 10-year-old children—had a highly individual reaction to the experience and left the island changed in small and large ways.

Would you like to see a 5,000-word article, "Islands Within Islands"?

I am an architect with articles published in both professional journals and consumer magazines.

Enclosed is a SASE for your response.

~

See also: COVER LETTERS, REPORTS, REQUESTS, SALES.

References and 38 Recommendations

A letter of reference vouches for a person's general character. It tells a third party that the person is a responsible, functioning member of society. A reference is a verification: "Yes, I've known this person for some time."

A letter of recommendation is more specific and focuses on the person's professional qualities. It's often written by someone who knows the applicant on the one hand and the prospective employer, college, club, or awards committee on the other hand. A recommendation is an endorsement: "Yes, this person would be an excellent candidate for your program."

Letters of recommendation and letters of reference are so closely related that guidelines for writing them are similar.

A letter of commendation, written to congratulate a person on an achievement, is a combination of appreciation and congratulations; see the relevant chapters.

Letters of Reference and Recommendations Include

- applying for club membership (see also ORGANIZATIONS)
- asking someone to write a letter on your behalf
- credit references (see CREDIT)
- recommendations: individuals/ideas/companies/projects/products/ services/programs/workshops/new procedures/managerial decisions/ plans of action/public office

- references: former employees/students/friends/family members/customers/neighbors/babysitters
- refusing to write (see also REFUSALS)
- requesting information from a previous employer or from a reference cited by an applicant
- thanking someone for writing (see also THANK YOU)

- Give the person's full name at the beginning of your reference or recommendation. Later refer to the person as Ms., Mr., or Dr. plus the last name for the first reference in each paragraph and "she" or "he" after that. Never use the first name alone.
- State your connection with the person (former employer, teacher, supervisor, adviser, associate, neighbor, mentor) and how long you've known them ("for five years").
- Focus on the person's character for a general letter of reference (trustworthiness, sense of responsibility, enthusiasm, tact). In a letter of recommendation, focus on job experience and skills (length of employment with you, special abilities and accomplishments, your sense of the person as a prospective employee). Support your statements with facts or examples.
- Close with a summary statement reaffirming your recommendation of or confidence in the person.
- Offer to provide further information, if appropriate. Include your name, address, and phone number if you are not using letterhead stationery.
- Give the reference or recommendation to the subject of the letter, leaving the envelope unsealed so the person can read it if they wish. If you've been asked to mail your letter directly to a personnel office, scholarship committee, or other inquiring agency, it is sealed. Occasionally you might be asked to sign your name over the sealed flap to insure confidentiality. Sealed letters are generally more persuasive than unsealed ones.

What Not to Say

- Don't use the trite "To whom it may concern" if you can help it. A memo format is appropriate: "To:/From:/Date:/Re:." Or, give your letter a suitable heading such as "Introducing Letitia Fillimore," "To: Prospective Employees," "Recommendation of Helena Landless," "Letter of Reference for William Einhorn."
- Don't be too lavish or use too many superlatives—it undermines your credibility. Focus on two or three qualities and give examples of them.
- Don't tell the prospective employer what to do: "I'd hire her in a minute if she were applying here," "If I were you, I'd snap this one up," or "I can't think of anyone more deserving of this scholarship." Most people resent being told their business. You supply the information; they make the decision.
- Avoid saying anything you can't prove. This is often not so much outright dishonesty as misplaced enthusiasm, but it can work to the subject's disadvantage.

Tips on Writing

~ Be brief. One page, at most two, is sufficient to convey the general picture without repeating yourself, using unnecessary and fulsome phrases, or boring the other person.

~ Be specific. Don't tell; show the reader. Instead of saying someone is honest, explain that the person had access to the cash register, and even when experiencing personal financial hardship, turned in accurate receipts. Instead of saying someone is compassionate, tell how they missed a dinner party to help a troubled co-worker.

~ When applying for a position, don't send letters of recommendation with your application letter or cover letter and résumé. Wait until they are requested.

Special Situations

~ When you want to list someone as a reference, call or write first and ask their permission.

∽ When asking someone to write a letter of reference or recommendation for you, give the person enough information to be able to emphasize what will be most helpful to you ("I am applying for a position as a claims examiner"). Help the person tailor what they know of you with what you tell them of the company's needs and requirements. Enclose either a SASE for a return to you or a stamped envelope addressed to the person who is to receive the reference. Express your appreciation. Allow two to three weeks for the person to write the letter.

∽ After thanking someone for writing you a recommendation or reference, share any news of your job search, membership application, or college admission efforts—or at least promise to let the person know what happens. Even if you don't get the position or choose not to take it, you will want to express your gratitude to the person for writing on your behalf.

∽ When you believe that writing a positive letter of reference or recommendation for a former employee is unjustified or, in some cases, irresponsible, you may decline to provide one. Most employee records are accessible to employees, who may be inspired to legal action if they do not care for what you have written. According to some surveys, many employers are so wary of lawsuits that they don't give any information on former employees without their written consent and indemnification. Some companies will never under any circumstances provide references; defending a defamation suit can cost hundreds of thousands of dollars, even if the company wins. Many companies and personnel departments have a policy of either giving information only over the phone (thus, putting nothing in writing) or sending a form letter that acknowledges that the person worked there and verifies the dates of employment. Such a form might add: "It is against our policy to discuss the performance of former employees."

∽ When recommending a service or product, relate your own experiences with it, but refrain from giving a blanket endorsement. Provide a few disclaimers: "This is only my opinion, of course"; "You may want to see what others think"; "It may not work for everyone, but we liked it."

∽ When formally recommending a course of action, a policy change, or a decision, include: a subject line or first sentence stating what the letter is about; a summary of your recommendations; factual support for your recommendations; your offer to accept further negotiation, to engage in further research, or to submit additional information. If your recommendation is critical or negative, word it carefully. Point out the benefits along with the disadvantages, stating that you think the latter outweigh the former.

Format

⁓ Letters of reference and recommendation are typed on letterhead paper.

⁓ Thank-you notes sent to people who have written letters of reference or recommendation are typed or handwritten on plain personal stationery or foldovers.

⁓ In-house recommendations dealing with matters of policy are typed on memo paper.

WORDS

admirable	effective	integrity	resourceful
approve	efficient	intelligent	respect
capable	endorse	invaluable	responsible
commendable	energetic	inventive	self-motivated
competent	ethical	loyal	sensible
congenial	excellent	meticulous	successful
conscientious	experienced	outstanding	suitable
considerate	first-rate	personable	tactful
cooperative	hardworking	praiseworthy	thoughtful
creative	honest	productive	trustworthy
dependable	imaginative	professional	valuable
diligent	indispensable	recommend	
discreet	ingenious	reliable	
dynamic	initiative	remarkable	

PHRASES

able to energize a group of people

acquits herself/himself well

asset to any organization

attentive to detail

broad experience/range of skills

can attest to

creative problem-solver

dependable/eager/hard worker

did much to improve/increase/
    better/upgrade

discharged his/her duties
    satisfactorily

distinguished herself/himself by

do not hesitate to recommend

energetic and enthusiastic worker

every confidence in

first-rate employee

for the past five years

gives me real satisfaction to

great respect for

happy to write on behalf

has three years' experience

have been impressed with

held in high regard here

held positions of responsibility

highly developed technical skills

I heartily/wholeheartedly/highly
recommend

in response to your request for
information about

many fine contributions

matchless record

nothing but praise for

one in a thousand

outstanding leadership abilities

rare find

recommend with complete
confidence

responsible for all aspects of security

satisfactory in every way

set great store by

skilled in all phrases of light clerical
duties

sterling qualities

take-charge person

take genuine pleasure in
recommending

takes pride in his/her work

vouch for

well thought of

SENTENCES

Although company policy prohibits my writing you the recommendation you requested, I certainly wish you every success with your career.

Ann Shankland has highly developed sales and marketing skills and has also proven herself invaluable in the recruiting, training, and supervising of an effective sales team.

Elizabeth Endorfield is one of our most knowledgeable people when it comes to custodial chemicals, equipment, and techniques.

Hiram G. Travers was in my employ for ten years.

I am proud to recommend Ellen Huntly to you—I always found her work, character, and office manner most satisfactory.

In response to your inquiry about Chester Nimmo, it is only fair to say that he seemed to need constant supervision and our association with him was not an altogether happy one.

I've known Richard Musgrove as a neighbor and employee for six years.

I would prefer not to comment on Jean Emerson's employment with us.

Mary Treadwell worked as an X-ray technician at Porter General Hospital from 1995 to 2001.

Mr. Tamson's record with our company was excellent.

Thank you for the wonderful and apparently persuasive recommendation you wrote for me—I've been accepted at the Maxwell School of Political Science!

To evaluate your suitability for the sales position you applied for, we need to speak to at least four former employers or supervisors—please provide names, addresses, and daytime phone numbers of people we may contact.

Working with you has meant a great deal to me and I'm wondering if I may give your name as a reference when I apply for my first "real" job.

PARAGRAPHS

Emily Wardle has asked that I write a letter of recommendation based on our professional association over the past several years. I've found Ms. Wardle to be intelligent and trustworthy as well as energetic in carrying out her duties. She is an asset to any organization. I would recommend her without reservation.

You asked what I thought of the Vanever-Hartletop contract. After looking into the matter, my best recommendation would be to return the contract unsigned with a request for renegotiation of the default clause.

In response to your request for information about Tasker Lithography, I must say that we've had nothing but exceptionally fine dealings with them for the past eight years. Deadlines were met, and the quality of their work has been superb. The few times we asked for changes, they were carried out quickly and cheerfully. It's possible that others have had different experiences with Tasker. I can only say that we are pleased with their work.

Nancy Lammeter-Cass is being considered for a position as pastry chef in our catering service, and has given your name as a reference. Will you please complete the attached form as soon as possible? Enclosed is a self-addressed stamped envelope for your reply. Thank you.

SAMPLE LETTERS

Dear Ms. Tartan,

You once offered to write me a letter of reference if ever I needed one. I would like to take you up on your kind offer now.

I am applying for a part-time teaching position in the Glendinning-Melville School District and have been asked to supply several letters of reference. In the hopes that you have the time and are still willing to write a letter, I'm enclosing an instruction sheet from the school district outlining what they need in a letter of reference as well as a stamped envelope addressed to the district personnel offices.

If for any reason you cannot do this, I will understand. Know that I am, in any case, grateful for past kindnesses.

Sincerely,

TO: Office of Admissions
FROM: Dr. Charles Kennedy
RE: Steve Monk
DATE: November 15, 2002

I have known Steve Monk for four years, first as a student in my earth sciences and biology classes and later as Steve's adviser for an independent study in biology. I am currently helping him with an extracurricular research project.

Mr. Monk is one of the brightest, most research-oriented students I have encountered in eighteen years of teaching. His SAT and achievement test scores only begin to tell the story. He has a wonderful understanding of the principles of scientific inquiry, a passion for exactitude, and a bottomless curiosity.

I am interested in Steve's situation and will be happy to provide any further information.

Dear Ms. Burnell,

You requested employment information about Dan Burke.

Mr. Burke was employed with us from 1996 through 1999 as a structural engineer. His work was satisfactory, and I believe he left us to pursue a more challenging job opportunity.

If we can be of additional assistance, please call.

Sincerely,

See also: APPRECIATION, EMPLOYMENT, INTRODUCTIONS, ORGANIZATIONS, REQUESTS, RESUMES, THANK YOU.

Refusals

39

Most people hate to say no—but not nearly as much as other people hate to hear it.

—DIANNE BOOHER

When we have no interest in an activity and also have an iron-clad excuse (being out of the country or out of money, for example), letters of refusal, regret, and rejection are easy to write. In all other cases, they are a challenge.

To write letters of refusal (also known as regrets and rejections), be certain that you want to say "no"; ambivalence will weaken your letter. A good reason for saying "no" is simply "I don't want to." When you have a specific reason for saying no, you can give it. However, the fact that someone wants you to do something confers no obligation on you to defend your decision. People who become angry with you for saying no, who try to manipulate you, or who make you feel guilty are confusing requests with demands.

Write a Refusal When Saying "No" to

- adjustment/claims requests
- applications: employment/franchise
- gifts
- invitations: personal/business
- proposals: contracts/bids/books
- requests: contributions/credit/introductions/time/volunteering/promotions/ raises/loans of money or possessions/appointments/meetings/interviews
- sales: presentations/offers/invitations
- wedding invitations (see WEDDINGS)

- Thank the person for the offer, request, invitation (which you describe or mention specifically).
- Make a courteous remark, agreeing with the person that the cause is worthy, the proposal well thought-out, the résumé impressive, or the invitation appealing.
- Say "no," expressing your regret at having to do so.
- If you wish, explain your position.
- Suggest alternate courses of action or other resources, if appropriate.
- Close with a pleasant wish to be of more help next time, to see the person again, or for success with their project, job search, or request.

- Don't leave any doubt in the other person's mind about your response; your "no" is firm and non-negotiable.
- Don't lie. It's too easy to be tripped up, and you'll be more comfortable with yourself and with the other person if you ground your refusal in some version of the truth.
- Don't offer lengthy, involved excuses and apologies; they are not persuasive, even when true. "Several excuses are always less convincing than one." (Aldous Huxley)
- Don't make personal remarks (about their appearance, personality, behavior, language skills) when turning down a person's request, job application, or proposal. Even if you think it would help the person in the future, leave this kind of comment to someone else in their life.
- Don't reply sarcastically to outrageous or inappropriate requests. It does you no good and angers the other person.

Tips on Writing

~ Respond promptly. "The prompter the refusal, the less the disappointment." (Publilius Syrus) In addition, most people asking for something or inviting you to an event need to know soon. By giving your refusal early, you allow them time to find another solution or invitee.

～ Be tactful. Avoid basing your refusal on the other person's résumé, program, invitation. Phrase it instead in terms of some inability or requirement on your part ("need someone who is bonded"; "another meeting that day"; "will be out of town"; or simply "will be unable to help").

～ Give your excuse before your refusal. The reader is thus prepared and the disappointment at your "no" doesn't keep them from "hearing" your reasons. Instead of saying, "I will not be able to attend your graduation because I'm going to be in California that week," say, "I am going to be in California the week of June 2, which means I won't, unfortunately, be able to attend your graduation."

～ Lessen the disappointment: offer to help at a later date; suggest someone who might be able to provide the same assistance; agree with them on some point; apologize for your inability to approve the request; indicate some benefit to them from your refusal; thank them for their interest/request/concern.

～ The inimitable Miss Manners (Judith Martin) wouldn't want you to completely lessen the disappointment, however. She points out that you can't reject someone without them feeling rejected; if they don't feel rejected they don't go away. A painless rejection isn't one, so don't give false hope. She advises writing refusals that are bland, routine, and unoriginal.

～ Occasionally, the way you turn down an applicant, proposal, bid, or other business matter can lead to legal problems. If you have concerns, consult with a lawyer before writing your letter.

Special Situations

～ When unable to attend, always respond with regret to an invitation marked "R.S.V.P.," "Please reply," or "Regrets only." This is mandatory, obligatory, required, compulsory, imperative, and essential. If the invitation is issued in the name of more than one person, mention all of them in your refusal and mail it either to the person listed under the R.S.V.P. or to the first name given. To decline an invitation, use the same format as the invitation itself: If it is handwritten, handwrite your reply. If business letterhead stationery is used, reply on your own business letterhead. When the invitation is worded informally, your reply is also informal. When the invitation is formal, your reply uses the same words, layout, and style as the invitation.

～ White House invitations include the phone number of the Social Office where you telephone your regrets or ask how to respond to the invitation. General guidelines are: reply within a day of receiving the invitation; write the reply yourself (don't have a secretary do it); handwrite it on plain or engraved personal stationery; use the same format and person (first person or third person) as the invitation. There are only four generally accepted excuses for not accepting a White House invitation: a death in the family, a family wedding, prior travel plans, illness. Your reply says, "We regret that owing to the illness/recent death of . . ."

~ When turning down an applicant for a position, include: your thanks for the person's application; a simple statement saying that you are unable to offer the person the position; if necessary or helpful, an explanation of the decision; positive comments on the person's credentials, abilities, interview, résumé; if applicable, an invitation to reapply at some later time; your good wishes for success in the person's search for a suitable position. Some companies don't notify a job-seeker whose application is unsuccessful. However, it is courteous as well as good public relations to write a brief, tactful letter. When replying to an unsolicited application, express your appreciation for thinking of your company, state that there are no positions open, offer to keep the résumé on file, and invite a later contact, if that is an option.

~ When you refuse a job offer, do so with thanks and complimentary remarks about the company, your interviewer, the human resources department. Express your regret. If appropriate, tell why you made the choice you did, but phrase it in terms of your needs and not the company's deficiencies. Close on a positive note that leaves the door open for the future.

~ When denying a requested promotion or raise or application for an in-house position (1) show appreciation for the employee's contributions, listing specific talents and strengths; (2) explain honestly and concretely why the request was denied; (3) offer suggestions on how the promotion or raise or other position might be obtained or, if your "no" depended on external factors (too many managers, budget shortfalls), what changes might affect a future request. The goal is to leave the employee feeling valued, motivated, and encouraged.

~ Refuse an adjustment or claims request in a way that maximizes the chances of keeping the customer. Be tactful and considerate. Offer an alternative or compromise solution when possible. Tell the customer that you understand their position, that their complaint has been given every consideration, and that you wish you could say "yes." Then give a credible explanation of your "no." Use facts or copies of documents to show that an adjustment is not warranted. Most customers are satisfied with a brief, clearly written refusal. A few will write back and argue, point by point. When that happens, write a firm "no" with no further explanations.

〜 Many companies and government agencies have codified procedures for handling bids. When you have a choice, notify bidders of your requirements as soon as possible. In rejecting bids, be courteous and supportive, and, when possible, explain briefly why the bid was rejected (especially if it concerned failure to follow directives or to stay within certain guidelines) or why the winning bid was accepted. Information like this is useful to your contractors. Close with an expression of appreciation and a reference to the possibility of doing business with them at a later date. You do not need to name the winning bidder.

〜 When refusing a request for credit or a loan, be tactful; the person is still a customer, a potential customer, or a friend. Thank the person for applying or asking. Express appreciation of the interest in your company or faith in your friendship. In the case of an application for a commercial loan or commercial credit, tell how you arrived at your decision (the application, employer's recommendation, background check, credit bureau file). Suggest ways of improving an applicant's credit standing, alternative sources of credit, or re-applying to you after a certain period of time or after resolving certain financial problems. In the case of a personal loan, omit the advice and simply state that you're unable to help at this time.

〜 Most manuscript rejections are made with form postcards or letters. Few are as witty as Samuel Johnson's: "Your manuscript is both good and original; but the part that is good is not original, and the part that is original is not good." When you write a personal letter, emphasize that the rejection is based on the needs and interests of your publishing house and that the situation at another publisher might be different. Assure the person that you've carefully considered the work, offer thanks for thinking of you, and send your good wishes for success in future endeavors.

〜 Most fundraising appeals are mass-produced and you will not reply if you are uninterested. However, when you receive a personal letter with first-class postage, written over the signature of someone known to you, you might want to respond. Compliment the person on the work the organization is doing, give a plausible excuse for not contributing, and offer good wishes. You don't have to give any more detail than you choose; a vague statement that you are currently overcommitted elsewhere is fine. If you are refusing because you disagree with the organization's goals or policies, say so.

〜 When terminating a business relationship, friendship, or dating relationship, aim for a no-fault "divorce": don't blame the other person or bring up past grievances. Help the other person save face by taking responsibility for the separation on yourself. Be as honest as is consistent with tact and kindness. Above all, be brief and unequivocal; over-explaining or "keeping your options open" can be fatal if you sincerely want to end the relationship. Conclude with an encouraging, complimentary remark.

~ Sometimes people are extremely persistent about wanting your company, your time, your money. When refusing their requests, your note is firm, simple, and unequivocal (the moment you waffle, they are back in the door). Give no explanations for your refusal ("I am sorry but I will not be able to" is sufficient). The moment you tell why you're refusing ("I'm very busy just now"), there will be an immediate response ("It will only take a minute"). When you offer another reason, there will be another rebuttal. Engaging you in wearying debate is part of the strategy; you wouldn't be the first person to say "yes" just to avoid being harangued. "I'm sorry, but no," repeated as many times as it takes, is the most effective response.

~ Sometimes you must refuse a gift—in business, for example, when you are offered an unacceptably expensive gift or the acceptance of gifts isn't allowed by your organization. Express your gratitude for the person's thoughtfulness and for the choice of gift. Explain why you must return it ("Employees are prohibited from accepting gifts from suppliers" or "I hope you will understand, but I would feel uncomfortable accepting such an expensive gift from a client"). Word your refusal so that it does not imply the person was guilty of poor judgment in offering the gift.

Format

~ Business letters of refusal are typed on letterhead stationery.

~ Personal letters of refusal are most often handwritten.

~ Form letters are used for routine refusals.

~ You may e-mail your rejection of queries, suggestions, or requests that were made by e-mail.

WORDS

awkward	doubtful	overstocked	unable
contraindicated	impossible	regretfully	unavailable
decline	impractical	reject	unfeasible
difficult	obstacle	reluctantly	unfortunately
dilemma	overextended	respond	unlikely

PHRASES

after much discussion/careful evaluation

although I am sympathetic to your problem/plight/situation

although the idea is appealing

appreciate your asking me/us, but

because of prior commitments

beyond the scope of the present study

company policy prohibits us from

current conditions do not warrant

difficult decision

disinclined at this time

doesn't qualify/warrant

don't have enough information

due to present budget problems

hope this will be of some help even though

I appreciate your asking me, but

if it were possible

I know how understanding you are, so I'm sure

I'm sorry to tell you

I must say no to

I regret that I cannot accept

it is, unfortunately, out of the question that

it's a wonderful program, but

it's currently impossible

I wish I could say yes, but

I would like to help, but

must decline/demur/pass up/ withdraw from/say no to

normally I would be delighted, but

not a choice I can make right now

not an option at the moment

not currently seeking

no, thank you

not interested at this time

previous commitments

puts me in something of a dilemma

regret to inform you

remain unconvinced of the value of

runs counter to

sincerely regret

sorry about this, but

unable to help/comply/grant/send/ contribute/offer/provide

we appreciate your interest, but

we find that we cannot

we have concluded with regret

we have now had a chance to review

your idea has merit, but

SENTENCES

Although we appreciate your interest in Dempsey Toys, we do not feel that your product is one we could successfully market.

Although your entry did not win, we wish you good luck and many future successes.

At this time there does not appear to be a position with us that is suited to your admittedly fine qualifications.

Fundraising is not one of my talents—is there anything else I could do for the committee?

I appreciate your offer but I want to try a few things before I go outside the firm for a solution.

I don't think this will work for us.

If you re-read your contract, specifically clause C1, you will see that we have no legal obligations in this regard.

I have taken on more projects than I can comfortably handle.

I hope this will help you understand why we are unable to furnish the additional funding you are requesting.

I know we'll be missing a wonderful time.

I'm sorry not to be able to give you the reference you requested in your letter of November 3.

I regret that I'm unable to accept your kind invitation—I will be out of town that evening.

I sympathize with your request and wish I could help.

It's possible we would be interested sometime after the first of the year.

I wish I could be more helpful, but it's not possible now.

I wish I didn't have to refuse you, Jerry, but I'm not in a position to make you the loan.

May I take a raincheck?

Our present schedule is, unfortunately, inflexible.

Regarding your request to use my name in your fundraising literature, I must say no.

Thank you, but we have had a regular purchasing arrangement with Burnside Office Supplies for many years.

The Board has, unfortunately, turned down your request.

The position at Locksley International for which you applied has been filled.

Unfortunately, this is not a priority for Pettifer Grains at this time.

We appreciate your asking us, and hope that we will have the opportunity of saying "yes" some other time.

We are unable to approve your loan application at this time.

We have decided to accept another proposal.

We have reviewed your credit application and regret to inform you that we are unable to offer you a bank card at this time.

We regret that your work was not selected for inclusion in the symposium.

We regret to inform you that Spenlow Paint & Tile is no longer considering applications for its sales positions.

We regret to say that a careful examination of your résumé does not indicate a particular match for our present needs.

Your request comes at a particularly difficult time for me—I'm over-scheduled for the next two months.

PARAGRAPHS

Dr. Gerda Torp regrets that because of a previous engagement she is unable to accept the kind invitation of Mr. and Mrs. Esdras B. Longer for Sunday, the third of June, at 8:00 p.m.

Thank you for your invitation to join Glowry Health Services as a pharmacy technician. The beautiful new facilities, the friendly staff members, and the good interview I had with you were all very persuasive. However, I have also been offered a position forty-five minutes closer to home. To have more time with my family, I plan to accept it. I thank you for your time, attention, and good humor. I hope our paths cross again someday.

Because we are financially committed to several charities similar to yours, we are unable to send you anything. However, please accept our best wishes for successful continuation and funding of your work—we certainly appreciate and admire what you're doing.

I've checked our production schedule and see no way of moving up your deliveries by two weeks. We are dependent on materials shipped to us by suppliers in other states who are unable to alter their timetables.

For a number of reasons, I am uneasy about writing you a letter of introduction to Sir Harrison Peters. I have discussed it with my superior, who would prefer that you find some other avenue of contact. I hope you understand.

We've just received your kind letter inviting us to Howards End. You can imagine how we'd enjoy seeing you again. However, Julia is graduating from college that weekend, so we have to say no this time. Thanks so much for thinking of us.

SAMPLE LETTERS

Dear Dean Arabin:

I regret that I am unable to represent Barchester College at the inauguration of Dr. Eleanor Bold as ne president of Century College on September 16. I was unable to reschedule a previous commitment for that day.

My wife is a graduate of Century, so I would have particularly enjoyed being part of the ceremony. Thank you for thinking of me. I was honored to be asked to represent the College and would be glad to be of service at some other time.

I hope you are able to make other arrangements.

Sincerely,

TO: Friends of the Library Committee

Thank you for your kind letter asking me to direct the annual fundraiser. I am flattered that you thought of me.

Because of several other time-consuming commitments, I am unable to accept your invitation. I would have enjoyed working with you and contributing in some way to our fine library system, but I feel sure that you will find the right person for this important project.

With best wishes, I am

Sincerely yours,

Dear Tony Cryspyn:

Thank you for submitting your work to us. As editors of the *Windsor Castle Review*, we have given your material careful consideration; every manuscript submitted to this office is read by one or more of us.

We regret that "The Ninth Son" is not suited to the current needs of the magazine, but we wish to thank you for having given us the opportunity of reading it. Unfortunately, the volume of submissions and the press of other editorial responsibilities do not permit us to make individual comments or suggestions.

Sincerely,

Dear Margaret Ivory,

We have appreciated having you as a patient these last two years. At this time, however, we feel that your best interests are not served by continuing treatment in this office. We would like to recommend that you make an appointment with Dr. Royde-Smith,

Dr. Owen, or a dentist of your choice. We will be happy to send along your dental records, including X-rays.

Let us know how we can facilitate this change in caregivers.

~

Dear Chris and David,

Thank you for sending us the information on your real estate trust investment opportunity.

Although it looks appealing, this is not something we are prepared to get into at the moment. I sent the prospectus on to my brother in Denver. It's possible he would be interested.

I'm sure you will find all the capital you need, and I wish you every success.

Best wishes,

~

Dear Mrs. Lanier,

We at Parker Investment Mortgage, Inc. understand and appreciate how difficult this past year must have been for you.

However, given your history of missed payments (June 2001, September 2001, November 2001, and February, March, and April 2002), the fact that your account is now three months past due, and our inability to arrange a meeting with you to discuss solutions, we are unable to grant you any additional time.

Unless we receive your unpaid balance by May 15, you will receive a foreclosure notice.

Sincerely,

~

See also: APPOINTMENTS, CREDIT, DISAGREEMENT, RESPONSES, SENSITIVE.

Reports and Proposals

40

*It may be said of me by Harper & Brothers, that although I
reject their proposals, I welcome their advances.*

—EDNA ST. VINCENT MILLAY

Standard proposals and reports aren't letters, but shorter ones are sometimes written as letters or memos. They use plainer language, do not have heads, sub-heads, and clauses, and are less formal and less complicated.

Proposals can be solicited (someone asks you for an estimate, bid, plan of action) or unsolicited (you want to sell your plan or service or program to someone who has not expressed a need for it). In either case, your proposal is a sales tool to persuade the other party that you are the best firm for the job (for a solicited proposal) or that it needs the service you are offering (for an unsolicited proposal).

Report and Proposal Letters Include

- acceptance of proposal/bid
- acknowledgment of receipt (see ACKNOWLEDGMENTS)
- bids and estimates
- book and article proposals (see QUERIES)
- compliance reports to government agencies
- credit reports (see CREDIT)
- investigative reports
- management, staff, policy, or recommendation reports

- progress/status reports
- proposals: products/grants/projects/programs/sales/services
- recommendations/suggestions
- rejection of proposal/bid/report (see REFUSALS)
- reports: annual/monthly/progress/management/staff/technical
- responses to inquiries/requests
- sales reports: weekly/monthly/annual

- Begin with a reference line that identifies the subject of the proposal or report.
- State why you are sending the report or proposal ("as requested," "for your information," "Charles O'Malley asked me to send you a copy," "in response to your request for a quotation").
- Describe the report in one or two sentences.
- The main body of the report or proposal—explaining the idea in detail, giving costs, specifications, deadlines, and examples of application—is organized into clear, logical units of information.
- Summarize the report in one or two sentences.
- Credit those who worked on the report or proposal.
- Offer to provide additional information and give the name and telephone number of the contact person.
- Tell what the next step is or what your expectations are ("call me," "sign the enclosed contract," "please respond with a written evaluation of the proposal").
- Thank the person for their time and consideration.

- Don't include other topics or business. The report or proposal is a focused document.
- Don't use jargon unless you're sure it's familiar to your readers.

Tips on Writing

~ Before preparing a report or proposal, know the answers to these questions: Who will read the document? What is its purpose? What material will it cover? How will the material be presented?

~ The main body of a letter proposal or report can be as short as a paragraph or long enough to be divided into one or more of the traditional report elements: title page; summary, synopsis, or abstract; a foreword, preface, introduction, history or background; acknowledgments; table of contents; a presentation of data, options, conclusions, and recommendations; appendix, bibliography, endnotes, references, and notice of any attached supporting documents.

~ Before mailing the proposal or report, ask someone knowledgeable about the issues (in some cases a lawyer) to read it for clarity and precision. Double-check a proposal to be certain that every item in the original request has been responded to.

~ If timing is important to your report or proposal, send it return receipt requested so you can verify the date it was received.

Special Situations

~ When writing grant proposals, three guidelines will boost your chances of success: (1) follow directions scrupulously—no allowances are made for deviations from stated formats; (2) present your material faultlessly—neatly typed on high-quality paper, error-free, well spaced; (3) the content must be your finest writing and slanted specifically to that funding organization—the identical material can seldom be proposed to two different groups. Artist resource groups offer help to grant applicants, and sometimes people in your field will critique your material.

~ Many progress reports have a codified format, but others may be written in narrative letter form. Include: what has been done during the reporting period; what is currently being done; what outstanding projects are waiting for attention; good news and bad news during the reporting period; other comments that give readers an appreciation of the progress of the student, employee, department, or company.

~ If it appears that your proposal will be acceptable to the other party, turn the proposal letter into a contract letter or binding agreement by adding at the bottom, "Read and approved on [date] by [signature and title]." If the proposal is part of a larger contract, add "pursuant to the Master Contract dated March 2, 2002, between Raikes Engineering and Phillips Contractors" (see also CONTRACTS).

Format

∽ Report or proposal letters are typewritten on letterhead or memo stationery.

∽ When time is an issue, reports and proposals can be faxed or e-mailed, but send hard copies too.

∽ Forms with blanks to be filled in are convenient for credit reports, school progress reports, routine production reports, and other reports that depend on numbers or short descriptions.

WORDS

abstract	display	judge	recommendation
advise	draft	layout	representation
agenda	establish	method	research
analysis	estimate	monograph	results
applications	evaluate	notification	review
appraise	exhibit	offer	statement
approach	explanation	opinion	strategy
assess	exploration	outcome	study
calculate	exposition	outline	subject
compute	findings	performance	suggest
conclude	forecast	policy	summary
conditions	gauge	preface	system
consider	guesstimate	preliminary	technical
critique	inquiry	presentation	terms
decision	inspect	procedure	text
design	instruction	program	undertaking
diagram	introduce	project	venture
disclose	investigation	projections	
discussion	issue	prospectus	

PHRASES

a considerable/significant/important
   advantage

address the problem of

along these lines

as you can see from the data

ballpark figure

close/exhaustive inquiry

copy of the proceedings

detailed statement

educated guess

estimated value

give our position on

gives me to understand

in-depth account of/look at

institute inquiries

make inquiry/known/public

map out

matter at hand/in dispute/under
   discussion/at issue

planning stages

plan of action

position paper

rough computation/calculation/
   draft/guess

subject of inquiry

summarizes the progress of

supplies/offers/provides some
   distinct advantages

take into consideration

take measures/steps

under consideration/discussion

SENTENCES

Data on in-line skating injuries in the United States during the past two
   years are charted below.

I propose that we set up a subcommittee to study flex-hours for all salaried
   employees.

Our annual report on homelessness in the six-county metro area reveals
   both good news and bad news.

Re: Acquisition of the Cypress Spa Products Corp.

Sperrit-Midmore Landscape Supply Center has had one of its most
   successful quarters ever—see below for details.

Subject: Proposed staffing changes in conference catering.

The following report was prepared by Robert Famish and Narcissa
   Topehall.

This report summarizes your benefits and any optional coverage you have
   chosen as of January 1.

PARAGRAPHS

A citizen task force composed of interested persons was formed last May and met almost the entire year to make recommendations to the Planning Commission, which, in turn, made its report to the City Council. Their report is summarized here.

Since our letter of September 3, in which we compared electroplating and sputtering for production of thin alloy films for recording, we have done some additional research on this subject. We have found that as long as the proper microstructure is achieved, both electroplating and sputtering are effective. It appears too early to exclude either of the processes. It may be helpful, however, to do a rough cost analysis either as more data from research in these two areas become available or by making a number of assumptions.

I've checked into the matter of buying versus renting an air compressor, and it seems far more cost-effective in the long run and convenient for us in the short run to buy a small portable air compressor rather than to rent one as needed. A study of our use of an air compressor suggests that although we need one only "infrequently," the rental charges and lost productive time in not having one immediately available outweight the cost of a new one. I suggest buying.

SAMPLE LETTERS

Dear Etta,

   Re: Proposed Budget for Design of Streets DRS – 821.01
   We have estimated the design cost to produce final plans for the relocation of Concannon Street from the bypass to the railroad tracks, and for Concannon Bypass from Blake Avenue to Nicholas. The design of Concannon Street is for a length of approximately 2,000 feet and consists of five traffic lanes, curb and gutter, and a raised median over 25% of its length. The Concannon Bypass design covers approximately 2,500 feet and includes curb and gutter along the outside lanes and median, pavement widening, intersection improvements, acceleration and deceleration lanes, and signals at three locations. The cost works out to $55,000, and we therefore propose that a budget for this amount be approved.

   Please call me if you have any questions concerning our estimate. Thanks.

                                              Sincerely,

To: Marketing Department
From: Stephen Rollo
Date: March 4, 2002
Re: Report on recent drop in sales

This memo report will serve as a summary of the attached 12-page in-depth report on what appear to be the mechanisms and underlying causes of the recent nationwide drop in sales at our restaurant equipment and supply outlets.

Based on these ideas, I'm planning experimental modifications to our outlets in Colorado Springs and Denver. If you have opinions on these ideas (especially if you disagree), I'd appreciate hearing from you.

The driving forces for sales to restaurants are of course need, immediate availability, accessibility, and price. We have isolated price as the critical factor in the recent downturn. Although our prices are, in fact, competitive with other suppliers, our prices do not *appear* to be competitive.

The report details the three potential ways of dealing with the perception that we are more expensive than our competitors. Please reflect, both individually and in groups, on our choices.

I will let you know the results of the planned changes in Del Mar and San Diego. In the meantime, I would appreciate getting as much feedback as possible (and as quickly as possible) on the attached report.

<div align="center">~~~</div>

Proposal
Marryat Insulation Systems, Inc.
54 Easthupp Boulevard
Frederick, IA 50501

Proposed work:

- Install fiberglass under boards in 900 sq. ft. attic area of two-story house.
- Remove and replace necessary boards.
- Install wind tunnels.
- Install 2 R-61 roof vents.
- Install fiberglass in sidewalls, approx. 2000 sq. ft.
- Drill siding and redwood plug, chisel and putty, owner to sand and paint.
- Remove and replace siding, drill above second floor windows only.
- Install 4 8" × 16" soffit vents, 2 front, 2 rear.

We propose hereby to furnish material and labor—complete in accordance with above specifications—for the sum of cash on completion, $2307.

All material is guaranteed to be as specified. All work to be completed according to standard practices. Any alteration or deviation from the above specifications involving extra costs will be executed only upon written orders, and will become an extra charge over and above the estimate. All agreements are contingent upon strikes, accidents, or delays beyond our control. Owner to carry fire, tornado, and other necessary insurance. Our work is fully covered by Worker's Compensation Insurance.

Note: This proposal may be withdrawn by us if not accepted within 10 days.

Date: May 3, 2003
Authorized signature: F. Marryat

Acceptance of proposal: The above prices, specifications, and conditions are satisfactory and are hereby accepted. You are authorized to do the work as specified. Payment will be made upon completion.

Date of acceptance: May 6, 2003
Signature: Jack Easy

See also: ACCEPTANCES, ACKNOWLEDGMENTS, COVER LETTERS, CREDIT, INSTRUCTIONS, MEMOS, REFERENCES, REFUSALS, RESPONSES, SALES.

Requests and Inquiries

41

Know how to ask. There is nothing more difficult
for some people, nor, for others, easier.

—Baltasar Gracián

Letters of request (when you want to ask for something) and letters of inquiry (when you want to know something) are critical in maintaining the flow of ideas and resources among individuals and organizations. Because they are often the first contact between businesses and potential customers, between those seeking something and the employers, publishers, and vendors they are seeking it from, these letters must be good ambassadors.

Most commonplace requests (to change a life insurance beneficiary, to claim insurance benefits, to apply for a VA loan, to purchase a home, for federal employment) are initiated by a phone call and completed with the appropriate forms. Only in the case of problems are letters required.

Write Letters of Request/Inquiry When You Want

- adjustments (see COMPLAINTS)
- advice (see ADVICE)
- appointments/meetings/interviews (see APPLICATIONS, APPOINTMENTS, EMPLOYMENT, RÉSUMÉS)
- assistance: business/personal
- bids and estimates
- contributions/donations (see FUNDRAISING)
- credit information (see CREDIT)

- documents or copies of business/personal records
- donation (see FUNDRAISING)
- extension of deadline
- favors: business/personal
- forgiveness (see APOLOGIES)
- goods/services: prices/samples/information/brochures/product literature
- information/explanations/instructions
- introductions (see INTRODUCTIONS)
- loan (see CREDIT)
- payment (see COLLECTION, CREDIT)
- permission to reprint/use copyrighted material
- raise in salary (see EMPLOYMENT)
- reservation (see TRAVEL)
- speakers for your conference/banquet/workshop
- to borrow money (see CREDIT)
- to check on an unacknowledged gift (see FOLLOW-UP)
- to interview for a job (see APPLICATIONS, COVER LETTERS)
- to learn if a company has job openings
- to query an editor about a book or article idea (see QUERIES)
- zoning changes

- State clearly and briefly what you're requesting, beginning with a courtesy phrase like "Please send me . . ." or "May I please have . . ."
- Give details to help the person send you exactly what you want (reference numbers, dates, descriptions, titles).
- If appropriate, and if it will help the person furnish you more precisely with what you need, briefly explain the use you intend to make of the material. (When writing the county pathologist for information on procedures in a murder case, it helps the person to know that you are a mystery writer looking for background rather than a prosecutor building a case or a physician in search of medical details.)
- State the specific action or response you want from your reader.

- Explain why your reader might want to respond to your request. "The best way to get on in the world is to make people believe it's to their advantage to help you." (La Bruyère)
- If appropriate, offer to cover costs of photocopying, postage, or fees.
- Specify the date by which you need a response.
- At the end, if your letter is a long one, restate your request.
- Express your thanks or appreciation for the other person's time and attention and close with a confident statement that the other person will respond positively.
- Enclose a self-addressed stamped envelope (SASE), if appropriate. Otherwise, tell where to send the information or where to telephone, fax, or e-mail the response.

What Not to Say

- Don't simply request "information." Be specific. Some companies have hundreds of brochures dealing with their products and services. A vague request for "information" may or may not net you what you need. If you don't know what other information might be available or useful, add, "I would appreciate any other information you think might be helpful."
- Don't be apologetic (unless your request is time-consuming or difficult to supply). Avoid phrases like "I hope this is not too much trouble" and "I'm sorry to inconvenience you." Indicate in passing your respect for the other person's time, talents, and resources ("I know how busy you are") but don't dwell on the negative. Everyone has requests, and the more matter-of-fact and courteous you are, the better your chances of getting a positive reply.
- Avoid a highhanded approach that implies you are entitled to the information, service, or favor. You are making a request, not a demand.

Tips on Writing

∼ Be brief, avoiding unnecessary explanations or asking the same question in two different ways. Reread your letter to see if your questions are easy to answer. Most people sitting at information-supplying desks have too much mail and too little time.

↜ Use a subject line to quickly orient your reader: "Subject: cellular phone service"; "Subject: horse transporting"; "Re: piano tuning rates"; "Subject: airbag safety information"; "Re: mountaineering and ice climbing expeditions in North America"; "Subject: recipes using cranberries." For simple, businesslike requests, no salutation is necessary; the subject line can stand alone.

↜ When you have several requests, number and place each one on a separate line (from most to least important) so that the recipient can tick off each item as it is responded to.

↜ Be precise about the information you want: mailing instructions for the return of a hard drive, how to petition a county court for a legal name change, availability and rates for the high season, absentee figures for the period January 1 to June 30. The more information you give, the more helpful is the information you receive.

↜ Several letterwriting authorities advise not to end a letter of request with "thank you" or "thanking you in advance" (because these expressions seem to signal an end to the exchange), but both have become common and acceptable in current usage. Some people like the brisk wrap-up sound of it and use it automatically. You can also end with "I appreciate your time and attention" or "I look forward to hearing from you."

↜ Make it easy for someone to respond to you: enclose a survey or questionnaire; provide a postage-paid postcard printed with a message and fill-in blanks; leave space under each question on your letter so the person can jot down replies and return it in the accompanying SASE. When the other person is doing you a favor, and one of you must bear the cost of postage, materials, or other assistance, it is, of course, you who should offer to pay. Include a SASE when asking someone to make an effort on your behalf. When requesting information of companies who hope to make a sale to you, this is unnecessary.

Special Situations

↜ When writing to ask if an unacknowledged gift was received, describe the item, tell when you sent it, and offer a face-saving excuse for the person ("I know you are especially busy just now"). You might say you're inquiring because you insured the package and if it did not arrive, you want to follow up on it, or that you are wondering if you should put a "stop" order on the check. You're not required to give a reason for your inquiry, but doing so is tactful.

~ When requesting reservations for facilities for conferences, meetings, sales presentations, and other business activities, begin your inquiries with a telephone call to determine rates, date availability, and description of facilities. When writing to confirm your arrangements, include: time, date, number of expected attendees, required equipment and supplies, refreshment arrangements, billing information, name of contact person in your organization (if not you), and any other agreed-upon items.

~ When requesting a pay raise in writing (as opposed to an interview), begin by identifying your position in the company and the amount of raise you want. List your reasons for thinking a raise is appropriate: longer hours, more responsibility, work successes, noteworthy results, new skills. Whenever possible, use figures ("increase of 10%"). Emphasize the work you've done since your last pay raise. It is not productive to point to other people in the department who do less than you and are better compensated. Repeat your strongest argument and close with good wishes and an expression of appreciation.

~ To request a copy of your military record, write: Personnel Records Officer, National Personnel Records Center, 9700 Page Boulevard, St. Louis, MO 63132-5100. Begin with a subject line that gives your service or social security number. State what you need ("discharge papers") and, if appropriate, why you need them or no longer have your copy of them. Give your mailing address and daytime phone number.

~ Your letter requesting a zoning change will become part of the public record, so it must be factual, accurate, unemotional, and businesslike. State your reasons for requesting the change, modification, or variance. Include as much information as you can showing that, first, a zoning change will not harm the environs and, second, that it has potential benefits. Attach statements from neighbors, petitions, assessments, and other documents that bear on the issue.

~ When requesting your physician to release your medical records to another physician, hospital, or insurance company, write: "Dear Dr. [name], I hereby authorize you to release my medical file to [name of recipient]. I will appreciate this being done as soon as possible. Thank you."

~ When requesting permission to reprint copyrighted material, make it easy to say "yes." Include two copies of either a form or your letter so that the person can sign and date them and return one to you. Include a self-addressed stamped envelope. State precisely what you want to use (title of book or article, page numbers, line or paragraph numbers, and a photocopy of the excerpted material). Tell how you plan to use the material (the name of your book or article, approximate publication date, publisher, price, expected number of copies to be printed, whether you want U.S. or world rights, and anything else that describes the anticipated audience and distribution). Include the credit line you will be using, and ask for their approval of it. Express your appreciation for considering the permissions request and, if you wish, your admiration for the person's work.

~ When asking someone to speak at your meeting or conference, give the following information: your organization's name; date, time, and place of the event, with directions or a map; desired length and subject of the talk; the reason or focus for the event; a description of the group's interests and backgrounds to give the speaker some sense of the audience; an estimate of the size of the audience; your expectations of when the speaker would arrive and depart; whether you are paying a fee and the speaker's travel expenses and lodgings; what equipment (microphone, overhead projector) is available; the name and phone number of a contact person (if this is not you).

~ When requesting estimates, bids, proposals, or price quotes, be specific: quantities, deadlines (for bid and for completion of work); special requirements; types, model numbers, colors; a list of everything you expect to be included in the total. To ensure that no important consideration is omitted, use the eventual contract that will be offered as a model for your letter.

~ To compare different services (office maintenance, lawn care, driving schools, carpet cleaning) send the same letter requesting information to all such services in your area.

Format

~ Business requests that go outside the company are typed, usually on letterhead stationery. Memo paper is used for routine in-house requests.

~ Personal requests may be typed or handwritten on business or personal stationery. The more personal the request (advice, favors), the more suitable it is to handwrite the note on a foldover or personal stationery.

~ Postcards are useful for one-line requests.

~ If you make the same type of request repeatedly, use a form letter or memo paper with blank space to fill in the title of the article or sample you're requesting.

~ E-mail is often used to make requests of companies with websites and can be used for some casual or routine requests.

WORDS

appeal	grant	products	refer
assistance	grateful	prompt	require
brochures	immediately	query	rush
expedite	information	question	seek
favor	inquiry	questionnaire	solicit
furnish	instructions	quickly	urgent
generous	problem	reconsider	

PHRASES

additional information/time

answer the following questions

anticipate a favorable response

apply/ask for

appreciate any information/your cooperation/your help

as soon as possible

by return mail

count on/upon

direct me to the appropriate agency

have the goodness to

hope you are able to

I'd appreciate having/receiving/ obtaining

if you can find time in your busy schedule to

if you think it might be possible

I'm writing to ask you

institute inquiries

interested in receiving information/ learning more about

it would be most helpful

I would appreciate your assessment of

I would be grateful/most grateful if/for

look forward to hearing from you

offer some assistance

of great help to us

on account of/behalf of

please call me to discuss

please let me have your estimate by

please provide us with/send details about

please reply by

reply by return mail

respectfully request

take into consideration

thank you for your efforts in/to

trouble you to/for

we would appreciate your taking a few minutes to

would you be willing to/ good enough to

your considered opinion

SENTENCES

Can you tell me which government agency might be able to give me
   background information on Minamata disease in Japan?

Do you remember that you once offered to lend me Grandma's pearl ring
   for a special occasion?

Enclosed is a self-addressed stamped envelope/an International Reply
   Coupon for your reply.

How can a private citizen be named to the task force on the Resolution
   Trust Corporation?

I am preparing a report for which I need annualized total returns for one,
   three, and five years through December 31—can you provide these by
   March 15?

I'd like to know how one goes about getting on your talk show.

I have a favor to ask you, but I take "no" very well!

I'm wondering if you have the time to give us a little guidance.

Is it true that it's possible to have stars named for people and, if so, how
   does one go about it?

I would be interested in seeing some of the material that went into the
   preparation of your most recent occupational titles handbook.

May I use your name as a reference when applying for a cashier position
   with Mawson's Country Inn?

Please forward this letter to the appropriate person.

Please send me any literature you have on antioxidant vitamins.

This is a formal request to you to make some other arrangements for your
   cats; your lease clearly states that animals are not allowed in the building.

We are contacting several industrial window cleaning firms to invite
   estimates.

We do not understand footnote (b) of Exhibit H—could you please explain it?

Will you please send me a copy of your current foam and sponge rubber
   products catalog along with information on bulk order discounts?

Will you please send me a list of those trash haulers in Willard County that
   contract by volume rather than by flat fee?

Your order forms, prices, and ordering instructions are oriented toward
   institutions—can you tell me how an individual can obtain your materials?

PARAGRAPHS

The flyer that came with this month's telephone bill describes a telephone answering system that is available for $8.95 per month. It is not clear to me whether this is an outright purchase (if so, how many months of payment are involved?) or a lease arrangement. Please send me complete information.

The Pallant County Arts Board is attempting to determine whether it is meeting the needs of county artists, writers, playwrights, and musicians. Would you be so kind as to take a few minutes to fill out the enclosed questionnaire and return it to us in the self-addressed, stamped envelope? Please do not fold the questionnaire as results will be tabulated by computer.

I was unable to attend your talk on "Texture Performance of Metals" but would greatly appreciate reprints or preprints of anything you have written in this area. Thanks.

Will you please place my name on your mailing list to receive all announcements, newsletters, and information regarding business mailing regulations and tips? If you have booklets or materials of general interest, I would appreciate copies. Let me know if there is a charge. Thank you.

I'm wondering if you could give me about five minutes of your time on the phone some time next week. I am writing a research paper on global economics, and think that you may have answers to some of my questions. I found when I interviewed other people that it takes from three to five minutes—no more. If you are unable to do this, I will understand. Enclosed is a self-addressed postcard—please indicate on it a time when I could call you.

I understand that the basement meeting room of the Oakdale Community Church is available for use by various small groups. Would it be possible for our study group to meet there one evening a month? Our own church does not have any such facilities, and we have found it difficult to move around to a different home each month. We could meet on nearly any Tuesday, Wednesday, or Thursday evening that is convenient for you.

We have just moved to the area and are interested in changing from our out-of-state insurance agent to someone local. Please send complete information for the following types of insurance: auto, home, whole life. We prefer that you do not follow up with a call or visit; as soon as we have studied the material, we will call you if we have questions or if we would like to schedule a meeting. Thank you.

I respectfully request to be excused from jury duty beginning Nov. 2. I am a veterinarian in a two-person practice. My partner will be in India (copies of airline tickets are attached) the entire month of November. The clinic would effectively be without a veterinarian, and I do not see how we could arrange for adequate care of our many patients during that time.

I will be calling on barbers in your area the week of June 4–June 11 to show a line of completely new Swedish barbering tools. Made of tempered steel, guaranteed for twenty years, and sold with a service contract at no extra cost, these implements have already won three first-place Mentions of Merit from the American Academy of Barbers. I would like to stop by The Hair Bear sometime during that week. Enclosed is a self-addressed, stamped post-card—please indicate a time that would be convenient for you. To thank you for your time, I will be bringing you a gift.

SAMPLE LETTERS

Dear Axel,

I plan to be on Sanburan Island in the near future, and am wondering if you could schedule a tour for me of the Tropical Belt Coal Company. Coal is one of my hobbies.

Enclosed is a self-addressed envelope and an International Reply Coupon for your response.

Thanks so much for your time and attention.

                                                   Sincerely,

Dear Mr. Babington:

I would like your permission to reprint the following material from your book, *Diplomacy Today*:

    page iv: paragraph 2: "Since 1701 . . . and nothing was said."
    page 294: final sentence: "If it appears that . . . only Henry VIII knows the truth."

This material would be used in my book, *The New Diplomacy*, to be published by Baines-Gandish in 2003. The book will retail for $16.95 and is expected to have a some-what limited market. I will send you a complimentary copy, and you would of course be given credit as follows:

Diplomacy Today (New York: Goddard Publishing, 1982), pp. iv, 294. Reprinted with permission from Spencer Babington.

I'm enclosing two copies of this letter. If you agree to grant me permission, please write "permission granted," sign and date one of the copies, and return it to me in the enclosed self-addressed stamped envelope.

I would appreciate being able to use those two excerpts. Your book was an eye-opener when it appeared, and it has remained a standard for me of fine writing, clear thinking, and inspired research.

Sincerely,

~

TO: Emmerick Demolition and Salvage

In September 2001 you submitted a bid to Brooker Real Estate to remove two structures, one at 1898 Stratfield and one at 1921 Cabell. Since that bid, two additional properties have been purchased by Brooker Real Estate that will require demolition this summer.

I invite you to submit a rebid to include the two additional sites plus tank removal at another site (please see attachment for description and addresses of sites).

Contact me if you will be submitting a bid as I would like to schedule a meeting to discuss this project further and to answer your questions.

~

Dear Morris,

I'm thinking of leaving Langdon Glass Works (I'll tell you why next time I see you) and am currently on the lookout for a good sales management position.

You seem to know everyone in the industry (and everybody knows you)—would you mind letting me know if you hear of any openings?

I appreciate being able to ask you this. Let's get together soon.

Sincerely,

~

TO: LeRoy Investment Services

Please send me information on investment opportunities for the small, independent investor. I would specifically like to know:

1. Requirements, interest rates, and other information on certificates of deposit, treasury bills, municipal bonds, mutual funds, and other investment programs.

2. The commission your company charges for handling such investments.

3. The performance records on your investment programs over the past two years.

4. The names of several people who have used your services recently.

~

TO: Zoning Commission
FROM: Barbara Topham
DATE: March 10, 2002
RE: Zoning File 9117, Children's Playschool

    I am writing to urge you to approve the Special Condition Use Permit sought by Children's Playschool. As we live directly across the street, we would be one of those most affected, and I believe it is important for you to know that the change would not appear to adversely affect the neighborhood.

⁓

Dear Archie,

    At the last meeting of the Open Door organizing committee, we discussed the need for new members. Your name came up several times as someone who has spent a good deal of time, money, and energy at the Food Shelf. We all felt you could add creativity, excitement, and inspiration to our efforts.

    Would you consider a one-year commitment to the committee? This would involve one general monthly meeting, one weekly subcommittee meeting, some telephone work, and your regular weekly volunteer hours. I think you are currently spending about ten hours a week at the center. If you need to cut down on those hours to devote time to the committee, that would be fine.

    Although this is something you'll need to think about, we are hoping to have your answer within the next two weeks so that we can publish the new roster in our year-end appeals. We are all hoping that you'll say "yes" but will understand if you cannot. In any case, we are grateful for the time and talent you have already given the center.

With best wishes,

⁓

TO: Metropolitan Council

    I understand that you are funding a special multi-family recycling program for those who live in apartments or condominiums with twenty or more units.

    I am writing on behalf of our neighborhood association, as we have a number of such buildings, and residents are interested in such a program. Please send information. We would also be interested in having someone from the Council speak at one of our meetings to explain the program.

Sincerely,

⁓

See also: APPOINTMENTS, COLLECTION, CREDIT, EMPLOYMENT, FUNDRAISING, INTRODUCTIONS, INVITATIONS, ORDERS, RESPONSES, SALES, THANK YOU, TRAVEL.

Responses

42

I was gratified to be able to answer promptly. I said I didn't know.

—MARK TWAIN

Prompt and thoughtful responses to incoming mail may be as important to your business as your carefully drafted sales letters. They are equally rewarding in your personal life. "A prompt response is a sign of vigorous and authentic concern; nothing could be more flattering or touching to the recipient." (Jennifer Williams)

When responding with a straightforward "yes" or "no," see ACCEPTANCES or REFUSALS.

Write Responses to

- announcements
- apologies
- complaints (see ADJUSTMENTS, APOLOGIES)
- congratulations
- expressions of sympathy
- gifts and kindnesses (see also THANK YOU)
- inquiries
- invitations (see also ACCEPTANCES, REFUSALS)
- letters addressed to someone temporarily absent
- requests: information/instructions/samples/introductions/ contributions/payments/letters of reference

353

- In the first sentence, state what you are responding to (a letter, invitation, memo) so the other person knows immediately why you're writing. In some cases, use a reference line ("Re: Order # 2K881").
- Briefly give all requested information.
- When you cannot respond completely to a request, include names, addresses, and phone numbers where more information can be obtained.
- If immediate action is not possible, tell what is being done and by what date results can be expected.
- If appropriate, offer further assistance.
- Let the other person know you appreciate them and are pleased to be responding.
- Close with good wishes, an expression of confidence in your product or service, or a remark about future contacts.

- Don't give more information than your reader requested. In most cases, this is unnecessary and unhelpful.
- Don't misspell the other person's name. It is immediately noticed and weakens the effect of your response.
- Don't allow an irritated tone to creep in, even when you consider the letter you're responding to offensive, uninformed, or inane.

Tips on Writing

∼ Respond promptly. "It should be the aim of every business office to answer all its mail the same day it is received." (Alexander L. Sheff and Edna Ingalls) That advice, written in 1942, may be an impossibility today, but it is still a good goal.

∼ When responding to a number of questions or to a complicated letter, organize your letter elements by using numbers, bullets, or asterisks and leave plenty of white space.

Special Situations

∼ Customer inquiries provide an unparalleled opportunity to promote your goods and services as well as your company. Handle them with the utmost respect, speed, efficiency, and good cheer—inquiries are generally forerunners of sales. Answer questions as completely as possible and enclose supplementary lists, articles, reports, brochures, flyers, or catalogs. Make it easy for the customer to follow up (place an order, find a local distributor, call a toll-free number).

∼ When responding to a job offer, express pleasure in your future association with the company; say something complimentary about the job interview and interviewer; restate, when appropriate, the conditions of employment; renew your confidence that you and the company are a good match; thank the person. Sometimes your response is a qualified one; you want the position but cannot accept some condition of employment (hours, salary, vacation time). Explain that they are your first choice except for that issue; can anything be done about it?

∼ Response to an invitation marked "R.S.V.P." or "Please reply" is mandatory, obligatory, required, compulsory, imperative, and essential. If you do not plan to attend, the same is true for "Regrets only." If your invitation includes no R.S.V.P., no "Regrets only," and no reply card, you need not respond. This type of invitation is used for large affairs—political gatherings, fundraising events, business cocktail parties, conventions. Guidelines for responding to an invitation: Reply within several days of receiving it. State clearly that you will or will not be able to attend. Mirror the invitation, using the same format, and almost all the same words. If you have cards with your name or personalized stationery, you can simply write under your name "accepts with pleasure the kind invitation of . . ." and repeat the kind of event, time, date, and place.

∼ Invitations (wedding, bar mitzvah, bat mitzvah) and announcements (engagement, graduation, birth, adoption) require a response (letter or congratulatory card with handwritten note), but if you don't attend the event or celebration you aren't expected to send a gift.

∼ Expressions of condolence require a response, which can take a number of forms, from handwritten formal notes of thanks (see THANK YOU) to printed newspaper announcements of appreciation (see ANNOUNCE-MENTS). In the case of a public figure, printed acknowledgments can be sent to large numbers of people who were not personally known to the family (see ACKNOWLEDGMENTS). Responses may be brief, may be sent up to six weeks following the funeral, and may be written by someone on behalf of the person closest to the deceased.

~ Responding to fundraising appeals does not often involve a letter, or even a comment from you; most organizations simply want your check, which you tuck into the provided envelope. If you write a letter, mention the sum you're donating, ask for a receipt (for tax purposes) if you wish, and attach a completed matching gift form if your employer participates in this program. If you are not familiar with the sponsoring organization, you can obtain (free) up to three reports on individual agencies by writing: National Charities Information Bureau, 19 Union Square West, New York, NYC 10003-3395. Enclose a # 10 self-addressed stamped envelope as it's a nonprofit organization. You can also visit them online at www.give.org.

~ Respond to an apology if only to acknowledge that you received it. What you do after that is your choice. "The person who can meet an apology more than halfway and forgive with a graciousness that makes the aggressor feel almost glad that the trouble occurred, but very certain that it shall never occur again, is the one who will make beautiful and lifelong friendships." (Julia W. Wolfe)

~ Birth and adoption announcements are responded to with cards or letters of congratulations. When writing about a child born with defects or a disability, avoid inappropriate or overly sympathetic remarks. Although this situation can entail difficulties and grief, it does not call for a sympathy letter. Until you know how the parents are feeling (devastated, concerned but basically optimistic, happy to have the child), do not reveal your own feelings—they may be wide of the mark. Do not write: "You're not going to keep it, are you?" "I think you should sue the hospital." "Is one of you a carrier for this?" "Maybe the baby won't live; that would be best all around." "Whose fault was it?" "Did you drink while you were pregnant?" "I guess it could have been worse." "God only sends burdens to those who can bear them." Instead, say that you've heard that they have a new little one and that you're thinking of them. You may want to avoid commercial "new baby" cards. Later, when you know how the parents are feeling, you can respond on a more emotional level.

~ In responding to flattering and enthusiastic congratulatory messages, say "thank you" first of all. Then be gracious. "A compliment is a gift, not to be thrown away carelessly unless you want to hurt the giver." (Eleanor Hamilton) Reflect the compliment back to the giver ("how nice of you to write," "your letter touched me," "how thoughtful of you").

~ When asked what you or someone close to you would like for a graduation, anniversary, birthday, or holiday gift, mention a broad gift category ("books," for example, but not "money") that will provide a range of prices for the giver.

Format

∾ Choosing a format for a letter or note of response is simple: do as you were done unto. If the original letter was typed, type yours; if it was handwritten, handwrite yours. If the invitation was formal, your response should be written in the third-person formal manner. If it was informal, first-person style on personal stationery, you respond similarly.

∾ If you use formal notes engraved or printed with your name, respond to invitations by penning in "accepts with pleasure" or "declines with regret" under your name. Add the date so that your recipient knows which invitation you're responding to.

∾ Forms are useful in responding to routine inquiries. Requests for information, materials, or samples can be handled with a printed card saying, "This comes to you at your request" or "Thank you for your inquiry. Enclosed are informational materials." Or, design a brief, general form letter that thanks the person for the inquiry and indicates what information is being forwarded. Include a checklist of publications so you can indicate those that you are enclosing or mailing under separate cover. You can also leave blanks: "Thank you for your inquiry about _____." Or design a form with every conceivable response and then check off the appropriate one ("Your order has been sent." "We are temporarily out of stock." "Please reorder in ___ days." "This is a prepaid item, and your payment has not yet been received." "Please indicate a second color choice.").

∾ Reply to an e-mail message with an e-mail. When letterwriters give an e-mail address in their letters, you may respond that way if your response is brief or routine.

WORDS

acknowledge	enclosed	inform	respond
appreciate	feedback	notify	return
confirm	grateful	regarding	send

PHRASES

according to your letter	as mentioned in your letter
appreciate your business	delighted to receive
appreciate your calling our attention to	enclosed you will find

for further information

happy to hear from you

I'm sending you

in response to your letter of

meant a great deal to me

pleased to be able to send you

thank you for your letter telling
  us about

to let you know

under separate cover

want to reply to your letter

we appreciate your interest in

we have carefully/thoughtfully
  considered your letter

your sympathetic/delightful/
  helpful/comforting/encouraging
  letter/note

SENTENCES

As requested, we are submitting a budget figure for construction surveillance for the water and sewer line project.

Here is the information you requested about the tank closure.

I have received your apology, and hope you will not give the matter another thought.

I hope this information is useful to you in resolving any remaining title issues.

In response to your request for sealed bids, a bid from Dale Heating and Plumbing is enclosed.

Letters like yours have been a great comfort to us all.

Mary Postgate has asked me to respond to your letter about the settlement agreement dated January 30.

Thank you for sharing with me the lovely memories you have of Father.

Thank you for taking the time to write, and please excuse my delay in responding to your letter.

Thank you so much for your kind words/for your letter.

This is to let you know that the report you requested will be mailed as soon as it is completed (Dec. 3).

We are pleased to send you the enclosed information about Weycock United Sugar Company.

We thank you for your inquiry, and are pleased to enclose a sample snack bar.

You have asked me to estimate the fees that would be required for our services.

PARAGRAPHS

Your book proposal has been read with great interest. We will want to have several other people read and evaluate it before submitting it for discussion at our weekly acquisition meeting. I will let you know as soon as we have made a decision.

Thank you for your inquiry about Gabbadeo Wines. Enclosed are several brochures describing our vineyards and products and a list of vendors in your area.

In response to your fax of June 3, I'm sending the three original contracts along with two copies of each, four pro forma invoices with two copies of each, and a bill of lading. Please let us know at once if everything is in order.

We received your impressive résumé today and look forward to meeting with you. Because of the large number of responses we received to our advertisement, however, it may be two or three weeks before you hear from us.

Thank you for your generous and sincere apology. I am entirely willing to put the incident behind me, and I look forward to continuing our old association.

In response to your letter of September 16, we have made a number of inquiries and are pleased to tell you that most of the staff here is agreeable to helping you with your research project. Please telephone the department secretary Arthur Eden to let him know what day or days you would like to spend with us.

SAMPLE LETTERS

Dear Ms. Stedman:

Thank you for your interest in our Quick Mail program. Due to an overwhelming demand, requests for our brochure and video cassette have far outpaced our supplies. However, a new shipment has been ordered, and we'll send you your materials as soon as we receive them.

Once you receive our kit, you'll learn all about the money-saving ideas that our program has to offer—reducing your mail float time, accelerating your cash flow, escalating your postage discounts, and still other techniques.

We'll look forward to hearing from you after you have had a chance to look over the materials.

Sincerely,

Dear Mr. Einhorn:

In response to your inquiry of December 3, I am sorry to tell you that Mr. Belton was with us for only a short time and our records do not indicate a forwarding address. I believe he used to also work for Lorraine Linens. You might try them.

⁓

Dear Barbara and Garnet,

Your love and support these past few weeks have been a great comfort to all of us. I am especially grateful for the way you took over with the children when I couldn't. And, Garnet, thank you for being a pallbearer. I know Edward would have wanted you there. I hope you have not exhausted your reserves of friendship, because I feel I am going to need your kindness and understanding for a while yet.

With love and gratitude,

⁓

Dear Louisa William,

I was delighted to receive and read your letter of August 3, 2005. Thank you for your kind remarks about the Alconleigh Suites and the excellent team that operates the hotel.

Louisa Kroesig, Sales and Catering Manager, is honored to receive this recognition for her staff. In addition, Christian Talbot, General Manager, on behalf of the entire hotel team, is pleased with your compliments about our meeting and exceeding the expectations of the Jassy/Radlett wedding group.

Thank you for allowing us to be your hotel of choice—both for hotel accommodations and for your wedding reception—and for providing us with the privilege of introducing our brand of hospitality to your guests from across the United States.

We look forward to being of service in the future and feel privileged to have earned your continued business.

Thanks again for sharing your satisfaction with us.

⁓

See also: ACCEPTANCES, ACKNOWLEDGMENTS, ADJUSTMENTS, APOLOGIES, COVER LETTERS, FAMILY, FOLLOW-UP, GOODWILL, REFUSALS, SENSITIVE, THANK YOU.

Résumés

43

*We judge ourselves by what we feel capable of doing,
while others judge us by what we have already done.*

—HENRY WADSWORTH LONGFELLOW

A résumé gives prospective employers a written summary of your qualifications and work history. It convinces the reader that you're a good candidate for the position and that you should be invited for an interview.

Although it lacks most of the features of a sales letter (few employers are dazzled by extravagant claims and catchy language), the résumé is a letter in which you are both the seller and the product.

When applying for a job, you might use one or two of the following: *résumé*, a businesslike summary of your work history, education, and career goals; *cover letter*, a brief letter written to accompany a résumé; *letter of application*, a combination cover letter and brief, informal résumé. See COVER LETTERS and APPLICATIONS for assistance with the second two.

Send a Résumé When

- applying for a franchise
- applying for a job or internship
- applying for membership in certain organizations
- applying to universities/degree programs
- inquiring about openings at a company
- responding to an employment ad

- Place your name, address, and daytime telephone number (and possibly e-mail address, fax number, and website address) at the top right or at the top center of your résumé (the top left position may get stapled or punched).
- State the position or kind of job you're seeking.
- Detail your work experience and job skills. There are two basic approaches.

  1. The traditional reverse chronological employment format starts by listing your most recent position and going back through time. This is the easiest format to use, but it has its weaknesses if there are gaps in your job history, if you're new to the job market, or if your previous jobs don't seem to relate well to the one you are seeking. The emphasis in this listing is on concrete information: dates of employment, name and full address of employer, job title, job duties, reason for leaving, if appropriate.

  2. The non-chronological résumé (also called a skills-oriented or functional résumé) stresses your qualifications and abilities. You group job experiences according to a specific skill. For example, under "Leadership Skills" you write, "Supervised night shift at Hooper & Co. for two years." Under "Interpersonal Skills" write, "As the mayor's troubleshooter, I was often called upon to intervene in disputes, negotiate contracts, and otherwise deal with constituents, politicians, and city personnel under difficult circumstances." "Organizational Skills" might include: "I was hired at Arnold-Browne to reorganize the accounting department, which was barely functioning at the time due to staff turnover, low morale, lack of department guidelines, and poor use of office space. At the end of two years, I was commended by the company president for 'unparalleled organizing skills.'"

  You can also combine the two approaches; under each job listed in reverse chronological order, group skills used in that position. Or, slant your résumé directly toward the job under consideration by listing the general qualifications and specific qualifications you have for it.

- Give the essential facts of your education: name of school, city and state where it is located, years you attended, the diploma or certificate you earned, the course of studies you pursued, special training, significant honors or memberships.
- List publications, if appropriate.

What Not to Say

- Don't include a photograph or personal information (age or birth year, weight, height, marital or financial status, children, ethnicity, disability, religious or political affiliation) unless it is pertinent to the situation you are seeking. For example, to apply for a position as a weight control group leader, a mention of your weight history is probably indicated. It is often illegal for prospective employers to ask questions about age, sex, race, and religion.

- Don't tell what you expect the company to do for you. ("This position is a wonderful opportunity to learn about the marketing side of the automotive industry.") Emphasize instead what you can contribute to the company.

- Don't present your accomplishments so that they say, "Here is what I've done." Instead, phrase them to say, "Here is what I can do for you." For example, "I have the experience and ability to help you increase production efficiency. While I was supervisor at Fortis & Co., department overruns decreased 32%."

- Don't tell every single thing you've done. Filler material detracts from a strong résumé. People who throw in all the extras on the theory that it "can't hurt" may be wrong. Don't include information on childhood, early schooling, hobbies, or interests (unless they relate directly to the position). Omit work you've done in the past that you don't want to do again, unless this would leave unexplained holes in your résumé.

- Don't embellish, exaggerate, tell half-truths, or, of course, lie. Many companies have résumé fact-checkers and if you're found out, you will be dismissed, will suffer embarrassment and humiliation, and may be liable for civil charges. Trying to make yourself sound better than you are is often a tip-off that you may not be well qualified for that particular position—or happy in it.

- Don't be too modest either by playing down your accomplishments. Have someone who knows you evaluate your final draft.

- Don't use "etc." It is uninformative and irritating and conveys excessive casualness.

- Don't use weak adjectives and adverbs. Remove every "very" you find and such lukewarm words as "good," "wonderful," "exciting." Use instead strong, perhaps even unusual, nouns and verbs. See lists of adjectives, nouns, and verbs in this chapter.

- Don't use jargon, long, involved phrases, a bookish vocabulary you don't normally use, or acronyms (unless the acronym is so familiar in your field that it would be insulting to spell it out).
- Don't mention salary in a résumé; this is better discussed in an interview (and then try to get your interviewer to mention a figure before you do).

Tips on Writing

∾ Before writing a résumé, assemble two kinds of information: facts about yourself and facts about your prospective employer and the position. Call the company to ask questions. Research the company at the library. Speak to people who work there or who know the company. When you tell a prospective employer what you can do for their company, the implication is that you've studied the company enough to know where you might fit in; this is appealing. Although you cannot change the facts of your employment history, you can emphasize certain skills and qualifications if you know that this is what the employer wants. The employer may want creativity, for example, and none of your previous jobs emphasized it. Check other areas of your life to see where you have shown creativity—art classes, hobby photography, teaching pottery. When prospective employers see a résumé that has obviously been written especially for them, they give it more than the sixty seconds that most résumés get. By presenting as clear a picture of yourself as you can in terms of the employer's needs, you make it easy for them to determine quickly whether there is a match.

∾ Your résumé may be skimmed by a human resources assistant, scanned into a computer, or screened by a recruiter. It must appeal to all three: short paragraphs and white space and good headings to catch the eye of the assistant; plenty of appropriate keywords (see below) for the computer; a logical and persuasive organization of material for the recruiter.

∾ Large companies use Optical Character Readers (OCRs) to scan incoming résumés. Software identifies keywords and stores the résumés in a large database. When a new employee is needed, the database is searched by keywords to identify applicants who have the needed skills. Some career counselors recommended a special keyword section with a listing of terms that might get your résumé pulled. Others point out that the computer will find the terms whether they are in one paragraph or spread out through the résumé. What is critical is that your résumé contain the words most likely to identify you for the position you want. Tips for scanned résumés: put only your name on the first line as that's what the software is expecting; use jargon, acronyms, and other words commonly used in your field, along with their logical synonyms; identify abilities specifically, for example, name the computer software you're familiar with (don't simply list "word-processing skills"); use variations of words ("administrator," "administered") so that the program will pick up either; be specific ("advertising manager" instead of "manager" so that no matter which is searched for, it'll be caught; use only one date for your education (the date you received your degree) or the program will assume you simply spent time there; use both "R.N." and "Registered Nurse" in case only one has been requested; check the advertisement you're responding to and be certain the words used in it appear on your résumé.

⌐∾ Your résumé is only as long as it needs to be. Most authorities recommend no more than one or two pages. In *The Smart Job Search*, Mark L. Makos says, "Unless it is not important to you to get a job, a one-page résumé is your only choice." However, for many academic and professional positions, you may need more than two pages—as many as twelve perhaps, if you have a long list of publications, patents, cases, conference presentations, or other itemizations. Whether one page or twelve, your résumé must be tightly written and readable: use simple, short sentences, keep paragraphs short, and leave plenty of white space and ample margins. "Think of a résumé as a sixty-second television commercial: that's probably all the time the reader is going to spend on it." (Lassor A. Blumenthal)

∾ Sample headings and divisions (you will generally have no more than five or six) that might be useful to you in constructing your résumé include:

Activities	Employment Objective
Additional Accomplishments	Executive Profile
Additional Experience	Experience
Awards, Honors, Offices	Extracurricular Activities
Background Summary	Highlighted Qualifications
Career Highlights	Interpersonal Skills
Career Objective	Job Objective
Career Summary	Key Qualifications
Communication Skills	Leadership Skills
Copywriting Experience	Management Profile
Editorial Experience	Managerial Experience
Education	Memberships

Negotiating Skills	Relevant Accomplishments
New Product Development Skills	Relevant Experience
Office Management Skills	Retail Sales Experience
Office Skills	Résumé
Organizational and Managerial Skills	Skills
Overview of Qualifications	Skills Summary
Professional Achievements	Special Skills
Professional Affiliations	Summary of Qualifications
Professional Background	Summary of Work History
Professional Experience	Supervisory Skills
Professional History	Systems Skills
Professional Profile	Technical Experience
Professional Qualifications	Training
Promotional Skills	Volunteer Work
Related Experience	Work Experience

~ Concentrate on your strengths; you don't have to include everything you've ever done. For each characteristic that you think your employer might want (leadership ability, problem solving, initiative), assemble examples from your work history.

~ There are three ways to refer to yourself in a résumé: (1) in the first person ("I managed the Midway Pro Bowl for three years, and saw it double in profits during that time"); (2) in the third person ("She has worked in a number of areas of radio broadcasting, including . . ." or "Dr. Patikar organized a new patient outcare service"); (3) without a pronoun ("Developed a new method of twinning steel"). Each style has advantages and disadvantages. The first can be wearying with all its "I"s (omit as many as possible), the second can appear remote and pretentious, and the third may seem abrupt. Use the style you feel most comfortable with, regardless of what you perceive as its benefits or disadvantages. In any case, do not refer to yourself as "the writer" ("The writer has six years' experience . . .").

~ Use strong, active verbs. Instead of the weaker "I did this" or "I was responsible for that," write "I managed," "I developed," "I directed." See the list of active verbs in this chapter.

~ Make all listings parallel in form: "I directed . . . I supervised . . . I increased . . ." Not: "I directed . . . I was a supervisor . . . I have increased."

∼ You will use two tenses in a résumé: the present tense for categories like career goal ("Desire position with . . .") and skills ("I am fluent in French, Italian, Spanish, and German"); the past tense for categories like work experience ("Headed all major advertising campaigns . . .") and professional accomplishments ("I won a six-state cabinetmaking competition").

∼ Use numbers to report successful outcomes of your work. Even if you were only partly responsible for increasing sales, decreasing expenditures, or coming in under budget for the first time in ten years, mention the figures. State how many people you supervised, how many copies of your books were sold, how many projects you oversaw, how much time or money you saved the company, the size of the budget you were responsible for, the percentage reduction in absenteeism in your department, the percentage increase in productivity at your station. Figures are persuasive.

∼ Resilience is an important qualification in a world where information and technology develop at high speeds. Emphasize your flexibility and ability to learn new tasks and adapt to new situations by making your past jobs sound different from each other. For example, if you've held several positions as an executive assistant, list under one position that you reorganized the filing system, under another that you trained employees in the use of the new telephone system, under yet another that you managed the office for three months while your supervisor was taking a leave of absence.

∼ Use only years, not months, when dating your work history.

∼ You need not mention the reason for leaving a position; if the employer wants to know, this will be brought up in the interview. Readily accepted reasons include: moving, returning to school, seeking a better position, unforeseen changes in your former job.

∼ The old résumé standby, "References available upon request," isn't necessary since it is taken for granted that later in the process references will be requested by them and supplied by you. Include the line only if you need to fill white space at the end of your résumé. Always ask people in advance if you can use them as references.

∼ Don't use the same boilerplate résumé for each job you apply for. Each résumé should be tailored to the particular company and typed or printed freshly (no photocopies).

∼ After you proofread your final draft, have at least two other people read it for you. The error that two of you miss will jump out at your prospective employer.

∼ Don't staple, glue, or seal your résumé into a binder or folder (unless requested to). The pages should be loose and paperclipped together; they are easier to handle. Mail your résumé and cover letter in a 9" × 12" envelope so they arrive unfolded and crisp-looking.

∼ In some situations include work samples, publications, or other supplementary materials.

∼ Check your library or bookstore for books devoted solely to résumé writing. Two suggestions: David F. Noble, *Gallery of Best Résumés: A Collection of Quality Résumés by Professional Résumé Writers*; Wendy S. Enelow, *Résumé Winners From the Pros* (includes names and addresses of professional résumé writers).

Special Situations

∼ If you prefer that your present employer doesn't know you're job-hunting, refer inquiries to your home phone or address and ask that references from your present employer wait until you and the prospective employer feel sure of the match.

∼ When given an application form to fill out for a job, you may attach a résumé to it.

∼ First-time job seekers encounter the classic frustration: They won't hire me because I don't have experience, and I don't have experience because they won't hire me. It is, however, possible to structure an appealing résumé without a significant work history. Summer jobs show dependability, initiative, responsibility. Extracurricular activities illustrate leadership potential, the ability to complete projects, and special interests. Awards, honors, GPA, elected offices, and scholarships indicate accomplishments and show that you have been singled out from your peers. Volunteer work, athletics, and organization memberships help define you and give you a profile. This type of résumé benefits from a skills orientation; you state that you are responsible, dependable, hardworking, a quick learner, or loyal and give illustrative examples.

∼ When asked to furnish a brief biographical sketch (or bio) for program notes, a newspaper article, or a company newsletter, your résumé will help you write it. A bio is written in narrative fashion, is far briefer and less specific than a résumé, and aims to capture the essence rather than the details of who you are professionally.

∼ When applying for a franchise, follow FTC guidelines. You may want a lawyer to help with some of the correspondence.

Format

~ All résumés are typed, printed, or machine-produced on good bond paper (white or off-white), on one side only, in sharp black elite or pica type (no script or fancy font). They look professional, conservative, and straightforward. In a few fields, you might obtain a job using a highly creative résumé with graphics, colored inks, and an offbeat design. For this approach, however, you must understand your market—to the point perhaps of knowing someone at the company who obtained a job that way. This type of résumé receives admiring looks, but is often passed over for the more "stable"-looking résumé.

~ When your résumé will be scanned: use only white paper; don't use graphic elements, small type, or unusual fonts (Times Roman or Ariel are good choices); don't use italics, underlining, or boldface; use asterisks instead of bullets as they are read as periods. OCRs like reading boring, homogeneous résumés; use this style only for them.

~ Fax your résumé only if you have been asked to do so or someone needs it at once. Faxed résumés don't look as good as those on résumé paper.

~ Résumés may be e-mailed in certain situations: the classified ad gives an e-mail address and asks that résumés be sent there; you find the job opening on the company website and they encourage sending your résumé by e-mail. Check with them first about any special e-mail requirements.

WORDS (ACTIVE VERBS)

accelerated	adjusted	amended	assembled
accentuated	administered	analyzed	assessed
accepted	adopted	anticipated	assigned
accommodated	advanced	applied	assisted
accomplished	advised	appointed	attained
accounted for	advocated	appraised	attended
achieved	aided	approached	augmented
acquired	allayed	appropriated	authored
acted	alleviated	approved	authorized
adapted	allocated	arbitrated	awarded
added	altered	arranged	balanced
addressed	amassed	articulated	began

bettered
bid
blended
boosted
bought
brought
budgeted
built
calculated
captured
carried out
carved
catalogued
categorized
caused
celebrated
centralized
chaired
challenged
championed
charged
charted
checked
chose
clarified
classified
cleared
closed
coached
collaborated
collated
collected
combined
commanded
commissioned

committed
communicated
compared
compiled
completed
composed
computed
conceived
conducted
confirmed
connected
conserved
considered
consolidated
constructed
consulted
contacted
continued
contracted
contributed
controlled
converted
cooperated
coordinated
corrected
corresponded
counseled
crafted
created
cultivated
cut
dealt
decided
decreased
defined

defrayed
delegated
delivered
demonstrated
deployed
designated
designed
detailed
detected
determined
developed
devised
diagnosed
directed
disbursed
discovered
dispatched
dispensed
displayed
disseminated
dissolved
distributed
diversified
divided
documented
doubled
downsized
drafted
drew up
drove
earned
economized
edited
educated
effected

elaborated
eliminated
emphasized
enabled
enacted
encouraged
enforced
engineered
enhanced
enlarged
enlisted
enriched
enrolled
ensured
entered
enticed
equipped
established
estimated
evaluated
examined
exceeded
exchanged
executed
exercised
exhibited
expanded
expedited
experienced
experimented
exported
extended
extracted
fabricated
facilitated

factored	heightened	invested	mended
familiarized	held	investigated	mentored
fashioned	helped	invited	merged
fielded	hired	involved	met
filed	hosted	isolated	met deadlines
finalized	hurried	issued	minimized
financed	identified	itemized	mobilized
finished	illustrated	joined	modeled
fixed	implemented	judge	moderated
focused	imported	justified	modernized
followed	improved	launched	modified
forecast	improvised	learned	molded
forged	incorporated	lectured	monitored
formed	increased	led	motivated
formulated	indexed	lessened	mounted
forwarded	influenced	leveraged	moved
fostered	informed	licensed	multiplied
fought	infused	liquidated	named
found	initiated	litigated	narrated
founded	innovated	located	narrowed
framed	inserviced	logged	navigated
fulfilled	inspected	lowered	negotiated
functioned as	inspired	maintained	netted
funded	installed	managed	nominated
furnished	instilled	mandated	notified
furthered	instituted	maneuvered	obtained
gained	instructed	manufactured	offered
gathered	integrated	mapped	officiated
generated	interacted	marked	opened
governed	interpreted	marketed	operated
grew	intervened	mastered	optimized
grouped	interviewed	masterminded	orchestrated
guided	introduced	maximized	ordered
handled	invented	measured	organized
headed	inventoried	mediated	originated

outdistanced
outlined
outsourced
overcame
overhauled
oversaw
paced
packaged
packed
parlayed
participated
partnered
perfected
performed
persuaded
piloted
pinpointed
pioneered
placed
planned
positioned
predicted
prepared
prescribed
presented
preserved
presided
prevented
printed
prioritized
processed
procured
produced
profiled
programmed

progressed
projected
promoted
proofread
proposed
protected
proved
provided
publicized
published
purchased
quadrupled
qualified
quantified
quoted
raised
ran
ranked
rated
reached
read
realigned
realized
rearranged
rebuilt
received
recognized
recommended
reconciled
reconstructed
recorded
recovered
recruited
rectified
redesigned

redirected
reduced costs
reengineered
referred
regained
registered
regulated
rehabilitated
reimbursed
reinforced
rejuvenated
related
remained
remedied
remodeled
rendered
renegotiated
renewed
reorganized
repaired
replaced
replicated
reported
repositioned
represented
reproduced
researched
reshaped
resolved
responded
restored
restructured
retained
retooled
retrieved

returned
revamped
reversed
reviewed
revised
revitalized
revived
revolutionized
rotated
routed
safeguarded
salvaged
satisfied
saved
scanned
scheduled
screened
searched
secured
selected
sent
sequenced
served
serviced
set strategy
set up
settled
shaped
shepherded
shipped
shortened
showed
signed
simplified
sold

solicited	submitted	tested	underlined
solidified	succeeded	topped	undertook
solved	suggested	totaled	underwrote
sorted	summarized	traced	unified
sourced	supervised	tracked	united
spearheaded	supplied	trained	unraveled
specified	supported	transacted	updated
speeded	surpassed	transcribed	upgraded
spent	surveyed	transferred	upheld
spoke	synchronized	transformed	urged
sponsored	synthesized	transitioned	used
stabilized	systematized	translated	validated
standardized	tabulated	traveled	verified
started	tackled	trimmed	viewed
steered	tallied	tripled	volunteered
stimulated	tapped	troubleshot	widened
streamlined	targeted	turned around	withstood
strengthened	taught	tutored	won
structured	tended	typed	worked
studied	terminated	uncovered	wrote

WORDS (NOUNS)

ability	experience	opportunity
background	goals	references
credentials	initiative	skills
education	objectives	

WORDS (ADJECTIVES)

adaptable	competent	dedicated	dynamic
ambitious	conscientious	dependable	eager
assertive	creative	determined	effective
capable	decisive	discreet	efficient

energetic   intelligent   pioneering   self-confident
enterprising   intuitive   practical   steady
enthusiastic   loyal   problem-solver   tactful
flexible   mature   productive   tenacious
friendly   methodical   professional   trustworthy
honest   motivated   progressive   versatile
imaginative   open-minded   qualified   well-organized
independent   optimistic   reliable
industrious   persistent   resourceful
innovative   persuasive   responsible

PHRASES

able to present facts clearly and
    succinctly
analytical and critical thinking skills
believe I could contribute/have a
    strong aptitude for
considered an enthusiastic worker
experience that qualifies me for
extensive experience with
good candidate/match for the job
good sense of/working knowledge of
in response to your advertisement
in this capacity
interested in pursuing a career with
may I have fifteen minutes of your
    time to discuss

my five years as
qualities that would be useful in
responsible for
serious interest in
sound understanding of
specialized in
supervisory abilities
take pride in my work
technical skills
well suited for
willing to travel
would enjoy attending/working/
    belonging

SENTENCES

I achieved a 19% capture rate on grants proposals submitted to local
    funders.
I am a skilled operator of the bridgeport mill and radial drill.
I have three years' experience in product development.

I met every deadline while working at Brooker Associates, some of them under fairly difficult circumstances.

In my last position I performed complex CNC turning operations on diversified parts with minimum supervision, and also had Mazatrol experience.

In my two years at Arrow Appliance, I helped increase productivity by approximately 25% and decrease absenteeism by almost 20%.

I successfully reduced stock levels while maintaining shipping and order schedules, resulting in lower overhead costs.

I was responsible for all aspects of store management, including sales, personnel, inventory, profit and loss control, and overseeing the annual budget.

My work skills include data entry, alphabetical and numerical filing, photocopying, typing skills, good organizational skills, an affinity for detail, and previous experience in a legal office.

PARAGRAPHS

Because my previous jobs have all involved public contact, I am comfortable dealing with people on many levels. As an academic adviser in the MBA program at McKeown College, I provided academic guidance and course selection assistance to adult graduate students and program applicants, recruited students, and promoted the program in talks and seminars.

I am highly skilled in the use and interpretation of specifications drawings and measuring instruments, generally knowledgeable about mechanical and electrical principles, and have experience in the construction, maintenance, and machine repair industries.

My responsibilities at Edwards International included invoicing, logging deposits, resolving billing problems related to data entry, managing four other accounts receivable employees, and filing a monthly report on the department.

I have analyzed malfunctioning machines and systems (electrical, hydraulic, pneumatic), recommended corrective action, and, upon approval, made repairs or modifications. I also have a working understanding of recovery equipment, instrumentation, systems, and facilities, know how to use complicated measuring and sampling equipment, and can repair machines and equipment, working from written or oral directions and specifications.

SAMPLE RÉSUMÉS

JOAN PENROSE

Present Address
14 Grace Lane,
Chance, UT 84623
801/555-2241

Permanent Address
#4 Route 9N
Fairfield, UT 84620
801/555-2789

OBJECTIVE

An entry-level management position in transportation and logistics with the opportunity to contribute to the efficient operation of a firm and to earn advancement through on-the-job performance.

EDUCATION

Bachelor of Business Administration, May 2002, from Merriam University, with a major in Transportation and Logistics and a minor in Psychology. Major G.P.A.: 4.0; cumulative G.P.A.: 3.4.

Coursework: Logistics Law, International Transportation and Logistics, Strategic Logistics Management, Transportation and Public Policy, Transportation Carrier Management, Transportation Economics; Accounting I and II, Business Communications, Business Law, Community and Regional Planning, Computer Science, Economics, Operations Management.

Financed 100% of college expenses through work, work-study programs, and grants.

EXPERIENCE

Merriam University Computer Lab, 1999–2002; supervised three other students; oversaw hardware repairs and updating of software library; assisted users with various software (15 hours/week, September to May only).

Swinney's Book Store, summers, 1998–2000: assembled and packed book, magazine, and giftware shipments; trained twelve employees (20 hours/week).

Creston Food Stores, Inc.: Deli Manager and Clerk, summers, 1998–2000; controlled all facets of delicatessen, including catering large and small events; worked at five different stores (20 hours/week).

Lorimer Industries, Salt Lake City, June and July 2001, Transportation/Distribution Intern: facilitated the relationship between Transportation and Customer Support Inventory Planning and Purchasing; assisted in the routing and controlling of inbound raw materials; gained experience in outbound logistics management, including warehousing and distribution.

Blaydon Logistics Case Study, August 2001: one of seven students selected to participate in logistics project at Blaydon Corporate Headquarters, San Diego; evaluated performance measures used in the areas of transportation, customs, and export administration; presented initial findings and suggested alternative measures.

STRENGTHS

Communication: communicate well when speaking and writing; able to act as liaison between different personality types; comfortable and effective communicating with both superiors and staff.

Leadership: able to motivate a project team; background in psychology provides wide range of interpersonal skills to encourage and instruct others.

Responsibility: accustomed to being in positions of responsibility; self-motivated and willing to set goals and work to achieve them; never assume "the other person" is responsible.

Organization: use time and resources effectively; consider efficiency, planning, and accountability very important.

Computer expertise: experienced in Lilypad 1-2-3, Savvy Pagemaker, WordAlmostPerfect 9.0, ELEMENTAL programming, Venus-Calc spreadsheets, Cambridge Graphics, MacroTough Advance, and Bytewise.

Other: willing to relocate anywhere; have traveled to Europe (three times) and to the Orient (once) and thus have a global awareness of business and politics; quick learner and trained in analytical problem-solving skills; solid work ethic that finds satisfaction and pleasure in achieving work goals; daily reader of *Wall Street Journal, The Journal of Commerce, Christian Science Monitor*, and *The Utah Times*.

ACTIVITIES

Treasurer, Transportation/Logistics Club
Member, University Finance Club
Campus Chest (student-operated community service organization), business manager, 1990, public relations, 1991
Member, Professional Women in Transportation, Utah Chapter.
Coordinator of the Business Council Peer Advisory to Transportation and Logistic Undergraduate Students

AWARDS

Creston's Employee-to-Employee Courtesy Award
Dean's List, eight semesters
Golden Key National Honor Society
National Collegiate Business Merit Award

FROM: Pip Thompson
TO: Raindance Film Festival
DATE: 4-9-2001
RE: bio for film festival program

Pip Thompson graduated magna cum laude from Yale University with a BA in Anthropology and Theater Studies. Two years in the film industry as script supervisor, production coordinator, and short-film director were followed by graduate school; she will receive her MFA in film (directing) from Columbia University in 2001.

Although Thompson admits her areas of specialization may seem unrelated to each other and a strange base on which to build a film career, she feels that anthropology, literally "the study of people," uncovers truths about human behavior while both theater and film convey those truths viscerally. Her viewfinder might not look like a microscope and her notebook contains storyboards, not observations on Inuit rituals, but she strives to direct films that give viewers insight into different cultures as a means of better understanding their own ways and the broader human experience.

A native of Minnesota, Thompson brought her interest in anthropology home with "The Windigo." Set in the preserved wilderness of northern Minnesota, the story derives its title and subject from a local Ojibwe Indian myth and dramatizes the misunderstandings that can arise between cultures. Gerard strives to emulate native ways, but he embodies a recent trend that appropriates Indian legends and beliefs without truly understanding them. Sandy, on the other hand, learns the hard way that he is biased in favor of laboratory wisdom. "The Windigo" examines ancient myths through the eyes of contemporary culture in order to shed light on the past and the present.

Regina Alving
1939 Norway Street
Cleveland, OH 44101
216/555-1234

OBJECTIVE
To obtain a position as an administrative assistant commensurate with my experience, capabilities, and need to be challenged

EDUCATION
2-year degree from Engstrand Technical College in office administration, 1999

WORK EXPERIENCE
Manders Realty, assistant to the president, 1996–present
Oswald Engineering Consultants, Inc., administrative assistant, 1993–1996
Ibsen Manufacturing International, assistant to the vice president, 1989–1993

SKILLS
All general office duties
Typing 65 wpm
Extensive experience with Microsoft Word, Access, Excel, Oracle Data Base, PowerPoint,
    Peachtree Accounting
Good oral and written communication skills
Fluent in written and spoken Spanish
Personal characteristics include being highly organized, able to take a multi-task approach to the
    workday, self-motivated, tactful, discreet

See also: APPLICATIONS, APPOINTMENTS, COVER LETTERS, EMPLOYMENT, FOLLOW-UP, REFERENCES, THANK YOU.

Sales Letters

44

*The advertisement is one of the most interesting and difficult
of modern literary forms.*

— Aldous Huxley

Almost every letter sent by a company, business, or organization is a sales letter. Even nonbusiness letters like sympathy notes, congratulations, thank-you letters, or apologies carry a second-level message that asks the recipient to think well of the firm. Courtesy, clarity, correctness, and persuasiveness are found in letters sent by successful companies.

Although computerized mailing lists have considerably reduced direct mail marketing costs, only about five out of every one hundred mailings are opened by the recipient. This has two implications: you use the envelope itself to entice the person to open it; you make those five opened letters so appealing that you obtain more than the average three out of five responses.

Sales letters aren't appropriate for all products and services, but they can get the reader to make the call or visit the store where the real selling can be done. Because they're effective and economical (compared to print and video advertising, for example), they're an integral part of most firms' marketing strategies. For many small businesses, they are the only affordable advertising tool.

Sales letters have become so sophisticated that many businesses no longer generate their own. The buzzword is "integration"—using full-service agencies to handle every aspect of advertising, including sales letters. Find such firms in the Yellow Pages under Direct Marketing, Advertising Agencies, or Public Relations Counselors.

Kinds of Sales Letters

- announcements: changes/new products
- asking for meeting/appointment (see APPOINTMENTS)
- congratulations: purchase/new account/payment
- direct mail advertising
- follow-up: inquiries/sales letters/sales
- form letters
- goodwill (see GOODWILL)
- introducing new products/services
- invitation: open house/sale/membership/new account
- questionnaires/surveys
- responding to inquiries
- special promotions/sales/gifts/free services
- thank you: sale/new account/revived account
- trial offers: products/programs/services/subscriptions

- Get the reader's attention with your opening sentence, question, anecdote, or statistic.
- Create an interest in what you're selling with a strong central sales message.
- Arouse the reader's desire for your product by using specific, vivid words as well as active power verbs. One word that never gets old is "new."
- Point out how your service or product differs from similar ones, emphasizing quality and dependability.
- Convince the reader that responding to your offer is a smart move, and offer "proof" (samples, testimonials, statistics).
- Tell how to obtain your product or service.
- Give a reason for acting immediately: limited supply, expiring sale offer, future price increase, early-response discount.
- State clearly what immediate action you want them to take: "Telephone now for an appointment"; "Order one for every family member"; "Call today to arrange a demonstration"; "Return the postage-paid reply card now"; "Send for your free copy of the planning guide."

- Close the sales letter by inciting readers to immediate action and telling them what you want them to do (order, call, mail a card, come to the store). Give them a good reason for acting right now: limited supplies, expiration date of sale offer, prices going up later, early-response discount. Make it convenient to respond: order blanks with postage-paid reply envelopes, prepaid form postcards asking for a sales rep to call or for additional information, a toll-free number to call for local distributors or to place orders, order now-pay later procedures, listing of store hours and locations. (Business reply mail, with the seller paying the postage, has a 10 to 20 percent higher response rate than courtesy reply, where the buyer pays the postage.)
- Finally, echo your letter opening in some way. If you began by quoting a celebrity, finish by saying something like, "And that's why So-and-So won't drive anything but a . . ."
- Add a P.S. to repeat your main point, to emphasize an important feature, or to offer a new and strong sales point such as a money-back guarantee, a time limit for the offer, an additional bonus for buying now: "P.S. To offer you these sale prices, we must receive your order by June 30"; "P.S. Don't forget—your fee includes a gift!"; "P.S. If you are not completely satisfied, return your Roebel Pager and we will cheerfully issue you a full refund." Lin Yutan wrote, "A letter is a soliloquy, but a letter with a postscript is a conversation."

What Not to Say

- Don't make too many points in one letter. Concentrate on your strongest one or two sales points, add one in the postscript if you like, and save the others for follow-up letters.
- Don't, in general, use numerous exclamation marks or exaggerated adjectives such as astonishing, revolutionary, incredible, sensational, extraordinary, spectacular. Describe instead concrete features, benefits, details, and product claims.
- Don't ask questions relating to the sale ("Can you afford to throw this letter away?" "Can anyone today get along without one?"). It's poor psychology to enlist readers in a dialogue in which they might not answer your question "correctly." Questions derail your reader from the one-way train of thought that leads to a sale and bring to full consciousness the idea of refusal.

- Don't say, "We never hold a sale! Our everyday prices are so low we don't need to." Human nature likes a sale. Even customers who regularly use your products or services and think they're reasonably priced are attracted by a bargain. By offering occasional discounts, sales, clearances, and special purchase promotions, you'll create a sense of excitement and willingness to buy in both old and new customers.

- Avoid jargon unless you're sure that your target audience is familiar with it.

- Don't threaten ("You'll be sorry if you don't order now"). It is off-putting and it tempts people to call your bluff. However, telling customers that their names will be removed from the mailing list if they don't order soon is sometimes effective because people fear missing out on something.

- Don't preach, scold, correct, or write down to customers ("you probably don't know this, but . . ."). Have others read your letter to be sure no patronizing tone has crept in.

- Avoid the first-name, pseudo-friend approach. Business columnist Louis Rukeyser received an impressive reader response after a column on form sales letters. According to him, "The artificially intimate stuff appears particularly irritating."

- Don't make assumptions: that your reader knows what you are talking about, is familiar with an industry term, can picture your product, agrees with your premises. Dale Carnegie wrote, "I deal with the obvious. I present, reiterate and glorify the obvious—because the obvious is what people need to be told."

Tips on Writing

~ Whether you're selling a product, service, idea, space, credit, or goodwill, the sales letter requires more work before you write than it does to actually write it. You need to know everything about your product or service. You need to know your reader, assembling as much data as possible. "Knowing something about your customer is just as important as knowing everything about your product." (Harvey Mackay) Pinpoint and develop a strong central selling point. Consider other factors (timing, design, length, developing a coupon or sample). Only after adequate preparation is a successful letter written.

~ Everyone agrees on the best way to begin a sales letter: with a bang! There's no agreement, however, on the type of "bang." Possibilities include: a surprising fact or statistic; a touching or dramatic anecdote; a personal story; significant savings; the offer of a gift, coupon, or booklet; a thought-provoking question or quotation; a joke or riddle; a celebrity endorsement, quote, or tie-in; a who-what-when-where-why paragraph; your strongest selling factor; a reference to something you have in common or to a previous contact or purchase; telling readers in a convincing way that they are special; asking or offering a favor; perhaps even a negative or unexpected statement.

~ It's hard to distinguish between the clever gimmick, hook, or attention-getter and the too-cute-for-its-own-good approach. When taking a risk with a novel overture, ask others to evaluate your letter. If it's clever, the rewards are great. If you stray on the side of coy or insensitive, the results can be fatal.

~ State the cost of your product or service. Customers ignore sales messages without prices, assuming they can't afford the item. Cost determines most purchases, and if the customer has to call to find out what it is, the extra trouble is often not worth it when a competitor's cost is available in its sales message.

~ Although both are necessary, emotional appeals tend to outpull intellectual appeals. Tie your message to some basic human emotion: love ("your child will have hours of fun!"); the need for love ("heads will turn when you wear this"); prestige ("your home will be a stand-out with . . . "); ambition ("learn new management techniques overnight"); security ("smoke-alarm with built-in battery tester"). Show how your service or product will bring the customer better health, popularity, pride of ownership or accomplishment, success, more money, improved appearance, more comfort and leisure, social and business advancement, loyalty.

~ From start to finish, the focus of a sales letter is on the prospective customer. Use the words "you" and "your" frequently, and describe the product in terms of benefits to the customers: how it relates to their needs, problems, and interests; how it can improve their lives, save them money, and make them feel more confident. The customer has only one question: "What will this do for me?" Persuade potential buyers that they need your product not so much because it's a great product, but because it is great for *them*.

~ Choose a consistent "voice" that complements your product or service and maintain it throughout your letter: friendly, neighbor-to-neighbor; serious and intellectual; humorous, lively, and fast-moving; brisk and businesslike; urgent and hard-hitting; sophisticated; soothing and reassuring; mysterious; technical or informational; emotional.

～ Use colorful descriptive words, strong verbs, appealing images. Sometimes sales letterwriters are so intent on either educating the prospective customer or building up a case with statistics, background information, and reports that they forget how boring and how un-client-centered such a message is.

～ Use repetition to emphasize a main point, clarify complicated material, and lend an attractive rhythm to your letter.

～ Sales messages can mimic other familiar letters: letters of congratulations, thank-you letters, announcements, invitations, letters of welcome, holiday greetings.

～ Create and foster credibility by means of testimonials, case histories, research studies, statistics, company reputation, product usage test results, comparison with similar products, free samples or trial periods, guaranties/warranties, celebrity endorsements, photographs of actual use, user polls. Whenever possible, guarantee the buyer's satisfaction in some way.

～ How long should a sales letter be? The key is that each word does its job, each word sells. A poorly written letter is in no way redeemed by being short, and some well-written long letters have enjoyed a high response rate. In general, however, shorter letters are better letters. Concentrate on what absolutely needs to be said—whether that takes one page, two, four, or ten. What needs to be kept short in any case are your paragraphs.

～ To increase the desirability of responding, offer discounts, bargain prices, special offers, delayed no-interest payments, gifts, in-store certificates, enclosures, coupons, brochures, samples, or trial period.

～ Attention-getting devices make your message more memorable: a message on the envelope that inspires the person to open it (studies show that mailers have about fifteen seconds to get customers to open the envelope or they lose them); handwriting part of the message (the P.S., for example); underlining certain words to look as though you personally emphasized the important points; yellow highlighting of key phrases; colored inks and papers; graphics; questionnaire or survey format; boxed information; italics, capital letters, quotation marks, unusual type faces; design elements such as heads, subheads, white space, short paragraphs, indented material, and bulleted lists. Attention-getting devices are not always appropriate; to sell bank cards, life insurance, healthcare services, or other sedate products and services, you want a more traditional format.

～ For more detailed advice on sales letters, see the excellent *Sales Letters That Sizzle: All the Hooks, Lines, and Sinkers You'll Ever Need to Close Sales*, 2nd ed., by Herschell Gordon Lewis (Chicago: NTC Business Books, 1999).

Special Situations

~ When responding to customer inquiries, the cover letter is a sales letter of the most potentially effective type because you've been given a focused opportunity to sell your product or service. Although the enclosure should sell itself (or the product it describes), the cover letter offers a strong sales message and additional incentives.

~ A series of letters is often effective. When a segment of the market is susceptible to your product (because of previous purchases, for example), contact them several times—but with a different focus each time: a new premium, an additional benefit of your product or service, time growing short with the offer expiring soon, two-for-one price, discount. Or, target customers buying one of your products with a sales letter promoting another product or service that, out of long habit, they don't "see" anymore. For example, customers who regularly use a hair salon may forget that they can also buy an extensive line of hair-care products, use tanning booths, or schedule manicures.

~ With a versatile product or service (or a number of different products in your line), you can reach different target audiences with letters tailored to their needs. A greenhouse manufacturer might write different sales letters to farmers, suburban homeowners, businesses, apartment dwellers, and even college students (the desktop miniature greenhouse).

~ Sales letters aimed at former customers emphasize your appreciation for past business, your desire to serve them again, products or services introduced since your last contact with them, your confidence that you can satisfy their needs. You could ask if there is a reason that they no longer bring their business to you. This may provide you with useful information. Or it may remind the customer that there is no particular reason.

Format

~ Most sales letters are computer-generated—either standard form letters or letters in which names, addresses, and salutations are personalized using a mass mail merge feature. The latter gives form letters a more personal look (unless you are also inserting the person's name here and there throughout the letter, which actually gives the opposite impression).

~ For highly select audiences, use good quality stationery, first-class postage, a real person's signature, and an individually typed address.

~ E-mail sales messages are a growing phenomenon. Although it's unknown how consistently successful they are to date, they may be appropriate for your product or service. If this is a new area for you, work with one of the e-mail suppliers. Internet sales are definitely generating dollars, if not yet significant profits, but this sales approach resembles a catalog or television commercial, not a letter, and requires expertise of its own.

WORDS

absolute	effective	low-priced	reward
acquaint	exceptional	luxurious	safe
adaptable	exciting	money-making	satisfaction
advanced	exclusive	natural	secure
advantages	expert	new	solution
affordable	exquisite	nostalgic	sophisticated
all-new	extensive	offer	spectacular
attractive	facts	opportunity	state-of-the-art
authentic	features	optional	stunning
benefits	flair	personalization	substantial
brand-new	flexible	pledge	successful
breakthrough	genuine	portable	super
choice	guaranteed	powerful	thrifty
classic	half-price	practical	tremendous
clever	handy	precision	trial
comfortable	helpful	premium	unbreakable
compact	high-quality	productive	unconditional
confident	immediate	professional	up-to-date
contemporary	indulge	profitable	urgent
convenient	inexpensive	proven	useful
dazzling	informative	quality	user-friendly
delightful	ingenious	rapid-action	valuable
demonstrated	innovative	reasonable	versatile
dependable	instant	rebate	warranted
details	invaluable	refund	waterproof
discovery	investment	reliable	wholesale
durable	lasting	results	
economical	low-cost	revolutionary	

PHRASES

add a new dimension to

advanced design

all for one low price

all-in-one convenience

as an added bonus

at a discount/a fraction of the cost/
    great savings/no expense to you

avoid worry/embarrassment/
    discomfort/risk

be more efficient

be the first to

both practical and
    beautiful/decorative

budget-pleasing prices

built-in features

business advancement

buy with confidence

can pay for itself in

carefree upkeep

choose from over 20 styles/cards/
    models/varieties

come in and try

compact design

complimentary copy

contemporary/gracious design

customer support

cutting edge

direct-to-you low prices

direct your attention to

discover for yourself

dramatic difference

easier and more enjoyable/
    comfortable

easier to use than ever before

easy/carefree maintenance

easy-to-follow instructions

elegant styling

engineered for dependability

exciting details/offer

exclusive features

experience the pleasure of

express your personality

fast, safe, easy-to-use

finely crafted

fit-any-budget price

fully automated/warranted

get full details

gives you your choice of

greater safety/convenience/
    pleasure/popularity

great gift idea

have the satisfaction of knowing

if not completely satisfied

if you accept this invitation/respond
    right away/send payment now

impressive collection

improved appearance

increased enjoyment

incredibly low introductory rate/
    price of

indulge yourself

influence others

in these fast-moving times

intelligent way to

invite you to

join millions of others who

just a reminder that

just pennies each

key to your peace of mind
lasting beauty
lets you enjoy more of your favorite
look forward to sending you
low, low prices
loyal customers like you
make it easy for yourself
makes any day special
many advantages of
money's worth
more advanced features
more money/comfort/leisure
more than fifty years of service
most versatile, powerful, and
    exciting study aid available
no matter which set you choose
no more mess/lost sales/
    typing errors/fuss/worry
no-risk examination
no strings attached
now for the first time
of particular importance to you
one easy operation
one of the largest and most respected
one reason among many to order
one size fits all
order today
our top-seller
outstanding features
over 50,000 satisfied customers
perfect gift for yourself or a loved one
pleased to be able to offer you
preferred customer/rates
previously sold for
price you'll appreciate
pride of accomplishment

privileges include
professional quality
prompt, courteous service
proven reliability/technology
provides the finest home hair care at
    the least cost
ready to spoil you with its powerful
    features
reasonably priced
reduced price
revolutionary approach
reward yourself with
risk nothing
rugged and dependable
satisfaction guaranteed
save money/time
security in your later years
see for yourself
simple steps
so unusual and striking that
special benefits/introductory
    offer/value
state of the art
step in the right direction
stop those costly losses with
supply is limited
surprise your special someone with
take advantage of this opportunity
take a giant step forward towards
take a moment right now to look
    over this
takes the gamble out of choosing
time is growing short
timeless elegance
time-tested
top of the line

treat yourself to

unconditional money-back guarantee

under no obligation to

under our simple plan

unequalled savings and convenience

unique limited edition creations

unique opportunity

urge you to

use it anywhere, anytime

we're making this generous offer because

what better way to

whole family can enjoy

with no obligation on your part

with our compliments

won't cost you a thing to

won't find better quality anywhere

world of enjoyment waiting for you

you can be proud of

you don't risk a penny

you'll be amazed to discover

you might expect these to cost as much as

your money back

you will appreciate the outstanding quality of these

SENTENCES

At this low price, every home should have one.

Be the first in your community to have one!

But act now—we expect a sizable response and we want to be certain that your order is processed.

Call today to arrange a demonstration.

Discover savings of up to 50%.

Discover the elegance of a genuine leather briefcase with discreet gold initials.

Don't miss out!

Do your holiday shopping the easy way.

Enjoy it for a 15-day home trial.

Every item is offered at a discount.

If you are not completely satisfied, simply return it for a full credit.

In order to make this offer, we must have your check by September 1.

It's a first!

It's a no-strings offer.

Join us today.

Just bring this letter with you when you come in to sign up.

Just what makes the Blount Filing System so great?

May I make an appointment with you next week to explain/show/ demonstrate our latest line of products?

Now there's a new magazine just for you.

Order one for every family member.

Please don't delay your decision—we expect a heavy demand for the Ellesmere filet knife.

P.S. To lock in these great rates, we must receive your deposit by October 15.

Returning the postage-paid reply card does not obligate you in any way.

Send for your free copy of the Bemerton planning guide.

Send today for free, no-obligation information on rates and available discounts, special services, and easy claims filing.

Take a look at the enclosed brochure for a sneak preview.

Telephone Sarah Lash, your personal representative, for an appointment.

The Art Deco look fits almost any decorating scheme.

There is absolutely no risk on your part.

There's no cost or obligation, of course.

These low prices are effective only until June 1.

This is just one more reason why our products have won such overwhelming acceptance.

Use the order form and postpaid reply envelope enclosed to receive your first Holiday Bell absolutely free.

We cannot extend this unusual offer beyond May 25, 2004.

We invite you to complete the enclosed reservation request form and return it now to confirm your choice of dates.

We're making this unprecedented offer to a select group of business executives.

We take all the risks.

We've missed you!

You can choose from over 150 different programs.

You can now acquire a two-line telephone for far less than you ever thought possible.

You'll appreciate these fine features.

You'll like our convenient evening and weekend hours; you'll love our brand-new equipment and experienced teachers!

You'll see that Rockminster China isn't like other china.

You may not have ever bought/invested/tried, which is why we are making you this no-risk trial offer.

You must see the complete series for yourself to appreciate how it can enrich your life.

PARAGRAPHS

If for any reason, at any time, you are not satisfied with your Haverley Air Cleaner, you can return it to us for a complete and prompt refund. No questions asked.

P.S. The cookbook of your choice and the lucite book stand are both yours free—without obligation. All you need to do is send in the enclosed form.

Send no money now. You will be billed at the time of shipment for any items ordered, plus shipping and sales tax (if applicable). You do not have to pay until you are totally convinced of the high quality and outstanding appeal of our lithographs and prints. If you are not delighted in every way, return your purchases within ten days, and you'll owe nothing!

There's one sure way to convince you that Bryerley Bath Beads are the last word in luxurious skin-softeners. We're enclosing sample packets of two of our most popular Bryerley scents, Gardenia and Lily of the Valley.

P.S. This is your last chance to buy the kits at these low prices. Rising material costs require a moderate price increase effective next month.

You want to give that special child in your life the finest reading—her or his very own books—but you don't have the time to look at thousands of children's books to find the best. That's where we come in.

Is a housecleaning service for you? We think so because you want the best for yourself and your family . . . and that takes time. Time you don't always have after working all week and meeting important family needs after hours. We can offer you thorough, reasonably priced, once-a-week housecleaning that will make a big difference in your life. Think about what you could do with the hours you now have to spend on housework. Think about walking into a clean house at night. And then think about giving us a call to schedule an estimate interview.

SAMPLE LETTERS

Dear Executive:

According to several management studies, the single most important characteristic of an effective executive is the ability to manage time.

Are you meeting your deadlines? Can you list your current projects in order of importance? Do you know where you're headed over the next week, month, year? Can you find things when you need them? Do you assign work in the most time-effective ways?

If you answered no to any of these questions, you're sure to benefit from our popular, effective Time Management Workshop.

In just two days you learn how to set priorities, how to use special tools to help you organize your time, and how to develop interpersonal skills to help you deal with unnecessary interruptions, inefficient staff, and group projects.

In fact, we don't want to be one of those interruptions, so we'll make this short. We simply suggest that you save time by making time for the next Time Management Workshop in your area. You can do this in under a minute by checking off a convenient date and signing the enclosed postage-paid reply card or by calling 800/555-1707 to register.

This is one workshop that won't be a waste of time!

Sincerely,

Dear Marietta Lyddon,

You were a member of the Atlas Fitness Club from March 15, 1996, to November 18, 2002, and according to our records you worked out regularly.

Whatever your reasons for not being with us the past several years, you may want to know about some changes that have taken place since you were last here:

New this year: Olympic-size pool with extended hours, 5:30 a.m. to midnight. A lifeguard is on duty at all times.

New this year: Membership packages designed to fit your use patterns. You may now choose between an all-use pass or a pass that specifies morning hours, early morning hours, after-five hours, evening hours, late evening hours.

New this year: Peripheral services that our members—most of whom are busy working people like yourself—have requested: a personal check-cashing service; yogurt, soup, and mineral water machines in the lobby; a telephone for the use of members making local calls; all-new padlocks for the lockers.

New last year: We have 50% more equipment in the weight lifting room, and three new Nautilus units.

If you liked us before, you'll love us now. I think it's worth a look, and I'm so convinced of this that I'm offering you a two-week membership for FREE.

Just bring this letter with you when you come to give us another look!

Sincerely yours,

See also: ANNOUNCEMENTS, APPRECIATION, CONGRATULATIONS, COVER LETTERS, CREDIT, FOLLOW-UP, GOODWILL, HOLIDAYS, INVITATIONS, ORDERS, REQUESTS, THANK YOU.

Sensitive Letters 45

When it comes to bombshells, there are few that can be more effective than that small, flat, frail thing, a letter.

—MARGARET DELAND

In some difficult situations, writing a letter is more effective than a face-to-face encounter. "Most people think better on their seat than on their feet." (Dianna Booher) When writing a letter, you have time to reflect on what has happened, to inform yourself of related or supporting facts, to choose your words so that they convey exactly what you want to convey, and to rewrite the letter as many times as you need to until it accurately presents your position.

Letters Require Sensitive Handling When You Must

- ask someone to return an engagement ring
- borrow money from a friend or family member
- break off a relationship
- claim credit for your work
- clear yourself of an unjust accusation
- deliver bad news
- inquire about a gift or check that hasn't been acknowledged
- offer unsolicited and probably unwelcome advice
- remind someone of an unpaid personal loan
- report a child's unpleasant behavior

393

- report sexual harassment
- reprimand an employee (see also EMPLOYMENT)
- respond to someone with a terminal illness (see "GET WELL")
- tell the other person they're wrong
- turn someone down for a job whom you know well
- uninvite guests

- Write promptly. Nothing will make a difficult letter more difficult to write than putting it off.
- Begin with a courteous expression about something, however small, that you can agree upon or that you have in common.
- Admit (if it's true) that you're uncomfortable with the situation.
- State the issue clearly and directly. Dressing up your message in big words, roundabout phrases, and conciliatory sentences only antagonizes the other person. If you have trouble writing this part of the letter, say your message aloud as though speaking to a friend. Boil down your "conversation" to a sentence or two that expresses the heart of the matter.
- Provide facts and details of the issue.
- Convey your understanding of the other person's position.
- Admit your role in the situation, if you have one. When you take responsibility for your contribution, others are more likely to own up to theirs.
- Examine your position for areas of negotiation. Can you trade one point for another? Can you accept anything less than what you originally wanted?
- State what you are asking or what solution you want.
- Close with a wish to put the matter behind you, with an expression of confidence that the situation will be resolved, with a statement that a satisfactory solution will benefit both of you, or with a sentence conveying your goodwill.

What Not to Say

- Don't tell people what to do (this sentence doesn't count). Words like "must," "ought," and "should" raise most people's hackles. Replace them with "might like to," "could consider," or other more open-ended phrases.

- Don't write unpleasantries. They live forever and you will not forget—or be allowed to forget—them.

- Don't use words that trigger negative reactions in the reader. Although almost any words, when strung together in the right order, could annoy a person, some are immediately inflammatory: "obviously" and "clearly" (of course it isn't obvious or clear, or the other person would have known it—are you saying they're stupid?); "you appear to think," "according to you," "you claim," and "if you are to be believed" (these belittle the other person's word); "you must agree" or "at least you will admit" (not so—these phrases make the person want to not agree and not admit).

- Don't use words like "problem," "argument," "battle," "disagreement" or those labeling a situation negative or adversarial.

- Don't exaggerate or dramatize: "You egregiously underestimated"; "In all my years as a coach I've never seen anything as reprehensible"; "I will never be able to forget what you did"; "You have contributed absolutely nothing to the department." When the words "never" and "always" appear, you are probably exaggerating or dramatizing. "Magnifying a matter is not the way to mend it." (Ivy Compton-Burnett)

- Don't be too "sensitive" when writing a letter about a sensitive issue: "I hesitated a long time before writing this . . ."; "I hate to write because I know how upset you get"; "Now don't be mad, but . . ."; "Promise me you won't take this the wrong way . . ." State calmly and neutrally what the issues are; leave the emotions (theirs and yours) out of it.

- Concentrate on facts instead of feelings. "I don't feel this is fair" does not carry as much weight as, "The guidelines for the competition stated clearly that . . ."

- Don't assume you have all the facts. Check your assumptions. Particularly when a number of people are involved, an issue can become muddled.

- Don't make a decision sound negotiable if it is not. It is kinder to be clear that the answer is no, the news is bad, the response is negative.

- Don't deal with other matters in a letter about a touchy situation; save them for later. Sometimes people try to hide the difficult part of the letter in a jumble of news, offhand remarks, or other distractions. It doesn't work.

- Don't try to teach people a lesson, lecture them, or label their behavior if you want to achieve a specific goal (the return of a tool, repayment of a debt, stopping a behavior, undoing a wrong). If you want to vent and don't care if you ever see the person again, it doesn't matter what you say.

- Don't put people on the defensive by attacking them or disparaging their personality, character, intelligence, or looks. People who have been made to feel stupid and little are not apt to give you what you want. Focus on the behavior, the facts, the central issue. Getting personal indicates a weak position and "anger is not an argument." (Daniel Webster)

- Don't threaten (lawsuit, loss of your friendship, some action). It won't solve the problem and it weakens your side of the issue. "Never give anyone an ultimatum unless you are prepared to lose." (Abigail Van Buren)

Tips on Writing

~ Think twice before offering unsolicited advice or "help." "It's awfully important to know what is and what is not your business." (Gertrude Stein)

~ Before writing the letter, finish this sentence: "I want them to . . ." Do you want a rebate, an exchange, repairs? Do you want an apology, a corrected statement, a credit? Do you want something redone? Do you want to convince the person that facts, statistics, opinions are wrong? Be clear about your goal.

~ Link some good news to the bad news. This shouldn't be artificial or inappropriate good news, but any upbeat items help put the unpleasant part of the letter in a more hopeful context.

~ When possible, help the other person save face. Set up the situation so that the person can do what you want and at the same time feel generous, gracious, powerful, and willing.

∼ We usually prefer active voice to passive voice. However, the passive voice is more tactful in a touchy situation. Instead of writing, "You did this," write, "This was done."

∼ You can say you are angry, disappointed, upset, distressed, appalled, or anything else you might feel. In fact, the more carefully you choose the words that describe your position, the clearer the communication will be. What is unacceptable is abusing the other person verbally. The difference often lies between "I" statements and "you" statements: "I am upset about the dent in my car door" is appropriate; "You are an idiot and they should take away your license" is not—unless, of course, you don't care if the person pays for the dent or if you ever see them again. Strive for a letter that is factual, dispassionate, considerate, and even-handed. When you write a letter in the midst of your anger, don't mail it; reread and rewrite your letter several times over a period of days.

∼ When writing a letter about a sensitive subject, ask someone you trust to read your letter before you send it.

Special Situations

∼ A profoundly bitter, prejudiced, hostile, accusatory, or hate-mongering letter requires careful handling. If you think the writer could be dangerous, consult with police or an attorney. In any case, you need never respond to an abusive letter. At the mild end of the spectrum, when the person simply seems to be letting off steam (and you think a response is called for), reply with "I am sorry to hear you feel that way."

∼ When writing to borrow money from a friend or relative, remain businesslike about how much you need, why you need it, and when you will repay it. Offer to sign an agreement. Reassure the person that you will understand if they have to refuse you.

∼ Sexual harassment consists of unwelcome, unsolicited, nonreciprocated sexual advances, requests for sexual favors, sexually motivated physical contact, or communication of a sexual nature, usually by someone who has power over another person. It includes comments, jokes, looks, innuendoes, and physical contact, and emphasizes a person's sex role over any function as a worker. It is against the law. If you are on the receiving end of such behavior, a good first step is a letter notifying the person that you consider the conduct sexual harassment. It used to be that saying anything about another's offensive behavior not only got you nowhere, but got you in trouble. This is no longer quite as true. Depending on your situation, a quiet warning note might be all that's needed. If you are the offender and have been called on it, (1) educate yourself about the issues until you feel sure you know where the boundaries are; (2) write a brief note of apology, thanking the person for letting you know and stating that you will comply with the request; (3) never repeat the behavior. Few reasonable people will bring a charge of sexual harassment against a one-time offender who didn't realize the original harm done and who is now apologetic and reformed.

~ In the case of a serious disagreement, begin by referring to the previous correspondence or to the event responsible for the present letter. Outline the two opposing views or actions. Give clear (perhaps numbered) reasons for your stand, using statistics, quotations from an employee handbook, supportive anecdotal material, and names of witnesses or others who agree with you (with their permission). If appropriate, suggest an intermediate stage of negotiation: a reply to specific questions in your letter; further research; a meeting between the two of you or with third parties present; visits to a lawyer, accountant, or other appropriate adviser. If the disagreement has reached the stage where you can effectively do this, finish by stating clearly the outcome you desire. End with your best wishes for a solution acceptable to both of you and a reference to good future relations.

~ When requesting a favor that makes you uncomfortable, admit it. You will make the request more easily if you can accept "no" for an answer, and if you make this clear to the other person.

~ When reprimanding an employee, begin with a positive or complimentary remark. Describe the employee behavior and tell why it is unacceptable. Mention how it came to your attention. Suggest how the employee can improve or change. Outline any previous history of the same behavior (documenting this with dated reprimands). State the consequences of continuing the behavior. Tell exactly what you expect the employee to do (apologize, take a class, speak to you, not repeat the behavior). Say that this letter will be placed in their file. Close with an expression of confidence that the situation will be successfully dealt with. You may want the employee to sign and date the letter to verify having read it. A reprimand is brief, respectful, encouraging, and positive (instead of writing, "Don't send out any letters with misspellings," write, "Please use your spellcheck function followed by a dictionary check of any questionable words").

Format

 Sensitive business matters are typed on letterhead stationery to convey formality and a certain neutrality. This will have a "cool" tone. When a business matter has personal aspects, handwrite it. This letter will have a "warm" tone.

 A sensitive personal matter is dealt with in a letter written by hand or typed on personal stationery.

 E-mail and fax are inappropriate for sensitive issues.

WORDS

ambiguous	distressing	negotiate	troublesome
annoyance	disturbing	object	troubling
arrange	embarrassment	oppose	unfavorable
bothersome	extent	predicament	unfortunate
burdensome	hardship	problem	unhappy
circumstances	impede	protest	unpromising
complex	inconvenient	puzzling	unsuccessful
difficult	inopportune	refusal	untimely
dilemma	intervene	regrettable	unwilling
discuss	involved	reluctant	upsetting
disinclined	mediate	thorny	worrying

PHRASES

agree to disagree	look forward to
apologize for my part	pleased to be able to discuss
appreciate your willingness to	rough going
come to terms	state of affairs
deal with	ticklish situation
difficult to understand	with your help
find a middle ground	work for a happy ending
give and take	work out a solution
happy to sit down and discuss	would like to hear your side
in the future	

SENTENCES

Do you have time to discuss this over a cup of coffee?

I feel sure you will make the best decision for all involved.

I hope you will understand that while I am in the early stages of recovery I simply can't be around some of my old friends—wish me well and I will call you when I can.

I understand you have some thoughts about my work, behavior, and looks, and I would like to discuss these with you directly instead of hearing them second-hand.

The language and tone of your last letter is unacceptable to us. Please forward our file to someone else in your organization who can handle this matter.

You don't have to understand where I'm coming from or agree with me or even like what I'm saying, but would you—as my good, dear friend—do me the great favor of not using crude language around me?

PARAGRAPHS

I'm sorry to have to write again about the $500 you owe me. I helped you with the clear understanding that the money would be repaid within two months. I've given you at least a month's grace, but I must insist on receiving the money before the end of the week.

I was surprised to learn last week from Miles MacPhadraick that you and he had been discussing your new alarm system. I suspect I misunderstood him because it sounded like the system I've been working on. You might be interested in seeing my record of invention (enclosed). I'd be happy to show you what I'm doing if you stop by the lab sometime.

Alert! Alert! Jay, I need my kayak. Now! Every time I've called I was sure we understood each other. Maybe a note will do the trick. Just keep saying to yourself: Kayak. Back. To Jack.

I'd like to set the record straight: it was not I who called you an ugly name. I don't know who it was. The person who ascribed it to me was mistaken. In any case, that's not my style—and I think you know that.

As you know, the Financial Commission has been very pleased with your work. Unfortunately, there is not quite enough of it. Your coffee breaks and lunch hours have been growing increasingly lengthy over the past few months. I realize it's tempting to slip out to run an errand or two or to go to the gym for a workout, but the company has a zero tolerance policy for short workdays. Please let us have a full measure of your fine work.

As you can imagine, I wish I had any other response to give you. I would have enjoyed working with you. The decision has been made, however, to hire someone with more experience in livestock production.

Christy and Ben tell me that Jimmy and Letty have been teasing them unmercifully about having two mothers instead of a mother and father. Some of the remarks sound oddly adult—not the sort of thing that preschoolers would come up with on their own. I know you have not been particularly happy to have us in the neighborhood, but we're sad to see the children involved this way. We'd like to invite the two of you and Jimmy and Letty for a couscous dinner one night next week. Perhaps we can find enough common ground to allow us to live in a neighborly way.

About your visit this weekend—Biddy is quite upset at the thought of having Pip in the house again. She isn't frightened of all dogs but Pip feels unpredictable to her. At any rate, we've made reservations for you at the Gargery Motel nearby. They welcome pets. Let us know if this is all right with you.

You're my brother and I love you, but please don't come to the house again when you've been drinking. It disturbs the children, and because they look up to you it sets an unfortunate example. You'll be welcome any other time. When you've been drinking, I will not be able to invite you in.

SAMPLE LETTERS

Dear Mrs. Tilford,

We all enjoyed Mary's stay with us last weekend. Because it was so pleasant, I'm sorry to be writing with this problem.

When I was a child, my father brought me back a small carved giraffe from Africa. As he died soon afterwards, I have always treasured this memento. I missed it Sunday evening and spent several days looking for it. Karen told me that Mary now carries it around in her schoolbag and freely admits to "finding" it here. In her six-year-old way, Karen demanded it back, but Mary was evidently not ready to let it go. I trust that you will find some good way of convincing Mary to return it.

Thank you for taking care of this.

Sincerely,

My dear Annie-Laurie,

I've lost the rhinestone necklace you lent me for the dinner dance last week. I am devastated. I've looked everywhere for it. I've called the hotel, the taxi company, everyone who was at the dance. Nothing. I'm not giving up (I'm putting an ad in the paper this week), but the situation is looking hopeless and I need to let you know what is going on.

I will of course replace it, but since it was your mother's, there's no way to make up for its sentimental value. I'll call you tomorrow to see what's the best way of going about this. My deepest apologies for an unforgivable loss.

My dear Bryn,

I've been doing a lot of thinking lately. I know you noticed because you've asked me several times what's wrong. What's wrong is that I've realized I don't have the kind of feelings for you that I want to have if we are to spend the rest of our lives together.

I think the world of you—and you know that's true—but I'm convinced my love for you is not a marrying kind of love. It's a friendship kind of love.

I waited to write this letter until I was very, very sure of my thoughts and feelings. You've done nothing wrong and there is nothing you can do to spark something that isn't there. I don't want to leave you with any doubts or hopes about what I'm saying.

I'm probably the last person who can be of support to you, but if there's anything I can do to make this easier, let me know. In the meantime, know that you are and will always be one of the dearest people in my life.

TO: Gus Parkington
FROM: Alice Sanderson
DATE: Nov. 13, 2002
RE: Request

I need to tell you that repeatedly touching my arm or putting your arm around my shoulder is inappropriate in a business setting (it would actually also be inappropriate outside the business setting because I don't welcome such gestures from people I don't know well). In the office, this is considered sexual harassment. I would appreciate keeping our exchanges on a professional level. Knowing how intelligent and quick-on-the-uptake you are, I feel sure we need never discuss this again.

Dear Lizzie and Jim,

We are still talking about your beautiful wedding! I meant to ask you if the singer was a friend of yours—his voice was stunning.

I'm wondering if you received my wedding gift. As it was rather fragile, I hesitate to pay my Cecil-Roberts charge balance until I am sure that (a) you did indeed receive it and (b) it arrived in one piece. I have visions of it having arrived damaged and you not knowing quite what to do about it.

Give my love to your mother when you see her, will you, Lizzie?

Fondly,
Bert

Dear Hamilton,

We are fortunate that in such a large, high-pressure office we all get along so well. You are one of the ones who keep the social temperature at such a comfortable setting. I don't know anyone in the office who is better liked than you.

You can perhaps help with this. The collection of contributions towards gifts for employees' personal-life events is becoming a little troubling. Certainly, the communal sending of a gift is justified now and then. In the past month, however, there have been collections for two baby shower gifts, one wedding shower gift, two wedding gifts, one funeral remembrance, four birthday gifts, and three graduation gifts.

It's not only the collected-from who are growing uncomfortable (and poor), but the collected-for feel uneasy receiving gifts from people who don't know them outside the office, who wouldn't even recognize their graduating children, their marrying daughters and sons, or their deceased relatives.

This is essentially a kind gesture (and one that people think well of you for), but the practice seems to have become too wide-ranging and feels inappropriate in today's office setting.

Thank you for understanding.

See also: ADJUSTMENTS, BELATED, COMPLAINTS, DISAGREEMENT, REFUSALS, SYMPATHY.

Letters of Sympathy

46

A good letter of condolence is like a handclasp, warm and friendly.

—LILLIAN EICHLER WATSON

Letters of condolence and sympathy are some of the most difficult to write. People who are shocked and saddened and who feel inadequate and tongue-tied are writing to people who are grief-stricken and vulnerable and who feel life is hardly worth living.

However painful they are to write, letters of sympathy are imperative if you have a personal or business relationship with the deceased's family or friends. It will not be easy for them to overlook your ignoring something as all-important as the death of a loved one.

Condolences are offered only in the event of a death; sympathy may be expressed for a death, but it is also extended to those who have suffered from a fire, flood, storm, or natural disaster; burglary, theft, or violent crime; a lost job, bankruptcy, personal reverses, or other misfortunes.

Send Letters of Sympathy in Cases of

- absence of a superior who would normally respond
- anniversary of a death (see also ANNIVERSARIES)
- death of a family member of friend/neighbor/relative/customer/ client/employee/colleague
- death of an employee (write to next of kin)
- death of a pet
- divorce
- hospitalization due to serious illness or accident (see also "GET WELL")

- miscarriage or stillbirth
- misfortune: loss of job/bankruptcy/burglary/violent crime
- natural disaster: flood/hurricane/drought/storms
- terminal illness (see also "GET WELL")

- Simply and directly express your sorrow about the other person's loss or trouble.
- Mention by name the person who died or the unfortunate event.
- Tell how you heard the news, if appropriate.
- Express your feelings of grief, dismay, loss.
- Offer sympathy, thoughts, prayers, good wishes.
- In the case of a death, mention what you liked or loved about the deceased; relate some happy memory, anecdote, favorite expression, or advice they gave you; mention the virtues, achievements, or successes for which they'll be remembered; tell about something they said or did that touched you. Especially welcome is recalling a complimentary or loving remark made by the deceased about the bereaved person. The more specific you are, the more memorable and comforting your letter will be.
- Close with a general expression of concern or affection or an encouraging reference to the future: "You are in my thoughts and prayers"; "My thoughts are with all of you in this time of sorrow"; "In the days ahead, may you find some small comfort in your many happy memories."

- Don't say too little (sending only a commercial card with your signature) and don't say too much (offering clichés, advice, or inappropriate comments).
- Don't use overly dramatic language ("the worst tragedy I ever heard of," "the dreadful, horrible, appalling news"). If you were shocked or appalled at the news, say so—but avoid being excessively sentimental, sensational, or morbid. A simple "I'm sorry" is effective and comforting.

- Don't discuss the philosophy of death and disaster or offer religious commentary unless you are certain that sympathy grounded in a shared philosophic or religious orientation is appropriate with this person. Avoid pious clichés, simplistic explanations of the tragedy, or unwarranted readings of God's activities, intents, or involvement.

- Don't give advice or encourage big changes (leaving town, moving into an apartment, selling the spouse's model ship collection). It's usually many months before survivors can make well-thought-out decisions.

- Don't make generic offers of help like "Let me know if I can help," or "Feel free to call on us." This requires a response from people who already have much to deal with; most people will not take you up on such vague invitations. Instead, just do something: bring food, have the dress or suit the person is wearing to the funeral drycleaned, put up out-of-town relatives, watch children for several hours, address acknowledgments, take over work duties for a few days, cut grass or shovel snow or water the garden, help clean the house. If you're not close to the bereaved, an offer of help will be seen for the empty gesture it is. If you are close, you will either know what is helpful or you know whom to ask (friend, neighbor) about what needs doing.

- Don't focus on your feelings: "I've been just devastated—I can't seem to keep my mind on anything"; "I start crying every time I think of him"; "Why didn't you call me?" In the chapter entitled, "P.S. Don't tell *me* how bad you feel!" of her best-selling book, *Widow*, Lynn Caine says most of the condolence letters she received were more about the writer's awkwardness, discomfort, and inadequacies than about her sorrow or their shared loss. She says many letters were "full of expressions of how uneasy the writers felt, how miserable the writers were—as if they expected *me* to comfort *them*." There is a fine line between expressing your sorrow and dramatizing your own reactions.

- Don't offer false cheeriness or optimistic platitudes. In a *Reader's Digest* article, "An Etiquette for Grief," Crystal Gromer says, "In the context of grief, clichés are simply bad manners. . . . 'At least he didn't suffer,' people say. 'At least he's not a vegetable.' Any time you hear 'at least' come out of your mouth, stop. Creating an imaginary worse scenario doesn't make the real and current one better. It trivializes it." C.C. Colton once said, "Most of our misfortunes are more supportable than the comments of our friends upon them." Avoid the following comments:

Chin up.

Be brave.

Don't cry.

You'll get over it.

It's better this way.

She is better off now.

Time heals all wounds.

He was too young to die.

Life is for the living.

Keep busy, you'll forget.

I know just how you feel.

God never makes a mistake.

Be happy for what you had.

He's in a better place now.

It's a blessing in disguise.

At least she isn't suffering.

You must get on with your life.

He was old and had a good life.

Every cloud has a silver lining.

I heard you're not taking it well.

She is out of her misery at least.

Be thankful you have another child.

At least you had him for eighteen years.

Don't worry, it was probably for the best.

I feel almost worse than you do about this.

God had a purpose in sending you this burden.

You're young yet; you can always marry again.

It's just as well you never got to know the baby.

You're not the first person this has happened to.

I have a friend who's going through the same thing.

God only sends burdens to those who can handle them.

Life must go on—you'll feel better before you know it.

Tips on Writing

∾ When your condolences are belated, send them anyway. A person can overlook tardiness, but it's almost impossible to overlook being ignored at a time like this.

∾ In most cases, be brief. A lengthy letter may be overwhelming in a time of grief. On the other hand, if your letter is lengthy because you are recounting wonderful memories of the deceased person, it will be comforting and welcome. A letter that is lengthy because it includes other news or because it dwells on your own feelings is not appropriate.

∾ Be tactful, but don't fear being honest—using the word *death* or *suicide*, for example. Circumlocutions like *passed on, passed away, departed, left this life, gone to their reward, gone to a better life, the deceased,* and *the dear departed* are no longer seen very often.

↷ Accept that nothing you write will take away the person's grief, grief that is a necessary part of the healing process. Too many people agonize about finding the words that will make everything right again. There simply aren't any.

↷ Observe the fine line between sympathy and pity. Sympathy respects the person's ability to survive the unfortunate event; pity suspects it has beaten them.

↷ Let the person know you don't expect a response to your note or letter. After writing thank-you notes for flowers, condolences, memorials, honorary pallbearers, and special assistance, there is often little energy left to acknowledge sympathy letters.

↷ If you're writing to one member of the family, mention the others in your closing.

↷ To ensure that you don't write anything awkward, pitying, or tactless, re-read your letter as though you were the one receiving it.

↷ For additional advice, see Leonard M. Zunin and Hilary Stanton Zunin, *The Art of Condolence: What to Write, What to Say, What to Do at a Time of Loss* (1991). For more general background reading, see Judith Viorst, *Necessary Losses* (1986).

Special Situations

↷ Miscarriages and stillbirths are devastating. Sympathize as you would for the death of any child. Avoid such unfortunately common remarks as: "You already have two lovely children—be grateful for what you have"; "This may have been for the best—there might have been something wrong with the baby, and this was nature's way of taking care of it"; "You're young yet—you can try again." And the worst of all: "Don't feel so bad. After all, it isn't as though you lost a child." The person *has* lost a child.

↷ In the case of a suicide, offer sympathy as you would to any bereaved family. Because many survivors experience feelings of guilt, rejection, confusion, and social stigma, they need to know that you're thinking of them. Although it is generally appropriate to say you were "shocked to hear about" someone's death, avoid the phrase in this case. Don't ask questions, speculate about how the death could have been prevented, or dwell on the fact of the suicide; what matters is that the person is gone and the family is grieving. Instead, talk about how the person touched your life, share a happy memory, or express sympathy for the bereaved's pain.

~ Those who live with AIDS are first of all your friends, neighbors, and relatives, and only second someone with a usually fatal illness. Write as you would to anyone with a serious illness. Don't assume the person's time is short. Some AIDS patients have good years ahead of them in spite of recurrent crises. It's more important to be supportive and to send a card than to say exactly the right thing. Focus on how special the person is to you rather than on their illness, their prognosis, the sadness of it all. Ask if they'd like company; because of the perceived nature of AIDS, some people are unwilling to visit and your friend may appreciate seeing you all the more.

~ Responding to news of a divorce or separation is difficult, unless you're well acquainted with the person you're addressing. Neither expressions of sympathy nor congratulations are entirely appropriate in most cases. However, whether the person is "better off" or not, such life changes are never without their sad aspects and mourned losses, and a message of sympathy and support is often welcome.

~ Don't hesitate to write to people experiencing a misfortune considered embarrassing (a family member convicted of a crime, for example); if friends and family are hurting, your warm message of support will be welcome.

~ When business associates, customers, clients, or employees lose someone close to them, write as you would for friends or relatives, although your note will be shorter and more formal. Avoid personal remarks; it is enough to say you are thinking about them at this time. Extend sympathy on behalf of the company and convey condolences to other members of the person's family. When writing to the family of an employee who has died, you can offer assistance in gathering personal effects, discuss the pension plan, or make a referral to someone in the company who can help with questions.

~ Those who are grieving the death of a companion animal will appreciate a note of sympathy. This loss can be devastating; whether one can identify with the feelings or not, expressing sympathy is a loving, respectful gesture.

~ When someone has lost a close family member, remember the person with a special note on the anniversary of the person's death and (in the case of a spouse) on the couple's wedding anniversary date. Don't worry about "bringing up sad memories." The person will hardly think of anything else on that day, and will be grateful for the supportive note that says somebody remembers. Those who plan class reunions might send cards or flowers to parents of deceased classmates to assure them that their children are remembered.

~ A letter to someone terminally or very seriously ill is more of a sympathy letter than a "get well" letter, but be careful not to anticipate someone's death. Avoid mention of imminent death unless the person has introduced the subject and shows a desire to talk about it. Instead, say how sorry you are to hear that the person is ill and that you are thinking of them. Instead of a "Get Well" card, choose one of the "Thinking of You" or no-message cards.

~ When sending flowers to a funeral home, address the accompanying small card's envelope to "The family of Emily Webb Gibbs." Insert a plain white card from the florist or your own visiting or business card with a brief message ("Please accept my sincerest sympathy" or "My thoughts and prayers are with you and the children"). If you make a donation to a charity in the deceased person's name, give the name and address of a family member as well as your own. The charity will send a notice of the contribution to the family and acknowledge to you that the donation was received.

Format

~ The personal letter of sympathy is always handwritten, unless a disability prohibits it. Use plain personal stationery or foldovers (no bright colors or fussy design).

~ Commercial greeting cards are acceptable as long as you add a personal line or two (or more).

~ Sympathy letters can be typed when writing a customer, client, employee, or colleague whom you don't know well but with whom you have business dealings. Use business-personal rather than full-size letterhead stationery.

WORDS

affection	distressed	mourn	sorry
bereavement	faith	ordeal	suffering
bitter	grief	overcome	sympathy
blow	hardship	regret	touched
comfort	healing	remember	tragic
commiserate	heartache	saddened	trouble
compassion	heartbroken	severe	trying
concerned	heartsick	shaken	unfortunate
consolation	heavyhearted	share	unhappy
devastating	hope	shocked	unwelcome
difficult	misfortune	sorrow	upset

PHRASES

although I never met

at a loss for words

beautiful/blessed/cherished
  memories

deepest sympathy

deeply saddened

during this difficult time

extremely/terribly/so sorry to hear of

family sorrow

feel fortunate to have known

feel the loss of

grand person

greatly saddened

greatly/sadly/sorely missed

grieved to hear/learn of your loss

grieve/mourn with you

heart goes out to

I remember so well

I was saddened to learn/so sorry to
  hear that

in your time of great sorrow

legacy of wisdom, humor, and love
  of family

long be remembered for

made a difference in many lives

many friends share your grief

no words to express my great/
  overwhelming/sincere/deep sorrow

offer most sincere/heartfelt/deepest
  sympathy

one of a kind

profound sorrow

rich memories

sad change in your circumstances

sad event/news/bereavement

send my condolences/our deepest
  sympathy

sharing in your grief/sorrow during
  this difficult time

shocked and profoundly grieved/
  saddened

sick at heart

sincere condolences

sorry to learn/hear about

so special to me

stunned by the news

terrible blow

touched to the quick

tragic news

trying time

upsetting news

warmest sympathy

wish to extend our condolences/
  sympathy

with sincere feeling/personal sorrow/
  love and sympathy/sorrow and
  concern

SENTENCES

All of us are the poorer for Patrick's death.

Dora was a wonderful person, talented and loving, and I know that you and
  your family have suffered a great loss.

How sad I was to hear of Hsuang Tsang's sudden death.

I am thinking of you in this time of sorrow.

I can still see the love in his face when he watched you tell a story.

I feel privileged to have counted Fanny as a friend.

I hope you don't mind, but Marion Halcombe told us about your recent bad luck and I wanted to tell you how sorry we were to hear it.

I know Phillip had many admiring friends, and I am proud to have been one of them.

I remember the way your mother made all your friends feel so welcome with her questions, her fudge, and her big smiles.

It seems impossible to speak of any consolation in the face of such a bitter loss.

It was with great sadness/sense of loss/profound sorrow that I learned of Ramona's death.

I was so sorry to hear that Mr. Golovin's long and courageous battle with cancer has ended.

I wish I weren't so far away.

I write this with a heavy heart.

Like so many others who were drawn to Yancy by his charm, courage, and warmth, I am deeply grieved and bewildered by his unexpected death.

Please extend our condolences to the members of your family.

Professor Bhaer will always remain alive in the memories of those who loved, respected, and treasured him.

The loss of your warm and charming home saddened us all.

The members of the Crestwell Women's Club send you their deepest sympathy.

The world has lost someone very special.

We always enjoyed Dr. Stanton's company and respected him so much as a competent, caring physician and surgeon.

We were grieved to hear that your baby was stillborn.

We were stunned to hear that you lost your job, but are hopeful that someone with your experience and qualifications will find something suitable—maybe even better.

We who knew and loved Varena have some idea of how great your loss truly is.

You and the family are much in our thoughts these days.

Your grief is shared by many.

PARAGRAPHS

We felt so bad when we heard about the burglary. Something similar happened to us, and it affected me much more deeply and took longer to get over than I would ever have expected. I hope you are not too undone. May we lend you anything? Help put things back in order? Type up an inventory of what's missing? I'll stop by to see what you need.

This will acknowledge your letter of the 16th. Unfortunately, Mr. Newman is vacationing in a wilderness area this week, but I know he will be most distressed to learn of your brother's death when he returns. Please accept my sympathy on your loss—Mr. de Bellegarde visited here only once, but he left behind the memory of a charming, generous man.

Helen's death is a sad loss for you and for many others at Zizzbaum & Son. We too will sorely miss her, both from a personal and from a professional standpoint. As you know, we could not have been more pleased with her work for us over the past five years. She made many good friends here, and we all send you our heartfelt sympathy.

It's been a year today since Hebble died, and I wanted to tell you that we think of him often and with great affection. You must still miss him very much. I hope you are keeping busy and managing to find small happinesses in everyday things. We will be passing through Cool Clary in March, and hope to see you then.

The staff and student body join me in extending our sympathy to you on the death of your father. I have heard the stories you tell about this delightful and determined man, and I am sure this is a great loss for you. A special donation has been made to the scholarship fund. Next year, one of the scholarships will carry his name.

There is no good time for a tragedy, of course, but I know that you were in the midst of completing plans for the national conference. Would it help if I tied up the loose ends for you? You are so organized I'm sure I'll have no trouble following your notes. Just say the word if this is something I could do for you. And, again, please accept my most sincere sympathies on your sister's death.

SAMPLE LETTERS

Dear Mr. Latch,

I was so sorry to hear of Mrs. Latch's death. Although I haven't seen you since I left Barfield, I have often thought with great affection and pleasure of those wonderful days we spent together at the races. Please accept my sympathy on your sad loss.

Yours truly,

~

Dear Mary and Jessie,

We were all so sorry to hear about your father's death. He was a fine man, and all of Cranford is in mourning for him. I remember seeing him take the two of you for a walk each evening after dinner when you were just little girls. I hope your memories of him will be some comfort to you.

Please accept our sympathy and good wishes.

Sincerely,

~

Dear Lydia,

I was shocked to hear of Noel's death; you must be devastated. You and Noel were always closer than any married couple I know. I can only hope that your years of happiness and your many good memories will enable you to live with this sad loss.

Affectionately yours,

~

Dear Dr. and Mrs. Primrose,

Please accept my sympathy on the fire that leveled your home. I understand you and your family are staying temporarily with the Thornhills. As soon as you begin rebuilding, please let me know—I would like to help.

My husband joins me in hoping that you and the children will soon be back in your own home.

With best wishes,

~

Dear Jody,

We were all sorry to hear the sad news. Flag was much more than a pet, I know, and you must be wondering if you'll ever feel happy again. I'm enclosing a picture that I took of you and Flag about a month ago. I hope it doesn't make you sad, but brings back good memories instead.

Love,

~

Dear Eden,

Harriet tells me that your divorce from Alayne is now final. Please accept my sympathies for the difficult experience this must have been. I also send my best wishes for a bright and happy future. I'll call you next week to see if you have time to get together.

Your friend,

Dear Ms. Abinger:

I was sorry to hear of the recent flooding you've had at the Corner Stores. It is one of those horror stories that haunt the dreams of self-employed businesspeople everywhere. I wish you all good luck in getting things back to normal as quickly as possible.

I wanted to assure you that although I will temporarily order my supplies elsewhere, I will be bringing my business back to you as soon as you are ready. I appreciate our long association and am looking forward to doing business with you again.

Sincerely,

Dear Leora and Martin,

Please accept our most heartfelt condolences on your miscarriage. I know how much you were both looking forward to welcoming this child into your lives.

Will you let us know the moment you feel up to a quiet visit? We would like to stop by with a couple of our warmest hugs.

With love and sympathy,

Dear Kitty and Chris,

We were stunned to hear the tragic news about Oliver. Everyone who knows you must be appalled and heartbroken at the loss of your bright, charming, lovable son. There are no words to adequately express our sympathy for the devastation and profound loss you must be feeling. Please know we are thinking of you and praying for you every minute.

In talking with Chris's mother, we learned that you are without a car because of the accident. We're leaving one of the demo cars for your use as long as you need it. Please let us do this; there is no need to call or to discuss it.

We'll be seeing you in the next couple of days. Until then, we send all our love and deepest sympathy.

Sincerely,

See also: ACKNOWLEDGMENTS, ANNOUNCEMENTS, BELATED, "GET WELL," RESPONSES, THANK YOU.

Thank-You Letters

47

*His courtesy was somewhat extravagant. He would write and thank people
who wrote to thank him for wedding presents and when he encountered anyone
as punctilious as himself the correspondence ended only with death.*

—EVELYN WAUGH

Thank-you letters enhance business and personal relationships and handsomely
reward those who make a practice of sending them. Despite this, people find
them difficult to write, which is perhaps why so many arrive late or not at all.

When you're unsure if a thank you is necessary, err on the side of "necessary." Even when you have graciously thanked someone in person, a written
thank you is often expected or required or, at the least, appreciated. In the business world, the thank-you note has become a must if you care about your
career. "Anyone too busy to say thank you will get fewer and fewer chances to
say it." (Harvey Mackay)

For wedding gift thank yous, see WEDDINGS.

Write Thank-You Letters for

- appreciation/congratulations/recognition
- contributions: fundraising drives/memorials/charities
- employee suggestions/outstanding efforts/jobs well done
- expressions of sympathy
- favors/kindness/assistance/special help/advice
- gifts: business/personal
- hospitality: business/personal
- job interviews

- money: gifts/bonuses/loans
- orders: new/unusual
- patronage: new account/first purchase/good customer
- referrals: customers/clients/patients
- requested information/materials/documents
- sales prospects
- wedding and wedding shower gifts (see WEDDINGS)

- Describe in some detail what you are grateful for (not just "the lovely gift" or "the nice present").
- Express your gratitude in an enthusiastic, appreciative way.
- Elaborate on your appreciation. Tell how useful or appropriate it is, how you plan to use it, where you have placed it, or how it enhances your life, home, office, wardrobe. Be specific about what pleased you.
- Close with one or two sentences unrelated to the object of your gratitude (expressing affection, promising to see the person soon, sending greetings to family members, saying something nice about the donor).

What Not to Say

- Don't dilute your thanks by including news, information, questions, and comments; save them for another time.
- When you receive duplicate gifts, don't mention this to the givers.
- Don't ask where the gift was purchased so you can exchange it.
- Some etiquette authorities say not to mention the amount of a money gift. They suggest instead speaking of the giver's kindness, generosity, or, perhaps, extravagance. However, if both you and the gift-giver are comfortable with a mention of the amount, this is an acceptable choice.
- A few letterwriting experts dislike the "Thanks again" that concludes so many thank-you letters and notes. However, it is a popular and benign way of reminding the reader of the purpose of the letter. If you like it, use it.
- "Never express more than you feel" is a good guideline, especially in thank-you letters, where we try to make up in verbiage what we lack in enthusiasm. A simple "thank you" is effective.

Tips on Writing

∼ Write soon. It's easier to find the words when you feel grateful than it is after your enthusiasm has cooled. It's also more courteous. Most givers don't need your thanks as much as they need to know if the gift arrived (especially if it was sent from a store) and if it pleased you. Some people think a thank-you note should be written within three days of receiving a gift. Certainly two weeks would be a maximum. For a stay in someone's home, write within one to three days, but certainly within a week; for dinners and other hospitality, within a day or two. When responding to expressions of sympathy, you have up to six weeks because of the special hardships involved. For "get well" gifts, wait until you are well enough to write comfortably (a friend can acknowledge gifts for you in the meantime).

∼ You are not obliged to write a thank you (although of course it is always in excellent taste and will be greatly appreciated if you do) for: a party at which you were not the guest of honor; a casual dinner, lunch, or cocktail party; birthday, anniversary, congratulations, and "get well" cards and greetings; favors and hospitality extended by people with whom you are close (a sibling, a neighbor) and with whom you have reciprocal arrangements. In these cases, thank the person by telephone or the next time you see them.

∼ Overnight hospitality always warrants a thank-you note—and usually a gift, which you bring with you or send afterwards (popular items are specialty foods, houseplants, flowers, something for the house, toys for the children). When you write a family, address the parents, but mention the children by name (and if you say something complimentary about them, you will have more than justified your invitation). If you write to only the one who invited you or the one who was primarily responsible for your comfort, extend your thanks to the other household members.

Special Situations

∼ A late "thank you" is harder to defend than any other delayed message, but it is better to write late than not at all. In his delightful manners book for children, *How Rude!*, Alex J. Packer tells them, "Thank-you notes get exponentially more difficult to write with each day that passes. By the second day, they are *four* times harder to write. By the third day, they are *nine* times harder, and if you wait twelve days, they are *144* times harder to write!" Don't spend more than a phrase or a sentence apologizing for the delay: "My thanks are no less sincere for being so unforgivably late." "I am sorry not to have told you sooner how much we enjoyed the petit fours."

~ Yes, you send a thank-you note for a thank-you gift, if for no other reason than to let the person know it arrived.

~ When someone donates money to a charity in your honor or in memory of a deceased relative, the charity will acknowledge the contribution to the donor, usually with a printed card or form letter, but you also write a thank-you note.

~ Although the guest or guests of honor at an anniversary party, birthday party, or shower always thank each friend warmly for gifts as they are opened, thank-you notes are still required. The party or shower host should receive a special thank you as well as a small gift.

~ An essential job-seeking technique as well as a gesture of courtesy is to thank the person who interviews you. Write a note immediately after the interview and before a decision has been made. State what you liked about the interview, the company, the position. Emphasize briefly and specifically your suitability for the job. Address concerns about your qualifications that came up during the interview. Mention any issue that you didn't have the opportunity to discuss.

~ Although business entertaining is often taken for granted, a thank you is appreciated and builds good relations. Notes to a colleague, client, employee, or supplier inspire loyalty, enthusiasm, and increased productivity. When you receive a gift from a business contact, write a thank you, even though you suspect hundreds of gifts were sent. When you are unable to accept a business gift, avoid any implied accusation of poor taste on the giver's part when you write your thank-you-but-I-must-refuse letter; explain simply that your firm doesn't allow you to accept gifts.

~ When gifts arrive early for an event, write thank-you notes after the special day.

~ When you receive a gift from more than one person, write personalized thank-you notes to each one. You don't need to do this when you receive a gift from a family (even when all five of them sign the card) or when you receive a gift from a group such as your bridge club, teachers at your school, your co-workers. You can write one letter to the group but circulate or post it so that everyone who contributed sees it.

~ After a death in the family, thank-you notes are written to people who sent flowers or donations, and to those who helped with hot meals, hosted dinners, put up out-of-town relatives, lent chairs, or were otherwise supportive. You also respond to those who sent notes of condolence (exception: those who sent printed cards with only a signature and no personal message). You may use the printed cards supplied by the funeral home if you add a personal note. When the person closest to the deceased is unable to manage the correspondence, a family member or friend writes thank-you notes on their behalf. The notes need not be long and, traditionally, you have up to six weeks after the funeral to send them. To keep track of who sent flowers, a family member or funeral home official should collect the attached cards and write a description of the flowers on them.

~ Send thank-you notes to sales prospects for the time they spend with you on the phone or in the office. Your notes—which take only minutes to write— will secure for you their good will and their increased willingness to speak with you next time. (You also may surprise yourself by liking this part of your work—after the first few notes anyway.)

~ For a few special gifts, you may want to write two thank-you notes, the first when you receive the gift (a check or a fondue set, for example) and the second when you use it ("we used your gift to enroll in a ballroom dancing class, something we've wanted to do for years" or "we invited the cousins over for fondue and told them that they could thank you too!").

Format

~ Thank-you messages are almost always handwritten on foldovers, note cards, or personal stationery. Typewritten thanks are acceptable when they are part of a long, personal letter to family or friends.

~ Use formal printed or engraved stationery to write thank-you notes for important events (weddings, for example).

~ Business thank yous are typed on letterhead stationery, personal-business stationery, or good bond paper. When you want a warmer tone, hand-write your note.

~ Commercial foldovers with "Thanks" or "Thank you" are convenient and acceptable; a handwritten note goes on the inside page. Contemporary thank-you cards with sentimental or humorous messages are also appropriate as long as a handwritten message is added.

~ When you need to thank many people, it is appropriate (and, in some areas, expected) to insert a thank-you notice in the local newspaper. The nurses, doctors, hospital staff, friends, and family who helped someone through a long and demanding illness are often thanked. The funeral of a public figure may inspire hundreds of notes of condolence, which are best acknowledged in a newspaper announcement. Recently elected public officials thank those who worked and voted for them. The wording is simple and warm: "We wish to thank all the generous and loving friends and family who sent cards and gifts on the occasion of our twenty-fifth wedding anniversary."

⁓ Can you e-mail your thanks? In most cases, no. Certainly e-mail is suitable for quick thanks between longtime friends for the loan of a book, a small favor, a light lunch. It can also be used as a down-payment on a "real" thank-you note, written primarily to say that the gift arrived and that a letter will follow. The point of a thank-you note is that it is personal. E-mail has many virtues, but graciousness and formality are not among them.

⁓ Miss Manners (Judith Martin of the *Washington Post*) warns against faxing a thank you to someone who has just bought your product. She points out that the recipient must pay for such a thank you (fax paper, the time the letter occupies the machine, machine depreciation).

WORDS

appreciate	favorite	lovely	sensational	thrilled
bountiful	flattered	luxurious	sophisticated	timeless
captivated	generosity	memorable	special	timely
charming	gracious	needed	spectacular	touched
cherished	grateful	one-of-a-kind	striking	treasure
classic	hospitable	overjoyed	stunned	treat
delighted	impressed	overwhelmed	sumptuous	unique
elegant	indebted	perfect	superb	useful
enchanted	invaluable	pleased	surprised	valuable
enjoyed	keepsake	priceless	tasteful	well-made
excited	kindness	remarkable	terrific	wonderful
fascinated	large-hearted	satisfying	thoughtful	

PHRASES

absolutely perfect choice for me
appreciate your confidence/interest/
   kind words/referral
a rare treat
cannot tell you how delighted I was
charming of you
consider me deeply in your debt for
convey my personal thanks to
   everyone who
deeply appreciate

derived great pleased from
did us good/our hearts good
enjoyable and informative tour
enjoyed it/ourselves enormously
excellent/splendid suggestion
felt right at home
from the bottom of my heart
generous gift
great gift for us

heartfelt/hearty thanks
how kind/dear/thoughtful/
     sweet of you to
how much it meant to us
I am indebted/very much obliged to
     you for
I have seldom seen such
I'll long remember
important addition to
I plan to use it for/to
I really treasure
it was a great pleasure
it was hospitable/kind of you to
I will never forget
made us feel so welcome
many thanks
meant a great deal to me
more people have remarked on the
more than kind
most sincerely grateful to you for
most thoughtful and generous
much obliged
one of the most memorable days
     of my trip
one of your usual inspired ideas
perfect gift/present
please accept my gratitude/our
     sincere appreciation

pleased as Punch
profoundly touched by
quite out of the ordinary
really appreciate your help
seventh heaven
so characteristically thoughtful
thoroughly enjoyed myself
tickled our fancy
truly a marvel
truly grateful
very special occasion
we want you to know how much
     we value
we were especially pleased because
we were simply thrilled/delighted/
     stunned with
what a joy it was to receive
will be used every day/often
with your usual inimitable flair/style
wonderful addition to
you made me feel so special by
you may be sure that I appreciate
you must be a mindreader
your generous gift
your gift meant a lot to me at this
     time because
your thoughtful/kind expression of
     sympathy

SENTENCES

All of us were touched by your thoughtfulness.

As soon as we decide what to do with your wonderful gift [money] we will
     let you know.

How dear of you—we are delighted!

How did you know we needed one?

I appreciate your advice more than I can say.

I can't remember when I've had a better/more pleasant/more relaxing/more enjoyable time.

I can't thank you enough for chauffeuring me around while my knee was in the immobilizer.

I'll cherish your gift always.

I love it!

I'm grateful for your help, and hope that I can reciprocate some day.

In the past several weeks, you have kindly referred Harvey Birch, Frances Wharton, and Judith Hunter to the Cooper Architectural Group—we are grateful!

I owe you one!

I plan to use your gift to buy a wok—we've always wanted one.

I treasure the paperweight—it will always remind me of you.

It was kind of you to let me know about the job opening—I'll keep you posted.

I very much appreciate your concern.

Madeleine will be writing you herself, but I wanted to thank you for knowing just what would please a nine-year-old.

More people have remarked on it!

On behalf of the family of Violet Effingham Chiltern, I thank you for your kind expression of sympathy.

Special thanks to the doctors and the nurses at Trewsbury County Hospital.

Thanks a million.

Thanks for recommending Bates Craters and Freighters—they've been as good as you said they were.

Thanks for the great advice on patio brick—I'm pleased with what we finally bought.

Thanks for thinking of me.

Thanks for your order and for the interest in Leeds Sporting Goods that prompted it.

Thank you for including me in this memorable/special event.

Thank you for opening a charge account with us recently.

Thank you for shopping regularly at Farrell Power & Light.

Thank you for your courtesy and patience in allowing me to pay off the balance of my Irving Products, Inc. account in small installments.

Thank you for your generous donation to the Dunstone Foundation in memory of James Calpon Amswell; he would have been pleased and I appreciate your comforting gesture very much.

Thank you for your kind hospitality last night; I have never felt less a stranger in a strange city.

Thank you so much for agreeing to speak to our study club.

The letter of reference you so kindly wrote for me must have been terrific— Goodman & Co. called yesterday with a job offer!

This is just a note to thank you for rushing the steel shelving to us in time for our event.

Visions of Paradise is a stunning book, and we are all enjoying it immensely.

We all thank you for the tickets to the science museum.

We are thrilled with the handsome brass bookends you sent!

We will never forget the autumn glories of the North Shore—thank you so much for inviting us to share your cabin with you last weekend.

You can see what a place of honor we've given your gift the next time you stop by.

You couldn't have found anything I'd enjoy more.

You shouldn't have, but since you did, may I say that your choice was absolutely inspired!

PARAGRAPHS

Thank you for agreeing to write a letter of recommendation for me, especially since I know how busy you are this time of year. I'm enclosing a stamped envelope addressed to the personnel officer at Strickland Construction. I will, of course, let you know at once if I get the job. In the meantime, thanks again for your kindness.

I want to thank you for all the time you put into coaching the Crossley-area baseball team this summer. It was a joy to watch you and your enthusiastic players model sporting behavior and team spirit to some of the younger teams. The assistance of our volunteer coaches is crucial to the survival of this program, and the Board of Directors joins me in sending you our admiration and thanks.

On behalf of the directors, staff, and employees of Mallinger Electronics, I want to thank you for your splendid arrangements for the Awards Banquet Night. Decorations, food, program, and hospitality were all first-rate. Please convey our admiration and thanks to your committee chairs.

If you can possibly face the thought, we'd like you to chair next year's celebration. The evening was an outstanding success in every way, primarily due to your organizational abilities, creativity, and interpersonal skills.

Thank you so much for the graduation check. As you know, I'm saving everything I earn for college, so when I received your card and gift, I knew right away what I was going to do with it! I've been needing and wanting a decent watch for a long time, and I can hardly wait to choose one. Every time I look at my new watch, I'll think of you with affection and gratitude.

It is my understanding that you wrote a letter supporting my nomination by the Department of Materials Science and Engineering as a Distinguished Professor. I am happy to inform you that I was indeed honored with this title on June 3, 2002. I am deeply appreciative of your kind support in this regard. Many thanks.

The kindness and generosity you showed to all of us at the time of Edgar's death are much appreciated. What a good idea to send a plant; we've put the chrysanthemums in Edgar's perennial garden. Thanks too for the hot meals, the touching letter that I know you put your whole self into, and for your constant support. We're blessed to count you as a friend.

What a wonderful engagement gift! We haven't even begun to think of planning our wedding as we've heard it's so much work and so complicated. With this marvelous book on wedding planning, I think we can quit worrying.

Your dad said you picked out my tie all by myself. Thank you! Aunt Belinda just took a picture of me wearing the tie and eating a piece of birthday cake. When we get the pictures developed I'll send you one so you can see how nice I look in my new tie.

I would like to thank one of your sales staff for being helpful, tactful, and speedy—all at the same time! I foolishly tried to buy a wedding gift on my lunch hour, and I am a poor shopper at the best of times. Within minutes, this young man helped me select the absolutely perfect gift at the price I wanted to pay. It was all done so smoothly that I was out of the store before I knew it—and before I thought to ask his name. The initials on my sales slip are R.J. Can you identify him and pass on my thanks?

Thanks for the Mozartkugeln! One of my favorite annual rituals is watching the Wimbledon tennis finals in bed (they start at 7:00 a.m.). The women's final was great, and that's when I ate the Mozartkugeln—they were deliciously decadent. When I lived in Salzburg, a shop near my apartment made them daily. They cost about a quarter each then, and every day after class I made my little journey there to get one.

Thank you for the assistance, information, and encouragement you offered us when Hannah was applying to the U.S. Air Force Academy. We're convinced that her acceptance was due in no small measure to your support and advocacy.

Thank you for your most welcome letter of September 28. I am impressed with your generosity in sending complimentary subscriptions of the magazine to our doctors and nurses presently working in Tanzania. They will make good use of then—they estimate that each copy of the magazine is held by over fifty pairs of hands!

I enjoyed this morning's discussion of the research position you want to fill. I was pleased to know that my advanced degree is definitely an asset. I've been "overqualified" for several jobs, and was beginning to wonder if my extra years of study were of any value in the job market. Thanks so much for your time and for the congenial interview.

SAMPLE LETTERS

Dear Mr. Hollingford,

Thank you for remembering my five-year anniversary with the company. I didn't think anyone would notice except me! I've enjoyed working here and plan to stay as long as you'll have me. Thank you, too, for the gift certificate to Sweeney Inn. I have another anniversary coming up (three years of marriage), and I know where we'll celebrate it.

                                        Sincerely,

Dear Aune Esther Koskenmaki Lilley,

Thank you so much for sending us a copy of your book, *Father Said, "Eat, Don't Giggle!"* You are quite right in thinking that our collection of folklore materials can benefit from your contribution, especially since Finnish folklore is of particular interest to our Folk Arts Division.

Again, thank you for your book.

                                        Sincerely,

Dear Agnes and Walter,

Thank you for the lovely silver piggy bank you gave Anabel. It's a classic, and I know she will treasure it all her life. In the meantime, it has a place of honor on her dresser, and we've gotten into the habit of putting our change into it at the end of the day.

Can you come by to see your new little grand-niece sometime next week? We're all feeling rested by now and would love to see you. Give me a call.

With much love,

⌒⁓⁓'

Dear Millicent,

The dinner party was elegant and memorable, and we were delighted to be included. I don't know anyone who has as much flair and style as you do when it comes to entertaining!

Fondly,

⌒⁓⁓'

Dear Vincent Crummles:

Thank you for your contribution of $200 to the Alumni Annual Giving Campaign. As stipulated on the donor card returned to this office, your gift will be designated for the Annual Giving Fund to be used where most needed.

We also appreciate your use of the Langdon Co. matching gifts program and look forward to receiving their one-for-one matching gift. This matching gift will also be directed to the Annual Giving Fund.

Thank you again for your generosity, which will make it possible for many young women and young men to have the advantage of a quality education.

Very truly yours,

⌒⁓⁓'

See also: ACCEPTANCES, ACKNOWLEDGMENTS, APPRECIATION, BELATED, RESPONSES.

Letters Related to Travel

48

A trip is what you take when you can't take any more of what you've been taking.

—ADELINE AINSWORTH

Today most travel arrangements (airline, car, hotel reservations; requests for tourist, passport, health information; cancellations) are made by phone, e-mail, or on the Internet. Occasionally, however, a letter or faxed letter is the best choice to outline complicated arrangements, confirm reservations, address special problems, or register a complaint.

Every letter that a travel business writes to customers—even a one-sentence response to a query for information—is a sales or goodwill letter and is courteous, positive, and presentable.

Write Travel Letters to

- airlines
- bus companies
- campground/RV facilities
- convention and visitors bureaus
- cruise companies
- customers of a travel business
- employers for travel reimbursement
- entertainment/amusement complexes
- friends and relatives

- hotels/motels/B&Bs
- national parks
- railroad companies
- resorts/spas/dude ranches
- tourist information centers
- travel agents

- Begin with your question or item of business.
- Include specifics: dates; number of nights, people, rooms, type of accommodation, extras, verification of information about accessibility, pool, cable TV, entertaining facilities; type of car, number of days, pickup and dropoff points; record, confirmation, or other locator number; credit card number; your address and telephone number; names of guests or passengers.
- Mention enclosed deposit or coupons.
- Repeat terms or information you were given over the telephone.
- Ask for a confirmation number.
- Close with a courtesy.

- Don't volunteer unnecessary personal information.
- Don't put your credit card number in a letter unless you know the company well.
- Don't assume anything. Ask for information when you are not sure about details.

Tips on Writing

∾ Aside from standard courtesies ("thank you for your assistance/attention"), you are brief when writing about travel arrangements.

~ Put each unit of information on its own line:

compact car

standard transmission

airconditioning

3 days, May 11–14

pickup: New York-JFK

dropoff: Boston-Logan

~ When requesting confirmation or a response from a non-U.S. hotel, resort, or travel bureau, especially one on the low-budget end, enclose an International Reply Coupon (available at post offices) to assure a response. If you don't have an IRC, suggest they e-mail or fax their response.

~ Take copies of all reservations, confirmation letters, etc., with you as you travel, along with notes on telephone arrangements.

~ To inspire you to write travel letters home, read Rudyard Kipling's *Letters of Travel*, Pierre Teilhard de Chardin's *Letters from a Traveller*, John Steinbeck's *A Russian Journal*, Michael Crichton's *Travels*. From Phillip Brooks' 1893 *Letters of Travel* and Gertrude Bell's 1894 *Persian Pictures* to Freya Stark's 1929 *Baghdad Sketches* to Joanne Sandstrom's 1983 *There and Back Again* and Erma Bombeck's 1991 *When You Look Like Your Passport Photo, It's Time to Go Home*, you'll find letters to inspire and entertain.

Special Situations

~ When making requests for hotel or motel reservations, include such information as the number of persons in your group, how many rooms you need and whether you want single or double beds, your times of arrival and departure, and any extras you'll need (crib, poolside room, connecting rooms, additional bed, nonsmoking room). Ask for confirmation of your reservation, and indicate how the rooms are to be billed—to you, to a credit card, to your company account—and if you are entitled to a discount of any kind.

~ When canceling a travel arrangement, repeat the information in your original letter. (Canceling has become more than courtesy; if you forget to cancel a reservation, your credit card may be charged for the first night.)

~ One can hardly say "travel" without thinking "postcards." If you choose the cards carefully, you will already have something to write ("Our hotel is right by this canal" or "We toured this castle yesterday" or "We went to the top of this mountain in a funicular"). A postcard shows recipients something colorful, interesting, or unknown to them. Your message focuses on your pleasure being there (nobody wants to hear that you've had trouble). Tell what you've liked best, a food you've eaten for the first time, an interesting fact or bit of history, the impact your trip is having on you.

~ For information and forms on obtaining or renewing a passport, write: National Passport Center, Federal Building, Chicago, IL 60604. The same information is available online at http://www.travel.state.gov and forms can be downloaded.

Format

~ Except for postcards and letters to family and friends, all travel correspondence should be typed to avoid errors.

~ Fax and e-mail are often used for travel arrangements.

WORDS

accommodation	deposit	nonrefundable	schedule
arrangement	directions	register	sightseeing
availability	discount	reimburse	tour
booked	excursion	rental	visa
cancel	fare	reservation	voyage
charter	lodging	roundtrip	

PHRASES

activities for children	hold for late arrival
advance purchase requirements	map of the area
areas of interest	nearby horseback riding
bed and breakfast (B&B)	sightseeing/tour package
discount for those over-55	sports facilities
eighteen-hole golf course	travel insurance
especially interested in	youth hostel
flexible schedule	

SENTENCES

Attached is a completed form about the luggage lost November 8 on flight # 78 as well as photos and descriptions of the missing luggage.

Enclosed are the reimbursable hotel, meal, and car rental receipts from my trip to Miami February 10–14.

Is your resort fully accessible to someone who uses a wheelchair?

I would like to dispute the $150 charge for changing the return date on my ticket.

Please send a brochure and rates for the Kokua Family Resort.

Sweeting-Nunnely Telecommunications is considering holding its annual shareholders' meeting in your area and would appreciate your sending us information on your convention center, hotels, area attractions, and any other material that would be helpful in making our decision.

This will confirm the cancellation of our reservation at the Doddington Dude Ranch.

We will be spending the month of July in Sundering-on-Sea and would appreciate receiving a map of the area, train schedules, a calendar of local events, and anything else that would help acquaint us with your area.

PARAGRAPHS

You asked about transportation between the airport and the hotel. We operate a free shuttle service that leaves the airport every half-hour between the hours of 7 a.m. and midnight from the Ground Transportation area. Look for the Crossley Hotels logo on the bus.

Your room will be billed on the group account for the convention so you do not have a confirmation number. However, at check-in give your name and say you are with Gammon, Quirk & Co.

As discussed in our telephone conversation this morning, we will arrive at the Lowborough Hotel at approximately 3 p.m., Thursday, August 31. Thank you for your willingness to reserve a parking space with orange traffic pylons for our 24' rental moving truck. I wouldn't like to depend on chance to find a parking place for a truck that size, especially in Boston!

I very much enjoyed my stay at the O'Reilly McMurrough International Hotel. However, I thought you'd like to know that when I tried to use the telephone, the "2" dialed 911. So did the "9." So did every other button. It was most disconcerting and a worrying nuisance for the emergency personnel on the other end of the calls. The iron also needs to be replaced; the plate is stained and it slightly damaged my dress.

Please accept this coupon good for one free night at the O'Reilly McMurrough International Hotel to apologize for the malfunctioning telephone and iron. We value your business and appreciate the courtesy of your letter.

We are planning to vacation in Seattle next June. Will you please send us information on hotels, a map of the area, descriptions of attractions, a list of events scheduled for that month, and a report of average June temperatures and rainfall?

SAMPLE LETTERS

Dear Mrs. Hawkins,

I would like to reserve a single room at the Admiral Benbow Inn for July 7–17. I will be arriving late on the evening of July 7 so please hold the room for my arrival. Enclosed is a check for the first night.

Thank you.

Sincerely,

TO: Granby Airlines
FAX: 212/555-1000
FROM: Julia Hazelrigg
DATE: Sept. 4, 2002
RECORD LOCATOR: # 4GMEN5
NUMBER OF PAGES: 2

In reference to today's telephone conversation, please cancel both reservations under record locator number # 4GMEN5.

My traveling companion was hospitalized suddenly yesterday for an indefinite period (attached is a note from the physician's office).

I understand that according to your policy for international flights, you offer a complete refund of all tickets in a party when one of the party must cancel due to illness.

I appreciate your compassion and prompt help at this difficult time.

Dear Knox Motor Inn,

I would like to reserve a no-smoking room in your hotel for two nights, June 19 and 20.

My husband and I have two sets of twins (ages six months and two-and-a-half years) so we will need four cribs and an extra set of sheets per crib. The room should also have two double beds since I spend much of the night nursing the infants and my husband spends much of the night comforting the toddlers.

We have lots of nighttime crying in our life just now so if you could please give us a room in a secluded wing of your hotel I'm sure your other patrons would appreciate it very much.

Please send confirmation of our reservation to our address as shown below.

Thank you!

$$\sim$$

See also: ACKNOWLEDGMENTS, ADJUSTMENTS, COMPLAINTS, FAXES, MEMOS, REQUESTS.

Wedding Correspondence

49

> *I joined a singles group in my neighborhood. The other day the president called me up and said, "Welcome to the group. I want to find out what kind of activities you like to plan." I said, "Well, weddings."*
>
> —LYNN HARRIS

All correspondence relating to weddings or commitment ceremonies, including engagements, is in this chapter. However, supporting advice may also be found in the chapters on ACCEPTANCES, ACKNOWLEDGMENTS, ANNOUNCEMENTS, BELATED, CONGRATULATIONS, INVITATIONS, REFUSALS, REQUESTS, RESPONSES, THANK YOU.

The only hard-and-fast rules for weddings and wedding correspondence today are those requiring courtesy, appropriateness, and common sense. The guidelines given below blend tradition and contemporary custom to provide you with a framework onto which you can sculpt your own individual tastes and circumstances.

Wedding Correspondence Includes

- acknowledging gifts
- announcements: printed/engraved/newspaper
- cancellation
- confirmation of arrangements
- congratulations on wedding
- families of wedding couple exchanging letters
- informing ex-spouse of remarriage

- invitations: showers/parties/dinners/wedding
- postponement
- responses: invitations/announcements
- selecting ceremony participants: attendants/presider/organist/
  musicians/reception helpers
- showers: invitations/thank yous
- thanking people for gifts/favors/greetings/assistance

- Engagement announcements can be made in one of four ways.
  (1) Handwrite individual letters to family and friends that include:
  name of the person you are to marry; wedding date (if known); if you
  choose, tell briefly how you met and how long you've known the
  person; some expression of your happiness; a personal comment (the
  other person is the first to know, you can't wait for them to meet
  your intended). (2) Insert an announcement in the newspaper that
  includes: your full names; hometowns; parents' names and hometowns; education backgrounds and places of employment; date of
  wedding or general plans ("a spring wedding is planned"). Some
  newspapers have requirements and deadlines for engagement
  announcements, and some will run either an engagement or a wedding announcement, but not both, so check beforehand. (3) Send
  formal printed or engraved engagement announcements: "Maria
  and Ernest Rockage announce the engagement of their daughter
  Phyllis to Stephen Newmark. An August wedding is planned."
  (4) Invite family and friends to a dinner party or other event at which
  the engagement is announced.
- Broken engagements need no announcement if no formal announcement was made. If you've written family and friends of the engagement, write the same type of personal note saying simply that you
  and the other person have broken your engagement; there's no need
  to explain why.
- When writing to ask friends or relatives to serve as attendants, state
  what you are asking and who pays for what. Offer them a graceful
  way of refusing so that they don't feel pressured. Express your appreciation for their friendship.

- Although many arrangements for weddings and commitment ceremonies are made by telephone, you often write letters of confirmation to the temple, church, or location where the ceremony is to be held; to the person who will officiate; to the sexton, organist, cantor, soloist, musicians; to your attendants, ushers, and others; to the photographer and videotaper; to the florist, jeweler, bakery; to hotels to make honeymoon arrangements; to the caterer or club for the reception; to order gifts for attendants, the aisle carpet, candles, ribbons, decorations. These different letters have three requirements in common: give all possible details; ask everything you need to know at the outset; keep copies of your correspondence.

- When hosting a wedding shower send handwritten invitations or commercial shower invitations that include: name of the honoree or honorees (bride-to-be, groom-to-be, the couple); type of shower (kitchen, tool, bath, garden, recipe, household); time, date, and place; R.S.V.P. or Regrets only; name, address, and telephone number of the host. Each guest is thanked for their gift at the shower, but thank-you notes are still sent to each person (even those who "went in together" on a gift) soon after the shower. The shower host receives a small gift as well as an especially warm thank you.

- Wedding invitations are engraved, printed, or handwritten. Many papers, typeface styles, inks, and designs are available at printers, stationery stores, and large department stores. The more formal the wedding, the more formal the invitations. Formal wedding invitations have two envelopes: the outer one is sealed for mailing, carries your return address, and is hand-addressed; the inner envelope, which contains the invitation (face up as you open the envelope), is unsealed (the flap has no glue) and carries the names of the invitees on the front. There may also be a sheet of tissue paper to protect the engraving, and enclosures such as at-home cards, reception cards, pew cards for a large wedding, maps indicating location of ceremony and reception, and admission cards if the ceremony or reception is held in a public place. Reply cards are inserted in envelopes addressed to you (printed or engraved) and stamped, and then placed in the inner envelope. Concern about our wasteful use of paper prompts some people to omit the inner envelope or to use recycled paper for their invitations. Reply envelopes are at least 5" × 3½" to comply with postal regulations. If you aren't using reply cards, include an address or telephone number below the R.S.V.P. so that guests know where to respond. For a small, casual wedding, handwrite invitations in black ink (perhaps a friend will offer calligraphy skills) on good-quality white or off-white notepaper or foldovers. Write in the first-person, in the same way that you would extend any informal invitation. Printed or engraved invitations are rarely sent for a small wedding. Your invitation includes: names of bride and groom; date, time, place; mention of hospitality to follow, if any; expression of pleasure at having guests celebrate with you. The invitation, whether formal or informal, may be issued by the couple, by both their parents, by the woman's parents, by the man's parents, or by a relative or family friend—in short, by whoever is hosting the event or whoever is most appropriate. A deceased parent is not named in the invitation as though it were being issued by her or him, but the person can be included if the invitation is sent by the bride and groom ("Jean Lucas, daughter of Martha Lucas and the late George Lucas, and Bruce Wetheral, son of Mr. and Mrs. John Henry Wetheral, request the honour of your presence . . .").

- Addressing invitations is an art in itself. On the outer envelope, list full names and addresses, with no abbreviations, if possible. On the inner envelope, repeat last names only ("Mr. and Mrs. Hollingrake"). Don't include young children's names on the outer envelope but list their first names under the parents' names on the inner envelope. (Never add "and family.") Older children (between thirteen and eighteen) receive their own invitations. Address one invitation using both full names to an unmarried couple living together. Your return address goes in the upper left-hand corner, unless you use embossed or engraved envelopes, in which case it is on the back flap. (Note that the U.S. Postal Service discourages placing return addresses on the back flap.) Use a good-quality fountain pen, felt tip, or narrow-tipped calligraphy pen to address the envelopes.

- Wedding cancellation announcements are similar in style and format to the invitations. If formal wedding invitations were sent, formal cancellation announcements are sent; they shouldn't be as lavish as the invitations, but should be of approximately the same quality. The message is simple: "Marjorie Corder and Theodore Honey announce that their marriage on the twenty-first of April, two thousand and three, will not take place."

- Printed, engraved, or handwritten announcements, modeled on the wedding invitation, are sent to those who weren't invited to the ceremony or reception. The same type of stationery is used, and the wording is similar. If formal invitations were sent, the announcements will also be formal; if the wedding was small and informal and invitations were handwritten, the announcements will also be handwritten. They are mailed as near the wedding date as possible (address them in advance), and may include at-home cards. The announcement is made by the bride's family ("Mr. and Mrs. Raymond Gray announce the marriage of their daughter Polly to . . ."); by the couple themselves ("Camilla Christy and Matthew Haslam announce their marriage on Saturday, the fifth of June . . ."); or by both sets of parents ("Evelyn and Peter Gresham and Bridget and Henry Derricks announce the marriage of their daughter and son, Audrey Gresham and George Derricks, on Friday, the third of April, two thousand and three, Emmanuel Lutheran Church, Golding, Nebraska").

- Reply to all wedding invitations. Use the formal reply card or, if there isn't one, use the same wording and degree of formality as the invitation to either "accept with pleasure" or "decline with regret." It is not improper to reply informally to a formal invitation. What is absolutely imperative is that you respond. (You need not respond if you are invited to the wedding ceremony only.) When accepting an invitation to a wedding reception, accept only for those people named on the invitation. If your children are not listed, they are not invited. It is highly improper to bring them to the reception. In the same way, if your envelope doesn't have "and guest" written on it, do not bring someone with you.

- Etiquette on thank-you notes for wedding gifts is inflexible: a handwritten thank you is sent for every gift, even if you thanked the individual in person or if you work with the person every day. Both newlyweds are responsible for thank-you notes; whoever writes mentions the other person ("Mae and I appreciate . . ."; "Hugh joins me in . . ."). Tradition allowed a month after the wedding to mail thank-you notes and contemporary authorities allow up to three months. However, the advice here is to send them immediately after the honeymoon. "The path of later leads to the house of never" (Donald E. Walker) and for many couples the three months turn into six, which turn into a year, which turns into embarrassment and denial and, finally, a guilty forgetfulness. Because everybody is busy today—even the people who found time to send you a gift—there's no excuse for not making a priority of sending wedding thank-you notes.

- Each thank-you note includes: a mention of the gift ("the silver bread tray," not "your lovely gift"); an expression of pleasure; a mention of how you'll use it, why you like it, how much you needed it; a sentence or two unrelated to the gift ("so good to see you at the wedding" or "hope you will come see our new home"). Don't mention dollar amounts of money gifts in your thank you, but tell how you plan to spend the money. Write separate and different thank yous to friends who sent joint gifts, unless the gift is from a large group, such as co-workers. If you use commercial thank-you foldovers or note cards, choose the plainest type. When a wedding gift is not to your taste, focus on the kindness of the giver rather than on the gift. For additional guidelines on writing thank-you notes, see THANKS.

- When you can't write immediate or at least timely thank-you notes (because of a large number of gifts, extended honeymoon, illness), send a handwritten or printed or engraved acknowledgment card for each gift. This lets the person know the gift arrived safely and assures them that you'll write a personal note as soon as you can. Acknowledgment cards in no way replace thank-you notes and are followed by them as soon as possible.

What Not to Say

- In formal wedding invitations and announcements, don't abbreviate anything except "Mr.," "Mrs.," "Ms.," "Jr.," and sometimes military rank. ("Doctor" is written out unless the name following it is too long.) In the case of initials in names, either supply the name for which an initial stands or omit the initial altogether. Write out "Second" and "Third" after a name or use Roman numerals ("Caspar Goodwood II"). There is no comma between the name and the numeral, although there is a comma between the name and "Jr." ("Caspar Goodwood, Jr."). The names of states are spelled out ("Alabama," not Ala. or AL) as are dates ("November third") and the time ("half past eight o'clock," "half past five o'clock"). All numbers under 100 are spelled out. No punctuation is used except for commas after the days of the week ("Saturday, the sixteenth of June") or periods after "Mr.," "Mrs.," "Jr." No words are capitalized except for people's names, place names, and days of the week or months. The year is not included on wedding invitations, but is usually included on announcements.
- When writing thank-you notes for wedding gifts, don't ask where a gift was purchased so that you can exchange it, and don't mention duplication of gifts.

Tips on Writing

∼ Traditionally "the honour of your presence" indicates a religious ceremony and "the pleasure of your company" is used for civil weddings or for wedding receptions.

∼ Watch for nonparallel forms when referring to the wedding couple in invitations, announcements, and other wedding correspondence—for example, "the marriage of Adela Polperro to Mr. Lucian Gildersleeve." Use honorifics for both (Ms. and Mr., for example) or for neither (neither is preferred). The phrase "man and wife" is "husband and wife" or "man and woman."

~ Timing: ask friends to be your attendants as soon as you have a date; order printed or engraved invitations at least three months before the wedding; begin to address invitations two months or more before the wedding (the envelopes can be picked up earlier than the invitations); mail all invitations at the same time—between three and six weeks before the wedding.

~ If you use reply cards, invitees will know how to respond. If you don't, insert an address or telephone number below the R.S.V.P. so they know where to send their responses.

~ In her 1941 book, Mary Owens Crowther tells readers mailing wedding invitations: "Do not use two one-cent stamps in place of a two-cent stamp. Somehow one-cent stamps are not dignified." Although her advice is dated, considering the appearance of your postage stamps is not; most invitations and announcements use attractive or meaningful commemorative stamps.

~ When you receive an engagement or wedding announcement, there is no obligation to send a gift, but it is customary to write your congratulations to the engaged or newly married couple. You may properly offer either one your "congratulations" or "best wishes." (These expressions used to be sex-linked; one was limited to use for the woman, one for the man.)

~ If you are late with your wedding congratulations, write anyway. Most people will understand and will be pleased that you remembered at all. Apologize only briefly for the delay.

~ Jot a brief description of the wedding gift on the back of the signed card that accompanies it. This has proved useful to more than a few newly married couples trying to determine which of the mystery gifts came from whom.

Special Situations

~ In today's over-scheduled world, many couples send "save the date" letters or even e-mails to notify family and friends of a wedding that may be a year or more in the future. Invitations are sent later in the normal way, six weeks before the wedding. While six weeks' notice was ample in the days when families and friends lived in the same small town and knew each other's news, today it is inadequate for making flight reservations, scheduling vacations around the date, or keeping the work calendar free for that day.

~ For a wedding announcement published in the newspaper, include as much of the following as allowed: bride's and groom's full names; date, time, and place of wedding; name of officiator or presider; names of members of the wedding party (and relation to the wedding couple); names, hometowns, and occupations or accomplishments of the couple's parents (and occasionally grandparents); information on the couple's education and careers; description of the flowers, music, and wedding party's clothes; where the reception was held; the couple's address after marriage. (If the woman keeps her birth name or if the couple adopts a hyphenated name, this is a good way to let people know: "Marian Belthem and Augustus F.G. Richmond will be living at 1871 Meredith.") Avoid nicknames and abbreviations. Call your newspaper in advance for guidelines on submitting wedding announcements. Some newspapers publish information about weddings only if there is news value. Others charge a fee for announcements. Some will publish either an engagement notice or a wedding announcement, but not both. And others will not print an announcement if it is "old news"—arriving more than several weeks after the wedding. Some want the information about three weeks before the wedding so that it can be run the day after the wedding. Wedding announcements can also be sent to employee newsletters, alumnae/alumni magazines, or other affiliation publications.

~ When the bride, the groom, or both are members of the military, it's customary to use their rank on invitations and announcements unless they are noncommissioned officers or enlisted personnel, in which case it may be omitted.

~ Prospective in-laws appreicate a gracious note of welcome by members of the family.

~ When you invite some people to the wedding and others to both wedding and reception, your wedding invitation mentions the ceremony only. Enclose a card (about 3" × 4", and of the same style stationery as the invitation) with an invitation to the reception. It is a shortened form of the wedding invitation: "Nora Hopper and George Trimmins request the pleasure of your company at their wedding reception [or: a reception following their wedding], on Saturday, the twelfth of June, Walter Village Inn, 55 North Walter Street. R.S.V.P." If all guests are invited to both the wedding and reception, you add, after the place of the wedding on your invitation, "Reception immediately following" or "and afterward at . . ." or "followed by a reception at . . ."

~ When prospective wedding guests indicate in their acceptance that they are bringing a friend or their children, whom you have not invited, write that you are pleased they can come to the wedding but that the reception is limited to those invited because of space or is for adults only. When you invite friends who may not know anyone at the reception, you can either call them for the name of a companion (so you can send a personal invitation) or add "and Guest" to their invitation.

~ To inform friends and relatives of your address after marriage, enclose an at-home card in your wedding invitation or announcement. It is usually the same style as your other wedding stationery, about 2¾" × 4": "Linda Condon and Arnaud Hallet will be at home after the sixth of June at 1918 Hergesheimer Road, Waunakee, Wisconsin 53597."

~ To let family and friends know that the woman plans to keep her birth name or that the couple is adopting a hyphenated or an altogether new surname, insert a small printed or engraved card (matching the wedding stationery) in the wedding invitation or announcement: "After their marriage, Clarissa Graham and Charles Belton will use the surname Belton-Graham," or "Clarissa Graham wishes to announce that following her marriage she will retain her birth name."

Format

~ Engagement or wedding announcement notices sent to newspapers are typed and double-spaced. If a photograph accompanies it, identify it on the back in case it gets separated from the announcement. (Use a return-address label or taped-on piece of paper; don't write directly on the back of the photo.)

~ Wedding invitations and announcements are engraved, printed, or handwritten. A bewildering variety of papers, type styles, inks, and designs are available at printers, stationery stores, and large department stores. Ecru remains the most popular color for invitations and social stationery. Your choice depends on the type of wedding—the more formal the wedding, the more formal the invitations and announcements. You can order matching name cards, thank-you notes, informals, notepaper, or other stationery at the same time.

~ Envelopes (for example, for reply cards and thank-you notes) must be at least 3½" × 5" to comply with postal regulations. And if your invitations are oversized or weigh more than an ounce (which happens with high-quality paper and two envelopes) they will need extra postage.

~ When responding to an invitation that contained no reply card, use formal notepaper or foldovers. If you have a card with your name on it, write underneath your name "accepts with pleasure" or "declines with regret" and then repeat the information about the event and the date.

WORDS

acknowledge	ceremony	marriage	ritual
announce	congratulations	matrimony	union
bless	happiness	nuptials	vows
celebrate	joy	pleasure	wishes

PHRASES

acknowledges with thanks the
   receipt of

groom's dinner

happy to announce/to invite
   you to

help us celebrate our wedding

invite you to celebrate with us

joined in holy matrimony

our fondest congratulations

rehearsal dinner

request the honour of your presence

request the pleasure of your company

share in the joy

united in wedlock

wedding party

we would be honored to

wish to acknowledge the receipt of

witness our marriage

SENTENCES

Aurelia and I were greatly touched by the beautiful family tea service you
   gave us for our wedding—we feel we're now connected to all the family
   that's gone before and all that is yet to come.

Best wishes on your wedding day!

Jane Vallens and Andrew Satchel gratefully acknowledge the receipt of your
   beautiful wedding gift and look forward to writing you a personal note of
   thanks at an early date.

Jesse joins me in thanking you for the oil painting you did especially for
   us—it is our first piece of original art!

Mary Llewellyn and Martin Hallam request the pleasure of your company
   at the marriage of their daughter Mary Frances.

Our very best wishes to you both for many years of happiness, health, and prosperity.

Please join us in celebrating the marriage of our daughter Sally to William Carter.

Thank you for your generous check, which will go a long way toward helping us buy the piano we have our eye on!

The ceremony will take place at 1:30 p.m., and a reception at the house will follow.

We're sorry, but we are limited in the number of guests we can have at the reception—we hope you'll still be able to come and that we can meet your cousin some other time.

We were delighted to hear of your engagement—Anita is an intelligent, beautiful, and kind young woman, and the two of you are beautifully matched!

We wish you every happiness as you celebrate the love you have for each other.

PARAGRAPHS

We would like to make an appointment with you to discuss the music for our wedding, which is scheduled for June 16 at 1:00 p.m. We have some ideas (and will bring some music with us), but we would appreciate some suggestions from you.

Julia and I will be married at our apartment on Saturday, June eighteenth at 5:30 p.m. It would mean a great deal to us if you would join us for the ceremony and for dinner afterwards.

You could not have chosen a more exquisite gift than the Waterford clock. I was deeply moved by your love and generosity. Unfortunately, Kit and I have canceled the wedding and we are returning all gifts. As you can imagine, I will never forget your thoughtfulness and I will always think of you whenever I see Waterford crystal.

Christina Hossett and Albert Edward Preemby were married June 18, 2002, at Wells First Christian Church. The Reverend Wilfred Devizes performed the ceremony. Parents are Mr. and Mrs. H.G. Hossett of Wells and Mr. and Mrs. A.E. Preemby, Sr., of Waynesville. Christina and Albert want to thank all the guests who celebrated with them. Both are employed at Stephens Insurance.

Bernice and I are absolutely delighted with the electric blanket. You must have been poor students yourselves once, living on the third floor of an old brownstone, hoping that perhaps today the heat might make it all the way upstairs. It's a beautiful, thoughtful, practical gift, and we're grateful.

SAMPLE LETTERS

The honour of your presence
is requested at the marriage of
Sybil Anstey Herbert
to
Harry Jardine
on Saturday, the tenth of October
at one o'clock
Lehmann Methodist Church
and afterward at
The New Lehmann Inn

R.S.V.P.
Sybil Anstey Herbert
20 Ianthe Court
Lehmann, OH 45042

~

Mr. Edmund Roundelay
regrets that owing to
the recent death of
Evelyn Ferguson Roundelay
the invitations to the marriage
of their daughter Crystal
to Maxwell Dunston
must be recalled.

~

Dear Lucy and Fred,

Christopher and I are so pleased you will be able to attend our wedding celebration. I'm afraid there's been a misunderstanding, however. You know how much we enjoy Freddy, Elsa, and Charles, but we are not planning on having any children at the reception. I hope you can find a babysitter so you can still come. Thanks for understanding.

Love,

~

Miss Laetitia Prism
regrets that she is unable to accept
the kind invitation of
Mr. and Mrs. Oscar Fairfax
to the marriage of their daughter
Gwendolyn Fairfax
Saturday, the sixth of June
two thousand and three
at 7:30 p.m.

～

Dear Marjorie,

Will and I have finally made the great decision—we're going to be married next August 19! And the really important question is: will you be my attendant? I can't imagine having anyone but you. However, if you can't get away—and what with your job, Richard's new business, and the children's activities, I know it will take some doing—I will certainly understand.

Enclosed is a sketch of the dress you'd wear. I want to pay for it, so don't worry about that. And of course you'll stay at the house, but unfortunately my budget won't run to your airfare. Will that be a problem?

I'll call next week after you've had time to think about this. In the meantime, Will sends his love along with mine.

～

Mr. and Mrs. Orville Jones
accept with pleasure
the kind invitation of
Belinda Jorricks
and
Charles Stobbs
to their marriage on
Friday, the tenth of May
two thousand and three
at 7:00 p.m.
St. James A.M.E. Zion Church
Reception following
Surtees Country Club
1838 Plains Highway

～

Christina Allaby and Theobald Pontifex
announce with great pleasure
their marriage on
Saturday, the twenty-third of June
two thousand and four
Butler, Maine

〜

Dear Grace and Harold,

Our dear Stella and Stanley Kowalski are being married on Saturday, September 4, at 3:00 p.m. in an informal ceremony at our house.

We'd love to have you celebrate with us, and stay after the ceremony for a small reception. Let me know if you can join us.

Fondly,

〜

Mimi Wynant and Christian Jorgensen
announce that their marriage
has been postponed from
Saturday, the third of June
until
Saturday, the sixth of August
at two o'clock
St. Anselm's Church
Webster City
Reception to follow
Webster City County Club

〜

See also: ACCEPTANCES, ACKNOWLEDGMENTS, ANNOUNCEMENTS, BELATED, CONGRATULATIONS, INVITATIONS, REFUSALS, REQUESTS, RESPONSES, THANK YOU.

Letters of Welcome

50

> Come in the evening, or come in the morning,
> Come when you're looked for, or come without warning.
> Kisses and welcomes you'll find here before you,
> And the oftener you come here the more I'll adore you.
>
> —THOMAS OSBORNE DAVIS

Because they're optional, letters of welcome are read with surprise, pleasure, and gratitude. They are a powerful sales tool for businesses, and a charming approach to smoothing and cementing interpersonal relations among neighbors, co-workers, and people with whom we have frequent dealings. For the naturally hospitable among us, they are a way of life and a joy to write.

Write Letters of Welcome to

- new business contacts/customers/clients
- new businesses in the neighborhood
- new co-workers/employees
- new members of club/organization/temple/church
- new neighbors
- new students/teachers
- potential customers/clients
- prospective in-laws

- State how happy you are to have the person join your company, store, division, club, family, group, neighborhood.
- Offer to help the person become acquainted with their new surroundings, duties, colleagues, neighbors.
- Tell something positive about the neighborhood, company, or organization the person is joining. If a special event is coming up, mention it to give the person something to look forward to.
- Suggest a possible future meeting, a store visit, an invitation to call you, or at least say that you're looking forward to meeting sometime soon. Assure the person you'll be glad to answer questions (include your telephone number)

- Don't refer to negative aspects of the person's new situation, for example, the mountains of unfinished work left by a predecessor or the roof problems that troubled the previous owner.
- Don't say "Good luck!" It implies that good luck will be needed.
- Avoid a strong selling message when welcoming customers.

Tips on Writing

∽ Send your welcome promptly; it is most appreciated when the new kid on the block still feels insecure.

∽ Find common ground between you or your organization and the person you're welcoming ("I understand you're a gardener—you'll be interested to know that many of us are!").

∽ The welcome letter is a fitting place to let the newcomer subtly know about any unwritten rules you might have. ("Although there's never time to chat during office hours, I'd like to get to know you better over lunch someday" or "We look forward to seeing you once you're settled in—but do give us a call first.")

Special Situations

∽ When welcoming new employees, include detailed terms of employment to avoid later misunderstandings: hours, duties, salary, title, starting date, supervisor. If the newcomer receives packets of information—building regulations, benefits, contact numbers—include a letter of welcome as the first sheet in the packet. A brief handwritten note from a superior, sent separately, is a powerful way to inspire loyalty and enthusiasm.

~ In late August, some elementary school teachers send postcards to welcome incoming students and to help them feel positive about returning to school. Mention a project that the class will enjoy or say, "I think we're going to have a great year." As this requires money for stamps and stationery, access to class lists, time, and energy, the parents of a child who isn't looking forward to the new school year might offer to help the teacher with welcome notes.

~ When welcoming a new business or new family to your market area, establish name-recognition and product-association in their minds. Offer a free service or product to introduce the potential customer to your goods and services and to encourage a visit to your office or store. Enclose a coupon for a small gift or a discount. A relatively inexpensive but useful gift to newcomers is information, for example, a card with phone numbers of area services, hospitals, day-care centers, schools, or hotlines. In a welcome letter, the sales message is more effective when it is unobtrusive and undemanding. A personal letter of welcome to potential customers over the manager's or president's signature will be more cost-effective than mass-produced flyers stuck between a door.

~ After a customer or client visits your place of business, follow up with a letter of welcome. If you have not done so earlier, you might now offer some sort of discount or coupon to encourage the customer to return a second time—the possible beginnings of a habit.

~ To invite prospective customers to an open house or to visit your new store or offices at their convenience, see INVITATIONS.

Format

~ Letters to new neighbors, prospective in-laws, and new students or teachers are handwritten on foldovers or personal stationery.

~ Welcome letters that carry a sales message and letters to new employees, colleagues, and organization members are typed on letterhead or business-personal stationery.

~ Postcards are often used to welcome new customers with a special offer or discount.

WORDS

community	greetings	meet	reception
congregation	hope	neighborhood	together
delighted	hospitality	organization	visit
excited	introduce	pleased	
future	invite	questions	

PHRASES

bid a cordial welcome	look us up
delighted to make your acquaintance	make yourself at home
eager to serve you	open arms/door/house
expect long and fruitful years of association	pleasure to welcome you
extend a welcome	so happy you can join
family circle	take great pleasure in
good place to pitch your tent	to help you get acquainted
help you get established	warm reception waiting
look forward to meeting/seeing you	welcome aboard/back
	welcome mat

SENTENCES

I look forward to a mutually satisfying business relationship.

I'm pleased to welcome you to the Board of Directors of the Margaret Peel Museum.

It is with the greatest pleasure that I welcome you to Paragon Photo Processing.

Let us know how we can help you feel quickly at home.

The door is always open to you.

The Packles & Son Theatrical Agency is pleased to welcome you to our select family of talented clients.

To introduce you to the faculty, there will be a welcome reception Thursday, September 8.

We believe you will enjoy meeting this challenge with us.

We hope you'll enjoy this area and the great neighbors as much as we have.

Welcome to the team!

We welcome you to Daphnis Wool and Textiles and look forward to a long, productive, and satisfying collaboration.

You've made a wonderful choice (in my opinion)!

PARAGRAPHS

It is my great pleasure to welcome you to the Rivermouth Centipedes. The enclosed preapproved membership card entitles you to all benefits and privileges of club membership.

We officially welcome Ottila Gottescheim as Director of Education on Friday, August 7 at 6:30 p.m. Please join us for services and an Oneg Shabbat in her honor.

Welcome to *SportsStory*, the best sports fiction published today! You will receive your first issue shortly. Don't forget to vote for your favorite story every month on our Internet site.

Nothing pleases us more than to be able to say "welcome back" when an inactive account is revived. We appreciate your return to our list of active accounts and look forward to serving you again.

Welcome to Plattsville! All of us here at The Tarkington Gift and Card Shop hope that you soon feel at home in your new surroundings and that you find much to enjoy and appreciate in Plattsville. To help acquaint you with your new town, we have put together a packet of information in conjunction with the chamber of commerce that we hope you will find helpful. Also enclosed is a coupon for 25% off your first purchase with us.

Welcome to Clyde Episcopal Church. I hope you felt "at home" with us at your first service last Sunday. On February 16 at 7:00 p.m. we are having a welcome party for new parishioners in the church hall. Newcomers have found it helpful to meet some of their neighbors and to hear about the programs we offer. We hope that the whole family will be able to come.

Thank you for your first purchase at Eyvind Hardware, and welcome to our store! We are more than "just a hardware store." You can ask any of us for advice and information on a wide range of topics—whether it's the most appropriate floor finish for your home, the differences between grades of sandpaper and steel wool, how to use our rental products, or the advantages and disadvantages of various grout cleaners. Bring us all your home maintenance questions. To show our appreciation for your business, we are enclosing a coupon good for a free pair of gardening gloves. Visit us again soon!

SAMPLE LETTERS

Dear Ms. Spenser-Smith:

It is with the greatest pleasure that we welcome you to the E.H. Young Literary Society. Enclosed please find: a list of members, a copy of our by-laws, a schedule of this year's meetings, minutes from the last meeting, and an annotated bibliography of the books we'll be reading this year.

Your mentor—to make your introduction into the Society as pleasant as possible—will be Ms. Hannah Mole. If you have any questions, please feel free to direct them to her or to me.

I am looking forward to visiting with you after the next meeting.

Sincerely yours,

Dear Mr. Jellyband:

The Dover Business Association welcomes you to one of the busiest and most successful retail areas on the south coast. Those of us who own or manage businesses here have been working together for the past eleven years to bring new business in and to promote the area. Enclosed is a description of the group's purpose and activities.

As the new owner of The Fisherman's Rest, you are cordially invited to join the Association. The next meeting will be held June 15 at The Crown and Feather. We hope you will enjoy doing business in Dover as much as we have.

Feel free to contact any of the listed members for information or assistance.

Sincerely,

Dear Dr. and Mrs. Townshend-Mahony,

Welcome to Buddlecombe! We're having a neighborhood barbecue/potluck dinner on August 3 at our place, and we would love to have you come. Most of the neighbors will be there, and we think you'll enjoy meeting them. If you'd like to bring something, a cold salad would be perfect.

Yours truly,

Dear Mr. Harness,

I am pleased to tell you that your six-month review shows that your work is more than satisfactory, your sales record is exceptional, and your relationships with managers, co-workers, and customers are all very cordial and productive. As of today, you are being upgraded from temporary to permanent employee status. Welcome to Trengartha Tin Plate Works.

With best wishes,

∽

Dear Godfrey,

Nancy just told us the good news, and we are both happy that she has chosen to spend the rest of her life with you, and you with her. We were not entirely surprised, as we've been hearing about you quite a bit lately! You already feel like part of the family, and we're looking forward to seeing you both at the end of the month. Welcome to the family!

∽

Dear Mr. and Mrs. Webb,

Welcome to Groves Corners. We sincerely hope you'll enjoy living in this friendly community. We at Thornton Furniture offer you a special welcome and invite you to come in and say hello to our friendly, courteous salespeople who are eager to serve you. To make your shopping even more convenient and enjoyable, we are pleased to extend credit privileges to you. Just fill out an application form the next time you are in the store.

We are always happy to answer questions, help you find what you need, or place special orders. Don't hesitate to ask. We pride ourselves on satisfying our customers!

Yours truly,

∽

See also: EMPLOYMENT, GOODWILL, NEIGHBORS, SALES.

Appendix I
Mechanics

*It was very pleasant to me to get a letter from you the other day. Perhaps I should
have found it pleasanter if I had been able to decipher it. I don't think that I mastered
anything beyond the date (which I knew) and the signature (which I guessed at).
There's a singular and a perpetual charm in a letter of yours; it never grows old,
it never loses its novelty.*

—Thomas Bailey Aldrich

Appendix I covers the concrete aspects of letterwriting, for example, types of
stationery, letter formats, envelope addresses, and postal regulations. For
assistance with the content of your message (tone, style, language, grammar),
see APPENDIX II.

STATIONERY

Business stationery

Traditionally, business stationery size is 8½" × 11"—for the practical reason
that odd-sized stationery is difficult to file. White, off-white, cream, light
gray, or other neutral shades are acceptable colors.

Twenty-pound rag bond paper is a popular choice for business stationery; for higher quality, go to a thirty-pound paper. Textures and finishes—
flat, matte, smooth, woven, linen-look, watermarked—are a matter of
personal taste; all are acceptable. Many businesses use recyclable paper, which
is good for public relations as well as for the environment.

All business organizations and many individuals use a letterhead on their
stationery, which includes the name of the firm (or the individual's name);
address including zipcode (ZIP + 4); area code and telephone number; option-
ally, fax number, e-mail address, website address, and telex number. The letterhead can also include a logo, an employee's name and title, a list of board
of directors or other governing bodies (if lengthy, this list is arranged along
the left edge of the page). A good letterhead is readable, informative, attrac-

tive, and not too insistent. Printers can show you many formats, inks, styles of type, papers, and engraving and printing methods. The most formal and conservative choice is black ink on white or off-white high-quality paper.

Second sheets are of the same quality as the letterhead paper. They are either plain or are printed or engraved with the company's name. The print is smaller than on letterhead and the address isn't included.

Envelopes match your stationery in color, weight, general style, and letterhead. Your return address always goes in the upper left corner of the front of the envelope. "The return address. Don't let your letters leave home without it." (Steve Sikora) The United States Postal Service (USPS) discourages return addresses on the back flap because sorting machines can't flip envelopes over to check for a return address.

Personal-business stationery

The size referred to as personal-business or executive stationery is 7" or 7½" × 10". Choose white, off-white, neutral, or pale shades of good-quality bond paper. The letterhead includes: the company name and address with the person's name, or name and title, set underneath or off to one side.

Although its use is declining, personal-business stationery is convenient for brief notes; when writing to someone as individual-to-individual rather than as company representative to employee or customer; when the information is casual; or for matters that cross over into the social or personal arena (congratulating a colleague on an award, for example).

Memos

Memos include anything from 8½" × 11" stationery to small pads of printed memo sheets. In white, off-white, neutral, or pastel colors, memo stationery matches the firm's regular business stationery but has only the company name at the top. Memos sent outside the company are printed with the company name, address, telephone and fax numbers. Some memo paper is labeled "Internal Correspondence" and at the top has "TO: FROM: DATE: SUBJECT:" with a space after each.

Personal stationery

You may need 8½" × 11" paper for some personal uses (complaints, household business matters), but personal stationery is generally 7–8" × 10½" or 5½" × 6½–7½" and has matching envelopes.

Formal stationery (for handwritten invitations, condolences, thank yous) is white, off-white, cream, eggshell, straw, beige, gray, or other neutral color with a self border, contrasting border, or no border. For informal use, almost anything is acceptable, with the exception perhaps of stationery that's perfumed, decorated with tiny objects, ruled, oddly shaped, or otherwise says too loudly, "Look at me!" On the other hand, nobody appears to have ever returned a letter because the stationery had too much personality.

If you use a letterhead, monograms, or other printing on your personal stationery, your second sheets have no printing but are the same color and quality as your first sheets.

One-page notecards and foldovers (at least $3\frac{1}{2}$" × 5" when folded) are of a heavier weight paper than stationery and are popular for thank-you notes, handwritten invitations, replies to invitations, condolences, and other formal and informal messages. They usually come with matching envelopes and may be engraved or printed. If your name, address, initials, or other printing appear on the front panel, write on the inside—beginning at the top of the two panels for a long letter or using the bottom panel for a short note. Otherwise, begin your note on the front panel. The Postal Servive discourages printing or engraving your return address on the envelope's flap. Letter-Sorting Machines (LSMs) cannot flip a letter to check the other side when it fails to find the return address on the front.

ENVELOPES

Business

The Postal Service says that for the best service you should use the optical-character-reader (OCR) format for your envelopes, a machine-readable style for rapid sorting. Type or machine-print all address information in capital letters, using black ink on white paper and sharp, clear print with no overlapping or touching letters. Problem fonts include extended fonts, italic fonts, condensed fonts, bold fonts, and stylized script-like fonts. Do not underline address information as that will interfere with character recognition. Scanners can read a combination of uppercase and lowercase characters but prefer all uppercase. Addresses appear flush left style, that is, the first letter of each line in the address should be directly under the first letter of the line above. Include as much address information as possible: apartment, floor, suite number, zipcode or ZIP + 4. Omit all punctuation (except the hyphen in the ZIP + 4). Use abbreviations preferred by the Postal Service (see list at the end of this Appendix). Leave at least one space between words and two spaces between word groups. Two spaces are preferred between city and state, and two spaces between state and zipcode (with no punctuation). Leave the bar code area free of any writing. Allow at least ½" on either side of the address and ⅝" from bottom of address to bottom of envelope. Every address must have a minimum of three lines and a maximum of five lines. If you have an attention line ("ATTN: Tom Bowling"), it goes on the second line (under the company name). If the address contains both a post office box and a street address, it will be delivered to whichever appears directly above the city and state. Hand-stamp or type mailing directions ("Airmail," "Third Class," "Special Delivery") under the area where the postage will go.

Personal

For all formal and many informal personal letters, handwrite your return address (upper left corner) as well as the addressee's (lower right). For less formal personal correspondence the envelope may be typed (single-spaced). Although formal personal stationery is sometimes engraved or printed with the person's name and address on the back flap, the Postal Service prefers the return address on the front. For the other person's address, use either block style (each line's left edge lines up with the others) or indented style (each successive line is indented one or two spaces). Formal correspondence traditionally does not use abbreviations for "Street," "Avenue," "Parkway," "Road," or state names. However, the Postal Service requests that, for optimum sorting and delivery, the address be printed all in capital letters, with no punctuation except the hyphen in the ZIP + 4, using approved two-letter state abbreviations. The European "7" is not recommended because of the possibility of its being confused by the scanner with f, h, p, or t. USPS guidelines differ from traditional addressing of personal correspondence. When Judith Martin ("Miss Manners") was asked if we must forgo etiquette rules on envelopes, she recommended following the USPS rules to ensure delivery, but suggested that the double envelope system (used for wedding invitations) can permit the writer to send a personal letter that is both prettily addressed and properly delivered.

ZIP codes

All letters need correct zipcodes to be delivered. When you know it, use the ZIP + 4 number; it indicates local routes and can speed your letter significantly. Use your ZIP + 4 on outgoing correspondence so that people use it when writing you. You can buy a national zipcode directory from your local post office, or look up zipcodes in the directory at the post office. For in-town mail, check your local phone book, which often lists zipcodes by street names.

The Postal Service prefers that there not be less than one full character space and not more than five full character spaces between city, state, and zipcode; it prefers two spaces between city and state, and two spaces between state and zipcode.

Note that there should be no information on the envelope below the zipcode line. This area is reserved for bar coding.

Folding and inserting

When inserting a sheet of 8½" × 11" paper into a # 10 envelope, fold it in horizontal thirds, and insert it with the back of the top third facing the flap so that the recipient pulls out the letter, flips up that third, and is ready to begin reading. When using window envelopes, letters need to be folded so that the name and address appear in the window.

When inserting a full-size sheet into an envelope smaller than a number ten, fold it in half horizontally and then again in thirds and insert it so that the open end is on the left and the top fold faces the flap. The recipient pulls it out, rotates it a quarter turn to the right, opens it, and is ready to read.

Personal stationery is folded once with the writing inside and inserted into its matching envelope, open edges down. The recipient removes the letter and flips up the top half to read.

When folding any size sheet of paper, the top and bottom edges are not perfectly even with each other (although the sides are). It is easier to unfold a sheet of paper if one end extends just slightly beyond the other.

No matter what stationery you're using, the salutation (which will be inside the folds) faces the flap of the envelope.

Enclosures

Flat enclosures (checks, folded flyers, business cards) are placed inside the folds of the letter. To safeguard against your reader overlooking them, add an enclosure line to your letter ("Enc.: subscription blank"). For larger enclosures, use an appropriately sized manila envelope (many businesses have their own imprinted larger envelopes). When a package contains a letter, the entire package must go first class. When there is no urgency about bulky or heavy enclosures, send them third class and advise your correspondent by first-class mail of the package being sent under separate cover.

WRITING, TYPING, PRINTING

Handwritten

Black or blue ink is preferred to other colors, and pencil is never used. Certain notes are almost always written by hand: thank-you notes, messages of sympathy, replies to invitations, invitations that are not engraved or printed. Write by hand to convey personal feeling or informality or, in the case of an interoffice memo, when you have a one- or two-line message.

Typewritten or computer-generated

Business correspondence is being word processed in almost all companies.

Engraved or printed

Acknowledgments, announcements, invitations, and response cards are commonly engraved or printed (engraving is more expensive). Printers can explain the differences between the types of engraving and printing, show you dozens of samples, and offer you a wide variety of papers, formats, type styles, and inks as well as advice on how to word your message.

ELEMENTS OF A LETTER

Personal letters

Date: The date is placed near the top of the right side of the page. When the person is unfamiliar with your address and you aren't using stationery with your address on it, start with your address in the upper right corner (usually two lines) followed by the date. The left edges of these three lines line up underneath each other.

Salutation: Begin the salutation a few spaces down and flush left. It is followed by a comma ("Dear Jean,"). You don't usually put the person's address above it, as you would with a business letter.

Body of the letter: Indent the first paragraph—five spaces if you are typing the letter, about ¼" if you are handwriting it. Indent all other paragraphs the same way.

Closing: The complimentary close ("Love," "Sincerely,") is set about one line below your last sentence and to the right, its left edge on a line with the left edge of your date. Sign your name on the line below the complimentary close.

If your letter is more than one page long, generally write only on one side of your stationery.

Memos

Headings: At the top of the memo are the headings, the to/from/date/subject lines, which replace the letter's salutation. The most common ways of arranging the headings on the page are:

TO:	Paul Rayley		TO:	Rowena Ravenstock
FROM:	Minta Doyle		FROM:	Max Tryte
DATE:	April 23, 2002		DATE:	November 1, 2001
RE:	Lighthouse repairs		SUBJECT:	Gouache supplies

~

TO: Martin Fenner   DATE: July 14, 2003
FROM: Owen Kettle   SUBJECT: Series on tuberculosis

Message or body of the memo: There are no rigid rules for spacing in a memo, but two or three blank lines are commonly left between the headings and the text, which is single-spaced. Each paragraph begins flush left and is separated from other paragraphs by a single line of space.

Notation lines: Notations such as "Enc.:" or "cc:" are placed flush left at the bottom, as in a letter.

No signature is necessary on a memo, but people often sign or initial it at the bottom or next to their name in the "From:" line. Some memos are arranged in two parts so that the recipient can respond on and return the second half.

Business letters

Return address: If you aren't using letterhead stationery, use the two lines immediately preceding the date line for your street address, city, state, and zipcode. Unless the letter is extremely formal, abbreviations ("Rd.," "Apt.," "NY") are acceptable.

Date: For dates use this format: "October 12, 2002." The month is not abbreviated, the day is not spelled out, and endings for numbers ("16th," "2nd") are not used. You may see "12 October 2002," particularly for international or government business. If you are typing in your return address, the date line goes directly beneath it. Otherwise, it is placed two to six lines below the printed address. When using the shortened date form ("10/12/2002") in a casual memo, remember that this is used primarily in the United States; in other countries the first number is the day, the second the month.

Confidential or personal notation: Indicate "Confidential" or "Personal" halfway between the date line and the inside address, flush left.

Inside address: The number of spaces between the date line and the inside address depends on the length of your letter. Balance the elements of the letter so that there's not too much white space above the inside address or below the last printed line. The inside address is always flush left and single spaced. If one line is long, put half of it on the next line, indenting two or three spaces. The person's name goes on the first line. A brief title follows the name, preceded by a comma. Otherwise the title goes on the second line or, if you need the space, can be omitted. When writing to two or more people, list them one to a line in alphabetical order. The company's name is on the next line, and the department or division is on the following line (unless space is a problem, in which case omit it). Information such as suite, room, floor, or apartment usually has its own line, unless it and the street address are short enough to fit on one line. It used to be standard practice to spell out all words of the inside address, but the use of two-letter state abbreviations has spread from the envelopes (where the Postal Service wants to see them) to the inside address, and if the letter is not formal, other abbreviations ("Ave.") may appear as well. Spell out compass directions that precede a street name but abbreviate those that follow it ("14 North Cedar," "14 Cedar N.W.").

Attention line: When you don't know the name of the individual to whom you are writing or you want to direct the letter to a particular person's attention, the attention line ("ATTN: Customer Service Representative") is placed below the inside address, leaving one line of space between them. You can also include an attention line as part of the inside address on either the first or second line (after the company name).

Subject line: To indicate the subject of your letter, type "Subject:" or "Re:" (for "regarding") between the salutation and the body of your letter or between the inside address and the salutation. A brief phrase follows it ("Subject: block and brick work" or "Re: vacation dates"). Many people replace the salutation with a subject line when writing an impersonal letter to an anonymous recipient (your credit card statement was incorrect, for example). The subject line is popular with people handling stacks of incoming letters, trying to quickly identify the purpose of each. It is not recommended when your letter deals with several subjects.

Reference line: When referring to an order number or to a reference number used either by your correspondent or by your firm, handle it like a subject line and place it between the inside address and the salutation or between the salutation and the body of the letter (leaving one line of space on both sides in each case). It may also be placed between the date line and the inside address.

Salutation: Leave one line of space between the inside address (or the subject line) and the salutation. The salutation is followed by a colon (which is more formal) or a comma.

Body of the letter: Leave one line of space between the salutation (or the subject line) and the body of the letter. In general, single space within paragraphs and leave a line of space between paragraphs. If your letter is brief, however, double-spacing (or even 1½ spacing) will make it look better on the page. Wide margins will also balance brief letters on the page just as narrow margins (but not less than 1¼") modify long letters. To indent paragraphs, start in five to ten spaces.

Do not justify the right margin.

If your letter runs to a second page, indicate the name of the recipient, the page number, and the date across the top of the page (about six lines below the paper's edge). When writing to two individuals, put both names on the left, one under the other, and on the right indicate the date with the page number under it. Then leave three to five lines before resuming the body of the text. There should be a minimum of three lines of type in addition to the signature block to justify a second page.

Complimentary close: Leave one line between the body of the text and the complimentary close ("Yours truly").

Signature: Your handwritten signature goes between the complimentary close and your typed name and title.

Name and title lines: Four spaces (or more, if your signature is large) below the complimentary close, type your name with the first letter directly beneath the first letter of the complimentary close. If you use a title, it is typed on the line beneath your name, and also lined up with the left edge of your name and the complimentary close. Omit the title if it appears on the letterhead.

Identification line: Leave one line of space between the name or title line and the identification line. Type the letter-signer's initials in capital letters flush left, followed by a slash or colon and the typist's initials in lowercase letters ("DCK/jp," "IN:pjm"). Or, since it is obvious who has signed the letter, the typist's initials appear alone. The identification line is no longer much used.

Enclosure line: Leave one line of space between the identification line or the name/title line and the enclosure line. Set flush left, this line begins with "Enc.:" and lists any enclosures in the order in which they are found in the envelope, one to a line. You may also use "Encl." or "Enclosures" followed by the number of items enclosed: "Enclosures (4)".

Copies line: Leave one line of space between previous material and the copy line. After "cc:" (from the old "carbon copy") list those receiving copies of the letter in alphabetical order, one to a line, either by their full name, initials and last name, or title and last name only. The person's address may also be included. If you don't want the recipient of the letter to know that copies were sent, indicate "bcc:" (blind carbon copy) with the names of those receiving copies on the office copy of the letter.

Postscript: A postscript, preceded by "P.S.," is typed flush left two spaces below the last typed line.

Mailing notation: Instructions for mailing (Special Delivery, Overnight Express) are noted on copies of the letter, but not on the original. This is rarely used today.

LETTER FORMATS

There is no "best" way to arrange the elements of a letter on the page (unless your company has a house style). You do, however, need to be consistent (if you indent one paragraph, you indent them all) and the layout must be readable and appealing. The following four formats are the most common, but any arrangement is acceptable if it makes sense, is readable, and is spaced nicely on the page.

Full-block letter

The easiest format for the typist, full block-style means that every line begins at the left margin—no exceptions. If you have a second page, the name of the recipient, the page number, and the date are typed flush left, one under the other.

CHANNING FURNITURE RENTAL
1927 James Avenue
Huntly, WI 53597

March 15, 2002

Confidential

Yorke Furniture Rental
ATTN: Constance Yorke
1862 Wood Street
Huntly, WI 53597

Dear Constance Yorke:

Re: bad checks

We spoke at the Huntly Business Association meeting last month about exchanging lists of customers who have written at least three unbankable checks. Enclosed is my list.

Yours truly,

[signature]

Hamish Channing
President

Enc.: list

P.S. I don't feel too bad about passing these names along because I keep this same list posted by my cash register.

Block letter

The block letter is identical to the full-block with two exceptions: the date line and reference line are typed flush right and the signature block (complimentary close plus signature plus name line and title line) are also set flush right or at least to the right of center. Otherwise, everything is flush left and there are no indentations. This format, which has a more traditional look than the full-block format, is used in the majority of business letters.

CHANNING FURNITURE RENTAL
1927 James Avenue
Huntly, WI 53597

March 15, 2002

CONFIDENTIAL

Yorke Furniture Rental
ATTN: Constance Yorke
1862 Wood Street
Huntly, WI 53597

Dear Constance Yorke:

Re: bad checks

We spoke at the Huntly Business Association meeting last month about exchanging lists of customers who have written at least three unbankable checks. Enclosed is my list.

Yours truly,

[signature]

Hamish Channing
President

Enc.: list

P.S. I don't feel too bad about passing these along because I keep this same list posted by my cash register.

Modified-block

Also known as the semi-block, this format is identical to the block format with one exception: it has indentations. All paragraphs are indented five to ten spaces. The subject line may also be indented. As in the block style, the date line, the reference line, and the signature block are all set flush right or at least to the right of center. This format, which appears a little warmer than the block formats, is probably the second most popular business letter format.

CHANNING FURNITURE RENTAL
1927 James Avenue
Huntly, WI 53597

March 15, 2002

CONFIDENTIAL

Yorke Furniture Rental
ATTN: Constance Yorke
1862 Wood Street
Huntly, WI 53597

Dear Constance Yorke:

Re: bad checks

We spoke at the Huntly Business Association meeting last month about exchanging lists of customers who have written at least three unbankable checks.

Enclosed is my list. I'll look forward to receiving yours when you have time to send it along.

Yours truly,

[signature]

Hamish Channing
President

Enc.: list

P.S. I don't feel too bad about passing these along because I keep this same list posted by my cash register.

Simplified

With its streamlined contemporary look, the simplified format is easily identified by its lack of salutation and complimentary close. Like the full-block style, all lines begin at the left margin. But it has a subject line (typed in capital letters) instead of a salutation. The letterwriter's name and title are typed in all capital letters.

CHANNING FURNITURE RENTAL
1927 James Avenue
Huntly, WI 53597

March 15, 2002

CONFIDENTIAL

Yorke Furniture Rental
1862 Wood Street
Huntly, WI 53597

RE: BAD CHECKS

As decided at the Huntly Business Association meeting last month, I am forwarding to other stores a list of my customers who have given me at least three unbankable checks.

Enclosed is my list. I'll look forward to receiving yours.

[signature]

HAMISH CHANNING
PRESIDENT

Enc.: list

UNITED STATES POSTAL SERVICE GUIDELINES

The United States Postal Service (USPS) offers services and publications useful to anyone who uses the U.S. mail. The free monthly "Memo to Mailers" for business mailers can be obtained by writing:

National Customer Support Center
United States Postal Service
6060 Primacy Pkwy Ste 101
Memphis, TN 38188-0001

Other services and publications include online or by-mail sale of postage stamps, automated telephone information on postal services, zipcode directories, brochures and videos on topics from a history of mailing and requirements for second-class mail to how to wrap packages and address envelopes. Check your phone book for a number to call to request publications, call the nearest USPS Business Center, ask at the post office, or look online (http://www.usps.gov).

Suggestions from the Postal Service on improving your mail handling include:

- Make sure your mail is readable by the Optical Character Readers (OCRs) used in automated sorting: use envelopes of standard size and shape (first-class mail must be rectangular—a square envelope, for example, will be assessed a surcharge); use only white, ivory, or pastels; avoid unusual features like odd papers or bright graphics; type the address IN CAPITAL LETTERS with no punctuation (except for the hyphen in ZIP + 4 codes), with one or two spaces between words, and with nothing but the address in the lower right part of the envelope.

- Don't use paperclips; they often jam the Letter-Sorting Machines (LSMs).

- Put your return address on envelopes; many people fail to do this.

- Use the two-letter state abbreviations and ZIP + 4.

- Set up a home postal center: obtain copies of USPS brochures listing postage rates, fees, and information; invest in a small postage scale; buy stamps of different denominations to keep in small nine- or fifteen-drawer organizers.

- Attend USPS workshops on such subjects as marketing with direct mail, professional mailroom management, and organizing mail for optimum service. The seminars are designed to help cut costs and improve efficiency by trying to match USPS programs to your company's needs. There is usually a small registration fee.

- Subscribe to *Domestic Mail Manual* and *International Mail Manual*. They may be too expensive (and unnecessary) for individual letterwriters, but many businesses find them indispensable.

- Use the Business Reply Mail Accounting System (BRMAS), which is available to customers who use Business Reply Mail.
- Bar code your mail. Using ZIP + 4 and bar codes gives you the largest postal discount available, and the bar coding equipment eventually pays for itself. If you are interested in bar coding your mail, contact an account representative at your local USPS Marketing and Communications office.
- Keep current with new publications, programs, rates, and services; the USPS constantly updates old services and introduces new ones.

ENVELOPE ABBREVIATIONS

Alabama	AL	Louisiana	LA
Alaska	AK	Maine	ME
American Samoa	AS	Marshall Islands	MH
Arizona	AZ	Maryland	MD
Arkansas	AR	Massachusetts	MA
California	CA	Michigan	MI
Colorado	CO	Minnesota	MN
Connecticut	CT	Mississippi	MS
Delaware	DE	Missouri	MO
District of Columbia	DC	Montana	MT
Federated States of		Nebraska	NE
Micronesia	FM	Nevada	NV
Florida	FL	New Hampshire	NH
Georgia	GA	New Jersey	NJ
Guam	GU	New Mexico	NM
Hawaii	HI	New York	NY
Idaho	ID	North Carolina	NC
Illinois	IL	North Dakota	ND
Indiana	IN	Northern Mariana Islands	MP
Iowa	IA	Ohio	OH
Kansas	KS	Oklahoma	OK
Kentucky	KY	Oregon	OR

Palau	PW	Utah	UT
Pennsylvania	PA	Vermont	VT
Puerto Rico	PR	Virginia	VA
Rhode Island	RI	Virgin Islands	VI
South Carolina	SC	Washington	WA
South Dakota	SD	West Virginia	WV
Tennessee	TN	Wisconsin	WI
Texas	TX	Wyoming	WY

～

Apartment	APT
Attention	ATTN
Building	BLDG
Center	CTR
Company	CO
Corporation	CORP
Department	DEPT
Division	DIV
Floor	FLR
Government	GOVT
Headquarters	HDQTRS
Hospital	HOSP
Institute	INST
National	NATL
Parkway	PKWY
Post Office Box	PO BOX
Room	RM
Rural Route	RR
Suite	STE

Appendix II
Content

I once read a survey that said the moment in the daily routine that people look forward to most is opening the mail.

—NANCY BERLINER

Appendix I tells *how* to put a letter on the page (and what kind of a page to put it on). Appendix II tells *what* to put on the page, discussing principles of good letterwriting and effective form letters; grammar and usage; respectful, unbiased language; names and titles; salutations, complimentary closes, and signatures; frequently misspelled words; superfluous words and phrases.

GENERAL GUIDELINES ON LETTER CONTENT

These guidelines apply primarily to business letters. For example, brevity is highly prized in a business letter, but it may not be appreciated by a dear friend. You aren't obliged to state your main idea (if indeed you have one) in the first sentence of a letter to a family member, whereas the business reader wants to know immediately what your letter is about. However, these suggestions will improve all your letterwriting.

- Before beginning to write, identify the purpose of your letter (to get a refund, to set up a meeting, to issue an invitation). Gather necessary information. Think about your reader—the more you know about the recipient of your letter, the more precisely you can tailor your message.
- State the main idea in the first or second sentence.
- Be brief. George Burns's advice on a good sermon applies equally well to letters: "a good beginning and a good ending . . . as close together as possible." Give brief explanations, instructions, reasons.
- Be specific. Nothing gives writing more power than details—not unnecessary details, but details that replace vague words and phrases. Readers want to know how much, what color, what date, what time, how big, how little. Re-read your letter and question every adjective—is it pulling its weight? Could it be more specific?

- Be pleasant, courteous, positive, and encouraging. For being so inexpensive, upbeat attitudes are startlingly effective.
- Be factual and avoid emotion in business letters. (It is fine—even desirable—in personal letters.) Your readers do not really care about your feelings; they want facts, they want to know outcomes, they want results, they want reasons. Don't exaggerate, or your message will lose credibility with your reader. It's better to mildly understate your case and let the reader take credit for seeing how wonderful it really is.
- Use (but don't overuse) the word "you" throughout your letter, and particularly in the opening sentences. The most important letterwriting rule is "Keep your reader in mind." Phrase your message in terms of your reader's interests, needs, and expectations. The "you" involves the reader in the letter. The exception to the use of "you" is the letter of complaint or disagreement, in which "you"-statements are perceived as (and often are) accusing and hostile. Phrase your message in terms of "I" statements.
- Use the active instead of the passive voice ("I received your letter last week," not "Your letter was received last week"). Use strong, direct, action-filled verbs ("is/are," "do," and "make" are not some of them). Use a thesaurus to find dynamic (but not unusual, unfamiliar, or unpronounceable) substitutes for your most overused words.
- Use a lively, conversational tone. Reading your letters out loud for several weeks will help you spot awkwardnesses.
- Choose a tone for your letter and stick to it. A letter might be formal or informal, cool or warm, serious or light-hearted, brisk or relaxed, simple or complex, elegant or down home. But it is, above all, consistent.
- Avoid overused words like "very" and "basically." Basically, neither of them means very much, and they become annoying to the reader.
- Avoid slang, jargon, clichés, buzz words, legalese, elitist language, and stilted usage like "I shall." Choose the familiar word over the unfamiliar.
- When writing abroad, keep sentences and syntax simple. Avoid slang, jargon, figures of speech, references to facets of American culture, the passive voice, and complex verb constructions. Keep to the present and simple past tenses. Instead of "If we had only known . . . ," say "We did not know . . ." If using numerals for the date, use day/month/year instead of month/day/year. If you know them, use social titles from the reader's own language ("Madame," "Signore," "Herr," "Señora"). Use the address exactly as given; it is most deliverable in that form. Letters from other countries often have ritualized closing sentences that express

the writer's respect and good wishes; take your cue from your correspondent's letter and reply in kind.

• Make it easy for your correspondent to reply: enclose a postage-paid reply envelope or a self-addressed stamped envelope.

FORM LETTERS

Form letters have done away with the numbing and time-consuming chore of typing the same letter thousands of times. They are invaluable in direct sales marketing and in the processing of routine business letters (confirmations, acknowledgments, cover letters, rejections).

Joseph Heller poked fun at form letters in *Catch-22*: "Dear Mrs, Mr, Miss, or Mr and Mrs Daneeka: Words cannot express the deep personal grief I experienced when your husband, son, father or brother was killed, wounded or reported missing in action."

To avoid this aspect of form letters, direct your message to the individual reading it. Inserting the person's name at intervals isn't the way to do this; too many spelling errors can creep in, and people do not in any case mistake this cheery and obviously phony friendship for real intimacy.

Personalize your letter by using "you" and using mailing lists of specific market targets. Then, if you are writing to members of a list who are all gardeners or who have all contributed to a charity within the past six months, you know how to frame your letter. For important mailings, use high-quality paper, sign each letter individually (there are people who look first to see if the signature is "real" or not and then either read the letter or toss it), and mail the letter first class.

GRAMMAR AND USAGE

Some common grammar and usage issues are outlined below. If you write more than the occasional letter, invest in a mini-library for your desk: dictionary, basic grammar, usage guide, style manual, thesaurus.

∼ Use **periods** at the end of sentences. Or sentence fragments. A period also follows an abbrev. Ellipsis points are used to replace missing words: three dots in the middle of the sentence, four at the end.

∼ **Commas** separate items or lists of things. It is correct either to use or not to use a comma before "and" in a series ("Milk, butter and eggs" or "Milk, butter, and eggs")—the only rule is to do it one way or the other consistently.

If you don't know when to use a comma, read the sentence aloud dramatically. The place where you pause to group a thought phrase together may need a comma. Commas are used before and after "etc.," years of a date ("On May 27, 1678, the sun rose . . ."), and academic degrees.

↜ Don't use **question marks** after indirect questions or requests ("He asked what went wrong" or "Please sweep up here after yourself"). Omit the comma after the question mark in cases like "Do you like it?" she asked.

↜ Except perhaps for sales letters, business correspondence doesn't need— and shouldn't have—**exclamation marks**. Be stingy with them in personal correspondence as well. J.L. Basford believed that "One who uses many periods is a philosopher; many interrogations, a student; many exclamations, a fanatic." Exclamations give your letters a certain manic look, like people laughing at their own jokes. At first, it will tear at your heart to remove them; by and by, you will be pleased to find that you can get along nicely without them.

↜ **Quotation marks** are used for quoted words and for the titles of magazine articles and TV and radio shows. All punctuation goes inside the quotation marks ("What?" "Egads!" "I won't," he said). Common sense ought to indicate the rare exceptions. If the punctuation in no way belongs to the quotation, you can leave it outside, as in the following sentence: How many times have you heard a child say "But I'm not tired"?

↜ **Parentheses** are used to enclose asides to your main train of thought. When the aside is an incomplete thought (incomplete sentence) it is placed in the middle of a regular sentence; the first word inside does not begin with a capital, nor is there any punctuation. (Sometimes, however, your thought is a complete thought, or complete sentence, in which case it is set inside parentheses and has its own initial capital letter and final punctuation.) When using parentheses within a sentence, all punctuation goes after the parentheses: Please order more ribbons, paper (30#), and file folders.

↜ In general, **hyphens** are used to help word pairs or groups form one easy-to-read thought group. Traditional exceptions are words ending in -ly ("newly appointed") and adjective groups that follow a noun ("well-known telecaster" but "she was well known"). The trend is to one word rather than hyphenated words or two separate words ("headlight," not "head-light" or "head light"). A quick check with a dictionary will give you the correct form for most words.

↜ Use **apostrophes** to replace missing letters ("isn't" = "is not") and to show possession ("Simon's"). The apostrophe most commonly shows up in the wrong place in "its" and "it's." If you can write "it is" in place of your word, it needs the apostrophe. If you have trouble with this pair, write only "it is" or "its" until you are comfortable with the difference. When more than one person is involved, show the plural possessive by placing the apostrophe after the "s" ("union members' votes" or "the parents' recommendations"). Omit the apostrophe when making plurals of number and letter combinations: Ph.D.s, the 1990s, the 2000s, the '50s, three 100s, IBMs.

~ **Colons** often precede a list or a long quotation ("We carry the following brand names: . . ." or "The hospital issued the following apology: . . ."). Do not use a colon when it unnecessarily breaks up a sentence (remove the colon in "Your kit contains: a lifetime supply of glue, four colors of paint, and a set of two brushes"). The colon is also used after a business or formal salutation ("Mr. President:").

~ **Semi-colons** tend to give a stuffy, old-fashioned look to a letter. However, they are still useful on occasion. When writing a long list that has internal punctuation, separate each element with a semi-colon ("New members for January: Rachel and Darke Solomon of Velindre, their children Peter, Jasper, Ruby, and Amber; Constantine Stephanopoulos; Catherine, Lize, and Fritz Steinhart"). You may also separate two independent clauses of a sentence with a semi-colon ("In prosperity our friends know us; in adversity we know our friends."—J. Churton Collins).

~ The overuse of **dashes** indicates a rather slapdash (you see where it comes from?) style. If you are a regular dash-user, check to see if other punctuation might not do as well. Dashes tend to mate in captivity, so once the dash habit takes hold, they proliferate on the page, giving a letter a rather forward-leaning, breathless quality.

~ A common grammar error involves **noun-verb agreement**. In complicated sentences in which the noun and verb become separated from each other, it's easy to make a mistake. When proofreading your letters, pick out long sentences, find your noun and verb, put them together, and see if they still make sense. Some nouns that look singular ("data") take a plural verb; some that look plural take a singular verb ("a series of books is scheduled for"; "the board of directors is investigating"). What do you do with "None of them has/have voted yet"? When in doubt, re-word the sentence ("Nobody has voted yet"; "Not one of them has voted yet") or ask what the sense of the phrase is. If you are speaking of only one person, use "has"; if the sense of the phrase indicates many people, use "have." "A number of accountants are signing up for . . ." but "The number of accountants is decreasing."

∿ **Underline or italicize** titles of books and movies; other titles go in quotation marks.

∿ One of the best things you can do for your writing is to become aware of **parallel structures**—from little things like capitalizing or not capitalizing all the words in a list to making sure each word in the list is the same part of speech. In long sentences, writers often forget that they started one phrase with "to interview . . ." but later used "calling the candidate" and ended up with "and, finally, you could meet with . . ." A parallel form would have "to interview . . . to call . . . to meet with . . ."

∿ Keep **paragraphs** short. Let each one develop a single idea. Start with your broadest idea and support it with detailed refinements. Or start with details and lead the reader to your final, topic sentence.

∿ The easiest way to decide whether you need **"that" or "which"** is to see if you need commas. Commas and "which" tend to go together: "The file, which eventually turned up on Frank's desk, had been missing for a week." "The file that had been missing eventually turned up on Frank's desk." Do not set off a phrase beginning with "that" with commas, but do set off a "which" clause with commas.

∿ "Howard and Paul had lunch together before he left." Which "he" left? Check pronouns ("who," "she," "they") to be sure the **antecedents** (the persons they refer to) are clear.

∿ **Dangling modifiers** consist of words tacked onto a sentence, front or back (sometimes even in the middle), in such a way that the reader doesn't know what they modify. In *Watch Your Language*, Theodore M. Bernstein gives several examples, among them: "Although definitely extinct, Professor Daevey said it had not been too long ago that the moa was floundering around his deathtrap swamps." "As reconstructed by the police, Pfeffer at first denied any knowledge of the Byrd murder."

∿ **"Between"** is generally between two people, no more. (And the correct expression is always "between you and me," "between Flory and me.") **"Among"** is generally for three or more: "We should have the necessary know-how among the four of us."

∿ Watch the placement of **"only"** and **"not only"**; they should go right next to the word they modify. Instead of "I am only buying one," write "I am buying only one."

∿ **"Whom"** and **"whomever"** do not occur nearly as often as people suppose. Use them only when you can show they are the object of a verb. The most common misuse of "whomever" occurs in a situation like this: "Please mail this file to whoever is elected secretary." "Whoever" is correct; it is the subject of the clause. If you are troubled by this construction, see a good grammar book; until then, it is perhaps enough to be aware of the problem.

TALKING ABOUT PEOPLE

Stereotypical language forgets that people are individuals. Exclusive language forgets to include certain people. When you invite customers to an open house and fail to say that the event is accessible, you exclude people with disabilities. When you begin your letter "Dear Sirs:" you forget that women might be reading it. When you refer to the "Judeo-Christian ethic" you exclude large numbers of highly ethical non-Jews and non-Christians. Words can exclude, stereotype, and discriminate against people on the basis of sex, age, ethnicity, disability, socioeconomic class, sexual orientation, and religion.

For information on using respectful people language, see *Talking About People* (Rosalie Maggio, The Oryx Press, 1997). The rationale is that it is good business; you can't sell anything or obtain any information or favors from someone whom you've just excluded or stereotyped. A few guidelines:

- The "people first" rule says we are people first, and only secondarily people who have disabilities, people who are over sixty-five, people who are Baptists, people who are Finnish-Americans. In your letters, decide first if you need to mention classifications such as sex, age, race, religion, economic class, or disability; most often they're unnecessary. When in doubt, omit them. Don't identify the whole person by part of the person. Madeline is someone who has paraplegia. Referring to her as "a paraplegic" identifies the whole Madeline by one part of her. People aren't "confined to a wheelchair"; they use wheelchairs.

- Check for parallel constructions: do you mention one person's marital status and not the other person's? One person's race, and not the other's? Identify some people as gay but not others as heterosexual? Is she Mrs. William Gostrey, but he is Ray Parker? Or he is Ray Parker and she is Sheila?

- Instead of "man" or "mankind" use words that include everyone, for example, people, we, us, humanity, human beings, individuals, human society, nature, planet earth, the world. Don't use "he" when you mean "he or she." Instead of "A mailcarrier has his work cut out for him today" use the plural: "Mailcarriers have their work cut out for them today." You can also rewrite the sentence to use "you" or "we." Sometimes "he," "his," or "him" can be omitted or replaced with a noun. Avoid the awkward "his or her" or "she or he." The centuries-old use of singular "they" ("to each their own"), which is found throughout this book, is accepted or endorsed by most language authorities, including *Oxford English Dictionary*; *Chicago Manual of Style*, 14th ed.; *American Heritage Dictionary of the English Language*, 3rd ed.; *American Heritage Book of English Usage*; the National Council of Teachers of English; *Random House Dictionary II*; *Webster's Third New International Dictionary*; Randolph Quirk et al., *A Grammar of Contemporary English*. With a few exceptions ("layperson," for example), words ending in *-person* are contrived-looking; good alternatives exist for almost all of them. Use *chair* instead of *chairperson*; *chair* is the older and tidier term. We use *head* ("the head of the department") and *headed* ("she headed the organization") without fearing a disembodied head; in the same way, no one mistakes the committee chair for what they're sitting on.

NAMES

There is only one rule about names: use whatever name your correspondent prefers. Guidelines include:

∽ Spell your correspondent's name correctly. It is worth the few minutes and the forty cents to call to obtain the correct spelling and current title of the person to whom you're writing.

∽ Although it is acceptable in some fields and in some parts of the country to call people by their first names, write "Dear Mr. Cokeson" rather than "Dear Bob" until you're sure the latter is welcome. Miss Manners says: "To prevent the unauthorized use of her first name, Miss Manners took the precaution of not having one." She says she is far from alone in cringing when strangers assume the privileges of intimacy by using her first name. When unsure about the degree of formality between you and a correspondent, choose the more formal approach.

∽ When ordering business cards or personal calling cards, spell out your full name. Social titles (Mr., Ms., Mrs., Miss) used to precede the name, but they are largely omitted today. Medical specialists use "Dr." or "Doctor" on social cards ("Doctor Christopher Bembridge"), but use "M.D.," "D.O.," "D.D.S.," "O.D." on business cards ("Muriel Eden, D.D.S."). Either "Joseph Farr, Jr." or "Joseph Farr II" is correct. When using "Esq." (short for Esquire) after a lawyer's name ("Marian Beltham, Esq."), omit all other titles (Mr., Ms., Mrs., Miss) before it.

～ For a woman, use the social title (also called courtesy title or honorific) she uses (see her last letter or call her home or office to check on the spelling of her name and to ask "Do you prefer Miss, Mrs., or Ms.?"). If there's no clue to her marital status (and remember that we've been addressing men for years without worrying about this), use her full name without a social title ("Dear Florence Churchill") or use "Ms." and her last name. The worst that can happen is that the letter you receive in return is signed by a "Mrs." or a "Dr." or some other title. Now you know. In business, women use their own first names. This used to indicate that a woman was single, divorced, or possibly widowed. Today it just means that that is her first name. Socially, some women use their husbands' names. Some may still sign a letter "Nelly Christie" but type underneath "Mrs. John Christie." Traditionally, married or widowed women used their husbands' names ("Mrs. Philip Halliday"), while divorced women used their own first name and either their family-of-origin name, their married name, or both. Single women were to use "Miss" or not, as they pleased. This marital coding system for women is no longer as reliable or as popular as it once was.

～ When addressing couples, use the form they use themselves: "Mr. and Mrs. Walter Evson"; "Adela and George Norrington"; "Dr. Guy and Mrs. Elizabeth Phillips"; "Katherine Halstead and Frank Luttrell"; "Dr. Linda and Mr. Arnaud Hallet." When addressing envelopes or typing the inside address, and each name is fairly long, put one to a line in alphabetic order.

～ When writing to more than one person, use each person's full name or use a social title plus last name for each. For single-sex groups, you may use "Mesdames" ("Mmes.") for women and "Messieurs" ("Messrs.") for men, although these terms have an old-fashioned ring to them. These titles are followed by the individuals' last names only. When addressing both women and men, use an inclusive salutation such as "Dear Friends," "Dear Co-chairs," "Dear Committee Members," or "To: (list names, one to a line in alphabetic order)."

SALUTATIONS, COMPLIMENTARY CLOSES, AND SIGNATURES

Salutations

The salutation (also referred to as a greeting) is set flush left. The first letter of the first word is capitalized but other modifying words are not ("My very dear Joanna"). All titles and names are capitalized. Use abbreviations for Ms.,

Mr., Mrs., Dr., but spell out religious, military, and professional titles such as Father, Major, Professor, Sister, Colonel. The salutation generally ends in a comma for personal or informal letters, and in a colon or a comma for business letters.

When possible, obtain the name of the person who is best suited to receive your letter and obtain the correct spelling of their name and verify their current title; call the company if necessary.

When you know the person's name, write: "Dear Neil A. McTodd" or "Dear Agnes Bailey" (full name with no social title) or "Dear Ms. Lee," "Dear Captain Crowe," "Dear Inspector Hopkins," "Dear Senator Burnside" (social title plus last name). The first convention is useful when you don't know the person's sex ("Audley Egerton") or which social title (Ms., Mrs., Miss) the person uses. Professional or academic titles (Dr., Representative) are always used instead of social titles (Mr., Miss).

When writing a form letter or when you don't know your correspondent's name, you can still write "Dear . . ." with nouns like: Neighbor, Subscriber, Friend, Motorist, Reader, Colleague, Student, Customer, Gardener, Client, Employee, Potential Employee, Parishioner, Collector, Cardholder, Concerned Parent, Initiate-Elect, Handgun Control Supporter, Member, Homeowner, Supplier, Executive, Aquarist, Equestrian, Do-It-Yourselfer. Or try job titles: Dentist, Copywriter, Electrician, Metallurgist, Customer Service Manager. Or use the company's name: Poulengay Upholsterers, Elliot-Lewis Stationers, Handford Lawn Care. You can also use an impersonal salutation like Good morning! Hello! Greetings! The best solution may be to replace the salutation with a subject line. (The outdated "Dear Sir or Madam" and "To Whom It May Concern" are not recommended.)

Complimentary Closes

The complimentary close follows the body of your letter, with one line of space between them. It always begins with a capital letter and ends with a comma. Words in between are not capitalized.

The most everyday, acceptable, and all-purpose complimentary closes are: Sincerely (used perhaps three-fourths of the time), Yours truly, Sincerely yours, Very sincerely yours, Very sincerely, Very truly yours. You cannot go wrong with one of these. Miss Manners (Judith Martin) says that business letters should close with "Yours truly"; "Can Miss Manners be the only person still alive who knows that?"

For a highly formal letter involving White House, diplomatic, judicial, or ecclesiastical correspondence, use: Respectfully yours or Respectfully. An informal letter in the same instances uses: Very respectfully yours, Yours respectfully, or Sincerely yours. In formal letters to members of Congress, senators, high-ranking politicians and government figures, priests, rabbis, and ministers, use: Yours very truly. The informal form is: Sincerely yours.

For most formal letters—regular business and personal—choose from among: Sincerely, Sincerely yours, Yours sincerely, Very sincerely yours, Very sincerely, Truly yours, Yours truly, Very truly yours, Yours very truly, Very cordially yours.

Informal closes include: Love, With all my love, Lovingly, Lovingly yours, Fondly, Affectionately, Yours affectionately, Sincerely, Sincerely yours, Cordially, Cordially yours, Yours cordially, Faithfully, Faithfully yours, Yours faithfully, As ever, As always, Devotedly, Yours, Best regards, Kindest regards, Warmest regards, Cheers, Your friend, Be well, Until next time.

Complimentary closes somewhere between formal and informal include: With all kind regards, Warm regards, Best regards, Best, Best wishes, With best wishes, With all best wishes, Cordially, Sincerely, All the very best, With every good wish, Warm personal regards.

After studying the above lists, choose one or two complimentary closes that reflect your letterwriting style and use them for most of your correspondence. It's rarely worth the trouble to fit a special complimentary close to each letter.

Signatures

Although there used to be many rules governing signatures, it's fairly simple today: use the version of your name that you want the person to use for you. If there is any ambiguity (for example, the person knows you only under your pen name, birth name, married name, or business name), put the name that might be more easily recognized in parentheses under your signature. Signatures rarely include social titles, so omit the "Dr.," "Ms.," or "Mr." (They may be typed on the name line, however.) In personal letters, your signature stands alone. In business letters, it is followed by your name and title (on one or two lines, depending on length). The name and title lines are typed four lines below the complimentary close—more, if you have a particularly sweeping signature. If your name and title are given on the letterhead, omit them under your signature. When signing a letter for someone else, put your initials just below and to the right of the signature, often after a slash. When you write a letter on someone else's behalf, sign your own name above a name line that identifies you: "Son of Christina Light" or "Secretary to Cavaliere Giacosa."

If your salutation uses the person's first name, sign the letter with your first name (although in a business letter, your full name and title will be printed below your signature). Nonparallel salutations and signatures can be insulting and offputting. If you write "Dear Fred," and sign it "Dr. Francis Etherington," you have assumed a superior position; writing it the other way around presumes an intimacy that may not exist. Except in rare cases, the salutation and signature should be strictly parallel: "Dear Rosa, . . . Love, Judy"; "Dear Thomas Eustick, . . . Sincerely, Margaret Kraft."

Index

belated, 87
children's behavior, 55
errors and mix-ups, 23, 24, 25, 55, 60,
   90
personal errors, 402
sexual harassment, 55
apostrophe, 476-477
application, letters of, 61-69
college/university, 64
designing job application form, 64
faxed, 196, 198
follow-up, 207
franchises, 64, 368
responding to, 174, 181
appointments, 70-76
accepting, 71
canceling or postponing, 71
changing, 71
confirming, 71
follow-up, 71, 202
missing, 60, 72
refusing, 71
requesting, 71
appreciation, letters of, 77-85
employee accomplishments, 77, 78, 80,
   83-84
fan letter, 80
goodwill, 79
neighbors, 287
See also congratulations, references and
   recommendations, thank-you notes
assistance. *See* advice, letters of; requests
   and inquiries; thank-you notes
associations. *See* organizations/clubs
attachments, 168-169
attendant, requesting someone to be, 436,
   447
attention-getting devices (sales letters), 384
attention line, 463
authorization of emergency medical care, 186

B
babies, adoptions, 18, 43-44, 51
birth announcements, 43-44
congratulations, 118
sympathy, 408, 415

banks, letters to. *See* credit, loans
bar mitzvah/bat mitzvah, 264
belated letters, 85-91
between/among, 478
biased language, 479-480
bids, refusing, 326
requesting, 346, 351
biographical sketch, 368
birth announcements, 43-44
birthday letters, 35-41
block letter format, 467
body of letter, 461, 462, 464
borrowing money. *See* credit, letters about;
   loans; requests and recommendations
brief bio, 368

C
cancellations, account,
   appointment, 71
   engagement, 436
   invitation, 265
   reservation, 430, 433
   wedding, 438, 446
canvassing. *See* fundraising
career-related letters. *See* cover letters;
   employment, letters dealing with;
   résumés
caregiver, letters to, 222
casual letters. *See* family and friends, letters to
catalog orders. *See* orders, letters dealing
   with
change of address, 44, 49, 443
cc:, 465
"chair"/"chairman," 301
charge accounts. *See* credit, letters about;
   refusals; requests and inquiries
charities. *See* fundraising
children, invitations to, 263
   letters to, 186-187
   misbehavior of, 288, 401
   pen pals, 187
   uninvited, 442-443, 446
churches/temples. *See* fundraising, organi-
   zations/clubs, requests and inquiries
claims. *See* adjustments; complaint, letters of

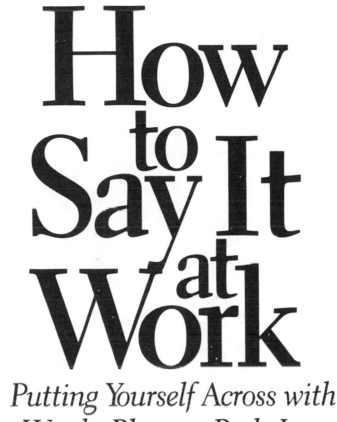

How to Say It at Work

*Putting Yourself Across with
Power Words, Phrases, Body Language,
and Communication Secrets*

JACK GRIFFIN

Why This Book Is for You

When you speak, speak as if your life depended on it. Because it does—at least when you're on the job. Maybe what you communicate will make the difference between being able to pay your rent this month and not. Maybe it will make the difference between paying rent and owning a house. Or perhaps it will be the difference between a job and a career: spending your time and drawing a check or turning time into self-fulfillment and satisfaction. In business, the way you put yourself across is always about getting something you need or something you want. It's about making a difference in your life and the lives of those who depend on you.

Putting yourself across. Nothing you do in business is more important. And you have to do it every day. Good thing you've gotten hold of this book: the *complete* guide to power words and phrases, body language, and communication secrets. With it, you can explore strategies and ready-to-use models of verbal and nonverbal communication designed to be effective for today's businessperson. *How to Say It® at Work* is a contemporary guide to persuasion, offering a minimum of theoretical speculation and a maximum of practical tips, advice, and examples taken *from* the real world for use *in* the real world.

REAL COMMUNICATION TOOLS FOR THE REAL WORLD

This book provides the tools for successful real-world communication and the techniques for applying them. Along the way, you'll also find diagnostic self-tests designed to save you time by helping you pinpoint just what skills you need to hone to make you consistently more effective as a communicator. Let's go back to that phrase "real world" for just a moment. Tools and techniques are fine, but they're not much use until they are actually *used*. At every step of the way, this book shows you how to apply the tools you acquire to specific business situations. The emphasis here is on practice rather than on theory.

The tools and techniques you'll acquire are of two kinds: equipment to *prepare* for communication and equipment you need when the time actually comes to put yourself across. In Part I you will find a special test to help you determine how effective your current verbal—and, just as important, your nonverbal—communications skills are. This book will introduce you to a core set of the words and phrases that should be a part of every business vocabulary.

SECRETS OF NONVERBAL COMMUNICATION

Effective communication is a lot more than a gift for gab. One of the paradoxes of our technically and culturally advanced civilization is that, as we have become more sophisticated, we have increasingly come to recognize how much in our highly mechanized, apparently abstract, and hyper-intellectualized daily lives is dependent on "primitive," "primal," or "unconscious" motives, forces, and signals. Of course, all of us learn at an early age that people sometimes say one thing while meaning another. Sometimes, when they do this, they actually believe they're telling the truth. Sometimes they're deliberately lying. And at other times still, we can just *look* at a person, and we know—we're convinced—he or she believes passionately and every word he or she utters. The person "looks convincing," we say, and maybe we wish *we* could always be assured of looking that way when we have something important to communicate. For it is a fact: The most effective, moving, and persuasive communication occurs when verbal and nonverbal signals are in perfect sync. The result is communication synergy. For this reason, Part I of *How to Say It® at Work* includes a special set of tools to help you build not only your verbal, but your *nonverbal* vocabulary, the looks and gestures by which we often telegraph our "real" message.

Part I concludes with a checklist for effective communication. Use it to assist you to define your objectives, clarify your goals, and illuminate your options *before* you open your mouth to speak. Complete it, and you're about ready to start talking. Go on to Part II.

HOW TO HANDLE SPECIFIC SITUATIONS AND PEOPLE

Part II—the rest of the book—shows you how to put yourself across in every major business situation and to all the key players in business: supervisors, colleagues, subordinates, clients and customers, vendors and suppliers, and creditors and investors. Included are full chapters devoted on getting a great job for yourself and to hiring a great employee for your firm. Each chapter begins with a brief and highly revealing opportunity to "Self-Test Your Savvy," so that you'll know where you are before you begin. Then, instead of making you slog through theory and speculation—you don't have the time for that—you get lists of power words and phrases that are specific to the person or situation covered in the chapter. Next come the words and phrases to *avoid*, the pitfalls that can sabotage any negotiation, deal, or critical conversation. Two concise discussions follow: "Body Language Strategy" and "Body Language to Avoid." As with the power words and phrases lists, both of these are carefully geared to the specific situations and persons treated in the chapter.

After covering these essentials, each chapter launches into an in-depth consideration of the most effective steps and strategies in a given situation. The emphasis is always on examples and ready-to-use models for communication. Wherever possible, brief scripts are included to help you do what great communicators have always done: prepare to be spontaneous.

Finally, because *How to Say It® at Work* is written for the real world, we confront the tough issues, ranging from overcoming indifference to handling hostility to dealing with inappropriate, unfair, even abusive behavior.

MASTERING THE MAGIC OF COMMUNICATION

Think of *How to Say It® at Work* as a manual of magic. Successful communication transforms your thoughts, will, and desires into action. It moves people. It transforms the thoughts, will, and desires of others. What better word for this process than *magic*?

But, as with most magic, there is really nothing supernatural about it. The apparent miracles of communication are worked by means of tools skillfully handled. And nearly anyone can acquire the tools and become proficient in the techniques of using them. It's a matter of knowing how to think through goals and objectives, then practicing how to become conscious of the combined effect of the words and the nonverbal signals we receive and broadcast every day. This book will guide you—quickly and practically—through that process of self-awareness. What I can promise you is that learning to put yourself across will be both personally and professionally profitable.

CHAPTER 1

How Good Are You at Putting Yourself Across?

SELF-TEST: GAUGING YOUR COMMUNICATION EFFECTIVENESS

The following is a simple diagnostic test. Its purpose is not to test your knowledge of communication theory or techniques, but to help you gauge how effectively you communicate in a day-to-day business context. For the most part, you will find it easy to guess the "right" answer. But getting the "right" answer is not the point of the test. Respond honestly, even if you feel that your response is not the best one possible. This is *not* a contest. The object is solely self-inventory.

SECTION ONE

1. I communicate effectively.	T/F	____
2. People really listen to me.	T/F	____
3. People enjoy talking to me.	T/F	____
4. I usually get my way.	T/F	____
5. People believe what I say.	T/F	____
6. People value my opinion.	T/F	____
7. I speak with confidence.	T/F	____
8. I feel good when I speak.	T/F	____
9. I like the sound of my voice.	T/F	____
10. I have no trouble saying what I mean.	T/F	____

11. I am persuasive.   T/F ____

12. I have a good vocabulary.   T/F ____

13. I look you in the eye when I speak.   T/F ____

14 I have a warm handshake.   T/F ____

15. I enjoy talking to new people.   T/F ____

16. I enjoy making small talk.   T/F ____

17. I look relaxed when I speak.   T/F ____

18. I feel relaxed when I speak.   T/F ____

19. I'm a good negotiator.   T/F ____

20. I enjoy talking about money.   T/F ____

21. I enjoy "haggling."   T/F ____

22. I enjoy friendly "haggling."   T/F ____

23. I usually get a good deal.   T/F ____

24. I usually get a fair deal.   T/F ____

Score 1 for each "True" response, 0 for "False":

TOTAL 1–24   ____

25. My voice is too high.   T/F ____

26. My voice is too soft.   T/F ____

27. I feel nervous when I speak.   T/F ____

28. I fidget when I speak.   T/F ____

29. I find it difficult to make eye contact.   T/F ____

30. I don't like shaking hands.   T/F ____

31. Sometimes I put my hand to my mouth when I speak.   T/F ____

32. Sometimes I touch my hair when I speak.   T/F ____

33. Sometimes I rub the back of my neck when I speak.   T/F ____

34. Sometimes I fold my arms across my chest when I speak.   T/F ____

35. Sometimes I speak with my hands on my hips.   T/F _____

36. Sometimes I gesture with clenched fists.   T/F _____

37. I get angry easily.   T/F _____

38. I take arguments personally.   T/F _____

39. I have an angry voice.   T/F _____

40. I bite my lip when I get nervous.   T/F _____

Score 1 for each "True" response, 0 for "False":

TOTAL 25-40   _____

SECTION ONE TOTAL (SUBTRACT TOTAL 25-40 FROM TOTAL 1-24)   _____

SECTION TWO

The following are my favorite business words (True or False):

41. analysis   T/F _____

42. answer   T/F _____

43. brainstorm   T/F _____

44. collaborate   T/F _____

45. collaborative   T/F _____

46. confer   T/F _____

47. control   T/F _____

48. cooperate   T/F _____

49. cooperative   T/F _____

50. good listener   T/F _____

51. guide   T/F _____

52. hear   T/F _____

53. helpful   T/F _____

54. huddle   T/F _____

55.	idea	T/F	_____
56.	learn	T/F	_____
57.	listen	T/F	_____
58.	manage	T/F	_____
59.	offer	T/F	_____
60.	open mind	T/F	_____
61.	productive	T/F	_____
62.	solve	T/F	_____
63.	synergy	T/F	_____
64.	team	T/F	_____
65.	team player	T/F	_____
66.	team up	T/F	_____
67.	thanks	T/F	_____
68.	together	T/F	_____
69.	work together	T/F	_____
70.	cost-effective	T/F	_____
71.	effective	T/F	_____
72.	emerge	T/F	_____
73.	evaluate	T/F	_____
74.	expedite	T/F	_____
75.	experience	T/F	_____
75.	feasible	T/F	_____
76.	improve	T/F	_____
77.	increase	T/F	_____
78.	productive	T/F	_____
79.	profitable	T/F	_____
80.	reduce	T/F	_____

81. smart	T/F	____
82. successful	T/F	____
83. valuable	T/F	____
84. value	T/F	____
85. vigorous	T/F	____

Score 1 for each "True" response, 0 for "False":

TOTAL 41–85   ____

The following words are part of my regular business vocabulary (True or False):

86. mine	T/F	____
87. you	T/F	____
88. yours	T/F	____
89. afraid	T/F	____
90. bad luck	T/F	____
91. blame	T/F	____
92. cannot	T/F	____
93. cheated	T/F	____
94. circumstances	T/F	____
95. cornered	T/F	____
96. crisis	T/F	____
97. delay	T/F	____
98. delinquent	T/F	____
99. demand	T/F	____
100. disaster	T/F	____
101. excuse	T/F	____
102. experiment	T/F	____
103. fail	T/F	____

104. fault   T/F ____

105. fear   T/F ____

106. final   T/F ____

107. forgot   T/F ____

108. frustrating   T/F ____

109. guess   T/F ____

110. hopeless   T/F ____

111. impossible   T/F ____

112. impractical   T/F ____

113. inadequate   T/F ____

114. insist   T/F ____

115. loser   T/F ____

116. loss   T/F ____

117. lost   T/F ____

118. make do   T/F ____

119. must   T/F ____

120. nervous   T/F ____

121. no   T/F ____

122. non-negotiable   T/F ____

123. one-time offer   T/F ____

124. overloaded   T/F ____

125. panic   T/F ____

126. relax   T/F ____

127. slipped   T/F ____

128. sorry   T/F ____

129. stupid   T/F ____

130. tired   T/F ____

131. unaware   T/F ____

132. unfair   T/F ____

133. unreasonable   T/F ____

134. wasted   T/F ____

Score 1 for each "True" response, 0 for "False":

TOTAL **86–134**   ____

SECTION TWO TOTAL (SUBTRACT TOTAL **86–134** FROM TOTAL **41–85**)   ____

GRAND TOTAL (ADD SECTION ONE TOTAL AND SECTION TWO TOTAL)   ____

(Note: A *negative* score is possible.)

WHAT IT MEANS TO YOU

This test is a quick-and-dirty diagnostic tool. Look at your Grand Total score. If it is

Higher than +50: You are probably a highly effective business communicator.

+35 to +49: You are probably often effective as a business communicator.

+20 to +34: You are probably sometimes effective as a business communicator.

+10 to +19: You are probably only occasionally effective as a business communicator.

+1 to +9: You are probably often ineffective as a business communicator.

Negative numbers: You are probably rarely effective as a business communicator.

I like to think that anyone can benefit from reading this book. Those who are likely to benefit most, however, are businesspersons who have scored below +50 points on this diagnostic test. Throughout this book, you will find additional diagnostic tests designed to help you gauge your effectiveness in specific areas of business communication.

CHAPTER 2

Building Your Basic Verbal and Nonverbal Communication Vocabulary

We could begin with the various theories of communication and persuasion. There are a great many of these—no end, it would seem. We could begin by discussing such issues as the credibility of the communicator, the role of self-interest and fear in creating persuasive appeals, the importance of organizing your arguments, the effect of group membership and identification on the success or failure of your appeal, the effect of personality on susceptibility to persuasion, and the effect of the passage of time on opinion formation and retention. All of these things are important—if you have the time for them.

But that is a very big *if.* Whom are we kidding? It's no *if* at all. You *don't* have the time, certainly not enough time to approach business communication by a tortuous theoretical route. Let's not even start with strategy. Instead, we begin with the building blocks of communication: the words.

THE 50 WORDS EVERY BUSINESSPERSON SHOULD KNOW AND USE

The first three are ridiculously easy words:

we

us

our

Or are they so easy?

Communication is essentially an exchange between an *I* and a *you.* Even as communication attempts to bridge the gap separating the *I* from the *you*, it continually defines and reiterates that gap. *I* want this, and *you* want that. The most basic step you can take to begin effective communication is to translate the *I* and the *you* into a *we*. Wherever possible and however possible, begin communication by defining areas of common interest, concern, and benefit. It doesn't take a rocket scientist to tell you that the person you are talking to is more interested in what he or she needs and what he or she wants than in what you need and want. One way to appeal to this other person is to forsake and forget your needs and wants and devote your communication to the person. This, of course, is not always desirable or even possible. A more realistic goal is to find common ground, the places where *I* and *you* can become *we*, where interests, needs, and wants can be seen as mutual. This is a powerful basis for all communication, especially in business, which is rooted in the exchange of value for value.

As you go through this book, in situation after situation, in putting yourself across to person after person, you will find that *we*, *us*, and *our* are among the most powerful words you can use.

- To the degree that you are able to translate *I* and *you* into *we*, you will become persuasive and your point of view will become compelling to the other person.

- To the degree that you are unable to effect this feat of translation, you and the other or others will remain separated by a gulf of differing concerns and needs.

From *we*, *us*, and *our*, let's go to the next essential word:

rapport

You may or may not have occasion actually to use the word in everyday business communication, but you should know it and consider it. *Rapport* is a relationship of mutual trust or emotional affinity. Typically, rapport develops over a long period of time between friends, between spouses, between business partners, between teachers and students. The more rapport you build in this way, the better. However, many—probably most— business relationships don't develop over years or even months. Many are brief exchanges defined by the length of a single conversation. Usually, then, you don't have the luxury of time over which to develop rapport. You have to move quickly.

The quickest way to create rapport is to use *we*, *us*, and *our* instead of *I*, *me*, and *you*. Here's an example. Let's say you are speaking to a sales prospect:

You: What do you see as your greatest need in the such-and-such area?

Prospect: Definitely fulfillment—getting the orders out on time.

You: I understand. Working together, *we* could solve *that* problem. I did X, Y, and Z for Acme Widget, and I believe *we* could apply some of those solutions here.

The rapport-building approach used here can be studied by looking at the word *we* in this brief exchange. Quickly, you move from *I* and *you* to *we*. You avoid telling the prospect, "*You've* got a real problem here." Instead, you take a share in ownership of that problem by using *we*. Notice that the problem becomes "*that* problem" rather than "*your* problem." It is something objective, which both you and the prospect will deal with. The prospect is no longer alone with the problem. It has, in fact, become the cornerstone on which your rapport will be built.

We, *us*, and *our* are words of inclusion, cooperation, coordination, and alliance—the very essence of rapport. Other words that cultivate rapport and that are, therefore, essential to your basic business vocabulary are:

analysis	idea
answer	learn
brainstorm	listen
collaborate	manage
collaborative	offer
confer	open mind
control	productive
cooperate	solve
cooperative	synergy
good listener	team
guide	team player
hear	team up
helpful	thanks
huddle	together
	work together

All these words convey the power, benefit, and value of working together, of taking joint ownership of problems, of in effect, translating *I* and *you* into *we*. Beyond these words, which emphasize the collaborative and cooperative aspects of the business relationship, are the words that focus on the exchange of value that is another key positive element in the productive business relationship. These words include:

cost-effective	productive
effective	profitable
emerge	reduce
evaluate	smart
expedite	successful
experience	valuable
feasible	value
improve	vigorous
increase	

Before we look more closely at some of these words, we'd better ask: Are these the only fifty words you need in business? Of course they aren't. But they are words you *should* use, because they build positive relationships, which are the bases for productive subsequent communication.

The words of the group beginning with *analysis* and ending with *work together* all convey the benefits of collaboration. Words such as *analysis, answer, control, guide, huddle, manage,* and *solve* emphasize control and management, the power of shared responsibility. Other words stress joint invention and cooperative creativity: *brainstorm, collaborate, collaborative, confer, idea, learn, productive, synergy, together,* and *work together*. A few more words are vital—*good listener, hear, helpful, listen, team, team player,* and *thanks*. These are necessary to demonstrate that, while you are eager to translate *I* and *you* into *we*, you are not about to forget that the "other" person is *another* person. You want to convey that you will listen to that person with gratitude and that you see the relationship not as one of dominance and submission, but as a relation between one team member and another.

The words of the next group, beginning with *cost-effective* and ending with *vigorous*, shift the communication to the bottom-line products of effective collaboration. These words emphasize cost-effectiveness, cost savings, productivity, and profitability. Notice that *price* and *cost* (except as part of the compound *cost-effective*) are not among these basic words. Why? Effective bottom-line communication guides the conversation away from mere price and cost to the far more relevant concept of *value*. Whatever your business, it is *value* that you are selling, not cost and not price. It is *value* that elevates a business transaction into a business relationship.

Before we go on to the 50 words the businessperson should avoid, let's consider for a moment the difference between business based on transactions and business based on relationships. Here's a question with at least one obvious answer: *What is a good salesperson?* The obvious answer is *A good salesperson makes sales.* And it's a good answer, as far as it goes. The trouble is that it doesn't go very far. While it is true that a good salesperson makes sales, a *great* salesperson makes customers. What is a sale, after all? An event that is soon over and done with, a transaction. What is a customer? A human being who may produce sale after sale and then tell others about you, thereby producing even more sales. This is a relationship. Obviously, then, it is beneficial to communicate in order to create relationships, not merely to generate transactions.

- The language of collaboration is all about creating relationships.

THE 50 WORDS TO AVOID—AND WHY

You probably don't need the list that I'm about to give you. I can tell you what words to avoid, even without listing them. Steer clear of negative words, of words that deny, of words that refuse, of words that turn away from, of words that close doors instead of opening them. Steer clear of limiting words.

This does not mean that you should avoid facing problems or use language that sugarcoats and covers up difficulties. On the contrary, the successful businessperson welcomes problems.

- She calls them challenges.
- She calls them opportunities.

What you should avoid is language that describes problems not as challenges and opportunities, but as causes of inevitable loss and limitation.

If *we*, *us*, and *our* are the words of choice, it might logically follow that *I*, *mine*, *you*, and *yours* should top the list of words to be avoided. Logical or not, and like it or not, it is obvious that you will have occasion to use these words; however, you should avoid them in all cases where *we*, *us*, and *our* can be made to work. So, yes, wherever possible avoid:

I

mine

you

yours

Avoid all language that divides and limits, that defines a winner and a loser, that pits an *I* against a *you*. This includes:

afraid	impractical
bad luck	inadequate
blame	insist
cannot	loser
cheated	loss
circumstances	lost
cornered	make do
crisis	must
delay	nervous
delinquent	no
demand	non-negotiable
disaster	one-time offer
excuse	overloaded
experiment	panic
fail	relax
fault	slipped
fear	sorry
final	stupid
forgot	tired
frustrating	unaware

guess   unfair

hopeless   unreasonable

impossible   wasted

The object is not to avoid reality, even unpleasant reality, nor to distort reality by disguising problems.

- The purpose of avoiding a vocabulary of limitation is to build business relationships.

"What's in a name?" Shakespeare asked. While most people call a problem or crisis or glitch an *obstacle*, you should think of it as an *opportunity*. Difficulties are opportunities to demonstrate problem-solving skills and to build business relationships, to forge teamwork, and to create a sense of partnership.

- Approach difficulties with language that defines them as opportunities, not as dead ends.

THE 12 ESSENTIALS OF NONVERBAL COMMUNICATION

In a famous 1971 study, psychologist Albert Mehrabian found that when listeners judge the emotional content of a speech, they give the most weight to the speaker's facial expressions and body movement: his or her "body language." Just how much weight? Fifty-five percent. This means that 55 percent of the speech's power of persuasion—its effectiveness—depends on visual, not on verbal, cues.

So only 45 percent of the effectiveness of a speech comes from the words?

No.

The next most important factor, according to Mehrabian's test audiences, were "vocal qualities"—not words, but tone of voice, voice pitch, and the pace of delivery. These accounted for 38 percent of the speech's effectiveness.

Now, add 55 and 38 percent. This gives you 93 percent. According to Mehrabian's study, 93 percent of the effectiveness of a speech—ostensibly a *verbal* presentation—has nothing to do with the meaning of the words used. The words themselves accounted for a mere 7 percent of the effectiveness of a speech.

The lesson of Meharabian's study applies to everyday communication as well as to formal speech: The business communicator ignores body language and quality of voice at his or her peril.

- Movement, expression, and tone speak volumes, regardless of the words that are used or not used.

Here are a dozen basic rules to help you think about, develop, and hone your nonverbal "vocabulary":

1. Make an Effective Entrance

"That woman sure knows how to make an entrance!"

How many times have you heard a comment like that? Too often, I suspect. It's become such a cliché that we don't think about what it really means. Too bad, because it means a lot. How you enter a room makes a powerful statement about who you are and who you think you are. For some, making a powerful positive first impression comes naturally and is easy. For others, awkward and uncomfortable practice is required. But even if making a positive entrance and effective first impression is difficult, it's a lot easier to put in the effort to make such an impression than it is to attempt to undo a bad first impression. In many situations, you may never have the opportunity even to try.

2. Walk Tall (Even if You're Short)

Nonverbal communication begins before a single word is uttered. When you make your entrance or approach the person or persons with whom you want to communicate, begin by walking tall. If you're on the short side, you won't like to hear that tall people tend to command greater authority than short people. This isn't fair, of course, and it is even disheartening that people attach so much value to something so arbitrary and superficial as physical stature. But it's the way things are.

Are men under six feet tall and women under, say, five-nine doomed to fail as effective communicators? Of course not. But they do approach the task with a disadvantage.

Must these folks then take their first steps toward effective communication in elevator shoes? Not necessarily, but it wouldn't hurt for shorter men to wear shoes with built-up heels and for shorter women to favor high heels. Moreover, it is a good idea for short men and women generally to dress in ways that appear to make them taller.

- Avoid boxy-looking tailoring.
- Avoid horizontally striped patterns.
- Shorter men should avoid baggy, loosely cut pants, and shorter women should favor longer hemlines.

3. Enter with a Purpose

Far more important than dressing to accent stature, however, is to practice walking tall. This means never entering a room or approaching another person in a cringing, stooped, or slouching manner. Concentrate on maintaining an erect posture as you make your entrance, and forthrightly, without hesitation, and with a purposeful stride.

How do you acquire a "purposeful stride"? Have a purpose, and know where you are going.

- Try always to approach any communication situation having already formulated the purpose and the objective of the communication.
- If you have to do your thinking as you make your entrance, chances are that you'll appear hesitant or absentminded. Work out your thinking as much as you can beforehand.
- The initial message you want to deliver is nonverbal, but it *can* be put into words: *I know how to carry myself.*

4. Smile

Close your eyes for a moment and summon an image of someone who walks tall. Maybe you know somebody personally. Maybe you already walk tall. Or maybe, just maybe, your mind's eye focuses on John Wayne. This movie star was—and remains—an American icon, a tall man who knew how to walk like a tall man.

Too bad that's not the way *you* should walk tall. Think of John Wayne, and you may think about walking tall. but you also think about a tight-lipped, unsmiling, taciturn presence: the so-called "strong, silent type" that Hollywood has long favored as the ideal of American manhood. Such a look works wonders on the screen, but in everyday business contexts, coming on strong and silent is usually perceived as hostile, threatening, and unsympathetic. It sets up barriers to communication rather than creating bridges.

- Walk tall, but walk in smiling.

A grim, closed-mouth negotiator can expect little success, a frowning salesperson probably won't make the sale, and the last public speaker to win over an audience without cracking a smile was Sir Winston Churchill. (But he was a great world leader, and there was a very nasty war on.)

A smile is an invitation. Anything less than a smile sends the message that you intend to offer little or nothing and that you are receptive to little or nothing. If you come on like a tough nut to crack, many of the people you approach will decide that you just aren't worth dealing with.

To some people, a smile comes naturally. Others must make a conscious effort to put one on. Everyone whose facial muscles and nerves are healthy can manage a smile, of course, but a phony smile is usually transparently fake and will turn people off. If you're not naturally a smiler, what can you do to acquire a *genuinely* genial and pleasant facial expression?

- Begin by relaxing. Before you make your entrance, glance downward, move your jaw around, then move your tongue around the inside of your mouth. Inhale deeply, hold it, then let out your breath forcefully. Repeat these exercises a few times.
- When your facial muscles feel relaxed, think about something or someone or some place you enjoy. Imagine pleasurable times, people, and places. Chances are that the combination of facial relaxation and a pleasant frame of mind will bring the easy, welcoming smile that is a tremendous communication facilitator.

5. Make Eye Contact

As soon as you walk into a client's, associate's, or boss's office or approach anyone you need to communicate with, look him or her in the eyes. This accomplishes two things. First, it is an unfailing token of openness and honesty. ("Look me in the eye and say that.") Second, eye contact instantly transmits energy. We've all heard people speak about the "sparkle" in someone's eye, as if that sparkle were an unusual thing, a thing that made the person in question seem special. Actually, *all* of us have a sparkle in our eyes, but it is rarely noticed because most people do not make full eye contact when they meet or speak, and full eye contact is required to make that sparkle visible. To exploit the sparkle in your eyes, to convey honesty and transmit energy, make eye contact—immediately, before the first words are spoken.

6. Give a Great Handshake

There was a time when all good fathers took their sons aside—back in the days when little boys, not little girls, were expected to enter the world of commerce—and solemnly explained the vital importance of a good, solid handshake. The right handshake was a key to commercial success, a kind of universal, all-purpose *open sesame*. A hearty handshake was regarded almost as a mystical thing. ("Son, *this* is important!")

Such a rite of passage may seem corny or at least quaint to us nowadays. We enjoy seeing ourselves as too "sophisticated" to put much stock in a ritual like shaking hands: *I'll shake your hand, but just cut to the chase and show me the bottom line.* The fact is that, try as we might to assert our "civilized," "intellectual," and "verbal" selves, physical touch and physical warmth continue to make a powerful *human* impression on us all—even in so-called professional or business contexts. If you want to test this proposition, think of a memorable handshake in your life. You'll soon discover this isn't as silly as it sounds. Most of us remember the handshake of some individual we have met, remember it because it was exceptionally warm and powerful or, perhaps, colder and deader than any cold, dead fish. Either way, it made an impression. We remember touch—contact—as much as we do words, and maybe even more.

Fortunately, it is not difficult to deliver a hearty handshake that conveys straightforward warmth, openness, and a willingness to communicate.

STEP 1:   Try to deliver a dry-palm handshake. It's a good idea to carry a handkerchief with you and use it to wipe your hands before you go into a meeting or conference that involves handshakes.

STEP 2:   Grasp the other person's hand fully, at the palm rather than at the fingers.

STEP 3:   Deliver a *moderately* tight grip. A firm handshake does not require a bone-crushing grip, but you should not offer a passive dead fish, either.

STEP 4:   Hold the other person's hand a few fractions of a second longer than you are naturally inclined to do. This conveys additional sincerity and quite literally "holds" the other person's attention while greetings are exchanged.

STEP 5:   While giving the handshake, do not look down at the clasped hands but, rather, into the other person's eyes.

STEP 6:   Start talking *before* you let go: "It's great to meet you" or "Glad to be here."

7. Think Before You Sit

Making an entrance often concludes with seating oneself in an office or at a conference table. Just how you do this tells those present something about your attitude and approach to business. Be aware that the people already in the room cannot help but watch you sit. Perhaps it's a throwback to our common mammalian heritage: we look intently at anyone who enters "our" territory. Whatever the reason, *you* tend to be the focus of attention when you enter the room and take a seat.

Don't rush to that seat. Doing so will make you appear anxious. More important, if others in the room are already seated, your standing will give you a few moments to be looked up to—literally. By standing in a room in which the others are seated, you take on an aura of authority, however temporary.

Give some thought, too, to where you sit. If you have a choice, choose a firm chair rather than a sofa or a very soft chair. You want a chair that keeps you upright and that allows you to maintain an erect posture, not a chair that swallows you whole.

If you are to be seated at a table, it is not appropriate for you to usurp the seat at the head of the table—unless, of course, you are running the meeting. Beyond this, be aware that there is a psychological power geography at work around any conference table.

- The greatest power position is, of course, at the head of the table.
- The second most dominant position is at the other end of the table.

- Perhaps surprisingly, the seats to either side of the head of the table are the weakest positions at the table and should be avoided, if possible.

8. Convey Relaxed Energy

Energy is a positive quality that is conveyed largely through nonverbal signals. But you don't want to give the impression of restlessness or nervousness. The ideal energy to convey is relaxed energy, a combination of enthusiasm and confidence that may be summed up in the word *poise.*

Relaxed energy—poise—begins with breathing. Now, we all have breathing patterns that are natural and comfortable for us. This is our normal state, a state in which breathing is thoroughly automatic, so that we are largely or entirely unaware of it. When you become upset, nervous, or scared, however, breathing typically becomes shallower, shorter, and faster. You often become conscious of the change in breathing pattern. More important, such changes are noticeable not only to you but, most likely, to any other astute observer.

There is no advantage to being perceived as short of breath and anxious, but, fortunately, it is possible to train yourself to breathe slowly and deeply, even when you are nervous. This requires some thought, but it can be done, and doing so will benefit you in two ways.

- Not only will learning to control your breathing keep your nervousness from being communicated, it will also actually cause you to feel less nervous.

Anxiety is a devilish thing. We feel scared, which creates certain physical sensations and symptoms; then, as we become aware of these sensations and symptoms, we become even more anxious, which, in turn, intensifies the sensations and symptoms. A vicious cycle is born.

9. Use Your Head (and Face)

Nothing "speaks" body language more eloquently than the head and face. Think about the messages you are delivering.

- The head tilted to one side indicates interest and close listening. This is a desirable gesture. Just make certain to vary it. No body language gesture is positive if it is held statically.

- A *slightly* out-thrust chin conveys confidence, but don't go overboard. Boldly thrust out your chin, and you will probably be perceived as arrogant.
- Nodding up and down conveys agreement, while shaking the head from side to side conveys disagreement. This should come as news to no one; however, it is all too easy to fall into the trap of sending mixed signals. We've all talked with people who *say* yes even as they—ever so slightly—shake their head *no*. Become conscious of your body language in order to prevent such garbled "transmissions."

10. Use Your Hands

Next to the head and face, the hands are the most fluent conveyors of body language. Many people worry about "what to do with" their hands. Why worry? You can use them consciously to help harness or drain off nervous energy. Feel free to gesture with your hands in order to help drive home your verbal points.

- Open hands, palms up, suggest honesty and openness.
- Rubbing the hands together communicates positive expectancy.
- Putting the fingertips together steeple-fashion conveys confidence.

11. Stick to the Basics When Speaking in Public

Most of the body-language basics that apply in everyday communications are also useful in more formal public speaking situations.

- In a formal speaking situation, maintain eye contact with your audience. This is not always easy when you have to look down at your typescript; therefore, rehearse the speech and practice looking up frequently. Each time you look up from your typescript, try to make contact with a specific person in the audience. Don't stare out blankly. Vary the targets of your gaze, but do pick a specific target each time.
- Smile as often as possible—unless the content of the speech makes this clearly inappropriate.
- Use hand gestures to underscore key points. Choreograph and practice useful, expressive gestures as required.

- Adopt a firm, upright, but comfortable stance at the podium. Soldiers required to stand at attention for extended periods quickly learn to appear rigid without actually standing rigidly. Do not lock your knees, but, instead, flex them slightly. This will have the effect of relaxing you without leading to a slouch position.

12. Communicate with Clothes

Another aspect of nonverbal communication is dress. The general rule is to make an effort to identify the prevailing "dress code" of the individual or group with whom you'll be communicating. Dress appropriately for that context. A casual look may be appropriate in one context, but inappropriate, even self-destructive, in another.

Many sales professionals make it a practice to dress "a notch above" their customers. This is a safe, conservative rule of thumb for nonverbal communication.

13. Learn to Use Your Voice

Just as tall people tend to command more authority than shorter folk, people with deep voices are generally perceived as more persuasive than those whose voices are relatively high pitched. This is true of women as well as men. If your voice is pitched in the higher registers, consider consciously trying to speak in a lower pitch. Practice until you are comfortable.

- Pitching your voice lower has the added benefit of producing a more pleasing tone. It also has the effect of slowing you down, thereby encouraging the more precise articulation of each word.

- Lowering pitch also tends to minimize any nasal vocal quality, which many listeners find annoying. (If you suffer from persistent allergies or chronic breathing problems, the state of your health as well as the effectiveness of your communication may benefit from a visit to the doctor.)

- In formal speaking situations, be sure to speak loudly enough. Don't strain, but be aware that a speaker can do absolutely nothing more annoying than fail to make himself or herself heard. How loud is loud enough? You should consciously enjoy the full, resonant sound of your own voice. When you have reached that point, you are probably speaking loudly enough.

• Whether in conversation or in a formal speaking situation, most speakers can benefit from making a deliberate effort to slow down. For public speakers, the rule of thumb is not to exceed 150 words per minute, which means that it should take you a full two minutes to read a double-spaced, typewritten page of text. The 150 WPM rule is too slow for most casual conversation, which usually proceeds at about 200 words per minute.

BEWARE OF THESE 25 NONVERBAL PITFALLS

If body language can help you communicate effectively, it can, unfortunately, also sabotage and undermine your intended message. Trouble often begins before a single word is spoken.

Hesitancy and Evasiveness

1. Avoid the tentative, hesitant, "aw shucks" entrance. When you decide to enter a room, a meeting, a conference, or even simply to approach someone with whom you want to speak, carry the action through smoothly and forthrightly. Know what you want and make an effort to move as if you know what you want.

2. Do not fail to establish eye contact quickly. Avoidance of eye contact will be interpreted as fear, indecisiveness, weakness, dishonesty, or any number of other negative things.

Handshake Problems

3. The limp, dead-fish handshake is never welcome and always a disappointment. There is an anticipated pleasure in a warm, firm grip. Fail to deliver this, and you will initiate communications with a failure of expectation.

4. The only thing more offensive than the dead-fish grip is the bone crusher. Give up the painfully childish idea of trying to dominate the other person with a display of your manual strength.

5. Many men automatically offer women a loose, overly delicate handshake. In a business context, an excessively soft handshake is likely to be perceived as patronizing or chauvinistic. Men should use the same *moderately* firm grip they would deliver to another man.

Nervous Energy and Anxiety

6. A feeling of energy is valuable in any communication; however, avoid displaying what is generally called "nervous energy." Learn to overcome and discard such activities as tapping feet, darting eyes, drumming fingers, and fingers that fiddle with necktie, jewelry, or hair.

7. If you are subject to anxiety in meetings and interviews, practice breathing deeply and regularly. The rapid, shallow breathing associated with anxiety will not only increase your anxiety—thereby creating a vicious cycle that will tend to make your breathing even more rapid and shallow—but will communicate your anxiety, fear, and uncertainty. It will make you that much less persuasive.

8. Avoid sighing. It will be interpreted either as a sign of distress or of boredom.

Dangerous Distractions

9. Avoid yawning. The reasons are obvious.

10. Scratching your head indicates confusion or disbelief.

11. Biting your lip signals anxiety.

12. Rubbing the back of your head or neck suggests frustration, impatience.

13. A lowered chin conveys defensiveness or insecurity.

14. Narrowing of the eyes communicates disagreement, resentment, anger, or disapproval. Marked narrowing may suggest puzzlement.

15. Avoiding eye contact conveys insincerity, fear, evasiveness, or, at the very least, lack of interest in what's being discussed.

16. Eye contact is great, but a steady stare suggests an arrogant need to control, intimidate, and dominate. At its worst, vacant staring seems weird and will alienate the person or persons with whom you are speaking.

17. Raising the eyebrows indicates surprise. Nothing wrong with that, if you want to communicate surprise. In some contexts, raised eyebrows suggests disbelief. You may inadvertently offend the speaker.

18. Peering over the top of your eyeglasses suggests doubt and disbelief.

19. Crossing your arms in front of your chest communicates defiance, defensiveness, resistance, aggressiveness, or a closed mind.

20. Using the hands to rub eyes, ears, or the side of the nose conveys doubt. This can really sabotage your verbal message.

21. Hand wringing is a strong sign of anxiety verging on terror. Avoid it.

22. Avoid holding head position and facial expressions for a long time or repeating any single gesture over and over. The idea is to look alive and lively!

Bad Habits

23. Learn to recognize and deal with tics and nervous habits. Here's what to watch for and avoid: continuous hand motions, rubbing your face, putting your hands anywhere near your mouth, repeatedly shrugging your shoulders.

24. In formal speaking situations, beware of nervously shifting your weight from side to side. This is highly distracting to your listeners.

25. Avoid ending declarative sentences on a rising note. This is a verbal habit more common to women than men. It makes a statement sound tentative, even doubtful, as if the speaker were continually seeking approval.

CHAPTER 3

Putting Yourself Across . . . to Get a Job

SELF-TEST YOUR INTERVIEWING SAVVY

The following is a simple diagnostic test. A smaller and more selective version of the self-test in Chapter 1, its purpose is not to test your knowledge of communication theory or techniques, but to help you gauge how effectively you communicate when interviewing for a job. For the most part, you will find it easy to guess the "right" answer. But getting the "right" answer is not the point of the test. Respond honestly, even if you feel that your response is not the best one possible. This is *not* a contest. The object is solely self-inventory.

1. I'm afraid I won't be able to answer the interviewer's questions.   T/F _____

2. I almost never have questions to ask at an interview.   T/F _____

3. I am prepared to answer the ten most commonly asked interview questions.   T/F _____

4. I am a good listener.   T/F _____

5. I come to the interview prepared with questions to ask .   T/F _____

6. I communicate high energy and vitality.   T/F _____

7. I dress to express myself. That's the most important thing.   T/F _____

8. I face interviews with dread.   T/F _____

9. I feel that the interviewer wants to trip me up.   T/F _____

10. I feel good about my interview wardrobe.   T/F _____

11. I feel I have little to offer an employer.   T/F _____

12. I feel confident that I can answer any question the interviewer asks.   T/F _____

13. I formulate objectives *before* going into a job interview.   T/F _____

14. I get bad "stage fright" at job interviews.   T/F _____

15. My greatest concern in the interview is salary.   T/F _____

16. I handle interview anxiety well.   T/F _____

17. I have nothing to say at job interviews.   T/F _____

18. I have prepared a list of accomplishments.   T/F _____

19. When I go into an interview, I know how much salary to expect.   T/F _____

20. During job interviews, I talk about *accomplishments*, not *experience*.   T/F _____

21. I know how to send the message that *I will fit in*.   T/F _____

22. I know how to send the message that *I can do the job*.   T/F _____

23. I know how to *help* the interviewer interview me.   T/F _____

24. I know how to do effective research on a prospective employer.   T/F _____

25. I know how to send the message that *I will deliver*.   T/F _____

26. I know how much salary I want/need.   T/F _____

27. I look at a job interview as a sales situation.   T/F _____

28. I perform well in a job interview.   T/F _____

29. I prefer "winging it" to preparing for job interviews.   T/F _____

30. I prepare effectively for interviews.   T/F _____

31. I present myself as a problem solver.   T/F _____

32. I want to get to the salary discussion as quickly as possible.   T/F _____

Total: _____

Score 1 point for each "True" response and 0 for each "False" response, EXCEPT for questions 1, 2, 7, 8, 9, 11, 14, 15, 17, 29, and 32. For *these questions only*, SUBTRACT 1 point for each "True" response. Record your total. A score below +20 indicates that you would benefit from practicing the communication techniques discussed in this chapter. (Note: It is possible to have a negative score.)

WORDS TO USE DURING INTERVIEWS

accomplishments	information
advise	initiated
anticipate	motivated
awake	profit
aware	reevaluated
built	responsive
consult	revamped
coordinate	revised
coordinator	revitalized
corporate	seek
created	self-starter
earned	sensitive
efficient	started
energetic	success
evaluation	successfully
goal	team
improved	teamwork

PHRASES TO USE DURING INTERVIEWS

accept criticism

corporate image

eager to take on additional responsibility

extra effort

eyes open
for the first time
goal-oriented
head on
in touch
make use of criticism
management team
nothing stops me
take direction
take charge
team effort
walk through walls for this job

WORDS TO AVOID DURING INTERVIEWS

bad
bored
depressed
frustrated
hard

incompetent
slow
tired
trouble

PHRASES TO AVOID DURING INTERVIEWS

dead end
didn't see eye to eye
disagreed with my boss
get away with
no future
terrible boss
too difficult
too easy
too many hours
too much work

BODY-LANGUAGE STRATEGY FOR JOB INTERVIEWS

The employment interview is a veritable showcase for body language. You are under intense scrutiny. While it is true that few interviewers are psychologists, amateur or professional, and therefore do not deliberately set out to "read" your body language, the average interviewers are far more sensitive to nonverbal signals than they realize. They may not consciously articulate how they admired the confidence, honesty, and energy communicated by steady eye contact, nor is it likely that they will report to a colleague that they couldn't trust you because you repeatedly rubbed the back of your neck when you spoke; nevertheless, such signals broadcast volumes, especially in an interview. Let's put the situation in its crudest, crassest terms. Manufacturers and retailers know the importance of creating appealing packaging to sell a product. The package is the consumer's first contact with the merchandise. Is packaging superficial? Yes, of course. By definition, packaging is superficial: external, on the outside. And it is important precisely because it is, in this sense, superficial. Body language and other aspects of nonverbal communication are likewise superficial. They are the equivalent of packaging and are vital to "selling" the "merchandise."

In a job interview, communication begins before a single word is spoken. How you enter the employer's shop, office, or conference room makes a powerful nonverbal statement about who you are and, even more important, who you think you are.

You can greatly increase the effectiveness of your communication if you begin by establishing objectives and *then* plan your strategy. The more you know about what the prospective employer is looking for, the more effectively and persuasively you will be able to communicate. "Preparing for the Interview: Plan to Be Spontaneous," later in this chapter, will help you learn about the target employers need and want *before* the interview begins. But there is one thing *every* employer needs and wants, and it doesn't take inside information or research to discover what that is. *Every employer wants an employee who can do the job.*

Simple? Not just simple; it's self-evident. And even novice job hunters understand that their chief task at the interview is to persuade the employer that they can do the job. Most job hunters—novices as well as those with more experience—think that this is a matter of having an impressive work history and an ability to present it impressively. Certainly, these things help. However, the persuasion begins before a word is spoken. The chief objective toward which you should direct your body language strategy is to send a nonverbal message that *you can do the job.*

Begin by making yourself as impressive a physical presence as possible. This includes your grooming and dress, which we'll discuss later in the chapter, but it also depends greatly on how you carry yourself. As was observed in Chapter 2, those lucky enough to have inherited "tall" genes have the edge on those of us who are on the middling to short side. Tall people are more readily perceived as leaders and self-starters. This isn't fair, this isn't good, and this isn't even rational. But it's the way things are.

- If you are tall, do nothing to compromise your physical stature.

- Practice good habits of posture. Do what your mother told you to do: Stand up straight.

TIP

Many tall women, in particular, grow up self-conscious of their height. As a result, some tend to slump or stoop in an unconscious effort to minimize their stature. Well, in the world of business, tall women have an advantage over shorter women, just as tall men enjoy an edge over short men. Like their male counterparts, tall women should exploit, not compromise, their stature.

Is it impossible for shorter men and women to become powerful executives? Of course not. And you don't have to wear elevator shoes, either. However, both men and women should dress in ways that enhance height.

- This means emphasizing the vertical dimension rather than the horizontal.

- Avoid boxy tailoring.

- Shoes? Shorter men can benefit from thicker soles and a somewhat built-up heel, and women might favor a reasonably high heel. (Moderation is the rule here, though, and we'll discuss this matter further in "Dressing for the Interview," later in the chapter.)

- Tall or short, you'll benefit from a display of erect posture. It broadcasts the message that you *know how to carry yourself, that you are self-confident, that you feel good about yourself,* that you take pride in yourself, that, in short, you are a competent, capable person.

Walking tall does not mean that you should present a stiff, humorless, unfriendly, disdainful, and aloof image. Nor should you come across with an equally humorless arrogance and swagger. There is no anatomical or physiological reason that you should be unable to maintain impressive posture and smile at the same time.

- A key part of your body-language strategy should be a smile.

If all employers want employees who can do the job, they also want to hire people who will fit in. After all, for at least 40 hours out of most weeks in the year, you will be living with your boss, colleagues, and subordinates. Make it clear, before a word is exchanged, that you are friendly, approachable, courteous, and considerate. All of this is conveyed in a smile. To be sure, an interview is a stressful situation, and a smile may not come naturally at the moment. Don't wait for your feelings to change (they probably won't); just smile. You'll probably receive smiles in return, and that in itself will help ease the tension. Moreover, your own smile should make you feel at least a little better. While it is true that happy feelings produce a smile, it is also the case that the act of smiling can induce some semblance of happy feelings: *I can't be all that scared. I'm smiling!*

What else can you count on an employer to look for?

- Someone who can do the job.
- Someone who's approachable, pleasant, and courteous.
- Someone who is honest, straightforward, and vital.

As with the other basic requirements, you can begin to communicate, nonverbally and from the outset, your ability to deliver. The key here is to establish and maintain eye contact. In fact, as soon as you walk into the room, target the principal interviewer (if there is more than one in the room) and look him or her in the eyes. The result will be an instant transmission of energy: an impression of vitality, openness, and honesty.

Start with a Strong Handshake

You've now made your entrance. Only a few seconds have elapsed since you appeared in the room. Those few seconds, however, have proven rich with messages and, more important, rich with the potential for powerful, positive, and persuasive messages. Yet not a word has been spoken. The culmination of these first few critical, but nonverbal, seconds of the interview comes with the handshake.

There once was a time when businessmen—and, back then, the world of business was almost exclusively male—gave a good deal of thought and even devoted considerable conversation to the subject of the handshake. A firm, warm grip was considered absolutely essential to success in commerce. These days, we hear little talk about the handshake. The subject seems quaint at best, corny at worst. True enough, it *is* possible to regard the handshake as a meaningless social ritual. But you can also rethink it, reflecting on the handshake as a powerful form of nonverbal communication. It is, after all, one of the few intimate acts our society endorses between strangers. Through the handshake may be transmitted strength and warmth, of course, but beyond this, a sense of confidence and openness as well. A weak or indifferent handshake, in contrast, transmits indecisiveness and coolness. It tends to create doubt in the other person.

Fortunately, it is not difficult to give a hearty handshake.

STEP 1:   Begin with dry palms. Taking into one's grip the cold, clammy hand of another is not a pleasant sensation. Moreover, it tells the other person that you are anxious, nervous, scared. Carry a handkerchief and use it to wipe your hands before you enter the interview room.

STEP 2:   Within a few paces of the interviewer, take the initiative and extend your hand as you walk toward him or her.

STEP 3:   Deliver a full, *moderately* tight grip.

STEP 4:   So far, nothing out of the ordinary. But here is a tactic that will elevate your handshake a cut above an ordinary greeting. Be certain to hold the other person's hand a few fractions of a second longer than you are naturally inclined to do. Then, while holding the other person's hand, look him or her in the eye.

STEP 5:   Before you let go, start talking: "It's great to meet you" or "Glad to be here."

Don't Rush to Sit Down

Interviews are not conducted standing up. However, when you enter the interviewer's office, do not rush to a vacant seat. Stand as you exchange greetings. You may then be *invited* to sit. If you are not asked to sit, do so after a few seconds. Just remember that, as long as you are standing, the interviewer or interviewers will see you at your full height. If they sit down first, there will be a moment or two in which you will be looked up to—literally. Standing in a room in which the others are seated is a powerful gesture. It imbues you with an aura of strength and authority. Temporary though this is, it makes a favorable nonverbal impression.

Convey Relaxed Energy

During the course of the interview, it is to your advantage to communicate a sense of relaxed energy, as discussed in Chapter 2. The elements of relaxed energy include:

- Measured breathing. Breathing patterns are a remarkably accurate barometer of the emotions. Anxiety disrupts our normal breathing patterns, typically rendering them short, rapid, and shallow. The result of this pattern is increased anxiety. Moreover, any careful observer will readily pick up on your short, shallow breaths and conclude that you are anxious. You can—and should—consciously slow down and deepen your breathing. You'll not only feel better for it, you will also communicate confidence rather than insecurity.

- Eye contact. Maintaining eye contact can be a challenge. To begin with, don't turn the valuable notion of eye contact into a blank staring contest. It is perfectly all right to look aside from time to time or to look downward for a moment as you compose an answer to a question. Do, however, focus on the other's eyes as often as possible, especially when you are making an important point. Continued eye contact helps maintain the energy level of the interview.

- Sit—relatively—still. This does not mean sitting rigidly or stiff as a board. We'll talk in a moment about what specific movements to avoid, but, in general, sit upright—don't slump—but do relax.

- Seated, your energy and acuteness of attention should be expressed chiefly through facial expression, the angle of the head, and the use of the hands.

- Smile as much as possible.

- Open your eyes wide to express heightened interest.

- Nod—gently—to communicate understanding and assent.
- Lean forward to express intensity of interest.
- Gesture with open hands, palms upward. This suggests openness, honesty, and acceptance.
- Steepling your hands—putting the fingertips of the left and right hands together in the manner of a church steeple—is a powerful gesture that suggests thought, confidence, and active, ongoing appraisal of what is being said.

BODY LANGUAGE TO AVOID DURING JOB INTERVIEWS

Body language that is self-destructive in an interview generally is of two kinds: gestures that communicate anxiety and gestures that communicate a closedness or failure to connect.

Watch Out for Signals of Fear

Let's begin with the body language that signals fear, but let's pause a moment to consider the nature of fear.

What's so bad about it? Surely, any sensitive, humane interviewer will forgive a certain amount of anxiety. It's only natural, after all.

Consciously, most interviewers are indeed charitable and decent. But the power of nonverbal communication lies in its appeal to the layer beneath conscious thought. Even the most forgiving interviewer will, at some level, react negatively to messages of anxiety. Remember, every employer wants to feel that he or she is hiring a person who can do the job. That feeling depends, in part, on the feelings *you* project. Anxiety is contagious. If your body language conveys fear, the interviewer will soon be "infected" as well—only his or her anxiety will be more narrowly and specifically focused: *I just don't feel as if this guy can do the job. I am* afraid *to hire him.*

Here are some of the "fear broadcasters" to recognize and avoid:

- You may dismiss swinging legs, tapping a foot, or pumping your leg like a piston—poising your foot on its toes and pumping your leg up and down—as mere "nervous energy." Well, that's bad enough. In any conversation, such fidgeting is annoying. However, it's worse than that. Leg or foot movement sends a strong message of anxiety. It communicates an urgent desire to get up and leave, indeed, to run away.

- Twirling the hair—a gesture more common to women than to men—not only suggests acute anxiety, it effectively transmits that anxiety to others. Nobody likes to feel anxious, and the last thing you want to do in an interview is make the interviewer feel bad.

- Aimless hand gestures. Many interviewees worry needlessly about their hands, having heard somewhere that it is a bad thing to "talk with your hands." This isn't true at all. Meaningful gestures, gestures that underscore important points or add needed emphasis, aid effective communication. Nor should you worry, as some do, that "talking with your hands" is overly "ethnic." As long as hand gestures add to the meaning of your words, they are valid and unobtrusive adjuncts to communication. However, avoid constant or meaningless use of the hands, gestures accompanying virtually each and every word. These suggest nothing more or less than sustained anxiety.

- Few gestures communicate more intense distress than hand wringing. This is a fatal signal to send an interviewer.

- Anxiety tends to dry out the mouth and lips. Repeated lip licking strongly signals fear. Like hair twirling, it is also a gesture that makes others uncomfortable.

- Touching the mouth or nose or, indeed, bringing the hands near the face suggests anxiety or dishonesty, as if you have something to hide. Many otherwise intelligent people make themselves look dumb by covering their mouths when they speak.

- Finger or nail biting sends an anxiety message that is fatal in an interview. This is not a subtle piece of body language. It screams: *Steer clear of me!*

It is worth devoting time and effort to eliminating the kinds of body language that broadcast anxiety, not only because these gestures send negative signals to the interviewer, but also because your own awareness of such movements, especially on a less than fully conscious level, fans the flames of fear. Anxiety produces the actions, but the actions confirm and reinforce the anxiety. Break the cycle, and you will feel better as well as perform more effectively.

Don't Convey a Failure to Connect

Anxiety is not the only negative message body language can transmit to an interviewer. If you consistently fail to make eye contact or if you go out of your way to avoid eye contact, you may be perceived as awkwardly shy and not self-confident. Even worse, you may be seen as evasive or dishonest, as if you were hiding something.

- Beware of bringing your hands near your face. Some gestures of this kind suggest anxiety. Others suggest deception, lack of trust, disbelief, or confusion.

- Stroking the chin suggests deception or disbelief.

- Running the fingers through the hair or rubbing the back of the neck suggests confusion.

- Touching the nose suggests disbelief.

- Crossing the arms across the chest suggests defiance, disbelief, or resistance to an idea or suggestion.

As important as positive body language is when you make your entrance, negative body language can undermine everything that follows. Here are a few *don'ts*:

- Don't avoid eye contact quickly. The idea is to demonstrate that you "belong" in this new "territory," and immediate eye contact is an effective way of staking your claim.

- Don't offer a limp, dead-fish handshake.

- Men, don't patronize a woman interviewer by offering her a gentle handshake. Use the same *moderately* firm grip you deliver to another man. In a business context, an excessively soft handshake is likely to be perceived as chauvinistic and offensive.

- Don't rush to take a seat. If there are other people in the room who have not yet taken seats, avoid the embarrassing slapstick of musical chairs by remaining on your feet until the others sit.

- If you have a choice, don't sit on sofas or soft, overstuffed chairs. The ideal interview chair is slightly uncomfortable, prompting you to sit straight up at all times. You do not want to occupy a chair that swallows you up and makes you feel (and perhaps look) immature or even foolish.

PREPARING FOR AN INTERVIEW: PLAN TO BE SPONTANEOUS

In many ways, the prospect of an interview is exciting, a challenge that is filled with opportunity. For many job hunters, however, it is a challenge they would just as soon forgo, if that were possible. If you are among those who face interviews with dread, you are not alone. But it is not only many candidates who cringe at the thought of an interview; employers—probably most of them—hate interviewing. Far from seeing the interview as an ego-boosting opportunity to play God with the fate of the interviewee, most employers see interviewing job candidates as an unwelcome intrusion into their daily routine. Other matters always seems more urgent, and they tend to resent having to put their day on hold to talk to a job candidate, no matter how badly they need the new employee. Beyond this, most supervisors and executives are simply uncomfortable with the interview process. They should be. Many—perhaps most—enter the interview unprepared or, at least, poorly prepared, having been too busy to review their needs thoroughly, let alone the details of the candidate's background and qualifications.

If you want to score interview points, prepare yourself with questions, comments, and issues *you* can raise during the interview, so that the interviewer doesn't have to do all the work. The easier you make it on the anxious and beleaguered interviewer, the more positive the impression you'll create.

- Forty-seven out of every one hundred job interviews lead to a job.

Too many job candidates confuse lying awake nights fretting about the upcoming interview with constructively preparing for it. Use the days or weeks before an interview to perform the following 12 tasks:

1. Learn about the organization to which you are applying.
2. Learn about the role of your target position (the job for which you are applying) within the organization.
3. Try to find out about the organization's special needs, goals, and problems.
4. Formulate some ideas about how you can fulfill the needs, help achieve the goals, and solve the problems you learn about.

5. Prepare a concise list of your accomplishments. Limit the list to specific accomplishments that are *relevant* to the target position.

Before we go on to the next seven items, let's pause a moment to look at the word *accomplishments*. Most job candidates believe that the employer is interested in their *experience*. In fact, much more compelling than experience are accomplishments.

- Experience is passive—"I had this job and that job and that job"— whereas *accomplishments* are active, creative, and individual: "I achieved this, I did that, I accomplished this."
- Prepare for the interview by making a list of your *accomplishments*— successes you "achieved"—rather than jobs you "held."

6. Formulate your salary needs. We'll discuss this in "Money Talk," later in the chapter.
7. Read "To Give the Right Answers, Get the Right Questions," later in this chapter. It will help you prepare answers for the ten most frequently asked interview questions and will suggest ten questions *you* should ask.
8. Create an Interview Kit, which we discuss in the next section.
9. Ensure that you have appropriate attire for the interview. This is discussed later in the chapter, in "Dressing for the Interview."
10. Be sure that you have accurate information covering all of the interview logistics, including the exact time and place of the interview.
11. Make certain that you know how to get to the interview and how long it will take to get there. If you need directions, ask.
12. Obtain and carry with you all necessary names and contact numbers. These include the names and numbers of everyone you may have spoken to on the telephone in connection with the interview. If your interview invitation came by letter, be certain to bring that letter along.

ASSEMBLING A STRONG INTERVIEW KIT

Make the interview most effective by bringing along something besides yourself. The Interview Kit is a kind of scrapbook, which may contain such items as the following:

- An additional three copies of your résumé
- An "executive briefing" summarizing your résumé in a single narrative paragraph
- Letters of commendation
- Awards
- Copies of (nonproprietary and nonclassified) business presentations you have made
- Photos of equipment you have worked with
- Other specific, graphic evidence of your accomplishments

You keep control of the Interview Kit. You may give the interviewer one of the copies of your résumé, if he or she asks for it, but the Interview Kit itself stays in your hands. Share it with the interviewer, but always convey the idea that the work it contains is yours, that it is of value, and that it is not up for grabs.

Think of the Interview Kit as a "conversation piece": something to spark and focus discussion. It will not only help you illustrate how your accomplishments can be applied to your prospective employer's needs, goals, and problems, it will also take some of the burden of the interview off the shoulders of the interviewer. The prop helps you, and it helps the interviewer. The beauty of this is that it allows you to come into the interview armed with precisely the solution to the employer's currently most pressing problem: how to get through the interview. And it is much more convincing to *demonstrate* your prowess as a problem solver than it is merely to *tell* the interviewer that is what you are.

DOING PREINTERVIEW RESEARCH

Before you walk into any meaningful communication, arm yourself with a clear understanding of your objectives. In no case is this more true than in the employment interview. Most job candidates concentrate on figuring out how much salary to ask for. To be sure, this is important, and "Talking Money During the Interview," later in this chapter, gives you some guidelines not only for deciding how much to ask for—as well as when *and when not to ask*—but also advises you on how to figure out, *before* the interview, how much salary you need. But salary is not the only objective you need to define before the interview. There are issues both broader and more profound, including:

- Career goals
- Fit with background and education
- Lifestyle considerations: hours required, type of tasks, travel requirements, and so on
- Opportunities for growth on the job
- Location

Do not go into the interview without having heeded the advice of the Oracle at Delphi, to "Know thyself." Set clear—perhaps flexible, but clear—employment objectives *before* you step across the interviewer's threshold.

Know thyself, yes, by all means. But, so far as the interviewer or interviewers are concerned, it is even more important to show that you know *them*. Many candidates manage to do a clear and convincing job of presenting their qualifications and their needs, only to fail to secure an offer. Why?

- The employer is interested in your accomplishments, qualifications, and needs, but he or she is *far more* interested in his or her own needs and requirements; therefore, it is critically important that you take the time to learn about the target organization, with particular emphasis on what issues and needs are likely to be of most concern to the interviewers.

At the least, demonstrating a thorough knowledge of the target company conveys to the interviewers the intensity of your interest and the high level of your initiative. Gratifyingly, it suggests that yours will be a smooth, low, and easy learning curve. You are likely to hit the ground running, proving yourself an immediate asset to the operation.

Great! What a great idea! Who *wouldn't* like to go into an interview loaded with inside information? But how do you come across it?

Getting Inside Information

Getting on the inside from the outside is less difficult than you might think. Let's say XYZ Corp calls you for an interview. Great! But don't sit back and put your feet up on the desk. Get to work, checking out the following:

- XYZ's annual report
- XYZ's catalogs, brochures, ads, and other published material
- Material supplied by XYZ's Public Relations and/or Customer Service departments
- Journals and newsletter articles covering XYZ
- Up-to-date books (often available in the public library) that mention XYZ or that discuss the industry of which XYZ is a part
- Online sources, including the Internet and commercial online providers, such as America Online, Csi (Compuserve), Prodigy, and others. It is even possible that XYZ maintains its own online BBS (electronic bulletin board service). You can usually find this out by first searching for an XYZ Web site on the Internet.

As determining a clear set of objectives should precede an interview, so a decision as to just what kinds of information to look for should be made before you plunge into researching the target company. You'll want to learn something about:

- The business of the company: What does it do or make?
- The scope of the company: How large? Where does it do business?
- The target company's competition: Who are they, and what is the target company's standing among them?

Before you venture too far afield—or even down to the local public library—to obtain information in these areas, be certain to try to get a formal job description from the target company itself. Some employers are sufficiently on the ball to send you one without having been asked. Such firms are in the minority, however. Always ask for a full job description when a company calls to schedule an interview.

This does not necessarily mean that you'll get one, for many organizations fail to prepare this very basic document. If this is the case, you'll have to take even more initiative by doing your best to assemble a description.

- Tactfully pump the employer for information. You are called for an interview. You ask for a job description and are told: "We don't have one." Don't let this end the conversation. Respond: "Well, I certainly understand what a widget analyst does in most organizations, but is there anything special and specific I should know about the position at XYZ? The information will help me prepare for the interview, so that I can give you a better idea of just who I am and how I can meet your needs."

Pause here a moment to take note of how the request for information is framed, not merely as something that will help the job candidate, but as a way that will help the job candidate perform more efficiently and productively at the interview *for the benefit of the employer*.

You might also go beyond the employer.

- Tap sources available in the public library.
- Contact people who do the job in question—but *not* anyone who works for the target company. If you are applying for the position of widget analyst, call friends and friends of friends who already are widget analysts. If you don't know any, call a widget company and ask to speak to a widget analyst. Introduce yourself, explain your situation, and ask for help. Why should this stranger help you? The surprising fact is that most people welcome the opportunity to be helpful.

DRESSING FOR THE INTERVIEW

No one can prescribe a foolproof interview outfit, but it is possible to establish at least one enduring principle: Dress in a way that makes you comfortable and expresses how you feel about yourself, but that is also appropriate to the field or industry in which you are seeking employment.

It is easy to overrate the concept of "dressing for success." If you think that finding the right combination of clothes will get you a job, you are almost certainly mistaken. However, it is also easy to *underrate* the concept. If you dress in way that *fails* to convey the message that you've been able to get yourself together in a professional manner, you will turn off potential employer after potential employer.

But "getting yourself together" may not be quite enough. A great many career fields and professions have unspoken dress codes. To the degree that you succeed in demonstrating an understanding of the code, you are likely to shine in the estimation of the interviewer, even before a word is exchanged. Whether or not you are hired depends in large part on the employer's perception that you can do the job. It is also based, in no small part, on his or her perception that you will "fit in." Approach the organization *looking* as if you are already a part of it, and you will begin the interview with a significant head start.

But how do you crack a particular company's dress code? Begin by recognizing that this is one code that is hardly kept secret. On the contrary, it's on exhibit every day. If possible, pay a casual visit to the target company and observe. Or, if the firm publishes a newsletter or other literature illustrated with photographs, look at these.

The "code" is important, but it is not the foundation of effective interview dress.

- Begin by ensuring that whatever you wear is sharp and clean. Suits, for men and women, should be dry-cleaned immediately before the interview, and shirts and blouses should be freshly laundered. You don't have to go out and buy a brand-new interview wardrobe, but make certain that whatever you wear is in impeccable repair.

- Take care to attend to personal hygiene as well. Shower or bathe, of course, and be certain to use deodorant, but avoid excessive use of perfume, cologne, or after-shave.

Some interviewers find sitting in a small office with a scent-soaked job candidate more than a little annoying. Some may even be mildly or severely allergic to perfume. But more important than this, if you use perfume, cologne, or after-shave liberally, you risk sending the psychological message that you are trying to "cover up" something. Olfactory sensation reaches far below the conscious, rational level and can provoke a strong, irrational response. Don't avoid scent; if you have a favorite perfume, cologne, or after-shave that makes you feel good about yourself, use it—sparingly. The scent should be *barely* perceptible.

- Another highly charged grooming issue is hair length, especially for men. This was an explosive issue in the 1960s, and although long hair for men or very short hair for women is no longer shocking, very long hair on men is still perceived in many quarters as a token of rebellion or, at least, unacceptable sloppiness, and some employers may find "mannish" female hairdos intimidating.

TIP

Even extremely short hair on men may raise employer doubts, evoking extremist images of the world of the "skinhead."

To be sure, certain "creative" industries—fashion, the arts, magazine work, and so on—invite and welcome a liberal array of hair fashions for men as well as women, but more traditional and conservative industries favor cuts that are strictly middle of the road.

- While it is true that, by federal law, no employer may discriminate in hiring on the basis of age, gender, or race, legislation cannot thoroughly regulate unthinking prejudice. Generally, the trend in business has been toward wider acceptance and even active development of ethnic and cultural diversity in the workplace; nevertheless, you may want to avoid "ethnic" hairstyles that represent significant departures from what is generally perceived as the cultural mainstream.

- The same applies to deciding whether to dye or tint hair to disguise gray. It is against the law for employers to discriminate on the basis of age, but many employers place a premium on youth and the appearance of youth. On the other hand, you may find that gray hair is an advantage, suggesting an image of seasoned wisdom.

If you find the preceding observations culturally obnoxious, well, the prejudices that make such observations necessary *are* indeed obscene, let alone obnoxious. The point is that, generally speaking, the "best" interview look is the safest. If you err, err on the side of conservatism and traditionalism.

- Dress appropriately for the position you seek, not for the position you currently have.

If you are an office assistant accustomed to wearing a sports jacket, shirt and tie, and jeans, invest in the best conservatively cut suit you can afford when you interview for the position of assistant account executive. Remember that fashion is communication, so set clear objectives for what you want to communicate to the interviewer. Let those objectives guide your fashion choices.

How to Say It with Clothes

The following is a brief "vocabulary" of general clothing choices and the messages they convey.

FOR MEN:

1. Dark colors convey authority, and dark blue conveys the greatest degree of authority.

2. If you do opt for dark colors, avoid black, which suggests mourning and death—hardly positive interview messages.

3. Choose natural fabrics. They look better than synthetics and do not retain body odors as readily. Even more important, natural fibers project an image of honesty—advocacy of the "real thing"—as opposed to synthetics, which might be perceived as suggesting phoniness.

4. Solids and subtle patterns are best for most suits. Muted, narrow pinstripes ("banker stripes") are appropriate to conservative finance and politics.

5. Loud-checked patterns suggest questionable taste and, as some see it, questionable ethics (summoning up images of sleazy old-timey salesmen).

6. Choose a suit cut to your build. Slender European cuts are fine if you have a slender build; otherwise, go with a fuller—and more conservative—American cut.

7. Wear only a long-sleeved shirt.

8. Choose solid white or solid pale blue for the shirt color. No patterns or stripes.

9. Avoid monograms. Many interviewers see monograms as pompous. It is even more important to avoid *designer* monograms, which convey insecurity about your own taste—as if you need the designer's seal of approval on what you choose to wear.

10. Choose a cotton shirt. Avoid synthetics.

11. The interview shirt should be professionally laundered, with medium-crisp starch.

12. Some experts say that, of all articles of clothing, the necktie makes the strongest initial impression.

13. For the tie, choose 100 percent silk.

14. The tie should complement the suit, but not match it.

15. Tie widths vary with changing fashion, but a safe rule of thumb is that the width of the tie should approximate the width of the suit lapels.

16. Choose a traditional pattern, such as a solid, foulard, stripe, or muted paisley. Avoid polka dots, pictures (animals, the heads of hunting dogs, and so forth), and sporting images (golf clubs, polo mallets). Also avoid designer logos, which suggest fundamental insecurity about your own taste.

17. It is important to tie the tie carefully and neatly. For some years now, fashion has favored a small, tight knot. The tied necktie should not extend below your trouser belt.

18. Don't wear a bow tie.

19. Shoes should be of black or brown leather only.

20. Europeans marvel at the American businessman's obsession with highly polished shoes. Better make certain yours are polished.

21. Heels should be even and relatively unworn.

22. Managers tend toward lace-up wing-tip styles, while accountant types seem to favor tasseled slip-on dress shoes. Only those interviewing for "creative" positions—such as advertising art director—should wear premium loafer styles.

23. The color of the socks should complement the suit; usually, this means a choice of blue, black, dark gray, or dark brown.

24. A simple and slim attaché is the best choice. Avoid anything that suggests a salesman's clunky sample case.

25. Carry a plain white cotton or linen handkerchief.

26. A leather belt should match or complement the shoes, and the buckle should be simple, small, and entirely unobtrusive.

27. Suspenders (or "braces") are less popular than they were in the 1980s; some interviewers find them pretentious.

28. Simple cuff links and a wedding band (if you're married) are safe jewelry choices for men. Everything else—neck chains, stickpins, bracelets, and pinky rings—should be avoided.

TIP

Some interviewers may find French cuffs, with their attendant cuff links, a bit pretentious. You may wish to play it safe with plain buttoned barrel cuffs.

29. Avoid wearing a topcoat, if possible—it gets in the way—but don't freeze yourself in cold weather, either. A wool camel hair or cashmere topcoat is most attractive and impressive.

Women do not have to be as conservative as men are in dressing appropriately for the employment interview; however, they are also under greater economic pressure to invest in current fashions. Whereas a man can get away with a two- or three-year-old suit, a woman cannot. Is this fair? Absolutely not. But it's the way it is.

FOR WOMEN, THEN:

1. In most interview situations, a suit is appropriate.
2. A woman's suit need not be an imitation of a man's suit in cut or color; but do note that a charcoal-gray suit with a white blouse is the safest interview combination.
3. Solids, pinstripes, and muted plaids in a variety of colors are all acceptable for women's suits.
4. For women's suits, natural-synthetic fabric blends are ideal. Given the styling of women's suits, all-natural fabrics tend to wrinkle.
5. Skirt length varies from season to season, but you and the interviewer will be most comfortable if you choose a more conservative length than what you might wear on a social occasion or even in an *everyday* business situation.
6. Choose a long-sleeve blouse. Completely avoid sleeveless blouses.
7. The blouse should be in a natural fabric, preferably cotton or silk.
8. Blouses in a wide range of colors are acceptable, but white, pale blue, or pearl gray are universally accepted in the business world.
9. Keep the blouse simple.
10. A beautiful scarf can add a dramatic accent to the interview wardrobe. Don't match the scarf with the blouse and avoid large polka-dot patterns; small polka dots are acceptable.
11. Wear simple, elegant shoes. A closed-toe pump with a one-and-a-half-inch heel is a safe choice.
12. Avoid very high heels, especially if you are not accustomed to them.
13. The color of the shoes should complement your suit and accessories.

14. Hosiery should be unobtrusive; neutral or skin tones are best.

15. Take along an extra pair of pantyhose or stockings in your briefcase or purse.

16. Briefcase or purse? You can't carry both. A briefcase projects more authority than a purse and creates a stronger image of professionalism. Why not put the essential contents of your purse in a small clutch bag, which you stow in the briefcase?

17. The belt should complement the shoes.

TIP

Think twice before you choose a belt made of unusual or exotic animal skin—snakeskin, alligator, lizard, and the like—that may offend an interviewer who happens to be sensitive to environmental issues. Plain leather is best.

18. With jewelry, less is more. It is best to limit the number of rings you wear. Thumb rings are out.

19. Wear small, discreet earrings, if you like.

20. Avoid all long, dangling jewelry, which may jangle irritatingly or catch on clothing.

21. Avoid gaudy jewelry.

22. Simple necklaces and bracelets are fine, but never wear an anklet to an interview. Avoid charm bracelets, which create a juvenile image, and avoid jewelry that bears your initials.

23. As with jewelry, the rule for makeup is simple: Less is more. The idea is to look natural, so if you are comfortable without lipstick, avoid it or apply a subdued shade only—and that sparingly.

TO GIVE THE RIGHT ANSWERS, GET THE RIGHT QUESTIONS

What makes most job candidates most nervous about the prospect of an interview are the questions. Many candidates fear that the interviewer has carefully stockpiled a list of questions designed to trip them up.

- The fact is that few interviewers go out of their way to concoct difficult questions. Nor do they have any desire to watch you squirm.

But if most interviewers don't *mean* to ask you hard questions, they may end up asking vague and poorly prepared questions that are open to so many possibilities that you may be overwhelmed if you do not prepare for them in advance.

- It's a good idea simply to assume that the interviewer won't be very well prepared for the interview. That's true more often than not.

Unfortunately, an interview conducted by an unprepared interviewer is a disappointment. What the interviewer will recall, as he or she evaluates your candidacy, is that the interview was unimpressive, which must mean that *you* are unimpressive. (You can bet that the interviewer won't blame himself or herself!)

It's up to you to help the interviewer make your interview an impressive event. Here's how:

1. Prepare. Learn as much possible beforehand about the company and the job, then come to the interview armed with topics of conversation related to currently hot issues, leading trends, major challenges faced by the company or the industry, and so on.
2. Based on your preinterview research, anticipate questions and prepare answers that will play to your strengths. The object is to direct the interviewer to subjects you know well and that will give you an opportunity to demonstrate your abilities, talents, accomplishments, and qualifications.
3. Again based on your research, prepare specific questions about the job and about the industry. These questions should demonstrate that you have given the job and the industry careful and creative thought.

TIP

If you take the time and effort to prepare, you will most likely create a more stimulating and persuasive interview, and you will earn the gratitude of the interviewer for taking much of the burden from his or her shoulders.

Ten Basic Questions Interviewers Ask

Comb the shelves of your local bookstore and you'll find any number of volumes that offer interview questions and answers. The truth is that no book can give you a really useful set of "canned" Q and A, because employer needs and wants vary greatly in detail. However, there are certain basic questions that almost all employers get around to asking sooner or later. Of the following ten questions, expect to be asked at least five in the course of an interview:

1. What can you tell me about yourself? This is as basic as it gets. But if you don't prepare for it, this apparently simple question will start the interview out with a grinding halt. Maybe you'll be able to pull yourself together sufficiently to ramble on with a drawn-out autobiography, but that's *not* what the interviewer wants to hear.

The secret to answering this question is twofold.

First, come to the interview armed with a *memorized* answer that fits the following formula:

- My name is _____.
- I've worked for *X* years as a [job title].
- Currently, I'm a [job title] at [company].
- Before that, I was [job title] at [company].
- I love the challenge of my work, especially the major strengths I offer, including [A, B, and C].

Simple? Yes. And that's the point. The danger of this question is that, by opening up so many possibilities and directions, it will overwhelm you, in effect swamping your thought process.

You can really turn this question into an opportunity for persuasion by taking a second step. After delivering the formula answer, *help* the interviewer by focusing the question: "But what about me would be most relevant to you and what this company needs?" This will help you focus your answer and will ensure that you give the interviewer the information he or she really wants.

2. Why do you want to leave your current job? Beware of questions that invite negative responses: "I don't get along very well with my boss," or "My supervisor is an uncreative slug who won't let me try out new ideas," and so on. Turn such questions into opportunities for positive response. Instead of letting the question focus your answer on why you want to *leave* your present company, explain why you want to *move to* the target company: "I am eager to take on more challenges, and I believe I will find them at Acme, Inc." The less negativity you project, the more positive the impression you will create.

If you have difficulty coming up with positive reasons for moving from one job to another, try the CLAMPS formula. It's an acronym that stands for

*C*hallenge

*L*ocation

*A*dvancement

*M*oney

*P*ride (or *P*restige)

*S*ecurity

Positive responses embodying any of these motivating factors should persuade the interviewer that you have a sound, intelligent, thoughtful reason for wanting to leave your current position.

3. What do you know about us?   This often comes at the beginning of an interview as an "icebreaker." There is no formulaic answer to this question, no substitute for having learned as much as you can about the target company before going to the interview.

4. How much experience do you have?   Here's another chance for preinterview research to pay off. Try to identify the target company's special needs and concerns, then marshal the experience you have that is relevant to these areas. But "experience" is really the wrong word. Translate "experience" into *accomplishments*—specific achievements, which will be much more persuasive in an interview. The more specific you can be the better.

Let's pause a moment to talk about being specific. The most specific you can get is to talk numbers, which is the very language of business.

- If at all possible, express your achievements in terms of money: money earned for your current or past employer, money saved, production increased, efficiency achieved—whatever. Try to quantify your accomplishments. Money, as the saying goes, talks.

But what if your research has failed to reveal any clear-cut areas of concern to the target company? Don't despair. Answer the question with a question in order to get the interviewer to define the areas of most concern to him or her:

- "Are you looking for overall experience or experience in some specific area of special interest to you?"

The interviewer's response should allow you to frame your answer in a way that will directly address the target company's needs.

5. What do you most like and most dislike about your current job?   Don't fall into the trap of emphasizing the negative. Even if you are very specific and honest in listing what you don't like about your current job, the interviewer will probably forget the details and remember only the negativity. The result: an *overall* impression of negativity, and that is not the impression you want to create. Even more important, while dissatisfaction with your current position may seem to *you* a very good reason to change jobs, it does not address the needs of the target *employer*. And while your needs are obviously important to you, it is the employer's needs that are most important in an interview. Your answers should always address those needs.

Your safest answer to this question? Pass up the negative part and just answer that you "like everything about my current position." Then go on to list the skills, abilities, and qualifications that your current or last position has given you or allowed you to hone these qualifications that you now offer the prospective employer. Conclude your answer with, "I'm now ready for a new set of challenges and an opportunity for greater advancement and greater responsibility."

6. How many hours a week do you need to get your job done?   This can be a difficult question to answer in a winning way. If you reply with something like 40 hours, you risk labeling yourself as a clock watcher, yet if you say 60, you may be implying that you're slow, inefficient, and easily overwhelmed. Your best course is not to reply with a specific number, but to deliver a more flexible and creative answer:

- "I try to plan my time efficiently. Usually, this works well. However, as you know, this business has crunch periods, and when that happens, I put in as many hours as necessary to get the job done."

7. How much are you making now and how much do you want?   A bit later in the chapter, we'll talk about negotiating salary, but the important principle to note now is that, in a salary negotiation, the first person who talks money is at a disadvantage. You have two objectives in responding to this question:

- First, *divorce* the first part from the second part. Don't let your current salary define or limit a salary offer.

- Then, for the second part of the question, you should do everything you reasonably can to avoid responding with a specific figure. If you ask for too much—or too little—you could disqualify yourself as a candidate for the job. And, certainly, you don't want to saddle yourself with a low figure and start a new job feeling disappointed.

Go ahead and answer the first part of the question, but don't allow the reply much significance: "I'm earning $28,000, but I'm not certain that helps you evaluate my 'worth,' since the two jobs differ significantly in their responsibilities."

TIP

How honest should you be about stating your current or most recent salary? The answer: very honest. Why? You might get caught if you lie. This said, however, make certain that the compensation figure you mention includes all benefits: insurance, profit-sharing, bonuses, commissions, and so on. Furnish the maximum figure you can honestly report.

Moving to the second part of the question, *avoid* stating a figure. Instead, reply by itemizing the skills, talents, abilities, and responsibilities the target position entails:

- "If I understand the full scope of the position, my responsibilities would include . . . Have I overlooked anything?" Then come to your eminently logical conclusion: "Given all of this, what figure did you have in mind for someone with my qualifications in a position as important as this?"

Here is another reply that sidesteps a figure:

- "I expect a salary appropriate to my qualifications and demonstrated abilities. What figure did you have in mind?"

TIP

"Talking Money During the Interview," later in the chapter, includes advice on what to do if the interviewer insists on obtaining a figure from you.

8. What's the most difficult situation you ever faced on the job?   This is a good question, and it invites an effective answer; however, avoid responding with a description of a situation so difficult that it resulted in personal failure or general disaster.

- Prepare in advance by thinking of a story of difficulty overcome, a tale with a happy ending—happy not only for you, but for your current or most recent employer.
- Under no circumstances should you answer this question with a discussion of personal or family difficulties.
- Also avoid discussing unresolved problems you've had with supervisors, peers, or subordinates.

TIP

Discussing a difficult situation involving a subordinate is fine, however, provided that the issues were resolved inventively and productively.

9. What are you looking for in this job?

- Remember: Regardless of how this question is phrased, the employer really is less interested in what *you* are looking for than in how hiring you can benefit *him or her.*

You may be "looking for" more money, more prestige, a nicer office—whatever. Mention none of these things. Instead, reply in a way that shows that you are looking for opportunities to serve the interests of the employer. Use such words as *contribute, enhance*, and *improve* in your response.

- "At XYZ, Inc., I discovered just how much one person could contribute to a company. As production supervisor, I increased efficiency an average of 16 percent, which meant a quarterly bottom-line increase of $29,000 in net revenue for our department. I'm looking to do even more for ABC Industries. *That's* what I'm looking for. *That's* what will give me satisfaction in this job."

10. Why should I hire you?   This little blockbuster is a favorite employer question. Whatever its tone, don't let it put you on the defensive. Treat it instead as the employer's request for help: "Help me to hire you."

- Keep your response brief.
- Recap any job requirements the interviewer may have enumerated earlier in the interview, then, point by point, match your skills, abilities, and qualifications to those items. The logic of such a reply is inescapable.

INAPPROPRIATE QUESTIONS (AND HOW TO ANSWER THEM)

Employers are forbidden by law to ask any questions bearing on your marital status, your sexual orientation, your age, your ethnic or national origins. Does this mean that you call the cops if you are asked one of these forbidden questions?

Well . . . not if you want the job.

Issues of discrimination are serious, but they are beyond the scope of this book. If you believe that you have been discriminated against, seek legal advice. Just be aware that discrimination cases are difficult, expensive, and time-consuming to prosecute. Right now, presumably, your objective is to secure employment, not to fight a legal battle. What follows, then, are suggestions for coping with inappropriate—even illegal—questions in ways that keep your candidacy alive.

- Obviously, if the employer's questions are truly outrageous or offensive, you should think very carefully before accepting an offer, if one is forthcoming.

1. **Are you married?**   The usual purpose of this illegal question is to determine if your family duties will interfere with your job. It may also be an attempt to assess your sexual orientation. If you are married, reply with something like this:

- "Yes, I am. My wife/husband and I are both professionals who have spent X years very happily keeping our professional lives separate from our family lives."

If you are not married, a simple no is sufficient.

2. **Do you plan to have children?**   Men are rarely asked this one. The employer most likely wants assurance that the woman he or she is interviewing will not quit soon after she is hired—and after the employer has spent time and money training and developing her—to raise a family. The question is inappropriate and at least verging on being illegal; however, the easiest course is simply to answer:

- "No, I don't currently have plans to raise a family."

If you do intend to have children, and you feel strongly inclined to answer frankly, you can still turn the question to your advantage:

- "Yes, eventually, I plan to raise a family. But these plans are directly dependent on the success of my career."

3. **What is your sexual orientation?**   There's no graceful way to respond to this illegal question. Politely ask the interviewer to "explain the relevance of the issue to the position" or just reply that you "don't think the question is appropriate."

4. **How old are you?**   Age discrimination is prohibited by law, and this illegal question exposes the employer to civil as well as criminal liability. But, again, do you really want to spend your time litigating, or do you want to find a job? If you want the job, find a way to answer the question positively:

- "Now that I'm in my forties, I've had more than a quarter century of experience in the widget industry."

Translate age into experience and youth into energy and flexibility.

5. Do you believe in God? What is your religious background? If you *want* to answer, it is best to keep specifics to a minimum.

- "I worship regularly, but I make it a practice not to involve any of my personal beliefs in my work."

If your religious activity involves charitable work, you should discuss that work here, especially if it involves organization, leadership, and administration on your part.
If you have no religious beliefs, don't make an issue of the fact.

- "My personal spiritual beliefs are very important to me, but I don't let them get involved with my professional life, and I make it a practice not to discuss them."

This response is also appropriate if you simply do not wish to discuss your spiritual beliefs.

6. Were you born in the United States? It is illegal to ask this question in the context of an employment interview, but if you were born in the United States, just say so. If not, but you are a citizen, reply:

- "No, but I became a citizen by very proud choice in [year]."

If you are not a citizen, you might want to reply:

- "No. I'm currently working toward becoming naturalized as a citizen."

TEN QUESTIONS YOU SHOULD ASK AT THE INTERVIEW

Perhaps the most self-destructive mistake you can make in an employment interview is to reply with a *no* to this question: "Do you have any questions?"

- Failure to ask questions at the interview tells the employer that you just don't care very much about the job or that you aren't very bright and are accustomed to accepting whatever anybody hands you. None of this bodes well for your chances of securing a job offer.

- Be certain to come to the interview prepared with relevant questions.

The key word is *relevant*. Do not ask off-the-wall questions or, even worse, questions to which you should already have the answer: "What does the telephone company do, anyway?"

Your interview questions should serve two purposes:

- To gather information that will help you evaluate a job offer
- To demonstrate—further—your qualifications, skills, and accomplishments

Here are some suggestions:

1. Have you had a chance to review my résumé?   Ask this early in the interview, and, please, phrase it in just this way. A great many interviewers fail to read your résumé before the interview or give it a glance so cursory that they might as well not have read it. Few interviewers, of course, will admit to this. Expect a response like this: "I haven't had the chance to review it as thoroughly as I'd like to."

Don't be offended or discouraged. Seize the opportunity to highlight your accomplishments: "Well, then, perhaps you'll find it helpful for me to hit the highlights of my qualifications."

2. Is there anything else I can tell you about my qualifications?   This is a good follow-up to the first question, or it may be asked as a stand-alone question toward the *end* of the interview. Not only does this question give you an opportunity to present yourself in the best possible light, it also requires the target employer to invest more time in you. The more time the interviewer invests, the more valuable you come to seem.

3. How would you describe the duties of this job?   Isn't this one of those obvious "questions to which you should already know the answer"? No. Even if you've received and read a job description, the question is still valuable. It asks the *interviewer* to describe the duties, to give you his or her take on the job, which, you may discover, is a far cry from what's in the official job description. Additionally, by asking the interviewer to describe the duties, you can get a better handle on which functions are perceived as most important and, therefore, really *are* the most important. This information will help you as you ponder an offer, and it will also furnish a springboard for launching a description of your particular skills and qualifications.

- "I'm glad to hear that you consider client contact so important in this position. For me, client contact means building a business, each and every day, one client at a time."

4. What are the principal problems facing your staff right now? To begin with, understanding the target employer's problems gives you an opportunity to present yourself as a solution to them. Second, the question may reveal some situation that might make you think twice about taking the job. This could avert a bad career move.

5. What results would you like me to produce? This would be a valuable question if it accomplished nothing more than to demonstrate your intention to *do* a job rather than *take* a job. It focuses on what most concerns the employer: *his or her* needs and *his or her* problems. Your object is to respond point by point to whatever list of requirements, tasks, or criteria the question elicits.

6. What do you consider ideal background and experience for this position? The chief purpose of this question is to get the interviewer to paint an outline into which you—verbally—can step. Try to show just how you fit in, as if the job were created with you in mind.

7. How would you describe the climate in this company? Stormy? This question may catch the interviewer slightly off guard and reveal problems or it may elicit a description to which you can respond, showing how you'll fit right into the work environment:

- "I like high-pressure situations. To me, nothing's more energizing."

8. Was the person who held this job before me promoted? This is a lot better than saying, "What happened to the last guy who had this job?" Phrased positively, this question aims to find out why the job in question is vacant. The question should also give you an opportunity to assess the prospects for advancement at this company and from this position.

9. **Could I meet with the person who held this job before me?** This request shows thoughtfulness and prudence, and your conversation with this person may provide valuable insight into the position.

Of course, it is possible that your request will not be honored. Perhaps the employee is no longer with the company. If the incumbent is still present, however, you may have reason to be suspicious of a negative response. Ask what the objections are.

10. **Based on what I've told you, don't you think I could deliver all that you need in this position?** This is what sales professionals would call a "closer." It invites—though certainly does not guarantee—a positive response.

FIVE STEPS TO GETTING A JOB OFFER

Question number ten should not be asked until you have reached the final stage of the interview. But what is the final stage of the interview? It is the point at which you believe you have made the "sale," the point at which you believe the interviewer is eager—is ready—to make an offer. It's the have-to-have point. There are five steps to getting there:

Step 1: *Listen.* During the early part of the interview, listen as much as possible. Listen to what the interviewer says about his or her company, its needs, its goals, its problems. Listen to what the interviewer says he or she needs. Formulate a response based on what you've heard. Soon, you will begin transforming yourself from a stranger looking for a job to a potential employee and colleague committed to the success of the enterprise.

Listening should not be an entirely passive activity. Provide feedback that tells the interviewer that you are listening. At intervals, underscore the interviewer's most important points by repeating and rephrasing them: "What I hear you saying is . . ." or "If I'm understanding you correctly . . ."

Step 2: *Arouse attention.* Remind the interviewer of why *he* or *she* called *you* in for an interview. Here's what you say: "I'm really excited to be here, since it seemed to me that my qualifications so closely coincided with what you need." Or: "I'm thrilled to be here. What I have to offer seems to me a perfect match for this company." The reason you were called for an interview is that you are the right person for the job. *Now* you have the interviewer's attention.

Step 3: *Transform attention into interest.* Develop the interviewer's interest in you as a prospective employee by demonstrating your value as a member of the employer's team. This is done by making an effort to turn everything you say into an expression of accomplishment, achievement, or qualification.

- Don't just heap praise on yourself. Be specific: "I specialize in handling the details and anticipating needs, so that you can be more efficient."

Step 4: *Transform interest into involvement.* At this point, be on the lookout for "buy signals." These may be obvious. The interviewer says:

- "That interests me," or
- "I like that," or
- "Great!"

More frequently, the buy signals are subtler, more neutral:

- "Tell me more about . . ." or
- "Can you be more specific about . . ."

It doesn't matter. A buy signal is a buy signal, an indication that you've pressed the right button. Once you detect a buy signal, focus on the point or issue that triggered the positive response. Develop that point further. Get specific—not so much about yourself, but about what you can do for the target employer.

TIP

Nothing develops the interviewer's involvement more strongly than money: money you will bring into the company and money you will save for the company. Money is the language of business. Whenever possible, speak this language. Quantify your accomplishments in dollars.

Step 5: *Push for action.* This is the moment to pose question number ten or its equivalent:

- "Based on what I've told you, don't you think I could give you all that you need in this position?"

However, if your sense is that you haven't quite connected with the interviewer—haven't reach the have-to-have point—try this alternative:

- "I've enjoyed talking with you, and I believe I can bring much of value to this company. Tell me, please, is there anything I haven't addressed to your satisfaction? What could I tell you that would prompt you to make an offer?"

If you've gone through the first four phases of the interview, the object is to push toward closure, toward action. The best outcome is a job offer. But action may be deferred. Perhaps you will be told that time is required for review, or the matter must be discussed by the "committee." Respond with thanks and ask when you should expect a decision:

- "Thank you very much. This has been a pleasure. When should I expect your decision?"

Closure—a push toward action—conveys a necessary urgency, creating an impression of your value. You cannot—and will not—wait indefinitely for a decision.

TALKING MONEY DURING THE INTERVIEW

Just as you need to prepare for the interview by learning as much as you can about the target company and industry, you should also establish your salary requirements and expectations. Two steps are involved:

Step 1: Establish your minimum cash requirements. "Minimum" means the least you need to feel reasonably secure and comfortable—not merely to subsist.

This is a very personal matter, but if you are looking for a starting point, total all your monthly obligations, add 3 percent, which is what you should save each month, and then add another 10 percent for emergencies. Experts advise a minimum of a three-month cash reserve on hand to ensure that you are never a paycheck or two from financial collapse.

Step 2: Once you have determined your comfortable minimum requirements, try to ascertain the going price of your qualifications and skills on the current market.

This may have emerged clearly as a result of homework you've already done. If not, consult the following:

- Obtain a copy of the latest report of the Bureau of Labor Statistics from the local office of the U.S. Department of Labor.
- Log on to the Internet and access the BLS at **http://www.bls.gov** or at **umslvma.umsl.edu.** (for *The Occupational Outlook Handbook*).
- Consult Les Krantz's *Jobs Rated Almanac* (New York: Wiley, 1995).
- Consult professional and trade journals in your field or industry; many of these periodically publish salary surveys.
- Pick up the *National Business Employment Weekly*, which runs salary surveys. Back issues are available through the publisher, or you might check your local library.

Before the interview, then, you should have two figures: the minimum salary you need and the average salary associated with your target position. Using these two figures, formulate a third: a reasonable salary requirement, which meets your requirements and falls within industry guidelines.

- What do you do if your requirements are far distant from industry standards? The answer is either to alter your lifestyle in order to change your requirements, or find a better-paying career.

Armed as you are with a salary figure, you may walk into the interview tempted to "cut to the chase" and commence a discussion of salary. This would be a mistake, since the first person to mention a figure is always in the weaker negotiating position. Indeed, try to delay discussion of salary until the final phase of the interview, by which time, if all has gone well, you have brought the interviewer to the stage at which he or she is eager to make an offer.

For a discussion of delaying tactics, review question number 7 in "To Give the Right Answers, Get the Right Questions," earlier in this chapter.

- Do not alienate the interviewer by being overly evasive. If he or she insists on your naming a figure, respond—not with a single target, however, but with a salary range. You can calculate it this way: Let's say you've decided that you need a minimum of $36,000. Your research suggests that the salary range for the target position is $33,000 to $41,000. You tell the prospective employer your range bracket so that it interlocks with the upper range of what you might expect as an industry standard and exceeds your own minimum requirement. In this case, a good range would be $38,000 to $43,000.
- Make certain that your low figure is still above your "real" minimum. You can always negotiate downward, but once you have established a floor, you cannot raise it.

Once you are ready to discuss salary—when you feel the interviewer has reached the have-to-have point—respond to the salary question by attempting to discover the ballpark:

- "This is the first time we've really broached the subject. Could you tell me what the authorized range is for someone with my qualifications?"

It is critically important that you maintain a poker face. Avoid looking disappointed or elated in response to the figure or range that emerges.

- Don't grimace.
- Don't smile.
- Don't look down.
- Don't squint or shut your eyes.
- Don't look up at the ceiling or roll your eyes.
- Don't cross your arms (it indicates defiance).
- Don't bring your hand to your face or mouth (it indicates insecurity).
- Just maintain neutral eye contact through the negotiation.

Once a salary range is on the table, you may:

1. Accept the range. Say: "The upper end of this range is in the ballpark."

2. Counteroffer with your own range, which overlaps the top end of the target employer's.
3. Respond with polite neutrality, thanking the interviewer for the information and asking for time to consider the figure. Be certain to agree on a specific time by which you will respond.
4. Reject the range.

The first alternative is the easiest, and there is nothing wrong with choosing it, if you are pleased with the offer. But you should know that most employers don't open with their best offer. They usually leave some negotiating room above the top end of the range. Assuming the employer is within your ballpark, it is probably worth the extra effort to respond with the second option. This may open up a somewhat higher range.

Now, don't expect the employer to give you what you want just because you asked for it. You'll have to work. Quickly hit the highlights of your qualifications; remind the employer of why you are worth top dollar. Add to this a demonstration of your knowledge of industry standards:

- "Based on my research into industry salary surveys, my range is reasonable. Since we're agreed that I have the qualifications that will more than satisfy your needs, I can say with confidence that I'll be up, running, and producing for you within a week. This is why I feel that compensation above your upper range is appropriate and fair—fair for me and, certainly, a fair value for you."

Hardball negotiation is what the fourth option represents. Backing the employer against the wall may get you the offer you want, but, more likely, playing hardball will get you thrown out of the game. The negotiation will end. Once you flatly reject an offer, it is difficult or impossible to reverse yourself. Therefore, the better alternative, if the offer is substantially below your range, is to ask for time to think over the offer. Set a specific time when you will call with your response—usually 24 to 48 hours hence—and use that time to evaluate, without pressure, the pros and cons of the job. Equally important, the employer will also have time to think and ponder that he or she is in danger of losing you.

You can get some idea of how much negotiating room you have by considering the position and salary level.

- At the lower levels, salaries are usually firmly fixed and least negotiable.

- As you go up in compensation, salary ranges increase in flexibility.
- At the highest ranges—above $60,000—there is often quite substantial room for negotiation.

Consider:

- Entry-level position—under $20,000 a year: fixed salary level
- Middle-level position—$20,000-$60,000 a year: may negotiate as much as 15 percent above the initial offer
- Upper-level position—$60,000+: substantial increases possible

Don't expect a smooth road in negotiation. Objections to your salary requirements are almost always variations on one of four themes:

1. "Your figure exceeds the range authorized for the position."
2. "Your figure is outside our budget."
3. "Others similarly qualified within the company don't make that kind of money."
4. "Your salary history doesn't warrant what you are asking for."

In entry-level positions, there may be little or nothing you can do to overcome the first objection. Characteristically, the specific salaries authorized for entry-level jobs are essentially carved in stone. Rather than offer you more money, the employer will simply go on to the next candidate. In all cases and at all salary levels, the other three objections tend to be less inflexible.

The key feature of these objections is that the most common of them focus on *cost*. It is your task to refocus the employer on *cost* versus *benefit*; that is, *value*. Your special qualifications, talents, and abilities are an investment in greater profitability. Perhaps you "cost" a little more than the employer had planned to pay, but the value you give is much greater:

- "I understand that you budgeted under $38,000 for this position, but I think that we're both agreed that I bring to the table special qualifications and skills, as well as a deep commitment to performance. Those things represent value for you and amply justify the $40,000 figure I'm asking for."

If you're told that others currently employed don't make the salary you're asking for, redirect the issue to your own performance. What the employer pays others is a matter between the employer and the others. What he or she pays you concerns only the employer and you:

- "I understand your concern, but, based on our conversation so far, I understood that my salary would be based on *my* performance and *my* qualifications and that it is not capped by what others in the organization earn."

From here, you can launch an even more aggressive negotiating maneuver:

- "In fact, this brings up another issue that I'd like clarification on. How will I be rewarded for performance? Are raises based primarily on a cost-of-living formula, or are they tied to performance?"

Your toughest obstacle may not be what others earn, but what you have earned in the past. The objective of negotiation in this case is to divorce the issue of prospective compensation from the record of what you earned in the past:

- "I don't understand what bearing my past salary has on the work I will do for you. I see performance—performance and my qualifications— as relevant to salary. I think that we're both agreed that I offer great value to the company. Wouldn't you also agree that a combination of the qualifications I offer and industry standards is a fair way of arriving at an appropriate salary figure?"

Negotiate the base money issues first, but be aware that straight salary is not the whole compensation package. Where employers may be unwilling or unable to budge on salary, you may be able to get improvements in such areas as:

- Performance-based bonuses
- Longer paid vacation
- Flex time
- Profit sharing

- Day-care services
- Professional membership dues
- Relocation expenses (including such items as moving, temporary housing, guaranteed purchase of your former residence)

Don't fail to negotiate, but do be aware that limits and brick walls exist. If you find that you and the employer are simply too far apart, either offer thanks, take your leave, and continue your job search elsewhere, or work on negotiating the *future*. Accept the employer's best offer now, but accept it with the proviso that your salary will be reviewed in six months in light of your performance.

WHAT IF YOU'RE ASKED TO TAKE A DRUG TEST?

These days, it is not uncommon to be asked to take a drug test as part of an employment-screening process. This issue has been tested in the courts, and, as of this writing, the courts have upheld an employer's right to require drug testing. Today, about half of the *Fortune* 500 companies include some form of drug testing, either during or after the hiring process. Of course, no employer can force you to take a drug test, but if you decline the test, you will almost certainly be found guilty without benefit of a trial. You won't get an offer. If, on the other hand, you indicate your willingness to submit to a test, the chances are good that no test will actually be administered. Only about half the candidates who agree to take a test are actually given one.

If you do submit to a drug test, make certain that the testing company fully explains the test and provides you with a complete list of foods, over-the-counter medications, and prescription drug items that may cause *false positive* results.

- The fact is that at least 5 percent of drug tests yield false positives due to the presence of perfectly innocuous, perfectly legal substances. (One authority places the false-positive figure at a staggering 14 percent!)

If you are the victim of a false positive, insist on being given a back-up test of a *different* type. Document your request in writing.

CHAPTER 4

Putting Yourself Across . . . to Supervisors

SELF-TEST YOUR SAVVY IN COMMUNICATING WITH YOUR BOSS

The following is a simple diagnostic test. A smaller and more selective version of the self-test in Chapter 1, its purpose is not to test your knowledge of communication theory or techniques, but to help you gauge how effectively you communicate with supervisors in a day-to-day business context. For the most part, you will find it easy to guess the "right" answer. But getting the "right" answer is not the point of the test. Respond honestly, even if you feel that your response is not the best one possible. This is *not* a contest. The object is solely self-inventory.

1. I accept praise and compliments easily. I like getting them.   T/F _____

2. I'm afraid to talk to my boss.   T/F _____

3. I allow my boss to motivate me.   T/F _____

4. I always assume the boss is right.   T/F _____

5. I am the victim of a slave-driving boss.   T/F _____

6. I am depressed when my boss criticizes me.   T/F _____

7. I am creative.   T/F _____

8. My boss respects me.   T/F _____

9. My boss is easy to talk to.   T/F _____

10. My boss isn't easy to talk to, but we manage to communicate.   T/F _____

11. My boss makes me feel guilty.   T/F ____

12. My boss is an idiot.   T/F ____

13. My boss welcomes my ideas.   T/F ____

14. My boss is bigger than life.   T/F ____

15. My boss makes me angry.   T/F ____

16. I can't talk to my boss.   T/F ____

17. I'm easily discouraged.   T/F ____

18. I effectively convey my ideas to my boss.   T/F ____

19. I feel threatened by my boss.   T/F ____

20. I focus on facts rather than on personalities.   T/F ____

21. I focus on responsibility rather than on blame.   T/F ____

22. I frequently ask my boss for advice.   T/F ____

23. I hate talking to my boss.   T/F ____

24. I hate to apologize.   T/F ____

25. I have a good relationship with my boss.   T/F ____

26. There is nothing I can do to change my boss.   T/F ____

27. I keep my ideas to myself.   T/F ____

28. I know how to appeal to my boss's self-interest.   T/F ____

29. I know how to do the necessary research to back up
    my request for a raise.   T/F ____

30. I know how to decline assignments gracefully.   T/F ____

31. I know how to "handle" my boss.   T/F ____

32. I learn from criticism.   T/F ____

33. I like to confront my boss.   T/F ____

34. I look my boss in the eye when I speak to him/her.   T/F ____

35. I look for the opportunities in crisis.   T/F ____

36. My motto: *Take this job and shove it!*   T/F ____

37. I never run away from a good fight.   T/F _____

38. I'm not afraid to fail—once in a while.   T/F _____

39. I respect my boss.   T/F _____

40. I see criticism as opportunity.   T/F _____

41. I take ownership of problems, not blame.   T/F _____

42. I think of my boss as a human being.   T/F _____

43. I've told my boss, "I deserve a raise."   T/F _____

44. I try to withhold immediate judgment of my boss's ideas. T/F _____

Total: _____

Score 1 point for each "True" response and 0 for each "False" response, EXCEPT for questions 2, 4, 5, 6, 11, 12, 14, 15, 16, 17, 19, 23, 24, 26, 27, 33, 36, 37, and 43. For *these questions only*, SUBTRACT 1 point for each "True" response. Record your total. A score below +23 indicates that you would benefit from practicing the communication techniques discussed in this chapter. (Note: It is possible to have a negative score.)

WORDS TO USE WITH YOUR BOSS

able	appropriate	careful
accept	approve	caution
accomplished	armed	change
achieved	asset	circumstances
acknowledge	aware	commitment
advice	balance	committed
advise	best	confidence
agree	better	confident
alter	can	consider
alternatives	capable	continue
amazed	care	contributed
appreciate	career	convert

WORDS TO USE WITH YOUR BOSS, *cont'd*

correct	faith	judgment
create	family	kind
creativity	feasible	knowledge
dedicated	firm	learned
delay	flabbergasted	loyal
delighted	formulated	manage
deserved	future	management
different	generosity	memories
difficulties	generous	methodically
discuss	goals	motivation
do	goodwill	negotiate
duties	grateful	new
effective	gratified	objectives
efficient	great	obstacles
encourage	happy	offer
encouraging	help	opportunity
enjoyed	helpful	performance
enthusiastic	helps	perspective
equipped	hope	plan
established	hurdles	planning
evaluate	idea	pleasant
excited	ideas	pleased
exciting	if	pleasure
expand	imagination	pointers
expedite	imaginative	positive
experience	improve	possibility
experienced	innovate	possible
expertise	innovative	potential
extend	input	prepared
fair	investigate	pride

WORDS TO USE WITH YOUR BOSS, *cont'd*

priorities	responsibility	suspend
problems	responsible	talent
productive	revamp	temporary
profitable	review	tested
propose	revise	thank
proud	revitalize	thankful
prudent	reward	thanks
qualified	rewarding	think
questions	rework	thrilled
reasonable	right	time
recognition	service	transition
reconsider	shocked	unstinting
record	skill fairness	untiring
redo	snags	valuable
reevaluate	solve	value
regret	source	weigh
reschedule	special	willing
resolve	strategy	wisdom
resource	strength	wonderful
resourceful	studied	workable
resources	stunned	
responsibilities	support	

PHRASES TO USE WITH YOUR BOSS

able to make decisions

achieved goals

adjust our priorities

apportion our resources

approval from someone I respect

PHRASES TO USE WITH YOUR BOSS, *cont'd*

>   best use of resources
>   best for the company
>   best for the team
>   best job possible
>   best for the project
>   better suited
>   big picture
>   both sides of the desk
>   break new ground
>   by all means
>   by the book
>   can we negotiate
>   can count on me
>   commitment to productivity
>   command decisions
>   commitment to the company
>   commitment to this department
>   consider the alternatives
>   cost in resources
>   cost in time
>   cover ourselves thoroughly
>   cut costs
>   delightful memories
>   difficulties to work out
>   do a creditable job
>   do it right
>   do a more thorough job
>   expanded territory
>   from bottom to top
>   from now on

PHRASES TO USE WITH YOUR BOSS, *cont'd*

gained experience

get your input

give full credit to

give me a day to review the assignment

give this a trial

given a great deal of thought to

good point

greatest admiration

happy to try it your way

helps me see

I appreciate

I look forward to working on this

I look forward to working with you

I know you'll be pleased with the result

I need your advice

I need your take on

I think you'll find

I'll be back to you with some questions

I'll get on it immediately

I'm going to enjoy this

I'm pleased

I've been preparing for this

improve the bottom line

increased market

increased productivity

in the future

invaluable experience

it would help me be more effective

know I'll have questions

make better use of

PHRASES TO USE WITH YOUR BOSS, *cont'd*

management team
minimum risk
more efficient
more flexibility
move forward
opens up possibilities
our company
our department
our mission
play to my strengths
problems to resolve
questions to answer
reaction has been good
really run with
reevaluate priorities
room to maneuver
run all the numbers
serious considerations
sink my teeth into
sink our teeth into
stronger in this area
take the ball and run with it
take time to weigh
take the upside
team player
thank you for this opportunity
thank you for asking me
the intelligent way to
think this through
this is great

PHRASES TO USE WITH YOUR BOSS, *cont'd*

this is helpful

this will be fun

time to review

time to evaluate

trial period

try something new

user-friendly

very excited about this

well-founded

win win situation

with great pleasure

without risk

you have a good point

you will appreciate

you can count on me

you can rely on me

your advice is welcome

WORDS TO AVOID WITH YOUR BOSS

afraid	can't	disaster
ask	cannot	doubt
backward	catastrophe	dull
bad	cheap	dumb
beg	cheated	embarrassed
better	confining	experiment
blame	crisis	exploded
bored	delay	fail
boss	demand	fault
brass	destroyed	fear

WORDS TO AVOID WITH YOUR BOSS, *cont'd*

final	mistaken	stuck
forgot	nervous	tedious
foul-up	non-negotiable	tired
frightened	overburdened	unappreciated
hopeless	overloaded	underpaid
impossible	panic	undeserved
inadequate	quit	unfair
incapable	refuse	unqualified
late	reject	unworkable
luck	ridiculous	unworthy
mess	risk	waste
misjudged	silly	wasted
mismanagement	snafu	won't
mistake	stodgy	worthless

PHRASES TO AVOID WITH YOUR BOSS

afraid to do it

back burner

bad pay

before you know it

beyond me

beyond repair

big mistake

big trouble

bit the big one

blew it

bombed out

can do better than this dead-end job

can't ask me to do something like this

PHRASES TO AVOID WITH YOUR BOSS, *cont'd*

can't be done

can't be fixed

can't do it

can't imagine how I could do it

cannot do it

doesn't thrill me

don't blame me

don't want to do it

doubt it will work

fatal error

get off my case

give me a break

give it a shot

have too many doubts

haven't got the experience

huge problem

I can't afford

I demand

I forgot

I can't

I insist

I need

I can't do any more

I can't do anything about it

I really don't deserve this

I was just lucky

I'll do the best I can

I'll have to quit

I'm fed up

I'm late

PHRASES TO AVOID WITH YOUR BOSS, *cont'd*

I'm only human
I'm overworked
I've had it
incapable of
it got by me
it was easy
it was a piece of cake
it was nothing
it slipped past me
just can't seem to get along
just don't have the qualifications
just one of those things
low wages
might work
my fault
no future
no opportunity
not my fault
not my problem
out of the question
quick and dirty
risk-adverse
save your compliments
screw up
set in our ways
struck out
take a risk for a change
take a chance
take a flier
that's my final word on the subject

PHRASES TO AVOID WITH YOUR BOSS, *cont'd*

there was nothing to it

think nothing of it

this is not negotiable

this is unfair

time flies

unavoidable error

unreasonable demand on me

waste of time

what can go wrong

what the hell

won't work that way

won't try it

worn out

wrong way

wrongheaded

you don't appreciate me

you expect too much

you have no choice

you have to

you must

BODY-LANGUAGE STRATEGY FOR COMMUNICATING WITH YOUR BOSS

Ask any number of people, and you will find many who confess to having a hard time "talking to the boss." No earth-shaking revelation here, but the fact is that *talking* is the wrong word. The trouble is not just talking to the boss, it's *communicating* with him or her. The difficulties actually begin before any words are spoken. Your attitude toward—your relationship with—your supervisor is typically telegraphed by your body language.

Before we look at the kinds of body language to avoid, which, alas, is the body language most people adopt in the presence of their bosses, let's look at the way things *should* be:

- Approach the supervisor politely, but as an equal.
- Knock on the door. When admitted, walk all the way in. Do not poke your head in the door. Do not linger on the threshold.
- Establish immediate eye contact.
- Maintain periodic eye contact, but do not stare.
- Shift eye contact to the forehead; that is, periodically focus your gaze just above the supervisor's eyes. This sends a subtle signal of domination.
- Do not rush to be seated. It is preferable to linger a moment or two standing in front of the supervisor's desk. He or she should look up to you. This puts you in a position of power.
- When seated, keep your hands fully visible. Use them to make gestures underscoring important points.
- Sit upright.
- Keep your hands away from your face, neck, hair, and mouth.
- Gesture frequently with an open, slightly upturned palm.

BODY LANGUAGE TO AVOID WITH YOUR BOSS

The basic desirable body-language strategy conveys both firmness and openness. Avoid stances and gestures that suggest the opposite:

- Avoid cringing. This includes poking your head in the doorway of the boss's office.
- Avoid looking down.
- Avoid looking to the side.
- Avoid rushing to be seated.
- Avoid slumping or slouching in the chair.
- Avoid leg movement when seated.
- Avoid bringing your hands anywhere near your face, mouth, neck, or hair. This suggests anxiety and evasion.

- Avoid crossing your arms in front of your chest. This suggests defiance.
- Avoid putting your hands in your pockets.
- Avoid aggressive gestures, including pointing, stabbing gestures, making a fist, pounding the desk.

SECRETS OF COMMUNICATING WITH EMOTIONALLY STUNTED SUPERVISORS

Communicating with a really competent supervisor is far easier than getting through to one who just doesn't have it all together. A supervisor's competence is in very large measure a function of his or her ability to facilitate communication. Unfortunately, most supervisors allow some particular aspect of their personality to dominate and control their interaction with subordinates. There are five major personality types among bosses.

- In the worst cases, the particular personality type completely takes over. There are, for example, plenty of supervisors who always act like a tyrant and are therefore tyrants, period.
- In most cases, the negative personality type emerges under pressure—such as the pressure of an unwelcome communication from a subordinate—and it can be said that the boss responds in the style of (for example) a tyrant.
- The object of communicating with the difficult supervisor is to identify what personality style is operative and respond to it. With luck, your response will get beyond the narrow personality style that has been adopted and will get through to the more fully rounded human being that lies behind it.

Type I: The Tyrant

Who is the tyrant? Well, he *thinks* he is your parent. This "parent" is not to be confused with your father or mother, who shows you love and concern, but with authority incarnate, absolute, commanding obedience and compliance, and never to be questioned. The tyrant's objective is to make you feel like a child in the narrowest and most negative sense: a *little* person wholly dependent on the parent and incapable of making decisions. To maintain this role, the tyrant relies on monologue and does what he can to avoid dialogue—though he may pepper you with lots of questions. The tyrant is interested in keeping you uneasy and unconfident. He wants you to feel that you are never doing an adequate job.

The tyrannical boss enjoys sitting behind a big desk, and his chair is always higher than yours, like that of a judge. He may have learned the trick of fixing his gaze not on your eyes, but on your forehead, which is a gesture of dominance. If he wears glasses, he may regard you by gazing over the top of his eyewear—another withering article of body language.

The tyrant boss is not subtle. He thrives on threats. That does not mean that he warns you daily about your performance or that he practices origami with a pink slip while he's talking to you. Expect to hear threatening phrases such as:

You'd better

Get a handle on

Get on top of

Get on the ball

Get on the stick

If, listening to the cliché-ridden speech of a tyrant boss, you get the feeling that he's speaking from a script, in a sense he *is*. The tyrant acts out of a hard-and-fast image of himself. He does not see *you*. Instead, he plays a role, and he expects you to respond by playing your role as well. If his role is that of the man in charge, yours is the obedient drone, the dependent, the victim.

- The most tyrannical bosses tend not to be those who really are in charge, such as owners of small businesses, but those with limited authority, who occupy a niche midway up the corporate food chain. While these bosses have power to wield, they also have pressure to bear, and the combination can bring out the worst in them. If the tyrant's boss knocks him, he's liable to pound you.

If all this sounds depressing, the good news is that the tyrant can be dealt with effectively, and you need not be his inevitable victim. Here's the most effective communication strategy:

STEP 1:   Cut the boss down to size. This most emphatically does *not* involve anything you say or do *to* him. Focus on some failing or foible that pierces the tyrant's image and pretension—the grosser and sillier the better: Perhaps he picks his nose when he thinks others aren't looking. Maybe he probes his ear? Perhaps his voice is high, or his grammar is bad. Or just imagine what he looks like in silly pajamas. We are all imperfect. Faced with a tyrannical boss, start by visualizing in your mind's eye all the flaws.

STEP 2:   If you can't find flaws, look harder.

STEP 3:   If you still can't find them, make them up.

STEP 4:   Practice these negative visualizations before you talk to your tyrant boss.

STEP 5:   Now, here comes the maneuver that gives you the most power. While you are still visualizing the boss's foibles, find something to compliment him on. Make your boss feel good about something relatively neutral—his choice of necktie, the color of his jacket—even while you are imagining how that necktie or that jacket will look when your boss spills his lunchtime marinara sauce all over it.

Why do all this? The object is to put you in control of the encounter. You are accustomed to thinking of yourself as the victim of a tyrant. Now turn the tables by allowing your imagination, your power of fantasy, to tyrannize over your boss, but, at the same time, remain in conscious control of the situation by deliberately playing the hypocrite, paying compliments and expressing your admiration.

STEP 6:   We're not through yet. Once you have imaginatively humbled your boss—in fact, fantasizing him as powerless—take steps to empower him *in his own eyes.* Do this by seeking his advice or asking his opinion. Show him that you value his thoughts. Suggest that you consider him someone from whom you have much to learn. This addresses his insecurity in a positive way. Instead of reinforcing the victimizer-victim relationship, it substitutes a more beneficent teacher-student relationship.

Your script: communicating with the tyrant

Here's an example of how a typical exchange with a tyrant might proceed:

Boss: I'm disappointed in you. I don't like what I see in your sales report for the northwest territory. I want my people selling out there.

You: I'm disappointed, too. Sales are not what I had projected. But I'm on top of it. I'm calling a meeting of the sales reps because I think it's time we took more control. I was about to come to you to seek your advice on the situation, which I'm sure is something you've handled plenty of times. Of course, I'd also like to get you in on the meeting, and I'd like to talk to you before the meeting so that you can help me clarify the issues and lay out the most effective approach. I want to expedite this. Can I see you at the end of the week and get your take on what I plan to do about the situation?

Note that the tyrant speaks like a parent: "I'm disappointed in you." He also verges on the vocabulary of a tin-horn dictator: "my people." These are his self-conceived roles. Don't reinforce his reality.

- Quietly and calmly decline to act the part of a naughty child or a downtrodden peasant.

- At the same time, however, as you dodge the tyrant's personal attack, address the *substance* of the issues he raised. If he's "disappointed," so are you.

- Conclude by showing that, although you are taking charge of the situation, you can do so far more effectively with the boss's advice and guidance.

Use caution. Be certain that, in empowering your boss, you don't give him the impression that you are not doing or cannot do your job. You are eager to present *your* plan and get *his* "take" on it. Empower your boss without relinquishing your own strength.

Negative responses to anticipate from the tyrant

1. Are you asking me to do your job for you?

Reply with:

No, I am not. But I *am* asking for your advice so that I can do my job more effectively.

2. This talk is all fine, but I'm just not sure you are motivated.

Reply with:

You don't have to worry about that. I promise you that I am motivated. I like to win, and I like to be on a winning team. That's why I want to take advantage of your experience.

3. Do you think you can get your people out there selling?

Reply with:

I know I can—especially with your help. We'll turn this situation around.

Type II: The Guilt Monger

The guilt monger boss gets you to do not just your work, but the work of two or three others. She is the mirror image of the tyrant boss. She makes no attempt to tower over you; instead, she shows you how you are tearing her down by your "unwillingness" to go "that extra mile."

- She will not threaten to fire you, but she will tell you (perhaps indirectly) that, unless "extra effort" is made, the company will collapse and you and everyone else will be out of work.
- She will not *tell* you to put in overtime, but she *will* look up from her desk at 5:30 and say something like, "Oh, no, don't stay late. You have more important things to do, like have dinner with your family. My family has gotten used to my working late by now."
- She'll use phrases like, "Somebody's got to do it—but don't you worry about it." Or: "I don't know where we're going to find the bodies to do this job, but we'll have to manage—somehow."

The guilt-mongering boss typically has a *passive-aggressive* personality, made evident through some of her favorite phrases:

Don't trouble yourself.

Think nothing of it.

No. We'll manage without you.

Oh—your *family* . . .

I can't remember the last time I had dinner at home on a weekday.

We'll find somebody to do it.

Well, if you're not available, you're not available.

I guess we'll manage.

I suppose you don't owe me any overtime.

The most effective strategy for dealing with the guilt monger is always to separate your commitment to your job from your relationship with your boss. Depending on how you feel about your work and what you realistically need to accomplish in order to do your job, you may have little choice about putting in overtime or pushing extra hard to meet a deadline. The crucial step is separating the unavoidable demands that come with the job from the emotional demands that come from a manipulative guilt monger. Then, once *you* have successfully distinguished between emotion and necessity, you need to help your boss do the same. There are two ways to accomplish this:

- If an unreasonable demand is made on your time and you have a legitimate excuse, use it: "Normally, I could work overtime, but today's our anniversary." Or: "I wish I could change my day off, but I have a medical appointment that would take months to reschedule." The problem with relying on such excuses is that, since the guilt-mongering boss is by definition chronic with her demands, you will soon run out of legitimate excuses.

- The second response to the guilt monger, then, is to administer a perspective-restoring dose of reality. Your boss says: "I suppose I'll just stay here and work on this report myself." You reply: "Do you think that's necessary? You know, I'll be completely available to you tomorrow. I could rough out a draft, and you could review it." Or: "Do you think it's a good idea to do something this important in such a hurry? Why don't we review it together first thing in the morning?" Provide real alternatives.

Your script: communicating with the guilt monger. The following is a typical exchange with the guilt-mongering boss:

Boss: I suppose we can manage—somehow—if we don't get this report out tomorrow. I'll make some excuse or other, I suppose.

You: I agree. It seems to me a lot better to take the time to do this thing right than to try to rush it through tonight. Tomorrow, I can give you all day. I'll rough out a draft, and we can go over it together. We need time to do a good job.

Note the two major elements of strategy here. First, the guilt monger works on emotion and expects you to respond emotionally. Choose not to. Instead, respond to the issues. The boss is insincere when she says "We'll manage," but you should take this at its face value and show her how, indeed, you *will* manage. Second, the pronoun *we* demonstrates that you are not deserting your boss. You are a member of the team, and committed to it.

NEGATIVE RESPONSES TO ANTICIPATE FROM THE GUILT MONGER

1. Well, I guess I'll just sit down and do what I can myself.

Reply with:
Why do that when I can give you all the help you want tomorrow? You deserve the night off.

2. It makes me nervous to work so close to a deadline.

Reply with:
That's why we need to approach this methodically, allowing ourselves time.

3. I guess it is unfair to ask you to do so much extra work.

Reply with:
It's not a question of fairness, but of making the most productive use of my time.

4. It would help if you could reschedule your appointments this evening.

Reply with:
I wish I could, but it's impossible on such short notice.

Type III: *The Merchant of Blame*

Some bosses take responsibility for their decisions and actions. Some do not. Some correctly, accurately, and fairly determine responsibility for problems and mistakes, and they make corrections appropriately; some do not. Some bosses deliberately dodge responsibility, while others just can't help responding with blame when a situation goes sour.

EFFECTIVE STRATEGY FOR COMMUNICATING WITH THE BLAMER

Let's pause a moment. Before we discuss strategies for verbally coping with the blamer, we must distinguish between those times when you are at fault and those times when you are not. If you have made a mistake, own up to it, confront it, deal with it, and repair it. Beyond this, distinguish between the boss who, on rare occasions, wrongly assigns blame and the habitual blamer, for whom blaming is an integral part of management style. The first case requires correction of a mistaken perception, the second is an issue of personality and style.

- Confronting the occasional accusation from an otherwise substantially stable boss calls for you to begin by getting the facts. Do not deny anything before you have the full story; that will just make you seem defensive.

- Collecting the facts will accomplish two things. First, it will calm your boss down by shifting his focus from personalities to events. Second, it will give you the opportunity not only to demonstrate your blamelessness, but might even lead to the resolution of the problem in question.

If you have the misfortune of working for a habitual blamer, begin the same way:

STEP 1:   Focus calmly on the facts. Confront the events rather than the boss's accusation.

Now, getting to the facts is not always easy when you are dealing with a habitual blamer. The blamer's object is to shift responsibility from himself to you. Actually, the last thing he is interested in is facts that may prevent him from accomplishing this shift. You do have a secret weapon, however:

STEP 2:   Offer a willingness to accept responsibility, not blame. Communicate that, while the snafu is not your fault, you are prepared to accept it as your problem and work to resolve it.

The blamer boss may resist your challenging him, but it is not likely that he will turn down your offer to take on the task of correcting a problem. While you have blocked the boss's attempt to fix blame on you, you have allowed him to feel as if he has won, because you have agreed to take on responsibility for resolving the problem.

YOUR SCRIPT: COMMUNICATING WITH THE BLAMER

Boss: Well, you've really done it this time. I turn my back for five minutes and everything goes to hell. The warehouse says it has no record of any of these orders. How do you think we make money? We take orders, transmit orders, and ship orders. How could you have screwed up so badly?

You: Mrs. Smith, this is the first I've heard of a problem. Please give me the details so that we can get to the bottom of it and arrive at a solution quickly.

Boss: How can this be the first you've heard about it? Where have you been all this time?

You: I've been right here, but you've been stuck with fielding this complaint. Tell me the details so that I can help get us back on track. After I get the whole story, I will do whatever is necessary to fix the problem.

Boss: I'm not confident that you can "fix" anything.

You: Mrs. Smith, it's true I can't if I don't know what went wrong. Let's go over this situation together

The blamer does not see *you*. He sees only a target. Begin bringing him back to reality by deliberately using his name; yet, even while you establish personal contact, avoid responding to any personal attacks. Focus—or refocus—the exchange on the facts of the situation in question. Get the story. Don't draw conclusions until you've collected the facts. But do, from the beginning, volunteer to find a solution.

NEGATIVE RESPONSES TO ANTICIPATE FROM THE BLAMER

1. Don't try to wiggle out of this.

Reply with:

That's the last thing I want to do. What I want is to get into this problem and start fixing it.

2. You have to take responsibility for this.

Reply with:

That is exactly what I want to do. Let me work with you to fix the problem. Let's begin by going over the facts, so that we can agree on a solution.

3. You'd better do it yourself and do it right now.

Reply with:

I'll give it top priority. It will save us both time if we begin by going over the facts now.

4. I'm too angry to go into details now.

Reply with:

I'll do what I can now, but I'm going to have to discuss this with you later. I'll drop by in an hour.

Type IV: The Dreamer

Some bosses are self-confident, some not. Working for an insecure boss is difficult, while working for one who has healthy self-confidence can be gratifying and rewarding—unless that self-confidence is without basis. The dreamer is the boss who is convinced that her every passing idea bears the seeds of greatness. The dreamer will call you into her office and declare: "While I was driving in this morning I hit a pothole. I thought, 'Why can't R & D come up with a sensor that will alert the driver to a pothole in time to avoid it?' We've got the technology, and we've got the marketing muscle. I want you to start working on this right away."

Suddenly you are swept away in your boss's stream of consciousness, the victim of an idea that happened to drift by. Now, by no means should you dodge every idea your boss comes up with. After all, it *is* possible that she might come up with something good, profitable, even brilliant. Nor can I tell you how to distinguish a good idea from an unworkable one. There are no general rules for determining this in all fields. And, alas, you may have no choice other than to act on whatever assignment your boss hands out. Depending on your position and the hierarchy of your company, it may not be your place to offer an opinion. Nevertheless, strategies are available to help you respond to the dreamer without getting sidetracked— or derailed.

We've all seen the ancient Hollywood movie cliché in which someone becomes hysterical, drifts off into his or her own world, and is brought back to reality with a sharp slap on the face. Some experts advise administering the verbal equivalent of the sharp slap in the case of ideas that seem doomed to fail. The problem with this approach is that it rarely pays for a subordinate to respond to a boss in this way, and, even if you do feel sufficiently secure in your job to deliver a harsh truth, the result is likely to be defensiveness and resistance. There is a more effective strategy available.

STEP 1:   Do not pass immediate judgment on the idea.

STEP 2:   Respond to the mechanics of your boss's request or direction: "What kind of priority do you want me to give this?" Or: "Should I put the XYZ account on the back burner to handle this?"

Emphasizing mechanics and logistics will help focus your boss on day-to-day reality, suggesting that certain business will have to be rescheduled, delayed, or sacrificed. This will put the idea in perspective and perhaps even take some of the wind out of the Dreamer's sails and some of the pressure off you. At the same time, it will convey the message that you are taking the idea seriously enough to concern yourself with scheduling action on it.

STEP 3:   Never say directly that you don't have time to act on the dreamer's idea. That dismisses both the idea and the person behind it.

STEP 4:   Buy time. Reply to the dreamer with, "This is very interesting. Give me some time to think about this. I imagine I'll have lots of questions for you."

STEP 5:   Take advantage of whatever bureaucracy your company has in place for dealing with new ideas, concepts, and programs. If you must fill out forms or write up a report, get your boss involved in this: "Okay. The first step will be a preliminary P and L. I'll get the paperwork started and bring it in tomorrow."

Remember, your object is not to avoid work but to avoid as much *unnecessary and wasteful* work as possible. It is also to head off the development of an unworkable idea that may soon become your responsibility and, ultimately, your failure. But your other, equally important, objective is to avoid alienating your boss.

Your script: communicating with the dreamer

Boss: I was watching television last night, and I got an idea. We should do our Annual Report as a music video. I mean it. Set those dry facts to music. It would get us publicity and stir up the investors. I want you to get this started.

You: I've got the XYZ project in stage four, and I'm pitching the ABC account. Do you want me to turn these over to someone else to clear the decks for the video? Or how should I juggle that? We're talking about a good deal of business there.

Boss: No. You'd better see those through.

You: Okay. Then I'll schedule the video project accordingly, but first let me think about it and rough out a list of questions and issues for you before we move ahead.

Don't address the unworkability of the proposed project. Instead, focus on the impact it will have on present reality. In effect, this will relieve you from the responsibility of shaking the boss back into reality. *Show* her the reality, and she will shake *herself.*

Negative responses to anticipate from the dreamer

1. I want you to give it your full attention.

Reply with:

Okay. But I'd better begin by giving you a report on my current projects, so that we can reschedule and reassign.

2. I don't want this to disappear into limbo. I want follow-through.

Reply with:

I need some time to review the idea, and then I'll prepare a list of questions and issues for you. I also need to discuss my current assignments, so that we can reschedule and reassign. I'm pretty heavily committed, and this is going to shake things up around here.

3. What do you think about this?

Reply with:

It is worth thinking seriously about. Let me give it some consideration and discuss it with you.

4. This is something we really need to be doing, and we need to move fast.

Reply with:

I'll start sketching out some ideas of the kind of resource commitment the project's likely to involve, and I'll get back to you with any questions.

Type V: The Volcano

Then there's the boss who just plain explodes. There's yelling, invective, ranting, finger jabbing, and fist pounding.

The emotional volcano is, by definition, a poor manager. While it is true that fear of the boss is a great motivator, what it motivates is passivity, the suppression of creativity, and the avoidance of communication. Perhaps most of all, it motivates a search for alternative employment. And, depending on many other factors associated with the job, that search may be your *best* alternative.

However, if you are stuck with an emotional volcano, you do have a variety of verbal strategies for dealing with him.

STEP 1:   Begin by understanding the basis of your boss's tendency to act on his feelings, and then think through your own response to those feelings. In most cases, the emotional volcano is driven by fear. What does your boss have to be afraid of? Plenty. If he has bosses to answer to, he suffers the same anxieties and pressures you do. If he owns the company, the consequences of failure, the sense that work is slipping, that profits are dwindling, that the business is leaking, triggers terrible emotions. In the anxiety-afflicted, insecure boss, any reversal—a late report, a lost sale—seems like the first step down the slippery slope not to a bad day, a poor month, or even a weak quarter, but to doom.

STEP 2:   Understand your own fear. The eruption of the emotional volcano creates two kinds of fear in you. One is the simple fear of losing your job: the thought that, in his rage, your boss will summarily fire you. Now, is this realistic? Well, people do get fired, but it is seldom an act of anger. Most employees are let go because of relatively long-term economic reasons, not as the immediate result of an emotional exchange.

   • Another source of fear is the prospect of actual violence. Of course, you may know in your head that the one thing your boss will *not* do is strike you, and the one thing you will *not* do is lash out at him. But at some level of consciousness you imagine an exchange between Neanderthals. Verbal violence is always a symbol of physical threat. Your boss represents power and authority. In a heated exchange, your imagination gives concrete shape to those abstractions. Your boss, you feel, has the power and authority to crush you. Equally anxiety provoking is the feeling you may have of wanting to fight back, perhaps even launch a preemptive strike. You *know* that none of this will happen, but you *feel* the associated emotions nonetheless.

STEP 3:   Fear is a primitive emotion. You can neither avoid nor escape it, but you don't have to be governed by it. Once the volcano erupts, it is best to let the lava flow around you. Force yourself to listen to the tirade—while standing, if possible, with your arms at your sides. Force yourself to look into your boss's eyes, as if you were having a regular conversation. At some natural pause—a lull in the storm—inject calm.

STEP 4:   Inject calm, but avoid telling your boss to "calm down." Never *tell* an angry person to do anything. It will only make him angrier. Nor should you tell him how to feel ("There's no reason for you to be so upset"), since meddling with another's emotions is also likely to elicit nothing but additional rage. Instead, acknowledge the other person's anger: "I can see that you are mad as hell, and I can't blame you, but . . ." The *but* is the point at which you introduce alternatives to the tirade: ". . . but I need to talk this through with you. Would it be better for me to come back and discuss this, or do you want to sit down and go over it now?"

STEP 5:   Rage narrows vision, preventing consideration of alternatives. Your objective in confronting the emotional volcano is to make the alternatives visible:

   A. *We can discuss this.*

   B. *We can resolve this.*

   C. *We can sit down together.*

   D. *We can do it now.*

   E. *We can do it later.*

TIP

Give your boss choices, alternatives. Compel him, in this way, to *think* for a moment rather than to *feel.*

STEP 6:   As for yourself, while you should not roll over to abuse, neither should you yield to the temptation to jump into a shouting match. Once *both* of you are yelling, *neither* of you is in charge. The emotion—anger—is in control. You won't win the struggle, and neither will your boss. Rage triumphs. Instead, listen unmoved. Let him vent. Then provide some choices and alternatives.

This strategy may work, but it is not foolproof. If your boss is on a roll, the tirade may not only continue, but intensify. At this point, the most effective move you can make is out. Separate yourself from your boss. Don't run, and certainly don't storm out of the office. Just excuse yourself as calmly and politely as possible: "Excuse me, Mrs. Smith. I understand how angry you are, and, because of that, I think it would be best if I went down to my office for a while. Why don't you buzz me downstairs when we can sit down and talk about this problem without yelling at one another."

Your script: communicating with the volcano

Here's what you might expect:

Boss: I'm tired of things going wrong around here. I'm tired of nothing getting followed up on. You and your department better shape up, because I'm getting tired of all of you. This is a tough, push, push, push business. And if you stop pushing, you don't survive. Well, let me tell you something right now. You're going down before I do, and that's a promise. I'm tired of being jerked around like this!

You: I understand that you're upset about sales this quarter. Well, so am I, but this is something we need to talk through. We can sit down now over this, or, if you like, I'll come back at a better time, when we can hammer out a strategy. It's up to you.

Take whatever verbal action is required to transform the situation from *me*-against-*you* to *us*-against-the-*problem*. Suggest postponing discussion until emotions have cooled.

Negative responses to anticipate from the volcano

1. I don't want to waste my time talking to you.

Reply with:
Then I'll go back down to my office. You can give me a buzz if you do decide to discuss this further.

2. I'm not finished with you yet.

Reply with:
I'm sure there's a lot more to say, but I'd prefer to come back at a better time. However, I'm willing to continue talking if we can conduct this as a conversation and not as a shouting match.

3. We have to hash all of this out right now!

Reply with:

Then I suggest that we sit down, calmly lay out the issues, and act on them accordingly. When we both have a clear idea of everything that's involved in this problem, I'm sure we can formulate a solution.

4. I don't want to hear any excuses.

Reply with:

And I don't have any excuses to give you. What I'd like is some time to review the problems you have brought up and come back to you with some suggestions for solving them.

5. You can't get away with sloppy work. I can't stand sloppy work.

Reply with:

I'm sorry that I've given you the feeling that I'm trying to get away with anything. Can we sit down and go over whatever problem areas you see? If I can get specifics, I can work with you on them one by one. Should I come back at a better time?

NEGOTIATING A RAISE

Here's a phrase not only to avoid saying, but one that you should expunge from your mind: *I deserve a raise.*

Your boss doesn't care. More important, you should not go into this negotiation thinking about what you deserve or don't deserve. Most of us are brought up with a false sense of modesty, which, at some level of consciousness, causes us to question whether we deserve anything good at all. Better not open that Freudian can of worms.

Well, then, what *do* you need a raise for? A new car? A new house? To make the payments on the house you've got? To send your kid through college?

Maybe your boss takes an interest in your needs. Maybe not. Personally, she may care about you very much. Personally, she may not. Whatever her feelings, if she's being at all professional about the matter, she will deliberately exclude your needs from her consideration of your salary. For one thing, a dozen other people in the company want a new car or new house or have a tough nut to make each month.

So, let's see. We've eliminated just deserts as a persuasive argument for getting a raise, and we've ditched personal needs as well. What's left?

- Answer: Your performance on the job. Period.

Now, this actually makes your task a lot easier, at least as far as your emotions are concerned. If it's hard enough to make a persuasive case for a raise based on your performance at work, think how much harder it would be if you had to justify the pitch on the basis of your whole life. (You see, your boss would be thinking, "Why does *he* need a new car? *I* don't have a new car. I can't afford a new car.")

Here's how to proceed. The first ten steps are preparation—don't stint on these—the rest is execution.

STEP 1:   Focus on how you meet—and exceed—the demands of your job.

Let's work on getting that focus razor sharp. Most novice communicators make the mistake of thinking that eloquence is a matter of commanding a range of beautifully descriptive adjectives. They incorrectly assume that punchy adjectives most effectively evoke emotion. The truth is that *people, things, events,* and *deeds* evoke far more emotion than words and that nouns and verbs—the kinds of words most directly connected to people, things, events, and deeds—therefore evoke more emotion than adjectives and adverbs, which are related to the real world less directly. The firmest foundation of eloquence is constructed of simple nouns and verbs, not flowery adjectives and sonorous adverbs. How can you make your focus razor sharp? Talk about people, things, events, and deeds.

Instead of trying to convince your boss that you're a "great" sales manager who has created a "dynamic" department, prove your case with the people, things, events, and deeds that make such adjectives as *great* and *dynamic* superfluous. For example:

> Last year at this time, when I took over, we were doing a volume of $75,000 in *X*, $55,000 in *Y*, and $45,000 in *Z*. Today, the numbers are $125,000, $78,000, and $55,000. I've also directed what looks like a great launch for product *A*—$35,000 in first-quarter sales alone—and I'm developing the staff not only to maintain but to better these numbers. Joe Blow, whom I brought on board in December, has made it his business to penetrate our traditionally weakest territories. In Chicago, for example, he's increased sales by 43 percent. . . .

The American poet William Carlos Williams told would-be writers that there are "no ideas but in things." He may have thought he was issuing a prescription for good literature, but what he was really doing was providing a formula for highly effective persuasion.

TIP

Show. Don't *tell.*

STEP 2: Make a list of highlights of your accomplishments during the preceding year or other period. Don't count on your boss's having dutifully kept score. In fact, you shouldn't even assume that she is on intimate terms with your job description. Make a list of your duties and responsibilities.

STEP 3: Research what others—in similar positions, with similar duties, and in similar companies—get paid. If the average is significantly higher than what you are getting, add the information to your arsenal. If you fall within the average, don't use the information; however, be prepared to emphasize the ways in which you outperform the average, just in case your boss brings up the subject of "industry standards of compensation." Finally, if you discover that you are getting paid substantially more than the average, you should either count yourself fortunate (and learn to live within your present budget for the time being) or think in terms of a promotion rather than a raise.

Just ahead, in the next section, we will discuss strategies for putting yourself across to secure a promotion. But pause a moment to think about that now. If your research does reveal that you are being "overpaid" in your current position, consider this bold approach:

> I want to level with you. I was planning on meeting with you to negotiate a raise. But I've done some research, and I've given the matter a good deal of thought. The fact is, you're paying me too much. The average sales manager in our industry takes home *X* dollars in straight salary. I'm getting *Y*. Now, before you think I've lost my mind, let me propose something that will be good for our division, the company—and, of course, good for me. Instead of paying *Y* dollars for a sales manager, why don't you pay *Z* dollars for a director of sales. I'm already doing *A*,

B, and *C*—all director's responsibilities—and I'm really ready for the move. The hike from salary *Y* to *Z* makes a lot more sense than maintaining me in a lesser position at *Y.*

STEP 4: Edit and digest your research. Go over it. Memorize the highlights—especially be able to tick off your stellar accomplishments. Carry to the meeting a neatly typed summary of the information, but don't read from it, and don't trot it out unless your boss asks to *see* facts and figures. Rehearse and memorize instead.

STEP 5: Do supplementary research to hold in reserve. You should be aware of how well (or how poorly) your company and department performed during the past year. If your company issues an annual report, read it. Supplement your research on industry standards of compensation for your position by determining if you are a professional in short supply or if the market for your position is well stocked or even glutted. Again: don't volunteer this information at the interview, but hold it in reserve, in case you meet resistance.

TIP

Taking the time to acquire the facts will not only directly help you make your case, it will also give you a depth of knowledge that will increase your self-confidence and will prepare you to answer questions and overcome resistance. Don't pummel your boss with the lock, stock, and barrel of your research, but be assured that having the facts on hand will suggest that you have depth and that you are committed to the company, to the industry, and to your career.

TIP

Where do you find the facts? Within most larger companies, salary information (except for company officers in publicly held corporations) is usually a closely guarded secret. In many firms, employees are even barred from discussing their salaries with others. You should not, therefore, base your research on what friends and associates tell you. That, after all, is gossip. Find cold, hard, dispassionate *published* sources. The best sources of industry-wide salary information are the compensation surveys published by trade organizations within your field.

STEP 6: Once you have found and digested the facts, take a few moments to "get your mind right." This means laying aside any self-doubt or questions about *Do I deserve a raise?* What you deserve or don't deserve should have no bearing on the task at hand. Nor should you let emotional—or financial—hunger take command. Focus on job performance. Period.

STEP 7: Formulate a target salary level. Based on your research, decide on what you can reasonably expect. However, as in any negotiation, you should not start by disclosing the figure. The best tactic is to elicit an offer from your boss and, depending on how that figure jives with what your research and desires tell you is appropriate, accept the offer or use it as the basis for further negotiation. The potential problem of laying all your cards on the table is not that the dollar amount you ask for will be too high, but that it will be too low.

STEP 8: Resolve not to *ask* for a raise. Psychologists who practice so-called "transactional analysis" say that each of us carries within our emotional selves a "parent," an "adult," and a "child." Ideally, two adults will relate to each other from the perspective of their "adult" selves. In actuality, many relations between adults involve the "child" in one relating to the "child" or the "parent" in the other. No matter how sophisticated we may believe ourselves to be, when we go to a supervisor to ask for a raise, we tend to cast ourselves in the role of the "child" and the supervisor in the role of the "adult." This emotional dynamic is more likely to result in resistance than in a raise. Avoid this counterproductive dynamic by *negotiating* for a raise, rather than *asking* for one.

What's the difference? It begins with attitude. You are not a charity case, out to get something for nothing. You are coming to the bargaining table with valuable skills and experience, for which you are trying to get the best price. Resolve to make this meeting a negotiation, a transaction, a bargaining session—not a hat-in-hand plea.

STEP 9: Dress for the part. Although the meeting is definitely a special occasion, don't pick this moment to change your customary wardrobe. Wear your usual business attire, taking extra care to ensure that your outfit is freshly laundered and dry cleaned and that it is in top repair. Avoid flamboyance or sexual provocation. Err on the conservative side. It is also a big mistake deliberately to "dress down" for the occasion, as if to suggest that you cannot afford to look your best. This will not garner sympathy, nor will it make your boss feel guilty about your current salary. What it *will* suggest is that you cannot manage your personal resources and that you are not giving your best to your job. It is likely to get your boss thinking that if you can't get it together personally how can you manage your job or your department effectively?

STEP 10:   Make the appointment. In some organizations, it is possible to see the boss without making an appointment. In others, an appointment is necessary. It is also possible that the subject of compensation can be discussed appropriately only at an annual or semiannual salary review. Even if you work in a firm in which a meeting with the boss is customarily spontaneous and casual, do make a specific appointment for this discussion. Moreover, be certain that your boss knows what the purpose of the meeting is. It is definitely not to your advantage to spring the salary negotiation on her. Don't let yourself believe that surprising your boss with a request for money will catch her off guard. Usually, a surprise proposition automatically elicits defensive resistance.

TIP

Your organization may or may not have a specific procedure for scheduling appointments with the supervisor. Whatever the details of the procedure, you should avoid "asking for" or "requesting" an appointment. Don't say, "Can I see you on . . ." but, "I need to meet with you to discuss a salary matter. Would Tuesday before 11 be good for you?" As in any sales situation (and you *are* selling your boss on the idea of compensating you at a higher level), your object is to move your "prospect" to act. The first act is agreeing to the appointment. Don't leave this up to your boss. Being specific and putting the request in the form of a statement rather than a question make it easy for her to act.

STEP 11:   Walk in and greet your boss as you normally would. Make strong eye contact and do your best to position yourself powerfully in the room. If she is behind her desk, pull a chair to the *side* of the desk, if possible, so that the desktop does not separate you. If this is not physically possible, sit as close to the desk as possible. Try to sit higher than or at the same level as your boss. In maintaining eye contact, be careful of your aim. From time to time, you may actually want to look slightly above your boss's eye level, a body-language signal that conveys subtle domination. Do not sustain this for too long a stretch, however, lest your healthy self-assertion be interpreted as arrogance.

STEP 12: Before getting to the point, begin with thanks for the meeting. This is not merely common courtesy (though it *is* that, too), it also reminds your boss that, in agreeing to the meeting, she has already invested something in you. Beginning with thanks enhances your value in her eyes.

STEP 13: Review the record. Then make your pitch.

YOUR SCRIPT: NEGOTIATING A RAISE

Here's a raise-seeking scenario:

You: Thanks for seeing me, Jane [if you customarily call her by her first name]. I've been with Better & Better for five years now—two years in sales and the past three in marketing. I believe you know the quality of work I've been doing here. I mean, for example, since I took over the Lummox account, we've penetrated two major new markets and at least one new territory. And the year's not over yet! I am confident that we'll see similar results with the Flummox account, which I've just taken on. You've given me a lot of creative freedom, and I've really been able to run with that.

I've also been able to put together a terrific team: I'm supervising four people on the Lummox account, and I plan to put together a six-person team on the Flummox job, at least through start-up.

It's true that I've advanced pretty rapidly here, but, then, I've had to take on a lot of responsibilities. I believe that it's time for my salary to catch up to my level of achievement and responsibilities. Certainly, it's time for my salary to get into step with industry-standard compensation for the kind of work I'm doing.

Jane, what do you think?

In brief compass, you've presented your case and you have hinted at a salary range (industry-standard) without limiting yourself to a figure that may be too low. Having demonstrated that your performance merits a higher level of compensation, you've also given your boss the feeling that she is a fair person and a shrewd judge of talent and ability ("You've given me a lot of creative freedom . . ."). In effect, you are reflecting to your boss what she already thinks. You are reminding her that she has invested in you. Your "rapid advance" will not be perceived as a reason to slow down now, but as a precedent for advancing you some more. Just as your pitch is aimed at (subtly) telling your boss that she already thinks you are great, the conclusion of your pitch should leave her feeling that the proposed raise is *her* idea. You've set up the context that makes it possible for your boss to respond positively. As in any effective sales pitch, you've also made it possible for her to act. The decision, of course, is ultimately hers. The question at the end of the pitch, however, does not merely acknowledge this immutable fact, it empowers her to make the decision you want her to make. Not: Will you give *me* more money? But: What do *you* think?

- Successful persuasion shifts the focus from you to your prospect. It translates your self-interest into terms of the self-interest of the other person.

Overcoming resistance to your raise request

The most common form of resistance you are likely to encounter is a delaying tactic, your boss telling you that she can't consider the request now or that it will have to wait until later. If your firm has an annual or semi-annual salary-review procedure, it may well be appropriate to reserve salary discussions until then. However, if an off-putting response is merely a delaying tactic, attempt to set a specific appointment date for the review:

- "I understand. When will it be appropriate to have this discussion?"
  or
- "I'd like to reschedule, then, in two weeks. Can we set that up now?"
  or
- "The sales meeting is on the twelfth. Does the fifteenth look good for rescheduling this discussion?"

Don't leave matters hanging.

HERE ARE SOME OTHER COMMON NEGATIVE RESPONSES:

1. If it were up to me, there's no question you'd get a raise at this time. I can make a recommendation, but I'm pretty much powerless to make the final decision.

Reply with:

Should I have a conversation with [name of boss's supervisor]? Can I count on your recommendation to him?

2. To be perfectly frank with you, a lot of people here are doing great jobs, and they're not getting the kind of increase you're talking about.

Reply with:

I'm only talking about myself and what is appropriate in my case.

It is also likely that a genuine negotiation will develop. For example:

3. I can't offer you a 15 percent increase. Three, maybe 5 percent is more like it.

Reply with:

[Say nothing, but don't leave—and don't glare. You're not angry. You are introducing a strategic silence in order to make your boss uncomfortable enough to make a better offer or, at least, to prompt further negotiation.]

After a protracted silence, your boss says: "I'm sorry, but this is final. Five percent is as high as I can go."

Reply with:

Okay. I appreciate your consideration, and I'll work at that salary, provided that we have a firm understanding that in three months we will review what I've done and where I've taken the department. I'm committed to this job, and I'm prepared to wait three months before reopening this subject.

TIP

Be certain to follow up with a memo summarizing your understanding of the agreement, including the scheduled review.

What if the answer is simply no (usually something like, "I can't accommodate you at this time")? You might respond with:

- "Is there something I've done or failed to do?"

  or

- "What can I do to change your thinking on this?"

  or

- "Tell me what would make it possible for me to get more appropriate compensation."

As is the case with most negotiations, even one that fails to produce the desired result can be productive nevertheless. Use a negative response to gain knowledge about how you fit into the organization, about your boss's needs as well as your own.

- The only truly unsuccessful negotiation is the one from which you fail to learn.

In the worst case, you may learn that you should seek a different employer. *Worst* case? That may actually turn out to be the best thing that ever happened to you.

NEGOTIATING A PROMOTION

Seeking a promotion is similar to negotiating for a raise in that your task is to sell your boss on your value, negotiating a deal rather than making a demand or asking for something in return for nothing. Indeed, in many cases, it is more appropriate to seek a promotion than it is to ask for a raise. Many positions have formal or informal salary ceilings, and the next step up the compensation ladder is through a loftier position.

Is it harder to get a raise or to get a promotion? That's the same kind of question as the classic posed to optimists and pessimists: Is the glass half empty or half full? The pessimist will tell you that it's harder to get a promotion because you are asking for *two* things, more money *and* more responsibility. By the same token, the pessimist might also tell you that it's harder to get a raise because you're asking for more money without doing anything more for it. An optimist, on the other hand, may opine that a boss is more likely to yield on money than on power. Or the optimist may tell you that a boss is more likely to tie a raise to a promotion because she feels she is getting a better bargain—paying more, but also getting more.

The pessimist/optimist debate may be useful for anticipating possible responses, but it is not worth worrying about. Just take an optimist's position; after all, it's the only viewpoint that will do you any good in a negotiation.

If you have a choice between asking for a raise or asking for a promotion, begin by deciding what you want. Most people will choose the promotion, and if that's what you want, here is the best way to begin:

STEP 1:   Adopt the attitude that you are offering to take on more responsibility in exchange for greater compensation. This not only has the potential for giving your boss positive feelings about parting with more money, even more important, it should allow you to feel less like a supplicant and more like a good businessperson: You are not simply asking for more, but you are offering value for value in a way that shows respect for yourself and a commitment to your company.

STEP 2:   If you are turned down for the promotion, you are still in a position to negotiate a raise in your present position. This is a key advantage of asking for a promotion rather than a raise. Had you begun by asking for a raise, you would have had no such positive fallback position.

STEP 3:   As with negotiating for a raise, it is far better to come into the discussion armed with a few solid accomplishments than with a collection of self-laudatory adjectives.

STEP 4:   Building on a base of accomplishment, suggest that you could be even more useful in a position of greater responsibility.

TIP

For most of us, it is emotionally very difficult to *ask* for things. It is also true that most people would rather receive than give. Therefore, secure your promotion by offering rather than asking.

Your script: negotiating a promotion

Here's a typical negotiation:

You: I've been on the selling floor now for just about four years. Three out of those four years I've been among your top three salespeople. I have learned a lot here, and not only about selling shoes, but also about what *moves* and what does not. I've also learned that I have a lot to offer—and not just on a customer-by-customer basis. I know that Mr. Jones is moving up from assistant buyer; well, I'm ready to move up to working more closely with you. I've had a long and successful record of customer contact, but I've been concentrating as much on the product as on the customers. I have a very fresh perspective on what is selling here—what moves, what doesn't—and I'd like to put that knowledge to work for us as our new assistant buyer.

The most important point to note here is how the applicant turns a request into an offer. He states the facts and establishes his record of achievement, not with the object of proving that he "deserves" a promotion, but with the goal of selling additional services to the company.

TIP

You don't have to sell your boss on the fact that a promotion will benefit you. She knows that. Your task is to sell her on the idea that promoting you will greatly benefit the company—and, therefore, her.

Negative responses to anticipate when asking for a promotion

1. I don't think you are ready yet.

Reply with:
What will it take for me to demonstrate that I *am* ready?

2. This is not the right time to talk about it.

Reply with:
When would be a better time? Can you pencil me in now?

3. You're doing such a good job where you are, that I'm afraid to move you out of the position.

Reply with:

Well, it sure is nice to be appreciated, but I'm confident that I can take the same skills and use them to greater advantage in an even more responsible position. I want to contribute as much as possible to our department.

5. I need to keep you where you are for at least another year.

Reply with:

I'd like to schedule a review before that time, to discuss my progress and my prospects. Can we plan on that now?

6. We're planning to fill that position with somebody from the outside.

Reply with:

Is that final? What would it take to change your mind? (Or: . . . to change company policy?) Can you tell me what it would take to get me in the running for this promotion?

PROMOTING AN IDEA OR PROJECT

It is difficult to prescribe any single strategy for promoting new ideas and projects, since the nurturing and reception of innovation are subject to the vagaries of a variety of corporate psychologies. Some bosses welcome and encourage new things, while others subtly or even actively discourage it.

- What is so intimidating about floating a new idea? The fear of meeting with hostility, discouragement, and derision.

The phrase that applies to this outcome is "shot down": *He shot me down. I was shot down.* Or even, *I went down in flames.* The vividness of the metaphor suggests the strength of the bad feelings associated with fear of rejection and humiliation.

If you happen to work in a corporate environment where innovation is indeed discouraged, nothing that can be suggested here will greatly affect your reality. If creativity and innovation are important to you, perhaps you should think about moving to an emotionally healthier company that welcomes these qualities. In the meantime, however, try to remember two things when you promote an idea or program:

1. If your boss habitually rejects innovation, *he's* the one with a problem, not you. Rejection of innovation is a sign of a very unhealthy manager. Unfortunately, your boss's illness also becomes your problem.

2. Painful as rejection can be, it is not really as painfully final as that "shot-down" figure of speech would suggest. I do not mean to minimize the bad feelings that rejection produces, but they are, after all, only feelings. They shouldn't be given the fiery gravity of death in aerial combat. You won't burst into flame.

TIP

What if you really *are* working for a company in which innovation can seriously threaten your job? If creativity is important to you, consider taking steps to move on to a different employer.

Bearing in mind that this situation presents a broad range of possible responses depending on varied corporate psychology, let's look at a best-case and worst-case scenario:

Best Case for Advancing Your Idea

The best case is promoting an idea or project to a boss who generally welcomes creativity.

STEP 1:   Prepare thoroughly. The presentation may range from an elaborate proposal prepared in accordance with prescribed company policy to an apparently spur-of-the-moment remark at a meeting. At either extreme, preparation is not only possible, but essential.

STEP 2:   If you present your boss with a ream of research material, give him some guiding remarks:

- "Here is the proposal for . . ."—then be as specific about the name of the project as possible.

- "As you look through the proposal, you might want to take special note of . . ."—then list a small number of *specific* highlights or key issues.

- "I'm especially concerned about . . ." Point out key issues you wish to discuss. Don't emphasize the negative.

- "It's been really exciting working on this, and I'd appreciate all the feedback I can get from you." (The object is not only to convey your own enthusiasm, but to let your boss know how much you value his response.)

STEP 3:   If the introduction of the new idea is done informally, on the spur of the moment, be sure to brief yourself on the agenda of the meeting at which you wish to introduce the idea.

STEP 4:   Arm yourself with notes. When you present an idea, you might preface it with a phrase such as, "This is something that just occurred to me," or "Here's something I think would be worth further thought," or "I just had a thought that might bear working up."

STEP 5:   Secure involvement and commitment from the others: "Help me out with this one," or "What do you think about," "What's your quick take on," and so on.

Worst Case for Advancing Your Idea

In the worst-case scenario, working in an environment that does not routinely welcome innovation, you need to augment these steps with a strategy that seeks to give your boss a tangible stake in your idea or project.

STEP 1:   You need to make your boss see himself as your partner in the project. For example: "As you look through the proposal, you might want to take special note of how I incorporated your thoughts in . . ." Or: "I'd like your take on what I did with the concepts you and I discussed last month."

STEP 2:   Put even more emphasis on the importance of the boss's help: "I'd really be grateful for help with such and such," or "Such and such needs a lot more work. I need your take on it."

STEP 3:   Make team-building statements: "It was great working with you on this."

YOUR SCRIPT: PRESENTING A NEW IDEA

Here's one way to introduce a new idea:

You: I'm very excited that I've completed the prospectus for the travel-book series I mentioned to you the week before last. Here it is. The potential here, I think you'll see, is in the combination of a fresh approach to a tested market and all the advantages of a series: a uniform design and format, a proven stable of authors, and a potentially unlimited number of titles. You'll see that I've run all the numbers here, and I'm confident you'll like what you see.

Now, I've given this a lot of thought, but I could really use your help with issues of format and size. This is one we can really run with.

- Communicate your enthusiasm and attempt to shape the desired degree of receptiveness. However, avoid bullying: "You're out of your mind if you don't go for this!"
- *Concisely* underscore the highlights of the proposal, giving specifics rather than adjectives; objective features rather than subjective attributes.
- Solicit your boss's input to get him on your team.

NEGATIVE RESPONSES TO ANTICIPATE WHEN PRESENTING AN IDEA

1. This one looks like a tough sell to me. I just don't know.

Reply with:
Well, they're all tough sells. What I ask is that you look over the proposal and look over the figures. *Then* let me know how tough it is. I'll trust your take on it.

2. I won't be able to get to this for a while.

Reply with:
I know you're busy here, but I'm confident you'll be excited by what you see in the proposal. It's worth making time for.

3. Look, we're putting all new projects on hold.

Reply with:
Even so, I'm so excited about this one that I'd really like to get your reaction to it and your advice on it—even if we can't act on it immediately.

4. We need to move cautiously. I don't want to rush into anything.

Reply with:

Neither do I. That's why I've taken time with the proposal, and that's why I don't want to rush it by you. I really need to get your response to it. Then I'll give it the time for all the revision and rethinking it may need.

RENEGOTIATING A DEADLINE

Bosses, even the most understanding of bosses, hate excuses, and nothing occasions more excuses than missing a deadline. Now, you might be able to get your boss to accept your excuse, but you will never be able to get her to like it. For that reason, it is best to give up on making excuses. Instead, recognize that extending a deadline is *buying* time, and like anything else you might "purchase," the buying of time is subject to negotiation.

STEP 1: Persuade your boss to "sell" you more time in exchange for value received: "To do the most thorough job possible on this, I'm going to need a week more. I don't think it will do us any good to try to rush it and end up neglecting x, y, and z." Make it clear what the additional time will buy—a more thorough, more satisfactory job.

STEP 2: Advise your boss as soon as possible of a time problem. No one likes to feel backed into a corner, and showing that you are on top of the schedule demonstrates that you are still in control, even if the deadline slips.

STEP 3: Present the problem with the deadline as a simple alteration in schedule rather than as a crisis.

STEP 4: Offer as many alternatives as possible. "I can get x done by Wednesday, y by Friday, and z early next week." Or: "If I postpone x, I can get you y and z by the original deadline." Avoid leaving your boss without choices.

Your script: changing a schedule.

Here's one approach:

You: I need to talk to you about altering the schedule for the XYZ project. All parts of the marketing report are scheduled for completion by March 15. I have enough information now to complete parts one through four by then, but a really thorough job on parts five and six is going to require an additional week of research. I don't see any point in throwing this together when, with a week's more time, I can do the job the way it should be done, and we'll have a document we can reasonably base decisions on.

TIP

Communicate control, the sense that altering a schedule is perfectly routine rather than something done in a hopeless emergency.

Negative responses to anticipate when renegotiating a deadline

1. This is a serious deadline. I need you to move heaven and earth to meet it.

Reply with:

I take the deadline very seriously. That's why I'm talking to you about it now. I can give you a job I'm 75 percent happy with by the deadline. Give me another week, and I can promise 100 percent. Yes, the deadline's serious, but so is the project.

2. How are you guys spending your time down there?

Reply with:

One thing we're doing is thinking through the nature of the project and just how best to use our resources. If we cut corners now, it will cost us time later. That's why I'm asking for the modification of the schedule—to build a solid foundation now, so that we don't have trouble further on. That's my judgment on the matter, and that's what I'm asking for.

3. Can't you move any faster?

Reply with:

Yeah, sure. But I'm not going to be comfortable with the results, and how can I expect you to be confident if I'm not comfortable?

4. Can you guarantee that this will be the last delay?

Reply with:

I can guarantee that we'll do everything possible to ensure that the schedule won't have to be altered again.

ACCEPTING AN ASSIGNMENT

The manner in which you accept an assignment is a lot like how you shake hands. It is an initial act of communication that conveys far more than may be at first apparent. A handshake is a chance to transmit strength, warmth, eagerness, loyalty, a willingness to get the job done. Grip too firmly, and you convey the insecurity of one who feels it necessary to demonstrate dominance. Proffer your hand limply, and you telegraph weakness and hesitation. The way in which you accept an assignment presents similar opportunities and potential hazards.

If you happen to be thrilled with the assignment, your communication task is simple: just go ahead and express your feelings. It will give your boss pleasure to know that he has assigned you something you are excited about doing. It will also give him the feeling that he has chosen the right person for the job.

But what if you have reservations about the assignment? Before you react, you must make an important decision. Do you have a choice about whether you will accept the assignment? If you are in a position to decline, and that is what you wish to do, read the next section. If, however, you decide that you have no choice, it is not necessary to counterfeit joy. What you do need to convey is the message that you will work enthusiastically and professionally to get the job done. Generally, this is all you should convey, and you should do so without qualification.

But what if your reservations run deep? What if you believe the project is doomed to fail?

STEP 1:   Neither feign enthusiastic confidence nor respond with panic-stricken negativity.

STEP 2:   Respond positively, but mention that you'll be back with some questions: "I'll start looking it over right away and be back to you with some questions."

STEP 3:   Give yourself time to review the pros and cons, the benefits and pitfalls of the project before you commit yourself to a definitive response. It is perfectly appropriate to buy time in this case, and it is certainly preferable to boxing yourself in with a thoughtlessly overconfident response on the one hand, or a rejection of the project on the other.

TIP

Even if you finally demonstrate the unfeasibility of an assignment, taking the time to consider it will still have conveyed your willingness to engage the task.

YOUR SCRIPT: ACCEPTING AN ASSIGNMENT

Here are several ways this discussion may go:

1. You: This is a very exciting opportunity. I've been preparing for just this kind of assignment, and I'll get on it immediately. I'm confident that you'll find my performance top-notch.
2. You: I'm prepared to get this under way now, and I know that you will be pleased with the results.
3. You: I'm very pleased that you've given this one to me. I've been wanting to work more closely with you on something, and now I have the opportunity. I look forward to it.
4. I'll look this over right away, and I should be back to you with some questions and issues over the next day or two.

- All of these responses are aimed at communicating enthusiasm and commitment that assure the boss that he has made the right choice.

Responses to Anticipate When Accepting an Assignment

1. Hey, hey. Don't let your enthusiasm run away with you!

Reply with:

I run *with* my enthusiasm. It's what drives me.

2. I'm counting on you.

Reply with:

I know you are, and I won't let you down.

3. Are you sure you're up to this?

Reply with:

You are making the right choice. I've prepared for this kind of assignment, I'm thrilled to get it, and I will make it work.

4. You seem to have some doubts.

Reply with:

What I have are some questions, and I need a day to review the assignment, formulate those questions, and come back to you with them.

5. I'd like to see more enthusiasm.

Reply with:

I'm being careful. I need to review the assignment, and I'll be back to you with any questions I have.

DECLINING AN ASSIGNMENT

You do *not* always have a practical choice about whether or not to accept an assignment. Just how much leeway you do have is something only you can judge at a given time and in a given situation. But observe this rule of thumb:

- If you are uncertain about an assignment, or even if you are certain you want to decline it, under most circumstances it is better to avoid an immediate negative response.

STEP 1: Faced with a distasteful or questionable assignment, respond that you will review it and that you will come back with any questions.

STEP 2: After you have reviewed the assignment, assuming that you are in a practical position to make the choice, decline.

Let's discuss the three ways to turn down an assignment:

1. You may attack the assignment itself, demonstrating that the project is unfeasible or unnecessary.

2. You may argue that, while the project is fine, you are not the best choice for it, either because of lack of qualifications, lack of experience, or because you are a resource better used elsewhere.

3. You may say that you prefer not to take on the project.

Each of these approaches has advantages and dangers. You'll need to exercise judgment.

Here are some guidelines to help you decide which strategy to employ:

- If you can demonstrate that a project is unworkable, you stand to save yourself as well as your company a lot of grief. But be strongly cautioned that the "if" here is a very big one. You should not protest the unworkability of an assignment just because you don't want to undertake it. This will benefit neither you nor your firm. If you are truly convinced that a project is doomed, present your well-reasoned doubts to your boss: "I mentioned that I'd be coming back to you on this project with some questions. I've reviewed the assignment, and, in fact, a number of very sticky points have come up. We'd better discuss and resolve these before we try to get this under way."

TIP

Note the transition from *I* to *we*. Don't deliver this message: "Wow! *You* have really stuck *me* with a turkey." Instead, express yourself this way: "*I* have reviewed the project and have discovered that *we* have problems."

- Don't toss the job back into your boss's lap or to make him feel as if you are shooting him down. It is one thing to criticize a project vigorously if you have been specifically asked to evaluate it. However, if your task was not evaluation but execution, you can safely assume that your boss thinks the assignment a good one and will be protective of it.

- Frame any criticism as positively as possible. Instead of rejecting the project out of hand, allude to "questions," "loose ends," "problems," "sticking points," and so on that need to be "resolved before proceeding." While this indicates that you are still engaged with the project, it also gives your boss an opportunity to acknowledge the difficulties for himself, which is better than your forcing the recognition on him.

What if there is nothing wrong with the project, but you are convinced that it is not right for you or, more accurately, you are not right for it?

STEP 1:   The object here is to get your boss to see things your way in this *single case*, without prompting him to question your competence generally.

STEP 2:   The safest course is to convince him that you are a resource better used on a different project. This, of course, is not always possible.

STEP 3:   If the alternative project strategy is unavailable to you, do not blurt out your lack of qualifications, but begin the process of declining the assignment by securing time to review it, promising to return with questions.

STEP 4:   Return armed with alternatives: "I've reviewed the project, and it seems to me that somebody in special sales would be better positioned to take this on. More than half the project, after all, depends on direct mail."

STEP 5:   Don't dwell on your unsuitability. Focus on suggesting alternatives. Remember, your boss is primarily interested in getting the job done, not in specifically getting *you* to do the job. Nominate someone else for the assignment.

What if there is no alternative? Proceed with caution. The best thing you can do in this case is to make a demonstration of frankness and mature self-evaluation. If you were accepting an assignment, you would do well to bring up some recent past success to suggest that you can achieve the same results now. In declining an assignment, you may also want to bring up a past success:

- First, to suggest your general competence—the present assignment is a *rare* instance for which you are not the right choice
- Second, to contrast the kinds of strengths previously demonstrated with what the present assignment calls for

Even if your work situation permits you sufficient leeway to turn down an assignment at will, it is still best to offer alternatives and to have a good reason for declining an assignment.

TIP

Frame your rejection in terms of doing what's best for the company: "I'd like to take a pass on this one. Somebody like Fredericks can take this kind of thing and really run with it. I'm better at the conceptual end. The project will move faster with someone who's got this stuff down cold."

YOUR SCRIPT: TURNING DOWN AN ASSIGNMENT

Here are a few typical scenarios:

1. You: I've reviewed the project we discussed, and, as I thought, it raises a lot of questions. There are some formidable hurdles we'll have to consider before we get under way. I'd like to go over them with you one by one.

2. You: After thinking this assignment through, I've reached the conclusion that I'm not the most effective choice to get the job done as efficiently as possible. Half the work is technical analysis, and my specialty is *market* analysis. *That's* the part of the job I should be doing. Have you talked to Smith? He's the technical expert. We'd save a lot of time using him on this.

3. You: I've looked at this thoroughly, and I'd like to take a pass on it. It's not the kind of assignment I can really sink my teeth into. I've got some alternatives to suggest, however . . .

TIP

Successful responses *decline* an assignment without *rejecting* it. The key is to provide alternatives.

RESPONSES TO ANTICIPATE WHEN DECLINING AN ASSIGNMENT

1. I *really* want you to do this.

Reply with:

I would be glad to do it, if I didn't think there were people here who could do it more effectively. I strongly feel that my taking on this assignment would not be the best use of our resources.

2. How can you turn something like this down?

Reply with:

It isn't easy, and I'm grateful for the confidence you've shown in me. That's why I'd like us to sit down and review the project once more. Until we've addressed the issues I've mentioned, I can't in good conscience tell you that I can accomplish what we both want from this assignment.

3. I'm not accustomed to being turned down like this.

Reply with:

I'm not turning you down. I'm just suggesting that you reconsider your choice for this assignment.

TAKING A COMPLIMENT—WITH GRACE

This should be easy. Your boss says something nice to you. You thank her. And you're both happy. End of story

For many of us, not quite the end.

If you have a hard time taking a compliment gracefully and comfortably, you're not alone. From childhood, many of us have been admonished to be "modest," and we've been warned that people who get too full of themselves will, sooner or later, fall flat on their faces. Unfortunately, such injunctions against feeling good about our accomplishments don't produce true modesty, but instead make us seem graceless and ungrateful when we are complimented. Learning how to accept a compliment gracefully not only lets us claim our just desserts with poise, dignity, and pleasure, but also allows us to show the appropriate generosity to the person who gave the compliment. And when you're dealing with your boss, that's important.

STEP 1:   Start with thank you. If you add the equivalent of "Coming from you, that really means something," you have a perfectly adequate response.

STEP 2:   Consider using the occasion to build additional goodwill and good feeling between you and your boss. Begin by expressing your pleasure and gratitude. Express your regard for your boss.

STEP 3:   Share the praise with others who deserve it. Name names. Recognize your colleagues and coworkers.

As important as it is to say the right things when you accept a compliment, avoid saying and doing the wrong things:

- Don't "confess" unworthiness. This does not make you look modest. It makes the person who paid you the compliment feel foolish.
- Don't respond with a long speech.

YOUR SCRIPT: ACCEPTING A COMPLIMENT

Here's a typical scenario:

Boss: Hey, Sarah, I want to tell you that I think you've handled Smith's problem very intelligently. That was good work.

You: Thanks. Coming from you, that's a real compliment. If there's one thing I've learned working in this department, it's to put the customer first. You've taught us to be good listeners, and that's the first step in customer relations.

TIP

Accept a compliment by giving a compliment—not just thanks.

RESPONSES TO ANTICIPATE WHEN ACCEPTING A COMPLIMENT

1. You deserve it.

Reply with:

I've had a good example set for me. You've given me a lot of support. It's meant a lot.

2. I don't give praise lightly.

Reply with:

I know you don't. That's why I'm thrilled with your remarks. They mean a great deal to me.

TAKING YOUR LUMPS—WITH DIGNITY

Let's face it: criticism from the boss is at best disturbing and, at worst, intimidating. Nevertheless, while you may never learn to welcome criticism, you can adopt strategies of responding to it in a constructive manner.

STEP 1: Accept criticism as an opportunity. All criticism, even unmerited criticism, is useful to you. Criticism, after all, may actually point out things you are doing ineffectively or poorly—things you could do better.

STEP 2: Fight the impulse to respond defensively. Listen and learn.

STEP 3: Realize that criticism is a perception, nothing more. Objective measurements—sales figures, for example—may indicate that you are doing a fine job, yet your boss may find something to criticize. Does this mean your boss is wrong or an ungrateful jerk? Quite possibly. But that conclusion should not prompt you to ignore the criticism. Explore, with yourself and with your boss, the reasons behind the criticism. Can you do something that will maintain the excellent sales performance you have achieved while also allowing your boss to *perceive* that you are doing a good job?

STEP 4: Do not meekly accept unjust or unfounded criticism, but don't reject it. Learn from it. Learn about creating more positive perceptions.

STEP 5: Seize the opportunity to respond to criticism, to communicate in a way that can strengthen and enhance your relationship with your boss.

STEP 6: While listening to criticism, demonstrate that you are hearing the criticism.

Send the right nonverbal signals to show that the criticism is registering with you:

- Make and maintain eye contact with your boss.
- Monitor your own signals of resistance, such as a hand placed over the mouth or on the forehead as if to shade—and partially conceal—the eyes, or arms folded across the chest. Such gestures are powerful signals of resistance that tell your boss you are determined *not* to hear her.

- If possible, both you and your boss should be seated during the discussion, since standing suggests and promotes face-to-face confrontation.

- If you must stand, it is best to keep your hands at your sides and to avoid the temptation to place your arms akimbo. This suggests defiance and sends a provocative message.

TIP

Your objective is *not* to appear passive, but open, willing to listen, to learn, to change, and to cooperate.

Your script: taking criticism

Some ways to profit from close encounters of the worst kind:

1. **Boss:** I don't want to run you down, but you should have been able to process those orders faster. Your trouble is that you need to delegate responsibility more effectively.

   You: I appreciate what you are saying. I'd be grateful for any advice you can give me on how to expedite these kinds of orders. I'm open to suggestion. I would certainly like to see the orders get out of here faster myself.

2. **Boss:** I have not been entirely pleased with the quality of the work coming out of your department. I want to talk to you about it.

   You: I wasn't aware of a problem, so it is very important that we talk and I get your input.

3. **Boss:** You've got some big, big problems here. A 2.5-percent reject rate is just too high. Let me tell you something, I just won't tolerate it.

   You: I'm aware of the problem, and I'd like to sit down and talk to you about it. I want to hear what you've got to say, and then I'll tell you how I plan to make improvements. It would be very helpful to get your opinion on the steps I plan to take.

TIP

Your boss may actually be spoiling for a confrontation. In all cases, your best verbal strategy is to avoid confrontation without, however, evading the underlying issues. Engage the issues rather than personalities. If you feel hurt, offended, or threatened, you'll just have to put those feelings on hold while you engage the issues.

RESPONSES TO ANTICIPATE WHEN TAKING CRITICISM

1. Look, you'd better shape up here.

Reply with:

I've heard your observations, and I need to review the problems you've pointed out. I'll come back to you with a plan that addresses these difficulties.

2. Generally, you do a fine job, but I hope that you can show improvement in the areas we discussed.

Reply with:

Well, your observations have been very helpful, and I'm confident that the problems you've noted can be resolved.

3. I hope you don't feel I'm picking on you.

Reply with:

If this is being picked on, I can use it. I need all the feedback I can get. To be frank, I don't agree with everything you've said, but you have given me a lot to think about. I'll review my methods and make some changes I think you will like.

4. I need to see significant improvement.

Reply with:

So do I. Let me review the situation. I have to say that my initial reaction is that you are overstating the degree of the problem, but I do agree that my department can perform at a higher level, and I will do everything possible to achieve that level. I appreciate your input, and we will do better. That I can promise you.

HANDLING SNAFU SITUATIONS

What was said about taking criticism applies as well to handling snafu situations. Yes, they're bad. No, nobody *wants* things to go wrong. But just about everything that happens in the workplace is an opportunity for communication, and communication can enhance relations between you and your boss.

- Most mistakes are not fatal or even beyond repair. Often, the more serious problem is the *feelings* mishaps produce. These can be truly destructive. Effective communication can minimize such damaging effect. In many cases, skillful communication can even produce positive feelings.

Accidents and errors contain at least one valuable element: the opportunity for forgiveness. If some of us derive satisfaction from affixing blame, it feels even better to forgive.

TIP

In apologizing for accidents and errors, never tell your boss (or anyone else, for that matter) how he or she should feel about it.

We'll deal with five major types of snafus, but all may be approached with the same basic strategy:

STEP 1:   Acknowledge the error.

STEP 2:   Let your boss know that he would be justified in getting angry, then thank him for his understanding and patience.

STEP 3:   Make positive suggestions for working together to repair any damage.

When the Problem Is Your Fault

Report the error as soon as possible, since it's better coming from you than if your boss discovers it on his own or, even worse, some third party makes the revelation.

STEP 1:   Do not run into the office in panic. The emotions you telegraph will strongly affect how your boss receives and interprets the news.

STEP 2:   Try to take time first to assess the nature and degree of the error.

STEP 3:   Try to prepare proposals for controlling and repairing the damage.

Armed with possible solutions, report the problem. However, it is not always the best idea to volunteer your assessment of the degree of damage. Use judgment before you deliver your assessment.

- An immediate assessment may be necessary for the good of the project or the company.
- If possible, however, report the particulars of error minimally. There is a strategic advantage in giving your boss the feeling that he is assessing the error for himself rather than having to take your "biased" version of it.

TIP

If you deliver a full report, try to go about it objectively. Avoid extremes— either bending over backwards to excusing yourself or beating your breast in a headlong rush to take all the blame.

Follow this overall plan:

1. Pause to assess the error.
2. Prepare potential remedies.
3. Report the error as concisely as circumstances allow.
4. Admit fault.
5. Acknowledge your boss's right to be angry.
6. Thank him for his patience and understanding.
7. Promise cooperation and swift action.

When It's Not Your Fault

When you encounter an accident or error for which you are not at fault, do not walk away from responsibility.

STEP 1:   If possible, find the person who is responsible for the problem and discuss the matter with him as helpfully as you can, always focusing on constructive solutions rather than on blame.

STEP 2:   If it is impossible or impractical to identify the responsible person, and assuming it is a problem you cannot address and solve entirely by yourself or on your own authority, report it to your boss.

TIP

Beware of two harmful tendencies when we report problems caused by others: We tend to exaggerate the seriousness of the problem. We also tend to harbor a certain self-satisfaction.

- The key strategy here is neither to ignore nor to revel in problems caused by others but, rather, to try to discover the opportunity within the problem.

It is to your advantage if your boss perceives you as a problem solver. You *need* a problem. Find one, report it, and suggest solutions.

It's Not Your Fault, But It Is Your Problem

Subordinates and others may cause problems for which you are not directly responsible, but which are, nevertheless, your problems.

STEP 1:   If you can handle such problems immediately, efficiently, and effectively without resorting to higher authority, by all means do so. Reporting such errors and accidents can be a delicate and tricky matter.

STEP 2:   When you must make a report, communicate your adherence to Harry Truman's universally respected motto: *The buck stops here.* You may assess fault—your subordinate failed to do something, a supplier failed to deliver, and so on—but you *must* demonstrate your willingness to take ultimate responsibility.

STEP 3:   Turn the event into something positive with a strong response that tells your boss that you are a problem solver.

When You're Baffled

It's bad enough when problems or errors occur. Bad as this is, it can get worse. Sometimes things go wrong for—as far as you can tell—no particular reason at all. You're baffled. You're in an uncomfortable spot. If you cannot get an immediate handle on the problem, you cannot instantly demonstrate mastery of the situation. This may scare you, and it certainly won't make your boss happy.

What you need is an ally.

And who would that be?

Your boss.

STEP 1:   Admit the difficulty calmly: "I need your help." This simple phrase is practically a magic formula, which even the hardest-hearted boss will find difficult to resist. "I need your help. We are missing three customer files. I don't know why, and I don't know where they could be. Rather than waste more time hunting for them, I'd like to call the clients. How do I do it without embarrassing us?"

TIP

Don't *dump* the problem in your boss's lap, but do enlist his aid. Suggest as much of a course of action as you can, but don't try to go it alone. Transform the situation from *I* to *we*. Work out a solution together.

What To Do When a Project Fails

Mistakes, errors, glitches. They happen. So does failure. A product line you've developed doesn't sell, a client you've courted doesn't buy, a contract you've angled for goes to someone else. In cases like this, depending on your employer and your track record, your job may or may not be on the line. Your ego, however, *certainly* is. And it is very hard to communicate strongly and positively when you are feeling bad about yourself. Yet it is essential that you do just that, salvaging whatever you can from the wreckage.

Much that you salvage is valuable. At the least, you may gather information that will help you learn from your mistakes. What you are salvaging—saving—is the future. And it is the future that constitutes the core of your strategy when you confront your boss in the wake of failure.

STEP 1:   Avoid such phrases as "should have," "wish I had," "if I had only," and so on.

STEP 2:   Use phrases like "next time," "in the future," "we"—not "I"—
           "learned a lesson for the future," "we won't do it this way next
           time," and so on.

STEP 3:   Accept responsibility for the present, but hold on to the future:
           potential and opportunity.

Your script: dealing with failure.

Here are some viable approaches:

1. **You:** I made a mistake in the report I submitted to our client. The figures for items two and seven are wrong. I tried to catch the documents
   before they went out of here, but I was too late. I've prepared a corrected report with a cover letter that I'd like you to read. Assuming you
   approve, I'll send this to our client by messenger. I'll call them to tell
   them it's coming. In the future, I see, we're just going to have to build
   in a full day's proofreading and fact-checking time.

   * This is the forthright approach. Error is admitted, and no excuses are
     offered. Nor is there any wallowing in guilt. The emphasis is on what
     to do in the future.

2. **You:** The figures are in on the client's promotional program. I'd be
   lying if I said I wasn't disappointed in the performance of what I
   thought would be a big sale. We worked hard on this, and it's rough
   on us all when things don't turn out as we had hoped and expected.
   I'd like to schedule a meeting with you to review the project and see
   what we can learn from it. I don't want to be disappointed the next
   time we promote our client's product.

   * In this approach, there is a willingness to learn. No excuses are offered,
     but perspective is maintained.

Responses to anticipate when admitting failure.

1. Don't be too hard on yourself.

Reply with:

Thanks. I appreciate that. Don't worry. I know that tearing myself up is not
going to keep this kind of thing from happening again. What I want to do

is take a good, hard look at the problem, analyze it, learn from it, and then discuss it with you.

2. Frankly, you're not being hard enough on yourself. You're letting yourself off too easy, I'm afraid.

Reply with:

I take full responsibility for what happened. If I thought an elaborate demonstration of remorse would do anything for our bottom line, I'd be in here with a cat-o'-nine-tails. I promise you that I will be very hard on whatever caused this error. That's what I'll devote my energy to. We won't let it happen again.

COMMUNICATING YOUR DECISION TO QUIT

Termination of employment—whether voluntary or not—shouldn't bring communication to an end. Depending on what you do for a living, the business world can be quite small, and it is possible that you and your boss will cross paths again. You may even return to the firm. Termination can be a positive event; don't let your words make it negative. But even when termination comes under bad circumstances, don't turn a bad thing into something even worse. Use words to keep your termination as open-ended as possible.

Quitting—either you make a decision to go into business for yourself or you've found another job.

- Before you announce your resignation, *think*. Do you absolutely want to quit?
- Or do you want to use the job offer you've just gotten as a bargaining chip with your present company?

Unless you are firmly bent on leaving, you should approach the "terminal" conversation *as if* you are willing to entertain (or are even seeking) a counteroffer from your boss.

STEP 1: Avoid beginning with something like, "I have accepted an offer from . . ." Instead, start with "I have *received* an offer from. . . . "

STEP 2: Give the particulars, including money and other conditions that make the offer attractive.

STEP 3:   Even if you are certain that you don't want to use the offer as leverage in your present position—that what you want is *out*, period—don't rush to slam the verbal doors behind you.

STEP 4:   Regardless of your reasons for leaving and your feelings about the job and the boss you are leaving, your "terminal" conversation should be framed as positively as possible. Don't lie, but do avoid concentrating on the negative reasons that have motivated your decision. Emphasize the positive: "I've decided to accept a position that offers me the kind of opportunities for advancement that, at least for now, we can't match here."

TIP

Use phrases such as "at least for now" or "at this time" to keep the door ever so slightly ajar. The object is not to soften the blow of your departure, but to demonstrate that you are a valuable person, a business asset, and that you are fully aware of your value.

STEP 5:   Plan your departure carefully, so that you can offer your boss something more than good words. Make it clear that you will do everything possible to ease the transition for your replacement. Engineering a smooth transition will go a long way toward defusing any smoldering resentment.

Your script: quitting your job

Some parting scenarios:

1. **You:** This is the hardest thing I've ever had to say to you, so I better just come out and say it. I've been offered a position as senior analyst with XYZ at a salary of $XX,000. As you know, that's more than we're in a position to ante up here. Add to that the way management is structured over there—well, I've got a faster track to account executive than what might be offered here. This place has been like family to me, but for the sake of my career I don't see how I can turn down the offer.

   • This is a good example of an opening that reflects a sincere intention to leave the company, coupled with equally sincere regrets about doing so, yet leaves the door ajar for a possible counteroffer.

2. **You:** I've been approached by XYZ Products with an offer of a position as assistant sales manager. I haven't said yes yet, but I've got to tell you that it is a very attractive offer—despite the loyalty I feel to our company and to you personally. The salary is XX percent higher, and the opportunities for advancement seem considerably greater. They want me to start in four weeks.

- This leaves the door open wider, more deliberately inviting a counter-offer.

3. **You:** I've worked here six years, and during that time I've gotten very close to a lot of people, including you. That's why it's not easy for me to tell you that I am accepting an offer from XYZ Printing Company as a press manager. The money, the hours, and the job security are just too inviting to pass up. Even with all that, it's a hard decision. I've learned a lot here, but it is time to move on to a position of broader responsibility.

- This approach closes the door firmly, though not rudely. Unless your boss is very devoted to you, this type of announcement will garner no counteroffer.

RESPONSES TO ANTICIPATE WHEN YOU QUIT

1. What would it take to make you change your mind?

Reply with:

I'll admit it. I would love it if you could make it impossible for me to take the offer. [Then list what you want: salary, hours, vacation, working conditions, position, etc.] That's what I would need to turn down the offer in good conscience.

2. You *can't* leave at a time like this.

Reply with:

I know this isn't the best time for the company. But it is when the offer came. For me, it is a case of act now or miss the opportunity, and this is an opportunity I cannot afford to miss. I've got three weeks. You have my assurance that I'll do whatever is necessary to ease the transition for you.

3. I feel betrayed. Stabbed in the back.

Reply with:

I'm sorry you feel that way. You must know that my leaving has nothing to do with you or with the company. It's a matter of opportunity for me. I don't see this as leaving ABC Company, but as doing what is necessary to build my career. If I could do it as effectively by staying, I would. It is very hard for me to leave.

4. I've enjoyed working with you, and I wish you the best of luck.

Reply with:

Thanks. Coming from you, that means a great deal to me. I know that we'll be staying in touch, and I am grateful to you for having made this a rewarding experience.

HOW TO RESPOND WHEN YOU'RE FIRED

People tell you that getting fired is not the end of the world. But when it comes, it might as well be. Your emotions may overwhelm you—feelings of failure, embarrassment, anger, and fear.

- The fact is that people are fired every day. It is a normal—not inevitable, but normal—phase of the employment cycle. Almost certainly, you will survive the experience, and you might even get a better job.

For the moment, your objective is to achieve effective verbal management—no small task when you are assailed by powerful emotions. Your strategy should be to make it possible for your boss to leave the door open—even just a crack—after she hands you your walking papers. How feasible that objective is depends on why you've been dismissed. If it's "for cause"—failure to do your assigned job, misconduct, excessive absenteeism, poor performance, and so on—the going will be rough. More often, however, dismissal comes as a result of economic conditions, corporate reorganization, or phase-out of a program. In these cases, do what you can to make reentry possible.

TIP

Dismissal for cause does not usually come out of the blue. It generally follows warnings and employee conferences. If you feel that you are being treated unjustly, plan to seek counsel from the appropriate union or professional or governmental agency. You may want to secure legal advice as well. At the time of dismissal, it is generally best to threaten nothing. Do, however, make clear your position that you are being treated unfairly, that you have endeavored to perform well for the company, and that you feel you deserve better treatment. You might ask, quite straightforwardly, if there is an alternative course available: temporary separation during a review process, for example.

STEP 1:   In cases where the dismissal is made without prejudice, perhaps even with regret, because of economic or other circumstances, respond by letting your boss know that while she has fired you, you have not dismissed her. You are greatly dismayed by the news, of course, since you have found working here such a rewarding experience.

STEP 2:   Determine, in conversation with your boss, whether the dismissal is permanent or temporary. Might you expect to be hired in this or another capacity at another time?

TIP

Beware of prompting false hope from the boss. She may tell you what you want to hear because she finds the experience of letting you go painful.

STEP 3:   Ask what circumstances would make continuation of this position—or hiring in another position—possible.

YOUR SCRIPT: HANDLING TERMINATION.

Some ideas for making the final scene less final:

1. **Boss:** I'm afraid that, due to corporate restructuring, we're going to have to let you go, effective two weeks from today. I wish there were something I could do about it.

You: I don't have to tell you, this is a shock. Let me digest this news for a day or two, and then I'd like to discuss the situation with you.

- If you have some advance warning, it is best to delay your response rather than stammer something while you are under the most pressure. When you return later for a conversation, raise the possibility of alternatives to dismissal or layoff, discuss the permanence of the layoff, and go over with your boss ways in which she is willing to help you find another job.

2. **Boss:** As you know, we have not been satisfied with your performance. I'm afraid at this point I have no choice but to let you go. The severance is effective immediately. I've prepared a severance check for you.

   You: I would be lying if I told you this is entirely unexpected. I had hoped, however, that we could work out some alternative to dismissal. I've enjoyed working here, and I believe I've given this company a lot. Since your decision does seem final, I'll leave without further discussion—except to tell you that you are losing an able, skilled, and loyal employee.

- When there is obviously no room to maneuver, leave with dignity, including a statement meant to set the record straight.

3. **Boss:** It's clear we're not getting along together, so I've decided to terminate our working relationship, effective two weeks from today.

   You: I am sorry you feel this way and, of course, even sorrier that you feel you must take such an extreme action. Since your decision seems to be based on feeling, it would help me very much if we could talk again before I leave. It would also be very helpful—and, I think, appropriate—if you could put your reasons for my dismissal more concretely and specifically, perhaps in the form of a letter. I have enjoyed working here, and I sincerely believe that I am good for this company. I don't want to leave without knowing exactly what went wrong.

- This response accomplishes three things: It leaves the door slightly ajar. It does not let your boss off the hook so easily, but compels her to review her decision. And it underscores your commitment to the firm.

RESPONSES TO ANTICIPATE WHEN YOU'VE BEEN FIRED

1. We have nothing further to discuss.

Reply with:

I don't agree. Other than knowing that you are somehow dissatisfied with my performance, I have very little idea of why I'm being fired. That is what we have to discuss, and I would like to discuss it.

2. I can't hold out much hope for another job here soon.

Reply with:

I'm not asking for much hope. I want to leave here with good feelings on all sides, and I want you to know that, no matter where I go from here, I'm always eager to hear of opportunities at XYZ.

3. The matter is closed.

Reply with:

For you it may be, but I have a lot of questions without answers. I would like to ask them, and I would like to hear the answers. I don't intend to argue. I just want to find out what went wrong.

CHAPTER 5

Putting Yourself Across . . . to Colleagues

SELF-TEST YOUR SAVVY IN COMMUNICATING WITH COLLEAGUES

The following is a simple diagnostic test. A smaller and more selective version of the self-test in Chapter 1, its purpose is not to test your knowledge of communication theory or techniques, but to help you gauge how effectively you communicate with your colleagues in a day-to-day business context. For the most part, you will find it easy to guess the "right" answer. But getting the "right" answer is not the point of the test. Respond honestly, even if you feel that your response is not the best one possible. This is *not* a contest. The object is solely self-inventory.

1. There's a lot of backstabbing that goes on where I work. T/F ____

2. I am open with my colleagues. T/F ____

3. I am pretty effective at getting my colleagues to cooperate with me. T/F ____

4. I am afraid my colleagues will steal my ideas. T/F ____

5. I ask my colleagues about what interests and concerns *them*. T/F ____

6. My colleagues respect me. T/F ____

7. My colleagues are jealous of me. T/F ____

8. I criticize issues and actions rather than people. T/F ____

9. I criticize only what I believe can be remedied, improved, or eliminated. T/F ____

10. I criticize constructively.   T/F ____

11. A dispute has a winner and a loser.   T/F ____

12. I don't make waves.   T/F ____

13. I dread making apologies.   T/F ____

14. I drink *lots* of coffee.   T/F ____

15. I enjoy the people I work with.   T/F ____

16. I enjoy conversation with my colleagues.   T/F ____

17. I feel like part of a team.   T/F ____

18. I get plenty of sleep.   T/F ____

19. I'm good at "brainstorming."   T/F ____

20. I handle stress well.   T/F ____

21. I have "championed" projects and ideas.   T/F ____

22. I have a happy home life.   T/F ____

23. I know my colleagues and their jobs, duties, and areas
    of expertise.   T/F ____

24. Our office is *very* political.   T/F ____

25. The people I work with waste my time with too much talk. T/F ____

26. I share ideas with my colleagues.   T/F ____

27. If someone gets angry, I tell them to calm down.   T/F ____

28. I think business meetings are a waste of time.   T/F ____

29. I try to respond fully and informatively to my colleagues'
    ideas and projects.   T/F ____

30. I usually get my way.   T/F ____

31. Sometimes you just have to holler and argue the
    other person down.   T/F ____

TOTAL T/F   ____

Score 1 point for each "True" response and 0 for each "False" response, EXCEPT for questions 1, 4, 7, 11, 12, 13, 14, 24, 25, 27, 28, and 31. For *these questions only*, SUBTRACT 1 point for each "True" response. Record your total. A score below +17 indicates that you would benefit from practicing the communication techniques discussed in this chapter. (Note: It is possible to have a negative score.)

WORDS TO USE WITH COLLEAGUES

adapt	merge
admire	modify
advice	objective
advise	open
agree	opinion
collaborate	our
combine	respect
confer	results
consult	rethink
contribute	reveal
contribution	revise
cooperate	straightforward
data	study
differ	suggestion
disagree	synergy
efficiency	talk
efficient	team
facts	tell me
feasible	thought
goal	thoughts
handshake	together
honest	us
input	we
may I	

PHRASES TO USE WITH COLLEAGUES

constructive criticism

get your opinion

get your take on

great idea

How would you like me to proceed?

let's talk about it

let's work it out together

pick your brain

seek your advice

team effort

value your opinion

value your thoughts

What do you need?

What would you like me to do?

work together

work this out

WORDS TO AVOID WITH COLLEAGUES

absurd

bad

can't

crazy

doomed

failure

impossible

incompetent

insane

refuse

ridiculous

stupid

unworkable

wrong

wrong-headed

PHRASES TO AVOID WITH COLLEAGUES

Are you out of your mind?

bad idea

don't know what you're doing

don't know what you're talking about

don't know your job

no good

won't work

you wouldn't understand

you're crazy

BODY-LANGUAGE STRATEGY FOR COLLEAGUES

The key element of body-language strategy in successfully working with colleagues is to establish openness. Look and act approachable. Generally, the more communication you invite, the better.

- Walk with arms at your sides.
- Smile.
- Make eye contact.
- Use open hand gestures—palms slightly upturned.

BODY LANGUAGE TO AVOID WITH COLLEAGUES

If the key strategic element is openness, obviously any postures and gestures that communicate standoffishness should be avoided.

Avoid:

- Walking with hands in pockets
- Walking with arms crossed
- Walking with head down; this suggests that you are "lost in thought" and do not want to be disturbed

- Averting eye contact
- Frowning
- Lip biting
- Gesturing with hands near mouth or face
- Shaking head "no"
- Pushing gestures—using the hands as if to push people or things away
- Sitting with hands to head

HOW EVERYONE CAN WIN WHEN COMMUNICATING WITH COLLEAGUES

Putting yourself across to your colleagues is more than just getting along with people—although that element is essential, and the body-language strategies just discussed will go a long way toward conveying, nonverbally, that "get-along" message. Beyond this, successful, persuasive communication with colleagues also requires creating an atmosphere in which everyone feels that something has been gained. Everyone needs to be a winner. If you look at communicating with colleagues as a zero-sum game, in which someone must lose if someone else wins, you make effective colleague communication almost impossible. If talking to you means losing, few will venture down that road.

Setting up a win-win communication environment depends on four principles:

1. *Demonstrate respect for your colleagues.*   You can think of this as the Golden Rule: Do unto your colleague as you would have him or her do unto you. Listen to coworkers. Hear what they have to say. Then demonstrate that you have heard them and that you value what they say.

TIP

Respect for colleagues may be shown in many ways, big and small. But it is the small gestures that are often the most cumulatively effective. Make clear how you value what your colleagues say by punctuating conversations with such phrases as "That's interesting," "It's worth thinking about," "I never thought of that before," "I see," and so on.

2. *Establish ground rules, define responsibilities, and refine and modify these definitions as necessary.* Human beings are territorial animals. Much workplace hostility and many barriers to communication are "turf" disputes. Indeed, it is amazing how many companies misuse—and also frustrate—their human resources by failing adequately to define responsibilities and areas of authority. This can happen even when so-called official job descriptions exist.

Create a relatively threat-free atmosphere by openly discussing your responsibilities and "turf" areas. Understand them and agree on them. Be sufficiently flexible to alter them as the demands of your business may require.

TIP

Consensus on responsibility is a key not only to efficient operation, but to successful ongoing communication.

3. *Don't suffer in silence. When necessary, "sound your horn."* Avoid unpleasant, even hurtful, encounters with coworkers by alerting them to any problems they may be causing you. If something bothers you, discuss it in a calm but firm and unmistakable way—a way that educates and informs rather than scolds or threatens.

4. *Make creative small talk.* Contrary to what all too many managers believe, small talk in the workplace need not be a waste of time. Indeed, it can be an important medium through which coworkers bond into an effective team by learning to appreciate and respect one another as human beings, not just as job titles. Demonstrate an interest in your fellow workers by asking about families, hobbies, interests, and outside activities. Small talk builds morale and improves cohesiveness.

TIP

Don't let small talk get out of hand. When enough is enough, and it's time to get down to the task at hand, terminate the small talk by politely and specifically pointing out what you have to do. Avoid saying, "Bill, I've got work to do." Instead, try: "Tom, you'll have to excuse me, but the XYZ report has got to get done by the ten o'clock meeting." If you don't have a pressing task, cite one that is as specific as possible: "Bill, I'm just settling down to catching up on my mail. Let's talk later."

SECRETS OF GETTING BIG RESULTS FROM SMALL TALK

"So now I have to *learn* to shoot the breeze?"

Of course not. But you may find useful some advice on shooting the breeze *effectively*. By "effectively" I mean using casual, day-to-day small talk to

- Help build a team.
- Establish and strengthen your position among your colleagues.
- Give you leverage to enable you to secure support and compliance.
- Generally make the workplace more harmonious.

All this from "shooting the breeze"?

Not quite. If you enjoy making conversation, ask yourself why. If the answer—the *honest* answer—is that you like to hear other people talk so that you can learn about them, congratulations. You are already well on your way to making *effective* small talk. But if most people answered this question honestly, they would say that their pleasure in small talk derives from hearing *themselves* talk. Now, there is nothing terribly wrong with this. Why shouldn't you get pleasure from holding court? But if you want to harness the power of small talk to enhance your position and influence among your colleagues and to improve the work environment, you're going to have give up some of that listening to yourself and start devoting more of your small-talk time to hearing others.

The easiest way to begin is to reduce the number of declarative sentences you utter and to increase the number of questions you ask.

Let's say you run into Joe Schmidt from accounting in the hall. You like Joe. Ordinarily, you might say something like this: "Hey, Joe! Listen, I just saw a movie over the weekend that you've got to get yourself to . . ." Friendly, warm—nothing wrong with that. But here's a more effective approach to small talk in the workplace: "Hey, Joe! Do you like movies?"

Now, let Joe talk. Let him tell you something about himself.

Is this just being polite? Well, it *is* considerate, and if being polite is making other people feel good, it certainly is true that showing interest in another person usually creates good feelings.

But asking questions is more than being polite. You already know what *you* like and don't like. You already know about yourself. You already know what you want and don't want. You already understand which are your hot buttons. Why waste valuable small-talk time going over what you already know? Instead, use it to learn something new.

Knowledge, the well-worn cliché goes, *is power*. The more you know about Joe Schmidt, the stronger your basis for communication with him.

- Small talk can be the key that unlocks the needs, wants, wishes, thoughts, and inclinations of those with whom you work. The more you know about your colleagues, the more effectively you can communicate with them.

Remember, effective communication—which, at its most effective, we call *persuasion*—depends on a perception of gain. It is difficult to persuade someone to act in a certain way or to do something if that person feels either that he will not gain from compliance or, even worse, will lose as a result of compliance. It is, therefore, to your advantage to appeal to the self-interest of others. Small talk can help you learn about that self-interest.

TIP

Use small talk to learn about your colleagues—what drives them, what upsets them, what pleases them, what interests them. Don't squander small talk on yourself—your own interests and needs.

GETTING INFORMATION OR HELP FROM COLLEAGUES

On a day-to-day basis, what you need most frequently from your colleagues is information and help. But before you ask for information or help, you need to identify the best sources. This may be obvious to you, but if it is not, ask yourself the following questions:

1. Who does what job?
2. Who seems to command influence and enjoy respect?
3. Who seems to be "in the loop"—communicating with upper levels of management most frequently and effectively?
4. Who has been climbing the corporate ladder?
5. Who answers questions frequently?
6. Who is frequently quoted?

7. Who makes the key decisions?

8. Who writes the significant memos?

9. Who runs the meetings?

Identify these people, get to know them, and cultivate them as your primary sources of information and aid.

Asking for information or help is, of course, *taking* rather than *giving*. So you need to find something to give in return for information and help. What you can always give is your interest.

STEP 1:   Cultivate the people you identify as key by taking an interest in what they do and say.

STEP 2:   Engage them in conversation about what interests them.

STEP 3:   If you run across an article or memo concerning a subject of interest to them, copy it or clip it and send it along to them.

STEP 4:   Building on the key person's interests is a great way to build an information-sharing and helping relationship.

Accelerate the development of the information-sharing relationship by *asking* for a conversation rather than demanding help or information. Use such phrases as:

- "I'd like a chance to speak with you."
- "What's a good time to talk about something?"
- "I need to find out ____, and I'd really like to talk to you about it. What's a convenient time for you?"
- "Mind if I pick your brain?"

SECRETS OF SUCCESSFUL MEETINGS

In business, it's difficult to make any statement that doesn't invite disagreement. Make this one, however, and you're likely to get closer to universal agreement than you ever thought possible:

Most meetings are a waste of time.

In fact, the chorus of assent is likely to be interrupted by only one thing: a call to the second, third, or fourth meeting of the day. The masochistic irony of it all is that, even while most of us decry and deride meetings, we call for them, set them up, attend them, and endure them, all the while complaining that, really, the best ideas come from informal discussions held in the corridor.

Well, sometimes that's true. And sometimes—maybe even most times—formal meetings are boring and unproductive.

But there is a big problem with corridor spontaneity. It's just so—well—*spontaneous*. You can't control it. You can't summon it up at will. Potentially, the greatest advantage a formal meeting offers is a forum and format for "forcing" spontaneity. Used this way, meetings can be transformed from hollow time wasters to exciting generators of ideas. You can work with your colleagues to effect this transformation. Here are some techniques:

1. *Problem polling.*   Gather an impromptu meeting in a room with a blackboard or the equivalent. Ask the participants to call out the problems and issues of greatest concern to them. Have someone write them on the board. Do not discuss the problems or issues. Do not analyze. Do not interrupt the flow until the flow stops. Then restate each concern in positive terms. For instance: "I'm worried about quality control" becomes "Our objective is to improve quality control in order to reduce returns by 15 percent."

2. *Brainstorming.*   This is a tried-and-tested method for generating ideas. It works in small peer groups—usually of eight participants or fewer. Define an issue, then ask for ideas. You objective is quantity rather than quality. Allow no discussion of the ideas. Allow no judgment or criticism or, for that matter, praise. Have someone write each of the ideas on a blackboard. After the flow of ideas peters out, begin to analyze the ideas, focusing on how to establish criteria for judging the value of each idea. In this way, you should be able to winnow the welter of ideas down to a few viable ones.

3. *Small-group discussion.*   Break larger groups into small groups (four participants is a good number), each of which is assigned a particular problem or issue to discuss. Appoint a leader of each group, whose job it is to keep the talk focused. Another participant should record the results of the discussion. After a period of time, reconvene the smaller groups into a larger group and ask the recorders to share the results of the individual discussions.

PROMOTING AN IDEA OR PROJECT TO YOUR COLLEAGUES

Whether within the context of a single meeting or a series of meetings, the key to promoting a project or an idea is to get your colleagues—not just your supervisors—to invest in it, to claim a stake in it. The successful devel-opment of ideas and projects requires a champion, someone willing to fight for the idea or project, pushing it through, over, and around the many orga-nizational and human obstacles that threaten to mire it in the muck of iner-tia. From among the ranks of colleagues and coworkers, the champion recruits "investors" in the idea or project.

What Is a Champion?

In the early 1950s, the U.S. Navy solicited proposals for the development of the Sidewinder missile. The Navy generated a long and stringent list of specifications. What William B. McLean, the physicist in charge of a missile-development team at the Naval Weapons Center, China Lake, California, understood, however, is that specifications suffer from a serious drawback: They force both customer and would-be contractor to presume they know the answers before they have any experience with the product. McLean, a scien-tist, wanted to get the answers first. Accordingly, he sheltered the Sidewinder program from internal critics and even from the "customer"—the U.S. Navy. He ignored the specs as issued and concentrated instead on developing con-cepts that his own actual experiments indicated would work.

McLean carried out these experiments on his own time, in his garage, in effect designing about 85 percent of the missile himself. Working with-in—as well as around—"The System," he scrounged money from other pro-jects, and he scavenged spare parts from wherever he could, including junk-yards in and around Pasadena. Once he developed a prototype, it failed. Actually, it failed 13 times—more than enough to kill the project. In fact, the Sidewinder officially ceased to exist. But McLean persisted, taking what he had learned from the 13 "failures" to make modifications and launch one more test, on September 11, 1953, which landed right on target. As quickly as it had been officially killed, the Sidewinder was officially reborn, and the Navy took an interest.

But now the Air Force balked. Not to be daunted, the Sidewinder's champion proposed a "shoot out" against the Air Force's favored Falcon missile. The challenge was accepted, the contest took place, and the Sidewinder won. First tested in 1953, it remains a key part of the U.S. arsenal, a weapon of incredible longevity. And it owes its existence to the man who championed it.

YOUR SCRIPT: CHAMPIONING AN IDEA

Here is an exchange in which a "champion" recruits a colleague "investor":

Champion: Sue, before we go into this meeting, I'd like to give you some advance information on the new widget idea. This is information you should have before it goes to a general discussion.

Note the approach. "Advance information" is made available exclusively to Sue. This makes her feel that her opinion is truly valued, that she is perceived as a special and powerful person within the company. This is a much more effective approach than simply saying "I need your support." "I need your support" is *asking* for something, whereas providing "advance information" is *giving* something.

Note also the phrase "the new widget idea." The champion avoids the possessive pronoun *my* and is careful to substitute the neutral article *the*. The object is to avoid laying claim to the idea or project. You want the "investor" to feel that she has a personal stake in the proposal.

Sue: Well, thanks. I'll look it over.

Champion: Great. This really needs not just your support, but your tender loving care. It needs your expertise. I want you in at a stage where you can contribute to shaping the project. Also, I know that, with you behind it, this thing will sail through the meeting to the next stage.

The champion continues to stress the value of Sue's involvement. She will make a genuine contribution. This is team building.

TIP

The champion must choose his allies wisely. Keep the group small enough to promote "ownership" of the project. A small group of "investors" is most effective in building reception of the project to critical mass, at which point consensus kicks in, and the project is in the best position to gain the support of management.

HANDLING DISSENT FROM YOUR COLLEAGUES

Working well with your colleagues is hardly about avoiding disputes, and when you champion an idea or project, you can count on at least some opposition. The key strategy here is not to suppress opposition, to ignore it, or to beat it down. Instead:

STEP 1:   Identify issues on which you differ and then separate these issues from the personalities behind them.

STEP 2:   Pit issue against issue, not personality against personality or ego against ego.

TIP

Focusing on opposing points of view on a particular issue or problem will not, of course, magically resolve the dispute, but it is essential to molding a cooperative team out of disparate personalities. Team members may have differing views, but they must be committed to common goals. Assuming your project goes into development, you do not want it subject at some later stage to sabotage, whether deliberate or unconscious, by disgruntled colleagues.

STEP 3:   In the course of a dispute, work toward shifting the focus from the disagreement to some alternative or set of alternatives on which agreement can be reached. Bring about a shift from a negative to a positive.

YOUR SCRIPT: HANDLING DISSENT

Colleague: Look, you're just out of your mind if you think the consumer will pay $25 for this widget.

The bait has been offered: "Out of your mind" is a provocative, offensive, and personal attack. You can take the bait and pitch the argument at an unproductive, even destructive, personal level, or you can shift the dispute productively to *issues*.

You: So you think the price point is wrong for the market?

No emotional, personal words here. Just business: "price point," "market." Note that the possessive pronoun *my* is also absent: not "my price point," but "*the* price point."

Colleague: That's right. Your idea will never sell.

The other fellow persists in keeping it personal: "*your* idea." Refocus.

You: Let's forget about the price point for just a minute. What about the product? What's your take on that?

Still refusing to take the bait, you look for some point of agreement.

Colleague: The product is fine—great—but what good is it if we can't sell it at $25?

With this point of agreement, you've got something to build on.

You: Maybe we *can* lower it. What if we increase initial rollout . . .

And so on. The keys to handling dissent are:

1. Keep the focus on the issues and away from egos.
2. Look for areas of agreement. Build on these.

But isn't point number two just evading the tough issues? What good is finding agreement if the obstacles remain?

The answer to the first objection is no, looking for areas of agreement is not simple evasion. However, there is no guarantee that, first, you'll find areas of agreement and, second, that finding them will bring about ultimate harmony and cooperation. But by finding areas of agreement and building on them, you prompt your colleague to make an investment in the project, which, in turn, motivates her to find a way to make the idea work.

TIP

Moving from 100 percent disagreement to 50 percent (or 20 percent, or 10 percent . . .) agreement is a positive step. It's now up to you to decide whether the glass is half empty or half full. Proceed accordingly.

RESPONDING TO THE IDEAS AND PROJECTS OF OTHERS

Just as it is important to secure the support and cooperation of colleagues for the ideas and projects that you champion, you owe it to those you work with—and to your company as well as to yourself—to respond fully and informatively to ideas and projects your colleagues may propose and champion. Effective responses fall into two categories: positive reinforcement and constructive criticism.

Providing Positive Reinforcement to Colleagues

In general, *all* of your responses to the ideas and projects proposed by others in your organization should be positive. This does not mean giving mindless, unqualified approval; however, the most effective response identifies positive elements of an idea or project and comments on them before identifying and criticizing problems.

TIP
_____

Once you reject an idea or project as 100 percent worthless, you and your colleague have very little reason to communicate and virtually no reason to communicate constructively.

Obviously, the task of communication is easiest and most pleasant when you *can* give unqualified approval to a project or idea. But, even in these cases, it is important to be specific.

- Responding to an idea or project with something like "That's great!" is not helpful or effective.
- Respond instead: "That's great! I'm especially excited about A, C, and E, which should greatly improve F, H, and I." Identify specific strengths in your response.

The more specific you are in your positive reinforcement, the more clearly you establish and demonstrate

1. The degree to which you value the project

2. The degree to which you are willing to cooperate to develop the project

Being specific also provides the basis for

1. Modifying parts of the project—emphasizing some aspects, reducing others
2. Providing criticism

The second point is especially important. The fact is that "unqualified" approval is rare in business. You may find an idea or project 99 percent wonderful, but it is to everyone's advantage for you to carve out a credible position that allows you to criticize that remaining 1 percent. Being specific about positive reinforcement earns you the right to be specific about criticism as well.

TIP

In contrast to most other business situations, providing positive reinforcement *should* take in personality and character. Praise the virtues of the project or idea, but also compliment the person or persons responsible: "This shows real creativity. You guys worked hard on this. It's great to be working with people like you."

The key to an effective positive reinforcement strategy is to think in terms of process rather than of product:

- Provide reinforcement at steps along the way of idea, project, or product development. The objective of reinforcing remarks is to further the process, increasing the prospects for the success of the next stage, and the stage, after that, and so on.
- Even if you are praising a finished product, look to the future—how the product fits into the ongoing process that is your business. Don't praise it as a done deed, a dead end.

TIP

Positive reinforcement should energize, encourage, and build. It should help to enable further achievement.

Here's an example of responding positively and effectively to an idea during the development of a product:

> **You:** I just want to congratulate you, Mary, and your team for coming up with the solution to problems A, B, and D. The scheme you've proposed for fast-tracking production is really innovative, but what's great about it is that, innovative as it is, it uses proven methods. I'm eager to work with you on this, and I'm confident that your team will now be able to come up with a satisfactory solution to C, which, I think, we're all agreed, still needs work in three areas . . .

Offering Constructive Criticism to Your Colleagues

Let's not kid ourselves. Responding *critically* to a colleague's idea or project is more difficult, more demanding, and more risky than providing positive reinforcement. But, like praise, criticism can also be positive. It can build relationships, foster a team spirit, and improve performance and productivity.

Constructive criticism is appropriate when:

1. Your colleagues are not functioning well.
2. A situation is threatening your working relationship with a colleague.
3. You have a sincere desire to upgrade a colleague's performance for the good of the organization.
4. A project or idea requires improvement or modification.

Even though criticism in these cases is justified and necessary and, therefore, positive, you may meet with negative responses:

1. You may be confronted with hostility.
2. You may be confronted with defensiveness.
3. You may be told that you have misunderstood the situation.

It is also possible that the criticism may be welcomed. If so, you'll hear responses like these:

- "I didn't realize I was doing that."

- "I didn't think there was a better way."
- "I was totally unaware of that."
- "You're right. I could be doing a better job if I approached the problem your way."

The objective of your criticism should be

- To correct or improve a problematic situation, faulty colleague performance, problems with ideas or projects
- To secure a positive response from the person or persons to whom the criticism is directed

You can maximize the chances for a positive reaction—and a positive outcome—by observing the following guidelines:

1. *Make certain the situation really does call for criticism.* You *should* be hesitant to offer criticism. Make certain that your criticism is motivated by a genuine problem or issue, not by your personal dislikes or frustrations. Make certain, too, that the problem or issue is serious enough to warrant criticism. After all, you are risking the creation of bad feelings. Make certain that the "cure" is not apt to be worse than the "disease."

2. *Don't go blundering into the criticism.* Practice finesse. Instead of opening up with your big guns, ask your colleague if she would *like to hear how* you feel about what she's doing. That is, ask her permission to offer criticism. This will help translate "criticism" into "feedback"—which is far more neutral and apt to trigger less defensiveness than criticism.

3. *Choose the right place and time.* Never criticize a colleague in front of others. Instead, find—or create—an appropriate time: "George, there's something I need to discuss with you. When would be a good time for us to have a few uninterrupted moments together?"

TIP

Avoid delivering criticism first thing in the morning—especially Monday morning. Avoid delivering it right before quitting time, especially before a weekend. You don't want to send a colleague home to stew about something you've said.

TIP

Don't deliver criticism in the heat of anger—for example, right after some incident has occurred. Try to cool down and reflect before offering criticism.

4. *Back up your criticism with substance.*   The most frustrating and enraging kind of criticism is delivered in vague generalities. Be concrete. Use specific incidents, instances, and events. Also, concentrating on specifics will help to keep the criticism from degenerating into a personal attack.

5. *Offer alternatives.*   It's easy to criticize, but much harder to come up with positive alternatives. Generally, you should not offer criticism to a colleague unless you are prepared to offer alternatives that will be helpful to him and to the organization.

6. *Be friendly.*   This does not mean that you should approach your colleague in a phony, sickeningly sweet, or patronizing manner. However, be considerate and sensitive. Don't tease or taunt. Don't raise your voice. Watch your vocabulary. Avoid such phrases as "you must," "you should," "you have to," "you never," "you always," and the like.

7. *Where possible, combine praise with criticism.*   This is not just to soften the blow, but to let your colleague know that you appreciate her value, her qualifications, and her abilities.

8. *Criticize only what can be improved or corrected.*   Make certain that you don't lay the blame for some essentially uncorrectable problem at the feet of your fellow worker.

9. *One at a time, please.*   Don't lay multiple criticism on anyone. Tackle one issue at a time.

10. *Follow up with positive feedback.*   If the situation improves or the issue is corrected, offer praise, congratulations, and thanks. Express your admiration.

Your script: giving construction criticism.

Here is an example of establishing a positive basis and maintaining the focus on issues rather than personalities or abilities:

You: What's working very well in this proposal is A, B, D, and F. These are cost-effective and, I think, very attractive in the present market. However, C and E pose serious problems. Here's what I mean: [explains the problems in detail].

With most of the proposal looking so sound and affording such advantages, we have to come up with solutions for C and E. Mary, you and your team have done wonderful things with A, B, D, and F. I would like to offer my support in resolving the problems with C and E.

APOLOGIZING FOR ERRORS AND MISUNDERSTANDINGS

If you find it difficult to apologize, you're hardly alone. Few people look forward to apologizing. Yet I would suggest that a revision in attitude is in order. While it is true that there is never anything to cherish about the reason for making an apology—that is, a mistake or misjudgment or misunderstanding—there is a good reason to value the apology itself as an opportunity for building and strengthening relationships with your colleagues.

It's relatively easy to get along with your colleagues when things are going well. The relationship is tested, however, when a crisis occurs. How you and your colleagues work together, help one another in the wake of an error or other crisis, is the test and the builder of effective coworker and colleague relationships.

When an apology is called for, observe the following:

- *Make it timely.* Don't wait to be asked for an explanation or apology. Be proactive. Take the initiative.
- *Be helpful.* Don't just apologize. Offer whatever help you can to make things right again. Such a response may not only repair damage, it can actually improve relations.

Common sense tells you that the most important component of an apology is the offer of a remedy. This is largely true, but of nearly equal importance is *how* you arrive at the remedy:

STEP 1:   Apologize; say that you are sorry.

STEP 2:   Sympathize; express understanding of the other's feelings.

STEP 3:   As you work toward a remedy for the situation, structure the conversation so that the words "you" and "I" become "we": "We'll repair this situation."

TIP

Your colleague will appreciate your apology. But make sure you give him what he probably needs most: help. Render aid, and you will become a hero, even if the problem was your fault to begin with.

TIP

Recognize the difference between an explanation and an excuse. You owe the wronged party an explanation—an outline of the facts and circumstances surrounding the error—but she will not want to hear an excuse: why the problem wasn't your fault. If the explanation—an outline of the facts—serves to exonerate you, great; if not, offer no additional excuse.

YOUR SCRIPT: APOLOGIZING TO A COLLEAGUE

Here's an apology for being late with information a colleague needs:

You: I'm very sorry that I was late with the report you needed. I know that put you in a tight spot.

Colleague: Well, yes, it sure did. The boss was angry.

You: I'm willing to explain to him that the problem was on my end. We didn't get the results back from the first three tests on time. There was nothing I could do about that, but I should have warned you that the problem was coming. I'd like to explain that to the boss.

Colleague: Well, I'd appreciate that.

You: Yeah. I know he can be pretty short-tempered about things like this. I'm sorry to have put you on the receiving end of *that* blast.

DEALING WITH AN IRATE COLLEAGUE

What if we could keep our emotions out of our work? Wouldn't that be wonderful? Sometimes. Expressions of outright anger in the workplace range from disturbing to downright frightening. Of course, if our work consistently failed to engage our emotions, if we just didn't care, the quality of what we do would suffer. Loud and visible anger in reaction to errors may result from passion about one's work, but other factors may also figure in the picture:

- A fight with one's spouse
- A fight with one's children
- A lingering disagreement with someone else at work
- A miserable morning commute in bumper-to-bumper traffic

Who knows what else? You cannot, of course, control all the stressful and enraging factors in your colleague's lives, but you can recognize that an enraged response from you in return will only fuel the anger. In contrast, a calm, businesslike response will make it that much more difficult for your colleague to maintain rage.

Successfully coping with the rage of others requires that you take steps to deal with the causes of stress in your own life. These nonverbal steps will help you deal more effectively with strong emotion in the workplace:

1. Get more sleep. Fatigue reduces your patience and tolerance, making you susceptible to angry outbursts.
2. Try to handle difficult colleague situations, such as apologies, after breakfast or after lunch—not when you or your colleague is hungry.
3. Moderate your intake of coffee. Caffeine heightens anxiety and rage levels.
4. Turn up the air conditioning. Too much heat makes most people more irritable.

5. Do what you can to make yourself more comfortable. Ditch the buzzing fluorescent tube. Get rid of the clock that ticks too loudly.

So much for what you can control. An error occurs. You are responsible. You apologize. Your colleague flies off the handle. Here's what you do:

STEP 1:   Start by doing little or nothing. Let the person vent.

TIP

It is difficult to sit and take it from an irate colleague, but doing so will allow him to bleed off some of that pent-up energy.

TIP

Avoid *telling* an irate colleague to "calm down." This will only stoke the fire. Avoid telling your colleague to do anything or to feel or behave in a certain way.

STEP 2:   After the first wave of rage has washed over, "play back" the gist of angry message—minus the rage: "If I understand you correctly . . ."

STEP 3:   If you believe that you have a satisfactory remedy for the colleague's issue, propose it—quickly.

STEP 4:   If no immediate remedy is available, lay the burden on your colleague: "How would you like to resolve this?"

TIP

Rage is directly proportional to a person's feeling of powerlessness. If you ask your colleague to tell you what he wants, you give him power and, therefore, reduce his feeling of powerlessness.

STEP 5:   If your colleague makes a proposal and you can agree to it, tell him that you will take the necessary action.

STEP 6:   If you are unsure that you can comply with the proposed remedy, ask for some time to consider and investigate. Arrange a specific time and place for a follow-up discussion.

STEP 7:   If your colleague's solution is unfeasible, negotiate an alternative: "I can't do that, but here's what I can do."

STEP 8:   Do what you can to transform "I" versus "you" into "we" versus "the problem."

TIP

If your colleague becomes abusive or threatening, remove yourself from the situation—immediately: "John, this is getting out of hand. I'm going to leave. I'll return in a half hour. Let's try to cool down and discuss this productively then."

CHAPTER 6

Putting Yourself Across . . . to Subordinates

SELF-TEST YOUR SAVVY IN COMMUNICATING WITH SUBORDINATES

The following is a simple diagnostic test. A smaller and more selective version of the self-test in Chapter 1, its purpose is not to test your knowledge of communication theory or techniques, but to help you gauge how effectively you communicate with your subordinates in a day-to-day business context. For the most part, you will find it easy to guess the "right" answer. But getting the "right" answer is not the point of the test. Respond honestly, even if you feel that your response is not the best one possible. This is not a contest. The object is solely self-inventory.

1. It's a bad idea to be friendly toward your subordinates.   T/F _____

2. I'm a leader because my boss says I'm a leader.   T/F _____

3. *Never* admit that you are wrong.   T/F _____

4. Employees *always* complain. You can't take it seriously. You just have to go on.   T/F _____

5. I am frank in assessing employees who are not performing up to par.   T/F _____

6. Questions are usually a waste of time.   T/F _____

7. Threats are not effective motivators.   T/F _____

8. I ask for feedback.   T/F _____

9. I ask permission to criticize.   T/F _____

10. You can't depend on your subordinates.   T/F _____

11. I care about my subordinates' personal goals, but they must mesh with the firm's.   T/F _____

12. Sometimes criticism is brutal. That's just the way it is.   T/F _____

13. My department is a democracy.   T/F _____

14. My department is a team.   T/F _____

15. I do issue verbal reprimands, but I summarize them afterwards in a written memo.   T/F _____

16. I don't *say* anything. I put it *all* in writing.   T/F _____

17. Insubordinate employees should be fired—quickly.   T/F _____

18. I expect my people to get it right—the *first* time.   T/F _____

19. I give *very* clear directions.   T/F _____

20. Subordinates have to be watched at all times.   T/F _____

21. We have an employee handbook with clear statements of workplace policy.   T/F _____

22. When I criticize a subordinate I hope to help him or her develop and improve.   T/F _____

23. I invite questions.   T/F _____

24. Criticism is part of mentoring.   T/F _____

25. Reprimand is a normal part of employee development.   T/F _____

26. Termination is a process, not an event.   T/F _____

27. It is quite possible to say no to an employee without alienating him or her.   T/F _____

28. Work is not fun.   T/F _____

29. Loyalty is important to me.   T/F _____

30. Call it what you want, criticism *is* finding fault.   T/F _____

31. Sometimes it is necessary to "terminate" an employee.   T/F _____

32. All management owes the employee is a paycheck.   T/F _____

33. I may be upset by the complaints of my subordinates, but I listen and try to learn.   T/F _____

34. I never get involved in disputes between subordinates. That's dangerous.   T/F _____

35. My people can do what I tell them to, or they can find other employment.   T/F _____

36. The people who report to me have to *perform*. Period.   T/F _____

37. I always resist requests for salary increases.   T/F _____

38. I see myself as a coach.   T/F _____

39. Some things just aren't worth criticizing.   T/F _____

40. When things go wrong, I try to offer not only an apology, but a remedy.   T/F _____

41. I try to combine criticism with praise.   T/F _____

42. Mature workers do not require profuse positive reinforcement.   T/F _____

TOTAL T/F   _____

Score 1 point for each "True" response and 0 for each "False" response, EXCEPT for questions 1, 2, 3, 4, 6, 10, 12, 13, 16, 17, 18, 20, 28, 30, 32, 34, 35, 36, 37, and 42. For these questions only, SUBTRACT 1 point for each "True" response. Record your total. A score below +20 indicates that you would benefit from practicing the communication techniques discussed in this chapter. (Note: It is possible to have a negative score.)

WORDS TO USE WITH SUBORDINATES

advice	future
advise	glitch
analyze	help
assist	invest
consider	lead

WORDS TO USE WITH SUBORDINATES, *cont'd*

control	learn
cope	lesson
counsel	manage
determine	navigate
discuss	plan
evaluate	reconsider
expedite	rethink
formulate	revise

PHRASES TO USE WITH SUBORDINATES

ask your advice

build on this

consult with you

create progress

create satisfaction

Do you understand?

full cooperation

get your input

give guidance

hear your take on this

How do you want to proceed?

How may I help you?

improve even more

join the team

make progress

realize our goals

team effort

What part is unclear?

What would you suggest?

WORDS TO AVOID WITH SUBORDINATES

blame

catastrophe

crisis

demand

destroyed

disaster

exploded

fault

force

foul-up

hopeless

idiotic

impossible

mess

misguided

must

snafu

PHRASES TO AVOID WITH SUBORDINATES

better shape up

can't do it

don't ask

don't come to me about it

don't want to hear it

don't worry about it

figure it out yourself

know what's good for you

no choice

not allowed

you wouldn't understand

you'd better

BODY-LANGUAGE STRATEGY FOR COMMUNICATING WITH SUBORDINATES

The basics of effective body language apply in conferences with subordinates:

- Make and maintain eye contact.
- Smile.
- Keep hands away from the face and mouth, but use many open-handed gestures.
- If you feel the need to achieve subtle domination, direct your glance to the subordinate's forehead rather than meeting his or her eyes directly.

Your approach is simple. It pays to come across as open and receptive. Of at least equal importance to the nonverbal cues you transmit is learning how to read those you receive. When you speak with a subordinate, how do you know that you are getting through? Do you know because the person *tells* you she understands? Or because he *promises* to do better "next time"?

In part, it's just this simple and obvious. *Ask* for feedback: "Am I making myself clear?" Or: "Is this helping you?" But you need to go beyond this.

- Particularly in situations in which you must deliver criticism and correction, you should expect instances of *verbal* compliance combined with the *nonverbal* signals of resistance.

Look out for:

1. Avoidance of eye contact, which suggests that you are not getting through
2. Hands to face or mouth, which suggests that the employee is not being fully honest with you
3. Arms folded across the chest or hands on hips, which suggests resistance, even defiance
4. Rubbing the back of the neck or, if the employee is seated, nervous leg movement, which suggests a desire to leave—*now*

If you pick up any of these nonverbal cues, try to bring the issue of communication out into the open:

STEP 1: Verbalize: "I get the feeling that I'm not communicating as effectively as I would like. Do you agree with such-and-such?" Or: "Does what I say disturb you? Does what I say seem inaccurate to you?"

STEP 2: Do not accuse the subordinate of *failing* to listen or *failing* to understand. In reacting to nonverbal cues, put the burden on yourself rather than the subordinate: "Am *I* making *myself* clear?"

BODY LANGUAGE TO AVOID WITH SUBORDINATES

Supervisors are notorious for telegraphing their emotions through frowns, narrowing of the eyes, pouting expressions, and so on. Endeavor to smile as much as possible, but when that is inappropriate, cultivate a neutral expression or "poker face." In addition, avoid:

- Gestures of hands over or near the mouth
- Running the hands through the hair or rubbing the back of the neck. These gestures transmit frustration
- Folding the arms across the chest—a gesture that indicates a closed mind or resistance
- Avoidance of eye contact
- Leg movement—which indicates a desire to be elsewhere, to get away
- Violent gesturing, including jabbing, pointing, and pounding fist

COMMUNICATING YOUR MANAGEMENT STYLE

You can choose to manage your department or your business like a dictator. In the short term, providing limited choices and unlimited threats may actually be effective. This style tends to produce immediate results; however, among those immediate results are employee dissatisfaction and, ultimately, a high turnover rate. Dictatorial managers do not create successful teams—certainly not for the long haul.

What about going to the other extreme? Giving little direction and communicating scant feedback can be effective if you have the right team assembled. But that is a big *if*. And to meet adversity with anything like passive resistance usually leads only to frustration—for you and your employees.

Generally speaking, the most effective managers resemble the legendary Notre Dame football coach Knute Rockne more than either Adolf Hitler or Mahatma Gandhi. They lead, but by inspiration rather than fear. They let team members discover the best within themselves, but they do so with positive criticism and encouragement rather than inscrutable silence.

The most effective managers are able to foster personal dedication not by persuading the staff that they work for a great and beneficent manager or company, but by convincing them that their personal goals mesh with those of the company; that is, personal success depends on the success of the corporate endeavor.

For the long term, showing the connection between personal goals and company objectives works well, but on a day-to-day basis an even more direct way to manage employees for optimum performance is to create in them a sense of personal loyalty to you. This is mostly a matter of communication, of conveying the following:

1. That you are accessible
2. That you are willing to hear—and respond to—grievances and complaints
3. Absolute clarity about your expectations
4. Generous positive feedback
5. Helpful and constructive criticism
6. A sense of fun and enjoyment in your directives

Listening to Complaints from Subordinates

Let's take a closer look at what it means to be willing to listen to complaints. It is a willingness that requires strength on your part. Most managers can get candor from their staff—at least once. It is how you respond to candor that determines whether the productive honesty will continue.

The most effective opening strategy is a what's-bothering-you-let's-talk-about-it approach.

STEP 1: "Sam, you look really upset about something. I want to hear about it. Go ahead. Don't pull any punches."

Just be certain that *you* can roll with those punches. The object is to learn from complaints, not to become enraged or offended by them. The most destructive thing you can do is ask for honesty, only to react to it with anger.

STEP 2: After the employee gets the gripe off his chest, try to translate the negative into a positive solution. If Issue A upsets Sam, ask him what can be done to resolve Issue A and improve the situation.

STEP 3: If no immediate solution is possible, indicate your willingness to work toward a solution.

Strive for Clarity in Your Communications

Effective management is not magic. Much of it is effective communication, and, in turn, effective communication consists largely of clear and precise directions.

1. Clarity is often best achieved by writing out your instructions in the form of a memo.
2. Use plain English. Quantify instructions wherever possible: how many, when, where, how much time, and so on.
3. Always invite questions.

Getting the Best from Your Subordinates

To cultivate the best in your team requires the development and nurturing of enthusiasm. Now, enthusiasm is not a robust commodity. Fragile, it is easily stifled by insensitive supervision and can be dissipated utterly by cynicism. The inspired manager circulates among her team, infusing it with enthusiasm. Upbeat, she

- Talks with team members
- Works closely with the group
- Suggests new approaches to stubborn problems

- Expresses empathy in difficult situations
- Tirelessly consults and coaches

Enthusiasm is a creation. Through frequent meetings and conferences, the manager

- Shares her observations
- Reinforces positive achievements and attitudes
- Continually corrects the team's direction and focus as required

You may hear "hard-nosed" managers protest that mature workers do not require profuse positive reinforcement. Look around: The world is full of rewards and awards and ceremonies of public recognition. Positive reinforcement is hardly a new idea, nor is it peculiar to the workplace. It is, quite literally, ancient history, and its utility is just common sense. Indeed, the effective manager should consider holding regular reinforcement meetings.

- Such meetings should be positive and upbeat; their objective is to reward, refresh, and, if necessary, refocus.
- Invite staffers to bring up their concerns, but defer full discussion of these to separate meetings if they threaten the upbeat tenor of the reinforcement meeting.
- Introduce an element of pleasure into each meeting. Serve refreshments, perhaps, or share a funny story.
- Greet your staff with kind and pleasant words: "You guys, as usual, look great!"
- Keep the tone of the meeting light, warm, and friendly.
- Be specific in your positive reinforcement. Invite the staffers you single out for praise to talk about their success.
- Spend less than an hour in the meeting—enough time to cite, in detail, several positive examples. Allow ample time for questions, discussion, and clarification.

TIP

Reinforcement meetings should not be lectures. Make them interactive.

In between reinforcement meetings, motivate your staff with continual feedback designed to reassure subordinates that you have confidence in their skills and abilities.

TIP

Be specific in your feedback. To the degree that it is possible to do so, stress the positive. Practice delivering feedback in a sincere tone. When you criticize, always suggest alternatives. Never simply demean an employee or reject his work.

TIP

The best managers enjoy what they do. Put some *fun* in your directives. Don't turn them into jokes, but feel free to use imagination when you give directions, discuss ideas, or deliver feedback.

Giving Constructive Criticism to Your Subordinates

Offering constructive criticism to subordinates is similar to criticizing your colleagues, except that you are in a more authoritative position with subordinates. This has its advantages as well as its liabilities. For while your subordinates are more likely to accept criticism—and to expect it—there is a greater potential for anxiety and, with anxiety, resentment of you. This can undermine your effectiveness as a manager and lead to resistance among your staff.

STEP 1:   Avoid creating resentment by communicating criticism in the manner of a mentor or a coach.

STEP 2:   Make it clear that you are committed not just to your department's or company's bottom line, but to the development of the employee as a long-term member of the team.

STEP 3:   Before you criticize, *be certain of your need to criticize*. Avoid using criticism merely to vent frustration, anger, or irritation.

TIP

If your remarks are not likely to improve the situation, don't make them.

STEP 4:   Ask permission to criticize. Asking permission to criticize will actually enhance the effectiveness of your remarks. Instead of starting out with something like, "You're not doing an effective job with so-and-so," begin with "We have a problem with so-and-so, which I would like to discuss with you."

STEP 5:   Be certain that the cure will not be worse than the disease. Even sensitively expressed, criticism can damage a fragile ego. Use judgment to decide whether the problem or issue is worth the risk that critical words entail.

STEP 6:   Do not criticize subordinates in front of others. Take the person aside—subtly. "Alice, I need to speak to you about an important matter. When is a good time for us to get together for a few minutes of uninterrupted time?"

STEP 7:   Avoid criticism first thing in the morning or at quitting time. Criticism is not a good way to start or end the day.

STEP 8:   Be specific and avoid issuing blanket criticism or generalized criticism. Cite specific issues and incidents.

STEP 9:   As far as possible, quantify your criticism objectively: "Turnaround time in your area is a good 15 percent more than we need it to be."

STEP 10:   Maintain your perspective. You are both on the same team; therefore, approach the subordinate not just as an employee, but as a member of *your* team. Be friendly.

STEP 11:   Always address issues, never personalities. Resist the temptation to tell an errant employee what you think of him. Focus on the issue.

TIP

If necessary, it is appropriate to focus on a particular negative or harmful behavior—just be sure it is a behavior in a certain circumstance or set of circumstances. Be specific.

STEP 12:   Combine as much praise as possible with the criticism. You might observe that, in general, you are pleased with the subordinate's work, but that, as regards issue A, an improvement needs to be made.

STEP 13: Limit your criticism to what can be changed. It does no good—and may do great harm—to criticize a subordinate for something over which she has little or no control.

STEP 14: Address one issue at a time. Avoid bombarding the subordinate with a cluster of faults and problems.

YOUR SCRIPT: GIVING CRITICISM TO SUBORDINATES

Here is an example of constructive criticism:

You: Mary, I liked the way you handled that customer's complaint. It was done quickly and politely.

Mary: Thanks.

You: May I just share with you a few observations, some points that might help you to deal with such complaints even more effectively?

Mary: Well . . . sure.

You: You came up with a course of action very quickly. There's a lot to be said for such decisive action; however, in cases where more than a few options are available, it would be more effective to ask the customer what he wants. Empowering the customer in this way increases your opportunity to create satisfaction. Am I expressing myself clearly?

Mary: I'm not sure. Are you saying I did something wrong . . . ?

You: No. Not at all. I want you to know that you handled that customer well, but there is an even more effective approach, I think. When you have choices to offer, give more power, more authority to the customer. Don't be too quick to propose a single solution. If the customer needs help deciding what to do, by all means, jump in.

Mary: But doesn't this take too much time?

You: That's a very good point, Mary. It *does* take time. But time spent with the customer in a case like this is valuable for us. It builds satisfaction. It turns a problem into an opportunity.

Note that the criticism, though expressed clearly and in detail, is softened by the generally positive context surrounding it. This boss offers positive reinforcement, then asks permission to offer criticism, then approaches the criticism as a mentor—not as a monitor.

WHAT TO SAY TO SUBORDINATES WHEN YOU ARE WRONG

Tyranny. Now *there's* a motivating force. It has sparked rebellion after rebellion, including our own American Revolution. Tyranny may be manifested in many ways, running the gamut of economic and physical oppression. But, at bottom, all tyranny is founded on injustice, a refusal either to recognize the differences between right and wrong or to admit wrong.

Supervisors and managers make mistakes. Sometimes those mistakes are hurtful, financially to the company or personally to an employee. Forgiveness may or may not be possible, depending on the problem, the magnitude of loss or harm, and the prevailing attitude of the company and the employees.

- But you can be certain of *not* being forgiven for one thing: a refusal to own up to the mistake, to admit error, and to work toward amends. That failure is tyranny.

STEP 1:   Assess the error, problem, and damage.

STEP 2:   Do not rush into a confession of guilt and do not wallow in remorse. Assess the degree of your culpability.

STEP 3:   Apologize and explain the problem or mistake.

STEP 4:   Listen to the affected employees. What do they need you to do?

STEP 5:   Empathize.

STEP 6:   Propose remedies.

STEP 7:   Explain and justify limitations to the remedies proposed.

Your script: telling a subordinate you're wrong

An employee submitted to you a request, with documentation, for travel-expense reimbursement. Three weeks after submitting this, he asks you about the status of his reimbursement. You tell him you'll look into it—and then discover that your accounting people never received the request from you. After further investigation, you realize that you've misplaced—*lost*—the employee's request and documentation. What do you say? What do you do?

You: Tom, I've traced the source of the delay in getting you your reimbursement.

Tom: Great!

You: Well, not so great. It's me. I don't know how it happened, but I have lost your request and documentation. Do you have any copies?

Tom: Well . . . I have a copy of the expense form, but I didn't make copies of the documentation.

You: Okay. Well, I really screwed up, and I'm sorry. This is what I propose to do. Give me the copy of the form. I will reimburse you out of petty cash immediately, and I'll submit the copy to accounting with an explanation that I have misplaced the documentation and have initiated a search. I'm really sorry to hang you up like this.

Tom: I'll get that copy to you right away.

You: And I'll draw the money for you. Again, sorry!

The employee does want to hear an apology, but what he wants even more is a fix for whatever went wrong. Offer the apology, but don't belabor it. Move as quickly as possible to the fix.

REFUSING REQUESTS—WITHOUT ALIENATING EMPLOYEES

In a perfect world, you would be able to grant the wishes of everyone who reports to you. Of course, in a perfect world, no one would ask you for anything. In our far-from-perfect world, they do ask, and sometimes you have to say no. The best you can do?

- Say no clearly and unmistakably.
- Say no gently.

- Provide a reason for your being unable—or unwilling—to meet the request.
- If possible and appropriate, offer alternatives.

TIP

Try not to emphasize what you can't do, but shift the focus to what you can do—even if this is substantially less than what you were asked for.

In general, take these steps to refuse a request without alienating the employee:

STEP 1: Listen without interruption—unless you need a point clarified.

STEP 2: Show that you have understood the request by rephrasing and summarizing it.

STEP 3: If there is any part of the request that you *can* satisfy in some degree, begin with that.

STEP 4: Express regret that you cannot satisfy the request or that you cannot satisfy it completely.

STEP 5: Explain why you cannot. This step is the most important of all.

STEP 6: Put the request in perspective; develop your negative response in the context of department or company needs and goals, which will ultimately benefit the employee.

STEP 7: Express your wish that your refusal will cause no great hardship or disappointment.

STEP 8: If possible and appropriate, suggest an alternative.

TIP

Be careful! In suggesting an alternative, beware of "volunteering" others to satisfy the request.

STEP 9: Offer *rational* hope. Are there conditions under which the request might be satisfied at some future time? Be as specific about this as circumstances allow.

STEP 10: Thank the employee for understanding.

TIP

Don't let the *no* cut off communication. Make it clear that you are responding negatively to the proposal, the request, or the idea—*not* to the *person* bringing you the proposal, request, or idea.

When a Subordinate Requests a Raise

Saying no to a request for a raise is one of the really hard things a manager has to do.

* Make the situation easier for you and the employee by establishing clear guidelines and policies, including annual or semi-annual performance reviews.

If you have to say no, your approach should be straightforward and unemotional. Avoid being either judgmental ("You don't deserve a raise!") or apologetic ("Aw, gee, shucks, darn it all . . .") Give a straightforward reason for your response and, if at all possible, offer rational, realistic, and clearly defined hope for the future.

Your script: handling a raise request

After four months on the job, Sally Smith wants a raise. She's doing a *very* good job, and the last thing you want to do is discourage her. But you can't give her a raise at four months. Offer praise and whatever promises you can honestly make:

You: Sally, I am thrilled with the job you've been doing for us in the four months you've been here. In that short time, you've already made a difference. But, look, it *has* been a *short* time. Policy is very clear: I can't even consider a raise before one year of employment. Now, that's the bad news. The *good* news is that you are not an "ordinary" employee. So here's what I would be willing to do: hold a salary review with you in May. You will have been here six months then. Assuming you maintain or even improve your level of performance, I will do whatever I can to secure an increase before the one-year mark.

Saying no to a request for a raise from an employee whose performance does not merit one can be a particularly difficult and unpleasant experience. However, try to look at it as an opportunity to help an employee improve performance and to develop professionally.

TIP

Keep this meeting as positive as possible. Avoid self-righteous outrage. Avoid threats.

Ostensibly, the object of the meeting is to deliver the bad news to the employee. It is more important, though, to use the occasion to outline the performance conditions that will make a raise possible in the future. Make this an educational experience.

You: Sid, before we can consider a compensation increase, we have to review your job performance. I have to tell you that your present level of performance does not merit a salary increase. I need to see improvement in three areas before I will consider a raise.

• Note the phrase "at present," which implies the possibility of improvement and the possibility of a raise later. Be certain to enumerate the three (or two or four or whatever) areas requiring improvement. Explain yourself. Make your requirements clear.

On this occasion or in a subsequent meeting, which you set up on this occasion, establish clear objectives and goals for each of the improvement areas you outline.

Conclude positively. The most positive—honest—conclusion you can reach is to reaffirm your bond with the employee.

You: Sid, I know that, together, we can bring your performance to a level that will merit an increase—and that will improve performance for all of us here and also increase your job satisfaction.

Perhaps even more painful for you are those occasions when a fine employee, whose work merits an increase, requests a raise, but your finances won't allow you to give her one. Even this cupboard-is-bare scenario can be turned to advantage. Emphasize to the employee that she has a real and immediate stake in the company's performance.

You: Esther, you deserve a raise. There is no question about that. The problem is that we, as a company, have not reached a revenue level this quarter that would make that raise possible. It's a tough one. I hope you realize how much I value your contribution to this team. While I'm sorry I can't increase your salary now, I do feel confident that, with your continued maximum effort, we will reach the level of revenue necessary to give you an increase. I promise that we'll review this situation at the end of the next quarter.

- Unless the employee in question is working under certain contract and union guarantees, regular periodic raises are not an unalienable right.

In the case of an employee who is doing a better-than-satisfactory job, you may not want (or be able) to grant a request for a raise if his compensation is already appropriate to his position. Saying no to a raise in this situation is an opportunity for mentoring, for developing the employee.

You: Ed, you do a wonderful job as production coordinator. That fact should be recognized and rewarded. And it *has* been. You are now at the top level of compensation for your position. If you want to grow financially, you're also going to have to grow in terms of the scope of responsibility you're willing to take on. Let's talk about how you can get to the next level.

TIP

Don't make the mistake of seeing salary issues in terms of an absolute yes or no. If you can't swing a raise in salary level, perhaps you can offer

- A compromise amount
- Enhanced benefits or perks
- Additional paid vacation
- Flexible hours

Be certain to respond positively. Don't stress what you *can't* do, but what you *can*.

You: "Helen, I am thrilled with your work. I agree that an increase is called for. But you have been with the company only a little over a year now, and the figure you propose is inappropriately high. I'm prepared to offer a 3 percent increase now, and at your two-year review we can revisit the matter.

When a Subordinate Requests a Promotion

Turning down a request for promotion may be even more difficult and trying than rejecting a bid for a raise. The dangers of offending pride, of injuring self-confidence, of implying that you do not appreciate the employee's accomplishments, or that you simply do not believe him capable of handling greater responsibility—all of these dangers are real and can be terrible for morale and motivation.

TIP

Avoid making the employee feel that he has reached a dead end and should seek opportunity elsewhere.

STEP 1:   Say no, but give a full an explanation for the no.

STEP 2:   If possible and appropriate, provide hope for the future. Be as specific as honestly possible. Lay out the conditions and performance expectations under which a promotion might be made in the future.

STEP 3:   Agree on mutual steps that may be taken to make the promotion possible at some future time.

STEP 4:   Without promising any action, do try to set a precise date for a new performance review.

Employees often want to move up faster than appropriate. Mary wants to move from associate to head widget inspector, even though she's been on the job for no more than six months. Your task is to respond prudently, but without curbing her ambition, enthusiasm, and commitment to the company or department.

You: I appreciate your ambition and enthusiasm, and it is clear to me that you are fully committed to this firm. I certainly see a move up to head widget inspector, and I don't think you need to stop there, either.

However, the earliest I could consider a promotion is in August. I promise we'll meet then.

Often, a promotion is simply not yours to give freely. Many companies operate in conformity to a seniority policy, which can be a source of great frustration both to staff and managers. If you must refuse a promotion due to seniority requirements, do your best to minimize the frustration.

STEP 1:　Do not use the phrase "company policy" to justify the refusal. This will be taken for exactly what it is: arbitrary and inflexible.

STEP 2:　Soften the blow with an encouraging, positive assessment: "Penny, I want to see that you grow here, and I want to accelerate that process. However, as you know, promotion here is guided by seniority status. You've done a great job in the time you've been here. However, right now, it would not be fair for me to put you ahead of others whose commitment and performance are comparable to yours. They've put in their time, and that counts for a lot. We reward commitment, and one of the chief measurements of commitment is, for better or worse, time."

In some cases, you may want to promote, but, for one reason or another, the firm is not filling the appropriate position at this time. Your challenging task becomes saying no without turning off a valuable member of your team. The most effective strategy is to *join forces* with the employee in mutual limitation.

You: I wish I could move you up to the position, but, at this time, management has made the decision not to fill it. Now, I don't believe this is a permanent situation. It will be reviewed, and I promise you that I'll let you know when the review takes place. At that time, you'll be very high on the list for that position, when it does open up.

When Subordinates Request Assorted Perks and Privileges

Outside of salary and promotion, employee requests range from the perfectly reasonable to the outlandish. Most requests fall somewhere in between. For example, one of the people you manage asks for a change in working hours. He's thinking—quite naturally—of himself, rather than of the needs of the team, the department, and the company. You are in no position to shuffle the staff around.

Of course, you can simply say no. You're the manager. But a more effective way to handle the matter is to position your no somewhere along the road to a solution.

> **You:** Gil, just now, we need you to be available as you are presently scheduled. I'm not in a position to shake up the entire department. But maybe *you* can do something about it. Why don't you discuss the matter with your colleagues? Perhaps one of them would be willing to swap hours with you. I would be open to that.

TIP

Demonstrate your willingness to take all requests seriously and in good faith. Employees may be disappointed if they don't get what they ask for, but they are downright enraged if they feel that their requests are dismissed out of hand by a boss who doesn't listen to them.

YOUR SCRIPTS: RESPONDING TO EMPLOYEE REQUESTS

1. **Employee:** The folks in the shop really want you to consider giving us an additional coffee break in the early afternoon. It's something we all need.

   You: Harry, a third coffee break would cut too deeply into our productive time. It's just not right for us. It won't work. Look, I understand that some of you may feel the need to get up and stretch and get a cup of coffee. Do it on your own, once in a while, and that's fine. But I can't afford the downtime of a third formal coffee break. That would just take too much time from everyone's schedule. It would impact the entire team.

2. **Employee:** Boss, I'd really like to get a new computer. Everyone else has one.

   You: I understand. But, actually, only two people in the department have computers purchased within the past six months or so. But, more important, Bill, your day-to-day needs don't call for a new computer. Look, you do very little word processing and no accounting. If you need faster Internet access from time to time, you can use the machine in the shipping department. That's open to everyone. I just can't justify the expenditure—based on what your job calls for.

Employee: Well, it doesn't seem fair . . .

You: Bill, if you can show me something in your job that I am overlooking, I'd be happy to reconsider. Why don't you give that some thought.

3. **Employee:** . . . So it seems to me about time that I got my own office. I could be much more productive.

   You: Claire, it wouldn't be appropriate for me to assign you a private office at this time. Here's why: First, your job doesn't require client conferences or other private meetings. Second, other staffers with positions equivalent to yours have not been assigned private offices. Third—and this is a big one—our building facilities are strictly limited, and we don't have the remodeling budget to fund additional private office space.

   Now, look, I'm sure you're not thrilled to hear all this, but I believe that you can appreciate my reasons for saying no.

4. **Employee:** Parking is a real pain. I really, *really* want to put in for a reserved space in the lot.

   You: I agree that parking is becoming a problem here, and we're working on it. The lot will be expanded within the next year and a half. For the present, however, reserved spaces are assigned on a seniority basis, period. I don't have the authority to override that. You're right, certainly, that, at present, we have far fewer reserved spaces than people who want them.

   All I can tell you is that I appreciate your willingness to tough it out until more spaces become available in about 18 months. The consolation I can give you is that you're not alone.

RESPONDING TO COMPLAINTS AND CRITICISM FROM EMPLOYEES

Being unreceptive to complaints and criticism will not make the sources of criticism and complaint go away. It merely puts you in the position of the proverbial ostrich: head uncomfortably in the sand, rear end dangerously exposed. Yes, complaints and criticism can be emotionally difficult to hear, but they give you valuable insight into what's working well and what isn't. In addition:

- Listening to criticism and complaints tells you about the morale of your company or department.
- It gives you the opportunity to affect—directly—morale.
- It gives you the opportunity to build or build up your team.

Listening to complaints and criticism does all this *provided* that

- You really do listen.
- You don't respond judgmentally.
- You don't respond defensively.

TIP

The worst thing you can do is to invite criticism—only to snap at a subordinate for accepting your invitation. If you ask for frank feedback, prepare to hear it and hear it out.

- Do not invite criticism and complaint if you have no intention of making any changes. Of course you do not have to act on each and every criticism and complaint—some will be groundless, and others will be impossible to remedy—but you do have to be willing to change what can and should be changed.

Unbearable Workload

Complaints about workload should be taken very seriously. They are rarely made idly, and they require action.

- Consider the possibility that your expectations of the employee in question are excessive or unrealistic.

- Consider the possibility that the workload would be burdensome to anyone. You may need to hire additional personnel.

Your overall strategy should be to present yourself to the employee as receptive and nonthreatening. Be certain to begin by expressing your appreciation of the employee's comments and his willingness to come to you with them. Here's how a typical conversation might go:

Employee: Boss, we've got to do something about handling the volume of work here. We're going to burn out sooner or later.

You: I agree that your work load is indeed heavy, and I have always greatly admired and appreciated your willingness to take it on. The problem we face is limited funding, which prevents our hiring additional personnel anytime soon.

Now, this doesn't mean that I intend to ignore the situation. Let's get together with the supervisors of the other departments to work out some strategies for making life more bearable around here.

Unpleasant Working Conditions

Managers are often all too quick to respond to complaints about working conditions by taking the attitude that the workforce is spoiled. But a physically comfortable and attractive working environment promotes productivity, communicates a high regard for quality, and generally increases employee satisfaction, which translates into better relations with customers and clients, resulting in greater customer satisfaction and a reduction in expensive employee turnover. It pays, then, to take complaints about working conditions seriously.

Again, as with other complaints, it may or may not be possible to remedy the problem. Serious problems that do impact on productivity and general employee satisfaction and well-being should be addressed, of course, but it is almost less important to remedy these problems than it is to listen and respond to the complaints. Communicating to your subordinates a feeling of teamwork, making them feel that they have a voice in the department or the company, is extraordinarily valuable in creating an effective workforce.

Your script: handling complaints about working conditions

Here is a typical working-conditions complaint scenario:

You: Hank, I'm very pleased that you and the others have taken the time and effort to report to me on the problems with employee facilities here at XYZ Company. I wish I could respond by telling you that I can address all of the issues you raise and totally refurbish the facilities. But I cannot. Our funding for the physical plant is far too limited to make all the improvements we would like. That said, I want to make it clear that I agree with you: Improve-ments are needed. This is what I suggest we do. The department staff should choose a delegation of three or four representatives to meet with me in order to determine which items on your "want list" are most pressing. Based on that evaluation and the available funds, we can determine just what changes can be made now, which ones can be put off until a later date, and which can be shelved at least for the time being. How does that sound to you?

Employee: It sounds like a good idea. I'm grateful.

You: Well, you folks decide on your representative group, and let's get started.

Differences with Coworkers

Managers are often reluctant to involve themselves in disputes between employees. Such managers argue that these matters should be resolved between the employees involved, that intervention from higher up will bring bad feelings on all sides. Certainly, there are risks associated with intervening in employee disputes.

- One party to the dispute may believe that you have shown favoritism to the other.
- *Both* parties to the dispute may believe that you have shown favoritism to the other.
- Employees may feel intruded upon.
- Employees may feel that their differences haven't been resolved—just ended by arbitrary authority.
- Resentment may be turned against you.

All of these risks are real. However, the consequences of failure to intervene can be far more devastating. They can, in fact, include all of the above, except that, instead of feeling intruded upon, employees may feel that you are indifferent to their problems. In addition, other negative feelings may result, including:

- Employee impression of weak or nonexistent authority
- Employee feeling that the workplace is unjust
- Poor performance
- Compromised productivity
- Increased frequency and volume of errors
- A poor, unprofessional image projected to customers and clients
- The creation of a hostile work environment

TIP

The phrase "hostile work environment" is all too familiar to anyone who has been involved in labor-related litigation. It is the language of harassment suits. If you allow a hostile work environment to develop, you expose your company to significant liability.

As with most management decisions, the decision whether or not to intervene in an employee dispute should involve a judgment of degree. Minor disputes probably are best left to the resolution of the employees themselves. But if you judge a dispute to be acute or critical, on the one hand, or chronic and long term, on the other, you should act.

STEP 1:   Avoid snap judgments.

STEP 2:   Meet with the employees involved and acknowledge the existence of a problem.

STEP 3:   Listen to all or both sides *without comment*. Interrupt only to seek clarification, but withhold judgment.

STEP 4:   After hearing all or both sides, ask those involved what *they* would like to see happen.

STEP 5:   Do not render a judgment now. Say that you need time to evaluate the problem. Set another meeting time.

STEP 6:   Assert the necessity of working cooperatively together—for the good of everyone. Don't *ask* for cooperation. Say that you *expect* it.

STEP 7:   Study the problem.

STEP 8:   Call another meeting and announce your decision. This may be in the form of suggestions or directives, as appropriate.

Your script: handling employee disputes

Here is an example of a response to an employee who brought a problem to the attention of the boss.

> **You:** Let me begin by telling you how pleased I am that you came to me to discuss the problems you and Fred are experiencing. I'm not saying I'm happy that you're having problems, but that you approached these problems rationally and productively by bringing them to my attention. Now, let's set up a meeting for Thursday. I want to speak with both of you.

Before the second meeting, review the records of both employees.

> **You:** I have reviewed your personnel files, and I have to say that you are both really top-notch performers. Everyone agrees on that. There is no record of any complaints or negative comments concerning either of you. This being the case, I am confident that the two of you can work your problem out together in the same rational spirit in which you approached me.
>   Now, I do have a few suggestions for how you may resolve your differences.

You give your suggestions.

> **You:** Do you have any thoughts on these suggestions?

After listening to the employees' remarks, continue:

> **You:** What outcome would you both like to see? Tell me, Fred, you first.

After listening to the employees' comments, conclude:

You: Look, you are both extremely valuable to this company, and I certainly enjoy working with you. I am eager for you to work well together. I am eager for this because we can't function as a team with any personal agendas in operation. It's bad for productivity, it makes a very bad impression on our clients, and it just makes the workplace—well—ultimately intolerable. That's why I am intervening. Here, at this company, a dispute is not just a personal, private matter. It *can't* be. Too many people depend on us.

Unsafe Conditions

Any report of an unsafe condition must be addressed immediately and taken seriously.

STEP 1:   Gather the facts.

STEP 2:   Ask employee(s) reporting the condition to do so in writing.

STEP 3:   Document your response in writing.

STEP 4:   Ensure that you follow company and governmental regulations concerning the condition.

STEP 5:   Act promptly.

TIP

Always express appreciation for prompt, accurate reporting of an unsafe condition. Encourage such reporting. Never let employees feel that making such reports constitutes grumbling or idle complaining.

REPRIMANDING YOUR SUBORDINATES

Reprimands should serve three important purposes.

1. They should furnish creative, constructive criticism to correct or improve a particular situation.
2. They should aid generally in the development of an employee.

3. The verbal reprimand, memorialized in writing, serves as a documentary record of employee performance.

Let's address this third point first.

- Verbal reprimands are more immediately effective than written reprimands.

- Verbal reprimands should always be followed up by a memo recording and summarizing the reprimand. The memo should note any action that is to be taken, including corrective action promised by the employee. The memo should also record any consequences of failure to remedy the situation.

- The written record of the verbal reprimand is valuable as a rationale for declining a request for a salary increase or promotion, for disciplinary action, or, in extreme cases, as backup for termination.

TIP

Ours is a most litigious age. Disciplining an employee is sometimes necessary—ideally, to improve performance, but also to build a case for termination. Failure to document this case—the progressive steps that led to termination—exposes you and your company to potentially expensive legal liability.

Assuming you wish to retain the employee, the tone of your reprimand should be as positive and constructive as the situation permits.

TIP

Never attack the employee personally. Never make threats—though you should, as appropriate, advise the employee of possible consequences if the problem is repeated or remains unremedied.

STEP 1:   If possible and appropriate, begin by acknowledging the generally positive nature of the employee's performance.

STEP 2:   Clearly state the nature of the problem, infraction, or issue.

STEP 3:   Explain the effect of the employee's error, bad behavior, or poor performance on the welfare of the company (on which, after all, his own welfare also depends).

STEP 4:   Suggest remedies and appropriate steps to resolve the situation.

STEP 5:   Ask the employee for comments and suggestions.

STEP 6:   Clearly advise the employee of consequences to himself if the infraction is repeated or the situation goes unresolved.

TIP

If termination is a realistic possibility, advise the employee of this; however, do not make idle threats.

STEP 7:   Assure the employee of your willingness to work with him to correct the problem.

Habitual Lateness or Early Departure

Failure to adhere to prescribed business hours is typically an insidious problem that comes on gradually. Coming in five minutes late or leaving ten minutes early becomes a habit. On occasion, the five or ten minutes grows to a half hour. The manager's task is to establish and enforce arrival and departure times without seeming (or being) petty and unreasonable.

STEP 1:   Ensure that arrival and departure times are clearly stated and understood.

STEP 2:   Establish definitions of what constitutes legitimate reasons for arriving late or leaving early.

STEP 3:   Establish a policy of clearing late arrival or early departure with a designated supervisor.

TIP

Of course you don't have to provide a reason for your on-time policies; however, you can expect greater compliance if you make clear the rationale behind enforcement of starting and quitting times: It is essential to productive operation that people be where they are expected to be.

Here is a statement of on-time policy, to be used in speaking with an employee who is habitually late or habitually leaves the workplace early:

You: Pat, I don't want to make you feel as if you've got to punch a clock. That's not the kind of work environment any of us here would be happy with. However, we *are* a team, and, as a team, we depend on all our people being where they are supposed to be when they are supposed to be there. I expect that, and so do the others. Starting time is nine, and quitting time is five. Do you anticipate any further problems with adhering to those times, Pat?

Absenteeism

If habitual tardiness or early departure are problems, even worse is absenteeism. As with late-arrival and early-departure problems, the most effective cure is prevention.

STEP 1:   Establish firm policies on sick days and personal days.

STEP 2:   Make it clear that everyone is essential to the team. Attendance is, therefore, critical.

Here is a typical corrective scenario:

You: Mary, you've been out X number of days during the past three months. We've missed you—I mean *really* missed you. It's critically important that you be here. We *need* you.

Mary: Well, I was sick a lot.

You: Well, Mary, I've never felt comfortable establishing a limit on the number of "sick days" an employee may take. After all, how can you predict how many days you might be sick? But I do rely on employees to use sick days only when absolutely necessary. Mary, if you're having a problem with chronic illness, we need to discuss it.

Look, you are a valuable part of this operation. I need to be able to depend on you—and that includes being able to depend on your being here.

Rude to Customers and Clients

The danger in reprimanding an employee for rude behavior is becoming rude oneself. Because you are addressing an issue of character and personality, it is difficult to keep from criticizing or attacking the employee personally. Difficult though it is, you must resist this temptation. Keep the conversation focused on a particular incident or incidents. Let the facts—deeds and words—speak for themselves.

YOUR SCRIPT: HANDLING RUDENESS TO CUSTOMERS

Here is one way to handle an issue of rudeness to customers:

You: Ben, I received a phone call yesterday, which disturbed me very much. One of your customers—who was (understandably) angry enough to take her business elsewhere—described some very rude treatment from you, including what I would consider abusive language. Now, that's her story. What's your take on this incident?

After listening to the employee, continue:

You: We are a service organization. We pride ourselves on treating each customer as someone who is special to us. *That* is the message we need to convey, one customer at a time. It's service, customer service, that gives us our edge. It's as important as any other product benefit we sell. Now, can you deliver courtesy?

Ben: Yes, I promise, I can.

You: I would like to suggest that you apologize to the customer. How do you feel about that?

Ben: Yes, I could do that.

You: Great. I'll leave it to you. Do you intend to call or write? I'd suggest a call. I know it's difficult, but I believe it would be more effective.

Insubordinate or Uncooperative Attitude

Insubordination and general lack of cooperation and compliance can be the result of many causes:

- Emotional instability
- Job dissatisfaction
- Personal crisis
- Failure to understand the nature of a job or assignment

Whatever the cause, the important thing is to recognize the insubordination or lack of cooperation, to call the employee on it, and to discuss with her the consequences of the behavior and acceptable alternatives to the behavior.

YOUR SCRIPT: DEALING WITH INSUBORDINATION

Here is a dispassionate, controlled response to an instance of insubordination:

You: When you started working here, Meg, you agreed to take direction from your supervisors. Now, yesterday, I asked you to do some filing. You refused because, you said, you didn't think the job was part of your job description.

Well, Meg, filing *is* part of your job description. But that's not nearly as important as the fact that here at XYZ Company we need to be able to rely on one another without a lot of discussion or second guessing. You need to do your job.

Meg: Well, it seems to me that you don't want the boat rocked. I mean, filing just isn't very creative. I thought a more junior person could do it.

You: Meg, the last thing we want here is an army of unthinking robots. If you're unhappy with your present position, let's talk about ways that you might move into something else. I'm also open to legitimate objections to certain things you might be asked to do, and I welcome alternatives. But a simple refusal to perform assigned work, well, that's insubordination, period. It's not acceptable.

Meg, I'm going to prepare a memo of this meeting. This is a reprimand, and it is a warning. If you are not willing to live up to the obligations, you must also be willing to recognize that we cannot and will not long retain your services.

The next move is yours. Where do you want to go from here, Meg?

Repeated Errors

Occasional mistakes are all too human, but a *pattern* of error is a quality-control problem, which you cannot afford to ignore.

STEP 1: Gather the facts.

STEP 2: Don't look for a person to blame, but do look for sources of the error.

STEP 3: Review procedures as necessary.

STEP 4: Do not criticize the employee(s) involved without also furnishing direction and alternatives.

STEP 5: Take a team approach. Work with the employee(s) involved in order to break the pattern of error.

YOUR SCRIPT: HANDLING REPEATED ERRORS

A meeting devoted to repeated errors must not be allowed to degenerate into a blame fest. Here's a productive exchange:

You: Ron, have you had an opportunity to look at the summary of error reports generated by customer service concerning your accounts?

Ron: Yes, I have.

Start out with facts—evidence. Avoid subjective assessments, which are subject to emotion-charged dispute. Focus on events and results, not on issues of skill, ability, talent, or character.

You: Taken in and of themselves, none of the errors is very serious. But it's the pattern of errors that bothers me. We shouldn't be making so many mistakes. Somewhere in our system and procedures, we're being sloppy. Now, since the errors fall into your area, you are the person who is going to have to be most responsible for creating improvement.

Let me give you my instructions, then I'll ask for your comments and suggestions.

First, I want you to review your customary processing procedures to ensure that your routine meets the requirements of company policy.

After you complete this self-review, I want to see a report to me no later than the fifteenth. Here's what I want in that report: First, describe what—exactly—has been going wrong. Second, why has it been going wrong? And third, what do you think you—and the rest of us—need to do to reduce the rate of error?

Ron, you are typically highly productive, which gives me confidence that once you enumerate and confront these errors head-on you will be able to improve overall performance.

Do you have any questions and comments?

Ron: I'm not so sure the situation is as bad as you think it is.

You: That's why I asked for the report. Let's assess it together.

Inadequate Record Keeping

As the pressure mounts to produce results *fast* and to turn out product *fast*, certain routine and superficially "nonproductive" functions may begin to suffer. Keeping files and records up to date takes time, and by putting on the pressure to produce, you may also be contributing to deficiencies in areas that are perceived to be secondary. Be aware of this when you speak to an employee about record keeping.

Your script: correcting record-keeping problems

You: Sarah, no one is more aware than I am that we move fast. No one is more aware of it, because I'm in large part responsible for setting the work pace. It is not tempting to cut corners, and I'm afraid I've even encouraged that. Well, the fact is that whatever else we must do to get the job done, there is one corner we cannot afford to cut.

Note that the boss includes himself in the "reprimand." If you are part of the problem, shoulder your fair share of the responsibility.

You: We must always take the time to keep accurate and full records in strict accordance with company policy. I have to tell you frankly that I was quite disturbed last week when I asked you for the file on the Jones account and found that a number of records were either missing or incomplete, including . . .

Be specific about what is missing or inadequate. Avoid mere subjective appraisal.

You: Sarah, you will need to set some time aside to begin reviewing your files, one by one, and bring each of them up to company standards in terms of completeness of records.

Look, don't drop everything to do this, but I do want to see a proposed schedule for completion. I'd like that schedule by Wednesday.

Disclosing Privileged or Proprietary Information

Information leaks can be highly destructive. The practical as well as legal strength of trade secrets depends on your company's ability to keep them secret. Other sensitive information may create critical problems if it falls into the wrong hands.

Communicating the seriousness of breaches in security or discretion is easier if you and your firm establish a clear policy on protecting privileged information, trade secrets, and other proprietary data. That is the first step to take. Beyond this, if a breach does occur, act swiftly.

TIP

It is critically important that you document verbal reprimands concerning disclosure of privileged information. The written record may figure in subsequent disciplinary or legal action.

YOUR SCRIPT: HANDLING SECURITY BREACHES. ACT SWIFTLY AND DECISIVELY

You: I am not happy to find myself obliged to remind you, Max, that you hold a position of significant sensitivity and confidence. I enjoyed seeing you at the annual trade convention reception last night, but I was alarmed to overhear you talking—even in the broadest terms—about our upcoming line of products.

You must know that, under no circumstances is such information to be considered a topic of casual conversation. To take such information outside the company is at the least squandering a portion of our investment in present research and future markets. At worst, Max, it is theft. It's grounds for dismissal.

Max: Oh, come on, boss! This was casual party conversation—not industrial espionage.

You: Max, it really is as serious as I say, and it will be taken that way.

Do not concede that the security breach was harmless. Indeed, make no judgment, other than pointing out the *fact* that sensitive information was inappropriately discussed.

You: Your careless conversation was improper, unwise, and dangerous. Max, I do not want this happening again. I am writing a memorandum of this conversation and placing it in the file. You will regard that as an official reprimand and as a warning. Future indiscretions will not be tolerated, and I will have no other choice than to act in strict accordance with company policy and the terms of your employment. Discussing privileged information with unauthorized persons is grounds for dismissal. Max, it really is that serious. Please, *please* be more discreet in the future. Is there anything I've said that is unclear to you?

Sloppy Appearance

Some managers find this a difficult subject to discuss. They feel that they are intruding into matters of personal taste and, perhaps, even matters of one's pocketbook.

STEP 1: Remove subjectivity from criticism of appearance by establishing (or working with your supervisors to establish) clear and specific guidelines for dress and grooming on the job.

STEP 2: When you discuss personal appearance with an employee, make it clear that your concern is essentially about communication: the message the employee's dress and grooming is transmitting to customers and clients.

YOUR SCRIPT: DEALING WITH SLOPPY APPEARANCE.

Approach this matter as specifically as possible.

You: Bob, I want to talk to you about something—about *confidence*. You know that whatever else we sell here, there is one "product" we must sell before we can promote anything else. That is *confidence*. Our customers have to feel comfortable dealing with us, and they can feel that way only if they believe in us.

We begin to sell confidence before we speak a word. We sell it by the way we present ourselves. It is important that we look professional and successful.

Now, Bob, we have never had a formal dress code at XYZ, but we have always depended on our employees to dress with taste and, above all, to dress neatly. It is all part of the package we are selling.

Taste is pretty subjective, Bob, but there are aspects of your appearance that aren't subjective at all. Lately, your clothes have been wrinkled, shirts occasionally unlaundered, tie loose. Look, I'm not saying that you go out and buy a new wardrobe, but I do ask that you make an extra effort to see to it that the clothing you wear is clean and neatly pressed. And, please, it is also important to the image we must create that you wear a necktie and that you keep it neatly tied.

Bob, you understand, I hope, that I'm not criticizing you personally. But I am concerned that we consistently send the right messages to our customers. Do you have any questions?

ACCEPTING RESIGNATIONS FROM SUBORDINATES

It's over, right? What more is there to say?

- Are you sure you want to go?
- Is there anything I can do that would change your mind?
- Congratulations!
- Let's stay in touch.

Moreover, accepting a resignation should never be casual. Document the event in writing. The employee should be asked to submit a written resignation, but if she does not, you should acknowledge the verbal resignation in a letter written to him and copied into your files.

TIP

It is extremely important to distinguish between a voluntary resignation and dismissal. Documentation of the voluntary resignation may be your only defense against severance claims and other legal actions.

In accepting the resignation, take the following steps:

STEP 1:   Acknowledge the resignation.

STEP 2:   Accept it with congratulations, regret, or whatever emotion is appropriate to the circumstances.

TIP

Keep the response as positive as possible. If you accept with regret, do not tinge that with personal bitterness. If you are happy for the employee, show it. If you are relieved to see her go, be as courteous as possible.

STEP 3:   If appropriate, share a memory, comment on years of service, and so on.

TIP

Why bother to personalize the moment? To begin with, there is nothing wrong with human decency and warmth in business. But, of more pragmatic import, the world of business can be remarkably small. You may well have dealings with this employee again. Let her leave with good memories of you and the company.

STEP 4:   If appropriate, invite reconsideration or later return.

STEP 5:   Wish the employee success in her new position or endeavor.

STEP 6:   Review the facts: date the employee wants to leave, status of projects, and so on. You may wish to set up a separate meeting for some of these matters.

Congratulating the Departing Employee

Accepting the resignation of an employee who is growing, going on to a well-deserved position that you are not in a position to provide, is the easiest of all resignation scenarios:

You: Well, Pete, I'm sorry to see you go. You know that. But this sounds like a great, great opportunity. I congratulate you on it.

Go on to Step 6, in the preceding section.

Asking the Employee to Reconsider

Inviting a resigning employee to pause a moment to reconsider can be a delicate matter, especially if you don't have a competitive incentive to offer.

STEP 1: Acknowledge the news.

STEP 2: Ask the employee what it would take for her to reconsider.

STEP 3: Negotiate, if you have the authority.

STEP 4: If necessary, ask for time to formulate a counteroffer.

STEP 5: If the employee does not want to entertain a counteroffer, offer your congratulations and proceed to clarify such items as last day, status of projects, and so on.

YOUR SCRIPT: ASKING THE EMPLOYEE TO RECONSIDER

An invitation to reconsider should never be a plea. It should be an *invitation*.

TIP

Do not appeal to feelings of guilt, even in jest.

You: Jane, I am not surprised that someone of your abilities should have attracted the attention of ABC Company. Would you entertain a counteroffer? I sure don't want to see you go.

Jane: Well, I . . . sure. I'd be willing to consider it. I'm flattered . . .

You: Okay. I need two days to formulate our counteroffer. Can I have that?

Jane: Yes.

Employee Resigning Under Unfavorable Circumstances

When an employee resigns under unfavorable circumstances—essentially to avoid dismissal—your task is as follows:

STEP 1:   Acknowledge the resignation.

STEP 2:   Maintain a neutral stance. Do not betray emotion.

STEP 3:   Do not comment on the employee's precarious position. To do so could render your firm liable for a severance settlement.

STEP 4:   State the procedure for the employee's departure, including the exact date, what to do with company property, company car, and so on. All of this should be furnished in writing.

STEP 5:   Ask for a written report on the status of the employee's projects.

YOUR SCRIPT: ACCEPTING THE RESIGNATION

You: Dan, I accept your resignation. Can we agree on March 3 as your last day?

Dan: Yes.

You: Please remove your personal belongings from your office by that time. I'll have Gail available to assist you, if you like. Now, Dan, your separation from us is subject to the policy set out in the Employee Manual. I will have a copy placed on your desk. On the day before you leave, I would like to get from you a report on the status of your projects. Do you have any questions?

Dan: No.

You: Very well. I wish you luck in your new endeavors.

Get no more emotional than a simple, polite "good luck" wish. Anything more intense than this may create an unwanted scene.

TERMINATING AN EMPLOYEE

Employee termination is usually a process rather than an event. It is often the culmination of "progressive discipline," a procedure that begins with supervisory counseling and progresses through warnings and, perhaps, a probationary period, ending at last in dismissal, if problems and deficiencies aren't cured.

TIP

The prospect of termination can be a powerful motivator. It should never be used as an idle threat, but a problem employee should be put on notice, in the course of progressive discipline, that termination is the ultimate consequence of failure to improve.

Of course, termination may be due to circumstances outside the employee's control, such as plant closings, layoffs, and so on. In such cases, sympathetic understanding is called for, but you should not put yourself in the position of apologizing for the company's actions.

Why expend much thought and energy on how you terminate an employee? After all, she is about to be history . . .

- Terminated employees do not vanish from the face of the earth. They move to other companies, and they talk about your company. For the sake of your firm's reputation and image, it pays to terminate with a sense of fairness and dignity.

- Losing a job puts a major dent in anybody's day. You can make feelings better or worse with words. Make them worse, and you may be more likely to find yourself with litigation on your hands.

- The world of business can be mighty small. You may want to rehire the terminated employee someday, or you may, in some capacity or other, end up working with him again. Don't create bad blood.

- Most of us want to behave as decent human beings. The process of termination affords ample opportunity to be decent and humane.

Communicating Probationary Status to an Employee

Management is frequently inclined to procrastinate when faced with a poorly performing employee. While it is true that termination need not be brutal and sudden, it is often well worth the effort to try more training, more coaching, and more counseling. But don't use these activities merely to prolong the agony for all involved. Make it clear to the employee that she is on probation and that how she performs and the degree of improvement she shows will determine whether she retains her job.

STEP 1:   Probation is partly about avoiding surprises. Even while you coach and train the employee, be clear with your criticism and be clear about the consequences of failure to improve:

- **You:** Pat, you are still performing below the minimum expected standards. We're going to continue with the training, but if we don't get a turnaround by August, I will need to release you from the company.

STEP 2:   State and define all of your expectations in specific, quantifiable, and measurable terms whenever possible:

- **You:** Pat, you turn around an average of five units per week. The departmental average is ten. I think you'll agree that five units is not an acceptable level of productivity. Is this the right job for you? How do you propose to increase your productivity?

STEP 3:   Document, document, document. Document performance in writing, using as many objective measurements as possible.

STEP 4:   Be specific about performance goals and about time lines.

STEP 5:   Make it clear to the employee that failure to achieve the goals will result in termination.

TIP

It's easy to call for immediate improvement, but not so easy to be explicit about the consequences of failure to improve. Tell the employee that he is in danger of losing his job.

YOUR SCRIPT: PUTTING AN EMPLOYEE ON PROBATION.

Here is a sample probationary statement:

You: Max, your performance is not improving. I don't think you are going to survive here. But this is what I propose to do. I will allow another 60 days for additional training. By the end of that period, I expect you to achieve the following: (lists goals). If you haven't achieved these goals by November 15, I will let you go.

Max, I suggest you do two things between now and then. First, work on achieving the goals we have just discussed. Second, use some of your time to explore other employment opportunities for which you may be better suited.

Now, just so that all of this is very clear, I will prepare a written summary of this conversation. You'll have a copy tomorrow.

- Notice that the tone is frank—humane but unapologetic. You owe it to your company and the employee not to disguise the gravity of the situation.

Dismissal "for Cause"

In contrast to dismissal for poor or inadequate performance, termination for cause is characteristically sudden. It is motivated by such problems as

- Simple failure to perform
- Failure to perform assigned tasks
- Gross insubordination
- Wrongdoing, such as theft, sexual harassment, drug use, and so on

In instances of dismissal for cause, your objectives are:

- To amass adequate documentation
- To separate the employee quickly and quietly

TIP
_____

If reasons for termination include possible criminal activity—drug use on the job, pilfering, embezzlement, theft, violence in the workplace, sexual misconduct, and so on, management must seek legal counsel. If you believe that you are dealing with a potentially dangerous person, the police and/or your company's private security officers should be present during the dismissal.

YOUR SCRIPT: DISMISSING FOR CAUSE.

Most terminations for cause do not result from dramatic instances of misconduct. Here is a typical scenario:

You: Gail, three days ago I brought to your attention discrepancies in your petty-cash records and asked that you prepare an explanation of them by this morning. I indicated to you that if the explanation was not satisfactory in all regards, you would face termination for cause. Have your prepared something for me?

Gail: No.

You: Then I have no choice but to tell you that you are released from the payroll effective immediately. I am asking security to meet you at your office while you remove your personal belongings. Within the hour, I will have a final check issued to you, which will include pay for unused vacation days and three days' additional pay in lieu of notice. You are to leave the building by five this afternoon.

Gail: I . . . I . . . Look, I'm sorry . . .

You: I understand that you are, but this decision is final. You are released from the payroll.

Gail: But can't I explain . . . ?

You: You had that opportunity. Now this is what must happen.

Gail: Are you going to call the police?

You: What legal action the company takes, if any, will be decided in consultation with our attorneys.

Gail: But I need to know.

You: Gail, I'm telling you all I know at this time. I am preparing a letter summarizing the terms of this dismissal. Please go to your office and collect your personal belongings now.

Keep the termination for cause as emotionally neutral as possible. Do not scold, do not lecture, do not express regrets. Above all, do not apologize. You have nothing to apologize for. Make no statements concerning future civil or criminal litigation.

Termination Due to External Circumstances

This is the most difficult termination scenario, both for the manager and the employee. Typically, you are in the position of having to lay off a good employee. It hardly seems fair, and it hurts.

Your strategy is to separate yourself and the employee from the action. "It" is happening. "It" is a fact. There is nothing either of you can do about it.

STEP 1:   Make a background statement: why layoffs are happening.

STEP 2:   Tell the employee he is being terminated.

STEP 3:   Give him the effective date of termination.

STEP 4:   Tell him any positive measures that can or will be taken on his behalf, including (for example) severance pay, salary for unused vacation, placement assistance, your willingness to write letters of recommendation, and so on.

STEP 5:   Provide instructions regarding collecting his final check, performance during the notice period, return of company property, and so on.

STEP 6:   Express sympathy, but do not apologize beyond remarking "I'm sorry this had to happen." Always stress the inevitable, unalterable nature of the layoff.

STEP 7:   An official notice must be submitted in writing.

YOUR SCRIPT: TERMINATING DUE TO EXTERNAL CAUSE.

Here is a typical conversation:

You: Cutbacks at the corporate level have made it necessary for XYZ Corporation to reduce personnel. Jack, you are among the employees being released from the payroll.

Your employment here will end on November 18. Your final check will be issued at that time. It will include any vacation pay you may have coming. There is also two weeks' severance pay.

The company offers a placement-assistance program, which you may find helpful in securing new employment. Personally, Jack, you know that you can come to me at any time for letters of recommendation or for a phone call to a prospective employer. I'll be happy to give you the fine recommendation you deserve.

Jack, I'm handing you a letter putting this termination in writing and spelling out the terms in detail. The letter also explains how you can continue health-insurance coverage and other benefits.

I'm sorry this had to happen, and I wish you all the luck in finding a great job.

CHAPTER 7

Putting Yourself Across . . . to Prospective Clients and Customers

SELF-TEST YOUR SAVVY IN COMMUNICATING WITH PROSPECTS

The following is a simple diagnostic test. A smaller and more selective version of the self-test in Chapter 1, its purpose is not to test your knowledge of communication theory or techniques, but to help you gauge how effectively you communicate with prospective clients and customers in a day-to-day business context. For the most part, you will find it easy to guess the "right" answer. But getting the "right" answer is not the point of the test. Respond honestly, even if you feel that your response is not the best one possible. This is *not* a contest. The object is solely self-inventory.

1. I always use a soft-sell approach.   T/F _____

2. I always use a hard-sell approach.   T/F _____

3. I always try to smile when I talk to a prospect on the phone. T/F _____

4. I approach the sales call systematically and step by step.   T/F _____

5. I care less about making a sale than I do about creating a customer.   T/F _____

6. Resistance is the customer asking for more information.   T/F _____

7. Don't let the customer ask questions. You'll lose the sale.   T/F _____

8. My main focus is to *make the sale*.   T/F _____

9. To make the sale, speak quickly.   T/F _____

10. I never "wing" a cold call. I prepare notes to work from.   T/F _____

11. I seek to *educate* my customer.   T/F ____

12. I sell value.   T/F ____

13. I sell price—the cheaper the better.   T/F ____

14. Never take *no* for an answer.   T/F ____

15. I try to get my prospects to ask questions—*lots* of questions. T/F ____

16. I want my customer to understand his or her choices.   T/F ____

TOTAL T/F   ____

Score 1 point for each "True" response and 0 for each "False" response, EXCEPT for questions 1, 2, 7, 8, 9, 13, and 14. For *these questions only*, SUBTRACT 1 point for each "True" response. Record your total. A score below +7 indicates that you would benefit from practicing the communication techniques discussed in this chapter. (Note: It is possible to have a negative score.)

WORDS TO USE WITH PROSPECTS

absolute	authorize	confirm
accessories	authorized	consider
accommodate	availability	convenient
act	available	convinced
acute	benefits	create
advise	choice	deadline
agree	choose	debate
alternative	client	decide
answer	close	decision
appreciate	comfort	demand
appropriate	commitment	demonstrate
approval	competitors	desire
assist	complacency	direct
assure	completion	directly
authorization	confident	disbelief

WORDS TO USE WITH PROSPECTS, *cont'd*

discerning	need	savvy
discuss	offer	schedule
do	okay	serve
enjoy	opportunities	service
enjoyable	option	smart
enjoyed	order	solution
ensure	our	solve
especially	partners	sophisticated
establish	percentage	special
expedite	personal	style
experience	pleased	substantial
extra	pleasure	successful
features	possible	supply
final	pressure	sure
fresh	price	talking
furnish	problem	target
generous	productive	terms
give	promise	testimonial
guarantee	quality	time
help	questions	trust
immediate	real	truth
immediately	relationship	try
information	reliability	understanding
inventory	require	unique
liabilities	requirement	value
listen	resolve	vendor
low	sale	welcome
minimum	satisfaction	winner
more	satisfied	yes
move	save	

PHRASES TO USE WITH PROSPECTS

always available

answer your objections

ask our advice

available for immediate shipment

best price

best effort

beyond my control

challenge the status quo

committed to you

confirm the availability

confirm that

confirm our understanding

count on the order

create a new market

deal direct

demand has been unusually high

do something good for yourself

do yourself a favor

don't cut any corners

enjoyed talking

exactly what you want

expect extra effort

expect more

expect your order

extend special terms

follow-up

generous terms

give us a try

go that extra mile

good news

PHRASES TO USE WITH PROSPECTS, *cont'd*

great product

greatest value for your dollar

have no choice

height of the season

here to serve you

hold the quantities promised

hold the prices promised

I think you'll agree

I understand completely

in the long run

industry leaders

lead time

let us help

let us help you

listen to you

little room for doubt

lock in your order

look forward to hearing from you

look forward to working with you

low prices

make certain

meet or exceed the specifications

no later than

no compromise on quality

our busy season

our situation

over the long haul

personal service

PHRASES TO USE WITH PROSPECTS, *cont'd*

price that's right for you

production times

prompt attention

proven winner

pure pleasure

put us on trial

put us to the test

ready to ship

reaping the benefits

right combination

self-indulgent

serve your needs better

special offer

special value

start-to-finish

target date

tell us what you need

to my attention

unique opportunity

very special price

we don't want you to get shut out

we won't leave you

we can

we can help

we care

we're here to help

we listen

what do you need?

you can talk to us

WORDS TO AVOID WITH PROSPECTS

bargain	costly
buy	cut rate
cannot	expensive
cheap	impossible
cheapest	sacrifice

PHRASES TO AVOID WITH PROSPECTS

be a fool to pass up

can't do it

cut to the bone

don't ask

I don't know

never again

no choice

once in a lifetime

think it over

BODY-LANGUAGE STRATEGY FOR COMMUNICATING WITH PROSPECTS

Let's begin by observing that, these days, much sales prospecting is done by telephone. Obviously, body language plays no role in that, right?

Well . . . wrong.

Consider adding two nonverbal elements to your prospecting calls:

1. Make the call standing up instead of sitting down. Talking while standing imparts more power and authority to your voice. (Few operatic arias are sung from a seated position!)

2. Smile as you talk. Even though the callee can't see your smile, she can *hear* it in your voice.

In addition, remember that, in general, the lower the pitch of your voice, the more conviction and authority it conveys. This is true whether you are a man or a woman.

- Pitch your voice lower than normal.
- Speak slowly and distinctly.

TIP

Some authorities advise salespeople to speak a little faster than at a normal conversational rate. Actually, it is advisable to speak a little more slowly than normal, especially during telephone calls. This not only makes your message clearer, it helps to defeat the negative image of the "fast-talking salesperson."

- Open your mouth when you speak into the telephone. Don't mumble.

In face-to-face sales situations, your object is to convey openness, trustworthiness, and honesty. Practice and apply the following:

- Establish and maintain eye contact.

TIP

In person-to-person sales situations, eye contact is the single most important nonverbal element of presentation. Eye contact conveys sincerity and character.

- Use open gestures, hands slightly spread, palms turned upward, as if offering something.
- When you stand, do so with feet slightly apart and firmly planted.
- Smile.
- Provide frequent nonverbal feedback. Gently nod to show that you are hearing and taking in what the prospect tells you.

BODY LANGUAGE TO AVOID WITH PROSPECTS

In general, avoid gestures that

- Suggest closedness, resistance, or that you are hiding something or "holding back"

- Convey nervousness
- Suggest evasiveness, shiftiness
- "Push" the prospect

Negative nonverbal gestures include

- Avoidance of eye contact
- Folding arms across the chest (suggests closedness or concealment)
- Hands on hips (suggests defiance)
- Shifting weight from side to side while standing (generally distracting and suggests that you don't want to be where you are)
- Leg movement when seated (distracting and suggests that you want to make a getaway)
- Hands near face or mouth (suggests evasiveness and concealment)
- Pointing, gesturing with a fist (coercive; likely to elicit resistance from the prospect)

FOUR-STEP FORMULA FOR BUILDING A CUSTOMER BASE

Working with a sales prospect can be broken down into four essential steps, which may be expressed in an operatic acronym: AIDA:

Attention

Interest

Desire

Action

Getting Attention from the Prospect

Get your prospect's attention. These days, we all swim in an ocean of information. Data stream by and around us. Is the result universal enlightenment?

Hardly.

The continual flux of information is often less enlightening than it is mind and emotion numbing. Your first task, then, is to get your prospect's attention. Here's an example of a telephone sales call:

You: Hello, Mr. Smith. This is Clara Barton at XYZ Company. I'm calling because we had a conversation a short time ago concerning high-performance widgets. I wanted to let you know that we are now stocking the brands we spoke about . . .

The caller gets the prospect's attention by recalling the past.

1. This is not a *total* stranger calling.
2. You and I had a conversation once.
3. You wanted something at that time.

Remind the prospect that he wants something, and you will get his attention. Identifying a need your callee has will also command attention.

Developing the Prospect's Interest

But attention is too brief to last through the close of a sale. You need to develop that attention into interest. Do this by showing your prospect how you can fill the need you've identified.

You: . . . and I think what we've got will suit your needs just perfectly. Even better, we're able to offer the widgets at a special introductory price. Are you interested?

TIP

Ask questions. Sales is not just about presenting information and speaking persuasively. It's about continued customer involvement, interactive feedback, opportunities for the customer to express himself and tell you what he wants.

Prospect: Yes, sure. I'm interested.

You: Great! I'll tell you about what we have.

Creating Desire in the Prospect

Interest certainly broadens attention, but it is still usually not enough to move the conversation along the road toward a close. This is the point at which you must make the merchandise attractive and irresistibly appealing.

TIP

The more you know about your prospect's taste, wants, and needs, the better chance you have of closing the sale.

You: Mr. Smith, in our earlier conversation you had mentioned (enumerate key points the prospect previously raised). The exciting news is that these widgets can do all of that—and more. For example: (enumerate key features).

Pause a beat to let this sink in. Then ratchet up the desire another notch:

You: But there's even more. Installation is *much* easier than it used to be for products of this type. Let me explain (explain improvements in installation).

One of your strongest selling points is value. You've built up desire. Now show that the desire *can* be satisfied:

You: Now, Mr. Smith, let me ask you something. How much have you been paying for widgets?

Prospect: (Answers with a figure.)

You: Here's a very pleasant surprise. The base price for these new widgets is $XX, with options extra. I think that you'll agree that this represents a spectacular value.

Prospect: Sounds pretty good to me.

You: Well, you won't pay that amount. We're offering a special introductory price, with the options package: $X! How does that sound to you?

This question is critical. Obtain a response to the price. This not only will further involve the prospect, bringing him closer to commitment, but will also allow you to gauge how close you are to closing the sale.

Prospect: I'm not sure . . .

You: Well, let me just add one other feature—our warranty. To begin with, warranties are quite good in this industry. Your typical widget warranty runs X years. *Ours* goes to XX years.

You know that our price is excellent, but you also know that price is meaningless without value. In terms of features, benefits, warranty, *and* price, well, you can't beat it, can you?

Prospect: It *does* sound good.

Moving the Prospect to Action

Once you receive a "buy signal"—an indication that the prospect is on the brink of commitment—move to close the sale. This critical point is not as difficult to reach as you may think. If the prospect is now ready to buy, all you have to do is make concluding the transaction easy.

TIP

Close the sale by making quick, easy, direct action possible.

You: Mr. Smith, the introductory pricing period will end on June 5. If you place your order now, I can guarantee units available at the price of $X. I can take a credit-card number right now.

MAKING THE SALE VERSUS CREATING A CUSTOMER

Sales professionals are typically told to concentrate on The Sale, and to make "one sale at a time." They are drilled in the ABC formula: *Always Be Closing.* The truth is that, for all the mystique and mystery in which selling is so often immersed, making "one sale at a time" is neither all that difficult—nor all that worthwhile. With practice and a halfway decent product to sell, you can probably close with a significant percentage of those you approach.

But why settle for that?

- Far better than the one-sale-at-a-time strategy is the one-customer-at-a-time approach.

A sales opportunity comes, you make the sale, and the event is over, finished. If, instead of making the sale, you create a feeling of trust and confidence in the customer, the sales *event* becomes a sales *process*. It doesn't just come and go. It develops. Approach selling as an opportunity to create satisfaction, to create, that is, customers.

- A sale is a one-shot event.
- A customer is a person who may generate sale after sale.
- Your best customers are your current customers.
- Your best advertising is the word of mouth of current customers.

Customers are a key asset. Develop the asset. Develop relationships. Develop trust. The payoff is plural sales, rather than *a* singular sale.

TIP

Not only are satisfied current customers great sources of word of mouth, they are often ideal consumers, consumers custom made for you. Cultivate them. Learn about what they want and don't want. Use this information to appeal to them, to make each sale that much easier.

ESTABLISHING AN EFFECTIVE COLD-CALL STRATEGY

A cold call is an unsolicited sales call: an attempt to sell someone something she hasn't asked for. At least, that's the simple and traditional view of the cold call. The cold call can be made more effective by preparation:

STEP 1: Don't make random calls to a random list of people you don't know.

STEP 2: Warm up cold calling by selecting names from special-interest lists you purchase or lease.

STEP 3: Call customers from your own data files.

STEP 4: Consider research efforts to identify potential customers; then call them.

Just as you should base your cold calling on some form of consumer research, prepare your presentation in advance.

TIP
_____

It is usually an exhausting mistake to attempt absolute spontaneity. Prepare.

Preparation for cold calling may include:

- Composing fully scripted pitches, which are read over the phone. Many direct marketers use this method. It is most practical for carrying out large-scale campaigns.
- For smaller campaigns that you handle personally, consider finding a middle ground between spontaneity on the one hand and a fully scripted pitch on the other.
- Prepare the "spontaneous" cold call by creating clear notes to yourself, including selling points, ways to meet and overcome objections, and so on.

Your phone notes should consist of fact sheets or "cue cards" listing the most important sales points of the merchandise or services you offer.

- The material on your cue cards should be just comprehensive enough to "hook" your customer. Avoid overselling, boring the prospect with details he doesn't want to hear.

TIP
_____

Avoid falling into the detail trap by asking the customer for feedback: "Do you want to hear more?" Or offer: "I can recite the whole spec sheet, if you like."

Should You Sell Soft or Hard?

Selling styles may be divided into two broad categories: soft sell and hard sell.

Soft sell is more conversational in tone than hard sell. It is a style that *pulls* the customer, gently, toward a close. Hard sell, in contrast, *pushes* the prospect, headlong, to a close.

Which approach is better?

This depends on the nature of the four major variables of any sales situation:

1. The perceived character of the seller
2. The skill of the seller
3. The needs and desires of the buyer
4. The intrinsic desirability—quality and value—of the product or service

In general, the more sophisticated these four variables are, the more appropriate is the soft-sell approach. The simpler these variables, the more likely it is that a hard sell will produce results.

YOUR SCRIPTS: MAKING COLD CALLS

Here's an example of soft-sell cold call:

You: Ms. Davidson, I'm taking the liberty of calling you at your office rather than your home to add yet one more call to your busy morning. Ms. Davidson, how many times has the phone rung this morning? How many problems have you handled? How many fires have you put out? How many meetings have you sat through? How many battles have you fought?

Prospect: Plenty . . .

You: If you're like most people in high-responsibility positions, you find it difficult to get through the day without taking some evidence of the pressure home with you: a knot in the stomach, an ache in the head, a pain in the neck.

Well, I won't use any more of your time to tell you how you feel. Let me get right to my offer: a place to go and work off all that tension. A place to do something kind and good and healthy for yourself.

XYZ Spa is a health club for professionals. We offer a complete gym, indoor track, two pools, sauna, and steam room. We're geared to offer you a vigorous breakfast-time workout before work, or fast and efficient lunchtime workout at midday, or something more when you have the time at the end of the day.

Ms. Davidson, what time is best for you?

Prospect: I really don't know.

You: Does the prospect of membership in a highly flexible and convenient health club interest you?

Prospect: I'm not sure.

You: Well, then, what you need is information. May I send you a brochure that describes our various programs? I think once you see the brochure, you'll be ready to pick a program that's right for you. You'll also find telephone numbers for fitness counselors, who can help you decide what would be best for you.

Here is a similar pitch, but done as a hard sell:

You: Mr. Tompkins, I'm calling to tell you to "Just do it."

Prospect: What?

You: Just do it. It's more than the slogan of a popular brand of running shoe. It's good advice. Especially now.
    Mr. Tompkins, have you ever thought about getting into better shape, or maintaining the shape you have, or just finding a time and place to unwind and have some fun?

Prospect: Are you trying to sell me a health-club membership?

You: Now is an excellent time to stop thinking and start doing.
    Yes, sir, I am offering an opportunity to join XYZ Club at special discount rates. Would you like me to explain?

Prospect: Yes, sure. Why not?

You: (Briefly outline the available plans, with promotional bargain prices.) Mr. Davidson, XYZ offers state-of-the-art facilities, including a Nautilus-equipped gym, indoor track, two pools, sauna, and steam room. We are located near your office, at First and Third Streets.
    You may be asking yourself, *Is there a catch?*
    Well, yes, there is. You must act now. This is a one-time telephone offer. To get the prices and services I just mentioned, you'll have to sign up today.

Now, we don't expect you to spend your money on blind faith. Here's the second part of the offer. Sign up and pay today, and you will be given a free 14-day trial membership. Here's how it works: If you join now, two weeks will be added—free—to your membership. If you join today and feel that you are not getting all that you had hoped for, just drop into our downtown office before November 12 and ask for a full refund. You risk nothing.

We've made it extra easy for you to "just do it." Just use your major credit card. Once you come into the club, you can put together your own health program, or you can talk with one of our fitness counselors. And remember: there is no risk. Try us for 14 days. If you don't like us, your money will be refunded—on the spot.

FOCUSING THE PROSPECT'S NEEDS

The great Chicago master of nineteenth-century retailing, Marshall Field, put his selling philosophy into a single phrase: "Give the lady what she wants." That is a fine philosophy—provided the lady, or the man, *knows* what she or he wants. In many selling situations, however, neither fulfillment of a clearly stated want nor persuasion of a need is called for. In many situations, selling is a process of education and discovery. It is up to the salesperson to help—yes, *help*—the customer focus his or her needs.

- In selling sophisticated or complex goods (personal computer equipment, for example), the educational component of the sales process may be especially significant.
- In selling high-ticket items, requiring a substantial investment from the customer, education plays a key role.
- In selling bulk items, it is often important to help the customer determine just what and how much of the product he or she needs.
- In selling merchandise intended to solve specific problems ("What flea shampoo is best for my dog?"), education is critical.
- In selling items that involve more than one purchase or financing option, education plays a key role.
- Selling merchandise incorporating new technologies requires educating the customer.

Salespeople of the old school—and salespeople who do not respect their product—discourage customer questions. They believe the salesperson should remain "in control," that questions bring on thought, thought brings on doubt, and doubt halts the momentum that makes a sale.

All of this is true—if you see the sales process as essentially cheating the customer out of his or her money.

If, however, you see sales as trading value for value, and, furthermore, if your objective is not merely to make a single sale, but to create a customer—a source of repeat business and word-of-mouth advertising—then you will make an effort to elicit questions from the customer.

TIP
_____

A question is an investment. It takes initiative, positive action, and effort to ask a question. The customer who asks questions has, in effect, made a down payment on the merchandise you offer.

The process of focusing needs typically begins when you pick up the phone and the caller tells you that she's looking for some "information" on the style and prices of widgets you carry. "I just want to get information," she warns, in an almost scolding tone, as if to put you on notice that she has no intention to make a purchase at this time.

Now, you may take this implied warning at face value. Or you may give it a little thought. While there are people who "window shop" on the phone, filling empty few moments with idle requests for information, it is more probable that the caller asking for "information" is really doing two things:

1. Shopping
2. Calling for help

The best way to handle the call is to offer:

1. Selling
2. Helping

If the caller's question is sufficiently specific, reply: "I can help you with that." If it is vague, ask questions to bring the caller's questions into clearer focus.

Better yet, let's establish a STEP 1 for focusing needs:

STEP 1:   When you pick up the phone, greet the caller, state your name, the company's name, and then ask: *How may I help you?*

Let's talk about this step. The phrase is important. It's not *May I help you?* or *What can I do for you?* but *How may I help you?* That single word *how* is a powerful tool for focusing the caller. The word prompts her to tell you what she wants. If all goes well, it will evoke a response such as, "I'm looking for a good, solid widget—not the cheapest, but I don't want to go overboard, either."

The *How may I help you?* approach is also very effective in face-to-face sales situations. In a retail setting, for example, you see a customer browsing certain items. The usual approach is to walk up to the customer and ask "May I help you?" There are two problems with this phrase:

1. It does nothing to focus the customer's needs.
2. It may be answered *yes* or *no* and is, therefore, quite possibly a dead end.

TIP

A good salesperson asks questions and invites questions, but avoids asking questions that can be answered yes or no. The object of a sales-oriented question is to define needs and to get the customer to invest time and effort in the sale, thereby increasing the customer's stake in the sale and the likelihood of the sale's coming to a close.

Once you have a response to *How may I help you?* begin to develop the response into a sale. Here, then, is STEP 2:

STEP 2:   Make the caller or browser feel that he has come to the right place. Now is the time for the *I can help you with that* response.

STEP 3:   Work with the caller or browser to develop the initial statement into whatever you need to make an informed and helpful response that will likely result in a sale.

TIP

Sales fail to close for many reasons. One of the most common is misunderstanding or inadequate understanding. This is a result of insufficient information, and that—let's face it—is *your* fault. It is up to you to ensure that the information you receive and supply is adequate and clear.

STEP 4: Be prepared to make an adequate commitment of time. It takes time to make a sale because it takes time to determine what information the customer requires, to provide that information, and to ensure that the customer understands the information. The time required to "persuade" the prospect is actually slight. Invest your time in information.

STEP 5: Do not avoid asking questions. This is how you gather the information you need to help the caller and to convert an "information-only" call into a sale.

YOUR SCRIPT: FOCUSING THE PROSPECT'S NEEDS

Here is a call-answering scenario. The phone rings, and you pick it up:

You: XYZ Company. This is Bill Smith. How may I help you?

Caller: I am interested in widgets.

You: I can help you with that. May I have your name?

Caller: Mary Clark.

You: Ms. Clark, we offer a wide variety of widgets. Let me just ask you a few questions so that we'll find just what you're looking for.

Be sure that you have at the ready a list of questions relating to the product you sell. Make it your business to know what buyers of your product are most interested in. In general, avoid talking about price until questions about product features and benefits have been answered.

You ask the questions, and the caller responds. After this, you continue:

You: Great. Now I have a clear picture of what you're looking for. Based on what you've just told me, I suggest that you consider either widget A or widget B. Both will do everything you've just told me you need; however, widget A also does (list additional functions). Would you like me to tell you more about those additional functions?

Caller: Well, what will they cost me?

The caller tries to introduce his own agenda. You don't want to give the impression that you are evading the question, but it is important for the caller to know more about the additional features *before* additional costs are discussed. If price is mentioned before interest in the additional features is developed, it will be difficult to develop that interest.

You: Let me quickly review these features in order to give you that information. (*After* explaining the additional features, the widget A price is given.) Now, widget B is priced at $XX, and widget A, with the additional features I mentioned, is $XXX.

I think you'll agree that both prices represent excellent value. Both widgets are of the same quality. The difference is in available features. If you want the additional features, the additional cost is certainly justified. But if you're looking for something more basic, which still fits the requirements you mentioned, you might want to spend less on widget B.

Is there anything more that I can tell you about the additional features—or the basic features, for that matter?

If there are more questions, handle them. Do not *push* the caller toward the more expensive product, but do make the additional features and value seem attractive. Once you have responded fully to the caller's requests for information, you have also set up a sale. Why not attempt to close? Ask:

You: May I take your order for widget A or widget B?

Maybe you'll get an order. However, if the customer hesitates or simply says that he is not yet ready to order, ask another question:

You: Is there any more information I could supply to help you make your choice?

TIP

Choice is a word you should always use in preference to *decide* or *decision*. *Decision* suggests compulsion, but *choice* connotes empowerment and freedom. It helps to put the sale in a positive context and gives the customer the feeling that he is in control.

You may have to be patient and review the information again. Be careful, though, not to bombard the caller with too many choices. This may lead to discouragement, the customer's feeling that he isn't sufficiently competent to make the decision. You may lose the sale. In complex sales situations, consider drawing up a "decision tree" or a "flow chart," with the yes and no responses branching from one decision to another, in order to help your sales staff "walk" customers through the options and help them clarify their needs.

GENERATING URGENCY IN THE PROSPECT

Generating a sense of urgency does not mean creating an aura of panic, hysteria, or ballyhoo. Rather, it requires demonstrating that *now* is the time to buy. Options for creating the sense of urgency include:

- There are price incentives.
- We can promise current availability of a high-demand item.
- You owe it to yourself to make the choice *now*.
- Why wait to begin enjoying the product benefits?

YOUR SCRIPT: GENERATING URGENCY.

Here are some examples of creating an appropriate sense of urgency:

1. **You:** There's a good reason to act now. I can deliver the widget to you for only $XX. That's a savings of $X. But this is a limited-time promotional price.

2. **You:** We sell an awful lot of these. Right now, I can guarantee immediate shipment. I can't promise *anything* about future orders. Demand is high, and production doesn't always keep up with it.

3. **You:** Why not do something good for yourself and buy now? You could own this widget today.

4. **You:** We're agreed that the widget will make your operations more efficient and cost-effective. My suggestion is that you put these product benefits to work for you right away.

OVERCOMING RESISTANCE BY THE PROSPECT

Resistance may be in the form of an outright "No, I'm not interested," but, more often, is expressed as "I don't know . . ." or some more specific phrase, such as:

- "Isn't that terribly expensive?"
- "I've heard those things don't work."
- "I've heard a new model is going to make that obsolete."
- "I've always used Brand X."
- "I don't have the staff to operate it."

Perhaps the most frequent expression of resistance is postponement:

- "Can you call me about it later?"
- "I've been too busy to think about it."
- "I'm not ready to buy yet."

The most effective strategy for overcoming resistance depends on the type of resistance you encounter. Answer the "I don't know" or more specific types of response by educating the prospect:

Prospect: It's too expensive.

You: You are right The widget does require an investment. But our experience has shown that it *is* precisely that: an *investment*—a cost-effective investment of resources. On average, in installations we've done for firms the size of yours, the initial outlay is amortized within less than a year. Of course, we also offer you a wide range of financing choices for you.

TIP
Resistance is not just something a customer puts up to thwart you. It is an obstacle that both you *and* the customer confront. Overcome resistance by showing your customer how to get around the obstacle. Never argue. That's negative. Instead, show the alternatives. These are positive.

The other type of resistance—postponement—may be overcome by exploring and removing some of the uncertainty that is typically at the heart of the resistance:

- "What can I do to help you make your choice?"
- "What additional information will help you move on to the next step?"
- "How can I help you define your options?"

WHEN TO WALK AWAY FROM THE PROSPECT

Old-time hard-sell sales forces were taught never to take no for an answer. This was thought to be a highly admirable approach. There are problems with it.

- Pursuing a nay-saying customer is exhausting and demoralizing for the sales staff.
- Pursuing this customer takes time away from more productive sales opportunities.
- Pursuing this customer will alienate him or her. *No* need not be a permanent state. Failure to make this particular sale is not a good reason to see to it that you lose this customer, who represents the possibility of *future* sales.

The key is to recognize the difference between resistance, hesitation, and uncertainty on the one hand and no on the other. It's really simple. If the prospect declares that she is "not interested" or that she is "not in the market for" your product, you may ask "Is there anything I can do that will change your mind?" If the answer is still no, *thank* the prospect for her time and stake a claim for the future: "Ms. Johnson, needs change over time, so I hope that you will think of us if you ever find that you do need to purchase a widget."

CHAPTER 8

Putting Yourself Across . . . to Current Clients and Customers

SELF-TEST YOUR SAVVY IN COMMUNICATING WITH CUSTOMERS

The following is a simple diagnostic test. A smaller and more selective version of the self-test in Chapter 1, its purpose is not to test your knowledge of communication theory or techniques, but to help you gauge how effectively you communicate with current clients and customers in a day-to-day business context. For the most part, you will find it easy to guess the "right" answer. But getting the "right" answer is not the point of the test. Respond honestly, even if you feel that your response is not the best one possible. This is not a contest. The object is solely self-inventory.

1. When a customer calls for information, I try to sell him something.   T/F ____

2. I am unable to resist a request for a favor.   T/F ____

3. I am willing to negotiate many things.   T/F ____

4. I ask the caller's permission before I put him or her on hold.   T/F ____

5. I call the customer if I know I will have a problem meeting a deadline.   T/F ____

6. Informing customers about new products and accessories is *helpful to them*.   T/F ____

7. A customer's call for information is a nuisance that should be quickly disposed of.   T/F ____

8. I don't panic when I'm going to miss a deadline.   T/F ____

9. I don't repeat back other ordering information a caller gives me. Too tedious.   T/F ____

10. I encourage the customer to order.   T/F ____

11. I *explain* costs and prices.   T/F ____

12. I feel good about asking for a favor.   T/F ____

13. I *hate* asking for favors.   T/F ____

14. *Everything* is negotiable.   T/F ____

15. I know how to upsell.   T/F ____

16. I know the products/services I sell.   T/F ____

17. I know how to turn informational calls into sales.   T/F ____

18. I let the customer know that I am eager and able to help him.   T/F ____

19. I never *demand* information from a customer. I ask.   T/F ____

20. I offer my customers guidance *and* choice.   T/F ____

21. Company policy is of supreme importance in dealing with customer requests.   T/F ____

22. I smile while I'm on the phone.   T/F ____

23. I sometimes try to avoid calls from customers.   T/F ____

24. I take the extra time to "error proof" orders.   T/F ____

25. I take customers' orders accurately and efficiently.   T/F ____

26. I try always to tell a customer what I *can* do, not what I *cannot.*   T/F ____

27. I understand rapport and how to establish it in the first few seconds of a phone call.   T/F ____

28. I won't take no for an answer.   T/F ____

TOTAL T/F   ____

Score 1 point for each "True" response and 0 for each "False" response, EXCEPT for questions 1, 2, 7, 9, 13, 14, 21, 23, and 28. For *these questions only*, SUBTRACT 1 point for each "True" response. Record your total. A score below +17 indicates that you would benefit from practicing the communication techniques discussed in this chapter. (Note: It is possible to have a negative score.)

WORDS TO USE WITH CUSTOMERS

able	exceptional	key
advance	excited	latest
answer	expect	money
answers	expected	new
anticipate	expedite	nominal
approach	experience	opportunity
assume	expertise	options
attention	extensive	outstanding
attitude	extra	personal
biggest	facts	please
client	features	pleasure
colleagues	figures	pledge
competitive	fine	prefer
complete	folks	pride
confidence	free	project
conversation	great	promised
customer	hope	prompt
deliver	impressive	provocative
delivery	improvements	purpose
detailed	include	quality
direct	inclusive	questions
discount	innovative	reaction
eager	inquired	ready
easier	interest	realize
enterprise	invite	requirements

WORDS TO USE WITH CUSTOMERS, *cont'd*

response	small	time
responsive	special	upgrade
review	specifications	warranty
save	standard	willing
send	style	winner
service	support	
shrewd	thanks	

PHRASES TO USE WITH CUSTOMERS

across the board

as you requested

bear in mind

brand-new

competitive edge

complete satisfaction

complete confidence

complete—with absolutely everything you need

comprehensive selection

compelling investment opportunity

cost savings

crystal-clear specifications

customer-support program

deeper level of service

detailed prospectus

discussed with you

drop by our showroom

even more useful

exceptional warranty

experience tells me

PHRASES TO USE WITH CUSTOMERS, *cont'd*

free customer support

full range of

give you

great numbers

just came in

just received

just gotten

key to success

let the document speak for itself

locked in and guaranteed

look forward to

many options

may I direct your attention

most popular

my direct line

no unwelcome surprises

not to be missed

nothing in this world is risk free

our relationship

our single most important product: ourselves

pass those savings on to you

personal attention

pleased to send

points of special interest to you

pride ourselves

prove it to yourself

ready, willing, and able

right away

risk free

save you plenty of time

see for yourself

PHRASES TO USE WITH CUSTOMERS, *cont'd*

significantly upgraded

special effort

special highlights

special offers

special price

special pride

talking with you

total commitment

trailblazing

uncompromising quality

very personal

virtually unlimited number of options

walk that extra mile

want very much to work with you

wide range

willingness to help

without risk

your bottom line

your thoughts on

WORDS TO AVOID WITH CUSTOMERS

bargain	expensive
buy	impossible
cannot	lost
cheap	sacrifice
cheapest	sidetrack
costly	unload
cut rate	wait
delay	

PHRASES TO AVOID WITH CUSTOMERS

back burner

be a fool to pass up

can't do it

check on you

cut to the bone

don't ask

haven't bought anything in a while

I don't know

inactive account

inactive customer

minimum purchase

never again

no choice

once in a lifetime

think it over

waiting list

BODY-LANGUAGE STRATEGY FOR COMMUNICATING WITH CUSTOMERS

The body-language strategy for dealing with current customers is the same as that for dealing with new customers and prospects, except that you might try to approach these current customers as you would acquaintances and friends. The approach may be informal, friendly. Make the customer feel that he or she has established a relationship with you.

BODY LANGUAGE TO AVOID WITH CUSTOMERS

See the discussion on this subject in Chapter 7.

BUILDING CUSTOMER RELATIONSHIPS BY PROVIDING INFORMATION

Most customer contact involves nothing more—or less—than conveying information. That's just fine. No matter what products or services your company sells, it deals in information. You need to know what your customers want, and they need to know what you have to offer, how much it costs, and how they can obtain it.

STEP 1:   Save timed by focusing informational calls with the question "How may I help you?" As discussed in the previous chapter, be sure that you include the *how* in this question. It will help the caller to focus her request, to be specific.

STEP 2:   When the caller answers that question, be prepared to focus it further. This may be done by echoing back to the caller what she has asked for, but modifying the statement to define it more precisely: "You want the *complete* price list, or the price list for the standard models only?"

STEP 3:   Once you have a clear understanding of what is being asked, provide the information.

TIP

If you must obtain information in order to handle a caller's request, *ask* permission to put the caller on hold: "May I put you on hold so that I can look up the answer? It will take about 30 seconds." Note that you should give the caller an accurate estimate of the amount of time she will be on hold.

TIP

If you are using a computer to obtain information, remember that your telephone customer cannot see what you are doing. Let her in on the action: "I'm going to search for that record right now. I'm typing it into the system . . . and it's searching . . . should be another few seconds. Yes. There. What's come up on my screen is a pair of orders from you, one dated June 5 and the other July 1."

STEP 4: If appropriate, conclude the call by asking for an order. "Will you be ordering those widgets today?"

STEP 5: If the customer does not want to order, ask "Have I answered all of your questions?"

STEP 6: Ask: "May I help you with anything else today?

STEP 7: Conclude the call by inviting future calls—directly to you: "Ms. Carlson, please feel free to call any time. Just ask for me. I'm Jake Barnes."

TIP
_____

Don't give *too much* information. Be sure to give the caller all the information she has asked for *plus* any information you judge necessary or useful, but do not overload the caller with marginally useful or confusing data.

Taking an Order from a Customer

Taking an order: It's the most basic exchange of information there is, right?

Absolutely. But taking an order should not stop with exchanging information. The process should also establish or build on a positive, business-growing relationship between your firm and the customer.

- Take the order quickly and efficiently while communicating an attitude of helpfulness, service, pride, and accountability.
- Do not use the caller's time to advertise your company.
- Review each order with the customer to ensure accuracy.
- Confirm verbal orders in writing.
- Create an order-taking process that has you doing the work, not the customer. That is, don't force the customer to look up item numbers or to memorize his account number or to perform any task. You should never be in the position of having to demand information from the customer.

Your script: taking a customer's order.

Here is the scenario for a straightforward order:

Caller: I want to order a dozen widgets.

You: I can help you with that.

In a single sentence you have told the caller that he has come to the right place and that you are ready to *help*. You are willing to serve. You continue:

You: We will need some information. May I have your name?

Here is that vital transformation that is at the heart of most successful business communication. Move the conversation from *I* and *you* to *we* as quickly as possible. This pronoun shift is the basis for rapport. Why do you need rapport? After all, *you* are filling an order at the *customer's* request. True. But, to fill this order, you must ask for information. See to it that this comes across as a gentle request that will benefit the caller. It should not come across as a demand. You continue after obtaining the information requested:

You: Mr. Smith, we're creating a customer profile for our database. That's what we're doing right now. It will help us to serve you most efficiently in the future. So if I may just get some more information from you . . .

After obtaining permission to ask more questions, you gather the database information that you need. Note that it is always most effective to explain what you are doing and to put it in terms that show how what you ask the customer to do will benefit the customer. Be sure to make any choices clear. Choice empowers the customer:

You: We usually ship via United Shipping Service, with a three- to five-day turnaround time. Do you have any other shipping preference?

After recording any responses to the "choice" questions, you continue:

You: Okay, the order. You want (quantity) widgets, correct?

Caller: That's right.

You: Those are available in white or black. Which do you prefer?

Be careful how you ask these kinds of questions concerning choice. Use words like *prefer* rather than *want*. *Prefer* emphasizes the customer's power of choice, whereas *want* suggests that you are impatient to have the customer make up his mind.

Caller: White—for all of them.

You: I've got that. We are shipping to you at (you repeat the shipping address you have been given) a dozen white widgets. Is that correct?

Caller: Right.

You: The total price, with shipping, is $XXX if you use a major credit card. For an added charge of $X, we will ship C.O.D. Which would you prefer?

Caller: I'll use my credit card.

You: Okay. I'm ready for the number.

Caller: (Gives the number.)

You: And that card expires . . . ?

Note that even here it is possible to do some of the work for the caller. Instead of demanding "Expiration date?" you start the caller's response for him.

Caller: (Provides expiration date.)

You: We are almost finished. Just let me read that credit card number back to you. (Does so.) Have I got it right?

Note that it is useful to keep the caller informed of the progress of the transaction: *We are almost finished.*

Caller: Correct.

You: We're finished. You'll have your dozen white widgets by Tuesday. Mr. Smith, may I help you with anything else today?

End the call with an offer of more help. Make it clear that you are *offering* a service, not demanding that the caller tell you if there is anything else he wants.

Caller: That's about all.

You: It's a pleasure doing business with you. Please call me, Jim Roberts, at 555-5555, if you have any questions. Have a good day.

A key to building a productive relationship with your customers is to make them feel comfortable with the order-taking process. Customers who place orders by telephone fear three things:

1. They will be tied up on the phone for a long time.
2. Errors will be made.
3. They will be assaulted by a sales pitch.

Here is a scenario showing how you might address these fears from the start of the call:

Caller: I am calling to order a dozen widgets.

You: I can help you with that. This should take us about five minutes. That will give us plenty of time to ensure accuracy. May I have your name? . . .

From here the order process continues. Anxiety is produced by the unknown, and giving the caller a time estimate reduces the unknown. Just be certain that you give a realistic estimate. Here the time estimate is combined with an assurance that errors will be avoided.

Occasionally, a customer may express her fears to you:

Caller: You're not going to waste my time with a lot of sales hype, are you?

You: Your time is valuable, and you know what you want. Let's get right to the order.

TIP

There is nothing wrong with informing the caller about additional merchandise. You must ensure, however, that the information is presented as *information*, something useful to the caller rather than a sales pitch, which the customer perceives as useful only to you.

Ask the caller's permission before providing more information. The best time to do this is after the order has been taken and while you are repeating back the essential items of the order: "We are shipping 40 standard widgets to you at 1234 Mockingbird Lane, Pine Barren, New Jersey, 09876. Have you considered purchasing an adjusting kit for the widgets? It makes installation much simpler. Would you like any information on the kit?"

Only if the caller expresses interest should you continue. If not, conclude the transaction and book the order as is.

Avoiding Errors with Customer Orders

How do you know when you've "put yourself across" successfully? How is the effectiveness of business communication measured? One objective and accurate measure is the absence of errors. Few things are more damaging to customer satisfaction than shipping the wrong order or an order that contains errors.

Take these steps to failure-proof all orders:

STEP 1:   Repeat information the customer gives you.

STEP 2:   If some part of the order doesn't seem right, question it. Don't cast yourself in the role of passive order taker. Guide the customer to satisfaction.

TIP

In questioning any part of the customer's order avoid injecting a line of challenge. "Are you *sure* you want that?" may sound to the caller more like "You *are* stupid, aren't you?" Keep it neutral and gentle: "I just want to confirm that you want such-and-such. Usually, so-and-so is better suited to the application you intend."

STEP 3:   If you are certain that the caller is making a mistake, intervene: "Mr. Thomas, that accessory will not work with the widget you ordered. The compatible accessory is . . ."

TIP

How do you know when the customer is making a mistake? There is no substitute for knowing your merchandise.

STEP 4:   Even if you know your merchandise, you may sometimes need to obtain additional information in order to help a caller order the correct item. Don't guess. Do what you have to do to obtain the information. If you must look something up, ask permission to put the caller on hold. Explain to the caller what you are doing and that you are doing it to *help him*. Give the caller an estimate of how long he will be on hold.

TIP

Never correct an error without advising the customer that you are doing so. Always confirm any corrections with the caller.

Informing Customers about Price Increases

Informing customers of price increases is both very important and quite delicate. In general, the preferable approach is proactive; that is, regular customers should receive mailings or even phone calls in advance of significant price increases. This serves three purposes:

1. It will avoid the sticker-shock factor at the time of an order.
2. It may make the customer feel that you are dealing decently and straightforwardly with him and giving him personal attention.
3. It may motivate preincrease sales.

TIP

Catalog and price list materials should always include disclaimers about price—that they are subject to change without notice.

Your script: telling customers about a price hike

Here's an example of a proactive call made to a regular customer, informing her of an impending price increase:

You: Hello, Jane. This is Max Morris at XYZ Company. In reviewing my customer profiles, I see that you currently use a Type B widget. Tell me, Jane, have you given any thought to upgrading to a Type H widget?

Jane: I've thought about it—and might do it some time in the future.

You: Well, the reason I'm calling is that in 60 days, prices will be going up across the board on widgets, including the Type H.

Jane: Oh, really . . .

You: We're talking about a XX percent increase, from $XX to $XXX. There is a 60-day window to purchase at the current price, so if you are thinking about upgrading any time soon, now would be the time to do it.

Jane: Are you *really* raising the price?

You: Yes. This call is intended as a service to you. The Type II widgets are very popular. We don't need any gimmick to move them. But the fact is that our cost of material has risen sharply, and we just don't have any choice in the price increase.

Jane: Do I have to place my order now?

You: Jane, I'm ready to take your order now, and, if you like, I can discuss with you financing terms and our trade-in policy on your current unit. Or we can set up another time to talk. The point is that after November 3 the Type H widgets will be priced at $XXX.

Potentially stickier is informing the customer of an increase at the time of the order. Here is a customer who is ordering from an outdated catalog:

Caller (having been informed of the higher price): Well, my catalog says $XX.

You: We have issued a new catalog, which includes certain price increases. Our cost of materials has risen sharply, and, unfortunately, we had no choice but to increase the price of the widget.

Caller: When did the prices go up?

You: About three months ago, on January 30.

Caller: It's only three months. Can't I get it at the old prices?

You: That wouldn't be fair to the others who have paid the announced price. Mr. Smith, if we didn't adjust the price, we would not be able to offer the widget. It was necessary.

Caller: Well, okay. It just doesn't seem fair.

You: It was necessary, given the increases in costs we incurred.

Informing Customers About Price Decreases

Obviously, price reductions will come to your customers as better news than an increase. Make the most of it.

- Do not announce a price reduction in advance.
- Consider promoting price reductions to move merchandise.
- Be prepared to cope with suspicions: "What's wrong with the widget? Why did you have to bring the price down?"
- Promote price reductions as evidence of your concern for and commitment to value.

YOUR SCRIPT: TELLING CUSTOMERS ABOUT A PRICE REDUCTION

A customer calls to order at the old price and gets the good news:

You: Are you aware of the new low price for the widget?

Caller: New low price?

You: That's right, $XX, down from $XXX.

Caller: Terrific! What's the problem?

You: No problem at all. This widget has been so successful that we have increased production and lowered our costs. We want to pass that savings on to you. That's the way we do business. We don't just make sales, we create customers.

WANT TO BUILD A RELATIONSHIP? ASK A FAVOR OF THE CUSTOMER

Most people hate asking for a favor. And they're right to feel this way—if they define *favor* as most of us do: asking for something in return for nothing.

Want to feel better about asking for favors? Then redefine the word. Think of the favor not as a bid to get something for nothing, but as providing your customer with an opportunity to help you.

Your Customers Love *Helping You*

Here's a revelation: most people enjoy helping others. Being asked to help empowers the helper. It is a flattering vote of confidence. It provides an occasion to feel good about oneself. Moreover, in the business world, many people rightly believe in a kind of commercial brand of karma: What goes around comes around. Doing a favor creates goodwill, which will ultimately benefit both the doer and the receiver of the favor.

There are four steps to asking a customer for a favor:

STEP 1: Establish the basis for the request. Usually, this is the fact of the business relationship itself: "We've worked together for so long that I feel comfortable asking you for a favor."

STEP 2: Be explicit and clear about what you want.

STEP 3: Explain how the favor will benefit you. This shows your customer just how much he will be able to help.

STEP 4: Express gratitude and thanks.

Getting Referrals and Recommendations

It's no secret that the best advertising for your business money cannot buy. And that, of course, is why it's the best. We're talking about word-of-mouth. Nothing is more convincing and compelling.

TIP

The value of word-of-mouth advertising is one reason why you should regard your current customers as your best customers. They are not only sources of additional sales, they can spread to others the good word about you.

Establish a mutually productive and profitable relationship with a customer and, chances are, she will be happy to recommend and refer your products and services to others. After all, she has positive motives for helping you:

- Doing so is an opportunity to do you a good turn, which makes the customer feel good and is good business.
- Doing so is an opportunity for the customer to build goodwill with one of her business associates by turning the associate on to a good thing.

Your script: ASKING A FAVOR OF A CUSTOMER

Here is a typical favor-requesting scenario. You call a favorite customer:

You: Bill, I'm calling to ask you for a favor. Now, we've had such a great working relationship that I've actually looked forward to making this request. Here's what I need: a brief letter of recommendation to the ABC Company to help us secure a major contract with them. Let me tell you what's going on for us.

Customer: Okay.

You: We've been asked to bid on supplying ABC with widgets and installation and maintenance services. I'm sure you realize that this represents very substantial business for us.

A recommendation from you would be absolute dynamite. Really, really valuable.

Customer: I'll be happy to do what I can—but I don't have a lot of time . . .

You: You don't need to devote any special time to this. I will ask ABC to call *you*. When they do, I'd appreciate whatever sell job you can do for us. The points I'd really like to get across to them are these three:

First, we give high value.

Second, we provide a very high level of first-rate client support.

And, third, we promise and deliver three-hour emergency response.

That's it. Would you like me to fax over those points?

- *Help* the customer to help you. He will not be offended if you supply him with a script. It takes the burden of spontaneity off him.

Getting More Time—Extending a Deadline with a Customer

Nothing in business is responsible for the creation of more excuses than missing a deadline. Face it:

- Telling your customer that you are going to miss a deadline will *probably* make her anxious and angry.
- Excuses about missing the deadline will *certainly* make the customer angry and will *probably* contribute to anxiety as well ("I'm working with somebody who can do nothing but make excuses . . .").

In view of this three steps are appropriate:

STEP 1:　Do whatever you can to avoid being late.

STEP 2:　When you know you are going to be late on completion or delivery of a project or product, inform the customer as soon as possible. Provide *timely* information when you cannot make *timely* delivery.

Advance warning of an impending schedule problem will give both you and your customer time to work out suitable alternatives. This should reduce panic and hysteria, thereby making the loss of the deadline seem less urgent and less serious. Advance word of deadline problems will give the customer the message that, despite the slip, you remain in control and "on top of things." It will also give the customer a sense of maintaining control as well.

STEP 3:   Avoid excuses.

Let's talk about Step 3. Instead of offering excuses for deadline slippage, realize that time is a commodity. You can buy more of it, and, as in any other sale, the purchase of time is negotiable. What do *you* have to offer in exchange for more time? What will you buy that time with?

- A better product
- A more successful result

Moving proactively, well in advance of the crisis, enhances the atmosphere of negotiation. In addition, avoid using crisis-creating language, words like:

cannot	neglected
crisis	no
delay	problem
due	slipped
forgot	trouble
impossible	unaware
late	unreasonable

Choose instead the vocabulary of negotiation, words that suggest choice and control:

alter	investigate
aware	manage
better	methodical
can	modify
care	possible
careful	priorities
caution	reschedule
expedite	resources
if	will

YOUR SCRIPT: ASKING A CUSTOMER TO EXTEND A DEADLINE

Here is a request for more time put in the form of a verbal progress report. No facts are withheld, but the tone of the request is matter-of-fact, conveying control, routine, nothing out of the ordinary. This is a phone call:

> **You:** John, I'm calling with a progress report on the Delta project. We have completed the first two phases as originally scheduled, but we are finding that the research for phase 3 is consuming more time than we had scheduled. I think you'll agree that this is *not* the stage for cutting corners, so we will need to alter the schedule, adjusting the completion date for the entire project from June 12 to September 1.

> **Customer:** That's a pretty big delay . . .

> **You:** I am confident that the results—and the resulting peace of mind you'll derive more than justify the extra time we are asking for. If we take the time to do it right now, you'll experience fewer start up glitches, and you'll be up and running to full capacity sooner.

OBJECTIONS TO OVERCOME WHEN ASKING FOR MORE TIME

Depending on *many* variables—the nature of the project, costs, lost revenue, the personalities involved, and on and on—asking for more time may be met with stiff resistance. Let's anticipate some of that here:

1. This is bad, bad for us. I was serious about that deadline. Now, look, you'd better just kick butt and get this thing in on time!

Reply with:

Mr. Perkins, I am very serious about the deadline, and that's why I'm talking to you about it now. This is the situation: I can give you a job you'll be 75 percent happy with if I deliver on deadline. Give me another week, and I can promise 100—percent satisfaction. The successful completion of the project is just as serious a matter as the deadline.

2. Look, what *do* you people do out there? I just can't understand it!

Reply with:

Ms. Garrison, we are moving ahead on the project. And one of the things we've just completed doing is an evaluation of the project in terms of how best to use our resources. We could cut corners, but that will only cost us time later. We'll have this conversation when the timeline's become a genuine crisis. We have control now. We have choices. That's why I want to modify the schedule—to build a better foundation now, so we'll avoid time-eating trouble later.

3. You have *got* to move faster than this!

Reply with:

Well, maybe we could. But neither of us would be comfortable with the results. And if we're not comfortable, how can we be confident?

4. Can you absolutely guarantee this will be the only delay?

Reply with:

I can guarantee that I will do everything possible to make certain that the schedule won't have to be altered again.

TIP

Answer with what you *can* do, not what you *cannot*.

Getting a Job Interview for a Friend or Relative

This is a frequently asked favor, but we conclude with it because it is also typical of the many miscellaneous favors you may ask a customer. With this favor request, as with all others, exercise thought before you call.

STEP 1:   Evaluate what you are asking. Can you and your customer live happily with the consequences of the favor? In this case, will your friend or relative be a credit to you?

TIP

Don't ask for favors casually. Remember, you have a relationship riding not so much on the request, but on the consequences of acting on that request.

STEP 2:   Acknowledge the magnitude of the favor. Doing the favor will require effort from the customer. Acknowledge this.

STEP 3:   Avoid *telling* the customer how he should feel about doing the favor: "Look, I know this is a real pain . . ." If it's a "real pain," why are you inflicting it? Let the customer decide.

STEP 4:   Do not falsely build up the job candidate, but do vouch for him. If you cannot recommend him for the job, you should not be asking for this favor.

STEP 5:   Express your appreciation, but do not emphasize how this favor benefits you. The customer should feel that, yes, he's doing you a service by interviewing your friend or relative, but also that you are doing *him* a favor by recommending a good employee.

YOUR SCRIPT: ASKING A CUSTOMER TO SET UP A JOB INTERVIEW

This scenario adds another element to the formal steps in requesting a job interview for a friend or relative: humor—a light, informal touch.

You: Kelly, I made a promise to myself years ago that I would *never* do what I'm about to do. I know you've been looking for an assistant, and I'd like to recommend and ask you to interview my nephew.

Customer: Ohhh . . . I don't know . . .

You: Now, come on, Kelly, you can stop groaning. The pleasant surprise in all this is that Jim, my nephew, is very bright, very eager, and a self-starter. He is just about to graduate from Midwestern University with a major in business, and he has a 3.4 grade-point average. He's also spent the summer interning at Smith and Company. They will furnish references.

But, Kelly, there's another thing. Jim's like me. You can't help but love him. He's just a great guy!

And, look, Kelly, you're too good a friend and customer for me to send you somebody I'm not proud of. Of course, you are under no obligations of any kind. You know that. But I would appreciate your talking with Jim.

Customer: Okay. Have him call me.

You: Kelly, I really appreciate it. I know you'll both enjoy the meeting.

HOW TO TURN DOWN A REQUEST WITHOUT TURNING OFF A CUSTOMER

It would make life easier if you could always say yes. Yes is easier than no.
For about three minutes.

The fact is that, without no, life would be impossible. Difficult and risky as it may be to decline a request, especially from a customer, doing so is sometimes absolutely necessary.

Five Secrets of Declining a Request for a Favor

1. Be certain that you should or must decline. If it is possible to say yes, do so. There is great relationship-building value in agreeing to perform a favor. Avoid knee-jerk nos.
2. If you must say no, begin by expressing regret.
3. Explain why you cannot perform the favor.
4. Apologize—but not profusely. Above all, do not waste the customer's time with a long apology. This comes across as a "punishment" for having asked a favor. It will discourage communication between you and the customer.
5. Offer something positive: the future. If it is possible and appropriate, suggest future circumstances and conditions that will enable you to perform the favor—the next time it is asked.

Avoiding a Flat-Out No

Saying no to a request doesn't necessarily mean having to say no to the *requester*. If possible, avoid an outright no and try to provide a no, but. This is nothing more than substituting a positive for a negative, emphasizing what you *can* do instead of what you *cannot*. Do this by providing alternatives to the customer's request.

- Be as specific as possible: "I can't deliver by Thursday, but I can deliver by the following Monday *and* expedite installation, which should save you three days on the back end."

TIP

Don't be vague about your alternative: "I can't. Maybe we can figure out something else." This is almost as frustrating as an outright no.

- If possible and appropriate, offer more than one *specific* and *helpful* alternative: "I can't deliver the entire order by Tuesday, but I can offer you a choice of alternatives. I can deliver a partial order by Tuesday, with the balance to come Friday, or I can prepare the complete shipment here for you to pick it up on Tuesday." Such choices empower the customer, making her feel less like someone who didn't get what she wanted and more in control.

TIP

Avoid overwhelming your customer with a laundry list of alternatives. If there really are multiple alternatives, provide guidance. Don't leave the customer to sink or swim on her own.

- No is a dead end. If you can't offer alternatives, perhaps you can offer a degree of no—which is, after all, also a degree of yes—rather than a final negative: "We can't extend to you the $70,000 line of credit you request, but we can offer an $18,000 line right now. As we do more business together, we can certainly revisit, and, I hope, revise this limit."
- Provide reasons for no. This is preferable to an arbitrary denial.
- If possible, state the conditions under which a yes would be possible: "We can't extend credit to you at this time, because of your history of slow payment. I would like to take another look at your credit picture in six months, which should give you time to catch up your open accounts. At that time, we'll reconsider the application."

Telling a Customer You Can't Change the Price

People who make their living by negotiating—salespeople, attorneys, professional mediators, and the like—insist that "everything is negotiable."

This is an example of hyperbole. While it is true that *more* is negotiable than most of us may believe, there are certain terms, amounts, and conditions that cannot be bargained. What happens when you have one of these absolutes and a customer approaches who is a believer in the everything-is-negotiable maxim? What happens when your price really is "carved in stone," but your customer insists on negotiating?

- The customer may yield and purchase the product.
- The customer may yield—grudgingly—and purchase the product. This time.
- You may lose the sale.
- You may lose the sale *and* the customer.

The preferable outcome, obviously, is the first. The strategy for arriving at it is to hold firm to what you cannot change and do one of the following:

- Offer alternatives in the case of items you can change.

  or

- Explain why the price cannot change (and hope the customer accepts the justness of the explanation).

YOUR SCRIPT: CONVINCING A CUSTOMER YOUR PRICE IS FIRM

This is a face-to-face encounter.

Customer: Okay, that's your *list* price. Now, what can you do for me?

You: We are not authorized to alter the price. We formulate a price we can live with—the most attractive price we can create for you. The margins are sliced thin, because we're interested in selling these in quantity. The advantage to you is that we come out with our best shot. The disadvantage of coming *out* with your best shot is that you don't have room to negotiate.

Customer: Come on. Everything's negotiable.

You: I can work with you to reduce installation charges, by giving you our preferred customer rate. I can offer an extended warranty at cost. I can give you our preferred customer rate on freight. These things do mean significant savings—$XX amount, if you took advantage of all of them. But the base price is our best price.

Watch your body language. Use open handed gestures and plenty of eye contact. Avoid gestures that signal defiance or closedness. Avoid gestures that suggest apology, particularly failure to maintain eye contact.

Customer: I might just try elsewhere.

Resist the temptation to "dare" the customer to do just this. The customer understands that the most persuasive negotiating tool he has is his feet. He can walk away. You have to be *willing* to let him do this, while keeping the offer open to him.

You: I am confident that you won't find a better price. But if you want to look, we'll be here to serve you when you come back. You won't find a better deal. Please remember that the deals I'm offering on extended warranty and freight, as well as installation amounts to $XX. I mean, that's money saved that would otherwise be coming out of your pocket.

Customer: Okay. I don't have the time to go elsewhere. Let's go with your price . . .

Explaining Why You Can't Extend Payment Terms

It is certainly not uncommon to renegotiate payment terms. Sometimes doing so is a matter of convenience for both parties involved. Sometimes the only alternative to such renegotiation is default and failure to collect anything. Again, therefore, the first step in responding to a request to extend payment terms is to avoid a knee-jerk no in favor of renegotiating terms. If, however, renegotiating is not an option, the no must be accompanied by sound reasoning that will seem fair to the customer.

TIP

It is a bad idea to appeal to such "authority" as "company policy" as a reason for not negotiating extended terms. Appeals to such abstractions frustrate the customer and make your firm appear rigid and without regard for customers and their needs.

YOUR SCRIPT: TELLING A CUSTOMER YOU CAN'T EXTEND PAYMENT TERMS

Here is an example of a no that relies on reasoned motives of fairness:

You: Mr. Thomas, this is Ellen James at XYZ Company. We spoke yesterday about renegotiating payment terms for your widgets. After reviewing the whole deal, Mr. Thomas, I find that I am unable to alter the terms. The prices you were given for the widgets were based on the terms to which you agreed. Changing that now would unfairly change the deal for us. We were able to offer you the widgets at the price you negotiated because of the terms to which you agreed. As part of the deal, I need you to adhere to those terms.

Denying a Customer's Request for Information

Information is usually easy to provide, and providing it on request goes a long way toward building an effective relationship with your customers. But if you find that you cannot provide requested information, you must take steps to ensure that failing or declining to satisfy the customer's request does not damage the relationship with that customer.

STEP 1:   Make clear the reason for not being able to furnish the requested information.

Acceptable reasons for not furnishing requested information include:

- You don't have the information.
- The information is proprietary.
- You have access to the information, but it is not in your control. (For example, another customer or client controls the information.)
- The information is confidential.

STEP 2:   Apologize.

STEP 3:   Thank the customer for his understanding.

Your script: turning down a request for information

Here is a response to a request for information you do not have:

You: I'm sorry, we don't have that information here. My suggestion is that you contact . . .

TIP
___
If possible, suggest alternate likely sources for information that you do not have.

TIP
___
Avoid sending customers or callers from your department to another in order to obtain information you don't have at your fingertips. If there is any way for you to obtain the information, do so. You—not the customer—should do the work.

Here is a scenario in which proprietary information was requested:

You: That information is proprietary.

Customer: Well, I don't want your corporate secrets. I just want to get those addresses.

You: The information is considered company property, and it is restricted to internal access only. I cannot transmit it outside of the company.

Customer: Is there someone else I could speak to?

You: For reasons of our security and the security of our customers, we do not share this information. I don't have any alternative suggestion.

You may be able to access information, but it is controlled by another customer or other third party.

You: That information belongs to our customer. I couldn't share it with you.

Customer: You have access to that information. What harm would it do to give me the information?

You: It would harm the property rights of our customer. We must respect and protect those, as we respect and protect yours. The information simply is not mine to give.

Keep your reply to requests for confidential information brief.

You: That information is confidential.

Customer: Oh, really . . . what harm can I do with it?

You: We must respect the confidentiality. We've promised to.

Explaining to a Customer That You Can't Lend Equipment

Lending equipment, when feasible, can be useful in building stronger relationships with your customers; however, it is not always possible or desirable to lend equipment, especially vital equipment, which you need to have on hand for your own purposes. Most customers will understand this, and there is no need to be overly apologetic. It is important, though, to explain why the equipment cannot be loaned. Don't let this decision come across as arbitrary. Above all, do not make mindless reference to "company policy." Give a current, pressing, immediate reason rather than a reference to a standing rule. As with other situations in which you find that you have to say no, try to offer alternatives.

TIP

Avoid complaining about your company's rules or saying something like "the boss won't let us." Such remarks are unprofessional and reflect well neither on you nor on your organization.

YOUR SCRIPT: TELLING A CUSTOMER YOU CAN'T LEND EQUIPMENT

You've been asked to lend equipment to a customer, who is willing to rent the equipment from you; however, the equipment is needed for your own current production.

You: John, I'm sorry, but that equipment is 100 percent in use on our own production.

Customer: I'm really in a bind.

You: I appreciate that. And that is exactly where my company would be if I took any of our equipment out of production right now. But maybe I can help in another way. I can give you some contact numbers to call. Some of these may have equipment available.

Turning Down a Request for Rush Order/Service

If you can embrace an opportunity to "go the extra mile" for a customer, do so. Nothing creates satisfaction more efficiently and effectively than a demonstration of extra effort. But, of course, resources are finite, and you can't stretch for every customer all of the time.

STEP 1: Express regret that you cannot provide the rush service requested.

STEP 2: Explain why you cannot.

STEP 3: Offer what you can.

STEP 4: Emphasize that you are being realistic, that you do not want to mislead the customer with empty, feel-good promises.

STEP 5: Thank the customer for her understanding.

YOUR SCRIPT: DENYING A REQUEST FOR RUSH SERVICE

A sample reply to a request for rush service:

You: Ms. Maxwell, XYZ is known for going the extra mile for its customers. I've tried to make arrangements to expedite shipment of your order for delivery before Thursday, but I have not succeeded.

This is our busiest season, and, making the situation even more difficult, we have been left temporarily shorthanded due to the illness of a number of our employees. This is just not a very promising time to try to expedite a shipment. Right now, we are working on an overtime schedule as it is.

Now, Ms. Maxwell, I am doing everything possible to shave some time off your shipping date, but I do not want to make you promises I cannot keep. Misleading you will do neither of us any good. I can promise you that we *will* do better than the original delivery date, but we will not make Thursday. I'll know by the end of the day just when your shipment will leave here, and I'll give you a call with that information.

Ms. Maxwell, I appreciate your understanding in this matter.

Explaining Why You Can't Provide an Odd Lot

In wholesale situations, it is often impractical to fill orders for odd lots. Company order forms should make this clear, and whoever is responsible for taking the customer's order should also be aware of odd lot policies. If, despite instructions, the customer insists on ordering an odd lot, you will need to be firm but neutral. Give the customer choices.

YOUR SCRIPT: TURNING DOWN AN ODD-LOT REQUEST

You: Mr. Wilson, I'm calling in regard to your order. As stated on our order form, the smallest order we can fill is for 12 dozen widgets. You've ordered half that number.

Customer: Why can't I order the quantity I want?

You: Our prices are based on wholesale orders in large lots. If we break them down, our prices go up. The prices we quoted you were based on our minimum wholesale order. It would be unfair to us and to other customers to make an exception. We just can't do business that way.

Now, I do have some options for you to consider. You can go ahead and put in the minimum order of 12 dozen. That's the easiest. Or you can put that order in, and we'd be willing to divide payment for a nominal carrying charge. How would you like to proceed?

- There is, of course, another alternative. The customer may cancel the order. You must assume that he is aware of that. Don't "dare" the customer to cancel, however, by pointing this out as one of his alternatives. *Assume* he wants to take delivery of the merchandise.

Telling a Customer You Can't Perform Requested Modification

Look for a way to satisfy the customer. If you cannot satisfy her on precisely her terms, look for the next closest thing. An example follows.

Your script: discussing modifications with a customer.

You: Brenda, I've looked over the list of modifications you want made to the Model 3 widget. Economically, we can't afford to tool up to make the modifications you requested on an order of fewer than a hundred units. The numbers just won't work.

I've discussed this with our design and engineering people, and we've come up with two alternatives: You could, of course, up the quantity of your order. At a hundred units, we can make the modifications at a price we all can live with. But, Brenda, have you given consideration to the Model 5 widget? It incorporates most of the features the modified Model 3 would offer. May I take a few minutes to go over them?

WHEN A CUSTOMER ASKS YOU TO "BEND" SAFETY RULES OR REGULATIONS

One type of customer "favor" is particularly unwelcome. It is the request that you shortcut or circumvent some safety procedure or regulation. Of course, this is one request you cannot grant.

- Exposing your customer to a safety hazard is no favor; in addition, you expose yourself and your firm to legal liability.

Enforcing safety regulations can be a thankless job. Your customers may or may not react well to it. You need to navigate a middle course that makes no compromise on issues of safety, but that does not alienate customers, either.

Your script: refusing to compromise on safety rules

You: I noticed as we walked by the widget we installed last year that the safety device had been disconnected. I would like to reconnect it for you before I leave.

Don't accuse anyone of anything. Eliminate pronouns (*"You* disconnected the safety device."). Just report neutral facts.

Customer: That's the way we want it. The safety device slows the machine down too much. We're all grown-ups here. We're careful.

You: That's right. *Careful.* We're both concerned with safety. That interlock can't be left unconnected.

Use *we* to create a community of interest and avoid an *I* versus *you* conflict.

Customer: Look, do me a favor. Just forget it. It's our machine. We'll take the responsibility for it.

You: Well, it's true that you bought the machine, but it does carry our brand name, and I did notice the safety device disconnected. I do need to reconnect the interlock. I must protect myself and my company from unnecessary liability exposure. I'll note in my service report that the safety device is disconnected and that you and I discussed the issue. I must explain that I offered to reconnect the device and that my offer was refused. We keep all communications in our files and send copies to our attorneys. If in the future—and we certainly hope this never occurs—someone is involved in an accident and our company is named as a party in a negligence case, we will use the letters to demonstrate that we were operating in good faith and made you aware of the risks you were incurring.

Customer: Aren't you taking things a bit too far here? You're threatening me with your lawyers!

You: No, not at all. I'm just telling you what I have to do. I am trying to keep you informed. You are my customer. You have a right to know what we must do.

CHAPTER 9

Putting Yourself Across . . .
When Handling Credit, Collection,
and Customer Complaints

SELF-TEST YOUR SAVVY IN COMMUNICATING ABOUT CREDIT, COLLECTION, AND COMPLAINTS

The following is a simple diagnostic test. A smaller and more selective version of the self-test in Chapter 1, its purpose is not to test your knowledge of communication theory or techniques, but to help you gauge how effectively you communicate about credit, collection, and customer complaints in a day-to-day business context. For the most part, you will find it easy to guess the "right" answer. But getting the "right" answer is not the point of the test. Respond honestly, even if you feel that your response is not the best one possible. This is *not* a contest. The object is solely self-inventory.

1. Ideally, a collection call is an effort to *help* the customer pay. T/F ____

2. I believe in giving my customers *positive* incentives for paying on time. T/F ____

3. I can honestly say that I *learn* from my mistakes. T/F ____

4. I can't always give the customer all the credit he wants. T/F ____

5. I avoid collection calls by riding herd on cash flow from the beginning. T/F ____

6. My company stands behind its products/services. T/F ____

7. Our credit process is self-explanatory. T/F ____

8. The customer is always right. T/F ____

9. Mature customers are not unduly upset by a credit rejection. T/F ____

10. I deal sensitively with my customer's money issues.   T/F ____

11. By definition, a collection call cannot be pleasant.   T/F ____

12. A delinquent customer is a *delinquent* and should be punished.   T/F ____

13. I don't have time for collections. I call an agency—or our attorneys.   T/F ____

14. You don't have to *sell* credit. It sells itself.   T/F ____

15. I emphasize what I *can* do, not what I *can't*.   T/F ____

16. I get angry when I'm owed money.   T/F ____

17. You have to be a hard-nosed negotiator.   T/F ____

18. Credit is something I give selected customers.   T/F ____

19. Sometimes it's cheaper just to give the customer what she wants—even if she's wrong.   T/F ____

20. I make collection calls at reasonable hours.   T/F ____

21. Cash-flow management involves continually communicating with customers.   T/F ____

22. I may decline credit, but I never reject a customer.   T/F ____

23. Credit means *investing* in your customers.   T/F ____

24. I never threaten my customers.   T/F ____

25. I promote the benefits of my company's credit programs.   T/F ____

26. I sell credit as I sell other merchandise. It's a product.   T/F ____

27. When something goes wrong, I apologize profusely.   T/F ____

28. I try always to offer my customers options and choices.   T/F ____

29. I walk customers through the credit-application process.   T/F ____

TOTAL T/F   ____

    Score 1 point for each "True" response and 0 for each "False" response, EXCEPT for questions 7, 8, 9, 11, 12, 13, 14, 16, 17, 18, and 27. For *these questions only*, SUBTRACT 1 point for each "True" response. Record your total. A score below +16 indicates that you would benefit from practicing the communication techniques discussed in this chapter. (Note: It is possible to have a negative score.)

WORDS TO USE FOR CREDIT, COLLECTION, AND COMPLAINTS

able	compelled	experience
accommodate	competitive	explain
active	confident	extending
advantage	confidential	fair
advise	configuration	features
agree	confirmation	force
agreeable	convenience	forced
allow	convince	frank
alternative	convinced	friendly
apologize	cooperate	frustration
appreciate	cooperation	glitch
appropriate	creating	grateful
assist	current	guaranteed
assistance	custom	happy
assume	delighted	help
assure	delinquent	immediate
assured	dependable	important
attention	disappointed	information
benefit	discount	inquiry
budget	doublecheck	investment
choice	easier	invite
choose	encouraging	invited
communicate	expect	issue
communication	expedite	latest
compel	expedited	maintain

WORDS TO USE FOR CREDIT, COLLECTION, AND COMPLAINTS *cont'd*

majority	prompt	serious
mistake	promptly	service
modify	proposal	significant
mutual	proud	solve
necessary	quality	sorry
opportunity	reason	special
optimal	reasonable	specified
optimum	refund	standard
option	reimburse	substantial
owe	reliable	support
patience	reminder	talked
payment	replace	today
performance	replacement	together
personal	resolve	unavoidable
pleased	respond	understand
pleasure	response	understanding
possible	responsive	unpaid
privilege	satisfaction	value
problem	satisfy	vital
program	save	waive
promise	savings	willing
promised	scheduled	

PHRASES TO USE FOR CREDIT, COLLECTION, AND COMPLAINTS

account back on track

added value

alternative-payment options

answers will help me determine

PHRASES TO USE FOR CREDIT, COLLECTION, AND COMPLAINTS *cont'd*

apologize for the inconvenience

apologize personally

appreciate your understanding

appreciate your business

as promised

avoid these charges

bear in mind

best case/worst case

best value possible

bottom line

continue providing

continue serving you

credit privileges

direct line

discount program

do everything possible

Do you happen to have your order number handy?

either/or

establish a pattern of prompt payment

expedite shipment

finance charge

formulate a payment plan we both can live with

good afternoon

good morning

grateful for your understanding

great customer

happy to hear from you

help us avoid

highest level

How may I help you?

PHRASES TO USE FOR CREDIT, COLLECTION, AND COMPLAINTS *cont'd*

I fully understand

I am calling to check

I estimate

I want to thank you

I'm sorry to hear

if you like

in business together

in good standing

is that agreeable

Is there anything else I can help you with today?

it will take

it's your call

leave the choice to you

legal counsel advises

let's work together

letter of agreement

making it possible

mutual satisfaction

my error

my mistake

necessary steps

no additional costs

no hidden charges

not too late

not carved in stone

offer will be good

on behalf of

packed with terrific features

partial payment

PHRASES TO USE FOR CREDIT, COLLECTION, AND COMPLAINTS *cont'd*

payment cycle

payment plan

payment schedule

personal attention

please help

prompt payment

prompt response

remains unpaid

resolve the problem

save yourself money

send your payment today

seriously delinquent

seriously past due

service and value

service charges

settle this account

settling the outstanding balance

shared your letter

small-company service

sorry you had a problem

sound to you reasonable

special offer

subject to an additional charge

substantial savings

suffer a blemish on your credit record

suspend your credit

take comments like yours very seriously

take advantage

thank you for paying promptly

PHRASES TO USE FOR CREDIT, COLLECTION, AND COMPLAINTS *cont'd*

thanks for your order

that information will speed things up

up to you

up and running

we make every effort

we work hard

we'll proceed accordingly

whatever is necessary

Which option would you prefer?

Which would you prefer?

within my power

without delay

you can help us

you can be certain

you may reduce

your satisfaction is our primary concern

WORDS TO AVOID IN CREDIT, COLLECTION, AND HANDLING COMPLAINTS

avoid	no
blame	poor
can't	sue
dumb	tough
fail	turf
fault	unfair
immediately	unreasonable
inadequate	won't
incompetent	wrong

PHRASES TO AVOID IN CREDIT, COLLECTION, AND HANDLING COMPLAINTS

accidents happen

can't be done

carved in stone

do something about it

get off my case

give me a break

I can't

I forgot

I'm only human

no can do

nothing we can do about it

out of luck

tough luck

What do you expect?

won't even try it

won't work that way

wrong way

you are insulting us

you have to

you have no choice

you're on your own

CREDIT, COLLECTION, AND HANDLING COMPLAINTS: BODY-LANGUAGE STRATEGY AND BODY LANGUAGE TO AVOID

The most effective body-language strategy is essentially the same as that discussed in Chapter 7. Be aware, however, that intense money issues can do some strange things to body language—both yours and your customer's.

- Eye contact becomes a problem. You may find in yourself a natural tendency to avoid eye contact when discussing money, especially the sometimes delicate issues of credit. More usually, you may find that your customer avoids eye contact. You should not read this as a sign of dishonesty or distrust, but as a natural gesture in these situations. Respond with reassurance. Smile. Adopt a pleasant tone.
- Smile. Making credit decisions is always a two-handed process. On the one hand, you are eager to make the credit arrangements that will allow this customer to do business—or more business—with you. On the other hand, you must be skeptical and cautious. These latter qualities do not usually express themselves in a smile. Nevertheless, it is a smile that is called for in this situation.

The key to body-language strategy during the credit process is to make your customer feel accepted, welcome. There is nothing to be gained by giving nonverbal expression to your skepticism or reserve. Obviously, however, you should make no *verbal* promises you cannot keep.

- Watch the customer's hands. Hands that stray near the face or mouth while the customer answers critical questions *may* signal that the customer is being less than thoroughly honest. Don't challenge, but do beware.
- Keep watching. A customer who runs his hands through his hair or who rubs the back of his neck with his hand is probably frustrated. This is an opportunity to provide reassurance or explanation.
- A customer who folds her arms across her chest is probably expressing resistance. This would be a good time for gentle leading questions: "Is there anything I can clarify for you? Anything we should discuss at this point?"
- Similarly, you should avoid such gestures as folding arms across the chest or standing with hands on your hips. These are gestures of exclusion.

CREDIT: INVESTING IN YOUR CUSTOMERS

This is not the time and place for an elementary lecture on credit. You know what it is. Just make sure that you *think* about what it is before you enter into a credit negotiation with a customer.

- Credit is an investment in a customer.

You make investments in people, companies, and things of value— people, companies, and things that you believe will return to you greater value than your original investment. Credit is not something you *give*. It is an investment. It represents value *to you*. Let these thoughts put you in the right frame of mind for the discussion.

Selling Your Credit Package to Customers

So approach the customer with a certain humility and gratitude; however, approach her also in the knowledge that you are offering additional value. The credit package is something of value and use to the customer. It is, in effect, an additional product benefit. Your most effective verbal strategy is to promote it as such.

Before you present the credit package to a customer, consider what a product *benefit* is. It is *not* the same thing as a product *feature*, which is merely an attribute of the product. For example, nonbreakable material is a *feature* of a certain coffee mug. A *benefit* is what good things the customer will derive from purchasing and using the product. Often, product benefits have a significant emotional content. Let's return to our cup. One of its chief features is that it is nonbreakable. The *benefit* this particular feature provides is security: You can enjoy your piping-hot coffee without worrying about the cup breaking.

- Explain the *features* of your credit program, but *promote* the *benefits*.

Benefits might include:

- Increased purchasing power
- Enhanced cash-flow management
- More control
- More flexibility

YOUR SCRIPT: PRESENTING YOUR CREDIT PACKAGE.

Keep the selling tone light.

You: The credit package we offer will not only give you increased purchasing power, but will help you manage your cash flow. Our terms are flexible enough to put you in charge.

TIP

If you offer a choice of packages, present the choices clearly and present the idea of choice as yet another product benefit. Nothing enhances the customer's feeling of control—and, therefore, well-being—more effectively than a sense of having choices.

Asking Credit Applicants the Right Questions

Credit information must be recorded in written form, of course, but you may find that it speeds up the application process if you *verbally* request certain items of information.

- Never *demand* information.
- Filling out a credit application requires labor; acknowledge this and express your appreciation for your customer's efforts.
- Emphasize the fact that the customer may speed the application process along by furnishing requested information fully, correctly, and promptly.

YOUR SCRIPT: ASKING FOR CREDIT INFORMATION

Here are some approaches to getting the credit information you need:

1. **You:** I need you to do me a favor. Please send me copies of your financial statements for the last three quarters, so that I can expedite your application and set up a line of credit right away.

2. **You:** Phil, I've got all the basic information I need to get your credit line set up—except for a copy of your latest financial statement. As soon as you send that to me, I'll be able to complete your application. Can you get that out by tomorrow?

3. **You:** Mary, to get your credit line set up I'm going to need financial statements for the past three quarters. You'll see on the credit application a request for two credit references. If you want to give those to me now—or call me with them tomorrow—I can really expedite this process and get you set up right away.

Reporting on the Progress of a Credit Application

If the credit-application process consumes more than a few days, expect to be peppered with calls asking for progress reports. Why not enhance your relationship with your customers by taking the initiative and calling *them* with a report first.

TIP

The actual substance of the report matters less than the mere fact that you are taking the time to make the call and give the report. Do not make or imply promises you may not be able to keep.

YOUR SCRIPT: REPORTING ON THE PROGRESS OF A CREDIT APPLICATION

Here is an example of a progress-report call:

You: Peter! This is (your name) from XYZ Company. I was calling just to let you know that we're in the home stretch along the way to setting up the line of credit you asked for. I don't see any problems at this point, so I *expect* the line to be established before the end of the week. I'll call you back then—sooner if we hit any snags.

Another:

You: Sarah, this is (your name). I'm just calling with a progress report on the line of credit you asked for. Our financial partners are looking over your paperwork now, and I expect to be calling you back by Thursday.

TIP

The progress report doesn't have to be detailed. Its principal purpose is to reassure the customer that his application *is* being processed and that you *are* working for him.

What to Say When You Can *Honor the Credit Application*

The tone to establish is one of welcome. Avoid sounding overly congratulatory, as this will come across as inflated and perhaps even offensive—as if you hadn't expected this customer to qualify. If you deliver the good news in person, a warm, hearty handshake is called for.

YOUR SCRIPT: HONORING THE CREDIT APPLICATION

You greet the customer who has walked into your office:

You (with a handshake): Welcome aboard! I'm delighted to sign you up for a line of credit of $XXXX. It's subject to the terms discussed on the application form. Do you have any questions about these? Would you like to review them together?

After answering any questions and reviewing terms, close with:

You: We look forward to working together. This line of credit will give you a lot of flexibility and cash-flow control.

TIP

Of course, *all* credit terms should be spelled out in formal letter of agreement or, preferably, a printed contract. It is critically important that nothing said verbally should differ from terms specified in writing.

Specifying Credit Limits and Conditions to a Customer

The limits, conditions, and terms of a credit agreement with a customer should be fully specified in writing. Normally, you should not have to cover these details verbally when you welcome the customer into your "credit family"; however, there may be cases where you want to point out special conditions or limitations or, most important, where you have granted credit amounts or terms that differ from what the customer had requested. In such cases, verbally preparing your customer can be quite useful.

As usual, the most effective strategy is to emphasize the positive—what you *are doing* for the customer—rather than stress what you cannot do. Keep the conversation as upbeat as possible.

YOUR SCRIPT: EXPLAINING CREDIT LIMITS AND CONDITIONS

While emphasizing the positive, provide reasons for giving the customer less than she asked for:

1. **You:** Ms. Young, we are prepared to extend to you a line of credit of $XXX at this time. The credit agreement I'm about to hand you explains the terms, which are those we discussed previously.

   Now, I know that $XXX is less of a credit line than you asked for, so let me explain what we've done. Your financial statements indicate a healthy business with a very promising future, but we have to weigh this against the fact that you have been in operation only 18 months. Ms. Young, as soon as you've crossed the two-year mark, we'd like to review your updated financials with an eye toward increasing your line.

2. **You:** Joe, I am setting up a credit line of $XXX for you at this time. That should give you some maneuvering room and purchasing power—even though it's not all that you had been looking for. I wish I could oblige with the full amount you requested. However, your financial statements suggest that, right now, you are just too heavily obligated for us to add to that burden beyond $XXX.

   Customer: Oh, man. This is a real problem for us. We really need a line of $XXXX.

   You: I understand. We can review your financials again next quarter and see where you are in paying down some of your open accounts. We certainly want to extend to you all the credit that we can.

3. **You:** Hank, welcome to our "credit family." I'm sure you'll find that this credit line will make it more convenient to do business with us.

   Hank, I know that the line is somewhat smaller than you had requested. So let's look at your next quarter's financial statement, and review your credit line with an eye toward increasing it.

What to Say When You Cannot Honor the Credit Application

There's no denying that it's much easier to welcome a customer to your "credit family" than it is to tell him that you must decline credit. There is no magic formula that will ensure that your action will not drive this customer away. It *is* possible that the customer will become angry and alienated. He may even find a vendor whose credit policies are more liberal than yours. Nevertheless, you can take verbal measures to minimize damage to your relationship:

STEP 1: Do not begin with an apology. Begin with thanks for the application.

STEP 2: Tell the customer that your company "is unable to extend the requested credit at this time."

STEP 3: If possible, offer hope for reconsideration.

STEP 4: Be specific about the conditions that must be met to make successful reconsideration possible.

STEP 5: Be specific about when the customer should reapply.

STEP 6: Make it clear that the customer is valuable to you, and that you value his business.

STEP 7: Assure the customer of continued top-notch service on a cash-with-order (or other) basis.

STEP 8: Thank the customer for his understanding.

TIP
_____

Declining the customer's credit application must be done in writing. Be careful to say nothing that adds to, modifies, or differs from the information contained in any written communication.

YOUR SCRIPT: DENYING THE CREDIT APPLICATION

You telephone the customer to deliver the bad news. It *is* a good idea for you to move proactively and make the call rather than wait for the customer to call in to check on the status of his credit application. Making the call conveys that you do value the customer, even if you could not oblige him in this instance.

1. **You:** Mr. Roberts, this is (your name) at XYZ Company. I wanted to thank you for applying for credit with us, but I must tell you that, at this time, your credit record shows a history of slow payment, and,

given your current obligations, we feel that it is appropriate to postpone acting on your request for three months in order to give you the time required to catch up on your open accounts.

We'll be pleased to look at your financials next quarter and reevaluate the application. For the immediate future, of course, we remain eager to serve you on a payment-with-order basis.

2. **You**: Ms. Thomas, this is (your name) at XYZ Company. I'm calling about your credit application. Thank you for your interest in us, but because you have only recently established your business, and in view of our own limited resources, we need some more experience with you as a "pay-as-you-go" customer before we can set up a line of credit.

What I'd like to suggest is that you reapply in six months, after we've worked together for a while on a cash basis. And do be assured that, during this period, we will continue to give you the very best prices and service in the industry. We appreciate your business, Ms. Thomas, and we look forward to working with you and to helping you establish yourself in our community.

The following script takes a situation that could be stated negatively— "You need someone to guarantee your credit"—and turns it into a positive statement of an alternative to an out-and-out no:

3. **You**: Pete, we'd very much like to work with you to set up a line of credit; however, the financial statements you sent indicated that you are undercapitalized at present, and we think this would make it difficult for you to meet payments on our terms. Now, my suggestion is that you find a person or firm to guarantee your open account with us. That would allow us to serve your credit needs as you become increasingly well established.

Of course, alternatively, we hope that you'll continue working with us on a cash basis and reapply for credit within, say, six months.

COLLECTING MONEY THAT'S OVERDUE

Maybe it's time to start thinking about the money you *don't* have. I don't mean the sales you haven't made yet, the customers you haven't called yet, the killer widget you haven't invented yet. I'm not talking about *making* money. That's what business used to be mostly about—*making* money. You sold something, you developed something, and you turned it all into cash. But among the many trends trendspotters spot in today's business environment, one stands out, even if it's seldom talked about. Business has been moving deeper and deeper into a twilight zone in which solid cash has dissolved into a vaporous ether called "accounts receivable." The business world used to be divided into

1. Customers who paid on time
2. Delinquent accounts
3. Out-and-out deadbeats

Nowadays, even your better accounts routinely let invoices go beyond 30 days before they pay. Worse, 60-, 90-, and 120-day remittances have come to seem as inevitable as the seasons themselves.

- Your customers and clients do not think it is permissible to wait one, two, three, or four months before they pay you, they think it is *normal*, practically a law of nature.

Now, one way to try to get the money that is due you is to make collection calls and write collection letters. Both of these can be tough assignments. After all, you don't want to alienate a customer—even a delinquent customer.

More effective is a communicative approach to your customers that seeks to avoid delinquency problems in the first place. This approach revolves around a single secret:

- *The people who owe you money actually want to pay you.*

Make no mistake: few people *like* to pay. But *everyone* enjoys being in a position to do so. Few people like to pay. But *nobody* relishes owing.

Some Verbal Secrets for Preventing Payment Problems

At its simplest, any business is a dynamic system that generates and expends cash. The concept of cash *flow* is useful, at least to a point. Cash flows into the business, where it is directed into the pipelines that run to the various mechanisms enabling the business to draw in more cash. To a certain extent, cash flow is similar to the operation of an automobile. In a car, fuel, a raw commodity, is taken in, processed, and converted into various specific actions aimed at keeping the vehicle going. If the fuel line gets clogged or suffers from vapor lock, or the fuel pump breaks down, or the carburetor malfunctions (in an older car), or the fuel injector gums up (in more recent models), or other mechanical systems break down, the car coughs, sputters, and rolls to a dead stop.

Now, there are two kinds of car owners: those who practice regular preventive maintenance and those who stare by the side of the road with blank incomprehension into the inert mass beneath the raised hood of the vehicle that has suddenly quit on them.

Managing cash flow is not unlike maintaining an automobile. There are those who

- Integrate cash flow into the daily management of their business, continually keeping in touch with customers, vendors, and lenders before, during, and after money changes hands

And those who

- Cut in some collection agency for a big chunk of what should have been profits because an account was allowed to break down

Talk to your customers. Get on top of *their* payment problems before they become *your* cash-flow problems.

- Old-style managers stress response to circumstances.
- New-style managers emphasize anticipation.
- Be a new-style manager.

Anticipate trends and needs in order to take advantage of potential opportunities for profit *and* to avoid or prepare for approaching liabilities. Address cash flow from the beginning of a business transaction. Don't wait for a problem.

'Tis Better to Help than to Extort

Think about how you felt the last time you were owed money by an unresponsive customer. Whatever your exact feelings, it is a safe bet that they were anything but friendly. In fact, the delinquent customer soon comes to seem a silent enemy, an adversary against whom you are willing to level the "big guns" of a collection agency or lawyer, though it cost you dearly.

Almost always, there is a more effective alternative than the adversarial, warlike approach.

STEP 1:   Begin by assuming that your customer wants to pay you (that is, doesn't want to *owe* you).

STEP 2:   Realize that you want to be paid.

STEP 3:   Conclude, therefore, that you and the customer share a common interest.

STEP 4:   Conclude further that people with interests in common should communicate with each other.

STEP 5:   Call the customer with an offer of help: You want to help her do what you both want—pay you.

TIP

Collection agencies and lawyers are a last resort. Be aware that once you bring them into the picture, you sever *helpful* communication with the customer.

Talking with the New Customer

Begin the conversation *before* any money is due, let alone overdue. In fact, you can begin talking even before a deal is concluded:

1. **You:** Hello, Mr. Garrison. This is (your name) at XYZ Company. I know how eager you are to get prices on the widget project, so I thought I'd give you a call to let you know that we'll have the bid prepared early this afternoon and fax it to you. We are cutting the numbers as close to the bone as we can—but I might point out to you that you can take an additional 3 percent off the top if you pay the invoice total within ten days of our invoice date. It'll give us both a break: You save a few dollars, and we keep our cash flowing. Keep that extra discount in mind when you review the figures, and do give me a call if you have any questions.

2. **You:** Hello, Ms. Jones. This is (your name) at XYZ Company. I'm calling to let you know that the proposal for the widget project will be faxed this afternoon. I know you're eager to get started, and I think you'll be pleased with the figures. We've built in an extra incentive discount for ten-day turnaround on our invoice, which is something you might want to think about when you're comparing our bid to others. We like to make it simple to cooperate—lower costs on your side and better ease cash flow on ours. I look forward to your call after you receive the proposal.

3. **You:** Hello, Bill. This is (your name) at XYZ Company. I thought I'd call to let you know that our proposal for the widget project was sent out to you this morning. I think you'll be pleased with the numbers—and you might want to bear in mind that, good as the prices are, they're based on payment within 30 days. We'll knock off an additional 3 percent for payment made within ten days of our invoice date. Do give me a call if you have any questions about the proposal or the incentive discount program.

The incentive discount for quick payment should be repeated in writing in such items as:

- Statements of bids
- Cover letters accompanying proposals
- Cover letters with payment schedules
- Inserts accompanying shipment
- Invoices or invoice fliers

COUNTERING A NEGATIVE RESPONSE TO YOUR DISCOUNT INCENTIVE

The discount incentive is a *positive* and *proactive* collections measure. Nevertheless, you may, from time to time, encounter a negative response from the cynical customer who sees the proverbial half-filled water glass as half empty:

You: You'll notice that we've invited you to take an additional 3 percent off the total for making payment within ten days.

Customer: What you really mean is that you tack on 3 percent for bills past ten days.

You: Not at all. Our standard terms are 30 days net. Beyond 30 days we do charge 1.5 percent per month, up to 90 days. After that, we consider the account delinquent. The 3 percent discount for prompt payment is a genuine discount off our best net price. It's not a hidden charge. It is, quite frankly, an incentive. We're a small company, and it's worth 3 percent to us keep as much cash coming in just as quickly as we can get it in here. That's the unvarnished truth. But don't feel pressured. We're just as happy to do business on the basis of 30 days net.

PUSHING THE INCENTIVE DISCOUNT

If you are serious about cash flow, you have to make a serious commitment to communication. Let's say you have a customer who doesn't take advantage of your incentive discount for a ten-day payment turnaround. You can hardly make a collection call at this point. The payment terms are, after all, 30 days. But you can make a *helpful* call. Just be certain to keep it helpful and friendly. Here's a bid for the future:

You: Hi, this is (your name) from XYZ Company. I was just looking over our customer list and noticed that your September 1 order is the first order you've placed with us. Were you aware of our 3 percent discount offer for accounts paid within ten days of our invoice date?

Customer: Yes, but I'm afraid I just haven't been able to get around to that invoice yet.

You: Well, it's no problem, of course. You account is on 30-day net terms. But I did want to alert you to our offer, just in case it had slipped by you. Maybe you'll want to take advantage of it on the next order.

As the account nears the 30-day mark, make another friendly call:

1. **You:** Hello, this is (your name) from XYZ Company. I thought I'd give you a friendly call to remind you that your account is approaching the 30-day mark, which means that we'll be tacking on a 1.5 percent finance charge beginning October 15. There's no problem with the account, of course, but it seemed to me that you might want to avoid paying even a few dollars extra. If you can get payment to us by October 20, we'll bill the account at net.

2. **You:** Hello, Bill. This is (your name) calling from XYZ Company. I had written a note to myself to give you a call before your account with us went beyond 30 days. Now there's absolutely no problem with the account, but I did want to remind you that a 1.5 percent finance charge kicks in after September 1. I thought you might want to be reminded in order to save yourself a few dollars.

You have received payment from a new customer. It is a week late on 30-day terms. Most companies would let this pass without comment. Certainly, this is not an occasion for a scolding telephone call. However, a timely, helpful, and friendly communication might expedite cash flow in the future:

You: Hello, Mary. This is (your name) from XYZ Company. I've just received your August payment on your account. Thanks. There's no problem as far as we're concerned, but are you aware that, since we received the payment after the due date, it's subject to a $20 service charge? I thought I'd call because the payment was only ten days behind the due date, and it seems a shame to incur service charges unnecessarily. If you can get us your next payment by September 15, you'll avoid a service charge on that one.

Once the new account has decidedly slipped past the 30-day net period, you might find a special new-customer incentive persuasive:

1. **You:** Hello, Ms. Reynolds. This is (your name) of XYZ Company. I was just going over some accounts and noticed that yours has passed the 30-day mark, which means that we're about to send you a new invoice with a $25 service charge tacked on. To tell you the truth, it's easier for me to make this phone call than to process and mail a new invoice. If you can settle your account now—get the check into the mail today—I won't have to do up another invoice and you'll save $25. You're a new customer, and I hate to hit you up with an extra charge.

2. **You:** Hello, Mr. Smith. This is (your name) of XYZ Company. I'm calling to save you some money. Your account with us has just gone past 30 days, which means that it is subject to a service charge of $25. To be frank, I'd much rather have that account paid in full at the present time than collect an additional $25 on it later. If you can get payment to me

by Monday, I will waive the service charge. I don't like having to charge extra—especially in the case of a brand-new customer like you.

3. **You:** Hello, Ms. Nelson. This is (your name) of XYZ Company. In looking over our accounts, I noticed that yours has passed the 30-day mark. Normally, we'd assess a service charge at this point, but since you are a brand-new customer, I'm willing to waive the service charge if you can get a check into the mail today.

Customer: I'd love to, but our cash-flow position isn't the greatest just now. I'm going to have to let the bill go for another couple of weeks and pay the service charge.

You: Well, that's not the end of the world, of course. And I certainly know what it's like to try to manage cash flow these days. Before we leave the matter, is there anything I can do to help? What I'm thinking is that, if you can send me a check for half of the current invoice now and pay the balance by the middle of the month, I'm still willing to waive the service charge. I like to make things as flexible as possible for my customers, especially the new ones.

Talking with the Established Customer

The most effective strategy for collection-related communication with an established customer is to think of the customer as a business partner. You have a relationship. You are in business together. You have interests in common. The key is to keep lines of communication open.

TIP

If a payment problem develops, communicate first and foremost your *concern* for the customer.

INSTALLMENT PAYMENT PROBLEM

One of the most frequently encountered payment problems with established customers involve missed installment payments. Emphasize the positive. Demonstrate that you are calling precisely because this glitch is exceptional:

You: Hello, John. This is (your name) from XYZ Company. Your payment of $XXX, which was due on Friday, hasn't arrived in our office. You're always so punctual with these payments, I was concerned. When did you send that out?

Customer: Well, I was planning on sending it out later in the week.

You: It was due on Friday. Can you get it into the mail today?

Customer: I'm not sure.

You: Well, I'll look for it by the first of the week. Does that sound all right with you?

Customer: Yes. Sorry about it. You'll have it then.

You: Great. If there is anything I can help you with, please give me a call.

Bounced checks

Bounced checks are another financial hazard, even in established customer relationships. It is best to approach the issue matter of factly, without alarm or emotion. If the customer apologizes, accept the apology gracefully.

You: Hello, Jill. This is (your name) from XYZ Company. We had an unwelcome surprise in the mail this morning. Your check, number 1234, was returned by the bank. I can go ahead and redeposit it, if everything's all clear on your end. I do need a check for an additional $25 to cover what the bank charges us and our own handling costs.

More serious payment lapses

Once an unpaid account approaches 60 days, it is time to get serious about helping your customer pay.

- Continue to use positive and negative incentives.
- Maintain communication in order to create the emotional as well as the business climate in which the errant account will positively entertain thoughts about paying you.

How do you convince someone to pay?

One strategy is to bully and threaten. This may work—once. After that, you will almost certainly have lost a customer. A much better approach is to *help* your customer make the decision to pay by demonstrating how it will benefit him.

STEP 1:   If you have a schedule of service/finance charges in place, you can make a phone call, reminding him how much is owed now and how much more will be due after a given date.

STEP 2:   Build on your relationship with the customer. Explain that prompt, personal service at the best prices requires the cooperation of the customer in the form of prompt payment, which keeps costs down.

STEP 3:   Point out that prices originally quoted and agreed to were based on net terms. In ordering from you, not only did your customer promise to pay promptly, but he also received in return for that promise the added value of the best possible prices.

TIP
_____

An appeal to fairness can be quite effective, if it is handled with a light hand.

The most common resistance you are likely to encounter is vagueness and evasiveness.

- Ask questions that can be answered, questions that relate to dates and amounts.
- If the customer tells you that now is a bad time to talk, remind him that *we* are running short of time and ask when it would be a good time to call back. Get a definite time.
- If the customer is vague about when she can pay, ask her to think the matter over, and tell her that you will call back at a specific time to get her response.
- If the customer passes the buck to his "accounting people," ask him if you should be talking to his accounting person yourself.
- If the customer is willing to negotiate, do so.

TIP

Once you have reached an agreement in principle, send the customer a memo summarizing your new understanding.

With accounts that have gone beyond the sixty-day mark, the primary task is definition and direction.

- Remind the customer of his obligation.
- Define the dates and the amounts involved in satisfying it.

In the case of payment due for commodity goods or services that are delivered or performed on an ongoing basis, discuss with the customer the following:

- There is the inevitable fact that the commodity or service delivery will be stopped unless payment is received by a certain date.
- There are the costs of discontinuing and restarting delivery or service.
- The fact that, in most cases, payment is made immediately after the service or commodity delivery is discontinued. Then extra costs are incurred. Why not avoid this by paying now?

Your scripts: handling serious payment lapses

1. **You:** Hello, Dick. This is (your name) from XYZ Company. I'm calling to talk to you about your account with us. It's approaching 60 days, and I'd like to ask you when we can expect payment. As you know, the prices we originally quoted you were based on 30-day net terms. Now that we're closing in on 60 days, you're looking at a $300 carrying charge on this account. Frankly, I'd rather have the account settled now than collect that charge. Can you get us a check by Friday?

   Customer: I'll have to talk to my accounting people.

   You: Is there someone in your accounting department that *I* should be talking to? I'll give him or her an opportunity to save you some money.

2. **You:** Hello, Jane. This is (your name) from XYZ Company. I'm calling to talk to you about your account with us. The prices we gave you were based on 30-day net terms, and we're now getting close to the 60-day point. We're a small company, and it's really very difficult for us to carry open accounts for any length of time. It would help us a great deal if you could pay the account in full.

   Customer: I'll look into it.

   You: May I call you at this time tomorrow to get a status report from you and, if necessary, to work out a payment plan together?

   Customer: Tomorrow is a bad time.

   You: Well, we are running short on time. After Tuesday, the account is subject to a $150 carrying charge, and I'd much rather work with you on a payment strategy that will save you that fee. When is a good time to call?

3. **You:** Hello, Carl. This is (your name) from XYZ Company. I'm calling to talk to you about your account with us. As you know, the prices we originally quoted you were based on 30-day net terms. We're approaching 60 days, which means that you will be paying us a $200 carrying charge on the account. Frankly, I'd rather have the account settled now than collect that fee. Can you get us a check by Friday?

   Customer: I'm in a real cash-flow bind just now. You know how it is.

   You: Unfortunately, I do. That's why I'd like to work with you on this. To help us both out. We need to come up with a plan that we can both live with. The balance due is $1,750. If I can get $650 by Friday, I'd be in a position to waive the carrying charges on the entire balance due—provided the account is completely settled by October 4. How does that sound?

   Customer: I just can't manage it at this time. I'll have to pay you later and just absorb the finance charges.

   You: Well, before we give up, can you tell me if I'm in the ballpark?

   Customer: You really want to get some money, don't you?

You: I told you that I know what it's like to have to manage cash flow carefully. Yeah, I can use all the cash I can get. What if we set up four payments and spread them out?

Talking with the Seriously Delinquent Customer

Even when an unpaid account remains open approaching 90 days, there is still room for such positive incentives as renegotiation of original cost incentives. This is also a good time to introduce such negative incentives as timely reminders of mounting service charges. Additionally, letters and telephone conversations at this point should direct the customer to ask himself why the bill has gone unpaid and what further delay will cost him, in terms of service charges as well as impact on credit history.

It may not seem so at the time, but at the 90-day point, the creditor is in a strong position.

- If a program of finance or service charges is in place, the creditor has more negotiating power at her command.
- Even if no external incentives are available, the delinquent account is usually more anxious to settle now than he was earlier.

TIP

Remember: the delinquent account can settle *only* if you keep the lines of communication open.

TIP

As the open account approaches 90 days, it is important not to issue threats or to give in to panic or anger. Now is the time for sound reasoning. This is your account's final opportunity to remain in good standing, and it is you who are giving him that opportunity.

As an account hovers near serious delinquency, your most effective collection strategy is to begin to separate yourself from such entities as *company policy, our accountants, our attorneys,* and the passage of time itself. It works like this: You would like to grant infinite extensions, but company policy (or our accountants or our attorneys) won't let you because time is running out.

TIP

Ordinarily, references to *company policy* are a bad customer-service idea; however, as a scapegoat in collections situations, company policy may come in handy.

This rhetorical strategy is intended to strengthen the cooperative bond between two people who have to work within certain rules. The subtle separation of the voice now on the phone—you—and "the company," "the rules," or "our policy" suggests that you and your customer are in control of the situation *now*, but soon, if positive action is not taken, other forces will take over. Credit will be suspended. Lawyers will take action. Things will get ugly. Choices will be few.

Note carefully that this approach is not a threat, and it should not be expressed as a threat. But unresolved debt is a serious matter, and it is time to let your customer become aware of this fact.

Your scripts: talking with seriously delinquent customers

Here are some scenarios using positive incentives:

1. **You:** Hello, Mike. This is (your name) at XYZ Company. I want to alert you to the next invoice you'll be getting from us. By the time you receive the statement, your account with us will have gone past 90 days, which means that you'll be assessed $175 in service charges. To be frank, I'm interested in getting your payment as soon as possible, and I'm willing to waive not only the 90-day charge, but the 60-day charge, which you, at this point, owe. That means that if you get a check into the mail today, you'll save $175. If you wait for the invoice, the $175 charge *will* apply.

2. **You:** Hello, Ms. Dinkler. This is (your name) at XYZ Company. I just put into the mail a statement of your account with us. You already have two statements from us, sent at 30 and at 60 days. I've sent this one a little early, because I wanted to give you the opportunity to beat the 90-day deadline and avoid paying a service charge of $150. Are you interested in saving some more money?

   Customer: I guess I am.

You: It's strictly your option, but if you can get a check into the mail today, you'll not only beat the 90-day service charge, I'll also waive the 60-day charge. You'll save a total of $150. How does that sound to you?

Customer: It sounds reasonable enough..

You: Then I should be looking for your check in the next day or two?

Customer: Yes.

3. **You:** Hello, Mr. Peterson. This is (your name) at XYZ Company. I just put a statement of your account with us in the mail. You already have two statements from us, sent at 30 and at 60 days. I've sent this one a little early, because I wanted to give you the opportunity to beat the 90-day deadline and avoid paying a service charge of $225. Are you interested in saving some more money?

Customer: I guess I am.

You: It's your decision, of course. But if you can get a check into the mail today, you'll save $225.

Customer: Look, it sounds fair enough, but I'm short on cash just now. I know you want to get paid, but with my cash flow, I'm afraid it will be another couple of weeks.

You: You're certainly right that I'd like to collect on this invoice. And I'd like to save you some money as well—without sending you to the poorhouse in the process. If you could manage to pay half now and the balance by the end of the month, which will put you beyond 90 days, I'd still be willing to waive the service charges.

Here are two ideas for using negative incentives:

1. **You:** Hello, Ms. Wallace. This is (your name) at XYZ Company. I was just going over some accounts here, and I noticed that yours is about to go past 90 days. Now that's not disaster, and I'm not calling to dun you, but I did want to alert you to the fact that the account is about to slip through another month unpaid. And what that means to you is a service charge of $150. If you want to avoid that charge, might I sug-

gest that you send out a check today? Once you slip past the fifteenth, I *must* assess the service charge.

Customer: I just don't have the cash on hand right now. Can you give me a grace period on that service charge?

You: When would you be paying?

Customer: In about two to three weeks.

You: Well, that's going to start getting close to 120 days, after which the account is delinquent. I'd like to accommodate you, but, you know, we're a small company, and we can't afford to carry an account that long without a service charge. If you can get me $1,200 by the twelfth, we can at least avoid letting the account slip into delinquency. Then we can work out together a schedule for the balance. How does that sound?

Is there a point at which you should give up hope? Once an unpaid account has passed 120 days, you have some important choices to make.

- Should you suspend the customer's credit? (The answer is, almost without reservation, yes.)
- Should you turn the account over to a collection agency or an attorney? (That depends on the amount involved and your relationship with the client or customer.)

Even more important are these questions:

- What more do I have to give?
- And what do I have left to gain?

You can still give your help, your offer to work with your customer to resolve his debt to you. This may seem difficult or impossible as you drift toward what neither of you can avoid perceiving as an adversarial relationship, perhaps even legal action. But this is where the tone and rhetoric of your communications play so important a role. At the 90-day mark, you began to separate yourself from the force of the inevitable and unmovable— company policy, our attorney, and the like. Now that separation should be made more dramatic. Hold yourself apart from the necessary steps that are impending. Remain available for discussion and negotiation.

TIP

Often, the first issue to address is lack of response. Accounts that have drifted this far tend not to reply to letters or take phone calls. Try to establish—or reestablish—contact.

STEP 1:   Open the lines of communication.

STEP 2:   Outline your customer's choices at this point.

STEP 3:   Make it clear that the choices are the customer's. You are running out of choices. In *X* number of days you will "have no choice" but to suspend the customer's credit unless he "chooses" to pay *X* amount by such-and-such a date.

Be aware that your customer feels that he has little power and that you are holding all the cards. It is true that you can take away his credit, and you can take him to court. The problem is that these will not help you resolve the situation quickly. Your strategy now should be to communicate in such a way as to empower your customer. Let him know that

- He can choose to settle.
- He can choose to help himself.
- He can choose to preserve his credit—with you as well as his credit record generally.

But to do all of these things, he has to work with you—*now*.

MORE SCRIPTS: TALKING WITH SERIOUSLY DELINQUENT CUSTOMERS

1. **You:** Hello, Ms. Thomas. This is (your name) at XYZ Company. I'm calling about your account with us. It has gone past 120 days for the second time this year. Ms. Thomas, I'm being pressured here to put your credit on hold and even turn the account over to a collection agency. Now, I'd rather not do that. I'd rather work with you to settle the account. Can you get me a check right away?

   Customer: I've been meaning to call you guys. I've got some real cash-flow problems that I'm trying to get out from under. Can I call you in a week or so to work this out?

You: The account is already 120 days past due, and, as I said, this isn't the first time. I know it's not going to help either one of us to press you for a snap answer now, but I can't really afford to put off the discussion for a "week or so," either. What if I give you a day to review your situation and then call back the day after tomorrow at about this time? My concern is to get this account settled, to work with you in settling it—to help you settle it—and to keep doing business with you in the future. So, may I call you Wednesday?

2. **You:** Hello, Mr. Samuels. This is (your name) calling from XYZ Company. I'm calling now to save us both a lot of trouble in the days and weeks to come. Your account with us has been outstanding now for more than 120 days. We've tried repeatedly to contact you about this, but we've received no reply. I'd like to avoid turning this over to our attorney for collection. Do you think we can work out payment on this account?

3. **You:** Hello, Ms. Ernst. This is (your name) calling from XYZ Company. I'm calling about your account with us. It's passed 120 days due, and I'm getting pressured here to turn it over to our lawyers. I was hoping that a simple phone call might make that unnecessary. The amount due is $1,800. Can you get a check to us today?

   Customer: Frankly, no. I've been meaning to call you. We've had some— uh—problems here, and I'm afraid I've had to let some accounts go longer than they should.

   You: Maybe I can help. The total due, as I said, is $1,800. What portion of this could you manage to pay *now*? I really want to hold off having to turn this over to collections—especially if you're in a crunch.

COLLECTION TALK VERSUS COLLECTION LETTERS

Talk, according to the cliché, is cheap. Should you spend time on the phone? Or would you be better off putting everything in writing?

The answer is not either/or, but both.

- Combine collection calls with letters.

- Confirm all verbal agreements in writing.
- Back up any verbal advisories or warnings with the same in writing.
- Take care not to contradict a written statement with a verbal one or vice versa.

A combination of verbal and written collection messages is more effective than either a verbal or written program alone.

CRITICAL ISSUE: AVOIDING THREATS AND HARASSMENT

The efforts you make to collect debts are subject to federal and state regulations. Doing any of the following is not only bad business, it may be illegal.

- Calling at unreasonable hours—early in the morning or late at night
- Attempting to pressure or embarrass the customer by discussing his indebtedness with anyone other than the customer himself
- Threatening the customer
- Using abusive language

Collection calls should be polite and businesslike. Their purpose should be to help the customer settle the debt, not punish him for his indebtedness or negligence.

HANDLING CUSTOMER COMPLAINTS

Nobody wants things to go wrong. But that doesn't mean you need to live in fear of mistakes, mishaps, and disasters. They will happen. Learn to make the best of them.

Seriously. The *best*.

How you respond to an error or mishap provides an opportunity to give your customer exceptional "extra-mile" service. From the disaster *can* come a satisfied customer.

If the widget your company sold to Ms. Smith fizzles, she *will* be more than a little annoyed. But what will happen if she calls your company and finds no help? Outrage, anger, fear, frustration, and feelings of abandonment. You will have lost a customer, whose negative word of mouth may lose you many more.

The answer? Be there for her.

- Responding to complaints is damage control.
- But it's more than damage control.
- Responding to complaints is satisfying warranty obligations and the like.
- But it is more than simply this.
- Responding to complaints demonstrates your company's willingness to stand behind its product or service.
- Responding to complaints should be a pledge to make things right again.

Effectively handled, your response to mistakes, mishaps, and disasters will not only redeem your company in the customer's estimation, it will actually build or strengthen a bond between your firm and the customer. Sure, Ms. Smith still won't like the fact that her widget blew up. But she will feel a whole lot better about your company. She may tell her friends about the widget problem, true enough, but she will devote most of her story to how the company mobilized its forces to *help her out*.

TIP

Responding to complaints is an opportunity to build and strengthen a positive relationship with your customer. It is an opportunity to turn a negative into a positive.

Reaping the Rewards of Utter Disaster: Ten Secrets Revealed

1. *Understand that your customer is anxious, frustrated, and angry.* These are intense feelings calling not for condescending assurances that "everything will be all right," but for a pair of urgent responses:

   - You are committed to help
   - You are able—competent—to help

2. *Begin by listening to the complaint, gathering as much information as you can.* You are trying to get facts. You want the customer to talk. Part of that talking may be more like venting. You will be tempted to react defensively. Resist that temptation. Let the customer reveal as much as possible.

3. *Acknowledge the complaint.* This does not mean admitting wrongdoing. Simply acknowledge that the product or service is not satisfying the customer.

4. *Express empathy, understanding, and concern:* "We're sorry that this has happened." Or: "We're sorry that the product is not performing to your satisfaction." Again, this is not the time to take on blame. Acknowledge the customer's feelings and respond—humanly and humanely—to them.

5. *If you know you can fix the problem, tell the caller what you propose to do.* The good news is that most problems can be fixed. Few require extensive investigation or creativity. Most have ready-made solutions available. If you can find and apply one of these, be certain to *explain* what you propose to do.

6. *Explain to the customer what she must do.* This includes whatever steps she needs to take to make the repair, replacement, or adjustment possible (for example, take the product to the nearest authorized dealer).

7. *Explain all necessary procedures*—not only what you are asking the customer to do, but what you (and your company) will do. How will the steps you propose to take fix the problem?

8. *Provide all of the information the customer needs*—such as a list of authorized repair facilities in his area. Follow up by mailing this list.

9. *Provide closure to the call by apologizing.* This does not mean making abject protestations of guilt. Do not dwell on the negatives, and certainly do not underscore your company's culpability. Instead, use your apology as a springboard to ending the call on an upbeat note.

10. *Emphasize your gratitude for the customer's patience and understanding.* Saying "I sure am sorry this has occurred" is not the same as saying "This is our fault, and we're terrible."

But what do you do in those relatively few cases where there is no quick fix?

- Do not abandon the caller: "There's really nothing I can do."
- Provide a plan of further action.

- Propose a set of alternatives.
- Suggest a temporary fix.

Dealing with a Variety of Customer-Complaint Scenarios

Here are some typical phone scenarios:

1. **Customer**: My name is John Smith. I purchased a widget from you, and I am not happy with it.

   You: I am sorry to hear that the widget isn't performing to your satisfaction, Mr. Smith. Can you describe the problem?

   Customer: (Describes the problem.)

   You: We can certainly fix that. Now, there are two ways we can work to resolve the problem and get you up and running as quickly and painlessly as possible. From what you describe, I'm pretty certain that the problem is with a bad converter. I can either send you a replacement converter, with full instructions for installing it. Or, if you prefer, you may return the entire unit to us, and we will replace the defective part. The first alternative is the quickest way to resolve the problem, but you may feel more comfortable having us perform the work. It's up to you.

   Customer: I'm all thumbs. You guys better do the work.

   You: I understand. Let me give you a few directions: First, please be careful to pack the unit in its original carton with all of the original shipping material. The carton and the shipping material are specifically designed to prevent damage. Send the unit to (give address) and mark on the carton the following return authorization number: 123456. Ship via (specify carrier). We will reimburse you for shipping costs.

   Customer: Okay, I got that. But what's your turnaround time?

You: Right now, I'd say ten days is a good bet. We might be able to better that a bit.

Customer: Okay.

You: Mr. Smith, I apologize for the inconvenience you have been caused, and I thank you for your patience and understanding. We'll resolve the problem as quickly as possible.

2. **Customer:** Yes, hello. My name is Mary Clark, and I'm really steamed about the Deluxe Widget, which I just bought. Your advertisements said that it would do (lists functions). Well, I can't get it do any of these things very well. I want my money back!

    You: I'm sorry to hear that you are disappointed with the Widget. Ms. Clark, the last thing we want to do is to mislead any of our customers. That's a terrible way to do business, and it certainly is not the way *we* do business. Ms. Clark, based on what you're telling me, I believe that you misread our advertisement. The product functions you are describing apply to our model 234, a significantly more feature-rich—and, therefore, more expensive—model. You've purchased the base model, 123.

    Customer: Ohhh . . . Then I guess I'm just stuck . . .

    You: Not at all. Here are two alternatives: First, if you like, I will authorize a full cash refund. Just repack the Widget in its original carton, including all accessories, and take it to the dealer from whom you purchased it. But, look, there was a reason you bought the Widget. You wanted to take advantage of all of its features. I can tell you more about model number 234, which does offer the features you describe— and more. You know, Ms. Clark, there are also some intermediate-range models you might want to know about. If you like, you may exchange your current unit for one of the more advanced models. You'll be given full credit for your purchase price. You'll just pay the difference. How would you like to proceed?

3. **Customer:** My name is Max Reger. The widget you sold me last month is nothing but trouble. I've brought it in for repair *twice*—in *one* month! I'm so unhappy with it that I not only want my money back, but intend never to do business with you again!

You: I can understand and appreciate your anger. The fact is that the widget failed you and, what's even worse, it failed you repeatedly. I'm sure that my telling you how rare such a failure is—let alone repeated failure—isn't much help to you. The point is that our product failed *you*.

Now, Mr. Reger, there's no problem with refunding the purchase price to you. If that's what you want, I will authorize it immediately. The refund will be sent out as soon as we receive your unit. But might I suggest another alternative?

Customer: I don't know. I'm not really interested . . .

You: Let me just *suggest* that you try a replacement unit. Don't give up on us just yet. If you like, I will send, without charge, a service representative to your site to supervise installation and to ensure that the unit is operating in an optimal environment.

What to Say When Your Customer Is Wrong

The customer, goes the old, old saying, *is always right.*
Like any number of "old sayings," this one isn't true. Yet there is something valuable to be learned from it:

- Never let the customer feel that he was wrong in having chosen to do business with your company.

And there is more:

- The customer may not be right, but you have to work with him.

When most customers complain, they have good reason. The complaints are usually valid. Sometimes the customer's lack of satisfaction arises from a problem with the product or service, sometimes from unrealistic expectations, sometimes from misunderstanding how the product operates or just what it is supposed to do. Sometimes, though, customer complaints are *unfounded*. The customer is just plain wrong.

Your objective in handling such calls is not to argue the customer into admitting that he is wrong, but to educate him:

1. To *demonstrate* that the complaint is without basis
2. To do this without alienating the customer

TIP

The most desirable outcome of these scenarios is for the customer to complete the call, having been pleased that what he thought was a problem has been solved.

Once you determine that a caller's complaint is unfounded, do the following:

STEP 1: Listen. Gather all the facts.

STEP 2: Tell the customer that you appreciate his concern.

STEP 3: Explain why the complaint is not valid.

TIP

Be careful with Step 3. Do not raise subjective issues such as taste or judgment. Keep the focus sharply on the product or service issue at hand.

STEP 4: Don't abandon the customer. Offer appropriate alternatives, including (for example), advice on using the product more effectively, sources of additional information, alternative products or accessories designed to make the product perform more nearly as the customer may wish.

STEP 5: Do not apologize. Neither you nor your product is at fault here. Moreover, apologizing in this circumstance is offensive, as if you are telling the customer, "I'm sorry I'm right and you're wrong."

STEP 6: Provide effective, positive closure by expressing your regret that the customer was less than fully satisfied.

STEP 7: Express your hope that the alternative(s) you propose will be of help to the caller.

ALTERNATIVE STRATEGY WHEN THE CUSTOMER IS WRONG

No law says that you must insist that you are right just because you are right. Many firms routinely take products back and refund the customer's money, even when the customer is absolutely wrong. Why? Such firms would rather let the customer abuse them now than bad-mouth them to others later. It may be cheaper and easier to give away a product or refund a sale than to counteract the consequences of negative word-of-mouth advertising.

YOUR SCRIPTS: HANDLING COMPLAINTS WHEN THE CUSTOMER IS WRONG

Here are some scenarios in which the customer is decidedly *not* right:

1. **Customer:** This is Peter Barnes calling. I bought a widget from your company, which I'm just not happy with. I want to get a full cash refund.

   You: I'm looking up your order on my computer now. It's just coming up onto the screen. Mr. Barnes, you purchased the widget on terms that specify no cash refund.

   Customer: I know. That's true. But I'm *really* unhappy. I just won't settle for anything less than a full refund. I don't intend to be a victim of your company's policy.

   You: Mr. Barnes, I understand your feelings, but these terms are not simply a matter of "company policy." They are part of the reason that we were able to offer the widget to you at such a low cost. The non-refund terms are part of the bargain you made with us when you purchased the widget.

   Customer: Well, I guess I see your point . . .

   You: However, sir, you still have options. You might exchange the widget for a different model or you can return it and accept a store credit, which has no time limit whatsoever. You can use it like cash here at the store. I think you'll agree that you still have quite a bit of flexibility, certainly enough to make a purchase decision you will be happy with.

2. **Customer:** This is Charlie Gobel. I recently purchased a Model 123 widget from you, plugged it into the power supply on my Acme AC, and the widget promptly burned out! I want a replacement unit.

   You: I'm very sorry this happened, but my company cannot take responsibility for the damage in this case. The Model 123 is designed for direct current only. By hooking it up to your Acme AC, you ran AC through it. Our spec sheet and warning labels clearly caution against doing this, explaining that alternating current will destroy the coils. That voids the warranty.

   Customer: What!? I can't believe it . . .

   You: Mr. Gobel, you do have some options here. Now, while I cannot make a warranty replacement in this case, I can offer to repair the motor. Most likely, the only damage is to the coil. That repair will run $50 plus $5 for shipping. If you prefer, you can take the unit directly to one of our authorized repair shops. The good news is that once the repair is made your original warranty will be reactivated.

3. **Customer:** What is the matter with your shipping department? I ordered model 12345 and received 34567 instead! I need to make an exchange as quickly as possible.

   You: Let me access your record. May I have your name?

   Customer: (Gives name and other information requested.)

   You: Okay. I'm calling up your record on my computer right now. It should come up on the monitor in just a second or two. Yes. There we are. Mr. Gaines, we clearly have an order here for model 34567.

   Customer: Yes. Well, if you do, that just means *you* took the order down wrong!

   You: That is not likely, Mr. Gaines, but, if you like, I can retrieve the paperwork. I can get your original purchase order. This will take about three minutes. May I put you on hold for that long?

Customer: Yes, go ahead. Let's get to the bottom of this.

You (returning): I have the purchase order here, signed by you, and it does specify model 34567. If you like, I'll fax you the document . . .

Customer: No. That won't be necessary. I guess I made a mistake.

You: Well, unfortunately, the model you ordered and received is a custom design, which means that I cannot simply exchange it for 12345. But I can offer you partial credit—$150—on your 34567 toward purchase of a 12345.

However, Mr. Gaines, have you considered just keeping what you have? You know, the 34567 should deliver satisfaction. Is there anything you don't like about it?

Customer: Well, not really. It's just not what I thought I'd ordered.

You: My suggestion is that you try the unit for a while. See if it does the job for you. If you're still unhappy with it in two weeks, give me a call, and I'll arrange the return for credit I just mentioned. How does that sound to you?

CHAPTER 10

Putting Yourself Across . . . to Vendors and Suppliers

SELF-TEST YOUR SAVVY IN COMMUNICATING WITH VENDORS AND SUPPLIERS

The following is a simple diagnostic test. A smaller and more selective version of the self-test in Chapter 1, its purpose is not to test your knowledge of communication theory or techniques, but to help you gauge how effectively you communicate with vendors and suppliers in a day-to-day business context. For the most part, you will find it easy to guess the "right" answer. But getting the "right" answer is not the point of the test. Respond honestly, even if you feel that your response is not the best one possible. This is *not* a contest. The object is solely self-inventory.

1. When a collection call comes, I just promise 'em anything.   T/F _____

2. I'm an impulse buyer.   T/F _____

3. Vendors are cheats.   T/F _____

4. I consider my creditor an ally, not an adversary.   T/F _____

5. I feel that, as far as overdue payables go,
   "Let sleeping dogs lie."   T/F _____

6. I give vendors verbal orders backed up by written orders.   T/F _____

7. A good vendor should feel like your partner.   T/F _____

8. When I have money trouble, I do what I can to avoid
   my creditors.   T/F _____

9. Service is important to me.   T/F _____

10. When I'm caught in a cash crunch, I get on the phone to the people I owe.   T/F ____

11. I like to talk to vendors.   T/F ____

12. I listen to what vendors tell me.   T/F ____

13. I make credit terms part of any negotiation.   T/F ____

14. My motto regarding vendors: "Give 'em hell!"   T/F ____

15. I negotiate for value rather than price.   T/F ____

16. I negotiate with vendors as I negotiate with customers.   T/F ____

17. I never get the best deal.   T/F ____

18. Vendors often cheat me.   T/F ____

19. I put my heart and soul into a deal. I get emotional.   T/F ____

20. I think it is important to create strong relationships with vendors.   T/F ____

21. I try to research the market before I settle on any one vendor.   T/F ____

22. I try to make vendors feel *good* about serving me.   T/F ____

TOTAL T/F   ____

Score 1 point for each "True" response and 0 for each "False" response, EXCEPT for questions 1, 2, 3, 5, 8, 14, 17, 18, and 19. For *these questions only*, SUBTRACT 1 point for each "True" response. Record your total. A score below +11 indicates that you would benefit from practicing the communication techniques discussed in this chapter. (Note: It is possible to have a negative score.)

WORDS TO USE WITH VENDORS AND SUPPLIERS

alternatives	careful
ballpark	comparison
best	deal

dependable

discuss

expect

expectation

lowest

negotiate

options

quality

reliable

responsive

select

service

specifications

value

PHRASES TO USE WITH VENDORS AND SUPPLIERS

Do you want to make the deal?

How firm is that price?

I have been looking

I'm listening

not an adequate value

not good enough

quite a bit more than I can spend/invest

real price

tell me what you can offer

Where can we go from here?

WORDS TO AVOID WITH VENDORS AND SUPPLIERS

absolute

bargain

cheap

excited

fair

good

great

immediately

now

terrific

wonderful

PHRASES TO AVOID WITH VENDORS AND SUPPLIERS

can't wait

give me the works

I don't know anything about this stuff

it's urgent

I'm in your hands

I'm desperate

money is no object

right away

will pay anything

BODY-LANGUAGE STRATEGY FOR VENDORS AND SUPPLIERS

The appropriate strategies are those of any sales situation. Use the strategies discussed in Chapter 7.

BODY LANGUAGE TO AVOID WITH VENDORS AND SUPPLIERS

Consult Chapter 7 for body language to avoid.

GETTING VENDORS TO GIVE YOU THEIR BEST

Businesses don't only sell goods and services to others, they also buy, and a good "buy" negotiation is really a good "sales" negotiation. When you make a business purchase, you need to *sell* your supplier on the notion of giving you super service, giving you the best deal possible, and supplying the highest-quality product. Let's face it, it you'll have a better shot at getting all of this if you are buying a lot of stuff or a lot of services from the vendor in question. Talk about communication? *Money* talks.

But making a big deal does not guarantee a good deal or great service, nor do you *have* to make a huge purchase to expect (or get) first-class treatment. The secret is communication.

STARTING OFF ON THE RIGHT FOOT WITH A VENDOR

Your "sales" pitch should commence when you solicit information from a vendor.

STEP 1: Begin by describing your business, emphasizing your reputation and special needs, and so on.

STEP 2: In a polite but straightforward way, *challenge* the supplier to measure up to the requirements of your business.

TIP

Don't be obnoxious about it. Pose the challenge in positive terms: "I've heard a lot of good things about you. I'm expecting to be dazzled."

STEP 3: Be as specific as possible about the kind of information you require from the vendor. You may want to submit a list of requirements.

If you take the next step with a vendor and solicit a bid, it is often helpful to back up your verbal requests with a letter or memo itemizing those specifications and requirements. In the case of complex specs, written documentation is absolutely necessary. This is also the case when you are soliciting competitive bids from more than one vendor.

- Even when you send a full spec sheet, consider augmenting this with a phone call.
- Begin the call by complimenting the vendor on his product and presentation.
- Let him know that *he* has persuaded you to expect great things from him.
- Use the call to highlight any points you may wish to emphasize in your spec sheet, or to ask for information that may have been omitted from the spec sheet (for example, "What is your customer-support policy?").
- Let the supplier know that you have solicited bids from other *excellent* companies.
- Close by inviting questions and establishing a firm deadline for submission of the bid.

YOUR SCRIPTS: APPROACHING VENDORS.

You might telephone a vendor with a message that runs something like one of these:

You: . . . We are a small maker of custom communication circuitry, known for the high quality of our work and the efficiency with which we carry out assignments. Let me lay it on the table: What we need is a supplier who can live up to our reputation. We've heard some very impressive things about you . . .

or:

You: . . . We are a small specialist marketing service with approximately 30 clients, for whom we drop about 200,000 national mailing pieces per month. We are currently looking to upgrade our list-maintenance software, which we run on a XYZ computer, using ABC Software. We want to replace the ABC software with something off the shelf. We've heard very good things about your pricing as well as your customer-support and training programs. What I'd like to see are spec sheets for all your relevant products, together with prices both for single and multiple users. Give us a detailed description of your customer support policy as well. One last thing: we need fast turnaround on this information. We plan to make the purchase as soon as possible.

Here is an idea for a call initiating a bid:

You: . . . We were all highly impressed by your presentation Friday, and we are confident that you can furnish the products and service we require. So, I'm going to put on the fax machine a formal request for a bid on the project. Now, I want you to know that we have solicited bids from a number of excellent suppliers. We intend to review them all intensively, so I must ask that you submit your bid no later than Wednesday. I can't give you any more time than this. You may call me directly at 555-5555 if you have any questions concerning the specifications. We look forward to receiving your bid.

TIP
_____

Avoid hinting at the vendor's standing vis à vis the other bidders. It is sufficient to alert him to the fact that there *are* others.

SECRETS OF NEGOTIATING PRICE AND TERMS WITH VENDORS

Who doesn't know someone who *always* seems to get the best prices? A haggler. A real wheeler dealer. And, knowing such a person, who doesn't envy her? How does she do it? What's her secret?

Doubtless, there are many "secrets" to negotiating the most favorable price, but there are only three that will *never* fail you:

- Know the competitive field. Know what others charge for the same or similar products or services. Do your research.
- Remember always that the object of negotiating is to buy the product or service you want at the best price you can get. Focus on the product or service, not on the personality of the individual from whom you are buying it.
- Go into a negotiation prepared to walk away, if necessary.

STEP 1: Step 1, then, is straightforward and begins before you open the negotiation. Do whatever research is required to become familiar with the competitive field. This may be as simple as consulting a few catalogues and price lists. Or it may involve more legwork, with numerous conversations with suppliers.

STEP 2: The more you know about the product or service you are buying, the less you need to rely on your ability to assess the honesty, integrity, and negotiating skills of the stranger with whom you have to deal. Know the competitive field and you can focus on value, not on the personality of the salesperson or vendor.

TIP

It is all too easy for a buyer to lose focus, turning the negotiation into a personality contest between buyer and seller. Such a contest may feel like real work. It is, after all, intense. But, if it *is* work, what's the point? To defeat another human being? The point *should* be to buy whatever needs to be bought and to buy it at the best price.

Everyone is familiar with the chief peril of buying an automobile: Cars appeal simultaneously to childlike fantasies and to an adult sense of self-indulgence. People really do "fall in love" with cars. The smell of the new vehicles, the bright lights of the showroom—these are seductive indeed, and the impulse is to buy and buy now.

In varying degrees, similar impulses can affect even business purchases. If you want to communicate and negotiate effectively, recognize and fight such impulses.

STEP 3:   Avoid impulse buying.

When dealing with high-ticket items—items that, for one reason or another, you covet—a good way to ensure that you do not yield to impulse is to enter into your initial conversation with a vendor determined *not* to buy, but to talk. Consider this part of the research stage. Teach yourself that a deal need not be consummated quickly.

TIP
_____

Impulsive is not a synonym for *decisive.*

STEP 4:   After you have gathered sufficient data, open negotiations with the vendor who seems to offer the best value.

Let's pause to discuss a key term. Too many purchasers focus on the *price* of the merchandise or service they want to buy. Now, price is an important element of the negotiation, but it is *only* an element, a component—a component of *value.* Value is a kind of equation:

Value = price/benefits

Value is an expression of price in proportion to benefits derived from the product or service. A cheap product—a product with a low price—may or may not be a good value. A "cheap" product that offers few benefits is a poorer value than a pricier product that offers many benefits—provided that these are benefits you want and can use. Targeting value will help you negotiate far more effectively.

STEP 5:   Use the best price you were quoted during your research phase as a starting point for getting an even better price.

Now, the hard part. If you and the vendor are far apart, it is time to use your most powerful nonverbal weapon: your feet (or just end the telephone conversation, if you are not negotiating in person).

STEP 6:   If necessary, walk away from the deal.

Unless the price gap is hopelessly wide, chances are that the vendor will follow you. If not, and you don't find a better deal elsewhere, call back. Recap what happened:

> **You**: Hi, this is (your name). We were talking about a price on three dozen widgets. You were at $XXX, and I offered $XX. Have you given any further thought to price?

See what happens. You may be able to meet somewhere in the middle.

There is one more alternative to walking away from the deal. Often, price is less of an obstacle than payment terms. Even if the price of goods or services remains steep, you may be able to negotiate sufficiently liberal terms to make the deal work. Generally, the best strategy is to settle on a price, then proceed to terms. If the vendor has been able to secure a price advantageous to him, he will be strongly motivated to arrive at terms that will make it possible for you to conclude the deal.

TALKING TO VENDORS ABOUT CREDIT

Talking to a vendor about credit is similar to talking to a bank or other financial institution about a loan in that your objective is to sell the vendor on the notion that she should have confidence in you. However, when applying to a vendor for credit, you have two advantages you do not enjoy when dealing with a bank:

1. Whether the bank wishes to believe it or not, the decision to lend you money is a decision to go into partnership with you. That is a fact, though a bank may choose not to think of it this way. A vendor, faced with the same fact, has no choice but to think of it this way. In order to make it possible for you to do business with him, the vendor knows that he must *find* a way to extend credit, to make you, in effect, his partner.

2. Vendors are not subject to anything like the restrictive regulations that govern banks. A vendor knows that he has to take risks in order to sell his product. The vendor *needs* to let you buy from him.

YOUR SCRIPTS: NEGOTIATING CREDIT TERMS

Here are some ideas for negotiating favorable credit terms. Seize on the positive—what you've been given—and work up from there. Do not emphasize what you lack.

1. **You:** Hello, Gary. This is (your name) from XYZ Company. I'm reviewing your bid for the widgets. Look, I think we're just about there, and I'm eager to sign, but I need either a break on the finance charge—down to X percent would work for us—or more space on the payment schedule. We need at least XX payments over XX months, not X payments over X months. We just don't have the cash flow for that.

    Basically, work with us on either of these options, and we're ready to sign.

2. **You:** Hello, Meg. This is (your name) from XYZ Company. I've just been looking over your bid on the widget project. Meg, I like what I see. Prices are good. Delivery schedule is fine. What I need to work on with you is the payment schedule. X payments over X months is going to hurt our cash flow. What would you say to XX payments over XX months? If you can live with that, I'm ready to make the buy.

3. **You:** Hello, Bob. This is (your name) from XYZ Company. I've had a chance to review your prices on the widget project. You've made the first cut. Now, what we need more flexibility on is your payment terms. We can do XX payments over XX months, but not the short-term schedule you propose.

    Vendor: Oh, I really don't know if we can stretch it out that far.

The pessimist would take this response as a no. The optimist seizes on the "really don't know" and the generally roundabout structure of the sentence as a plea for a little more convincing. Proceed positively:

You: Well, if you find that you can stretch that little bit, I'm inclined to sign right now. So, would you give it some thought and call me back later on today? We're ready to get moving.

Vendor: I'll try to get back to you today.

You: That would be good, because we've got to get started here with somebody. So I'd appreciate your pushing on it.

3. **You**: Hello, Sam. This is (your name) from XYZ Company. I've got your bid on the merchandise . We've enjoyed doing business with you in the past, and your prices look pretty fair this time around. The only serious problem I've got is with the payment schedule you've proposed.

Vendor: It's pretty standard. I mean, it's what we set up before.

You: I understand that, but, you know, one of the things we've liked about working with you is that we've never felt you were nailing us to a boilerplate. You've been willing to accommodate. And what I'm asking for is nothing radical in any case. Instead of X payments over X months, we need to spread XX payments over XX months. Sam, we can live with the finance charge, but I can't be tying up $XXX every month. Can you meet me halfway on this? I want to move forward with this project.

HOW TO GET SPECIAL TREATMENT FROM A VENDOR

Everyone wants special treatment. You don't go to a vendor and ask to be treated like a number. But how do you persuade a vendor to treat you well?

The most effective strategy is the same strategy to use whenever you want something for yourself. Appeal to the *other* person's self-interest.

STEP 1: Be pleasant and professional.

Coming on like a hard-nosed, impossible-to-please, fiercely demanding individual will tend to alienate rather than ingratiate.

STEP 2: Be specific about what you want.

Clear objectives and goals reduce anxiety, which makes the vendor feel good about working with you.

STEP 3: Make it clear that you want to establish a working relationship.

You already know that a key to success in a sales-oriented business is *not* making *a* sale, but in *creating a satisfied customer* who will generate repeat business and positive word of mouth. Appeal to the vendor's self-interest by letting her know that you want to be just such a customer for her. You are interested in finding a business "partner," not just someone to supply a single piece of merchandise or do a single job.

TIP
_____
Do not make false or empty promises. Don't "guarantee" loads of business "if you treat us right." Just make it clear that you want to establish a stable, dependable, mutually productive working relationship.

YOUR SCRIPT: GETTING SPECIAL TREATMENT

Here's a bit of face-to-face conversation with a vendor:

You: We buy about a hundred widgets each quarter. That's a good chunk of business. Price is important, of course, and I do like your prices. But we also need a supplier who will *be there* for us, who will go the extra mile when we need him to. That means expediting delivery and being available for quick-turnaround odd-lot orders from time to time. That also means accuracy in filling our orders. I just don't have a lot of time to waste.

If we can establish a stable, solid working relationship, well, as long as that's true, you've got my business.

REJECTING A VENDOR'S PROPOSAL—WITHOUT REJECTING THE VENDOR

Perhaps the single greatest lesson one can learn about putting oneself across in business—communicating effectively in the context of commerce—is *convincingly* to separate issues from personalities. Almost every difficult, unpleasant, or sensitive business communication is made easier or more effective by such a separation. In no case is this more true than when you must say no to a vendor.

Now, you may think: *This guy is in business. If his feelings are going to be hurt by rejection, that's* his *problem.* And you'd be right. Business is all about deals made and deals *not* made, and the businessperson who takes it all personally does, indeed, have a problem. However, if feelings are hurt, it's not just the other person's problem: it's yours as well.

- You may want or need to call on the rejected vendor again, at another time. You want him to have positive feelings about you and your firm.
- Rejection can serve a positive purpose. It can deliver a strong message to a vendor, telling him what he *must* do to get your business. But this message will be heard only if the relationship between you and the vendor continues. If rejection ends the relationship, the value of rejection is lost.

TIP

No law says that you have to explain to a vendor why you're turning him down; however, you will probably benefit from taking the time to do just that. Giving a concise reason for choosing one proposal over another is not only polite and decent—both essential to creating or preserving a positive relationship with a potential future supplier—it also helps to educate the supplier as to how he might serve you better in months or years to come. This will benefit both of you.

YOUR SCRIPTS: REJECTING VENDORS' PROPOSALS

Here are some scenarios in which proposals and bids are rejected, but relationships preserved.

1. Remember: Say no to the proposal, not to the vendor.

   You: Your proposal for our project was very impressive, Bill, and it has triggered a lot of thought here. However, the approach outlined is just too costly, and we are going to go with a scaled-back version. But I want to thank you for a terrific effort, and I will certainly be calling on you in the future. I'm glad to have met you and to have seen what your company can do.

2. If possible, offer hope, not misleading encouragement. Your object is to get the vendor to perform for you.

   You: We've finished reviewing your proposal for supplying the equipment, but unfortunately what you propose is not up to spec. Obviously, we're looking at other suppliers, but there is still a month before we close out on bids. Maybe you would like to take another look at our spec sheet and submit a revised proposal by the twelfth of next month?

3. A vendor has replied to your RFP (request for proposal) with a bid that was so far outside of the ballpark that you've not even *responded* to it. The danger of not responding is that you'll be caught short by a surprise phone call. He's on the line now. Your feelings in the matter? Based on the response to your RFP, you don't anticipate wanting or needing to do business with her in the future. Nevertheless, you are well aware that, in the business world, what goes around comes around. How do you say no firmly, but decently?

   You: Charlotte, your proposal came in *40 percent* over our target cost figures. That's a gap I couldn't see even *asking* you to close. I went with a proposal that was much closer to the target.

TIP

Focus on your quantifiable, objective target versus the proposal. Avoid judgmental statements relating to capability, talent, or personality.

COMPLAINING PRODUCTIVELY TO A SUPPLIER

"Give 'em hell!" says your boss. She's referring to that shipment of widgets from the new supplier. Wrong colors. Wrong quantities. Wrong everything. "Give 'em hell!"

And *then* what?

What is your objective here? To vent your rage? Your boss's rage? Or is it to correct a problem?

If, on sober reflection, you decide in favor of the latter, try this approach:

- Rather than get angry, express disappointment. You want to send a message that you expected better things from such a fine vendor.

Sticking with this strategy may not be easy. At the least, it probably does not come naturally. After all, the emotion that motivates a complaint is not disappointment, but anger—or, at least, irritation. Giving vent to anger may make you feel better for a while, but then what are you left with? The original problem *and* an alienated and resentful vendor, who may no longer be particularly inclined to remedy the problem.

Complaining effectively is easier if you take these steps:

STEP 1:   Clearly state the problem. As TV's Sergeant Joe Friday used to say, "Just the facts, ma'am." Make no accusations. Don't guess at motives or motivations. Just enumerate such details as the duration or frequency of the problem or error, as well as the *material* (not emotional) effect of the problem or error.

TIP

Whenever possible, quantify the consequences of the problem: "Late shipments this month have cost us upwards of $3,300."

STEP 2:   Either propose a solution or ask for one.

STEP 3:   Conclude by converting *I* and *you* into *we*. Affirm that you want to work *with*—not in opposition to—the vendor.

Shipment or Service Overdue

The most common complaints against vendors are related to time. Deadlines are missed. Schedules fall apart.

Your scripts: complaining about overdue shipments

1. Begin gently, if you can. Secure cooperation. A shipment arrived late enough to have an impact on manufacturing. You call the vendor, who offers some explanations and excuses. How do you say no to the excuses without cutting loose a vendor who has offers you favorable prices?

You: I understand the problems you are facing, but *we*—you and I— are facing a problem, too. We need to work out a reliable schedule. This can't happen again. We can't absorb a delay again. Let's work together on the problem and agree on a new shipping plan to prevent late deliveries in the future.

TIP
_____

Translate the *I*-versus-*you* situation into a *we*.

Here's a simpler situation:

You: Hello, Tom. This is (your name) at XYZ Company. We ordered a gross of widgets from you on April 3 and paid with the order a deposit of $XX. A month has gone by, and we have yet to receive the merchandise. I know you received the order, and you folks deposited our check. We were promised a three-week turnaround. What's happening?

Vendor: I'll look into it and get back to you.

You: Tom, when will I hear from you? Because, look, we're up against it here. Unless we get delivery by the 14th, we will cancel the order and recall our deposit.

Vendor: Well, I'll get back to you as soon as I can.

You: Tom, I don't *want* to have to cancel this order. We want the merchandise. And I'm sure you don't want to lose the order. Please work with us now to avoid something neither of us wants. Please give me a definite time when you will get back to me.

Vendor: You'll have the information this afternoon before five.

You: That would be great. Thanks.

2. Sometimes late is just *too* late. If you must cancel an order, make certain the vendor knows why. The call *must* be followed up with a written cancellation and repudiation of the order.

You: Tom, this is (your name) over at XYZ Company. You know that old saying, "Better late than never"? Well, unfortunately, it doesn't apply this time. Tom, we ordered a gross of widgets from you on March 15. At that time, we paid in full. You've deposited the check. Now, when we failed to receive the goods by April 15, I called you, asking for immediate delivery or return of our money. You promised immediate delivery. We're still waiting—and we can't wait any longer. Tom, I just sent you a fax canceling the order because of nondelivery, and I expect our money returned within the week.

Vendor: I think you're being unreasonable. I can look into it . . .

You: Tom, it's just too late, and there is nothing to be done now but cancel the order and return the money. When will you send out that check?

Repeated Errors by the Vendor

Repeated errors are, of course, especially frustrating. Calling to complain about such problems may involve two objectives:

1. To make it clear that the situation is unacceptable and cannot continue

2. To offer help, advice, or suggestions in an effort to improve the vendor's system problems

Again, address issues, not personalities or character.

YOUR SCRIPTS: COMPLAINING ABOUT REPEATED ERRORS

The following are two approaches to opening up discussion of repeated errors.

1. **You:** . . . We've been doing business with you for a long time now, and I feel I can speak frankly with you. The performance of your shipping department over the past three months has been unacceptable from our point of view. It's just this simple: Of 25 shipments we received since date, five have been late by at least three days; eight

have been incomplete; and three have included items we did not order. Bill, your shipping department's errors have cost us time and effort, and they have often inconvenienced our customers. These errors have to stop.

I am very interested to hear your take on this situation. It might be productive for us to speak further about it. Maybe I can even make some suggestions you would find helpful.

2. **You:** . . . Edwina, as you know, I've been installing your product for some five years now. Most of the time, I've had no reason to be anything less than delighted. My customers were happy. I made money. Installations went smoothly. But since April, I have received 15 complaints from my customers, and I've had to replace eight units.

   I don't think either of us can avoid the conclusion that too many faulty units are being shipped. I have to think that you have a problem in your quality-control procedures.

   Vendor: I'm not aware of any problem. I mean, this is the first I've heard of this.

   You: I can't keep making my customers unhappy. Are you willing to review your quality-control procedures?

   Vendor: Sure . . . we'll review them.

   You: We do a lot of business together. I would like to meet with you after you've made your review and go over what steps you are taking to ensure that I'm not shipped an unacceptably high number of defective units.

WHAT TO SAY TO THE VENDOR IF YOU HAVE PAYMENT PROBLEMS

What are the hardest apologies to make? Other than incidents culminating in physical injury, the most difficult mishaps to apologize for concern money. And, in business, most apologies concern just that: late payments, missed payments, neglected bills, errors of addition or subtraction, even bounced checks.

Difficult? Yes. But, surprisingly, a straightforward, honest admission of financial error or problem gives you a certain strength to exploit.

- The admission and apology are often received with respect. It takes character to admit being wrong or to accept responsibility for dealing with a situation resulting from your financial error or difficulty.
- Admitting a problem and asking for assistance or patient indulgence empowers the creditor-vendor, giving him an opportunity to be gracious, understanding, and human—in short, giving him a chance to strengthen his partnership with you.

TIP

There is certainly no guarantee that the vendor will seize the opportunity to be decent. But if he responds with anger, good communication is even more important.

The old saw "Let sleeping dogs lie" is extremely destructive in business. If you want to ensure that your creditor will go ballistic, just give her the impression that you're blowing her off. Don't communicate. Don't answer phone calls. Throw those frantic letters in the wastebasket.

If, however, you want to avert a full-blown crisis and resolve financial problems to your advantage, go out of your way to communicate and to keep the lines of communication open. As soon as you anticipate a payment problem:

STEP 1: Advise your lender, vendor, or supplier.

STEP 2: Explain to the vendor the nature of the problem.

STEP 3: Explain how your problem will affect payment to the vendor.

STEP 4: Explain how you propose to deal with the problem.

STEP 5: Tell the vendor what you would like her to do to help *both* of you.

Let's face it, it is not always possible to anticipate cash-flow problems. On these occasions of unforeseen crisis, your only available option is an after-the-fact apology. This should not be a simple "I'm sorry," but

- Should explain the nature of the problem

- Should explain how you propose to deal with it
- Should outline how the vendor can help

TIP

If at all possible, the after-the-fact apology should be accompanied by some proposal for a solution. Even better, it should be accompanied by some *step toward* a solution. If, for example, the problem is a late payment, send the apology with a check for whatever portion of the money due you can pay.

Advising a Vendor of a Payment Problem

Telling a vendor about an impending payment problem can be emotionally difficult, but the occasion is an opportunity to take charge of a problematic situation and to demonstrate that you *have* taken charge and that the problem will not spin out of control.

The most effective strategy to formulate is one that incorporates an element of apology, but that conveys even more dominantly a tone of calm control rather than anguished contrition. If you cry *mea culpa* too loudly and too long, the vendor will believe you, conclude that you really are *terribly* at fault, and may therefore decline not only to forgive you but, more important, may choose not to take the necessary actions that will benefit you both.

TIP

Don't take the opposite tack, backing the vendor into a corner by self-righteously daring her to grant 30 days' grace on a receivable. Just don't put yourself across as a guilt-tormented sinner, either.

STEP 1: Strike the even-handed, middle tone by refraining from emotion-charged language. Avoid such words as *terrible, awful, dreadful, unfortunate, disaster, crisis,* and the like.

STEP 2: Present the facts straightforwardly.

STEP 3: If you have a specific request to make, do so directly after explaining the situation.

STEP 4: While you may conclude with an apology, do not apologize for the request or requests you make.

TIP

Avoid emotional words that tell your correspondent how to feel. Also take care to avoid telling your correspondent how he should judge your request. If you say something like, "I know this is a lot to ask," the vendor is likely, either consciously or unconsciously, to agree with you: *He is asking a lot!* Don't sandbag yourself. Make the request, and let the vendor decide just how big a favor you are asking.

STEP 5:   Do not shift the focus to yourself by telling the vendor how bad you feel about the problem. Of course you feel bad. Why should your creditor be made to feel bad, too? Isn't it enough that she's not getting her money on time?

Your scripts: renegotiating payment terms

Here are two phone scripts for renegotiating terms—*before* payment problems actually develop:

1. **You:** . . . I don't usually quote the presidents, Jane, but Abe Lincoln, you know, advised against changing *horses* in midstream. Now, as far as I know, he had nothing against changing *payment terms* to make your customer's life easier. So I hope you'll hear me out.

    We want to extend payments on our account an additional three months, reducing our monthly payment from $XXX to $XX, *but* retaining our present rate of interest. Jane, I really would like to clear this debt as quickly as possible, but our operating costs have increased faster than our client list, and we have embarked on a program designed to reduce our overhead.

    That's what *we* get out of the deal. For you, you collect another three months interest—and our undying gratitude and good will.

There is nothing wrong with a light touch—a bit of humor—just don't drown content in an attempt to get laughs at the vendor's expense.

2. **You:** Hello, Ken. This is (your name) at XYZ Company. I'm very pleased that you can take us on as a credit customer, and I've just been looking over the final forms. Everything is fine—except for the payment due date. I'm hoping you can be flexible on that. Instead of the

first of the month, we'd like to pay on the fifteenth. This works out much more smoothly with our payment-and-collection cycle. I won't have to hassle my clients each month, and, more important, it will keep the money flowing into your operation without any problems.

Here are some ideas for advising vendors of impending problems:

1. **You:** Hello, John. This is (your name) at XYZ Company. I'm calling in reference to our account with you—that's account number 12345. I am hoping you can help us over what looks to be a rough patch. We've just had some equipment breakdowns and, consequently, a number of heavy and unanticipated expenses. It would be a great help in managing cash flow if we could reschedule our payment due dates for the next six months. We currently pay on the first of each month. I would like to push that back to the twentieth. The rescheduling will help us out of a tight spot.

2: **You:** . . . We are digging out from under a number of emergency expenses that have been heaped on us this month, and I'm calling to advise you that we will be ten days late in getting a check to you for the widgets you shipped on March 5. Is this delay going to pose any serious problem for you? You *will* have the check by the twenty-fourth.

3. **You:** . . . I need to ask for your help—or, at least, for your patience. We're navigating some ticklish cash-flow situations here, and it would help me a great deal if I could defer paying off your account for 20 days. Is that going to present you with a serious problem? If not, it would sure help me out.

4. **You:** . . . I'm calling to let you know that we're going to be 20 days late getting a check to you. I'm hoping this doesn't present a problem for you.

   Vendor: Normally, it wouldn't. We usually have some flexibility. But, this month, it's not news I wanted to hear.

   You: We are talking about 20 days, but would it help if I could get you $XX by the 1st and the balance on the twentieth?

5. **You:** . . . I'm calling to let you know that we're going to be 20 days late getting a check to you. I'm hoping this doesn't present a problem for you.

Vendor: Unfortunately, it *does* present a problem.

You: I wish I didn't have to put you in this position. Given our situation, however, I don't see any way to avoid a late payment. I can come up with $XX now, if that would make it easier for you to accommodate us.

6. **You:** . . . I'm calling about our account with you, Jack. It looks as if we're going to be late with this month's payment. We've had some emergency expenses. I can hand-deliver a check on the twelfth, which will put us less than two weeks past due. I hope you can help us out with some flexibility this month. It's an unusual circumstance, which I don't anticipate happening again.

7. **You:** . . . I'm calling in reference to our account. I am anticipating a delay in paying next month's installment, and I'd like to work out an arrangement to defer that payment for 20 days.

Vendor: That's something I just can't do. I suggest you try to defer another of your expenses.

You: This is a unique circumstance, which will not be repeated. I suppose I could have just skipped the payment and taken the consequences, but I want to maintain a good working relationship with you. What would make it possible for you to assist me?

Vendor: I could speak to my credit manager . . .

You: I would really appreciate that. I don't believe in evading responsibility. I'd like us to reach an understanding that will get us both through next month. Will you call me after you've spoken to your credit manager, or should I call you?

Here are a pair of phone calls advising the vendor of a partial payment. It is not a good idea to send partial payment without advising the vendor of this.

1. **You:** . . . I just put into the mail for you a $XXX check. Before you congratulate me, let me point out that your invoice is for $XXXX, and it's about due. I've run into some cash-flow problems here, and I

thought you'd rather have a portion of the payment now than wait another 20 days or so for the whole thing. I will be sending you the balance by the twenty-fifth. Is this going to work out for you?

2. **You:** . . . You're about to get less than you deserve—and I wanted to be the first to tell you. I just sent off to you a check for $XX, which is one third of the total we owe on your last invoice. I just got hit with some unexpected emergency repair costs, which have thrown my cash position way off. I'm hoping you can see your way clear to help me out by giving me a little breathing space on this invoice. $XX is on the way to you. Another $XX will go out on the fifteenth, and the balance will go out at the end of the month. Unless my whole office goes up in smoke, I can guarantee those dates. Can you live with them?

Apologizing for Late Payment or Other Financial Glitches

If you can't advise of upcoming problems, you can apologize for problems that have already occurred.

STEP 1:   Begin by realizing that the mere fact of formally apologizing for a late payment or a missed payment or other financial glitch goes a long way toward defusing a potentially destructive situation.

STEP 2:   Make it clear that you *are* apologizing. Use such phrases as "I hope you will accept my apology," "I'm sorry," and the like.

STEP 3:   Include with the apology some positive steps toward remedying the error. Enclose a check, if appropriate and possible, either for the full amount or a partial amount. At the least, propose a definite plan for settling your account or rectifying the error.

STEP 4:   Include a brief and direct explanation of whatever has caused the problem.

STEP 5:   Include the vendor in the solution. Ask what *she* would like you to do. Use phrases like, "How do you want to proceed?" "What would be best for you?" "What would be least inconvenient?" "I suggest doing such and such, but how do you want to move on this?"

TIP

Depending on your relationship with your correspondent, don't be afraid to keep the tone lighthearted, even humorous—especially at your own expense. Honesty is disarming. If you tell your correspondent that you made a "dumb" mistake, she will respect your hard-nosed self-assessment and admire your willingness to cut through any pretense of corporate bureaucracy by taking responsibility for your actions.

YOUR SCRIPTS: APOLOGIZING FOR LATE PAYMENT

Simple is often the best:

1. **You:** Hello, Frank. This is (your name) at XYZ Company. I've just put into the mail a check for $XX, which, I'm afraid, is overdue. I wanted to let you know that the money is on the way, and I wanted to apologize for being late with it. It won't happen again.

2. **You:** . . . You know, you really ought to print your invoices on bigger paper—maybe the size of a poster—for confused folks like me who shuffle sheets on their desks until something gets lost. Your invoice, which I see is dated March 10, got buried on my desk, and now, I'm embarrassed to say, is overdue. I've made the check out and I'm putting it into the mail now. I'm very sorry for the slip-up, and I appreciate your not hollering at me, which you have every right to do.

Sometimes a little more explanation is required:

3. **You:** . . . Things got a little hectic here, and I've been hustling to get my payables out the door. I just sent you a check for $XX, which, I know, is late.

   Vendor: Yes, it *is* late. I was about to call you.

   You: Well, as the saying goes, the check is in the mail.

   Vendor: I've heard *that* one before.

   You: I bet you have. But I wanted you to hear it from me—personally. And I wanted to apologize for the delay. It will not happen again.

4. **You:** . . . It has been a very rough couple of weeks—very hectic and a lot of pressure. The good news is that I've just sent you a check for $XX. The bad news is that it's two weeks late. I thought I'd call to let you know that it's on its way and to beg—on bended knee, no less— your forgiveness.

Vendor: Oh, really, it's no problem. These things happen.

You: Not to me, they don't. I don't make it a practice to pay late. I really do appreciate your understanding.

Responding to Collection Calls

Despite your best intentions, a bill can go unpaid, and a vendor—or a collection agency—can make a collection call. Depending on the tone of the caller, such a call can rattle even the most experienced business person. In responding, try these tactics:

- You will be asked for immediate answers. Don't feel compelled to give them. If you need time to review a billing situation, say so—but give your caller an exact time when you will get back to him, and do not fail to do as you promised.
- Apologize directly, but not abjectly.
- Negotiate. If, for example, your caller demands payment in full and you are not in a position to make it, suggest a partial payment, using a phrase such as, "Would X amount help now?"
- Express appreciation for the caller's patience, understanding, and willingness to cooperate.
- Ask your caller how she would like to proceed, what would be best for her, and so on.

TIP

If your caller is really steamed—and, even among professionals, this can happen—resist the temptation either to cave in, just saying what the caller wants to hear, or to respond with anger yourself. Use the caller's name; make sure he knows he is dealing with a person to whom courtesy is due.

Do not be in too great a hurry to agree with collectors.

- Determine the facts.
- Compare balances due, dates, and so on.
- If you conclude you are in the wrong, admit it, apologize, and (if possible) negotiate an *immediate* interim action such as a partial payment.

TIP

If the situation is really hot, it may be best to cool things off by playing for time. Tell your caller that you recognize the problem and that you will take care of it, but you have to review the matter with your bookkeeper *immediately*. Give your caller an exact time when *you* will call him back.

YOUR SCRIPTS: RESPONDING TO COLLECTION CALLS

Here are some collection response scenarios:

1. **Vendor:** I'm calling about your account with us. We're showing that $XX was due on the fifteenth.

   You: You're right. I should have called. We've had some emergency expenses here, and I delayed sending out some of my payables. I can get payment in full to you by the twentieth of next month. Will that work for you?

   Vendor: I really don't like to wait that long.

   You: Would it help if I got $X out to you now, and the balance by the twentieth? I can manage that.

   Vendor: That's better for us.

   You: I appreciate your understanding, and I'm sorry—both for being late and for neglecting to give you a call earlier.

2. **Vendor:** I'm calling about your account with us. We're showing that $XXX was due on May 13.

   You: Let me look at my book. My ledger shows that a check for that amount was mailed to you on May 4. It's our check number 12345. You should have gotten it by now.

Vendor: No, it's not here.

You: I see. How would you like to proceed? I can put a stop on the check we sent and send you out a new one today. Or we can wait until the end of the week.

Vendor: I think it would be best to get a new check.

You: Okay. Let me confirm your address. I'll get that right out to you, and I'm sorry the check went astray.

3. **Vendor:** I'm calling about your account with us. Do you intend to pay it?

You: Am I speaking to Pete Williams (name of usual contact)?

Vendor: Yes, this is Pete.

You: Pete, of course we intend to pay the amount due. I am showing a balance due of $XXX. Is that what you've got?

Vendor: Yes.

You: And you're right. We're late. I am very sorry. I am not prepared at this time to pay the full balance due. I can send you $XX now, and the balance by the end of February.

Vendor: I wish you had called me earlier, if there was a problem.

You: Pete, I agree with you. I should have asked for your help on this to begin with. It would have made the situation easier for you and, certainly, for me. I apologize. And I hope we can work together on the basis I suggested: $XX now, and the balance by February 28.

THANKING A VENDOR AND GIVING REFERRALS

Saying Thanks to a Vendor

When a vendor goes the extra mile for you, expressing thanks not only acknowledges that fact and makes the vendor feel good, it makes you feel good, too. But thanks is not only an act of courtesy. It is also a means of *reinforcing* positive action and building a relationship in which extra-mile service can become the norm. Behavioral psychologists have long known that positive reinforcement is much more effective than negative reinforcement (threats and the like) in creating desired behavior or action. But what makes the difference between a perfunctory, formal thank you and a truly meaningful expression of thanks?

Specificity. Facts. Details.

The strategy for making an effective thank you call is to stick to the facts.

STEP 1: State exactly what you are thanking the vendor for.

STEP 2: Say something about the positive effect of the vendor's extra-mile action.

STEP 3: Close with an expression of appreciation.

TIP
_____

The key to an effective thank-you call is to be specific, expressing thanks and then explaining how valuable the service, favor, whatever is. You don't need to exaggerate the good consequences of the act. Just be as specific as possible.

Being specific about the effect of the extra-mile action satisfies the human urge to see, to realize, the results of effort. It is a strong means of reinforcing positive behavior. Remember to

- Keep the thanks straightforward
- Use verbs and nouns—specifics—instead of adjectives
- Let the warmth of your voice come through in your message

YOUR SCRIPTS: EXPRESSING THANKS TO VENDORS

Here are some spontaneous thank-you calls to vendors.

1. **You:** Frank, your guidance in upgrading our software saved us at least $XXX in direct software and training costs. That means a lot to us. We're very grateful for the time and care you took with us.

2. **You:** Betty, you saved the day when you managed to expedite shipment of the Johnson order. You don't know how close we came to losing a major customer, but, thanks to your extra-mile effort, we delivered on time and ended up strengthening that relationship. We're very
grateful to you for your hard work and commitment to us.

Giving Vendor Referrals

Referral calls should be a pleasure to make. They not only present an
opportunity to help a deserving vendor, they also directly benefit your interests.

- It is worthwhile to extend your influence and judgment throughout the
  business community.

- Sending a good vendor to a colleague builds a positive relationship
  with that colleague as well as with the vendor.

- A good referral is a favor to two people: the vendor and the colleague.

As with thanking a vendor for extra-mile service, the key to making
effective referrals is to be as specific as possible.

- Avoid vague adjectives.

- Mention specific events, projects, and accomplishments relating to the
  vendor you are recommending.

TIP

Do not make the referral unless you can do so without reservation. If
you have any doubts about the vendor, decline the vendor's request for
a recommendation.

TIP

If a vendor asks you to call a colleague with a recommendation, you can
make the call easier by asking the vendor to tell you what he'd like you
to mention.

Your script: giving vendor referrals

Here's an example of a vendor referral:

You: Norma, Sarah Coates at WXY Widgets asked me to give you a call to tell you something about her and her company. We've been doing business with WXY for three years, and I wouldn't think of going to any other supplier. Not only are WXY's prices fair—I think unbeatable—the service is personal, direct, and responsive. Just a few days ago, I need an odd-lot assortment of widgets for a rush job. I called Sarah. She had an up-to-the-minute inventory on everything, and the *single* time she didn't have on one hand, she got it for me that same day. And this isn't an isolated case. This is the kind of responsiveness I expect from WXY. So, I'm very happy to recommend her company to you.

CHAPTER 11

Putting Yourself Across . . . to Lenders and Investors

SELF-TEST YOUR SAVVY IN COMMUNICATING WITH LENDERS AND INVESTORS

The following is a simple diagnostic test. A smaller and more selective version of the self-test in Chapter 1, its purpose is not to test your knowledge of communication theory or techniques, but to help you gauge how effectively you communicate with lenders and investors in a day-to-day business context. For the most part, you will find it easy to guess the "right" answer. But getting the "right" answer is not the point of the test. Respond honestly, even if you feel that your response is not the best one possible. This is *not* a contest. The object is solely self-inventory.

1. If a prospect fails to return my calls, I try, try again. T/F ____

2. I always use a soft-sell strategy. T/F ____

3. I am willing—personally—to explain and defend my credit history. T/F ____

4. I am confident that I have the expertise to get the job done. T/F ____

5. Investors and lenders generally have confidence in me. T/F ____

6. Going back to an original investor for more money is easier than finding new sources. T/F ____

7. No business plan should exceed five or six pages. T/F ____

8. I don't ask for more without offering more. T/F ____

9. I don't say anything. I put it all in writing. T/F ____

10. I highlight my written business plan with a verbal
    send-off.   T/F ____

11. There is nothing wrong with hiring a consultant to help
    with the business plan.   T/F ____

12. It is better to renegotiate terms before your account
    becomes delinquent.   T/F ____

13. Everyone lies on loan applications.   T/F ____

14. Banks loan you money only if you can prove you
    don't need it.   T/F ____

15. I make follow-up calls to ensure that the prospect has
    all the information he needs.   T/F ____

16. Loan officers are busy. I don't annoy them with
    follow-up calls.   T/F ____

17. I often follow up with prospects who have turned
    me down—just in case.   T/F ____

18. Business plans should be extremely detailed.   T/F ____

19. I present investment as an opportunity.   T/F ____

20. Investment prospects are annoyed by follow-up calls.
    I try not to make them.   T/F ____

21. I see the business plan as a *real* plan, not just a sales tool. T/F ____

22. I sell the future.   T/F ____

23. I want prospective investors to ask a lot of questions.   T/F ____

TOTAL T/F   ____

Score 1 point for each "True" response and 0 for each "False" response,
EXCEPT for questions 2, 7, 9, 13, 14, 16, 18, and 20. For *these questions only*,
SUBTRACT 1 point for each "True" response. Record your total. A score
below +13 indicates that you would benefit from practicing the communication techniques discussed in this chapter. (Note: It is possible to have a
negative score.)

WORDS TO USE WITH LENDERS AND INVESTORS

advice
advise
aggressive
alternatives
caution
checklist
evaluate
expertise
explain
growth
issues
negotiate
opportunity
options

outline
plan
potential
precise
precisely
present
problem
proceed
quantity
safe
safety
satisfaction
strategy

PHRASES TO USE WITH LENDERS AND INVESTORS

best guess
best-case scenario
give me the percentages
how confident are you
issues to address
lay out for you
make a list
next move
pin down
pros and cons
what are the odds
what's the probability
worst-case scenario

WORDS TO AVOID WITH LENDERS AND INVESTORS

basically	generally
broke	must
desperate	shyster
desperation	urgent

PHRASES TO AVOID WITH LENDERS AND INVESTORS

get on the stick
hurry up
in general
let me talk to you
now or never
once in a lifetime
take all the time you need
take it or leave it
tell me what I should do
What's my next move?

BODY-LANGUAGE STRATEGY FOR COMMUNICATING WITH LENDERS AND INVESTORS

Review Chapter 7 for a discussion of body-language strategy that is appropriate for working with clients and customers as well as lenders and investors. In addition, keep uppermost in mind two objectives of nonverbal communication with lenders and investors:

1. To communicate honesty and trustworthiness—"character"
2. To communicate confidence

Accordingly, review in particular comments in the "Body-Language Strategy" section of Chapter 7 covering the handshake and posture. Communicating with lenders and investors benefits from a firm, warm handshake and from an upright posture. Use open gestures. Establish and maintain eye contact.

People tend to associate a lower-pitched voice with authority and honesty. If you can cultivate the lower registers of your voice, do so. This advice applies to men and women alike. Deliberately pitching your voice a bit lower than normal should also help slow your speech and improve your enunciation. The more clearly you speak, the more confident you seem, and the more confidence you inspire in others.

BODY LANGUAGE TO AVOID WITH LENDERS AND INVESTORS

Avoid gestures that express

- Evasiveness
- Timidity
- Uncertainty
- Vagueness
- General nervousness

The following body language may kill a deal:

- Avoidance of eye contact
- Bringing the hands to the mouth
- Rubbing the face
- Shielding the eyes
- Running hands through hair or manipulating your hair
- Rubbing the back of the neck
- Rubbing the eyes
- Scratching yourself—anywhere
- Licking the lips
- Biting the lips
- Slouching
- Shifting weight from side to side (standing)

- Leg movement (sitting)
- Shaking the head *no*

SECRETS OF SELLING YOUR FUTURE TO LENDERS AND INVESTORS

Why doesn't everybody with at least a little money to invest clean up on the stock market?

There are undoubtedly many plausible answers to this question, but the most meaningful answer is simple:

- *Few people understand what it means to invest in the future.*

Putting money in a *relatively* mature company is *relatively* safe but also *relatively* unprofitable. The future of a mature company will probably be little different from its present; therefore, investments will probably enjoy only modest growth.

Your strategic objective in communicating with investors and lenders is to educate them about your future and, once they are sufficiently educated, to *sell* them a share of that future.

Selling. That is what communicating to investors and lenders is. As in most other sales situations, there are two broad approaches:

1. *The soft sell.* This approach appeals to reason and intellect. Usually, the soft sell appeals to the more sophisticated investor, the person accustomed to making up his or her own mind.
2. *The hard sell.* This approach makes its case more directly, often bypassing the intellect in order to appeal to the emotions. If a soft sell is a word to the wise, a hard sell is an impassioned plea.

Both soft-sell and hard-sell strategies can be effective. Choosing between them depends on the nature of your business and on the kind of investor you are after.

- The soft sell is an attempt to open the door to further discussion.
- At its most extreme, the hard sell tries to open the door, enter the room, make the sale, and leave with the cash.

TIP

Be careful. In most jurisdictions, soliciting investment money requires a full-disclosure prospectus. Make certain that you are thoroughly familiar with all applicable laws governing the solicitation of investments. The laws vary from business to business and jurisdiction to jurisdiction.

- The hard sell will often provoke a more definite response from the prospect, which, depending on the type of investment and the type of investor, may be a more definitely *positive* or a more definitely *negative* response.
- The soft sell is less definite, but also less risky. Knock politely on a door, and you may be refused admittance, but at least you won't get *kicked* out.

For all their differences, the soft-sell and the hard-sell approaches typically must achieve seven objectives to be successful:

1. Give the prospective investor or lender a good reason for your having approached him.

TIP

When approaching investors, you may want to identify the prospect as a member of an elite group—one of a group of historically successful investors, for example.

2. Make a case for the investment opportunity; that is, identify a hitherto unmet need for which there is a lucrative market.
3. Explain how your project or company will meet this need.
4. Persuade the investor of your personal ability to meet the need, that you are qualified to run the company or project.
5. Enumerate the benefits—to the investor or lender—of the investment or loan.
6. Outline a course of action.

In a hard sell, outlining a course of action may involve prodding the prospect with provocative questions (which you always answer for him) and announcing that you will follow up personally to solicit a response. The soft sell, in contrast, merely lays the groundwork for a follow-up, then asks for an invitation to follow up.

7. Invite questions.

Never be afraid of questions. Not only is it up to you to demonstrate that you have nothing to hide, but questions in and of themselves represent an investment in your company or project. The more interactive the prospect is willing to be, the better your chances of making the sale.

Your scripts: communicating with lenders and investors

Here are some ideas for conversations with potential investors or lenders. We begin with a soft-sell approach:

1. **You:** . . . Mr. Perkins, I've always believed that when I needed help, it's best to go right to the top. That's why I'm calling you, a leader of this city's business and cultural community.

    Last year, some 650 small presses in the United States and Canada published some 3,500 books intended to appeal to the general reader. Unfortunately, few of these presses had access to a decent distribution service, and, therefore, the "general reader" never saw the majority of these books, let alone had the opportunity to buy them.

    I have a plan to change this situation with a company I call Bookserve, Inc., a distribution-and-warehouse service for independent and small presses. The publishers are crying out for such a service.

    But, Mr. Perkins, the small presses are not the only ones who will profit from the enterprise. Bookstores will gain access to vast, enticing new stocks. And readers everywhere, of course, will benefit.

    And then there is you. Investors in Bookserve, Inc., should realize profits within three to four years after start-up. How do I know? I've been in book distribution for more than 20 years and am currently general manager of XYZ Company, one of the nation's most successful distributors.

    I know I can make Bookserve, Inc., a major success, and I would like to set up—at this time—an appointment to speak with you in person and present to you a detailed business plan.

2. **You:** . . . Ms. Deacon, we all like to win. Too often, however, one person's triumph comes at the cost of another's defeat.

   But not this time.

   I'd like the opportunity to talk with you about an investment opportunity in which everyone involved will win.

   Last year, some 650 small presses in the United States and Canada published some 3,500 books intended to appeal to the general reader. Unfortunately, few of these presses had access to a decent distribution service, and, therefore, the "general reader" never saw the majority of these books, let alone had the opportunity to buy them.

   My plan is to change all this with a company called Bookserve, Inc., a distribution-and-warehouse service for small presses. After working more than 20 years in book distribution (I'm currently general manager of XYZ Company, one of the nation's most successful book distributors), I know I can make this company a winner.

   I know, too, that it will make winners of small presses, bookstores, and readers. And it will make winners of those who invest in Bookserve, Inc.

   I want very much to introduce myself to you in person and to present a detailed business plan. I will be in your city on . . .

3. **You:** . . . When Bill Johnson at EFG Company told me that you are an avid reader *and* a shrewd investor, that was all I needed to hear. I knew that I had to call you.

   Mr. Nelson, last year, some 650 small presses in the United States and Canada published some 3,500 books intended to appeal to the general reader. Unfortunately, few of these presses had access to a decent distribution service, and, therefore, the "general reader" never saw the majority of these books, let alone had the opportunity to buy them.

   My plan is to change all this with a company called Bookserve, Inc., a distribution-and-warehouse service for small presses. After working more than 20 years in book distribution (I'm currently general manager of XYZ Company, one of the nation's most successful distributors), I know I can make Bookserve, Inc., work—for small presses, for book dealers, for the reading public, and for you, the investor.

   I'm going to be in your town from May tenth through the twelfth, and I am eager to set up an appointment to introduce myself in person and to present you with a detailed business plan, which you can study at your leisure.

4. **You:** Ms. Kelly, your name appears in some of the best places, especially the annual reports of numerous small innovative entrepreneurial firms. That's why I am calling you right now.

 I've started a company called Bookserve, Inc., a distribution-and-warehouse service for small presses. Last year, some 650 such presses in the United States and Canada published about 3,500 books intended to appeal to the general reader. Unfortunately, few small presses have access to a decent distribution service and, therefore, the "general reader" never sees the majority of these books, let alone has the opportunity to buy them.

 With the help of investors like you, Bookserve, Inc., will change all that. The small presses will profit, bookstores will profit, readers will profit, and, of course, investors will profit.

 I look forward to speaking with you, meeting you in person, telling you more about myself, and presenting a detailed business plan for Bookserve, Inc.

And now, for comparison, some hard-sell approaches:

1. **You:** . . . Mr. Williams, I know of 650 companies that need your help and that are willing to give you a fair share of their profits for helping them.

 Let me explain.

 Last year, some 650 small presses in the United States and Canada published over 3,500 books they intended for the general reader. Because few of these presses had access to a decent distribution service, the "general reader" never saw the majority of these books, let alone had the opportunity to buy them.

 My plan is to change all this with a company called Bookserve, Inc., a distribution-and-warehouse service for small presses. After working more 20 twenty years in book distribution (I'm currently general manager of XYZ Company, one of the nation's most successful distributors), I know I can make Bookserve, Inc., work—for small presses, for book dealers, for the reading public, and for you, the investor.

 Shall I go on?

Prospect: Sure. I'm listening.

You: I want to introduce myself in person and show you a detailed business plan, which explains how you can expect to realize a profit on your investment in just three to four years. I want to explain how, with your help, we will revolutionize an industry, perform a cultural service, and make money in the bargain. I will be in town . . .

2. **You:** . . .You've heard about the notion of doing well by doing good, haven't you?

Prospect: Yes.

You: Well, cynics say things just don't ever really work that way. But how many wealthy cynics do you know? Look, there are 650 small companies in this country and Canada that need your help—and that will share their profits with you to get it.
   Should I tell you more?

Prospect: I'm interested in hearing your story.

You: Then let me explain. Last year, some 650 small presses in the United States and Canada published approximately 3,500 books they intended for the general reader. Because few of these presses had access to a decent distribution service, the "general reader" never saw the majority of these books, let alone had the opportunity to buy them.
   My plan is to change all this with a company called Bookserve, Inc., a distribution-and-warehouse service for small presses. After working more than 20 years in book distribution (I'm currently general manager of XYZ Company, one of the nation's most successful distributors), I know I can make Bookserve, Inc., work—for small presses, for book dealers, for the reading public, and for you, the investor.
   Mr. Larson, I'd like an opportunity to introduce myself in person and to present a full business plan. I'll be in town . . .

3. **You:** . . . Everybody wants to make more money. That's not news. But let me get specific. I can name right now about 650 entrepreneurial CEOs who want to make more—and who are willing to share their profits with you in order to do so.
   There are just about 650 small presses in the United States and Canada turning out terrific books intended to appeal to the general

reader—some 3,500 titles last year alone. Unfortunately, the "general reader" rarely sees or even hears of these books (let alone buys them) because small presses have never been able to get the kind of distribution they desperately need.

I want to change that with a company called Bookserve, Inc., a warehouse-and-distribution service for small presses. And I want you to help me now so that you can share in the profits later—not *much* later, just three to four years.

Twenty years in book distribution (I'm currently general manager of XYZ Company, one of the nation's most successful distributors) makes me confident that Bookserve, Inc., will work spectacularly well.

I'm also confident that you, a literate investor accustomed to making the right decision, will want to see me when I will be in your area. I'll be armed with a detailed business plan.

4. **You:** I've got a question *and* an answer for you. What would you do if you had a terrific product you couldn't sell? Here's the answer: You'd pay somebody to sell it for you.

The fact is that there are about 650 fine companies out there who are looking for that somebody. And that somebody could be you.

I am creating a company called Bookserve, Inc., a warehouse-and-distribution service for small presses. Last year, some 650 of them in the United States and Canada published approximately 3,500 books they intended for the general reader. The trouble is that the "general reader" neither saw nor heard of most of these books (let alone bought them) because small presses have never been able to get the kind of distribution they desperately need.

Bookserve, Inc., is meant to change all that. It will help small presses sell books, open up a vast array of new suppliers to book retailers, provide readers with a treasure trove of unique and worthwhile books, and, for a few shrewd investors, generate revenue.

Twenty years in book distribution (I'm currently general manager of XYZ Company, one of the nation's most successful distributors) leaves no room for doubt in my mind that I will make Bookserve, Inc., work. I also have no doubt that you'll be interested enough in the project to allow me the opportunity to meet with you in person next week. I want to show you a detailed business plan. . . .

PRESENTING A PROSPECTUS OR BUSINESS PLAN

Once you have sufficiently interested a prospect in your company, project, or venture, it is time to follow up—and follow up quickly—with a detailed business plan. Now, *How to Say It at Work* is not a book devoted to creating a business plan. There are plenty of books—as well as software for the personal computer—to help you there. Two good general volumes to consult are

- James B. Arkebauer's *McGraw-Hill Guide to Writing a High-Impact Business Plan* (McGraw-Hill, 1994)
- Joseph Covello and Brian Hazelgran's *Your First Business Plan* (Small Business Source Books, 1993)

And if you prefer working with PC software, Tim Berry's *Business Plan Pro* (Palo Alto Software) is a good choice. Whatever books or computer programs you use, just remember that there is no one-size-fits-all prescription for writing a business plan. Suit the plan to:

- Your business, venture, or project
- The kind of investor you are going after

TIP

It is imperative that, once the investor's interest is piqued, the business plan is presented without delay. Momentum is one of the keys to unlocking capital.

Let's say you're an inventor or the developer of new products. Why not just call on your local venture capitalist with a prototype in hand? What could be more persuasive (provided the darn thing works, of course)?

The truth is that the savvy investor *will* look at the prototype—at some point. But what he'll want to see first is your business plan. The plan you present should serve four basic purposes:

1. It should be a tool to pry loose money.
2. It should be obviously and clearly usable as a guide to running the business once the funding is in place. That is, it *really* should be a business *plan*—not just something to show to investors.

3. It should serve as persuasive evidence of your ability to think, to organize, to plan, to anticipate, to create.

Finally, *for yourself:*

4. The business plan should turn up any problems and issues that need
to be resolved. Review your plan carefully. Redraft and redraft it until
the problems *are* solved.

However you decide to structure and pitch your business plan, observe
the following:

- Don't skimp, but do strive to be concise. The plan should be readable
in a single sitting—which means about 20 to 30 pages for most projects
or ventures.

- Avoid vagueness and pie-in-the-sky, but do not smother the investor in
details.

TIP

Detailed breakdowns, test-market results, focus-group numbers, and so
on should be available in a backup document for the investor who asks
to see these things.

In addition to a business plan, you should be prepared to furnish a
more specifically detailed marketing plan, a document that will cover, at
minimum, ten key issues.

1. The customer
2. The product or project
3. The market: size? growth potential?
4. A strategy for distribution of the product or service
5. A strategy for pricing
6. A strategy for promotion

7. How your company and product relate to the established industry

8. How you propose to compete—and win

9. The environment: political and regulatory, legal, cultural, economic

10. The technological context

TIP
_____

Don't rule out hiring a consultant to help you prepare your business plan. If bringing an expert on board saves time and speeds your proposal to investors and lenders, it's worth it.

YOUR SCRIPTS: PRESENTING YOUR BUSINESS PLAN

If you don't present your business plan in person, a phone call alerting the prospect to its arrival is a valuable step to take:

1. **You**: . . . I am happy to tell you that the business plan for Bookserve, Inc., is on its way by overnight mail. Although it speaks for itself, you might want to look for these highlights: probable return on your investment within six months, profit on start-up capital within three to four years, a client base of 450 to 650 firms, and diversity within a focused, targeted market. It has been a pleasure speaking with you about this project, and I look forward to your response to the business plan. I will call you early next week to get your reaction to it.

2. **You**: . . . After our conversation yesterday, I'm not surprised you asked to see the business plan. You should have it later today. Once you've read through it, you will see why I'm so excited about the company. Now, it is true, as you pointed out, that small presses cannot afford to put much money behind promotion. As I mentioned to you, however, the key to selling books is not advertising but distribution. And that, of course, is what we are all about. You might also bear in mind a few other highlights as you read through the prospectus: probable return on investment within six months, profit on start-up capital in three to four years, client base of 450 to 650 firms, and diversity within a focused, targeted market. It's a winner—but you'll see that for yourself. I'll call you early next week to discuss.

PRESENTING AN ANNUAL REPORT: SECRETS OF KEEPING THE IDEA ALOFT

Shouldn't an annual report speak for itself? The answer is *yes, but* . . .

Telephoning key investors in advance of sending the annual report can accomplish three things:

1. It personalizes the report, reinforcing the impression that you regard this investor as a key player and partner in your enterprise.
2. It draws attention to highlights and achievements of the year.
3. It explains—or puts into perspective—any disappointments.

Your scripts: enhancing the annual report

Examples of calls you might make just before the annual report is issued:

1. **You:** . . . I've just sent out to you the first annual report of Bookserve, Inc. You will find it both interesting and, I am happy to say, highly *enjoyable* reading. Like any good investor, you'll go right to the bottom line, of course, and I know you'll like what you see there. But I also respectfully direct your attention to the growth of our client list, which exceeds the prospectus numbers by 14 percent, and our retail penetration, which is right on target.

   George, I am grateful for your support during this past year and trust that you look forward to the next year as much as I do. Give me a call if you have questions about the report.

2. **You:** . . . Fay, I just sent our first annual report out to you. Now, you don't need that report to tell you that we have come through a rough start-up year. But take a good look at the numbers in that report. You'll see that the growth of our client list is right on target, and while our retail penetration has fallen 5 percent behind what we expected, it has picked up with each quarter. For now, in this rocky retail climate, the very good news is that we *have* come through. For the future, the numbers suggest a pattern of increasingly rapid growth.

   Fay, I'm proud of this report, and I greatly appreciate your support during a challenging period. Together, I am confident we can look forward to a brighter future. Call me if you have any questions.

FOLLOWING UP (GO EASY ON THE SPURS)

Following Up with Investor Prospects

Follow-up calls can be valuable in the following situations:

- In the interval between initial contact with a prospect and the next contact, a personal interview, or the transmission of a business plan
- When a prospect fails to return your calls
- If a prospect declines to invest

YOUR SCRIPTS: FOLLOWING UP WITH PROSPECTIVE INVESTORS

The following call would be useful to keep the level of the prospect's excitement high:

You: It was a pleasure speaking with you on the telephone yesterday, and I look forward to our meeting a week from Thursday.

Your questions were stimulating, challenging, shrewd, and entirely appropriate. I am confident that the business plan I will present when I see you answers them all.

What really excites me is that our conversation convinced me that you are the kind of investor Bookserve needs—one who does more than simply throw money at a project. See you Thursday next week.

Here is a follow-up aimed at encouraging the prospect to read a prospectus, business plan, or other material that was left with him:

You: Thanks for giving me the opportunity to present the business plan for Bookserve. It's apparent that you are a careful investor and that you will subject the material I left to a rigorous review. So much the better for Bookserve.

As you do work your way through the proposal, please keep the following points in mind: You can distribute your investment capital over eight quarters, with the option to pull out at any time; your voting privileges on the board of directors are proportional to your investment; you always retain the right to review the list of publishers and titles we will carry; and most important, you are contributing to a 100 percent win-win enterprise. Six hundred fifty deserving companies will profit from your investment. Book retailers will profit from your investment. The book-buying public will profit from your investment. And, yes, *you* will profit from your investment.

Anyway, I'll call back next week, after you've had ample opportunity to review the proposal in depth. In the meantime, of course, don't hesitate to call with questions.

The following scenario is useful when you are met with indifference. This is a message left on the prospect's voice mail:

You: . . . Hello, Carol. You're not one to dodge a call, so I assume you've been too swamped to get back to me on the Bookserve proposal. It's a winning proposition, and I'd hate to see us both lose just because we couldn't make contact. I'll call again early next week. In the meantime, I hope you'll have an opportunity to examine the business plan I left with you.

When you meet with a no, it may or may not be time to move on to another prospect. Follow up with a call if you aren't certain that you gave the initial pitch your best shot:

You: . . . I appreciate the time you gave me to present my proposal for Bookserve, Inc. Of course, I'm disappointed by your decision not to invest in the enterprise. I can't help thinking that, in my zeal to present a detailed plan, I caused you to lose sight of a few essential points that might otherwise have influenced your decision. Did I make the following clear?

First, that you can distribute your investment capital over eight quarters, with the option to pull out at any time. Second, that your voting privileges on the board of directors are proportional to your investment. And, third, that you always retain the right to review the list of publishers and titles we will carry. Are there any questions I left unanswered? I appreciate the time you've given me. Of course, I'd appreciate even more any time you might devote to reconsidering the proposal.

Following Up with Lenders

In the case of loan applications, a follow-up call may be necessary to get the loan officer off the dime. It is unfortunate that banks are justly notorious for crawling just when you need them to sprint. A judicious follow-up call can help speed things up.

STEP 1:   Begin by letting the loan officer know that you realize how busy he is.

STEP 2:   Go on to explain (without the least trace of whining) why you need a prompt answer.

TIP

The loan officer should feel that you are asking for help not from a faceless bureaucrat, but from an individual who is about to become your de facto business partner. It is amazing, as well as gratifying, to discover that business people welcome opportunities to be helpful. Keeping this fact of human nature in mind makes the chore of follow-up calls much easier.

STEP 3:   Gently goad the loan officer into action by giving him an opportunity to be helpful.

YOUR SCRIPTS: FOLLOWING UP WITH LENDERS

Here are some approaches to sluggish bankers:

1. **You:** . . . It has been *X* days since I submitted my application for this loan. I faxed you on the fifteenth, but I received no reply. I realize that processing a business loan can be painstaking and time-consuming, but I am confident that you appreciate the impossibility of maintaining responsible financial management in the absence of financial information. Mr. Thomas, I need an update on the status of my loan application.

2. **You:** . . . In *X* days, Ms. Donaldson, I face the quarterly chore of advising my backers as to the financial state of my company. Right now there is a disturbingly large question mark looming over "funds available." You, Ms. Donaldson, have it in your power to remove that question mark. Please: Where are we on my loan application? Is there any additional information you need from me?

3. **You:** . . . Silence, they say, is golden, Mr. Kern, but this is taking the virtue a bit far. I first met with you on May tenth and filed my loan application on May fourteenth. Since that time, I have had no substantive word on the status of my application. Is there a problem? If there is, let me in on it, so that we can work together to resolve it. If there is no problem, I need an answer to this application.

HOW TO PUT THE PAST INTO PERSPECTIVE (CREDIT-HISTORY GAFFES AND GLITCHES)

Sorry, but no matter how well you put yourself across, you're not likely to convince any bank or conventional lending institution to give you cash unless you have a decent balance sheet, prospects for a bright future—*and* a reasonably clean credit history. The good news is that "reasonably clean" is a matter of some judgment and, as such, may be colored by the way you present that history.

Most banks and conventional lending institutions will request a formal letter explaining any questionable episodes in a loan applicant's credit history. But even before you put it in writing, you should be prepared with a calm, reasoned *verbal* explanation of credit gaffes and glitches.

STEP 1: Don't be in *too* great a hurry to explain.

This is one time when it does not pay to be overly proactive. Unless the blemish on your credit history is very substantial and very obvious, let the lender decide whether it is worth discussing. Don't volunteer your opinion that an incident or incidents *require* explanation. Wait to be asked. In the case of "substantial and obvious" credit-history problems, such as the following, you *should* consider speaking with the lender when you discuss terms or at the time that you file your application.

- Bankruptcy
- Legal judgments against you
- Obviously heavy debt load
- Substantial losses

STEP 2: If you are asked about specific episodes of your credit history, respond calmly. Adopt an even, businesslike tone.

TIP

Avoid defensiveness. Avoid a confessional tone. Avoid such telltale negative body language as failure to make eye contact, biting of the lips, bringing the hands to the face or mouth, and head shaking. Avoid nervous laughter.

STEP 3: Make no obvious attempt to minimize or dismiss the incident in question. The lender *believes* it may be important.

You'll have to *show* that the episode is not significant. If you merely assert that it is not, the lender will tend to assume the opposite, and you will likely be denied the loan.

STEP 4: Provide a concise explanation of the episode, including all mitigating circumstances.

TIP

Be careful that what you say verbally does not conflict with anything you have put in writing or plan to put in writing. Remember, even if you give a persuasive verbal explanation of credit-history gaffes and glitches, you will almost certainly be asked to provide a written explanation as well. You are speaking for the record.

STEP 5: Put the glitch into perspective. Picture it as a small blotch on the otherwise exemplary credit history of a prosperous company.

TIP

Putting a credit-history glitch in perspective—in context—may be the most persuasive tactic available to you. But you *must* work within the facts. You cannot lie. Doing so may, at the least, result in the loan being denied or, even worse, repudiated later. At its worst, giving false information on a loan application is criminal fraud.

STEP 6: End by announcing your availability to answer further questions.

How effective is a good verbal explanation of credit-history difficulties? The effectiveness depends on the gravity of the financial or credit problem in question. If you make it a habit not to pay your bills, no amount of explaining is likely to get you a loan.

YOUR SCRIPTS: HANDLING QUESTIONS ABOUT YOUR CREDIT HISTORY

Here are typical verbal responses to questions about irregularities in credit history. While the answers should never be vague or evasive, do not smother the loan officer in details. Keep the response concise. If the loan officer needs more information, she will ask you. Remember, too, that you will almost certainly be asked subsequently to embody the verbal explanation in a formal letter of explanation.

1. **Lender**: I see that you had a late payment on your corporate credit card last quarter.

    You: That's right. From May 10 to June 5, both principals of our company were out of the country. The explanation for this *single* tardy payment is that neither my partner nor I was present when the bill arrived, and in the backlog of work that had accumulated by the time of our return, this bill was shuffled to the bottom of the heap. That was careless, but it was an accident. I mean, you'll note that the payment was made only 10 days beyond the 30-day limit. We've held the credit card for X years, and this is the single instance of a late payment.

2. **Lender**: I am troubled by three late payments noted in the credit report we secured in processing your loan application.

    You: You will note that all of the late payments occurred during the March to May period. During that time, we lost two of our major clients: ABC Company failed to secure anticipated funding for a project contracted with us, and DEF Company petitioned for Chapter 11 bankruptcy at the end of March. Consequently, our available cash was unexpectedly low for the period. We contacted the credit officers at the three firms in question and arranged deferred payments. I can furnish, in writing, the details of these arrangements, as well as the names of the contact people we worked with. Most important, all of those accounts are now currently up to date.

The following is phone-call response to a query made earlier by the loan officer:

3. **You:** . . . I was surprised and distressed to hear that the SOL Credit Reporting Agency reported late payments to ABC Company. Mr. Larson, this report is in error. I have contacted SOL to advise them of their error and to demand that they correct it. I have also contacted Claire Peters at ABC Company, who has agreed to send you directly a letter confirming that the credit report is indeed in error and affirming our good payment record with them. She'll fax that to you, following it up in the mail with hard copy.

     Mr. Larson, I will call again early next week to confirm that you have received Ms. Peters's letter, and I trust that this credit reporter's error will not delay processing our application.

4. **You:** . . . We have made no secret of the financial problems we experienced last year. The delinquent accounts to which you refer, however, have been settled. I am faxing the relevant documents.

     Ms. Flint, I think you'll agree that our most recent financial statements amply demonstrate that our difficulties are well behind us, and we are in a period of growth and increased profitability. Since June, our credit record—with banks as well as with vendors—has been without blemish. We're not only a good risk, we're a good investment.

WHEN THINGS GO WRONG: RENEGOTIATING TERMS

Sometimes temporary cash-flow problems make it desirable or necessary to renegotiate the terms of a loan. This is a common situation, and it should be met with routine rationality. However, when *Homo sapiens* find it difficult to meet monthly obligations, the species' prime and primal instinct is to run and hide.

The *last* thing he wants to do is contact the lender.

This behavior, instinctive though it may be, is, in fact, very self-destructive.

*   The most important time to maintain close communication with a lender is precisely when you are having difficulty paying him.

If you fail to communicate, the lender will naturally assume that you are evading her (because you are) and that you are trying to get away with something (which is exactly what you are trying to do). If, on the other hand, you communicate effectively, you are assuring the lender that, though you have problems and those problems are affecting her as well as yourself, you have no intention of dodging your responsibility. On the contrary, you are anxious to work things out together.

- It is even better to initiate this process of communication *before* your account becomes delinquent.
- If you know that you are going to be unable to meet a payment, advise the lender of this difficulty in advance, proposing, as you do so, a realistic alternative—usually deferred payment.

STEP 1:   Advise the loan officer of the problem.

STEP 2:   Explain the reason for the problem, stressing the (anticipated) temporary nature of the difficulty.

STEP 3:   Propose an alternative.

STEP 4:   Put the problem in perspective: This is a glitch in an otherwise profitable business relationship; it is the exception and most definitely not the rule.

STEP 5:   Apologize, fully acknowledging that your difficulty is creating an "inconvenience" for the lender, and thank the lender for her anticipated "understanding" and "cooperation."

TIP

Where more complex repayment solutions are called for, it is best to enclose a detailed plan with a cover letter, which thanks the lender for her willingness to consider renegotiating the terms of the loan and which also may point to highlights of the proposed plan that benefit the lender.

YOUR SCRIPTS: RENEGOTIATING PAYMENT TERMS

Here are some phone scripts for advising a lender of an *anticipated* payment problem:

1. **You:** . . . Because of cash-flow problems resulting from the sudden loss of a major client, we cannot make the May 15 payment before the end of the month. I anticipate that the current shortfall will have been made up by July, so subsequent payments should be on time.

    Because we've enjoyed such a good relationship, I feel comfortable asking you to bear with us for two weeks. I'm sorry for any inconvenience this may cause, but I am very grateful for your assistance.

2. **You:** . . . Payment of receivables due us from several clients by June 1 will be delayed until approximately August 1. This situation is beyond our control, and, unfortunately, it really impacts on our cash flow. I'm going to have to defer a payment due you on June 15. I will be able to make the payment by July 15. Can you live with this?

    Lender: It's not news I wanted to hear. We'll need the request in writing, and I will have to assess a service charge.

    You: I understand. I'll get a letter off to you immediately, and I'm sorry for the inconvenience to you. Thanks for your understanding.

3. **You:** . . . Jill, I have to tell you that, like many businesses in this community, we have been hit hard by the slump in the local economy. Orders this quarter have been off by 24 percent. We are expanding our sales efforts, but I don't see substantial improvement soon.

    We want above all to avoid bankruptcy and to maintain an excellent and equitable relationship with our creditors. To do this, I need to speak with you about renegotiating the terms of repayment of our loan. . . .

4. **You:** . . . You may have heard about the fire in our office, on Friday. The damage from flames and smoke was bad enough, but the water! It's done a number on our hard-copy as well as our computer files. Now, insurance pays for the physical damage, but not for the time lost and revenues deferred as we scramble here to sort out shipping orders, invoices, payments due, and the like. I would be very grateful if you would grant us a thirty-day extension on our payment due this month. This will give us the breathing space we need to clean up here and to collect receivables due us.

HOW TO GET MORE MONEY FROM INVESTORS AND LENDERS

When you return to original investors or lenders with a request for additional funds, you have two good reasons *not* to face your task with dread.

- Experienced salespeople know that their *best* customers are their *current* customers. Repeat business is generally easier to get than new business. The same principle applies to investors. Once an investment commitment is made, it is easier to obtain additional investments than it is to campaign among new prospects.
- Don't ask to be *given* more. Instead, *offer* more. Amplify and increase the opportunity.

The most effective strategies are based on the current investor's commitment and the offer of additional benefits.

YOUR SCRIPTS: GETTING MORE MONEY FROM AN INVESTOR

Here are some approaches to broaching the subject of additional investment:

1. **You:** . . . So you've had an opportunity to read our first quarterly report?

Investor: Yes, I have.

You: As you can see from the numbers, our initial client base is larger than anticipated. That, of course, is great news. But accommodating these added clients requires another $XXXX in start-up funding than we had originally projected. I am sending to you a detailed breakdown of what we need and how an additional investment is likely to increase your returns. We have an opportunity to acquire clients even more quickly than we had originally projected, and I need your help to take advantage of this opportunity for *your* company.

2. **You:** . . . Marsha, I'm very grateful for your offer to invest $XXX in the project. You know, my father used to tell me that, after you make a sale, it's time to shut your mouth. But I can't quite bring myself to do that. Before I go ahead and ask you to send us your check, I would

like you to think more about your investment and to think about value received.

The investment you propose entitles you to XXX shares in the project. An additional $XXX buys XXX more shares. That's an X percent stake in the enterprise.

Marsha, I am delighted to accept any investment you care to make, but I am also eager to ensure that you will be satisfied that you have made the best deal.

Index